EARLY CHILDHOOD EDUCATION TODAY

EARLY CHILDHOOD EDUCATION TODAY

FIFTH EDITION

George S. Morrison

Florida International University

Merrill, an Imprint of
Macmillan Publishing Company
New York

Collier Macmillan Canada, Inc.
Toronto

Maxwell Macmillan International Publishing Group
New York   Oxford   Singapore   Sydney

Cover photograph copyright Deborah Davis/Photo Edit.

Administrative Editor: Linda A. Sullivan
Developmental Editor: Kevin M. Davis
Production Editor: Peg Connelly Gluntz
Production Buyer: Pamela D. Bennett
Art Coordinator: Raydelle Clement
Photo Editor: Gail Meese
Text Designer: Connie Young
Cover Designer: Brian Deep

This book was set in Garamond.

Photo credits (t = top, b = bottom, l = left, r = right):
Nancy P. Alexander, pp. 72, 141, 180(tl, b), 186, 227, 320(b), 468(b); American Montessori Society, p. 80(bl); Sandra Anselmo/Merrill, pp. 185, 191, 320(tl); AP/World Wide Photos, p. 457; Art Resource, p. 25; Bettman Archive, p. 40(b); Don Birdd/Merrill, p. 257; Andy Brunk/Merrill, pp. 214(bl), 221, 230, 336(b), 492(br, t), 501, 504; Jerry Bushey/Sunrise Trinity Photos, p. 19; Ben Chandler/Merrill, pp. 12, 50, 86, 88, 94, 95, 127, 142, 223, 225, 234, 473; Children's Hospital, Columbus, Ohio, p. 472; Paul Conklin, pp. 33, 40(tl, tr), 274, 292(br); Rohn Engh/Sunrise Trinity Photos, pp. 69, 436(r), 439; Envision/Ben Asen, p. 362; Kevin Fitzsimmons/Merrill, pp. 116(tl), 388(t, br); Girl Scouts of the U.S.A., p. 345; Jo Hall/Merrill, pp. 60, 80(t), 153; Tom Hubbard, p. 475; Tom Hutchinson/Merrill, p. 340; Bruce Johnson/Merrill, pp. 55, 108(bl), 201, 246(tr, l), 342, 436(t); Joanne Kash, p. 381, 420(l); Korver/Thorpe Ltd., p. 56; Lloyd Lemmerman/Merrill, pp. 136(br), 183, 189, 199, 214(tl), 259, 365, 397, 399, 410, 468(tl), 495; Little Bighorn Photos/Jean McKean, p. 336(t); Gail Meese/Merrill, facing p. 1 (tl, r), pp. 80 (br), 84, 101, 103, 214(r), 292(bl), 325, 428, 497; Robert Meier/Sunrise Trinity Photos, p. 54; Merrill, pp. 108(tl), 306, 322, 336, 416(br); George Morrison, pp. 3, 5, 64, 158, 281, 285, 286, 329, 369, 463; Norma Morrison, p. 416(l); NEA/Joe Didio, p. 356; Timothy O'Leary, p. 43; Harvey Phillips, p. 92; Christopher Reddick, p. 416(tr); Michael Siluk, pp. 29, 47, 73, 116(b), 229, 246(br), 308, 320(tr), 453, 503; Jan Smith/Merrill, p. 352(bl); David Strickler, pp. 392, 436(b), 449; Mary Elenz Tranter, p. 420(r); Ann Vega/Merrill, p. 180(tl); Ulrike Welsch, pp. 36, 52, 108(r), 114, 116(tr), 119, 136(l), 263, 388(bl), 506; Randall D. Williams, p. 352(t); J. Wishbe/C.S.U., p. 352 (r); Charles Wolfgang/Merrill, p. 309; Allen Zak, facing p. 1 (bl), pp. 152, 462; Gale Zuker, pp. 45, 61, 62, 136(l), 146, 292(t), 299, 379, 468(tr), 471, 492(bl).

Macmillan Publishing Company
866 Third Avenue, New York, NY 10022

Collier Macmillan Canada, Inc.

Library of Congress Catalog Card Number: 90-61400

International Standard Book Number: 0-675-21342-8

Printing: 1 2 3 4 5 6 7 8 9   Year: 1 2 3 4

This book is affectionately dedicated to B.J., a very able helpmate

PREFACE

The world of early childhood education is one of constant change. Just as we professionals make important transitions in our lives, so must we be prepared to help young children make transitions in their lives. The 1990s promise to be exciting and challenging for children, parents, and teachers. This period of transition from one millennium to another will provide many opportunities and rewards for early childhood educators. And it is hoped that the fifth edition of *Early Childhood Education Today* will help prepare teachers to rightfully, knowledgeably, and confidently assume their role in educating young children of the twenty-first century.

GOALS AND COVERAGE

Early Childhood Education Today provides educators with a thorough introduction to the field of early childhood education by offering an up-to-date and comprehensive overview of current programs and practices, the historical foundation of early childhood education, and recent trends and issues in the field. One of the central aims of this book is to familiarize students with and help them understand theory so that they can implement exemplary practice. After being given developmental information and developmentally appropriate practice for infants to eight-year-olds, students can under-

stand and evaluate for themselves what is developmentally appropriate. Chapter-length coverage is given to each of the key issues of involving parents, guiding children's behavior, and teaching students with special needs. Concepts, activities, and practices described in this book are developmentally appropriate, multiculturally inclusive, and child centered.

Early Childhood Education Today seeks to promote the competence and effectiveness of all early childhood professionals, teachers, and caregivers in child care settings, infant and toddler programs, nursery schools, preschools, kindergartens, the early primary grades, and Head Start programs.

NEW IN THE FIFTH EDITION

The fifth edition of *Early Childhood Education Today* has been extensively revised. Following are some of the key changes in this edition:

☐ A chapter on future trends in early childhood education (Chapter 16) has been added, encouraging students to think about where early childhood education is headed and what is currently affecting its course.
☐ The information on child development has been updated throughout the book, particularly in the child care, preschool, and kindergarten chapters. These three chapters

have also been expanded to include new material related to teaching and child care practices.

☐ New program vignettes illustrate real-life applications of current educational theory and help the reader translate theory into practice.

☐ Contemporary issues of concern to early childhood educators have been added— including stress in young children; AIDS; homelessness; the effects of crack-cocaine on the unborn, newborn, and developing child; disease control in child care programs; and drug prevention programs.

☐ This edition better emphasizes the continuity of education from birth to age eight.

ACKNOWLEDGMENTS

Like earlier editions, this fifth edition has been written with a deep sense of pride in all who teach, care for, and parent young children. I agree with Froebel, Montessori, and Dewey that teaching is a redemptive calling and that early childhood educators should strive to achieve their best to help children and their families. This view of teaching is echoed in the portraits of Teachers of the Year in Chapter 15.

During the revision process, I met and talked with many people who are deeply committed to educating young children. I am always impressed and touched by the openness, honesty, and unselfish sharing of ideas that characterize these professional colleagues. Those who shared of themselves and their ideas were Virginia Boone, Beverly McGhee, Miriam Mades, Marsha Poster, Natalie Kaplan, Donna McClelland, Patricia Boyles, Mary Wilson, Brenda McDaniel, E. Dollie Wolverton, Gina Barclay-McLaughlin, Ann Dehan, Harriet Midget, Sally Schur, John Staley, Glenna Markey, Etta Mae Swalm, Gail D. Gonzalez, Robert A. Rodriguez, Keith Osborne, Robert Keiser, Michael W. Jones, Yvonne Hatfield, Harriet Egertson, Connie Iverson, Ruth Cripps, Shirley Crozier, Jamie MacIntyre-Southworth, Louisa Birch, Bernice Gehrls, Isabelle L. Buckner, Shawn Michaud, Nira Changwatchai, Kathie W. Dobberteen, Sara P. Grillo, Maria de La Torre, Elizabeth Sears, Linda S. Lentin, Cathy Gust, Harriet Paul Jonquiere, Andrea Rochelle Willis, Gail C. Hartman, Virginia Varga, and Carole Wolfe Korngold.

Any major revision of a text requires the committed involvement of very special people. This fifth edition is as comprehensive and up-to-date as it is because of the extraordinary involvement of the following people.

Cynthia H. Haralson, Ph.D., is a child development specialist with the Dade County Public Schools and adjunct professor of early childhood education at Florida International University. Cindy provided many excellent examples to help clarify textual material, and contributed the Chapter 15 vignette, "Growing from a Student to a Professional." She also facilitated the creative process and injected a sense of vitality and dedication to the sections on developmentally appropriate curricula.

Silvia La Villa is director of curriculum development at Holy Cross Child Care Center in Miami Florida and a doctoral candidate at Florida International University. She provided excellent advice and information regarding migrant education and the CDA process and helped ensure that multiculturalism would be a dominant theme throughout the fifth edition. Silvia also provided editorial assistance and advice about current programs and ideas.

Cristina M. Larrea, a mechanical engineering student at Florida International University, provided outstanding assistance in research, organization, and compilation. When facts and dates were needed, Cristina always found the most appropriate and up-to-date source.

José Mario Gonzalez Granados, an electrical engineering student at Florida International University, is a master facilitator and coordinator of human and material resources. He provided invaluable assistance in research and compilation.

I would like to also thank the reviewers of the previous four editions as well as the following people who offered helpful comments on this edition: Elizabeth Engley, Jacksonville State University; Anne Federlein, University of Northern Iowa; Joseph Lawton, University of Wisconsin–Madison; Lorraine Shanoski, Bloomsburg University of Pennsylvania; and Irma Van Scoy, James Madison University.

Finally, I want to thank all the professionals at Merrill who helped with this book: Molly Kyle for her efficient copy editing, Peg Gluntz for so ably handling all the necessary production details, and Kevin Davis for his helpful and professional manner and for caring enough to make this edition better than all the rest.

CONTENTS

CHAPTER 1
Interest and Issues:
What's All the Fuss About?   1

Popularity of Early Childhood Education   2

Continued Interest in the Early Years   2

Parents and Early Childhood   3

State Involvement in Early
Childhood Programs   4

Corporate Dissatisfaction with the
Results of Public Schooling   4

Giving Parents Choices   5

Cocaine Babies   5

Terminology of Early Childhood Education   6

The Ecology of Early Childhood   12

Observing Children's Behavior   15

Public Policy   16

The Disappearance of Childhood   17

Views of Children   18

Children's Rights   23

Contemporary Influences on Early
Childhood Education   26

The Public Schools and Early Education   35

Further Reading   37

Further Study   38

Notes   39

CHAPTER 2
Historical Influences:
People, Events, and Accomplishments   41

Martin Luther   42

John Amos Comenius   44

John Locke   47

Jean Jacques Rousseau   48

Johann Heinrick Pestalozzi   49

Robert Owen   51

Friedrich Wilhelm Froebel   53

Maria Montessori   59

John Dewey   60

Jean Piaget   63

The Recent Past   65

Modern Implications   70

The Teacher's Role   71

Recurring Themes   73

Further Reading   77

Further Study   77

Notes   78

CHAPTER 3
Maria Montessori:
The Start of It All   81

Principles of the Montessori Method   82

The Role of the Teacher   87

The Montessori Method in Practice   87

Selecting a Montessori School   104

Further Reading   105

Further Study   105

Notes   106

CHAPTER 4
Jean Piaget:
A New Way of Thinking
About Thinking   109

Intellectual Development
and Adaptation   110

Educational Curricula Based on Piaget   121

Common Themes of
Piaget-Based Curricula   132

Further Reading   133

Further Study   134

Notes   134

CHAPTER 5
Child Care:
Taking Care of the Nation's Children 137

Popularity of Child Care   138

Types of Child Care Programs   140

Federally Supported Child Care   146

Employer-Sponsored Child
Care Programs   147

Ill Child Care   158

Before- and After-School Care   160

Military Child Care   160

The Nanny Movement   161

Training and Certification for
Early Childhood Personnel   161

What Constitutes Quality Child Care?   164

Finding Child Care: Information
and Referral Systems   167

Child Care Issues   168

Future Trends in Child Care   174

Further Reading   175

Further Study   176

Notes   177

CHAPTER 6
Infants and Toddlers:
Rediscovering the Early Years   181

Physical Development   182

Motor Development   182

Intellectual Development   185

Language Development   190

Psychosocial Development   196

Curricula for Infants and Toddlers   200

Further Reading   210

Further Study   211

Notes   212

CHAPTER 7
The Preschool Years:
Readiness for Learning   215

History of Preschool Education   216

The Growing Popularity of Preschools   217

Who Is Preschool For?   218

Who Is the Preschooler?   219

Preschool Play   222

The Preschool Curriculum   229

Preschool Goals   230

The States and Preschool   232

The Daily Schedule   235

Selecting a Good Early
Childhood Program   237

Effectiveness of Preschool Programs   239

Issues of Preschool Education   240

Further Reading   242

Further Study   243

Notes   244

CHAPTER 8
Kindergarten Education: More Than ABC's 247

Kindergarten Education: History and Future Direction 248

Who Is Kindergarten For? 249

School Readiness: Who Gets Ready for Whom? 250

What Happens When We Retain a Child? 254

Developmental Kindergartens 256

Transitional Classes 256

What Should Kindergarten Be Like? 256

Assessment in the Kindergarten 268

Computers in the Kindergarten 269

Reading in the Kindergarten 275

Literacy and the Nation's Children 277

Bilingual Education 284

Kindergarten Children and Transitions 287

What Lies Ahead? 288

Further Reading 288

Further Study 289

Notes 289

CHAPTER 9
The Primary Years: The Process of Schooling 293

What Are Primary Children Like? 294

Significance of the Primary Years 297

Reasons for the Back-to-Basics Movement 298

Curriculum for the Primary Grades 299

Computers in the Primary Grades 307

Characteristics of a Good Primary Teacher 309

Issues in Primary Education 311

Home Schooling 312

The Future of Primary Education 315

Further Reading 316

Further Study 317

Notes 318

CHAPTER 10
The Federal Government and Early Childhood Education: Helping Children Win 321

Head Start: History and Operating Principles 323

Head Start Components 326

Head Start Improvements and Innovations 335

Migrant Education 343

Chapter 1 344

Federal Support for Early Childhood Programs 345

Further Reading 348

Further Study 348

Notes 349

CHAPTER 11
Teaching Children with Special Needs: Developing Awareness 353

Special Needs Children 354

Teaching in the Mainstream 355

Interest in Special Needs Children 357

Function of the IEP 362

Teaching the Handicapped 364

Making Transitions 376

Gifted Children 377

Children with Multicultural Heritages 380

Involving Special Needs Families 383

Further Reading 383

Further Study 386

Notes 387

CHAPTER 12
Guiding Behavior:
Helping Children Become
Responsible   389

Behavior: What Is It?   390

Discipline Defined   390

Principles of Behavior Modification   394

Reinforcing Behavior   399

Teaching by Precept and Example   403

Further Reading   412

Further Study   413

Notes   414

CHAPTER 13
Parent Involvement:
Key to Successful Programs   417

Parent Involvement—A Process
Whose Time Has Come   418

Who Is a Parent?   418

What Is a Family?   418

Implications of Family Patterns for
Early Childhood Educators   419

What is Parent Involvement?   422

Involving Single Parents   428

Language Minority Parents   429

Teenage Parents   430

Involving Fathers   430

Involving Other Caregivers   431

Family Support Programs   431

Community Involvement   431

Further Reading   432

Further Study   433

Notes   434

CHAPTER 14
Contemporary Concerns:
Educating Children in a
Changing Society   437

Children of Poverty   438

Child Abuse and Neglect   439

Missing Children   447

Sexism and Sex Role Stereotyping   448

Making Early Childhood
Programs Humane   451

Homeless Children   453

Children with AIDS   455

Prevention   460

Childhood Stress   460

Health Issues   462

Further Reading   464

Further Study   465

Notes   466

CHAPTER 15
Responsible Caregiving and Teaching:
Becoming a Professional   469

Qualities of the Early
Childhood Educator   470

Preparing for a Career in Early
Childhood Education   470

Developing a Philosophy of Education   477

Becoming a Professional   485

Further Reading   489

Further Study   490

Notes   491

CHAPTER 16
Future Trends in Early
Childhood Education:
Where Do We Go From Here?   493

Why Are Trends Important?   494

The Nature of Trends   494

Current Trends and Their Significance   495

Where Do We Go From Here?   510

Further Reading   510

Further Study   511

Notes   512

APPENDIX A–CDA Competency
Goals and Functional Areas   513

APPENDIX B–The Key Experiences   515

APPENDIX C–Sample Individualized
Family Service Plan   521

APPENDIX D–The National Association for
the Education of Young Children   531

APPENDIX E–Journals and Associations
Concerning Early Childhood Education   537

INDEX   541

THE AUTHOR   549

CHAPTER 1
Interest and Issues
What's All the Fuss About?

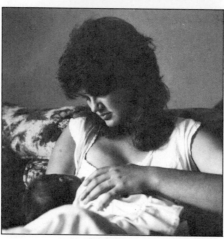

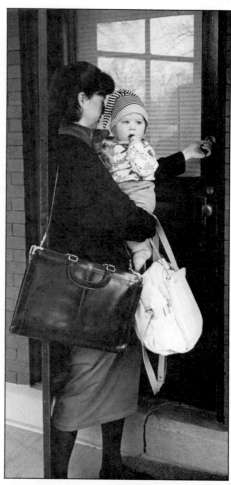

As you read and study:
- ☐ Identify contemporary influences that create interest in early childhood education.
- ☐ Understand and use the terminology of early childhood education.
- ☐ Identify and describe types of early childhood education programs.
- ☐ Recognize the importance of the ecology of early childhood education.
- ☐ Analyze the influence of the concept of "the competent child" on child rearing and education.
- ☐ Consider influences that hurry, pressure, and encourage children to grow up too soon, too fast.
- ☐ Understand the need for public policy and how public policy is developed.
- ☐ Examine adults' views of children and explain the implications these views have for rearing and educating children.
- ☐ Examine social, political, economic, and educational issues that influence child rearing, teaching, and policy development.
- ☐ Understand how the public's desire for basic education influences early childhood education programs.
- ☐ Review the procedures for observing children and plan to apply and use the observational guidelines in your work with young children.

POPULARITY OF EARLY CHILDHOOD EDUCATION

In 1965, with the beginning of the Head Start Program (see Chapter 10), early childhood education entered its modern period. Over the past three decades, the field of early childhood education has been enormously popular, and interest in the field is at an all-time high. For all early childhood professionals, the years that close the 20th century and act as a prelude to the 21st century promise to be exciting and challenging. Early childhood education will continue to be in the spotlight; however, the challenges, issues, and opportunities of the past quarter-century will little resemble those of the next decade. While all areas of early childhood education continue to capture attention, the area most in the spotlight is the period from conception to age six.

More parents—and the public at large—recognize the importance of the early years to learning and later development. Many upwardly mobile parents believe they have only a few years to set the course of their children's development and futures. They are extremely goal-directed about their careers and their children. Given this attitude, it is likely that the popularity of early childhood education and interest in the early years will continue unabated.

Problems such as child abuse and the numbers of children who live in poverty are perennial sources of controversy and concern, to which early childhood professionals continue to seek new solutions. Topics such as infant stimulation and infant child care have caught early educators' attention. The continual emergence of new ideas and issues relating to the education and care of young children and the quest to provide educationally and developmentally appropriate programs keeps the field in a state of disequilibrium by constantly challenging early childhood professionals to determine what is best for young children and their families.

CONTINUED INTEREST IN THE EARLY YEARS

Evidence of the public's interest in early childhood education is all around us. The April 17, 1989, cover story of *Newsweek* was devoted to "How Kids Learn." The article emphasized how children learn through play and self-discovery and generally won the praise of early childhood professionals, who applauded it as a vindication of their beliefs that parents and public school educators should not rush young children into early academics.

Daily newspapers also provide ample evidence of the nation's interest in young children. These are a few newspaper headlines that called attention to stories and articles about young children and their parents.

"Congress Shows Signs of Spending to Fight Infant Deaths" (*The New York Times*, May 21, 1989)

"Infant IQ Pigeonholing" (*The Christian Science Monitor*, May 24, 1989)

"Infant Mortality: A National Disgrace; Each Child Has A Right To Adequate Prenatal Care" (*The Los Angeles Times*, April 21, 1989)

"Parents Cautioned on Low-fat Baby Diets" (*The Los Angeles Times*, March 30, 1989)

"U.S. and States Faulted on Child Care" (*The New York Times*, January 9, 1990)

"A Primary School Tests for Drugs: Program at Catholic Academy in Chicago May Be a First" (*The New York Times,* January 21, 1990)

"A Test for AIDS Infection in Newborns" (*The New York Times,* June 22, 1989)

"Tiny Miracles Become Huge Public Health Problem" (*The New York Times,* February 19, 1989)

Mass media magazines such as *First,* designed to address parenting and other questions asked by contemporary adults, *Working Mother,* which provides child-rearing and work-related information, and *Parenting* help quench the insatiable desire of parents and the public for information about child care and rearing. Many hospitals have jumped on the bandwagon, and they too are providing parent-oriented publications to meet parents' needs and longing for information.

PARENTS AND EARLY CHILDHOOD

More parents have more disposable income and are willing to spend it on enriching their and their children's lives. Parents enroll themselves and their infants and toddlers in self-improvement programs promoted as physically and cognitively stimulating. Courses designed for expectant parents, new parents, and harried parents are now a standard part of the curriculum of many community colleges and schools. During one semester at a local community college, parents could select from these courses:

As more women enter the work force, quality child care becomes an even greater necessity. Caregivers who provide quality child care help assure that children will have an appropriate foundation for later life and learning.

Parent/Infant Enrichment, Play Activities with the Preschool Child, Discipline Strategies That Work, Movement and Play Activities, Creative Learning-Storytelling/Drama, Toilet Learning, Choosing a Preschool for Your Child, Building Your Child's Self-esteem, and Developmental Screening for Infants. Many of the courses required registration of both parents and their young children!

Parent groups discuss prevention of child abuse; how to reduce stress in children's lives; the demise of childhood; how to nurture in the nuclear age; ways to develop curricula for peace; how to extend more rights to children; and how to parent in these increasingly stressful and permissive times.

Stimulation/enrichment programs help popularize the importance of the very early years. Infant-parent stimulation programs catch the fancy and serve the needs of young parents, especially upwardly mobile parents. They want "the best" for their children and are willing to spend time, effort, and money to see that they get the best. This, in turn, makes it possible for early childhood educators to address the importance of the early years. It also creates a climate of acceptance for very early education and an arena in which early childhood educators are heard. Infant stimulation programs stimulate more than infants.

STATE INVOLVEMENT IN EARLY CHILDHOOD PROGRAMS

All the states of the nation are taking a lead in developing programs for young children. State initiative is stimulated by several factors. One is the continuing federal cuts in funds for early childhood and other human services programs. As federal dollars dry up, states are responding by initiating programs of their own, funded from many sources—from lottery monies to taxes on commodities such as cigarettes.

Second, instead of giving monies directly to specific programs, federal monies are consolidated into what are known as "block grants"—sums of money given to states to provide services according to broad general guidelines. In essence, the states control how the money is spent and the nature of the programs funded, not the federal government. As federal support for early education continues to decline, the states continue to fund replacement, alternative, and substitute programs. This involvement will grow and strengthen as the states make greater commitments to child care and early education programs, especially for children from low-income familites. Over 31 states have appropriated monies for prekindergarten programs to serve at-risk four-year-old children[1]. This trend will continue and accelerate. With direct funding comes control. When agencies contribute funding for programs, they also help determine the direction the programs will take, the policies that govern them, and what children and families they will serve.

CORPORATE DISSATISFACTION WITH THE RESULTS OF PUBLIC SCHOOLING

U.S. corporations are increasingly dissatisfied with the products of the nation's schools. Many companies find that they must spend millions of dollars teaching potential employees to read and write. Faced with the prospect of an undereducated and untrained work force, corporations are stepping in to assist the public schools. In addition to providing money and expertise, corporations are pressuring schools to improve attendance, drop-out rates, and reading ability. Because it is in the early years that attitudes toward school and life are formed, corporations are willing to spend money and develop cooperative relationships to support preschool and other intervention programs. (We will discuss this trend further in Chapter 16.)

GIVING PARENTS CHOICES

Choice is one of the current themes throughout education, from grades K–12. More and more parents and others—especially politicians—want to choose where children will attend school and the types of programs in which they will participate. The rationale for choice is based on a number of thoughts.

First is the belief that parents want to choose the school their children will attend. Second is the recognition that students learn in different ways and teachers teach in different ways, and that choice can create a match between these two. Third is the use of choice as a means for integrating schools. The idea here is that parents will choose to send their children to good schools or schools that promote a particular program, and integration will result. In Minneapolis, for example, parents have a choice of five types of elementary schools: Fundamental, Contemporary, Montessori, Continuous Progress, and Open. (This parental choice is also evident in the vignette about the Magnet Art School in Kansas City in Chapter 16.)

Although it is difficult to argue with the concept of choice, there are problems in implementation:

- Not all parents want to choose—often because they don't know all the options available to them.
- Not all parents are comfortable with the available choices. A particular school may be farther away than they want to send the child, or may have a much larger enrollment than the parents are comfortable with (some elementary schools have enrollments of over 1000 students).
- As to child care, the nation cannot take care of all infants and toddlers in center care; in fact, parents who work often prefer home care.

So the topic of choice is not as simple as we might first think.

COCAINE BABIES

One consequence of the war on drugs is what happens to babies who are born to cocaine-using mothers. Called "cocaine babies," these infants require special care to reduce the risks they face. School districts and community agencies are developing programs to help reduce the effects of being born cocaine-addicted and to help these infants and their parents live drug-free and productive lives. (Chapter 14 offers additional information.)

In short, young children have captured the attention of the nation. They compete with budget deficits, nuclear arms treaties, and summit meetings for media attention. Young children are prime-time subjects. Consequently, early childhood educators must learn more about how to care for, educate, and rear children so they can advise parents, legislators, and those who formulate public policy when they look to them for guidance in determining what is best for the nation's children.

TERMINOLOGY OF EARLY CHILDHOOD EDUCATION

Terminology is frequently a problem when discussing early childhood education. Early childhood educators are not always clear with terms they use in their work, so it is important to have some knowledge of common definitions, and a command of the terminology used by the National Association for the Education of Young Children (NAEYC) and most early childhood professionals.

Throughout this text, *early childhood* refers to the child from birth to age eight. This is a standard and accepted definition used by the NAEYC.[2] (At the same time, professionals recognize that prenatal [before birth] development is also important.) The term frequently refers to children who have not yet reached school age, and the public often uses it to refer to children in any type of preschool.

Early childhood settings provide "services for children from birth through age eight in part-day and full-day group programs in centers, homes, and institutions; kindergartens and primary schools, and recreational programs."[3]

Early childhood education consists of the services provided in early childhood settings. It is common for educators of young children to use the terms *early childhood* and *early childhood education* synonymously.

Other terms frequently used when discussing the education of young children are nursery school and preschool. *Nursery school* is a program for the education of two-, three-, and four-year-old children. Many nursery schools are half-day programs, usually designed for children of mothers who do not work outside the home, although many children who have two working parents do attend. The purpose of the nursery school is to provide for active learning in a play setting. In some instances the kindergarten curriculum has been pushed down into the nursery school. As a result, a child-centered program in an informal play setting that characterizes a good nursery school has been replaced by a formal teacher-centered setting. *Preschool* generally means any educational program for children prior to their entrance into kindergarten.

When a public school or other agency operates one program for five-year-olds and another for four-year-olds, the term *kindergarten* is applied to the former and *nursery school* or *preschool* to the latter. Public-school kindergarten is now almost universal for five-year-old children (see Chapter 8), so it can no longer be thought of as "preschool"—kindergarten is now considered part of the elementary grades K–6.

The term *prekindergarten* is growing in usage to refer to a program for four-year-olds attending a program prior to kindergarten. Another term, *transitional kindergarten,* designates a program for children who are not ready for kindergarten and who can benefit from another year of the program. The term *transitional* also refers to grade-school programs that provide additional opportunities for children to master skills associated with a particular grade. Transitional programs do not usually appear beyond the second and third grades.

Junior first grade or *pre-first grade* are transitional programs between kindergarten and first grade developed to help five-year-olds get ready to enter first grade. Not all children are equally "ready" to enter first grade because of the wide range of mental ages and experiential backgrounds, and children frequently benefit from such special programs.

Preprimary refers to programs for children prior to their entering first grade; *primary* means grades first, second, and third. With increasing frequency, primary

The majority of children in many of today's early childhood programs are from what were once thought of as minority groups.

children are being taught in classes that include two grade levels. In these *split* or *nongraded classes,* first and second graders and second and third graders are taught in a single class. Split classes are seldom composed of upper-elementary children. Reasons for split classes are decreasing school enrollments, influences of open education practices, and teacher contracts that limit class size.

A *parent cooperative* preschool is a school formed and controlled by parents for their children. Programs of this type are generally operated democratically with the parents hiring the staff. Often, some of the parents are hired to direct or staff the program. Being part of a cooperative means parents have some responsibility for assisting in the program.

The term *child care* encompasses many programs and services for preschool children. The more common term is *day care,* but most people engaged in the care of young children recognize this as outmoded. *Child care* is more accurate because it focuses on the children themselves. The primary purpose of child care programs is to care for young children who are not in school and for school-age children of working parents before and after school hours. Child care programs may have an educational orientation, or may offer primarily babysitting or custodial care. Many programs have a sliding fee schedule based on parents' ability to pay. Quality child care programs are increasingly characterized by their comprehensive or full-range services that address children's total needs—physical, social, emotional, creative and intellectual. Today, there is a general understanding on the part of parents, the public, and the profession that *child care* means physical care *and* educational programs.

A large number of *family day care* programs provide child care services in the homes of the caregivers. This alternative to center-based programs usually accommodates a maximum of four or five children in a *family day care home. Home care* programs were formerly custodial in nature, but there is a growing trend for caregivers to provide a full range of services in their homes.

Church related or *church-sponsored* preschool and elementary programs are quite common and becoming more popular. These programs usually have a cognitive, basic skills emphasis within a context of religious doctrine and discipline. The reason for the popularity of these church-sponsored programs, which often charge tuition, is their emphasis on the basic skills and no-nonsense approach to learning and teaching.

Head Start is a federally sponsored program for children from low-income families. Established by the Economic Opportunity Act in 1964, the program is intended to overcome the effects of poverty. *Follow Through* extends Head Start programs to children in grades 1 through 3, and works with school personnel rather than apart from the schools.

There are not as many federal programs providing services to children, parents, and families as there were in the 1970s, but these programs have had a tremendous influence on early childhood education. For example, *Home Start* was a demonstration program within Head Start designed to deliver a comprehensive program of services to children and parents in the home. Today, many Head Start programs provide children and families a *Home Base* option for delivery of services. Table 1–1 delineates the purposes of the various types of early childhood programs.

Public and private agencies, including colleges, universities, hospitals, and corporations, operate many kinds of *demonstration programs.* Many colleges and universities with schools of education have a *laboratory school* used primarily for research in teaching methods, demonstration of exemplary programs and activities, and for training teachers. Many of these schools also develop materials and programs for children with handicaps and learning disabilities.

As the name implies, a *toy library* makes toys and other learning materials available to children, parents, child care providers, and teachers. Toy libraries are housed in many different settings, such as libraries, shopping malls, churches, preschools, and vans. Many toy libraries are supported by user fees and parent and community volunteers.

TABLE 1−1 Types of Early Childhood Programs

Program	Purpose	Age
Early childhood	Multipurpose	Birth to third grade
Child care	Play/socialization; babysitting; physical care; provide parents opportunities to work; cognitive development	Birth to 6 years
Employer child care	Different settings for meeting child care needs of working parents	Variable; usually as early as 6 weeks to the beginning of school
Corporate child care	Same as employer child care	Same as employer child care
Industrial child care	Same as employer child care	Same as employer child care
Proprietary care	Provide care and/or education to children; designed to make a profit	6 weeks to entrance into first grade
Nursery (public or private)	Play/socialization; cognitive development	2–4 years
Preschool (public or private)	Play/socialization; cognitive development	2½–5 years
Parent cooperative preschool	Play/socialization; preparation for kindergarten and first grade; babysitting; cognitive development	2–5 years
Babysitting cooperatives (Co-op)	Provide parents with reliable babysitting; parents sit for others' children in return for reciprocal services	All ages
Prekindergarten	Play/socialization; cognitive development; preparation for kindergarten	3½–5 years
Junior kindergarten	A prekindergarten program	Primarily 4-year-olds
Senior kindergarten	Basically the same as regular kindergarten	Same as kindergarten
Kindergarten	Preparation for first grade; developmentally appropriate activities for 4½- to 6-year-olds	4–6 years
Developmental kindergarten	Same as regular kindergarten. Often enrolls children who have completed one or more years in an early childhood special education progam	5–6 years
Transitional kindergarten	Extended learning of kindergarten; preparation for first grade	Variable
Preprimary	Preparation for first grade	5–6 years
Primary	Teach skills associated with grades 1, 2, and 3	6–8 years

TABLE 1–1   *continued*

Program	Purpose	Age
Toy lending libraries	Provide parents and children with games, toys, and other materials that can be used for learning purposes; housed in libraries, vans, or early childhood centers	Birth through primary years
Lekotek	Resource centers for families who have children with special needs; sometimes referred to as a *toy* or *play library* (Lekotek is a Scandinavian word that means *play library*)	Birth through primary years
High school child care programs	Provide child care for children of high school students, especially unwed parents; serve as an incentive for student/parents to finish high school and as a training program in child care and parenting skills	Six weeks–5 years
Drop-off child care centers	Provide care for short periods of time while parents shop, exercise, or have appointments	Infancy through the primary grades
Infant stimulation programs (also called parent/infant stimulation programs)	Programs for enhancing sensory and cognitive development of infants and young toddlers through exercise and play; activities include general sensory stimulation for children and educational information and advice for parents	3 months–2 years
Pre-first grade	Preparation for first grade; often for students who "failed" or did not do well in kindergarten	5–6 years
Interim first grade	Provide children with an additional year of kindergarten and readiness activities prior to and as preparation for first grade	5–6 years
Transitional or transition classes	Classes specifically designed to provide for children of the same developmental age	Variable
Multiage grouping	Groups of children of various ages who work at their own pace	Variable
Junior first grade	Preparation for first grade	5–6 years
Split class	Teach basic academic and social skills of grades involved	Variable, but usually primary
After school care	To provide child care for children after school hours	Children of school age; generally K-6

TABLE 1-1 *continued*

Program	Purpose	Age
Family day care	Provide care for a group of children in a home setting; generally custodial in nature	
Head Start	Play/socialization; academic learning; comprehensive social and health services; prepare children for first grade	2-6 years
Private schools	Provide care and/or education	Usually preschool through high school
Departments of Children, Youth, and Families	A multipurpose agency of many state and county governments; usually provides such services as administration of state and federal monies, child care licensing, and protective sevices	All
Health and Human Services	Same as Dept. of Children, Youth, and Families	All
Health and Social Services	Same as Dept. of Children, Youth, and Families	All
Follow Through	Extend Head Start services to grades 1, 2, and 3	6-8 years
Home Start	Provide Head Start service in the home setting	Birth-6 or 7 years
Laboratory school	Provide demonstration programs for preservice teachers; conduct research	Variable; from birth through senior high
Child and Family Resource Program	Deliver Head Start services to families	Birth-8 years
Montessori School (preschool and grade school)	Provide programs that use the philosophy, procedures, and materials developed by Maria Montessori (see Chapter 3)	1-8 years
Open education	Child-centered learning in an environment characterized by freedom and learning through activities based on children's interests	2-8 years
British primary school	Implement the practices and procedures of open education	2-8 years
Magnet school	Specializes in subjects and curriculum designed to attract students; usually has a theme (e.g., performing arts); designed to give parents choices and to integrate schools	5-18 years

Good early childhood programs offer a variety of stimulating and enriching activities that are developmentally appropriate.

Early Childhood Labels

Professionals in early childhood education use certain labels to refer to children of different ages, as outlined in Table 1–2. Just as professionals use certain terms to refer to children, so, too, there are labels for the various adults who work with young children, as shown in Table 1–3.

THE ECOLOGY OF EARLY CHILDHOOD

Ecology is the study of how people interact with their environments and the results and consequences (good and bad) of these interactions. There is growing interest in how children interact with their environments—home, child care center, and school— and the effect of these interactions on children. Early childhood educators realize they must pay greater attention to children's environments.

Early childhood ecological considerations apply at three levels. The first level is an examination of the environments and how they are structured and arranged to promote children's maximum growth. For example, early childhood educators are more aware than ever of the role the child care environment has in influencing health, safety, and physical and intellectual development. Sensitive professionals seek ways to structure environments so they are less stressful, more healthful, less dangerous, and more accommodating to children's developmental needs.

TABLE 1–2   Labels for Children

Label	Description	Age
Baby	Generic term referring to a child from birth through the first two years of life	Birth to two years
Neonate	Child during the first month of life, from Latin term *neo* (new) *natus* (born); usually used by nurses, pediatric specialists, and people working in the area of child development	Birth to one month
Infants	Children from birth to the beginning of independent walking (about 12 months of age)	Birth to one year
Toddlers	Children from the beginning of independent walking to about age four; the term *toddler* is derived from the lunging, tottering, precarious balanced movement of children as they learn to walk	Thirteen months to three years
Preschoolers	Children between toddler age and age of entrance into kindergarten or first grade; because kindergarten is becoming more widespread, it is customary to refer to four-year-olds as preschoolers	Three to five years
Child/Children	Generic term for individuals from birth through the elementary grades	Birth to eight years
The very young	Used to identify and specify children from birth through preschool	Birth to five years

At a second level, early childhood educators focus on how environments interact with each other. Educators are part of children's environments, and how they interact with parents, who are also part of children's environments, affects children. Urie Bronfenbrenner, a leading proponent of the importance of ecological studies in education, says "A child's ability to learn to read in the primary grades may depend no less on how he is taught than on the existence and nature of ties between the school and home.[4] Early childhood educators demonstrate their attunement to the importance of interactions between educational settings and homes when they initiate programs of parent involvement and family support.

Political and social environments represent a third, more abstract, level of inter-action. For example, in Florida, kindergarten is compulsory for all children five years of age as of September first. What effects does such political policy have on young children? Some people worry that children who are five by September first are "too old" when they enter kindergarten. Others are concerned about the cost and trauma Parents undergo to find quality child care because their children were born a month or a day too late. Others see an advantage to the September first age limit in that children are older when they come to school, and therefore will be "ready" to learn.

Ecological considerations are of interest to early childhood and child development researchers in another way. They want to know how children's natural environments— their homes, families, care centers, peer groups, and communities—influence their behavior. Say, for example, that a researcher is interested in knowing more about the factors that influence young children's toy selection. She designs a laboratory experiment, gathers data, and arrives at certain conclusions. But these conclusions may not be equally valid for explaining how young children select toys in their homes. This is one reason there is so much interest in ecological settings by those who are

TABLE 1–3   Adults Who Work with Young Children

Label	Description
Early childhood educator	Works with young children and has committed to self-development by participating in specialized training and programs to extend professional knowledge and competence
Early childhood teacher	Responsible for planning and conducting a developmentally and educationally appropriate program for a group or classroom of children; supervises an assistant teacher or aide, usually has a bachelor's degree in early childhood, elementary education, or child development
Early childhood assistant teacher	Assists the teacher in conducting a developmentally and educationally appropriate program for a group or classroom; frequently acts as a co-teacher, but may lack education or training to be classified as teacher (many people who have teacher qualifications serve as an assistant teacher because they enjoy the program or because the position of teacher is not available); usually has a high school diploma or associate degree and is involved in professional development
Early childhood associate teacher	Plans and implements activities with children; has an associate degree and/or the CDA credential; may also be responsible for care and education of a group of children
Aide	Assists the teacher and teacher assistant when requested; usually considered an entry-level position
Director	Develops and implements a center or school program; supervises all staff; may teach a group of children
Home visitor	Conducts a home-based child development/education program; works with children, families, and staff members
Child Development Associate	Has completed a CDA assessment and been awarded the CDA credential*
Caregiver	Provides care, education, and protection for the very young in or outside the home†, includes parents, relatives, child care workers, and early childhood teachers
Parent	Provides the child with basic care, direction, support, protection, and guidance‡

*CDA National Credentialing Program, *Child Development Associate Assessment System and Competency Standards* (Washington, D.C.: CDA National Credentialing Program, 1985), p. 551.

†George S. Morrison, *The Education and Development of Infants, Toddlers, and Preschoolers* (Boston: Little, Brown, 1988).

‡George S. Morrison, *Parent Involvement in the Home, School and Community* (Columbus, Ohio: Merrill Publishing Company, 1978), p. 28.

searching for answers to why children behave as they do. The point is that members of the early childhood profession, parents, social workers, legislators, and others are beginning to care about such ecological relationships, which will undoubtedly play an even more important role in early childhood as the years go by. An important factor in making decisions about ecological relationships is skill in observing.

OBSERVING CHILDREN'S BEHAVIOR

Often when teachers and parents look at children, they don't really see what they are doing or understand why they are engaged in a particular behavior or activity. Many behaviors provide insight into the child, but because teachers don't observe in any systematic way, the significance and importance goes undetected. It is thus important for early childhood educators to understand the importance of using observation to gather data about young children.

Observation is the systematic examination, noting, or conscious attention to a child, setting, program, or situation for the purpose of gathering information on which to base a judgment, make a recommendation, or develop a plan or strategy. Observation is an intentional activity for the purpose of influencing behavior or programs; observation as used for data gathering and informational purposes is entirely different from the casual and unsystematic "looking" we use in daily interactions with children. A child care worker may notice that there is a new child from Vietnam in the center attended by Hispanic and Anglo children, but through systematic observation she will be able to determine the attitudes of children to children of other races and then plan accordingly.

Advantages of Observation

There are a number of reasons for and advantages to gathering data through observation.

☐ Observation provides for intentional and systematic gathering of data.
☐ Observation enables the observer to gather data that cannot be gathered by paper-and-pencil tests or by questioning a young child. If we want to study the reactions of four-year-old preschoolers to a new room arrangement, for example, observation will probably provide us with more valid data than other methods. Observation enables educators to gather information directly that could otherwise be gathered only indirectly.

Steps in Observing

A credible and professional job of observing requires several steps.

Step 1. Planning the Observation.   This step includes developing and stating your goals for observation. These goals state *why* you want to observe and help direct your efforts to *what* you will observe. Stating goals provides direction for your observation and helps focus your attention on the observational process. A goal for observing might be "To determine the effectiveness of activities used to mainstream (see Chapter 11) handicapped children into the day care program." Another goal might be "To determine what modifications will be necessary in the classroom setting to facilitate the mainstreaming of handicapped children."

Step 2. Conducting the Observation.   In conducting your observation, it is important to be objective, specific, and as thorough as possible. For example, during your objective observation you may write, "Dana states that she is going to color a picture for her daddy. There is not enough room for Dana's wheelchair to fit between the art table and the easel so she can have access to the art shelf. She had to ask someone to get the crayons for her."

Step 3. Interpretation.   All observations can and should result in some kind of interpretation. Interpretation serves several important functions. First, interpretation puts our observations into perspective; that is, in relation to what we know. Second, interpretation helps us make sense of what we have observed. Third, interpretation has the potential to make us grow. For example, interpreting the lack of access of the handicapped child to crayons raises the legitimate question, "Should Dana have access to all parts of the learning environment that other children have access to?" To answer this question, you will probably need to extend your knowledge of laws and practices relating to handicapped children in regular classrooms. Fourth, interpretation is the foundation for implementing results of observation. Without interpretation of some kind, it would be difficult to do much about what you observed. You may interpret your observations this way: "The fact that a wheelchair-bound child cannot reach an integral part of the classroom without assistance indicates that the room arrangement must be modified."

Step 4. Implementation.   The implementation phase means that you will do something with the results or "findings" of your observation. Of course, how you use your observational results will depend largely on why you observed in the first place. Most often, observation is done for a specific reason. In our case, you could implement the findings several ways. You could write up your results in the form of a paper in which you recommend activities and classroom settings appropriate for handicapped children such as Dana. Or, you could meet with Dana's teacher and share your observational results. Perhaps Dana's teacher will seek your further help and cooperation in making her classroom more accessible for handicapped children. The Observational Guide shown in Figure 1–1 will help you with observations you may want to conduct as you read this text.

PUBLIC POLICY

Public policies in the field of early childhood education are policies that affect and influence the lives of children, parents, and families. The public policies are implemented through official statements, pronouncements, and legislation. Many child care programs and most public schools, for example, have policies that require full immunization against childhood diseases. This is a public policy regarding immunization of children. As you might suspect, there are many public policies that determine what ages children can enter school, how child care programs should operate, and how to provide appropriate care and education for special needs children. Throughout the text, you will find many instances in which public policy outlines specific kinds of programs for children and the circumstances and funding under which they will be delivered.

Observer's Name: _____

Children Observed (e.g., Cindy H., Silvia L.): _____

Children's Ages (e.g., 4–5 or kindergarten): _____

Observation Setting: _____

Date and Time of Observation: _____

Observation Goal—Purpose of Observation: _____

Objective Observation:

1.

2.

3.

4.

Interpretations:

Implementation Recommendations:

FIGURE 1–1   Observational Guide

As early childhood professionals become increasingly involved in advocacy activities, they and their professional organizations issue position papers designed to influence public policy prior to its enactment and implementation. Child advocacy agencies are drafting position papers on topics ranging from developmentally appropriate curricula for young children to the pros and cons of developing public school programs for four-year-olds. A leading professional organization, the National Association for the Education of Young Children, is a strong advocate for developmentally appropriate practices in early childhood programs. Agencies have also influenced and are influencing national legislation for child care such as the Act for Better Child Care. (In Chapter 15, you will learn more about your professional roles and responsibilities in advocating for public policy that supports children and their families.)

At no time in American history has there been so much interest and involvement on the part of educators in the development of public policy. This political reality is beneficial to all—children, parents, families, and early childhood professionals—for it helps to assure that children's best interests will be considered when decisions are made that affect them.

THE DISAPPEARANCE OF CHILDHOOD

There is growing concern that childhood as we knew it or remember it is disappearing. Children are often viewed as pseudoadults; they even dress like adults, in designer jeans, tops, and running shoes. Some believe that childhood is not only endangered, but already gone. Neil Postman deals with the demise of childhood in his book, *The Disappearance of Childhood.* Postman says that before the Renaissance, there was no such period as childhood. The invention of the printing press and books brought childhood into being, because children now had to earn their right to adulthood by learning to read, so as to gain access to adult information and knowledge. With the advent of books came schools, where children were taught to read and prepared to become literate adults. Postman says the hundred-year period from 1850 to 1950 represents the highwater mark of childhood, and was also the period during which the stereotype of the "modern" family developed. The introduction of television assured the end of childhood, because television presents information that is available to all in an undifferentiated form. The whole family—infants, toddlers, teenagers, and parents—watch the same programs together.

> We may conclude, then, that television erodes the dividing line between childhood and adulthood in three ways, all having to do with its undifferentiated accessibility; first, because it requires no instruction to grasp its form; second, because it does not make complex demands on either mind or behavior; and third, because it does not segregate its audience. . . . Given the conditions I have described, electric media find it impossible to withhold any secrets. Without secrets, of course, there can be no such thing as childhood.[5]

Vance Packard expresses alarm over "a deep malaise" that has come over child rearing in America. Packard believes that changes in the family have contributed to an overall deterioration in the quality of parenting. He finds these societal forces responsible:

1. An antichild culture that confronts children with a cool, hard world outside their homes
2. The surge of married women—including millions of mothers—into jobs outside the home
3. An increase in the splitting up of parents and the reverberating impact on the millions of children involved[6]

Perhaps even more disturbing, Packard detects a growing sentiment against children. He believes that many people are consciously deciding not to have children, and a childless lifestyle is viewed by some as the "ultimate liberation." Children are no longer considered emotionally necessary to the fulfillment of an individual lifestyle or married life. On the contrary, children are perceived as obstacles to fulfillment, obstacles to a career, an economic burden, and impediments to marital happiness. People who consider children unnecessary to their own fulfillment and as obstacles and economic burdens are less likely to be concerned about the welfare of children in general. They will be less inclined to consider programs for children a top national priority.

VIEWS OF CHILDREN

Views of children determine how people teach and rear them. As you read about the different views of children, try to clarify and change what you believe. Also identify social, environmental, and political factors that tend to support each particular view. Sometimes, of course, views overlap, so it is possible to synthesize ideas from several views into a particular personal view.

Because children's views of themselves result partly from how society and adults view them, it is important that society's view is positive, to help children develop to their fullest potential.

Miniature Adults

What early childhood educators and parents identify as childhood has not always been considered a distinct period of life. During medieval times, the notion of childhood did not exist; little distinction was made between children and adults. The concept of children as miniature adults was logical for the time and conditions of medieval Europe. Economic conditions did not allow for a long childhood dependency. The only characteristics that separated children from adults were size and age. Children were expected to act as adults in every way, and they did so.

In many respects the twentieth century is no different, because children are still viewed and treated as adults. In many third world countries of Latin America, Africa, and Asia, children are, of necessity, expected to be economically productive. They are members of the adult world of work at the ages of four, five, or six.

In the United States, where child labor laws protect children from the world of adult work and exploitation, there are those who advocate allowing children to enter the workplace at earlier ages and for lower wages. In some rural settings, the young child still has economic value. Approximately one million migrant children pick crops and help their parents earn a livelihood (see Chapter 10). At the other end of the spectrum, child actors and models engage in highly profitable and what some call glamorous careers. National publicity about child abuse and drug use dramatizes the extent to which young children are involved in prostitution and drugs.

Encouraging children to act like adults and hurrying them toward adulthood causes conflicts between capabilities and expectations, particularly when early childhood educators demand adultlike behavior from children and set unrealistic expectations.

The Competent Child

The decade of the 1960s ushered in a renewal of interest in very young children and how they learn. Many research studies (see Chapter 2) focused on the importance of the early years and challenged educators and parents to reconsider the role early learning plays in life-long learning. A result of this renewed interest in the early years was that parents placed great *intellectual* importance on early learning. This change in parental attitudes toward early learning resulted in what David Elkind calls the "concept of the competent infant." Elkind believes the image of the competent infant is promoted and reinforced by such social conditions as divorce, increasing numbers of single parents, and two-career families. According to Elkind, "The concept of the competent infant is clearly more in keeping with these contemporary family styles." Contemporary social forces and lifestyles create a need to view children as competent. As Elkind explains,

> A competent infant can cope with the separation from parents at an early age. He or she is able to adjust with minimal difficulty to babysitters, day care centers, full day nursery schools and so on. If some parents feel residual pangs of guilt about leaving their young offspring in out-of-home care, they can place their youngster in a high-pressure academic program. If the child were not in such a program, the parents tell themselves, he or she would fall behind peers and would not be able to compete academically when it is time to enter kindergarten. From this perspective, high pressure academic programs are for the young child's "own good."[7]

Many parents embrace the concept of the competent infant as compatible with what they want to achieve in their own lives. An upwardly mobile career parent wants a child who can achieve at an early age. Parents want to begin early to assure success and advancement for their competent children. Susan Littwin sums up the new attitude toward child rearing:

> What the child care experts did do, at least indirectly, was create the idea of the professional parent. With all the advice available on television talk shows and in magazines and paperback books, raising children could no longer be something that you did by tradition or whim or common sense. There was a right way and a wrong way to put a child to bed, to leave him with a baby-sitter, to get him started at school, to have a friend over. Being a parent was a career; the harder you worked the more you gained.[8]

The Child as Sinful

Based primarily on the religious belief in original sin, the view of the child as sinful was widely accepted in the fourteenth through eighteenth centuries, particularly in Colonial North America during the Puritan era of the sixteenth and seventeenth centuries. Misbehavior was a sign of this inherent sin. Making children behave and using corporal punishment whenever necessary was emphasized. Misbehavior was taken as proof of the devil's influence, and beating the devil out of the child was an acceptable solution.

This view of inherent sinfulness persists, manifested in the belief that children need to be controlled through rigid supervision and insistence on unquestioning obedience to and respect for adults. Educational institutions are perceived as places where children can be taught "right" behavior. The number of private and parochial or religious schools that emphasize respect, obedience, and correct behavior is growing because of parents' hopes of rearing children who are less susceptible to the temptations of crime and drugs.

Blank Tablets

The English philosopher John Locke (1632–1704) believed that children were born into the world as *tabula rasa,* or *blank tablets.* After extensive observations, Locke concluded: "there is not the least appearance of any settled ideas at all in them; especially of ideas answering the terms which make up those universal propositions that are esteemed innate principles."[9] Locke believed that children's experiences, through sensory impressions, determined what they learned and, consequently, what they became. The blank tablet view presupposes no innate genetic code or inborn traits; that is, children are born with no predisposition toward any behavior except what is characteristic of human beings. The sum of what a child becomes depends upon the nature and quality of experience; in other words, the primary determinant of what a person becomes is environment.

The blank tablet view has several implications for teaching and child rearing. If children are seen as empty vessels to be filled, the teacher's job is to fill them—to present knowledge without regard to needs, interests, or readiness for learning. What is important is that children learn what is taught. Children become what adults make of them.

This view of children deemphasizes individual differences, and assumes that as children are exposed to the same environmental influences, they will tend to behave and even think the same. This concept is the basis for many educational beliefs and practices in socialist countries. Children begin schooling early, often at six weeks of age, and are taught a standard curriculum that promotes a common political consciousness. They are expected to behave in ways that are consistent with and appropriate to how a citizen of the state should behave.

Growing Plants

Another viewpoint is that of children as growing plants. The role of the educator or parent is similar to that of a gardener, and classrooms and homes are greenhouses where children grow and mature in harmony with their natural growth patterns. A natural consequence of growth and maturing is that children *unfold,* much as the bloom of a flower unfolds under the proper conditions. In other words, what children are to become results from natural growth and a nurturing environment. Two key ingredients of this natural growth and unfolding are *play* and *readiness.* The content and process of learning are included in play, and materials and activities are designed to promote play.

Children become ready for learning through motivation and play. This concept prompts teaching subjects or skills when children reach the point where they can benefit from appropriate instruction. Lack of readiness to learn indicates that the child has not sufficiently matured; the natural process of unfolding has not occurred.

Belief in the concept of unfolding is evident in certain social and educational policies, such as proposals to raise the age requirements for entry into kindergartens and first grade so that children have more time to mature and get ready for school. Many people also believe each child's maturation occurs in accordance with an innate timetable; that there is a "best time" for learning specific tasks. They believe it is important to allow time for children's inner tendencies to develop, and that teachers and parents should not "force" learning. This maturation process is as important, if not more so, than children's experiences. Many contemporary programs operate on the unfolding concept, whether or not it is explicitly stated.

Evidence for the widespread view of children as growing plants is poignantly illustrated by one father's reflections on and about the results and implications of his son's kindergarten screening test. This father was struck by the fact that his son had performed adequately, but not perfectly, and wondered what relevance the kindergarten screening test actually had to his son's future school performance.

> We then went upstairs to water some late seedlings that go into our garden for fall. Radicchio (sorry, but it is good, so expensive and you do bring some urban addictions to the country), broccoli, lettuce and cauliflower. Noah ran his finger over the sprouts and giggled. They tickled. There they were, uncounted dozens of sprouts, all green, all about the same height.
> And it came to me.
> As I nurture and fertilize and pull the weeds that will want to clog this boy's growing-up years, he, too, will come to fruition. I'll have some control over that—some, not total, I realize. He may turn out to be the finest of the group, the biggest broccoli, the finest head of radicchio. He may command respect, praise and a high price in the marketplace of life.[10]

Property

The view has persisted throughout history that children are the property of their parents or of institutions, justified in part by the idea that, as creators of children, parents have a right to them and their labors. Children are, in a real sense, the property of their parents. Parents have broad authority and jurisdiction over a child. Few laws interfere with the right of parents to control their child's life.

Laws (although difficult to enforce) protect children from physical and emotional abuse. Where there are compulsory attendance laws, parents must send their children to school. Generally, however, parents have a free hand in dealing with their children. Legislatures and courts are reluctant to interfere in what is considered a sacrosanct relationship. Parents are generally free to exercise full authority over their children. Within certain broad limits, most parents feel their children are theirs to do with and for as they please. Parents who embrace this view see themselves as decision makers for their children and may place their own best interests above those of their children.

Investments in the Future

Closely associated with the notion of children as property is the view that children represent future wealth or potential for parents and a nation. Since medieval times, people have viewed child rearing as an investment in the future. Many parents assume (not always consciously) that, when they are no longer able to work or must retire, their children will provide for them. Consequently, having children becomes a means to an end. Seeing that children are clothed and fed assures their future economic contribution to their parents.

Over the last several decades, many social policies in the U.S. have been based partly on the view that children are future investments. Many federal programs were built on the underlying assumption that preventing problems in childhood leads to more productive adulthood. An extension of this attitude is that prevention is less expensive than curing a problem. Many local educational programs emphasize identifying the problems of children and their families early, so as to take preventive rather than remedial action. The rationale is that it is less costly in the long run to prevent in the preschool and primary years than it is to remediate in the high school or later years. As educators, we also know that besides being more expensive, remediation is not as effective as prevention.

Particularly during the 1960s, many federal programs were based on the idea of conserving one of the country's greatest resources—its children. Head Start, Follow Through, and child welfare programs are products of this view, which has resulted in a "human capital" or "investment" rationale for child care and other services. As expressed by the Research and Policy Committee of the Committee for Economic Development,

> The most important investment this nation can make is in its children. Although many institutions influence our children's education and development—the family, the community, the church, the media—the focus of this policy statement is on the institution in which the public plays a direct and dominant role: America's public schools.

> •   •   •

> We are convinced that the earliest stages of educational development are where we will receive the best return on our investment in education. This means a stronger focus on the elementary schools and on well-designed preschool programs for children from disadvantaged backgrounds.[11]

The public believes a primary goal of education is to develop children who will be productive and will help protect the nation against "foreign" competition. Therefore, the early education of young children in "good" programs is seen as one way to strengthen the U.S. economically. Thus, the country's best defense against outside forces is a well-educated, economically productive population. From this perspective, then, investing in children is seen as an investment in the United States. T. H. Bell, former Secretary of Education, has stated that "Education is the prime source of economic strength of the country. It produces the intellectual skills which produce the goods and services." For Bell, then, the view that children are our greatest wealth is a focus of his concern that we not continue to waste this potential.[12] Some believe, however, that this view of children as an investment in the future fails to consider children's intrinsic human worth. Trying to make a nation stronger through its children tends to emphasize national priorities over individuals.

CHILDREN'S RIGHTS

A contemporary legal and humanistic view recognizes children as individuals with rights of their own. While children are often still treated as economic commodities and individuals who need protection, their rights are beginning to be defined. Since children are not organized into political groups, others must act as their advocates. Courts and social service agencies are becoming particular champions and defenders.

The International Year of the Child, sponsored by the United Nations in 1979, helped focus attention on the UN's view of the basic rights of children as adopted by the General Assembly. The UN Declaration of the rights of the child included these points:

- [ ] The right to affection, love, and understanding.
- [ ] The right to adequate nutrition and medical care.
- [ ] The right to full opportunity for play and recreation.
- [ ] The right to a name and nationality.
- [ ] The right to special care if handicapped.
- [ ] The right to be among the first to receive relief in times of disaster.
- [ ] The right to learn to be a useful member of society and to develop individual abilities.
- [ ] The right to be brought up in a spirit of peace and brotherhood.
- [ ] The right to enjoy these rights, regardless of race, color, sex, religion, national or social origin.
- [ ] All children, without any exception whatsoever, shall be entitled to these rights, without distinction or discrimination.

Many professions and child advocacy groups also have goals and statements that advocate extension of certain basic rights to children. The National Child Health Goals of the American Academy of Pediatrics are an example:

- [ ] All children should be wanted and born to healthy mothers.
- [ ] All children should be born well.
- [ ] All children should be immunized against the preventable infectious diseases for which there are recommended immunization procedures.
- [ ] All children should have good nutrition.
- [ ] All children should be educated about health and health care systems.
- [ ] All children should live in a safe environment.
- [ ] All children with chronic handicaps should be able to function at their optimal level.
- [ ] All children should live in a family setting with an adequate income to provide basic needs to insure physical, mental and intellectual health.
- [ ] All children should live in an environment that is as free as possible from contaminants.
- [ ] All adolescents and young people should live in a societal setting that recognizes their special health, personal and social needs.[13]

Societal attitudes toward children's rights are often ambivalent. Child abuse laws tend to protect children from physical and emotional abuse; on the other hand, the courts do not consider corporal punishment of school-age children cruel and inhumane treatment. Contemporary advocates of children's rights, such as Richard Farson, feel that society does not recognize the right of children to full humanity:

> Our world is not a good place for children. Every institution in our society discriminates against them. We all come to feel that it is either natural or necessary to cooperate in that

discrimination. Unconsciously we carry out the will of a society which holds a limited and demeaned view of children and which refuses to recognize their right to full humanity.[14]

Some children's rights supporters believe children need advocates to act on their behalf because they are politically disenfranchised, economically disadvantaged, have passive legal status, are the personal property of their parents, and because their lack of experience makes them vulnerable to abuse and exploitation. On the other hand, many people, including parents, feel they should be allowed to raise their children as they think best, free of interference.

Rights are being extended to children in ways that would not have been thought possible ten years ago. Particularly in the area of fetal rights, parents are encountering conflicts between their rights and the lives of their unborn children. Many localities require places that sell liquor to post a sign that says: "Warning: Drinking alcoholic beverages during pregnancy can cause birth defects." Major controversies are arising between the right of the unborn and the rights of pregnant women. Questions such as "What rights of the pregnant woman supersede those of her unborn child?" and "Does the government or other agency have the right to intervene in a woman's life on behalf of her unborn child?" are not easy to answer. Controversy continues between

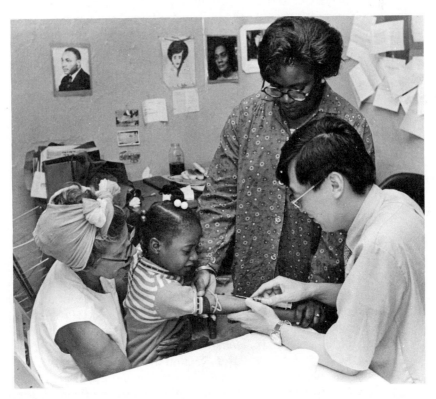

Only about half the states have immunization requirements for child care centers. This oversight represents a serious health problem for the nation's children and denies them a basic right—freedom from preventable diseases.

those groups that advocate for the rights of the unborn fetus and groups that advocate for a mother's rights, including privacy, emotional and physical integrity, and self-determination. Questions as to whose rights take precedence—the fetus's or the mother's—are becoming increasingly polarized.

Generally speaking, people who teach and care for young children are more accepting of laws that extend children's rights. In a survey of early childhood educators, Kerckhoff and McPhee found that 78 percent favored laws giving children more protection, 67 percent favored giving children more rights, 72 percent favored providing an advocate for children, and 51 percent favored making it illegal to sell war toys for children. Further, 41 percent of those surveyed favored providing children with attorneys when their parents are divorcing, and 42 percent favored making it illegal for parents to ridicule their children.[15]

The debate will undoubtedly continue as the rights of children become further defined and clarified through the judicial system. The rights of all children will be examined, and more special interest groups will join the trend to gain even more rights for children.

A review of the ways we see children leads to some intriguing questions. In this generation, are parents and teachers as child-centered as they should be? Are early childhood educators interested in helping children receive the best so they can realize their best? What we know we should do and what we do are often two different things. Public and social policies often supersede our interest in children. Wars, national defense, and economics sometimes take precedence over questions of what is best for children.

CONTEMPORARY INFLUENCES ON EARLY CHILDHOOD EDUCATION

The field of early childhood education is constantly changing as a result of social, political, and economic conditions. These areas influence not only how children are taught, but where and by whom. Economic influences often determine whether we can afford to teach and provide basic care for children. A number of forces and topics influence the nature of early childhood. Some have exerted influence for many years; others are only now emerging, and the exact nature of their influence is yet to be determined.

Women's Movement

The women's movement has had a tremendous and long-lasting influence on young children and early childhood education. A major reason for the interest in infants and infant care is that women want quality out-of-home care for their infants. The National Organization for Women (NOW) is working for a federally funded, 24-hour child care program. True equality for women depends partly on relieving them of the constant care of children. As women have more choices about how best to conduct their lives and the lives of their children, we find more women entering the work force, more divorces, single parenting, and demand for more and better comprehensive child care. The women's movement has helped enlighten parents regarding their rights as parents, including helping them learn how to advocate on behalf of themselves and their children for better health services, child care, and programs for earlier education.

Previously, the public supposed that because parents conceived children, they knew how to provide experiences that would promote intellectual, social, and emotional growth. Today, more people seek help to become effective parents because of the programs and efforts of the women's movement.

Working Parents

More and more families find that both parents need employment to make ends meet. Over 50 percent of mothers with children under six are currently employed or are actively seeking employment, creating a greater need for early childhood programs (see Figure 1–2). This need has brought a beneficial recognition to early childhood programs and prompted early childhood educators to try to meet parents' needs. Unfortunately, the urgent need for child care has encouraged people who are ill-prepared and who do not necessarily have children's or parents' best interests in mind to establish programs. Demand is high enough that good programs have not had a chance to drive inferior programs from the child care marketplace.

For their part, some parents are not able or willing to evaluate programs and select the best ones for their children, which also encourages poor quality programs to stay in operation.

Rising Incomes

Ironically, while the need for two incomes generates interest in early childhood, rising incomes are also a factor. Many parents with college degrees and middle-level incomes

FIGURE 1–2   Increase in Percentage of Mothers in the Labor Force (Source: Bureau of the Census, *Statistical Abstract* 1989.)

are willing to invest money in early education for their children. They look for nursery schools and preschool programs they feel will give their children a good start in life, and many Montessori schools and franchised operations have benefited in the process. In the last several years, the Montessori system has experienced a tremendous boom, both in the number of individuals seeking Montessori teacher training and in preschool enrollments. Many parents of three- and four-year-olds spend almost as much in tuition to send their children to good preschools as parents of eighteen-year-olds spend to send their children to state-supported universities.

Single Parents

The number of one-parent families is increasing, as shown in Figure 1–3. In 1988, more than 25 percent of American families with children were headed by a single parent. People become single parents for a number of reasons. Half of all marriages end in divorce. Some people choose single parenthood; others, such as teenagers, become parents by default. Liberalized adoption procedures, artificial insemination, surrogate childbearing, and general public support for single parents make this lifestyle an attractive option for some people.

No matter how people become single parents, the reality and extent of single parenthood has tremendous implications for early childhood educators. Early childhood programs are having to develop curricula to help children and their parents deal with the stress of family breakups, and teachers are called upon to help children

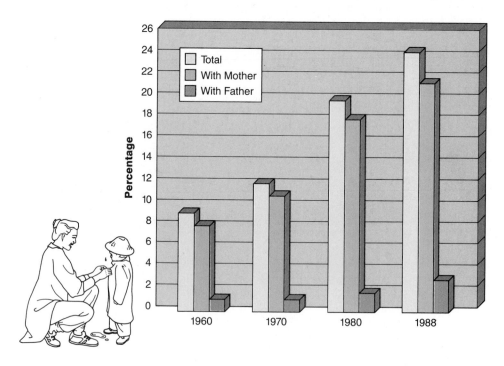

FIGURE 1–3   Increase in Single-Parent Families (Source: Bureau of the Census, *Statistical Abstract* 1989.)

The growing demand for child care services creates interest in early childhood programs and helps raise public expectations about the nature and quality of the programs.

adjust to the guilt they often feel and to their altered family pattern. In addition to child care, single parents frequently seek help in child rearing, especially in regard to discipline. Early childhood educators are often asked to conduct seminars to help parents gain these skills.

A decade ago, early educators were not as concerned about how to help and support single parents and children from single-parent families, but today they recognize that single parents want and need their help. How well early educators adjust to accommodate the needs of single parents may well make the difference in how successful many single parents are in their new roles.

Awareness of the growing number of single-parent families is not enough; we must also understand that within the population as a whole, certain cultural groups are disproportionately represented in single-parent families. Figure 1–4 shows the rapid increase in single-parent families among Hispanics and African-Americans. That increase is attributable to a number of factors. Pregnancy rates are higher among lower socioeconomic groups, and many Hispanics and African-Americans live below the poverty level. Part of the national effort to deal with issues of single-parent families and teenage pregnancy must address economic solutions that will give more people opportunities to be economically self-sufficient and maintain decent standards of

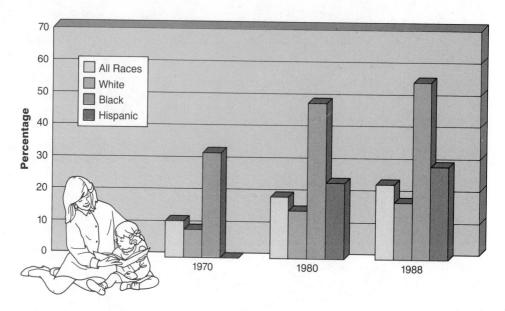

FIGURE 1—4   One-Parent Groups, Mother and Child (Source: Bureau of the Census, *Current Population Reports,* Series P-23, No. 163.)

living. Second, the teenage pregnancy rates in the Hispanic and African-American populations are much higher because of poorer education, economics, and lack of opportunities.

It should come as no surprise that with the rise in single-parent families, there is a reciprocal decline in the number of two-parent families, as shown in Figure 1–5. Part of the increase in single parenting can be attributed to choice and divorce. More educated women are choosing to be single mothers; for example, a director of a major social service agency in a large city who wished to become a parent without the constraints of marriage chose to be artificially inseminated. Other single women choose adoption. Figure 1–6 shows the rising level of education of women who are single parents.

Fathers

A continuing change in early childhood today is that fathers have rediscovered the joys of parenting and working with young children. Men are playing an active role in providing basic care, love, and nurturance to their children. The definition of father has changed; a father is no longer stereotypically unemotional, detached from everyday responsibilities of child care, authoritarian, and a disciplinarian. Fathers no longer isolate themselves from child rearing only because they are male. Men are more concerned about the role of fatherhood and their participation in family events before, during, and after the birth of their children. Fathers want to be involved in the whole process of child rearing. Because so many men feel unprepared for fatherhood,

FIGURE 1–5 Decrease in the Number of Two-Parent Families (Source: Bureau of the Census, *Current Population Reports,* Series P-23, No. 163.)

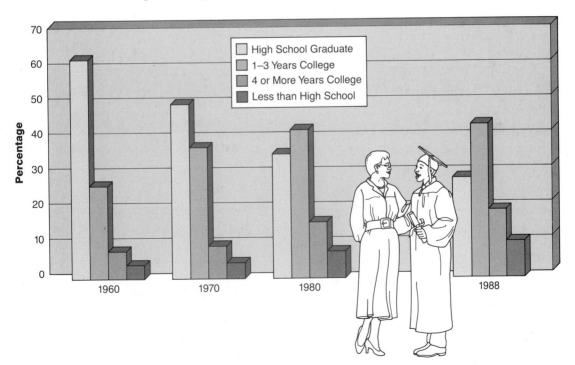

FIGURE 1–6 Years of Education Achieved, Mother-Child Families (Source: Bureau of the Census, *Current Population Reports,* Series P-23, No. 163.)

agencies such as hospitals and community colleges are providing courses and seminars to introduce fathers to the joys, rewards, and responsibilities of fathering.

Fathers no longer quietly acquiesce to giving up custody of their children in a divorce. Men are becoming single parents through adoption and surrogate child-bearing. Figure 1–7 indicates the percentage of single families headed by fathers. Fathers' rights groups have tremendous implications for the family court system and traditional interpretations of family law. Fathers are also receiving some of the employment benefits that have traditionally gone only to women. Paternity leaves, flexible work schedules, and sick leave for family illness are just a few examples of how fathering has come to the workplace.

Early childhood educators are having to readjust their thinking. They are learning how to work with and involve both parents and single fathers. In particular, they are learning how to help fathers overcome cultural stereotypes and prejudices. While one dad who provides family child care or one househusband doesn't create the attention it might have several years ago, taken collectively, males are a strong influence and a definite sign of a growing trend toward equality in parenting roles.

Teenage Parents: Children Having Children

Teenage pregnancies continue to be a problem. Each year one out of ten teenagers—1.1 million—become pregnant. These facts about teenage pregnancy dramatically demonstrate its extent and effects:

☐ One out of ten girls between the ages of 15 and 19 becomes pregnant each year
☐ Fifteen percent of all pregnant teenagers will become pregnant again within a
   year

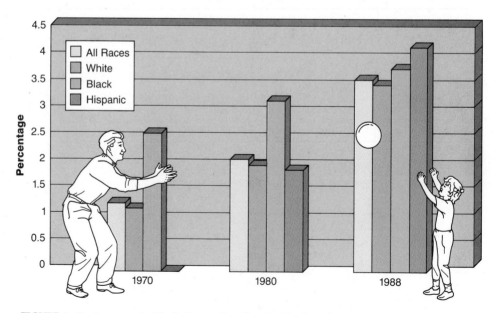

FIGURE 1–7   Increase in Single-Parent Families in Which Father is Present (Source: Bureau of the Census, *Current Population Reports,* Series P-23, No. 163.)

Fathers have rediscovered the joys of parenting and working with young children and are being encouraged and supported in their new roles of shared parenting.

☐ Many teenagers are emotionally and physically unprepared for parenthood

☐ Becoming a teenage parent often means a sudden drastic change in lifestyle

☐ Complications during pregnancy are more likely among teenage girls because their bodies may not be physically mature

☐ Children born to mothers under 18 face greater hazards than those born to older mothers

☐ Many teen parents are forced to reconsider career and educational plans in trying to fulfill the role of parents[16]

☐ The U.S. is among the world's top six developed countries with the highest teenage birthrates

☐ There are 1.3 million children living with 1.1 million teenage mothers; two-thirds of these 1.3 million children were born to mothers age 17 and younger

☐ An additional 1.6 million children under age 5 are living with mothers who were teenage mothers when they gave birth

☐ The risk of infant death is nearly twice as high for teen mothers as for mothers in their early twenties

☐ Of the 1.1 million teenage mothers, two-thirds have not completed high school[17]

Concerned legislators, public policy developers, and national leaders view teenage pregnancy as further evidence of the breakup of the family. They worry about the demand for public health and welfare services; envision a drain on taxpayer dollars;

and decry the loss of future potential because of school dropouts. From an early childhood point of view, teenage pregnancies create greater demand for infant and toddler child care and the need to develop programs to help teenagers learn how to parent. The staff of an early childhood program must often provide nurturance for both child and parent, because the parent herself may not be emotionally mature. Emotional maturity is necessary for a parent to engage in a giving relationship with children. When teenage parents lack parenting characteristics of any kind, early childhood educators must help them develop them.

The Federal Role in Social Service and Education Programs

Beginning about 1980, the federal government began cutting many program budgets, and private agencies and state governments had to take over support of some programs. Other programs had to close, so that some families and children must cope with reduced services or no services at all. Federal monies had a stimulating effect on early childhood programs in the 1960s and 1970s, but cuts have had a dampening effect. Federal budget cuts that affect early childhood and related programs are likely to continue, and federal officials suggest that support from private agencies, contributions, and volunteerism constitute legitimate alternatives to federal funds.

Critics of the declining federal presence in early childhood programs maintain that the results are harmful for women, children and families; they cite increases in the number of women and children living in poverty and a higher infant mortality rate. Reduced funding for early childhood programs requires early childhood educators to be strong advocates on behalf of children and their families. Early educators should be in the vanguard of efforts to influence public policy and develop public awareness about providing for children in the early years.

There is growing evidence that such advocacy is beginning to pay off, as reflected in new efforts to pass federal legislation supporting child care and family support programs. Programs that commit to and depend on federal monies must recognize their vulnerability to shifts in political attitude and swings, both up and down, in federal support. Agencies that provide money can also take away money. Part of the solution to this dilemma is strong advocacy for and development of programs based on multiple funding sources rather than a single source.

The Basic Education Movement

The basic education movement in early childhood advocates early teaching of the basics—reading, writing, arithmetic, and the skills and concepts associated with learning them. While writing might not actually be taught to preschoolers, skills such as holding a pencil, making straight and curved lines, letter identification, and eye-hand coordination activities would be included in the curriculum. The same would be true for reading and mathematics.

The basic education movement has tended to create a sense of urgency in parents, and an accompanying tendency to start schooling at an earlier age, which some people cite as evidence of hurrying, pressuring, and making children grow up too fast.

The issue of what to teach often polarizes between advocates of basic education on the one hand and of progressive education on the other. The basic education viewpoint is the belief that certain basics should receive priority—reading, writing, arithmetic, and cultural heritage. Those who support this point of view generally advocate a no-nonsense approach to education that includes, among other elements, homework, tests, memorization, and strict discipline. The school is a place where hard work and obedience to teacher authority are expected, and the functions of the school are to impart factual knowledge, preserve the cultural heritage, promote basic values such as hard work, and guard the status quo.

Those who believe the school should be child-centered advocate a curriculum based on the "whole child" and developed out of his interests and abilities. John Dewey is credited with fathering the progressive education movement. The progressive curriculum currently finds expression in the open education method.

It is possible to teach just about anything (content) with just about any methodology (process). For example, it is possible to teach basic skills (content) in an open education setting (process) and in a traditionalist or back-to-basics classroom (process). Some parents and educators feel that a particular process precludes teaching a particular content, but this is not so.

THE PUBLIC SCHOOLS AND EARLY EDUCATION

Traditionally, the majority of preschool programs were operated by private agencies or by agencies supported wholly or in part by federal funds to help the poor, unemployed, working parents, and disadvantaged children—but times have changed. Now working and single parents exert great pressure on public school officials and state legislatures to sponsor and fund additional preschool and early childhood programs. The public schools of 14 states provide some degree of funding for programs for four-year-olds. Consequently, public school programs for four-year-olds are a growing reality.

Parents lobby for public support of early childhood education for a number of reasons. First, because working parents cannot find quality child care for their children, they believe the public schools hold the solution to child care needs. Second, the persistent belief that children are a nation's greatest wealth makes it seem sensible to provide services to young children to avoid future school and learning problems. Third, many people believe that early public schooling, especially for children from low-income families, is necessary if the U.S. is to promote equal opportunity for all. They argue that low-income children begin school already far behind their more fortunate middle-class counterparts, and the best way to keep them from falling hopelessly behind is for them to begin school earlier. Fourth, many parents cannot afford quality child care. They believe preschools, furnished at the public's expense, are a reasonable and cost-efficient way to meet child care needs.

A fifth reason for the demand for public school involvement relates to the "competent child." Parents want academic programs for their children at an earlier age, and look, naturally, to the public schools to provide programs that will help their children succeed in life. Sixth, baby-boom parents are the best educated in American history. One in four men and one in five women have college degrees.[18] These well-educated parents are causing a boom in preschool programs that emphasize earlier and more comprehensive education for young children.

Television has given today's children a door to the world of adulthood. Television offers entertainment and educational benefits, but also exposes children to violence and a degree of sophistication that earlier generations did not have to deal with.

There have been discussions at the federal level about how to link programs such as Head Start more closely to the public schools. With continuing cuts in educational programs, there may be greater effort to effect such linkages, and many public schools have already moved into the area of child care. There are several arguments in favor of a realignment. First, some educators don't think it makes sense to train nonteachers for preschool work when trained teachers are available. Second, some educators think it is reasonable to put the responsibility for educating and caring for the nation's children under the sponsorship of one agency—the public schools. For their part, public school teachers and the unions that represent them are anxious to bring early childhood programs within the structure of the public school system.

There is by no means consensus that there should be universal public schooling or even anything approaching it. Critics of the effort to place preschool programs in the public schools cite three reasons against such a policy. First, they cite the failure of public education to do a good job of teaching young children. They ask how public schools can handle an expanded role if they have not done a good job with what they are already supposed to do. Second, some critics say that public school teachers are not trained in the specific skills needed in Head Start, child care, and other preschool programs. A third, more convincing argument relates to money: the cost of having the public schools assume the responsibility of preschool programs would probably cost over several billion dollars, which taxpayers are unlikely to be willing to pay.

FURTHER READING

Brooks, Andrée Aelion. *Children of Fast-track Parents: Raising Self-sufficient and Confident Children in an Achievement-oriented World* (New York: Viking, 1989)

Brooks identifies a new American childhood, populated by baby-boom parents whose drive for success and accomplishment has created a generation of angry and distressed children. The author provides specific suggestions to counteract the effects of the resulting alienation.

Cleverley, Joan, and D.C. Phillips. *Visions of Childhood: Influential Models from Locke to Spock,* Revised Edition (New York: Teachers College Press, 1986)

Updated focus on major ideas and theories of child rearing and educational practices. Examines major contributions of Freud, Piaget, Dewey, and many others; provides solid foundation of philosophy and fundamentals of early childhood education.

Davidson, J.I. *Children and Computers Together in the Early Childhood Classroom,* ed. Jay Whitney (Albany, N.Y.: Delmar, 1988)

Topics include why to have computers in the classroom, how to set up computers, how to select software, and activities for computer use. Written primarily for the novice.

Galinsky, Ellen, and David, Judy. *The Preschool Years: Family Strategies that Work from Experts and Parents* (New York: Time Books, 1988)

A contemporary view of parenting that recommends strategies for balancing commitments of parents to child rearing, home, and careers. Includes information on child and parent development, models for problem solving, and insights into conflicts between parents and preschoolers.

Greenberg, Martin. *The Birth of a Father* (New York: Continuum, 1985)

The author states, "The event of fatherhood is a momentous occurrence in the life cycle of man. It inevitably triggers . . . emotions that are multi-faceted and often tumultuous." Prospective parents need to read Greenberg's book.

Littwin, Susan. *The Postponed Generation: Why America's Grown-up Kids Are Growing Up Later* (New York: William Morrow, 1986)

Explores the "startling trend" of a generation of young people who are postponing the responsibilities and autonomy of adulthood and the social, economic, and emotional factors that have caused this turnabout in traditional expectations.

Hochschild, Arlie, and Machung, Anne. *The Second Shift: Inside the Two-job Marriage* (New York: Penguin, 1989)

Based on interviews with 50 working families, the authors maintain that women are in the midst of a stalled revolution. Their work outside the home has resulted in little change in the home. Women are still primarily responsible for parenting and housekeeping during the second, or domestic, shift.

Postman, Neil. *The Disappearance of Childhood* (New York: Delacorte Press, 1982)

Postman argues convincingly that childhood is disappearing at "dazzling speed." He credits the Renaissance with creating childhood as a social structure and psychological condition, and blames electronic media for the disappearance of childhood.

Osborne, Philip. *Parenting for the '90s* (Intercourse, Pa.: Good Books, 1989)

This book cuts through many of the trendy ideas of the last decade and provides parents with a meaningful framework for parenting. Helps parents help their children grow within the parents' value system.

Schorr, Lisbeth B. and Schorr, Daniel. *Within Our Reach: Breaking the Cycle of Disadvantage* (New York: Doubleday, 1988)

A valuable book that has created a great deal of interest in what works and doesn't work in national efforts to break cycles of poverty and dependency. Suggests many "progressive" solutions to social and educational problems in the '90s.

FURTHER STUDY

1. Would you consider sending your own child to a nursery school (or any type of care setting) at age four? Why or why not?
2. Interview parents who are actively involved in children's programs and others who are not. Are there noticeable differences in their children or in the parents?
3. Research the theories of children as "growing plants" and as "property." How have these theories influenced today's views of children?
4. Contact different agencies to gather information about single parenting, teenage parenting, legal separation rights, and custody of young children. How are these social forces affecting early childhood education programs in your state and local community?
5. Identify and define terms that summarize how young children are viewed in today's society.
6. Observe parent-child relationships in public settings such as supermarkets, laundries, and restaurants. What do these relationships tell you about parent-child interactions and how parents rear their children? What implications do these relationships have for how the child is taught in school?
7. Critique the issues presented in this chapter. What issues are most significant? What other issues do you feel should be included? Defend your selections.
8. Given a limited amount of community resources to spend on education for young children, how would you spend it? Establish priorities for services.
9. Find out what problems teachers in your schools face as a result of divorce, abuse, and other types of stress in children's lives.
10. Find out what types of nursery school programs are available in your community. Who may attend them? How are they financed? What percentage of the children who attend have mothers who work outside the home?

11. Find advertisements for child care in the classified ads of newspapers and the yellow pages of the telephone directory. Call or visit one of these programs. Based on the information you obtain, tell why you would or would not send your child to the program.
12. Visit attorneys, legal aid societies, juvenile courts, and other agencies. List the legal rights children already have. Do you think children have some rights they should not have? Which ones? Why?
13. List certain rights that children do not have that you think should be extended to them. Justify your response.
14. List factors that support the argument that childhood is disappearing or has disappeared. Then make a list to support the opposite viewpoint— that childhood is not disappearing.
15. What actions do you think government, schools, and other agencies could take to curtail the disappearance of childhood?
16. What useful purposes does childhood serve?
17. Ask parents and early childhood educators about their views of the very young. How do their views differ from yours? What implications do your data have for parenting and child care?
18. List at least five social, political, and economic conditions of modern society and explain how these conditions influence how people view, treat, and care for the very young.
19. Use specific descriptions to illustrate how views discussed in this chapter influence caregiver practices.
20. List at least five significant contributions you believe good early childhood education programs can make in the lives of young children.
21. Over a period of several weeks or a month, collect articles from newspapers and popular magazines relating to infants, toddlers, and preschoolers. Then, (a) Categorize these articles by topics; for example, child abuse. What topics were given the most coverage? Why? (b) What are the emerging topics or trends in early ed-

ucation, according to newspaper and magazine coverage? (c) Do you agree with everything you read? Can you find instances in which information or advice may be inaccurate, inappropriate, or contradictory?

22. The emphasis on early education has prompted some critics and experts to charge that parents and early childhood educators are making children grow up too soon, too fast. (a) Interview parents and preschool teachers to determine their views on this topic. (b) How do you agree or disagree with the data you gathered?

23. Recall your own childhood. Do you think your parents pushed you through childhood too quickly? Or did you have a relaxed, unhurried childhood?

24. Interview single parents and determine the following: (a) What effects and influences does single parenting have on children? (b) In what ways is single parenting stressful to parents and children? (c) How can early childhood programs support and help single parents?

25. Review early childhood literature and daily newspapers to identify statements of public policy and issues relating to public policy. (a) What are the issues involved in each? (b) In what ways do you agree or disagree with these policies?

NOTES

1. Anne Mitchell, "Old Baggage, New Visions: Shaping Policy for Early Childhood Programs," *Phi Delta Kappan,* 70 (1989), p. 666.

2. National Academy of Early Childhood Programs, *Accreditation Criteria and Procedures* (Washington, D.C.: National Association for the Education of Young Children, 1984), p. x.

3. National Association for the Education of Young Children, *Early Childhood Teacher Education Guidelines* (Washington, D.C.: NAEYC, 1982), p. xii.

4. Urie Bronfenbrenner, *The Ecology of Human Development* (Cambridge, Mass.: Harvard University Press, 1979), p. 3.

5. Neil Postman, *The Disappearance of Childhood* (New York: Delacorte Press, 1982), p. 80.

6. Vance Packard, *Our Endangered Children: Growing Up in a Changing World* (Boston: Little, Brown, 1983), p. xx.

7. David Elkind, "Formal Education and Early Education: An Essential Difference," *Phi Delta Kappan* 67 (1986), p. 634.

8. Susan Littwin, *The Postponed Generation: Why America's Grown-up Kids Are Growing Up Later* (New York: William Morrow, 1986), p. 21.

9. John Locke, *An Essay Concerning Human Understanding* (New York: Dover Publications, 1959), pp. 92–93.

10. Paul Wilkes, "The First Test of Childhood," *Newsweek,* 114 (1989), p. 8.

11. Committee for Economic Development, *Investing in Our Children: Business and the Public Schools* (New York: The Committee, 1985), pp. 1, 9.

12. T.H. Bell, Distinguished Visiting Professor Series. Miami Dade Community College, March 2, 1989.

13. AAP Child Health Goals, *News and Comment,* vol. 29, no. 3, March 1978. Copyright © American Academy of Pediatrics 1978.

14. Richard Farson, *Birthrights* (New York: Macmillan, 1978), p. 1.

15. Richard K. Kerckhoff and Jeffrey McPhee, "Receptivity to Child-Rights Legislation: A Survey," *Young Children* 39:58–61.

16. "What You Should Know About Teen Parenthood," © 1982; "What You Should Know About Teenage Pregnancy," © 1983, Channing L. Bete Co., Inc., South Deerfield, MA 01373.

17. United Nations Children's Fund, *UNICEF Facts and Figures* (New York: UNICEF, 1989).

18. Brad Edmondson, "The Education of Children," *American Demographics* 8 (1986):28.

CHAPTER 2
Historical Influences
People, Events, and Accomplishments

As you read and study:

☐ Identify why it is important to know about the ideas and theories of great educators.

☐ Analyze and develop a basic understanding of the beliefs of Luther, Comenius, Locke, Rousseau, Pestalozzi, Owen, Froebel, Montessori, Dewey, and Piaget.

☐ Understand how the beliefs and ideas of great educators have influenced and continue to influence early childhood programs.

☐ Identify basic concepts that are essential to high quality early childhood programs and education.

☐ Develop an appreciation for others' professional accomplishments and contributions to the field of early childhood education.

☐ Develop knowledge of and respect for events that have had significant influences on the field of early childhood education.

☐ Understand how people, agencies, and legislation influence early childhood education.

There are at least five important reasons to know about the ideas and theories of great educators who have influenced the field of early childhood education. First, by reading of the hopes, ideas, and accomplishments of people your profession judges famous, you will realize that today's ideas are not necessarily new. Old ideas and theories have a way of being reborn. Topics such as individualized instruction, compensatory education, open education, behavior modification, and basic education have been discussed since the 1400s. Maria Montessori, for example was a proponent of open education, which was popular in the '70s and is now being renewed in the '90s. We can more fully appreciate the premises of open education and other programs in early education if we have at least a rudimentary understanding of Montessori and the thinkers who influenced her, such as Pestalozzi and Froebel. Montessori's influences, in turn, are found in many modern materials, activities and programs.

Second, many ideas of the earlier educators are still dreams, despite the advances we think modern education has made. In this regard, we are the inheritors of a long line of thinkers as far back as Socrates and Plato. We should acknowledge this inheritance and use it as a base to build meaningful teaching careers and lives for children and their families.

Third, ideas expressed by the early educators help us better understand how to implement current teaching strategies. For instance, Rousseau, Froebel, and Montessori all believed children should be taught with dignity and respect. This attitude toward children is essential to an understanding of good educational practice and often makes the difference between good and bad teaching.

Fourth, theories about how young children grow, develop and learn decisively shape educational and child rearing practices. Some parents and teachers may not realize, however, what assumptions form the foundations of their daily practices. Studying and examining beliefs of the great educators helps parents and early childhood educators clarify what they do and gives them insight into their actions. In this sense, knowing about theories liberates the uninformed from ignorance and empowers professionals and parents. As a consequence, they are able to implement developmentally appropriate practices with confidence.

Fifth, exploring, analyzing, and discovering the roots of early childhood education helps *inspire* professionals. Recurring rediscovery forces people to examine current practices against what others have advocated. Examining sources of beliefs helps clarify modern practice, and reading and studying others' ideas makes us rethink our own beliefs and positions. In this regard, the history of the great educators and their beliefs can keep us current. When we pause long enough to listen to what they have to say, we frequently find a new insight or idea that motivates us to continue our quest to be the best we can be.

MARTIN LUTHER

While the primary impact of the Protestant Reformation was religious, other far-reaching effects were secular. Two of these were *universal education* and *literacy*, both topics very much in the news today.

In Europe, the sixteenth century was a time of great social, religious, and economic upheaval, due partly to the Renaissance and partly to the Reformation. Great emphasis was placed on formal schooling to teach children how to read, the impetus for which is generally attributed to Martin Luther (1483–1546), the father of the Reformation.

The question of what to teach is an issue in any educational endeavor. Does society create schools and then decide what to teach, or do the needs of society determine what schools it will establish to meet desired goals? In the case of European education, the necessity of establishing schools to teach children to read was an issue raised by Martin Luther. Simply stated, Luther replaced the authority of the hierarchy of the Catholic Church with the authority of the Bible. Believing that each person was free to work out his own salvation through the Scriptures meant that people had to learn to read the Bible in their native tongue.

This concept marked the real beginning of teaching and learning in the people's native language, the *vernacular,* as opposed to Latin, the official language of the

The great educators believed that parents were their children's primary teachers. Teaching parents to read is as important as teaching their children to read, so that parents will be able to provide an intergenerational basis for literacy.

Catholic Church. Before the Reformation, only the wealthy or those preparing for a religious vocation learned to read or write Latin. One of the early tasks undertaken by Luther was the translation of the Bible into German; the Bible thus became available to the people in their own language, and the Protestant Reformation, under the impetus of Luther, encouraged and supported popular universal education.

Luther believed the family was the most important institution in the education of children. To this end, he encouraged parents to provide religious instruction and vocational education in the home. Throughout his life Luther remained a champion of education. He wrote letters and treatises and preached sermons on the subject. His best known letter on education is the *Letter to the Mayors and Aldermen of All the Cities of Germany in Behalf of Christian Schools,* written in 1524. In this letter, Luther argues for public support of education.

> Therefore it will be the duty of the mayors and council to exercise the greatest care over the young. For since the happiness, honor, and life of the city are committed to their hands, they would be held recreant before God and the world, if they did not, day and night, with all their power, seek its welfare and improvement. Now the welfare of a city does not consist alone in great treasures, firm walls, beautiful houses, and munitions of war; indeed, where all these are found, and reckless fools come into power, the city sustains the greatest injury. But the highest welfare, safety, and power of a city consists in able, learned, wise, upright, cultivated citizens, who can secure, preserve, and utilize every treasure and advantage.[1]

Out of the Reformation came other religious denominations, all interested in preserving the faith and keeping their followers within the fold of their church. Most of the major denominations such as Calvinism and Lutheranism established their own schools to provide literacy and knowledge about the faith. Education and schooling were considered not only socializing forces, but also means of religious and moral instruction. Many religious groups have always had rather extensive school programs, for this is one way to help assure that children born into the faith will continue in the faith. Religious schools are a means of defending and perpetuating the faith as well as a place where converts can learn about and become strong in the faith.

JOHN AMOS COMENIUS

Comenius (1592–1670) was born in Moravia, a former province of Czechoslovakia, and became a minister of Moravian faith. Comenius spent his life serving as a bishop, teaching school, and writing textbooks. Of his many writings, those that have received the most attention are *The Great Didactic* and the *Orbis Pictus (The World in Pictures),* considered the first picture book for children.

Just as Luther's religious beliefs formed the basis for his educational ideas, so too with John Comenius. In fact, throughout this discussion of the influence of great men and women on educational thought and practice, you will see a parallel interest in religion and education. It has always been obvious to religious followers that what they believe gives shape, form, and substance to what they will teach, and to a large degree, what is taught determines the extent to which the religious beliefs are maintained and extended.

Comenius believed that humans are born in the image of God. Therefore, each individual has an obligation and duty to be educated to the fullest extent of one's abilities so as to fulfill this godlike image. Since so much depends on education, then, as far as Comenius was concerned, it should begin in the early years.

> It is the nature of everything that comes into being, that while tender it is easily bent and formed, but that, when it has grown hard, it is not easy to alter. Wax, when soft, can be easily fashioned and shaped; when hard it cracks readily. A young plant can be planted, transplanted, pruned, and bent this way or that. When it has become a tree these processes are impossible.[2]

Comenius became an advocate of universal education that began at an early age and continued through adulthood. He also believed in the essential goodness of man. Because one of his fundamental beliefs was that people are essentially good, he believed that education should be a positive learning experience that includes freedom, joy, and pleasure. This contrasts sharply to the concept of education as discipline, consisting partly of a rigid, authoritarian atmosphere designed to control children's natural inclination to do bad things. In modern terms, the argument is whether children learn better in an authoritarian setting characterized by traditional classrooms, or in a child-centered setting that encourages autonomy and self-regulation.

Another of Comenius's basic beliefs was that education should follow the order of nature. Following this natural order implies a timetable for growth and learning, and early childhood educators must observe this pattern to avoid forcing learning before children are ready. This belief is reflected in Montessori's concept of sensitive periods,

Play is the basis for learning in early childhood. All great educators encouraged development of programs that provide for play.

Piaget's stages of development, and the perennial issue of readiness and learning. Comenius also thought that learning is best achieved when the senses are involved, and that sensory education formed the basis for all learning.

> Those things, therefore, that are placed before the intelligence of the young, must be real things and not the shadows of things. I repeat, they must be *things;* and by the term I mean determinate, real, and useful things that can make an impression on the senses and on the imagination. But they can only make this impression when brought sufficiently near.
>
> From this a golden rule for teachers may be derived. Everything should, as far as is possible, be placed before the senses. Everything visible should be brought before the organs of sight, everything audible before that of hearing. Odours should be placed before the sense of smell, and things that are tastable and tangible before the sense of taste and of touch respectively. If an object can make an impression on several senses at once, it should be brought into contact with several.[3]

We see an extension and refinement of Comenius's principle in the works of Montessori and Piaget and in contemporary programs that stress manipulation of concrete objects.

Comenius gave some good advice when he said that the golden rule of teaching should be to place everything before the senses. Because of his belief in sensory education, Comenius thought children should not be taught the names of objects apart from the objects themselves or pictures of the objects. His *Orbis Pictus* helped children learn the names of things and concepts through pictures and words. As the name implies, *Orbis Pictus* pictured the world as it was during Comenius's time. Comenius's emphasis on the concrete and sensory is a pedagogical principle early childhood educators still try to fully grasp and implement. Many modern programs, such as those derived from Montessori's ideas, stress sensory learning. Many early childhood materials use learning activities that promote learning through the senses.

A broad view of Comenius's total concept of education can be gained by an examination of some of his principles of teaching:

> Following in the footsteps of nature we find that the process of education will be easy
> (i) If it begins early, before the mind is corrupted.
> (ii) If the mind be duly prepared to receive it.
> (iii) If it proceed from the general to the particular.
> (iv) And from what is easy to what is more difficult.
> (v) If the pupil be not overburdened by too many subjects.
> (vi) And if progress be slow in every case.
> (vii) If the intellect be forced to nothing to which its natural bent does not incline it, in accordance with its age and with the right method.
> (viii) If everything be taught through the medium of the senses.
> (ix) And if the use of everything taught be continually kept in view.
> (x) If everything be taught according to one and the same method.
> These, I say, are the principles to be adopted if education is to be easy and pleasant.[4]

There is a noticeable trend in education today to make learning, as Comenius suggested, easier and more pleasant. Probably the two most significant contributions of Comenius to today's education are textbooks with illustrations and the emphasis in most early childhood programs on training the senses. We take the former for granted, and naturally assume that the latter is necessary as a basis for learning.

JOHN LOCKE

As mentioned in Chapter 1, John Locke (1632–1704) popularized the *blank tablet* view of children. This and other of his views influence modern early childhood education and practice. Indeed, the extent of Locke's influence is probably unappreciated by many who daily implement practices based on his theories. More precisely, Locke developed the theory of and laid the foundation for *environmentalism*—the belief that it is the environment, not innate characteristics, that determine what a person will become.

Locke, born in Somerset, England, was a medical doctor, philosopher, and social scientist. His ideas about education were first applied when his cousin and her husband asked him for child rearing advice. His letters to them were published in 1693 as *Some Thoughts Concerning Education*. Many of his philosophical ideas that directly relate to education are also found in *An Essay Concerning Human Understanding*. Locke's assumption of human learning and nature was that there are no innate ideas, which gave rise to his theory of the mind as a blank tablet or "white paper." As Locke explains,

> Let us suppose the mind to be, as we say, white paper void of all characters, without ideas. How comes it to be furnished? Whence comes it by that vast store which the busy and

Although parents and the environment are not the only influences on children's development, as Rousseau maintained, they and other caregivers do have a powerful role in shaping the course of their development.

boundless fancy of man has painted on it with an almost endless variety? Whence has it all the materials of reason and knowledge? To this I answer, in one word, from *experience;* in that all our knowledge is founded, and from that it ultimately derives itself.[5]

For Locke, then, the environment forms the mind. The implications of this idea are clearly reflected in modern educational practice. The notion of the primacy of environmental influences is particularly evident in programs that encourage and promote early education as a means of overcoming or compensating for a poor or disadvantaged environment. Based partly on the assumption that all children are born with the same general capacity for mental development and learning, these programs also assume that differences in learning and achievement are attributable to environmental factors such as home background, early education, and experiences. Programs of early schooling, especially the current move for public schooling for four-year-olds, work on the premise that children's differences arise because disadvantaged children fail to have the experiences of their more advantaged counterparts that are necessary for school success. In fact, it is not uncommon, as evidenced by Head Start and programs in Texas and Florida, to limit early schooling to those who are considered disadvantaged and to design it especially for them. Because Locke believed that experiences determine the nature of the individual, sensory training became a prominent feature in the application of his theory to education. He and others who followed him believed that the best way to make children receptive to experiences was to train their senses. In this regard, Locke exerted considerable influence on others, particularly Maria Montessori, who developed her system of early education based on sensory training.

JEAN JACQUES ROUSSEAU

Jean Jacques Rousseau (1712–1778) was born in Geneva, Switzerland, but spent most of his life in France. He is best remembered by educators for his book *Emile,* in which he raises a hypothetical child from birth to adolescence. Rousseau's theories were radical for his time. The opening lines of *Emile* not only set the tone for Rousseau's educational views, but for many of his political ideas as well. "God makes all things good; man meddles with them and they become evil."[6]

Rousseau advocated a return to nature and a natural approach to educating children, called *naturalism.* To Rousseau, naturalism meant abandoning society's artificiality and pretentiousness. A naturalistic education would permit growth without undue interference or restrictions. Indeed, Rousseau wanted Emile to admire and emulate Daniel Defoe's Robinson Crusoe as an example of a resourceful person living close to and in harmony with nature. Rousseau would probably argue against such modern practices as dress codes, compulsory attendance, minimum basic skills, frequent and standardized testing, and ability grouping, because they are "unnatural." There is some tendency in American education to emphasize naturalism by replacing practices such as regimentation, compulsory assignments, and school-imposed regulations with less structured processes.

According to Rousseau, natural education promotes and encourages qualities such as happiness, spontaneity, and the inquisitiveness associated with childhood. In his method, parents and teachers allow children to develop according to their natural abilities and do not interfere with development by forcing education upon them or by protecting them from the corrupting influences of society. Rousseau felt that Emile's education occurred through three sources: nature, people, and things. As Rousseau elaborates,

> All that we lack at birth and need when grown up is given us by education. This education comes to us from nature, from men, or from things. The internal development of our faculties and organs is the education of nature. . . . It is not enough merely to keep children alive. They should learn to bear the blows of fortune; to meet either wealth or poverty, to live if need be in the frosts of Iceland or on the sweltering rock of Malta.[7]

Rousseau believed, however, that although we have control over the education that comes from social and sensory experiences, we have no control over natural growth. In essence, this is the idea of *unfolding,* in which the nature of children—what they are to be—unfolds as a result of maturation according to their innate timetables. We should observe the child's growth and provide experiences at appropriate times. Some educators have interpreted this notion as a *laissez-faire* approach.

Educational historians point to Rousseau as dividing the historical and modern periods of education. Rousseau established a way of thinking about the young child that is reflected in innovators of educational practice such as Pestalozzi and Froebel. His concept of natural unfolding echoes Comenius and appears in current programs that stress readiness as a factor of learning. Piaget's developmental stages reinforce Rousseau's thinking about the importance of natural development. Educational practices that provide an environment in which children can become autonomous and self-regulating have a basis in his philosophy. The common element in all the approaches that advocate educating in a free and natural environment is the view of children as essentially good and capable of great achievement. It is the responsibility of teachers and parents to apply the right educational strategy at the right period of readiness for this potential to be fulfilled.

Perhaps the most famous contemporary example of the laissez-faire approach to child rearing and education is found in A.S. Neill's book, *Summerhill,* which is also the name of his famous school. Neill presents a strong case for freedom and self-regulation. He and his wife wanted "to make the school fit the child—instead of making the child fit the school." Therefore,

> We set out to make a school in which we should allow children freedom to be themselves. In order to do this, we had to renounce all discipline, all direction, all suggestion, all moral training, all religious instruction. We have been called brave, but it did not require courage. All it required was what we had—a complete belief in the child as good, not an evil, being. For almost forty years, this belief in the goodness of the child has never wavered; it rather has become a final faith.[8]

JOHANN HEINRICK PESTALOZZI

Pestalozzi (1746–1827) was born in Zurich, Switzerland. He was greatly influenced by Rousseau and his *Emile.* In fact, Pestalozzi was so impressed by Rousseau's back-to-nature concepts that he purchased a farm that he hoped would become a center for new and experimental methods in agriculture. While engaged in farming, Pestalozzi became more and more interested in education and, in 1774, started a school called Neuhof at his farm. At Neuhof, Pestalozzi developed his ideas of the integration of

Activities of daily living offer young children opportunities to learn responsibilities, develop self-confidence, and practice skills associated with schooling.

home life, vocational education, and education for reading and writing. Because the cost of trying his ideas was much greater than the tuition he was able to collect, this educational enterprise went bankrupt.

Pestalozzi spent the next twenty years writing about his educational ideas and practices. From such writings as *Leonard and Gertrude,* which was read as a romantic novel rather than for its educational ideas, Pestalozzi became well known as a writer and educator. He spent his later years developing and perfecting his ideas at various schools throughout Europe.

Rousseau's influence is most apparent in Pestalozzi's belief that education should follow the child's nature. His dedication to this concept is demonstrated by his rearing his only son, Jean Jacques, using *Emile* as a guide. His methods were based upon harmonizing nature and educational practices.

> And what is this method? It is a method which simply follows the path of Nature, or, in other words, which leads the child slowly, and by his own efforts, from sense-impressions to abstract ideas. Another advantage of this method is that it does not unduly exalt the master, inasmuch as he never appears as a superior being, but, like kindly Nature, lives and works with the children, his equals, seeming rather to learn with them than to teach them with authority.[9]

Unfortunately, Pestalozzi did not have much success rearing his son according to Rousseau's tenets, as evidenced by Jean Jacques's inability to read and write by the age of twelve. This may be due either to his physical condition (he was thought to be epileptic), or to Pestalozzi's inability to translate Rousseau's abstract ideas into practice. Pestalozzi was able, however, to develop his own pedagogical ideas as a result of the process.

Probably the most important lesson from Pestalozzi's experience is that if learning is to occur, educators cannot rely solely on children's own initiative. Although some children can teach themselves to read, others have created the climate and conditions for that beginning reading process. To expect that children will be or can be responsible for learning basic skills by themselves is simply asking too much.

Pestalozzi believed all education is based on sensory impressions, and that through the proper sensory experiences, children would reach natural potential. This belief led to "object lessons." As the name implies, Pestalozzi thought the best way to learn many concepts was through manipulative experiences, such as counting, measuring, feeling, and touching. Pestalozzi believed the best teachers were those who taught children, not subjects. He also believed in multiage grouping. Pestalozzi anticipated by about 150 years the many parent programs that teach parents to work with young children in the home. He believed mothers could best teach their children and wrote two books, *How Gertrude Teaches Her Children* and *Book for Mothers,* detailing procedures for doing this. He felt that "the time is drawing near when methods of teaching will be so simplified that each mother will be able not only to teach her children without help, but continue her own education at the same time."[10]

ROBERT OWEN

As is so often the case, people who affect and influence the course of educational thought and practice are visionaries in political and social affairs as well. Robert Owen (1771–1858) is no exception. Owen's influences on education resulted from his entrepreneurial activities associated with New Lanark, a model mill town he managed in Great Britain. Owen was an *environmentalist*; that is, he believed that the environment in which children are reared is the main contributing factor to what they believe and how they behave. Consequently, Owen maintained that society and persons acting in the best interests of society can shape children's individual characters. Owen and other *Utopians* like him believed that by controlling the circumstances and consequent outcomes of child rearing, it was possible to build a new and perhaps more perfect society. Such a deterministic view of child rearing and education pushes free will to the background and makes environmental conditions the predominate force in directing and determining human behavior. This is how Owen explained it:

> Any character, from the best to the worst, from the most ignorant to the most enlightened may be given to any community, even to the world at large, by the application of proper means; which means are to a great extent at the command and under the control of those who have influence in the affairs of men.[11]

Owen believed that good traits were instilled at an early age and that a child's behavior was influenced primarily by the environment. Thus, in Owen, we see influences of both Locke's theory of blank tablet and Rousseau's theory of innate goodness. To implement his beliefs, Owen opened an infant school in 1861 at New Lanark, designed to provide care for children while their parents were working in his mills. Part of Owen's motivation for opening the infant schools was to get the children away from their uneducated parents. Indeed, to provide for the education of his workers and transform them into "rational beings," Owen opened a night school for the workers.

Owen's infant school included activities of dancing, singing, and listening to and reciting rhymes written by James Buchanan, who directed the school. This is one of the rhymes:

> Hark to me and silence keep,
> And you will hear about the sheep;
> For sheep are useful and you know
> That on their backs the wool does grow.
> The sheep are taken once a year,
> And plunged in water cool and clear
> And there they swim and never bite
> While men do wash and clean them white.[12]

Owen also had Utopian ideas regarding communal living and practice. In 1824, he purchased the village of New Harmony, Indiana, for a grand experiment in communal living. Part of the community included a center for 100 infants. The New Harmony experiment failed, but Owen's legacy lived on in the infant schools of England. These eventually developed into kindergartens, influenced by European educators.

A consistent theme of the great educators is that play enhances children's growth and development. Today's early childhood educators are charged with bringing meaningful play into their programs.

Several things about Owen's efforts and accomplishments are noteworthy. First, Owen's infant school preceded Froebel's kindergarten by about a quarter of a century. Second, Owen's ideas and practices influenced educators as to the importance of early education and the relationship between education and societal improvements, which is an idea much in vogue in current educational practice. In addition, not unlike Owen's time, early childhood educators and other professionals today are seeking through education to reform society and provide a better world for all humankind.

FRIEDRICH WILHELM FROEBEL

Born in Germany, Froebel (1782–1852) devoted his life to developing a system for the education of young children. While his contemporary, Pestalozzi, with whom he studied and worked, advocated a system for teaching, Froebel developed a curriculum and methodology. In the process, Froebel earned the distinction of "father of the kindergarten." As a result of his close relationship with Pestalozzi and of reading the works of Rousseau, Froebel decided to open a school and put his ideas into practice. Like some other great people, Froebel was not eminently successful in either his personal or professional life. Some reasons for the lack of recognition during his lifetime were his inability to find educators who were interested in his ideas and accompanying personal problems. In his early years, Froebel was supported both financially and emotionally by his brother's widow, who as a result of this support had expectations of marriage. When this union did not materialize, Froebel's relatives mounted an attack on him and his ideas. This animosity lasted throughout his life and prevented, in several instances, the adoption of his ideas by others. It was only at the end of his life that he and his methods received the recognition they so richly deserved.

Froebel's primary contributions to educational thought and practice are in the areas of learning, curriculum, methodology, and teacher training. His concept of children and how they learn was based, in part, on the idea of unfolding, held by Comenius and Pestalozzi before him. The educator's role, whether parent or teacher, was to observe this natural unfolding and provide activities that would enable children to learn what they are ready to learn. The teacher's role, in essence, was to help children develop their inherent qualities for learning. In this sense, the teacher was a designer of experiences and activities. This notion of teacher as facilitator would be reinforced later by both Montessori and Piaget, both undoubtedly influenced by Froebel, who believed that:

> Therefore, education in instruction and training, originally and in its first principles, should necessarily be *passive, following* (only guarding and protecting), *not prescriptive, categorical, interfering.*
>
> Indeed, in its very essence, education should have these characteristics; for the undisturbed operation of the Divine Unity is necessarily good—cannot be otherwise than good. This necessity implies that the young human being—as it were, still in process of creation— would seek, although still unconsciously, as a product of nature, yet decidedly and surely, that which is in itself best; and, moreover, in a form wholly adapted to his condition, as well as to his disposition, his powers, and means.[13]

Consistent with his idea of unfolding, comparable to the process of a flower blooming from a bud, Froebel compared the child to a seed that is planted, germinates,

Froebel compared the child to a seed and likened caregivers to gardeners. As discussed in Chapter 1, the view of children as growing plants and of their development as unfolding is a prevalent and powerful one in contemporary society.

brings forth a new shoot, and grows from a young, tender plant to a mature fruit-producing one. He likened the role of educator to that of gardener. In his kindergarten, or "garden of children," he envisioned children being educated in close harmony with their own nature and the nature of the universe. Children unfold their uniqueness in play, and it is in the area of play that Froebel makes one of his greatest contributions to the curriculum of the preschool.

> Play is the purest, most spiritual activity of man at this stage, and, at the same time, typical of human life as a whole—of the inner hidden natural life in man and all things. It gives, therefore, joy, freedom, contentment, inner and outer rest, peace with the world. It holds the sources of all that is good. A child that plays thoroughly, with self-active determination, perseveringly until physical fatigue forbids, will surely be a thorough, determined man, capable of self-sacrifice for the promotion of the welfare of himself and others. Is not the most beautiful expression of child-life at this time a playing child?—a child wholly absorbed in his play?—a child that has fallen asleep while so absorbed?
>
> As already indicated, play at this time is not trivial, it is highly serious and of deep significance. Cultivate and foster it, O mother; protect and guard it, O father! To the calm, keen vision of one who truly knows human nature, the spontaneous play of the child discloses the future inner life of the man.
>
> The plays of childhood are the germinal leaves of all later life; for the whole man is developed and shown in these, in his tenderest dispositions, in his innermost tendencies.[14]

Learning and socializing are and should be joyful activities, as they can be when children have caring adults and meaningful and appropriate experiences.

Froebel knew from experience, however, that unstructured play represented a potential danger and that it was quite likely, as Pestalozzi learned with his son Jean Jacques, that a child left to his own devices does not learn much. Without guidance and direction, and a planned environment in which to learn, there was a real possibility that no learning or the wrong kind of learning might occur.

According to Froebel, the teacher is responsible for guidance and direction so children can become creative, contributing members of society. To achieve this end, Froebel developed a systematic, planned curriculum for education of the young child. The basis for his curriculum were "gifts," "occupations," songs he composed, and educational games. Gifts were objects for children to handle and use in accordance with the teacher's instructions, so they could learn shape, size, color, and concepts involved in counting, measuring, contrasting, and comparison. The first gift was a set of six balls of yarn, each a different color, with six lengths of yarn the same colors as the balls. Part of the purpose of this gift was to teach color recognition.

Froebel felt that the ball (meaning a round, spherical object) played an important role in education; consequently, he placed a great deal of emphasis on its use. He also believed the ball was a perfect symbol for humankind's unity with the divine, a concept he felt was important but is difficult for us to understand. Froebel said of the ball:

> Even the word *ball,* in our significant language, is full of expression and meaning, pointing out that the ball is, as it were, an image of the all; but the ball itself has such an extraordinary charm, such a constant attraction for early childhood, as well as for later youth, that it is beyond comparison the first as well as the most important plaything of childhood especially.[15]

These modern reproductions of some of Froebel's "gifts" attest to the renewed interest in Froebelian ideas and materials.

The second gift was a cube, a cylinder, and a sphere. The directions for the use of the second gift give an insight into Froebel's educational methods and philosophy.

The importance of the consideration of the presence and absence of an object and its utilization for play, and in playing with the child, has been already noticed (with the ball, see first gift). With this we will now add a continuation to the play; for repeating the same experience in different ways with the same object serves to develop as well as to strengthen the child. Hence the mother hides the cube in her hand while she sings to her child:

I see now the hand alone.

Where, oh, where can cube be gone?

The mother thus leads the gaze and attention of the child to her hand, which he will therefore watch intently; the gaze, and even the little hand of the child, will make an effort to find the cube. As if yielding to this effort, the concealing hand opens, and the mother says or sings to the child:

Aha! aha!

My hand has hid the cube with care,

While you looked for it everywhere.

See, it is here!

Look at it, dear.

By this play the child is not only again made to notice that the cube fills space, but his attention is also called to the precise form of the cube; and he will look at it sharply, unconsciously comparing it with the hand, to which his eyes were first attracted. But the form of the cube appears to him, up to this point, as too large a whole, and composed of too many kinds of parts; the child's view of it must therefore be clarified by single perceptions.

Therefore the mother or nurse clasps the cube again in her hand, but so that one surface is still perceptible, singing to the child:

Only one side here you see

Where can now the others be?[16]

"Occupations" were materials designed for developing various skills, primarily psychomotor, through activities such as sewing with a sewing board, drawing pictures by following the dots, modeling with clay, cutting, bead stringing, weaving, drawing, pasting, and paper folding. Many of the games or plays Froebel developed were based on his gifts.

The following "Taste Song" from Froebel's *Mother's Songs, Games, and Stories* is typical of how he felt mothers could talk to, play with, and provide their children with sensory impressors. Froebel wanted mother and child to actively engage in the process of learning.

Through the Senses, Nature plainly speaks to Baby here:
Mother, see that he finds Nature through their accents clear.
Through the Senses, there's a pathway to the inmost door;
But the mind must light this pathway, light on darkness pour.
In the Senses, Baby's soul lies open, fair and pure;
Train the Senses truly, Mother, with a hope that's sure.
You may hope that little Baby will avoid much pain,
And for clearness, joy and gladness may prepare the reign.

For in Nature's every word
God's own Father-voice is heard.
A Child's sense we must early rouse to trace
The inner meaning in the outward face.
Once let a Baby this connection seize,
He'll find his own way to his goal with ease.
He to whom Nature Law and God reveals,
Finds that about him God's own peace he feels.

I

Open your mouth, my little Pet!
Something very nice you'll get.
Bite this soft, ripe, purple plum;
Use your tongue in tasting some.
What's the taste? Dza, dza! it's nice!
Sweet things will the tongue entice.

II

Bite this rosy apple here!
It is also eaten, Dear.
Oh! your mouth is drawn like paper,
When it's burnt in fire or taper.
"Sour!" you say. "'Tis sour, I find.
Give me sweet things, Mother kind!"

III

Bitter almond kernel try;
You will like it by-and-by.
Bitter things do good, I think,
Though your mouth will rather shrink.
Bitter things you'll often meet,
But Life soon will make them sweet.

IV

If you eat harsh, unripe things,
Pleasure after-evil brings.
Unripe things you must not touch, Dear;
They will hurt you very much, Dear.
Nothing, Dear, is good for you,
That is not quite ripe all through.[17]

These are some of Froebel's explanations and comments about the "Taste Song":

What is more important, Mother, for your child than the improvement of the senses, and especially the improvement of the sense of Taste, in its transferred moral meaning as well? Who likes to be accused of having "common and low Taste," and who is not glad when it can be said of him: "He has fine, elevated, good Taste?"

Now, why is it that people praise the improvement of a man's Taste? Because it is Taste that proclaims and reveals the inner part, the essence, the soul, the mind of the thing, its principle of life or death.

If even at this early age, it is important to improve the senses, whether of Sight, or more especially of Smell and Taste, in order to avoid much that is harmful and unwholesome, this improvement is above all important for the development and ennobling of the disposition and mind, and for the awakening of the will for activity.

For since it is in the senses that the soul, the very spirit's own activity, lies open, even in a child, so it is the senses which are, in their turn, like leaders to our knowledge of what is most intellectual—above all, the sense of taste, physical as well as intellectual taste.[18]

Froebel is not called the "father of the kindergarten" simply because he coined the name, but because he devoted his life to developing both a program for the young child and a system of training for kindergarten teachers. Many of the concepts and activities of the "gifts" and "occupations" are similar to activities that many kindergarten programs provide.

Froebel's recognition of the importance of learning through play is reinforced by modern teachers who intuitively structure their programs around play activities. Other features of Froebel's kindergarten that remain are the play circle, where children arrange themselves in a circle for learning, and singing songs to reinforce concepts taught with "gifts" and "occupations." Froebel was the first educator to develop a planned, systematic program for educating young children and the first to encourage young, unmarried women to become teachers. This break with tradition caused Froebel no small amount of criticism and was one reason his methods encountered opposition.

All the educators discussed so far have had certain basic premises in common. First, they believed strongly in the important role of the family in educating the child and providing the background for all future learning. Second, they felt it was important to begin educating the child early in life. Consequently, they advocated schooling either in the home or in a school setting. Third, they felt that parents needed training and help to be good teachers for their children. They recognized that for education to begin early in life, it was imperative that parents have materials and training to do a good job. (As we will discuss in Chapter 13, there is a growing public interest in procedures for involving parents in children's learning experiences.)

Educators and politicians are rediscovering how important parents are in the educational process. Parent involvement is being encouraged in public schools and other agencies, and we are learning what great educators knew all along—that parents are their children's first, and perhaps best, teachers.

MARIA MONTESSORI

Maria Montessori (1870–1952) was born in Italy, and devoted her life to developing a system for educating young children. Her system has influenced virtually all subsequent early childhood programs. A precocious young woman who thought of undertaking either mathematics or engineering as a career, she instead chose medicine. Despite the obstacles to entering a field traditionally closed to women, she became the first woman in Italy to earn a medical degree. Following this achievement, she was appointed assistant instructor in the psychiatric clinic of the University of Rome. Since it was customary not to distinguish between the mentally retarded children and the insane, her work brought her into contact with the mentally retarded children who had been committed to insane asylums. Although Montessori's first intention was to study children's diseases, she soon became interested in educational solutions for problems such as deafness, paralysis, and idiocy.

At that time she said, "I differed from my colleagues in that I instinctively felt that mental deficiency was more of an educational than medical problem."[19] Montessori became interested in the work of Edouard Seguin, a pioneer in the development of an educational system for mentally defective children, and of Jean Itard, who developed an educational system for deaf mutes. Montessori credits Itard and Seguin with inspiring her to continue her studies with mentally retarded children. Of her initial efforts at educating children, she says:

> I succeeded in teaching a number of the idiots from the asylums both to read and to write so well that I was able to present them at a public school for an examination together with normal children. And they passed the examination successfully.[20]

This was a remarkable achievement, which aroused interest in both Montessori and in her methods. Montessori, however, was already considering something else:

> While everyone else was admiring the progress made by my defective charges, I was trying to discover the reasons which could have reduced the healthy, happy pupils of the ordinary schools to such a low state that in the intelligence test they were on the level with my own unfortunate pupils.[21]

While continuing to study and prepare herself for the task of educating children, the opportunity to perfect her methods and implement them with normal school-age children occurred quite by chance. In 1906 she was invited by the director general of the Roman Association for Good Building to organize schools for young children of families who occupied the tenement houses the association had constructed. In the first school, named the *Casa dei Bambini,* or Children's House, she had the opportunity to test her ideas and gain insights into children and teaching that led to the perfection of her system.

Montessori was profoundly religious, and a religious undertone is reflected throughout her work. She often quoted from the Bible to support her points. For example, at the dedication ceremonies of the first Children's House, she read from Isaiah 60:1–5, and ended by saying, "Perhaps, this Children's House can become a

Montessori's philosophical and pedagogical ideas are evident in many early childhood programs. As much as any other single individual, Montessori influenced the nature and direction of American preschool education. One of her concepts, daily living skills, has found its way into almost every early childhood program.

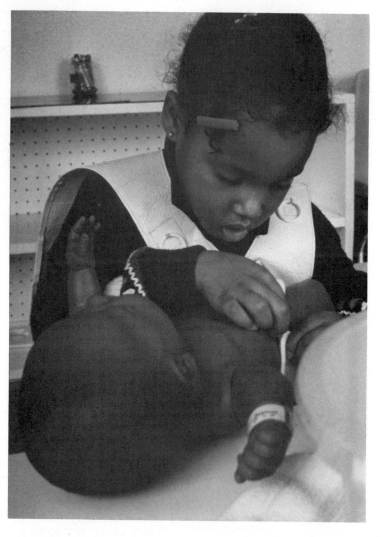

new Jerusalem, which, if it is spread out among the abandoned people of the world, can bring a new light to education."[22] Her religious dedication to the fundamental sacredness and uniqueness of every child and subsequent grounding of educational processes in a religious conviction undoubtedly account for some of her remarkable achievements as a person and as an educator. Thus, her system functions well for those who are willing to dedicate themselves to teaching as if it were a religious vocation.

JOHN DEWEY

John Dewey (1859–1952) represents a truly American influence on American education. Through his positions as professor of philosophy at the University of Chicago

Educators must meet the challenge to provide humane and meaningful care for children. All children are entitled to environments that promote optimum development.

and Columbia University, his extensive writing, and the educational practices of his many followers, Dewey did more to alter and redirect the course of American education than any other person.

Dewey's theory of schooling, usually called *progressivism,* emphasizes the child and his interests rather than subject matter; from this emphasis come the terms *child-centered curriculum* and *child-centered schools.* The progressive movement also maintains that schools should be concerned with preparing the child for the realities of today rather than for some vague future time. As expressed by Dewey in *My Pedagogical Creed,* "education, therefore, is a process of living and not a preparation for future living."[23]

What is included in Dewey's concept of children's interests? "Not some one thing," he explained, "it is a name for the fact that a course of action, an occupation, or pursuit absorbs the powers of an individual in a thorough-going way."[24] In a classroom based upon Dewey's ideas, children are involved with physical activities, utilization of things, intellectual pursuits, and social interaction. Physical activities are expressed through running, jumping, and other autonomous activities. In this phase the child begins the process of education and develops other interest areas. The growing child learns to use tools and objects. Dewey felt that an ideal expression for this interest was daily living activities or occupations such as cooking and carpentry.

To promote an interest in the intellectual—solving problems, discovering new things, and figuring out how things work—the child is given opportunities for inquiry and discovery. *Social interest* refers to interactions with people; Dewey believed this interest was encouraged in a democratically run classroom.

While Dewey believed the curriculum should be built on the interests of children, he also felt it was the teacher's responsibility to plan for and capitalize on opportunities to weave traditional subject matter through and around the fabric of these interests. Dewey describes a school based on his ideas:

Dewey believed that working on projects helps children learn many useful social virtues, such as cooperation, consideration for others, the dignity of labor, and concentration— values that are worthy of promotion today.

> All of the schools . . . as compared with traditional schools . . . [exhibit] a common emphasis upon respect for individuality and for increased freedom; a common disposition to build upon the nature and experience of the boys and girls that come to them, instead of imposing from without external subject-matter standards. They all display a certain atmosphere of informality, because experience has proved that formalization is hostile to genuine mental activity and to sincere emotional expression and growth. Emphasis upon activity as distinct from passivity is one of the common factors.[25]

Teachers who correlate subjects, utilize the unit approach, and encourage problem-solving activities are philosophically indebted to Dewey.

There has been a great deal of misinterpretation and criticism of the progressive movement and of Dewey's ideas, especially by those who favor a traditional approach that emphasizes the basic subjects and skills. Actually, Dewey was not opposed to teaching basic skills or subject matter. He did believe, however, that traditional educational strategies *imposed* knowledge on children, whereas their interests should be a springboard for involvement with skills and subject matter.

> The accumulation and acquisition of information for purposes of reproduction in recitation and examination is made too much of. "Knowledge," in the sense of information, means the working capital, the indispensable resources of further inquiry; of finding out, or learning, more things. Frequently it is treated as an end itself, and then the goal becomes to heap it up and display it when called for. This static, cold-storage ideal of knowledge is inimical to educative development. It not only lets occasions for thinking go unused, but it swamps thinking. No one could construct a house on ground cluttered with miscellaneous junk.

FROM LUTHER TO PIAGET: BASIC CONCEPTS ESSENTIAL TO GOOD EDUCATIONAL PRACTICES

As They Relate to Children

Everyone needs to learn how to read and write.

Children learn best when they use all their senses.

All children are capable of being educated.

All children should be educated to the fullest extent of their abilities.

Education should begin early in life.

Children should not be forced to learn, but should be appropriately taught what they are ready to learn and should be prepared for the next stage of learning.

Learning activities should be interesting and meaningful.

As They Relate to Teachers

Teachers must show love and respect for all children.

Teachers should be dedicated to the teaching profession.

Good teaching is based on a theory, a philosophy, goals, and objectives.

Children's learning is enhanced through the use of concrete materials.

Teaching should move from the concrete to the abstract.

Observation is a key means for determining children's needs.

Teaching should be a planned, systematic process.

Teaching should be child-centered rather than adult-centered or subject-centered.

Teaching should be based on children's interests.

As They Relate to Parents

The family is an important institution in education and in the education and development of children.

Parents are their children's primary educators.

Parents must guide and direct young children's learning.

Parents should be involved in any educational program designed for their children.

Everyone should have knowledge of and training for child rearing.

Pupils who have stored their "minds" with all kinds of material which they have never put to intellectual uses are sure to be hampered when they try to think. They have no practice in selecting what is appropriate, and no criterion to go by; everything is on the same dead static level.[26]

Dewey not only influenced American educational thought and practice, but also exerted a strong influence on the educational thought and practice of other countries who embrace his concept of incorporating work and education. We find the idea of "socially useful education" particularly evident in contemporary China, Russia, and other socialist countries.

JEAN PIAGET

Jean Piaget (1896–1980) was born in Switzerland. He was a precocious child who published his first article at the age of ten. He received his baccalaureate degree from college at eighteen and earned his doctorate three years later. His training in biology was influential in the development of his ideas about knowledge, and forms the primary basis for his theory of intellectual development.

Piaget studied in Paris, where he worked with Theodore Simon at the Alfred Binet laboratory, standardizing tests of reasoning for use with children. (Binet and Simon developed a scale for measuring intelligence.) This experience provided the foundation for Piaget's clinical method of interviewing, used in studying children's intellectual development. As Piaget recalls, "Thus I engaged my subjects in conversations patterned after psychiatric questioning, with the aim of discovering something about the reasoning process underlying their right, but especially their wrong, answers."[27] The emphasis on this method helps explain why some developers of a Piaget-based early childhood curriculum emphasize the teacher's use of questioning procedures to promote thinking.

Following his work with children in Paris, which established the direction of his lifework, Piaget became associated with the Institute J. J. Rousseau in Geneva and began studying intellectual development. Piaget's own three children played a major role in his studies, since many of his consequent insights about how children develop intellectually are based on his observations and work with them. Using his own children in his studies caused some to criticize his findings. His theory, however, is not only based on his research, but on literally hundreds of other studies involving thousands of children.

Although Piaget's work has been known in Europe since the early 1930s, it was not until the 1960s that it began to receive the attention it deserved in the United States. Based on his research, Piaget came to these conclusions about early childhood education:

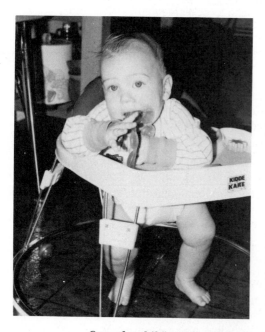 

One of a child's earliest behaviors is sucking, which begins at birth. In infancy, sucking contributes to sensorimotor intelligence; however, the boy on the right is using the thumb-sucking as a means of self-pacification.

□ Children play an active role in their own cognitive development
□ Mental and physical activity are important for children's cognitive development
□ Experiences constitute the raw materials children use to develop mental structures
□ Children develop cognitively through interaction with and adaptation to the environment
□ Development is a continuous process
□ Development results from maturation and the *transactions* or interactions between children and the physical and social environments

Piaget also popularized the age/stage approach to cognitive development and influenced others to apply the theory to other processes such as moral, language, and social development. He encouraged and inspired many psychologists and educators to develop educational curricula and programs utilizing his ideas and promoted interest in the study of young children's cognitive development that has in turn contributed to the interest in infant development and education.

THE RECENT PAST

To fully understand the basis for the public interest in the field of early childhood education and young children, we need to look back almost half a century to three significant events. The first event was the general acceptance of claims that the public schools were not successfully teaching reading and related skills. The second event was the boycott of city buses by blacks in Montgomery, Alabama, on December 1, 1955. The third event was the launching of the Sputnik by the Soviet Union on October 4, 1957.

These three events changed early childhood education in two important ways. First, in and of themselves, they influenced specific policies, programs, and legislation affecting young children and their families. Second, they influenced people's attitudes toward and ways of thinking about what is best for young children. How America educates its children and how well the schools fulfill their appointed tasks are always topics of national discussion and debate. Hardly a day passes that the schools are not criticized in some way. Schooling and public criticism go hand in hand. During the 1950s a host of articles and books detailed "why children couldn't read," followed in 1955 by the publication of Rudolf Flesch's *Why Johnny Can't Read*. Flesch criticized the schools for the way reading was taught. Critics and parents began to question the methodology and results of the teaching of reading and other basic skills. Parents demanded schools and programs that would teach these skills. Many parents felt that traditional play-oriented preschools and public school programs that emphasized socialization were not preparing their children for college or for earning a living. Preschools that stressed cognitive learning became popular with parents who wanted to give their children both an early start and a good foundation in learning.

Flesch's criticism of reading methods laid the groundwork for introducing the phonetic approach to reading, a system based on having children learn that letters represent sounds. As children learn such skills as initial consonant sounds, blends, digraphs (a pair of letters representing a specific speech sound), silent consonants, and medial and final consonants, they can "sound out" the majority of words they encounter. This phonetic method, championed by Jeanne Chall, replaced the "look-say" or "whole-word" method popular at the time. As you might expect, given the inevitable swing of the education pendulum, the phonetic approach is currently encountering criticism and challenges in the name of *whole language* and *emerging literacy*, which we discuss in Chapters 7 and 8.

The Montgomery bus boycott set in motion a series of court cases and demonstrations for civil rights and human dignity. The fight for civil liberties spread quickly to the school arena. As a result, the rights of children and parents to public education were and are being clarified and extended. Many of the new federal and state regulations and laws that deal with handicapped, disadvantaged, and abused children are essentially civil rights legislation rather than purely educational legislation. Included in this legislation, and undoubtedly the two most important for early childhood, are P.L. 94-142, *The Education for All Handicapped Children Act*, and P.L. 99-457, *The Education of the Handicapped Act Amendments*, both of which extend rights to educational and social services to special needs children and their parents and families. Both laws, with their tremendous educational implications, also broaden and extend civil rights. Consequently, children have been granted rights to a free, appropriate, individualized education, as well as to humane treatment.

Spurred by the Soviet Union's early lead in space exploration, the U.S. government in 1958 passed the National Defense Education Act to meet national needs, particularly in the sciences. As a result of the renewed interest in our educational system, Americans became more interested in other educational systems, including that of the Soviet Union. What made it possible for the Soviets to launch Sputnik? Examination of the Soviet educational system led to the conclusion that it provided educational opportunities at an earlier age than did the U.S. public schools, and some educators began to wonder if we could have more intelligent adults if we taught children at a younger age.

Research

At the same time that Soviet space achievements brought a reappraisal of our educational system, research studies were also influencing our ideas about how children learn, how to teach them, and what they should learn. These studies led to a major shift in basic educational premises concerning what children can achieve. This shift is attributed in part to works by B.S. Bloom and J. McV. Hunt. One of Bloom's conclusions was as follows:

> When a number of longitudinal studies are compared with each other and allowances are made for the reliability of the instruments and the variability of the samples, a single pattern clearly emerges. . . .Both the correlational data and the absolute scale of intelligence development make it clear that intelligence is a developing function and that the stability of measured intelligence increases with age. Both types of data suggest that in terms of intelligence measured at age 17, about 50% of the development takes place between conception and age 4, about 30% between ages 4 and 8, and about 20% between ages 8 and 17.[28]

In *Intelligence and Experience,* Hunt draws these conclusions:

> In view of the conceptual developments and the evidence coming from animals learning to learn, from neuropsychology, from the programming of electronic computers to solve

problems, and from the development of intelligence in children, it would appear that intelligence should be conceived as intellectual capacities based on central processes hierarchically arranged within the intrinsic portions of the cerebrum. These central processes are approximately analogous to the strategies for information processing and action with which electronic computers are programmed. With such a conception of intelligence, the assumptions that intelligence is fixed and that its development is predetermined by the genes are no longer tenable. In light of these considerations, it appears that the counsel from experts on child-rearing during the third and much of the fourth decades of the twentieth century to let children be while they grow and to avoid excessive stimulation was highly unfortunate. . . .

Further in the light of these theoretical considerations and the evidence concerning the effects of early experience on adult problem-solving in animals, it is no longer unreasonable to consider that it might be feasible to discover ways to govern the encounters that children have with their environments, especially during the early years of their development, to achieve a substantially faster rate of intellectual development and a substantially higher adult level of intellectual capacity.[29]

We can draw four inferences from this research. First, the period of most rapid intellectual growth occurs before age eight. The extent to which children will become intelligent, based on those things by which we measure intelligence and school achievement, is determined long before many children enter school. The notion of shaping intelligence implies that children benefit from home environments that are conducive to learning and early school-like experiences especially for children from environments that place children at risk for developing their full potential.

Second, it is increasingly evident that a child is not born with a fixed intelligence. This outdated concept fails to do justice to people's tremendous capacity for learning and change. In addition, evidence supports developmental intelligence. The extent to which individual intelligence develops depends upon many variables, such as experiences, child rearing practices, economic factors, nutrition, and the quality of prenatal and postnatal environments. Inherited genetic characteristics set a broad framework within which intelligence will develop. Heredity set the limits, while environment determines the extent to which the limits will be achieved. For example, the child's genetic makeup carries the capacity for language development, but a child who is reared in an environment devoid of opportunities for conversation with adults will probably not be as linguistically competent as the child who has conversational opportunities.

Third, children who are reared in homes that are not intellectually stimulating may also lag intellectually behind their counterparts reared in more advantaged environments. Hunt's implications concerning the home environment are obvious. While questions have been raised about how well school achievement indicates real life achievement and success, experience shows that children who lack an environment that promotes learning opportunities will be handicapped throughout life. On the other hand, homes that offer intellectual stimulation tend to produce students who do well in school.

A fourth conclusion implied by the studies is this: If 80 percent of children's intellectual development occurs by the time they are eight, then the environment will have its greatest impact during the first eight years. If intelligence does develop at the rates and in the proportions Bloom states, then the concepts, attitudes, and ways of looking at the world that children learn early in life will essentially remain with them for life. The things children learn early in life, especially from their parents, are hard to change later. A child reared in an environment of noncommunication may well experience difficulty in communicating. Enrichment of the child's life, therefore, should be undertaken earlier than the age of six, the traditional age for admittance to school.

More contemporary studies of the influence of family background tend to support the earlier research of Hunt and Bloom. Christopher Jencks and his colleagues analyzed the effects of inequality of opportunity and concluded:

> We found that family background had much more influence than IQ genotype on an individual's educational attainment. The family's influence depended partly on its socioeconomic status and partly on cultural and psychological characteristics that were independent of socioeconomic level. The effect of cognitive skill on educational attainment proved difficult to estimate, but it was clearly significant. We found no evidence that the role of family background was declining or that the role of cognitive skill was increasing. Qualitative differences between schools played a very minor role in determining how much schooling people eventually got.[30]

Another study that supports the role and influence of the family in the educative process was conducted by Mayeske and his associates; they concluded:

> This study has demonstrated that family background plays a profound role in the development of achievement, not only through the social and economic well-being of the family but through the values its members hold with regard to education, and the activities that parents and parental surrogates engage in with their children to make these values operational.[31]

After examining the influences of people and the environment on young children, Burton White drew this conclusion:

> In our studies we were not only impressed by what some children could achieve during the first years, but also by the fact that the child's own family seemed so obviously central to the outcome. Indeed, we came to believe that the informal education that the families provide for their children *makes more of an impact on a child's total educational development than the formal educational system.* If a family does its job well, the professional can then provide effective training. If not, there may be little the professional can do to save the child from mediocrity. This grim assessment is a direct conclusion from the findings of thousands of programs in remedial education, such as Head Start and Follow Through projects.[32]

There are dangers in assuming that preschool experiences totally determine a child's achievement. It becomes too easy to adopt a fatalistic and uncaring attitude toward a child. This attitude usually results in blaming the home for the child's lack of achievement, and can also lead to a deterministic point of view that not much will help the child; the damage has already been done. My response to this attitude has always been that if the teachers of the world are not optimistic about and hopeful for children, then who will be?

Schools are a basic social service. The manner and extent to which this service is provided makes a difference in how well and how much children achieve. The quality of education depends on the interest of professional educators in providing it to all children who come to school: the handicapped, the gifted, the poor, the slow learner, the quick learner, and all those children we label "average."

How should we respond to the research that seems to indicate the family has an extremely powerful influence on the child's achievement? As with so many controversies, the middle ground is often the best position. We cannot ignore or minimize the influence of the family. Schools and society should do everything possible to involve parents in schooling and help do the best job of nurturing, rearing, and educating. On the other hand, schools and teachers must be willing to respond creatively and with a broad range of services to all children without blaming anyone or any institution for a poor job. The responses of the school to family conditions and their effects on the child is critical in determining how well schools fulfill the functions of education and socialization.

Poverty

During the 1960s, the United States rediscovered the poor and recognized that not everyone enjoyed affluence. In 1964, Congress enacted the Economic Opportunity Act. The EOA was designed to wage a war on poverty on several fronts. Head Start, one of the provisions of the EOA, attempted to break generational cycles of poverty

One of the problems facing a growing number of the nation's children is that they are living in, or are affected by, poverty. Helping children and their families overcome poverty requires more than education; it also requires assistance with employment, housing, and social services.

by providing education and social opportunities for the preschool children of poor families (see Chapter 10).

Head Start has probably done more than any other single force to interest the nation in the business of educating the young child. Although programs for children had been sponsored by the federal government during the Great Depression and World War II, these were primarily designed to free mothers for jobs in defense plants. Head Start marked the first time that children were the intended beneficiaries of the services.

MODERN IMPLICATIONS

To what extent are we influenced by the great educational thinkers of the past? While it is difficult to ascertain exactly in what areas and to what degree, it is obvious that we can find evidence of their thinking in current educational practices. Although much of today's jargon would be alien to Froebel, many of the strategies would not. Terms such as *open education* and *individualized prescribed instruction* are merely new names for old methods.

Open Education

Open education is an attempt to restructure preschool and primary classrooms into settings that support individuality, promote independence, encourage freedom, and demonstrate respect for children. In this context, open education is a logical extension of many of the ideas of Montessori, Dewey, and Piaget. Open education is an attitude that encourages children to become involved in their own learning, and teachers allow children to make choices about how and what they learn. Teachers can conduct an open program regardless of the physical, social, or financial setting of the school or community.

Open education is an environment in which children are free from *authoritarian* adults and *arbitrary* rules. Contrary to popular misconception, children are not free to do everything they choose. Within broad guidelines, however (ideally established by teachers, students, and administrators), children are free to move about the room, carry on conversations, and engage in learning activities based on their interests.

Open education is child-centered learning. Adults do not do all the talking, decision making, organizing, and planning when it is children who need to develop these skills. Open education seeks to return the emphasis to the child, where it rightfully belongs.

Historical Influences

We can trace the foundations of open education to Pestalozzi, Froebel, Montessori, and Dewey, although they did not use the same terminology. Montessori might be called the first modern open educator, because she allowed children to enjoy freedom within a prepared environment. She also encouraged individualized instruction, and most important, insisted on respect for children.

Interest in open education in the U.S. began in the 1960s when many educators and critics called attention to the ways schools were stifling student initiative, freedom, and self-direction. Schools were compared to prisons; critics described students sitting apathetically in straight rows, passively listening to robotlike teachers, with little or no real learning taking place. In short, classrooms and learning were assumed to be devoid of enthusiasm, joy, and self-direction. Educators and schools were challenged to involve students in learning and abolish policies and procedures that were detrimental to students' physical and mental health. In essence, schools were challenged to become happy places of learning.

Concurrently, school reformers in the U.S. discovered the British Primary School, a comprehensive education program characterized by respect for children, responsiveness to children's needs, and learning through interests. The terms *open education, open classroom, British Primary School,* and *British Infant School* are often used interchangeably.

THE TEACHER'S ROLE

Just as Montessori conceptualized a new role for the teacher, so does open education encourage redefinition of the role. The teacher who believes that open education is possible has surmounted the first obstacle—many teachers are afraid to try it. An open education teacher respects children and believes they are capable of assuming responsibility for their own learning. The teacher considers herself primarily a teacher of children, not of subject matter, and feels confident with all students in all subject areas. Like the Montessori directress, she is a keen observer, for many of the decisions regarding instruction and activities depend on thorough knowledge of what the children have accomplished. Adjectives that describe the teacher's role include *learner, guide, facilitator, catalyst,* and *director.*

The Death and Rebirth of Open Education

As is so often the case, the pendulum of change has swung toward a "back to basics," subject-centered, teacher-centered, highly organized system, and away from a child-centered, activity-centered program characterized by freedom and open education. How long before the pendulum swings back toward concepts embodied in open education remains to be seen. The open education concept was always most popular and successful with preschool educators, perhaps because of a combination of young children's natural ability to work well in an open setting and the fact that preschool teachers are generally comfortable in an informal classroom atmosphere. It seems that the graded concept for older children is difficult to dislodge from educators' hearts and minds. So, once teachers and children enter a graded program, teachers tend to adopt the style and habits associated with the graded approach.

Open education is full of excitement and challenge for teachers who are willing to dedicate themselves to it. The opportunities for an individualized, self-paced program, operated within a context of freedom, respect for children, and relevance, ought to appeal to the teaching profession; however, the failure of open education is attributable to several factors:

1. Many educators have never understood the concept of open education or how to implement it.
2. Teachers were not trained for the transition from the graded teaching approach to open education concepts.

Many of the concepts of open education advocates are coming back into fashion, including child-centered learning, multiage grouping, and freedom of activity in the classroom.

3. Many teachers in open education programs did not emphasize or sufficiently explain to parents how the program worked or the progress of their children.
4. Education colleges as a whole did too little or were too late in developing training programs to support open education.

A child-centered form of education will probably regain popularity in the coming years; in fact, it is possible to detect public sentiment for educational practices that are developmentally consistent with young children's needs and maturation.

There is a familiar saying in the worlds of fashion, design, and education: "If it's good, it will be back in ten or fifteen years"—of course, the time frame may be more or less. Sometimes, good educational practices such as open education just don't catch on; in a sense, their time hasn't come. But open education and its accompanying practices seem to be on the verge of rebirth. Encouraging signs are these:

Interest in discussing and implementing developmentally oriented curricula and practices designed to meet children's developmental needs (see Chapter 6)

Interest in whole language, emergent literacy and other practices designed to integrate processes of reading, writing and speaking (see Chapters 8 and 9)

Cooperative planning between teacher and child promotes autonomy, responsibility, and self-directed learning.

Renewed interest in child-centered versus teacher- and subject-centered teaching and learning

The growing interest in teaching/learning processes and curricula associated with open education methodology and teaching is also accompanied by a renewed interest in the philosophies and ideas of those who encouraged child-centered education, particularly Montessori, Dewey, and Piaget.

RECURRING THEMES

Certain ingredients are common to good teaching regardless of time or place. Respecting children, attending to individual differences, and getting children interested and involved in their learning are the framework of quality educational programs. Reading about and examining the experiences of great educators helps keep this vision before us. Interestingly, many early educators tended to make schools resemble a family situation, a tendency evident today in some open classrooms where children are grouped as "families," with children of different ages who share responsibilities and arrive at decisions after discussion among "family" members. Grouping children into families provides not only structure, but an identity and security in which to learn. In addition, the emphasis on parent involvement underscores the historical importance of the family as a context in which to conduct education.

All great educators have believed in the basic goodness of children; that is, that children by nature tend to behave in socially acceptable ways. They believed it was the role of the teacher to provide the environment for this goodness to manifest itself. The young child learns to behave in a certain way according to how he is treated; the role models he has to emulate; and the environment he has to grow in. The child

TIMELINE—THE HISTORY OF EARLY CHILDHOOD EDUCATION

1524   Martin Luther argued for public support of education for all children in his "Letter to the Mayors and Aldermen of All the Cities of Germany in Behalf of Christian Schools"

1628   John Amos Comenius's *The Great Didactic* proclaimed the value of education for all children according to the laws of nature

1762   Jean Jacques Rousseau wrote *Emile,* explaining that education should take into account the child's natural growth and interests

1780   Robert Raikes initiated the Sunday School movement in England to teach Bible study and religion to children

1801   Johann Pestalozzi wrote *How Gertrude Teaches Her Children,* emphasizing home education and learning by discovery

1816   Robert Owen set up a nursery school in Great Britain at the New Lanark Cotton Mills, believing that early education could counteract bad influences of the home

1817   Thomas Gallaudet founded the first residential school for the deaf in Hartford, Connecticut

1824   The American Sunday School Union was started with the purpose of initiating Sunday schools around the United States

1836   William McGuffey began publishing the *Eclectic Reader* for elementary school children; his writing had a strong impact on moral and literary attitudes in the nineteenth century

1837   Friedrich Froebel, known as the "Father of the Kindergarten," established the first kindergarten in Blankenburgh, Germany

1837   Horace Mann began his job as secretary of the Massachusetts State Board of Education; he is often called the "Father of the Common Schools" because of the role he played in helping to set up the elementary school system in the United States

1837   Edouard Seguin, influenced by Jean

Itard, started the first school for the feeble-minded in France

1856   Mrs. Carl Schurz established the first kindergarten in the U.S. in Watertown, Wisconsin; the school was founded for children of German immigrants, and the program was conducted in German

1860   Elizabeth Peabody opened a private kindergarten in Boston, Massachusetts, for English-speaking children

1869   The first special education class for the deaf was founded in Boston

1871   The first public kindergarten in North America was started in Ontario, Canada

1873   Susan Blow opened the first public school kindergarten in the U.S. in St. Louis, Missouri, as a cooperative effort with William Harris, superintendent of schools

1876   Model kindergarten shown at Philadelphia Centennial Exposition

1880   First teacher-training program for teachers of kindergarten, Oshkosh Normal School, Philadelphia

1884   The American Association of Elementary, Kindergarten, and Nursery School Educators founded to serve in a consulting capacity for other educators

1892   International Kindergarten Union founded

1896   John Dewey started the Laboratory School at the University of Chicago, basing his program on child-centered learning with an emphasis on life experiences

1905   Sigmund Freud wrote *Three Essays of the Theory of Sexuality,* emphasizing the value of a healthy emotional environment during childhood

1907   Maria Montessori started her first preschool in Rome, Italy, called Children's House; her now-famous teaching method was based on the theory that children learn best by themselves in a properly prepared environment

1909   First White House Conference on

Children convened by Theodore Roosevelt

1911   Arnold Gesell, well known for his research on the importance of the preschool years, began child development study at Yale University

1911   Margaret and Rachel McMillan founded an open-air nursery school in Great Britain, where the class met outdoors and emphasis was on healthy living

1912   Arnold and Beatrice Gesell wrote *The Normal Child and Primary Education*

1915   Eva McLin started the first U.S. Montessori nursery school in New York City

1915   Child Education Foundation of New York City founded a nursery school using Montessori's principles

1918   The first public nursery schools were started in Great Britain

1919   Harriet Johnson started the Nursery School of the Bureau of Educational Experiments, later to become the Bank Street College of Education

1921   Patty Smith Hill started a progressive, laboratory nursery school at Columbia Teachers College

1921   A.S. Neill founded Summerhill, an experimental school based on the ideas of Rousseau and Dewey

1922   With Edna Noble White as its first director, the Merrill-Palmer Institute Nursery School opened in Detroit, with the purpose of preparing women in proper child care; at this time, the Institute was known as the Merrill-Palmer School of Motherhood and Home Training

1922   Abigail Eliot, influenced by the open-air school in Great Britain and basing her program on personal hygiene and proper behavior, started the Ruggles Street Nursery School in Boston

1924   *Childhood Education,* the first professional journal in early childhood education, was published by the International Kindergarten Union (IKU)

1926   The National Committee on Nursery Schools was initiated by Patty Smith Hill at Columbia Teachers College; now called the National Association for the Education of Young Children, it provides guidance and consultant services for educators

1926   National Association of Nursery Education (NANE) founded

1930   IKU changed name to Association for Childhood Education

1933   The Work Projects Administration (WPA) provided money to start nursery schools so that unemployed teachers would have jobs

1935   First toy lending library, Toy Loan, was founded in Los Angeles

1940   The Lanham Act provided funds for child care during World War II, mainly for day care centers for children whose mothers worked in the war effort

1943   Kaiser Child Care Centers opened in Portland, Oregon, to provide twenty-four-hour child care for children of mothers working in war-related industries

1944   *Young Children* first published by NANE

1946   Dr. Benjamin Spock wrote the *Common Sense Book of Baby and Child Care*

1950   Erik Erikson published his writings on the "eight ages or stages" of personality growth and development and identified "tasks" for each stage of development; the information, known as "Personality in the Making," formed the basis for the 1950 White House Conference on Children and Youth

1952   Jean Piaget's *The Origins of Intelligence in Children* published in English translation

1955   Rudolph Flesch's *Why Johnny Can't Read* criticized the schools for their methodology in teaching reading and other basic skills

1957   The Soviet Union launched Sputnik, sparking renewed interest in other educational systems and marking the

continued

beginning of the "rediscovery" of early childhood education

1958   The National Defense Education Act was passed to provide federal funds for improving education in the sciences, mathematics, and foreign languages

1960   Katharine Whiteside Taylor founded the American Council of Parent Cooperatives for those interested in exchanging ideas in preschool education; it later became the Parent Cooperative Preschools International

1960   The Day Care and Child Development Council of America was formed to publicize the need for quality services for children

1964   At the Miami Beach Conference, NANE became NAEYC

1964   The Economic Opportunity Act of 1964 was passed as the beginning of the war on poverty and was the foundation for Head Start

1965   The Elementary and Secondary Education Act was passed to provide federal money for programs for educationally deprived children

1965   The Head Start Program began with federal money allocated for preschool education; the early programs were known as child development centers

1966   Bureau of Education for the Handicapped was established

1967   The Follow Through Program was initiated to extend the Head Start Program into the primary grades

1968   B.F. Skinner wrote *The Technology of Teaching,* which outlines a programmed approach to learning

1968   The federal government established the Handicapped Children's Early Education Program to fund model preschool programs for handicapped children

1970   The White House Conference on Children and Youth

1971   The Stride-Rite Corporation in Boston was the first to start a corporate-supported child care program

1972   The National Home Start Program began for the purpose of involving parents in their children's education

1975   P.L. 94-142, The Education for All Handicapped Children Act, was passed mandating a free and appropriate education for all handicapped children and extending many rights to parents of handicapped children

1979   International Year of the Child sponsored by the United Nations and designated by Executive Order

1980   The first American LEKOTEK opened its doors in Evanston, Illinois

1980   White House Conference on Families

1981   Head Start Act of 1981 (Omnibus Budget Reconciliation Act of 1981, P.L. 97-35) was passed to extend Head Start and provide for effective delivery of comprehensive services to economically disadvantaged children and their families

1981   Education Consolidation and Improvement Act (ECIA) was passed, consolidating many federal support programs for education

1985   Head Start celebrated its 20th anniversary with a Joint Resolution of the Senate and House "reaffirming congressional support"

1986   The U.S. secretary of education proclaimed this the Year of the Elementary School, saying "Let's do all we can this year to remind this nation that the time our children spend in elementary school is crucial to everything they will do for the rest of their lives"

1986   Public Law 99-457 (the Education of the Handicapped Act Amendment) established a national policy on early intervention that recognizes its benefits, provides assistance to states to build systems of service delivery, and recognizes the unique role of families in the development of their handicapped children

1987   Congress created the National Commission to Prevent Infant Mortality

does not emerge from the womb with a propensity toward badness, but tends to grow and behave as he is treated and taught.

A central point that Luther, Comenius, Pestalozzi, Froebel, Montessori, and Dewey sought to make about our work as educators, no matter in what context—parent, classroom teacher, or child care worker—is that we must do it well and act as though we really care about those whom we have been called to serve. We cannot teach a child how to read unless we care for him.

FURTHER READING

Day, D. *Open Learning in Early Childhood* (New York: Macmillan, 1975)

> For teachers and administrators who are developing an open education program, but also useful for parents. Useful activities and learning games for communication/language arts, fine arts, home living, creative dramatics, science, math, movement, and outdoor play; valuable reference for parents of children attending an open education school

Dewey, John. *Experience and Education* (New York: Collier Books, 1938)

> Dewey's comparison of traditional and progressive education.

Dropkin, Ruth, and Arthur Tobier, eds. *Roots of Open Education in America: Reminiscences and Reflections* (New York: The City College Workshop Center for Open Education,1976)

> Papers that grew out of a 1975 conference at Lillian Weber's Center trace roots of open education back to the Mohawk nation. Settlement houses, one-room schoolhouses, Dewey, and Progressivism are cited for their significant or in some cases overrated contributions.

Winsor, Charlotte, ed. *Experimental Schools Revisited* (New York: Agathon Press, 1973)

> Series of bulletins published by Bureau of Educational Experiments, a group of professionals dedicated to cooperative study of children, from 1917 to 1924; document roots of modern education, relate first serious attempts to provide educational programs for toddlers and experiences based on children's maturational levels. Chapters dealing with Play School and Playthings demonstrate philosophical and methodological bases for learning through play.

FURTHER STUDY

1. Compare classrooms you attended as a child to early education classrooms you are now visiting. What are the major similarities and differences? How do you explain the differences?
2. Do you think most teachers are aware of the historical influences on their teaching? Is it important for teachers to be aware of these influences? Why or why not?
3. Teaching has been compared to the ministry; according to this view, teaching is a vocation to which one is called. Discuss this concept as a class activity.
4. Many teachers of young children are more Froebelian in their approach to teaching than they realize. Can you find evidence to support this statement?
5. Some critics of education feel that schools have assumed (or have been given) too much responsibility for teaching too many things. Do you think certain subjects or services could be taught or provided through another institution or agency? If so, which ones? Why?
6. Reflect on your experiences in elementary school. What experiences were most meaningful? Why? What teachers do you remember best? Why?
7. Visit a parochial preschool and primary school. How are they similar to and different from public school programs? What strong points did you observe? What weaknesses?
8. Interview the parents of children who attend a parochial school. Find out why they send their children to these schools. Do you agree or disagree with their reasons?
9. Reexamine Comenius's ten basic principles of teaching. Are they applicable today? Which do you agree with most and least?

10. Is it really necessary for children to learn through their senses? Why or why not?

11. To what extent do religious beliefs determine educational practice? Give specific examples from your own experiences and observations to support your answer.

12. Why has society in general and education in particular failed to follow the best educational practices advocated by many great educators?

13. Why is it important that teaching be guided by goals and objectives? Can you cite instances where you observed teaching that was not guided by goals and objectives?

14. Have you observed instances where children were left to their own whims in a laissez-faire school environment? What were the results and why did they occur?

15. Suppose the Russians had not launched a satellite before the United States. Do you think our educational system would be different? If so, how?

16. Educators attach different meanings to openness and open education. Interview teachers, principals, and parents to determine their ideas and definitions of open education, and compare them to those of your classmates. How many different meanings did you find?

17. Visit both a traditional classroom and an open classroom. List activities children participate in. Compare the activities to the models discussed in this chapter.

18. Do you believe open education is a good idea? Why or why not?

19. Besides the recurring themes of the great educators presented in this chapter, are there others you would list? Tell why you selected other themes.

20. List people, agencies, and legislation that are influencing early childhood education. Give specific examples. Do you think the influences will be long-lasting or short-lived?

21. What evidence can you find that Piaget has influenced a program in your area? Cite specific examples.

22. List ways you have been or are being influenced by ideas and theories of the people and events discussed in this chapter. Do schools make a difference? Or, as Jencks and Mayeske suggest, do families and other institutions make a greater difference? Support your answer.

NOTES

1. From *Luther on Education* by F.V.N. Painter, © 1928 by Concordia Publishing House. Used by permission, pp. 180-81.

2. John Amos Comenius, *The Great Didactic of John Amos Comenius,* trans. and ed. M.W. Keatinge, 1896, 1910 (New York: Russell and Russell, 1967), p. 58.

3. Comenius, *The Great Didactic,* pp. 184-85.

4. Comenius, *The Great Didactic,* p. 127.

5. John Locke, *An Essay Concerning Human Understanding, ed. Peter H. Nidditch* (Oxford: Oxford University Press, 1975), p. 104.

6. *Emile; Or, Education,* by Jean Jacques Rousseau. Trans. Barbara Foxley, Everyman's Library Edition (New York: E.P. Dutton, 1933), p. 5.

7. Jean Jacques Rousseau, *Emile,* trans. and ed. William Boyd (New York: Teachers College Press, by arrangement with William Heinemann Ltd., London, 1962), pp. 11-15.

8. Alexander S. Neill, *Summerhill* (New York: Hart, 1960), p. 4.

9. Roger DeGuimps, *Pestalozzi: His Life and Work* (New York: D. Appleton, 1890), p. 205.

10. DeGuimps, *Pestalozzi,* p. 1691.

11. S. Ramford, *Passages in the Life of a Radical* (London: London Simpkin Marshall & Co.)

12. Margery Browning, "Owen As an Educator," in *Robert Owen: Prince of Cotton Spinners,* ed. John Butt (Newton Abbot: David and Charles, 1971), p. 65.

13. Friedrich Froebel, *The Education of Man* (Clifton, N.J.: Augustus M. Kelley, 1974), pp. 7-8.

14. Friedrich Froebel, *The Education of Man,* trans. M.W. Hailman (New York: D. Appleton, 1887), p. 55.

15. Friedrich Froebel, *Pedagogics of the Kindergarten,* trans. Josephine Jarvis (New York: D. Appleton, 1902), p. 32.

16. Froebel, *Pedagogics,* pp. 83-84.

17. Friedrich Froebel, *Mother's Songs, Games, and Stories* (New York: Arno Press, 1976), pp. 20-21.

18. Froebel, *Mother's Songs,* pp. 136-37.

19. Maria Montessori, *The Discovery of the Child,*

trans. M.J. Costelloe (Notre Dame, Ind.: Fides Publishers, 1967), p. 22.

20. Maria Montessori, *The Montessori Method,* trans. Anne E. George (Cambridge, Mass.: Robert Bentley, 1967), p. 38.

21. Montessori, *The Discovery of the Child,* p. 28.

22. Montessori, *The Discovery of the Child,* p. 37.

23. Reginald D. Archambault, eds., *John Dewey on Education—Selected Writings* (New York: Random House, 1964), p. 430.

24. Henry Suzzallo, ed., *John Dewey's Interest and Effort in Education* (Boston: Houghton Mifflin, 1913), p. 65.

25. Archambault, *John Dewey on Education,* pp. 170-71.

26. From *Democracy and Education* by John Dewey. Copyright 1916 by Macmillan Company; Copyright renewed 1944 by John Dewey. Reprinted with permission of Macmillan Publishing Co.

27. Edwin G. Boring et al., eds., *A History of Psychology in Autobiography*, vol. IV (Worcester, Mass.: Clark University Press, 1952; New York: Russell and Russell, 1968), p. 244.

28. Benjamin S. Bloom, *Stability and Change in Human Characteristics* (New York: John Wiley, 1964), p. 88.

29. J.McV. Hunt, *Intelligence and Experience* (New York: The Ronald Press Company, Copyright © 1961), pp. 362-63.

30. Christopher Jencks et al., *Inequality: A Reassessment of the Effect of Family and Schooling in America* (New York: Harper and Row, 1973), p. 254.

31. George W. Mayeske et al., *A Study of the Achievement of Our Nation's Students* (Washington, D.C.: U.S. Govt. Printing Office, 1973).

32. *The First Three Years of Life* The Revised Edition by Burton L. White, copyright 1985. Reprinted by permission of the publisher, Prentice Hall Press, New York, NY.

CHAPTER 3
Maria Montessori
The Start of It All

As you read and study:

☐ Understand the key factors in Maria Montessori's career that influenced her educational methods

☐ Compare and contrast the Montessori philosophy with those of other early childhood education programs

☐ Identify the basic Montessori principles that explain how children learn

☐ Examine, understand, and critique the basic characteristics of a good Montessori program

☐ Learn the main philosophical and pedagogical principles of the Montessori program

☐ Become familiar with materials used in a Montessori program and understand their purpose

☐ Develop a rationale for explaining contemporary support and popularity of the Montessori method

☐ Describe the role of the directress (teacher) in a children's house

☐ Describe the role of children in the Montessori program

☐ Identify and describe features of the prepared environment that are unique to the Montessori method

☐ Explain how the Montessori system can be adapted to a regular classroom setting

If we were to single out any one person to credit with the revival of early childhood education, it would be Maria Montessori. From day care centers to PTA meetings, it is usually possible to find someone discussing the pros and cons of her methodology. Nearly every town large enough to support one has a Montessori school. What is so attractive and mesmerizing about the Montessori system? It is intriguing for a number of reasons. First, Montessori education is often identified with the wealthy and upwardly mobile. If parents can afford to give their very young child a preschool education, frequently that education is a Montessori program. Identification with the upwardly mobile gives Montessori education an aura of respectability and elitism. Second, parents who observe a *good* Montessori program like what they see—orderliness, independent children, self-directed learning, a calm environment, and *children* at the center of the learning process. Third, Montessori's philosophy is based on the premise that education begins at birth, and, as we read in Chapter 1, the idea of early learning is popular with parents.

For these reasons, then, Montessori is popular; in fact, Montessori is so popular, and its appeal of quality education so enticing, that many public school systems have adapted and modified Montessori techniques in their kindergarten and first grade programs. Inclusion of Montessori in the public schools is a way of giving parents choices in the kind of program their children will have at a particular school, and it is also a means of desegregation. Montessori would probably smilingly approve of the contemporary use of her method to once again help change the nature and character of early childhood education.

PRINCIPLES OF THE MONTESSORI METHOD

The following principles by no means constitute all the ideas and practices Montessori stressed. They are based on my synthesis of the system from reading Montessori's writings, working with Montessori teachers, and observing in many Montessori settings.

Respect for the Child

The cornerstone on which all other Montessori principles rest is respect for the child. Montessori said,

> As a rule, however, we do not respect children. We try to force them to follow us without regard to their special needs. We are overbearing with them, and above all, rude; and then we expect them to be submissive and well-behaved, knowing all the time how strong is their instinct of imitation and how touching their faith in and admiration of us. They will imitate us in any case. Let us treat them, therefore, with all the kindness which we would wish to help to develop in them. And by kindness is not meant caresses. Should we not call anyone who embraced us at the first time of meeting rude, vulgar and ill-bred? Kindness consists in interpreting the wishes of others, in conforming one's self to them, and sacrificing, if need be, one's own desire.[1]

Because each child is unique, education should be individualized for each child:

> The educator must be as one inspired by a deep *worship of life,* and must, through this reverence, respect, while he observes with human interest, the *development* of the child life. Now, child life is not an abstraction; *it is the life of individual children.* There exists

only one real biological manifestation: the *living individual;* and toward single individuals, one by one observed, education must direct itself.[2]

Children are not miniature adults, and should not be treated as such. Montessori was firm in her belief that a child's life must be recognized as separate and distinct from that of the adult. She attributed most of the responsibility for hampering the education of young children to adults who impose their ideas, wishes, and dreams, failing to distinguish between children's lives and their own.

> In their dealings with children adults do not become egotistic but egocentric. They look upon everything pertaining to a child's soul from their own point of view and, consequently, their misapprehensions are constantly on the increase. Because of this egocentric view, adults look upon the child as *something empty* that is to be filled through their own efforts, as *something inert* and helpless for which they must do everything, as *something lacking an inner guide* and in constant need of direction. In conclusion we may say that the adult looks upon himself as the child's creator and judges the child's actions as good or bad from the viewpoint of his own relations to the child. The adult makes himself the touch stone of what is good and evil in the child. He is infallible, the model upon which the child must be molded. Any deviation on the child's part from adult ways is regarded as an evil which the adult hastens to correct.
>
> An adult who acts in this way, even though he may be convinced that he is filled with zeal, love, and a spirit of sacrifice on behalf of his child, unconsciously suppresses the development of the *child's own personality.*[3]

Educators and parents show respect for children in many ways. Helping children do things for themselves, for example, encourages and promotes independence. At the same time, it also demonstrates a basic respect for their needs as individuals to be independent and self-regulating. When children have choices, they are able to develop the skills and abilities necessary for effective learning and for autonomy and positive self-esteem. These practices are so much more respectful of children than always doing for them or insisting that they do things as adults want them to. (The theme of respect for children resurfaces in our discussion of guiding behavior in Chapter 12.)

The Absorbent Mind

Montessori believed that no child is educated by another person; rather, one must *educate oneself:* "It may be said that we acquire knowledge by using our minds; but the child absorbs knowledge directly into his psychic life. Simply by continuing to live, the child learns to speak his native tongue."[4] There are unconscious and conscious stages in the development of the *absorbent mind.* From birth to three years, the *unconscious absorbent mind* develops the senses used for seeing, hearing, tasting, smelling, and touching. The child absorbs everything.

From three to six years, the *conscious absorbent mind* selects sensory impressions from the environment and further develops the senses. In this phase the child is selective in that he refines what he knows. For example, the child in the unconscious stage merely sees and absorbs an array of colors without distinguishing among them; however, from three on, he develops the ability to distinguish, match, and grade colors. Montessori challenged the teacher to think through the concept of the absorbent mind:

Maria Montessori emphasized sensory training. Here one child helps another to identify cloth swatches by texture. This is the second stage of the activity, in which child performs the task while blindfolded.

How does a child, starting with nothing, orient himself in this complicated world? How does he come to distinguish things, by what marvelous means does he come to learn a language in all its minute details without a teacher but merely by living simply, joyfully, and without fatigue, whereas an adult is in constant need of assistance to orient himself in a new environment to learn a new language, which he finds tedious and which he will never master with the same perfection with which a child acquires his own mother tongue?[5]

Montessori wants us to understand that children cannot help but learn. Simply by living, children learn from their environment. Jerome Bruner expresses this idea when he says that "learning is involuntary." The child learns because he is a thinking being. What he learns depends greatly on the people in his environment, what they say and do, and how they react to him. In addition, available experiences and materials also help determine the type and quality of learning—and thus the individual.

Sensitive Periods

Montessori believed there were *sensitive periods* when children were more susceptible to certain behaviors and could learn specific skills more easily:

A sensitive period refers to a special sensibility which a creature acquires in its infantile state, while it is still in a process of evolution. It is a transient disposition and limited to the acquisition of a particular trait. Once this trait or characteristic has been acquired, the special sensibility disappears.[6]

A child learns to adjust himself and make acquisitions in his sensitive periods. These are like a beam that lights interiorly or a battery that furnishes energy. It is this sensibility which enables a child to come in contact with the external world in a particularly intense manner. At such a time everything is easy; all is life and enthusiasm. Every effort marks an increase in power. Only when the goal has been obtained does fatigue and the weight of indifference come on.

When one of these psychic passions is exhausted, another area is enkindled. Childhood thus passes from conquest to conquest in a constant rhythm that constitutes its joy and happiness.[7]

The secret of using sensitive periods in teaching is to recognize them when they occur. While all children experience the same sensitive periods—for example, a sensitive period for writing—the time at which the periods occur is different for each child. Therefore, it becomes the role of the directress (as Montessori teachers are often called) or the parent to detect these times of sensitivity for learning and provide the setting for optimum fulfillment. Observation thus becomes crucial for teachers and parents. Indeed, many educators believe that observation of children's achievement and behavior is more accurate than the use of tests (see Chapter 1).

The sensitive period for many learnings occurs early in life, during the period of intellectual growth. The experiences necessary for optimum development must be provided at this time. Through observation and practice, Montessori was convinced the sensitive period for development of language was a year or two earlier than originally thought.

Once the sensibility for learning a particular skill occurs, it does not occur again with the same intensity. For example, children will never learn languages as well as when the special sensitivity for language learning occurs. Montessori says, "The child grows up speaking his parent's tongue, yet to grownups the learning of a language is a very great intellectual achievement."[8]

Teachers must do three things: recognize that there are sensitive periods; learn to detect them; and capitalize on them by providing the optimum learning setting to foster their development. Much of what early childhood educators mean by *readiness* is contained in Montessori's concept of sensitive periods.

The Prepared Environment

Montessori believed the child learns best in a *prepared environment*. This environment can be any setting—classroom, a room at home, nursery, or playground. The purpose of the prepared environment is to make the child independent of the adult. It is a place where the child can *do things for himself.* The ideal classrooms Montessori describes are really what educators advocate when they talk about open education; in many respects, Montessori was the precursor of the open classroom movement.

Following a teacher's introduction to the prepared environment, children could come and go according to their desires and needs, deciding for themselves which materials to work with. Montessori removed the typical school desks from the classroom and replaced them with tables and chairs where children could work individually or in small groups. In a modern Montessori classroom, much of a child's work is done on the floor. Montessori saw no reason for a teacher's desk, since the teacher should be involved with the children where they are doing their work. She also

The concept of a prepared environment is a critical ingredient in a Montessori classroom. Organization and arrangement determine, in part, how children behave and what they learn.

introduced child-sized furniture, lowered chalkboards, and outside areas where children could, at will, take part in gardening and other outdoor activities.

Her concept of a classroom was a place where children could do things for themselves; where they could play with material placed there for specific purposes; and *where they could educate themselves.* She developed a classroom free of many of the inhibiting elements in some of today's classrooms. An essential characteristic of the prepared environment is freedom. Since children are free, within the environment, to explore materials of their own choosing, they absorb what they find there.

Many adults fear the child will automatically abuse freedom through destructive acts. When a Montessori teacher anticipates destructive acts, she quickly diverts the child's attention to other materials or activities. Although the Montessori teacher believes in freedom for the child and the child's ability to exercise that freedom, the child is not free to make unlimited choices. For example, the child must know how to use materials correctly before he is is free to choose materials. The student is free to choose within the framework of choices provided by the teacher. Choice, however, is a product of discipline and self-control.

Self- or Auto-Education

Montessori called the concept that children are capable of educating themselves *auto-education:*

> The commonest prejudice in ordinary education is that everything can be accomplished by talking (by appealing, that is, to the child's ear), or by holding one's self up as a model to

be imitated (a kind of appeal to the eye), while the truth is that the personality can only develop by making use of its own powers.[9]

The child who is actively involved in a prepared environment and exercising freedom of choice literally educates himself. The role freedom plays in self-education is crucial:

> And this freedom is not only an external sign of liberty, but a means of education. If by an awkward movement a child upsets a chair, which falls noisily to the floor, he will have an evident proof of his own incapacity; the same movement had it taken place amidst stationary benches would have passed unnoticed by him. Thus the child has some means by which he can correct himself, and having done so will have before him the actual proof of the power he has gained: the little tables and chairs remain firm and silent each in its own place. It is plainly seen that the *child has learned* to command his movements.[10]

Our universal perception of the teaching-learning act is that because the teacher teaches, the child learns—which overlooks that everyone learns a great deal through one's own efforts. Through the principle of auto-education, Montessori focuses our attention on this human capability. The art of teaching includes preparing the environment so that children, by participating in it, educate themselves. Think of the things you learned by yourself and the conditions and circumstances under which you learned them. Your reflections will remind you of the self-satisfaction that accompanies self-learning and the power it has to generate further involvement.

Obviously, it is sometimes quicker, more efficient, and more economical to be told or shown what to do and how to do it. Teachers and parents need to understand, however, that auto-education should have a more dominant role in education than we have been willing to give it. In this sense, education should become more child-centered and less teacher-centered.

THE ROLE OF THE TEACHER

The Montessori teacher must have certain qualities to implement the principles of this child-centered approach. The role of the teacher includes

1. Making the children the center of learning. As Montessori said, "The teacher's task is not to talk, but to prepare and arrange a series of motives for cultural activity in a special environment made for the child."[11]
2. Encouraging children to use the freedom provided for them.
3. Observing children so as to prepare the best possible environment, recognizing sensitive periods, and diverting unacceptable behavior to meaningful tasks.

Montessori believed, "It is necessary for the teacher to *guide* the child without letting him feel her presence too much, so that she may be always ready to supply the desired help, but may never be the obstacle between the child and his experience."[12]

THE MONTESSORI METHOD IN PRACTICE

In a prepared environment, certain materials and activities provide for three basic areas of child involvement: *practical life* or motor education, *sensory materials* for training the senses, and *academic materials* for teaching writing and reading. All these activities are taught according to a prescribed procedure.

Practical Life

The prepared environment emphasizes basic, everyday motor activities, such as walking from place to place in an orderly manner, carrying objects such as trays and chairs, greeting a visitor, walking on a line, and being silent. A new observer to a Montessori classroom is always fascinated by the "dressing frames" designed to perfect the motor skills involved in buttoning, zipping, lacing, buckling, and tying. The philosophy for activities such as these is to make the child independent of the adult and to develop concentration. Water activities play a large role in Montessori methods, and children are taught to scrub, wash, and pour as a means of developing coordination. Practical life exercises also include polishing mirrors and shoes, sweeping the floor, dusting furniture, and peeling vegetables.

Montessorians believe that as the child becomes absorbed in an activity, he gradually lengthens his span of concentration; as he follows a regular sequence of actions, he learns to pay attention to details. They believe that without concentration and involvement through the senses, little learning takes place. Although most people assume

Practical life activities help children learn about and practice everyday activities such as folding napkins, polishing silver, cleaning carrots, polishing shoes, buttoning, buckling, snapping, and washing hands.

that we learn practical life activities incidentally, a Montessori teacher shows children how to do these activities through precisely detailed instructions, with emphasis on sensory materials. Verbal instructions are minimal; the emphasis in the instructional process is on *showing how*.

Montessori also believed children's involvement and concentration in motor activities lengthened their attention span. In a Montessori classroom, it is not uncommon to see a child of four or five polish his shoes or scrub a table for twenty minutes at a time!

Practical life activities are taught in four different types of exercises. *Care of the person* involves activities such as using the dressing frames, polishing shoes, and washing hands. *Care of the environment* includes dusting, polishing a table, and raking leaves. *Social relations* include lessons in grace and courtesy. The fourth type of exercise involves *analysis and control of movement* and includes locomotor activities such as walking and balancing. Figures 3–1, 3–2, and 3–3 are directions for some of

FIGURE 3–1 Pouring (Source: E.G. Caspari, 1974.

Materials: Tray, rice, two small pitchers (one empty, the other containing rice)

Presentation: The child must be shown how to lift the empty pitcher with the left hand and with the right, raise the pitcher containing rice slightly higher. Grasping the handle, lifting, and tilting are practiced. The spout of the full pitcher must be moved to about the center of the empty pitcher before the pouring begins. Set down both pitchers; then change the full one to the right side, to repeat the exercise.
When rice is spilled, the child will set the pitchers down, beside the top of the tray, and pick the grains up, one at a time, with thumb and forefinger.

Purpose: Control of movement.

Point of Interest: Watching the rice.

Control of Error: Hearing the rice drop on the tray.

Age: 2½ years.

Exercise: A container with a smaller diameter, requiring better control of movement. Control the amount of rice for the smaller container.

Note: Set up a similar exercise, using colored popcorn instead of rice.

Rice or Popcorn

Materials: Apron, green-leafed plant, sheet of white freezer paper, basket with small sponge, caster, bottle of plant polish, orange stick, cotton ball.

Presentation:
1. Lay out all the material in order of use from left to right.
2. Bring a plant to the table and place it on the paper.
3. Dampen the sponge at the sink and gently wipe off the top side of the leaf with forward strokes. Hold the leaf on the underside with the other hand. Stroke several leaves to remove the dust.
4. Pour small amount of polish into caster.
5. Wrap a small portion of the cotton ball on the orange stick.
6. Dip the stick in the polish and again stroke gently on the leaf in the manner described above.

Clean up:
1. Remove cotton from the stick and put it in the wastebasket.
2. Take the caster to the sink and wash and dry it.
3. Wash the sponge and bring it back to the table.
4. Place the material back in the basket.
5. Replace the plant on the shelf.
6. Fold the paper. Discard only if necessary.
7. Return basket and paper to the shelf.

Purpose: Co-ordination of movement; care of plants.

Point of Interest: Seeing the leaves get shiny.

Control of Error: Dull leaves and polish on white paper.

Age: 3 years and up.

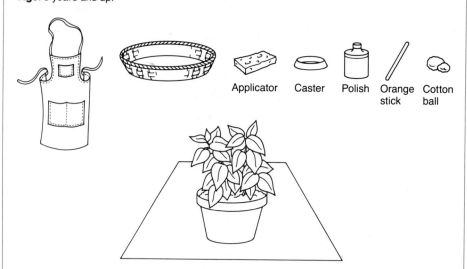

Applicator   Caster   Polish   Orange stick   Cotton ball

FIGURE 3–2   Plant Shining (Source: © E. G. Caspari, 1974. All Rights Reserved.)

Materials: Basket with a duster, soft brush, and feather duster; table to be dusted

Presentation:
Look for dust, with the eyes at the level of the surface of the table. Start with one half of the table, the one immediately in front of you.
Wipe the surface first, as most of the dust will be lying on the top and will give the greatest result.
Always dust away from the body, starting at one end working progressively to the other end, using circular movements.
After the top dust the sides, after the sides dust the legs. Don't forget the corners, the insides of the legs, and underneath the tabletop. The brush is to be used for the corners.
Shake the duster over the wastebasket or outdoors.

Purpose: Coordination of movements, care of the environment, indirect preparation for writing

Point of Interest: The dust to be found in the duster; shaking the dust off the cloth

Control of Error: Any spot of dust left behind

Age: 2½ to 4½ years.

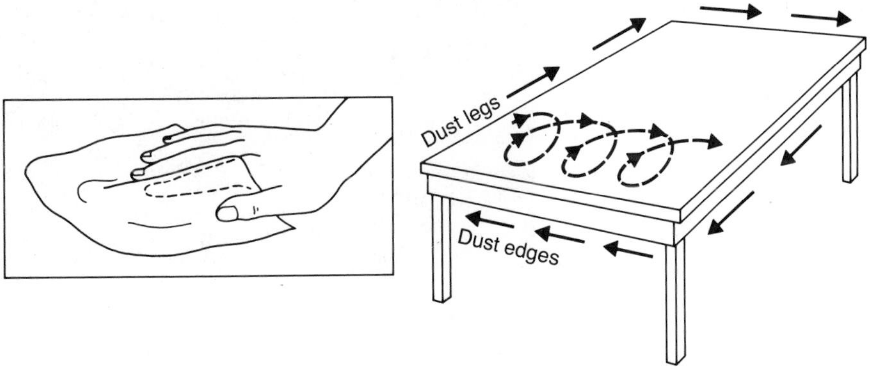

FIGURE 3–3 Dusting (Source: © E. G. Caspari, 1974. All Rights Reserved.)

the practical life activities in a Montessori classroom. Notice the procedures and the exactness of presentation.

Sensory Materials
These are materials in a typical Montessori classroom (the learning purpose appears in parentheses).
☐ Pink tower (visual discrimination of dimension)—ten wood cubes of the same shape and texture, all pink, the largest of which is ten centimeters cubed. Each succeeding block is one centimeter smaller. The child builds a tower beginning with the largest block.
☐ Brown stairs (visual discrimination of width and height)—ten blocks of wood, all brown, differing in height and width. The child arranges the blocks next to each other from thickest to thinnest so the blocks resemble a staircase.

Sensory training involves identifying the quality of objects. It includes motor and sensory experiences with color, sound, dimension, form, texture, taste, and smell.

☐ Red rods (visual discrimination of length)—ten rod-shaped pieces of wood, all red, of identical size but differing in lengths from ten centimeters to one meter. The child arranges the rods next to each other from largest to smallest.

☐ Cylinder blocks (visual discrimination of size)—four individual wood blocks that have holes of various sizes; one block deals with height, one with diameter, and two with the relationship of both variables. The child removes the cylinders in random order, then matches each cylinder to the correct hole.

☐ Smelling jars (olfactory discrimination)—two identical sets of white, opaque glass jars with removable tops through which the child cannot see but through which odors can pass. The teacher places various substances, such as herbs, in the jars, and the child matches the jars according to the smell of the substance in the jars.

☐ Baric tablets (discrimination of weight)—sets of rectangular pieces of wood that vary according to weight. There are three sets, light, medium, and heavy, which the child matches according to the weight of the tablets.

☐ Color tablets (discrimination of color and education of the chromatic sense)—two identical sets of small, rectangular pieces of wood used for matching color or shading.

☐ Sound boxes (auditory discrimination)—two identical sets of cylinders filled with various materials, such as salt and rice. The child matches the cylinders according to the sound the materials make.

☐ Tonal bells (sound and pitch)—two sets of eight bells, alike in shape and size but different in color; one set is white, the other brown. The child matches the bells according to the tone they make.

☐ Cloth swatches (sense of touch)—the child identifies two identical swatches of cloth according to touch. This activity is performed first without a blindfold, but is later accomplished using a blindfold.

☐ Temperature jugs or thermic bottles (thermic sense and ability to distinguish between temperatures)—small metal jugs filled with water of varying temperatures. The child matches jugs of the same temperature.

Materials for training and developing the senses have these characteristics:

1. Control of error. Materials are designed so that a child can see if he makes a mistake; for example, if he does not build the blocks of the pink tower in their proper order, he does not achieve a tower effect.
2. Isolation of a single quality. Materials are designed so that other variables are held constant except for the isolated quality or qualities. Therefore, all blocks of the pink tower are pink because size, not color, is the isolated quality.
3. Active involvement. Materials encourage active involvement rather than the more passive process of looking.
4. Attractiveness. Materials are attractive, with colors and proportions that appeal to children.

Basic Purposes of Sensory Materials. The sensory Montessori materials are often labeled *didactic* (designed to instruct). One purpose of Montessori sensory materials is to train the child's senses to focus on some obvious, particular quality; for example, with the red rods, the quality is length; with pink tower cubes, size; and with bells, musical pitch. Montessori felt is was necessary to help children discriminate among the many stimuli they receive. Accordingly, the sensory materials help make children more aware of the capacity of their bodies to receive, interpret, and make use of stimuli.

Montessori also thought that perception and the ability to observe details were crucial to reading. She believed children should sharpen their powers of observation and visual discrimination before learning to read.

A third purpose of the sensory materials is to increase the child's ability to think, a process that depends on the ability to distinguish, classify, and organize. Children constantly face decisions about the sensory materials: which block comes next, which color matches the other, which shape goes where. These are not decisions the teacher makes, nor are they decisions the child arrives at by guessing; rather, they are decisions made by the intellectual process of observation and selection based upon knowledge gathered through the senses.

Finally, all the sensory activities are not ends in themselves. Their purpose is to prepare the child for the occurrence of the sensitive periods for writing and reading. In this sense, all activities are preliminary steps in the writing-reading process.

In addition, the sensory activities should not be isolated from the real world. If a child is asked to deal with color only when he works with the color tablets, there is no assurance he will have a meaningful understanding of color. Examples in the classroom should call the child's attention to color. The activity enriches the child's ability to learn only as he uses color as a basis for more learning.

Materials for Writing, Reading, and Mathematics

The third area of Montessori materials is *academic;* specifically, items for writing, reading, and mathematics. Exercises are presented in a sequence that encourages writing before reading. Reading is therefore an outgrowth of writing. Both processes, however, are introduced so gradually that children are never aware they are learning to write and read until one day they realize they are writing and reading. Describing this phenomenon, Montessori said that chiildren "burst spontaneously" into writing and reading.

Montessori believed many children were ready for writing at four years of age. Consequently, a child who enters a Montessori system at age three has done most of the sensory exercises by the time he is four; it is not uncommon to see four- and five-year-old children in a Montessori classroom writing and reading. These are examples of materials for writing and reading:

This child is using Montessori's pink tower and brown stairs to learn concepts of seriation and mathematics.

☐ Ten geometric forms and colored pencils that introduce the child to the coordination necessary for writing. After selecting a geometric inset, the child traces it
on paper and fills in the outline with a colored pencil of his choosing.

☐ Sandpaper letters, each letter of the alphabet outlined in sandpaper on a card,
with vowels in blue and consonants in red. The child sees the shape, feels the
shape, and hears the sound of the letter, which the teacher repeats when introducing it.

☐ Movable alphabet, individual wooden letters. The child learns to put together
familiar words.

☐ Command cards, a set of red cards with a single action word printed on each
card. The child reads the word on the card and does what the word tells him to
do; for example, *run, jump*.

Examples of materials for mathematics are:

☐ Number rods—a set of red and blue rods varying in length from ten centimeters to one meter, representing the quantities one through ten. With the help of
the teacher, the child is introduced to counting.

☐ Sandpaper numerals—each number from one to nine in sandpaper on a card.
The child sees, touches, and hears the numbers. He eventually matches number
rods and sandpaper numerals. The child also has the opportunity to discover
mathematical facts through the use of these numerals.

☐ Golden beads—a concrete material for the decimal system. The single bead
represents one unit. A bar made up of ten units in a row represents a ten; ten of

*A Montessori environment is characterized by orderliness, with a place for everything and
everything in its place. The low shelving gives children ready access and encourages use
of the materials.*

the ten bars form a square representing one hundred; and ten hundred squares form the cube representing one thousand.

Additional Features

Other features of the Montessori system are mixed age grouping and self-pacing. A Montessori classroom always contains children of different ages, usually from two-and-a-half to six years of age. This strategy is becoming more popular in many class-rooms and has long been popular in the British Infant Schools. Advantages of mixed age groups are that children learn from one another and help each other; a wide range of materials is available for all children; and older children become role models for younger children. Contemporary instructional practices of student mentoring and cooperative learning all have their roots in and are supported by multiage grouping.

In a Montessori classroom, children are free to learn at their own rate and level of achievement. The child determines which activities to participate in and works at his own pace. Do not assume, however, that the child is allowed to dally at a task. Through observation, the teacher determines when a child has perfected one exercise and is ready to move to a higher level or different exercise. If a child does not perform an activity correctly, the teacher gives him additional help and instruction.

Table 3–1 outlines the basic characteristics of a good Montessori program. Examine it in detail, and use it as a guideline when you observe Montessori programs. Perhaps you can add other criteria you think make a good program. You will be able to

TABLE 3–1   Basic Characteristics of a Montessori Program for Three- to Six-year-old Children

Growth in the Child	Program Organization	Adult Aspects
Independent	Ungraded mix of three-year age span	Professionally educated and certified Montessori educator
Self-directed		
Responsible group member	Enrollment age between 2.6 and 3.6 years	Regularly scheduled staff meetings
Self-disciplined	Policy of three-year cycle of attendance	Ongoing inservice training for auxiliary classroom personnel
Self-accepting		Parent education programs
Enjoys learning	Five-day week with a minimum daily three-hour session	
A unique individual	Separate, small groups; specially designed orientation program for new children	
	Observational records of the individual child and classroom life	
	Public observation policy	

Source: American Montessori Society. Copyright September 1976. Published in New York, New York.

understand further what Montessori education is all about when you read "A Day in a Children's House." Keep in mind that although details of educational programs vary from center to center, the basic constructs of the Montessori program do not.

Criticisms of the Montessori Method

The Montessori system is not without critics. One criticism deals with the didactic nature of the materials and the program. Critics say the system teaches a narrow spectrum of activities in which concepts are learned in a prescribed manner, following prescribed methods, using a prescribed set of materials.

Critics also claim the Montessori classroom does not provide for socialization. They cite the lack of group play, games, and other activities normally present in traditional kindergarten programs. This accusation, of course, is no truer for a Montessori setting than for any other classroom. No method or teacher can stop social interaction unless the teacher is a dictator or the children are afraid of her, which could happen in any classroom. Many Montessori activities promote and offer opportunities for task sharing, cooperation, collaboration, and helping. Also, outdoor time and lunchtime (where children eat in pairs, threes, or small groups) afford ample opportunity for social interaction.

A related criticism is that children do not have opportunities to participate in dramatics, make-believe, and pretending. Montessori felt that children two-and-one-half to six years of age were not mature enough to handle the demands put on them

Learning Environment	Program Emphasis	Administrative Support Systems
Full range of sequentially structured developmental aids	Auto-education	Organized as a legally and fiscally responsible entity
Minimum of thirty-five square feet per child indoors, above space for furnishings and storage	Intrinsic motivation	Nondiscriminatory admissions policy
	Process, not product	Regular administrator
	Cooperation, not competition	Published educational policies and procedures
Adequate outdoor area	Fostering autonomy in the child	Adherence to state laws and health requirements
Lightweight, proportionate, movable, child-sized furnishings	Fostering competencies based on success	Membership in professional national society
Identifiable ground rules	Spontaneous activity	
	Peer teaching	
	Sensorimotor preparation for intellectual development	
	Natural social development	
	Biological basis for support of developmental needs	
	Responsible freedom	

A DAY IN A CHILDREN'S HOUSE[13]

Billy Smith arrives at the Alexander Montessori School at 8:30 a.m. He is left off at the entrance to the school by his mother, who is on her way to work as a secretary at the headquarters of a national airline.

Billy is greeted by one of the classroom aides as he gets out of the car. Billy has gained a great deal of independence in his year and a half at the school, and goes into his classroom by himself. If a child is new to the school, he is escorted to his classroom, or children's house, by an aide until he is able to go by himself. Billy, who is four years old, has a brother and a sister. He will attend the school until he is six, when he will enter first grade in a Montessori elementary or a local public school.

Billy is greeted by his teacher, Frances Collins, as he enters the classroom. "Good morning, Billy. How are you this morning?" Mrs. Collins greets Billy while shaking his hand. She engages him in a brief conversation about his baby sister.

The previous day, Billy checked out, by himself, a book from the children's house library. This morning, Billy goes to the library card file and finds the card to the book he checked out. He places the card in the book and returns the book to the library. Billy does all the checking out and in of books, including writing his own name, without help. The key to this independence is the arrangement of the library. Mrs. Collins has the library, book cards, and the check-out and check-in systems arranged so the children can do all these things themselves.

In Mrs. Collins's class of thirty-three children, ages range from two-and-a-half to five-and-a-half years. Mrs. Collins has two aides to help her.

Since Billy is the first child to arrive in the children's house this morning, he takes the chairs down from all the tables. He also puts down pieces of carpeting (approximately 2' x 3') on the floor for each child, and places a name card for each child on each piece of carpet. When the children come into the class, they will find their name card, pick it up, and place it on a pile. This is one way Mrs. Collins takes roll and, at the same time, helps the children learn their printed names.

FIGURE A   Geometric Inserts.

Next, Billy goes to the language area, takes a set of geometric insets to a table (writing is always done on a table), and uses the frame and insets to make a geometric design, of his choice, on a sheet of paper. When his design is finished, he fills in the design with straight lines using colored pencils (see Figure A). Billy uses an ink stamp to stamp lines on the back of his paper, writes his name on the paper, and files his paper in his own file. The materials in his file will be made into a booklet that will be sent home at the end of the week.

Billy is in the sensitive stage for writing, which means his motor skills make him capable of writing on paper, and he is always eager to write. Billy goes to the other side of the language corner to the movable alphabet cabinet and takes a set of word pictures to the carpet. Using the movable alphabet, he constructs a sentence using the picture card and movable alphabet letters. Billy's sentence is: "The king is fat" (see Figure B). After he has constructed his sentence, Billy takes paper and pencil and goes to a table where he writes this sentence. After he finishes writing, he puts the paper in his file.

At about 10:15 a.m., Billy takes a break for juice. The snack in the Montessori house is on an "as needed" basis, and Billy helps himself, pouring his own drink. Sometimes he and one of his friends take their break together. No attempt is made to force children to take a break or take it all at once or in groups.

After his snack, Billy goes to the practical life area and polishes a table. This activity takes about fifteen minutes. Billy gets all the materials needed for the activity, completes the task, and puts things away by himself. Through exercises of practical life, Billy develops good work habits and extends his span of concentration. Polishing the table involves him in a gross motor activity which has to be performed in a certain way—setting up the material in a specific sequence (from left to right) and then polishing the table. When he has finished polishing, it is Billy's responsibility to replace the materials and return everything to the shelf.

After polishing the table, Billy goes to the math center. Here he and another student set up the addition strip board and see how many

continued

FIGURE B **Writing.**

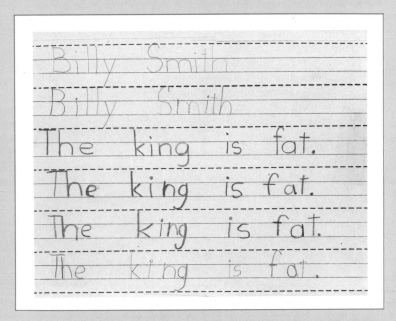

A DAY IN A CHILDREN'S HOUSE *continued*

ways they can make "nine." This activity usually takes about ten minutes. After he finishes in the math area, Billy goes to a directed lesson shared by Mrs. Collins and a group of six children. Each child is given a reading booklet (published by a major publishing company), and they discuss the pictures. The children who can, read the story, while those who can't, follow along. Emphasis in this activity is on listening, sequencing, and comprehension. This activity usually lasts from ten to fifteen minutes.

From 11:00 to about 11:20, the children go outside, where they engage in free play for about ten minutes, then have a directed movement lesson consisting of jumping rope, throwing, or catching. In addition to free or directed play, this outdoor time may be used for nature walks and other kinds of field experiences.

When Billy comes in from outdoor play, he joins the other children in a circle activity with Mrs. Collins to learn songs and sing songs previously learned. The songs are usually based on a monthly theme selected by Mrs. Collins. In addition to a song, the children will also do finger plays, recite poems, and use rhythm band instruments. In the circle time (the children sit on a circle or ellipse marked on the floor), Billy holds the flag while the children say the Pledge of Allegiance; another child leads the group in song about good health habits; and each child is given an opportunity to share an experience that is important to him. Billy tells about his cousin visiting him over the weekend. The circle time also provides an opportunity to talk about matters of interest to the whole group. A child is free to join the circle time as he wishes. The teacher respects the child's personal independence and concentration on the task he is working on, so no one need stop what he is doing just to join the circle time. Because the circle time activities are so interesting, however, children generally want to join. The circle time provides an opportunity to all the children, who have been working at their own pace all morning, to come together.

When circle time is over, usually after about

twenty minutes, the children eat their lunch. Each child washes his hands, gets a paper place mat, places it on a table, and sets his lunch pail on it. At Billy's children's house, all the children bring their own lunch. Sometimes a child or several children who did not go outside during the recess time will set the tables.

Billy is responsible for helping clean up the table where he eats. In a children's house, a child does everything he might normally do in his own house: cleaning up, setting the table, getting his own snack. After lunch, he can take part in games and songs. This activity is directed by the teacher. Lunchtime usually lasts about an hour. During lunchtime, the children are also free to visit with each other and use materials of their choice.

After lunch, Billy checks his folder to see if there is any unfinished work. If there is, he finishes it. If there is no work to be finished, the teacher suggests several things for him to do. On this particular day, Billy chooses to work with the geometry cabinet. This activity involves matching a set of cards to their corresponding geometric shapes. This matching activity takes Billy about twenty minutes. After he puts his materials away, Billy chooses easel painting. Again, Billy is responsible for putting on his own apron, getting the paper, putting it on the easel, and painting his own picture. This activity also encourages creativity.

In Billy's children's house, there is no special time for rest. A child rests when he feels a need for it. Even with the two-and-a-half-year-olds, there is no attempt to force a nap time or rest period. The two-and-a-half and three-year-old children go home for the day at noon, so there are only four- and five-year-olds in the school during the afternoon. Billy and his classmates, as a general rule, don't rest.

When his art activity is finished, Billy's teacher offers him a new lesson with the hundred board. Billy is invited to a table and the teacher brings the materials to the table. Part of Billy's task is to pay attention to the directed lesson so he will know how to do the lesson independently. When the teacher feels he is

The Montessori environment is designed to promote independence and enable children to learn on their own.

ready, Billy can begin to participate, and he gradually takes over the activity. This does not mean that Billy has entirely absorbed the lesson. If his teacher thinks it is necessary, she will give him another, or a more directed, lesson. This directed activity usually lasts about half an hour.

The last activity of the day is a birthday party for one of the classmates. The day ends at 3:00 p.m. Mrs. Collins says good-bye to Billy and tells him she is looking forward to seeing him tomorrow. Billy goes to the area where the children are picked up by their parents or other caregivers. Billy is picked up by a caregiver.

There is really no such thing as a "typical" day in a children's house. On any particular day, a child may work only in the areas of math and practical life. Also, if a child is undecided about what to do at any time, he will check his work folder to get ideas about what to do, or to see what he needs to finish. He will also confer with his teacher to get direction.

How Billy's Teacher Keeps Her Records

Each child has a work folder with his name on it. Inside are four sheets listing the lessons from each of the four areas or avenues (practical life, sensorial, math, and language) of the Montessori system. Mrs. Collins marks each lesson with a yellow marker when she presents it to the child. When the child has mastered the lesson, she marks it in red, indicating that the child is ready to go to another lesson.

All written work, such as words, sentences, numbers, geometric shapes, and tracing, is kept in the child's work folder. When the child has completed five papers of each activity, Mrs. Collins makes it into a booklet to take home. Reports to parents are made both in conferences and in writing. The Montessori program is explained to the parents before their children are enrolled. Periodic parent programs are also conducted to keep the parents informed and involved.

MONTESSORI KINDERGARTEN PROGRAM: NATCHEZ-ADAMS SCHOOL DISTRICT, NATCHEZ, MISSISSIPPI*

In 1970–71, the Natchez Public School System began searching for a kindergarten approach that would serve the needs of children with a wide range of abilities and from various socioeconomic backgrounds. After visiting schools with different kindergarten programs, the decision was made to implement an adapted Montessori approach for the kindergarten in our school district. The Montessori curriculum was chosen because it provides individual instruction for students of varied learning abilities; it fosters an enhanced self-concept for students; it encourages classroom interactions and peer-teaching; students compete only with themselves; and it encourages independence.

Children

Students who are five years of age on or before September first are eligible for kindergarten. Students enter school on a staggered schedule to allow for individual or small group orientation to the environment. The teacher and assistant work with five to eight new students each day while the students from previous days practice materials that have already been introduced. *The Montessori Matters*, published by Sisters of

Notre Dame de Namur, Cincinnati, Ohio, is used as a curriculum guide.

Staff

Each classroom is staffed with one teacher, a full-time state-funded assistant, and a half-time Chapter I assistant. Physical education, music, and library personnel also serve the kindergarten. A district Chapter I resource teacher helps coordinate the kindergarten program throughout the district. The staff works with classes no larger than 27 students.

Environment

Classrooms are set up with activities according to Montessori guidelines for a *prepared environment*. Centers include practical life, sensorial, language, math, science, social studies, and art. These centers meet the state curriculum guidelines for kindergarten in Mississippi.

Parent Involvement

Workshops are held for parents to help them understand the Montessori philosophy and materials. Parents are enthusiastic about the Montessori kindergarten. As one parent comments, "Montessori helps with prereading skills, coordination, and self-concept. In addition, my child helps at home more now and he has learned to share with others and respect others' rights."

*Contributed by Etta Mae Swalm, director of Instructional Support Services, and her staff.

by a make-believe world, so she did not provide for it in her system. This does not, however, resolve the question of the appropriateness of these activities for young children.

The charge is frequently heard that Montessori schools represent an elitist or middle-class system. This claim likely stems from the fact that most Montessori schools are private or are operated by individuals for profit or by parochial school systems. Whereas this seems to be the case, the Montessori program is now used in many Head Start, day care, and public school programs.

One reason many parents and teachers feel the Montessori program is rigid is that her ideas and methodologies are so detailed. Another reason is that they have nothing to compare this system to other than the free play programs they are more accustomed

A Montessori program offers many opportunities for socialization. Mealtime is one of these.

to. When parents and teachers compare the Montessori system, which organizes the environment and learning experiences in a specific, precise way, to a free play setting, there is a tendency to view the Montessori setting as rigid. Parents and teachers need to focus instead on the results of the systems.

In some Montessori programs that enroll children with limited language development and skills, teachers must make special efforts to provide for children's language needs. These children will need more language stimulation, experiences and opportunities to engage in adult/child and child/child dialogues than they would probably have if they were involved only in Montessori activities in which teachers demonstrate the use of materials. A good teacher will supplement and enrich whatever program she is using.

SELECTING A MONTESSORI SCHOOL

Parents who want a Montessori program for their preschool child face the problem of finding out if the school that calls itself a Montessori school really is one. Unfortunately, there is no guarantee that the program of studies will be of the kind and quality advocated by Maria Montessori. Selecting a Montessori preschool is no different from other consumer choices; the customer must beware of being cheated. No truth-in-advertising law requires operators of a Montessori school to operate a quality program. Because the name has such appeal to parents, some schools call themselves Montessori without either the trained staff or facilities to justify their claim.

Not only do some schools misrepresent themselves, but some teachers as well. There is no requirement that a teacher must have Montessori training of any particular duration or by any prescribed course of instruction. The American Montessori Society (AMS) approves training programs that meet its standards for teacher training, and the Association Montessori Internationale (AMI) approves teacher training programs that meet the standards of the international organization.

To decide whether a Montessori school is a good one, parents should consider these points:

- ☐ Is the school affiliated with a recognized Montessori association (AMS or AMI)?
- ☐ Is the teacher a certified Montessori teacher?
- ☐ How many characteristics outlined by the AMS does the program have?
- ☐ Are practices of the Montessori method part of the program?
- ☐ Contact parents of former students to determine their satisfaction with the program; ask "Would you again send your child to this school? How is your child doing in first grade? How was the Montessori program beneficial to your child?"
- ☐ Compare tuition rates of the Montessori school to other schools. Is any difference in tuition worth it?
- ☐ Ask yourself why you want your child to attend a Montessori school. Is it social status? prestige? Do you feel your child will achieve more by attending a Montessori school? Visit other preschool programs to determine if a Montessori program is best for your child.
- ☐ Interview the director and staff to learn about the program's philosophy, the curriculum, rules and regulations, and how the program differs from others that are not Montessori.
- ☐ If you enroll your child, pay attention to his or her progress through visits, written reports, and conferences to be sure the child is learning what will be needed for success in the first grade.

More Information.   Information about becoming a Montessori teacher can be obtained by writing to The American Montessori Society, 150 Fifth Avenue, New York, New York 10011. Requests for information about the International Association should be addressed to AMI/USA, 170 West Scholfield Road, Rochester, New York 14617. Generally, Montessori training takes one year to complete and results in a certificate to teach in Montessori settings. This certification does not generally substitute for public school certification. A bachelor's degree may or may not be required for AMI or AMS training, depending on the level of the courses.

FURTHER READING

Hainstock, Elizabeth G. *Teaching Montessori in the Home: The Pre-School Years* (New York: Random House, 1971)

Makes Montessori ideas understandable to parents and practical for use in the home.

_____. *Teaching Montessori in the Home: The School Years* (New York: Random House, 1971)

Companion to *Teaching Montessori in the Home: The Pre-School Years.* Extends concepts of early learning and emphasizes mathematics and language development. Encourages parents to take responsibility for their children's learning, and outlines the three-period lesson.

Kramer, Rita. *Maria Montessori* (New York: G. P. Putnam's Sons, 1976)

Well-researched and documented biography.

Lillard, Paula Polk. *Montessori, A Modern Approach* (New York: Schocken Books, 1977)

Good account of what happens in the Montessori classroom. Begins with the life of Montessori, concludes with a description of current practices.

Montessori, Maria. *Spontaneous Activity in Education* (New York: Schocken Books, 1965)

Continuation of ideas and methodologies begun in *The Montessori Method.* Deals with concepts of attention, intelligence, imagination, and moral development, and discusses provisions for them in a Montessori setting.

Montessori, Mario M., Jr. *Education for Human Development: Understanding Montessori,* Paula Polk Lillard, ed. (New York: Schocken Books, 1976)

Written by the grandson of Maria Montessori,

essays in this book provide fresh insight into many Montessorian concepts. Addresses some traditional criticisms of the Montessori method and gives a modern approach to the Montessori system. Should be read after one has a knowledge of Montessori and her ideas.

Orem, R. C., ed. *Montessori: Her Method and the Movement* (New York: G. P. Putnam's Sons, 1974)

Layman's guide to the Montessori philosophy and method; includes questions and answers.

_____. *Montessori Today* (New York: G. P. Putnam's Sons, 1971)

Survey of the philosophies and actual programs of Montessori schools in the United States.

Orem, R. C., and Marjorie Coburn. *Montessori Prescription for Children with Learning Disabilities* (New York: G. P. Putnam's Sons, 1978)

Applies and adapts Montessori methods to the needs of the child with learning disabilities. Deals with current trends; gives parents a major role in its program outline.

Standing, E. M. *The Montessori Revolution in Education,* 6th ed. (New York: Schocken Books, 1971)

Excellent reference; easy-to-read, understandable description of activities, with illustrations.

Montessori in Perspective, ed. Publications Committee of the National Association for the Education of Young Children, 1966.

Collection of articles by educators about the history and method of the Montessori system. Should be read with a knowledge of Montessori and after reading at least one of her own books.

FURTHER STUDY

1. In what ways has Montessori influenced early childhood educational practice?
2. Compare Montessori materials to those in other kindergartens and preschool programs. Is it possible for teachers to make Montessori materials? What advantages or disadvantages would there be in making and using these materials?
3. What features of the Montessori program do you like best? Why? What features do you like least? Why? What features are best for children?

4. After visiting a Montessori classroom and talking with teachers, evaluate the criticisms of the system mentioned in the chapter. Are the criticisms valid? Are there any you would add? Why?
5. If a mother of a four-year-old asked your advice about sending her child to a Montessori school, what would you tell her?
6. From your observation of children, give specific examples to support your opinion that there are or are not sensitive periods of learning.
7. Read one of Montessori's books and give an oral

report to your class. Include your opinion on the book and its implications for modern education.

8. Interview public and private school teachers about their understanding of the Montessori program. Do they have a good understanding of the program? What are the most critical areas of understanding or misunderstanding? Do you think *all* early childhood teachers should have knowledge of the Montessori program? Why or why not?

9. Do you think the Montessori method will ever be a dominant program in the public school system? Why or why not? Explain why the Montessori program has remained mainly in the private schools. Interview a public school kinder-garten or preschool teacher and a Montessori teacher on the topic. Compare their opinions to yours.

10. Review several recent studies that deal with the effect of the Montessori method on preschool children's behavior and achievement. Do the findings differ from what you expected? How? Does this change your opinion of the Montessori method?

11. Why is Montessori education so popular?

12. Interview a Montessori school director to learn how to go about opening a Montessori school. (a) Determine what basic materials are needed and their cost. (b) Tell how a particular community would determine how one would "market" the program.

NOTES

1. Maria Montessori, *Dr. Montessori's Own Handbook* (New York: Schocken Books, 1965), p. 133.

2. Maria Montessori, *The Montessori Method,* trans. Anne E. George (Cambridge, Mass.: 1967), p. 104.

3. Maria Montessori, *The Secret of Childhood,* trans. M.J. Costello (Notre Dame, Ind.: Fides Publishers, 1966), p. 20.

4. Maria Montessori, *The Absorbent Mind,* trans. Claude A. Claremont (New York: Holt, Rinehart and Winston, 1967), p. 25.

5. Montessori, *The Secret of Childhood,* p. 48.

6. Montessori, *The Secret of Childhood,* p. 46.

7. Montessori, *The Secret of Childhood,* p. 49.

8. Montessori, *The Absorbent Mind,* p. 6.

9. Montessori, *The Absorbent Mind,* p. 254.

10. Montessori, *The Absorbent Mind,* p. 84.

11. Montessori, *The Absorbent Mind,* p. 8.

12. Montessori, *Dr. Montessori's Own Handbook, p. 131.*

13. The account of a day in a children's house is based on the program and activities of the Alexander Montessori School, Miami, Florida. There are nine directresses at the Alexander School, some of whom are AMI or AMS trained. Two of the staff come from Cuba, one from Italy, one from Hungary, and five are natives of the U.S.

CHAPTER 4
Jean Piaget
A New Way of Thinking About Thinking

As you read and study:

☐ Critically examine and develop an understanding of Piaget's theory of intellectual development

☐ Identify the cognitive processes that Piaget considered integral parts of intellectual development

☐ Understand Piaget's stages of intellectual development

☐ Understand the characteristics of children's thinking at each stage of intellectual development

☐ Learn the terminology necessary to understand Piaget's theory

☐ Analyze Piaget's stages of intellectual development in their relationship to children's development of knowledge

☐ Identify the major features and common concepts of educational curricula based on Piaget's theory

☐ Explain the role of autonomy in children's learning

☐ Discuss issues and controversies associated with Piaget's theory

The Swiss epistemologist Jean Piaget (see Chapter 2) developed the *cognitive theory* approach to learning. An epistemologist is one who studies how knowledge is acquired. Piaget was interested in how humans learn and develop intellectually, beginning at birth and continuing across the life span. He devoted his life to conducting experiments, observing children—including his own—and writing about his theory. Because of Piaget, our knowledge about children's thinking is greatly enriched, and his influence on early childhood education continues to be significant.

Generally, "intelligence" suggests intelligence quotient or IQ—that which is measured on an intelligence test. This is not what Piaget means by intelligence; for him, intelligence is the cognitive, or mental, process by which children acquire knowledge—hence, *intelligence* is "to know." It is synonymous with thinking in that it involves the use of mental operations developed as a result of acting mentally and physically in and on the environment. Basic to Piaget's cognitive theory is the active involvement of children through direct experiences with the physical world. A second point is that intelligence develops over time, and a third premise is that children are *intrinsically* motivated to develop intelligence.

To adequately understand and appreciate Piaget's cognitive theory, you must understand that his early training as a biologist permeates and influences his thinking and ideas. He conceives of intelligence as having a biological basis—that is, all organisms, including humans, adapt to their environments. You are probably familiar with the process of physical adaptation, whereby an individual, stimulated by environmental factors, reacts and adjusts to that environment; this adjustment results in physical changes. Piaget applies the concept of adaptation to the mental level and uses it to help explain how intellectual development evolves through stages of thinking. Humans mentally adapt to environmental experiences as a result of encounters with people, places, and things; the result is *cognitive development*.

INTELLECTUAL DEVELOPMENT AND ADAPTATION

To Piaget, the adaptive process at the intellectual level operates much the same as at the physical level. He sees the newborn child as lacking intelligence, except the intelligence expressed through reflexive motor actions such as sucking, grasping, head turning, and swallowing. Through the process of adaptation to the environment via these reflexive actions, the intelligence of the young child has its origin and is developed.

> Adaptation is for Piaget, the essence of intellectual functioning, just as it is the essence of biological functioning. It is one of the two basic tendencies inherent in all species; the other is organization, the ability to integrate both physical and psychological structures into coherent systems. Adaptation takes place through organization; the organism discriminates among the myriad stimuli and sensations by which it is bombarded and organizes them into some kind of structure.[1]

Through this interaction with the environment that results in adaptation, the child organizes sensations and experiences. The resulting organization and processes of interaction are what is called *intelligence*. Obviously, therefore, the quality of the environment and the nature of the child's experiences will play a major role in the development of intelligence. For example, the child with various and differing objects available to grasp and suck, and many opportunities for this behavior, will develop differentiated sucking organizations (and therefore an intelligence) quite different from that of the child who has nothing to suck but a pacifier.

The Process of Adaptation

Piaget believed the adaptive process is composed of two interrelated processes, assimilation and accommodation. On the intellectual level, *assimilation* is the taking in of data through sensory impulses via experiences and impressions and incorporating them into knowledge of people and objects already created as a result of these experiences.

> Every experience we have, whether as infant, child, or adult, is taken into the mind and made to fit into the experiences which already exist there. The new experience will need to be changed in some degree in order for it to fit in. Some experiences cannot be taken in because they do not fit. These are rejected. Thus the intellect assimilates new experiences into itself by transforming them to fit the structure which has been built up. This process of acting on the environment in order to build up a model of it in the mind, Piaget calls assimilation.[2]

Accommodation, on the other hand, is the process by which the individual changes his way of thinking, behaving, and believing to come into accord with reality. For example, a child who is familiar with cats because she has several at home may, upon seeing a dog for the first time, call it a cat. She has assimilated dog into her organization of cat. However, she must change (accommodate) her model of what constitutes "catness" to exclude dogs. She does this by starting to construct or build a scheme for dog and thus what "dogness" represents.

> Now with each new experience, the structures which have already been built up will need to modify themselves to accept that new experience, for, as each new experience is fitted in to the old, the structures will be slightly changed. This process by which the intellect continually adjusts its model of the world to fit in each new acquisition, Piaget calls accommodation.[3]

The twin processes of assimilation and accommodation, viewed as an integrated, functioning whole, constitute *adaptation.*

Another term in Piaget's theory of intelligence is *equilibrium.* Equilibrium is a balance between assimilation and accommodation. An individual cannot assimilate new data without to some degree changing his way of thinking or acting to fit those new data. People who always assimilate without much evidence of having changed are characterized as "flying in the face of reality." Yet, an individual cannot always accommodate old ideas to all the information he receives. If this were the case, no beliefs would ever be maintained. A balance is needed between the two. Diagramed, the process would look something like that in Figure 4–1.

Upon receiving new sensory and experiential data, the child assimilates or fits these data into her already existing knowledge (scheme) of reality and the world. If the new data can be immediately assimilated, then equilibrium occurs. If she is unable to assimilate the data, she tries to accommodate and change her way of thinking, acting, and perceiving to account for the new data and restore equilibrium to the

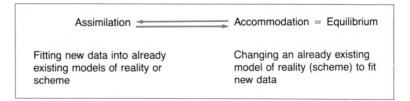

FIGURE 4–1   The Adaptation Process.

intellectual system. It may well be that she can neither assimilate nor accommodate the new data; if so, she rejects the data entirely.

Instances of rejection are common if what the child is trying to assimilate and accommodate is radically different from her past data and experiences. This partially accounts for Piaget's insistence that new experiences have some connection or relationship to previous experiences; for example, present school experiences should build on previous life experiences.

Even more importantly, a teacher must try to assess children's cognitive structures and determine the suitability of school tasks in promoting cognitive growth. Before giving a child activities in classification, for example, a teacher must determine at what level the child is functioning in relation to classification structures. It is also imperative that the teacher not assign (or demand, as is so frequently done) the child to do tasks for which she lacks the cognitive structure. Undoubtedly, some of the reasons for school failure can be attributed to teachers who insist that children engage in tasks for which they have no experiential background and consequently lack the necessary cognitive structure. For example, a child must "know" what a circle is before being able to "find something shaped like a circle in the room"; and, of course, she should not be asked to separate red beads from blue and yellow beads if she cannot yet discriminate among colors.

Schemes

Piaget used the term *scheme* to refer to units of knowledge the child develops through the adaptive process. (In reality, the child develops many schemes.) A newborn has only reflexive actions. By using reflexive actions such as sucking and grasping, the child begins to build her concept and understanding of her world. When the child uses primarily reflexive actions to develop intellectually, she is in what Piaget calls the *sensorimotor stage,* which begins at birth and usually ends between eighteen months and two years. Reflexive actions help her construct a mental scheme of what is suckable and what is not (what can fit into her mouth and what cannot), and what sensations (warm and cold) occur by sucking. She also uses her grasping reflex in much the same way to build schemes of what can and cannot be grasped.

Why do some children develop or create different schemes? This depends upon the environment in which the child is reared and the quality of the child's experiences in that environment. If the environment establishes parameters for the development of intelligence, the child who is confined to a crib with no objects to suck or grasp is at a disadvantage in building mental structures through the adaptive process utilizing sensorimotor responses. The child who has a variety of materials has more opportunity to develop alternative schemes. Children who have a variety of materials and a caring adult to help stimulate sensory responses will do even better. By the same token, as the child grows and matures, she will have greater opportunities to develop intellectually in an environment that provides for interaction with people, objects, and things.

In this process of adaptation, Piaget ascribed primary importance to the child's physical activity. Physical activity leads to mental stimulus, which in turn leads to mental activity. Thus it is not possible to draw a clear line between physical activity and mental activity in infancy and early childhood. Settings should enable children to explore their physical environment and to interact with people and objects in this exploration. A child who is confined to a playpen without opportunities for manipulating objects and for social interactions is limited in adaptive opportunities.

Everyone recognizes that children should play, but we have not always recognized the importance of play as the context in which the child constructs mental schemes to form a basis for all other schemes. Play, to Piaget, becomes a powerful process in intellectual development. Parents seem to sense this intuitively in wanting their children to play, particularly with other children. Many kindergarten and first-grade teachers also have an intuitive sense of the importance of play and include many opportunities for play in their curricula.

Constructivism and Intellectual Development

The constructivist concept is central to understanding Piaget's theory. Children literally construct their knowledge of the world and their level of cognitive functioning. "The more advanced forms of cognition are constructed anew by each individual through a process of 'self-directed' or 'self-regulated' activity."[4] The constructivist process "is defined in terms of the individual's organizing, structuring and restructuring of experience—an ongoing lifelong process—in accordance with existing schemes of thought. In turn, these very schemes become modified and enriched in the course of interaction with the physical and social world."[5] Children continuously organize, structure, and restructure experiences in relation to existing schemes of thought. Experiences provide a basis for constructing schemes.

In explaining the role of constructivism, Constance Kamii, a leading Piaget scholar, states, "Constructivism refers to the fact that knowledge is built by an active child from the inside rather than being transmitted from the outside through the senses."[6]

Maturation and Intellectual Development

Piaget believed maturation, the child's development over time, also influences intellectual development. Factors that in turn influence maturation are (1) genetic characteristics peculiar to the child as an individual, (2) the unique characteristics of the child as a human being, and (3) environmental factors such as nutrition. Maturation helps explain why a child's thinking is not the same as the thinking of the adult, and why we should not expect a child to think as an adult does. A child who has adults to interact with, as through conversation that solicits and promotes the child's involvement, has the opportunity to develop schemes that differ from those of the child who lacks this involvement.

Play provides children with the means and opportunity to be physically and mentally involved. Piaget believed that physical activity is necessary for mental development in the early years.

Social Transmission and Intellectual Development

Piaget felt social transmission is important because some information and modes of behavior are best transmitted to the child by people rather than by other methods, such as reading. (When discussing environmental influences, I include people; Piaget considers them a separate factor.) Examples of social transmission include behavior appropriate to certain situations, such as not running in front of cars, and many curriculum skills involving the 3Rs. From the cognitive-development viewpoint, however, there is a difference between being told what something is ("this block is large") and understanding what "large" means as a result of playing and experimenting with blocks of different sizes. Telling a child that something is large involves no thinking processes on the child's part; to develop thinking processes one must provide the child with many experiences to perform operations—for example, stacking, sorting, seriating, experimenting, and building with blocks.

Stages of Intellectual Development

Table 4–1 summarizes Piaget's developmental stages and will help you conceptualize stage-related characteristics. Piaget contended that the developmental stages are the same for all children, including the atypical child, and that all children progress through each stage in the same order. The ages are only approximate and should not be considered fixed. The sequence of growth through the developmental stages does not vary; the ages at which progression occurs do vary.

TABLE 4-1   Piaget's Stages of Cognitive Development

Stage	Characteristics
Sensorimotor (Birth–18 months/2 years)	Uses sensorimotor system of sucking, grasping, and gross body activities to build schemes. Begins to develop object permanency. Dependent on concrete representations. Frame of reference is the world of here and now.
Preoperational (2–7 years)	Language development accelerates. Internalizes events. Egocentric in thought and action. Thinks everything has a reason or purpose. Is perceptually bound. Makes judgments primarily on basis of how things look.
Concrete Operations (7–12 years)	Capable of reversal of thought processes. Ability to conserve. Still dependent on how things look for decision making. Less egocentric. Structures time and space. Understanding of number. Beginning of logical thinking.
Formal Operations (12–15 years)	Capable of dealing with verbal and hypothetical problems. Ability to reason scientifically and logically. No longer bound to the concrete. Can think with symbols.

Sensorimotor Stage.   During the period from birth to about two years, children use senses and motor reflexes to begin building knowledge of the world. They use their eyes to view the world, their mouths to suck, and their hands to grasp. Through these innate sensory and reflexive actions, they continue to develop an increasingly complex, unique, and individualized hierarchy of schemes. What the child is to become both physically and intellectually is related to these sensorimotor functions and interactions. Furth says "An organism exists only insofar as it functions."[7] This important concept stresses the necessity of an enriched environment for children. Major characteristics of the sensorimotor period include these:

☐ Dependency on and use of innate reflexive actions
☐ Initial development of object permanency (the idea that objects can exist without being seen)
☐ Egocentricity, whereby the child sees herself as the center of the world and believes events are caused by her
☐ Dependence upon concrete representations (things) rather than symbols (words, pictures) for information
☐ By the end of the second year, the child relies less on sensorimotor reflexive actions and begins to use symbols for things that are not present. (We will discuss intellectual development in infants, toddlers, preschoolers, and primary-grade children in more detail in later chapters.)

Preoperational Stage.   The preoperational stage begins at age two and ends at approximately seven years of age. The preoperational child is different from the sensorimotor child in these ways:

☐ Language development begins to accelerate rapidly
☐ There is less dependence on sensorimotor action
☐ There is an increased ability to internalize events and to think by utilizing representational symbols such as words in place of things

Piaget's theory has many implications for how teachers and caregivers interact with children and design learning experiences for them. Among the implications are that children think differently at different stages of cognitive development and that their thinking is not like adult thinking and should not be compared to it.

The preoperational child continues to share common characteristics with the sensorimotor child, such as egocentricity. At the preoperational level, egocentricity is characterized by being perceptually bound, the outward manifestation of which is making judgments, expressing ideas, and basing perceptions mainly on an interpretation of how things are physically perceived by the senses. How things look to the preoperational child is in turn the foundation for several other stage-related characteristics. First, a child faced with an object that has multiple characteristics, such as a long, round, yellow pencil, will "see" whichever of those qualities first catches her eye. A preoperational child's knowledge is based only on what she is able to see, simply because she does not yet have operational intelligence or the ability to think using mental images.

Second, absence of operations makes it impossible to conserve, or determine that the quantity of an object does not change simply because some transformation occurs in its physical appearance. For example, show a preoperational child two identical rows of matching toy soliders (see Figure 4–2). Ask the child if there are the same number of toy soldiers in each row. She should answer affirmatively. Next, space out the toy soldiers in each row, and ask the child if the two rows still have the same number of toy soldiers. She may insist that there are more toy soliders in one row "because it's longer." The child bases her judgment on what she can see, namely the spatial extension of one row beyond the other row. This is also an example of reversibility; in this case, the child is not capable of reversing thought or action, which would require that she mentally put the row back to its original length.

The preoperational child acts as though everything has a reason or purpose; that is, she believes every act of her mother, father, and teacher, or every event in nature, happens for a specific purpose. This accounts for the child's constant and recurring questions about why things happen, how things work, and the corresponding exasperation of adults in trying to answer these questions.

Preoperational children also believe everyone thinks as they think and therefore act as they act for the same reasons. Because the preoperational child is egocentric, she cannot put herself in another's place. To ask her to sympathize or empathize with others is asking her to perform an operation beyond her developmental level.

Preoperational children's language illustrates their egocentrism. For example, in explaining to you about a dog that ran away, a child might say something like this: "And we couldn't find him . . . and my dad he looked . . . and we were glad." In this case, because of her egocentrism, she assumes you have the same point of view she does and know the whole story. The details are missing for you, not for her. Young children's egocentrism also helps explain why they tend to talk at each other rather than with each other. This dialogue between two children playing at a day care center reveals egocentrism:

> Jessica: My mommy's going to take me shopping.
> Mandy: I'm going to dress this doll.
> Jessica: If I'm good I'm going to get an ice-cream cone too.
> Mandy: I'm going to put this dress on her.

The point is that egocentrism is a fact of cognitive development in the early childhood years. Our inability to always see clearly someone else's point of view is evidence

All toy soldiers should be equal in size, dimension, and color. When asked if there are the same number of toy soldiers in each row, the preoperational child will answer yes. However, when one row is spread out, so that the correspondence of being exactly opposite from each other is destroyed (below), the preoperational child will say there are more toy soldiers in the bottom row because it is longer.

FIGURE 4–2   Perceptions of a Preoperational Child.

that egocentrism in one form or another is part of the cognitive process across the life span.

Concrete Operations Stage.   Piaget defined *operation* as follows: "First of all, an operation is an action that can be internalized; that is, it can be carried out in thought as well as executed materially. Second, it is a reversible action; that is, it can take place in one direction or in the opposite direction."[8] Unlike the preoperational child,

Classroom activities should help children develop an understanding of how things are related, through ordering, classifying, and seriating.

whose thought goes in only one direction (using the body and sensory organs to act on materials), children in the concrete stage begin to use mental images and symbols during the thinking process and can reverse operations. Although children are very much dependent on the perceptual level of how things look to them, development of mental processes can be encouraged and facilitated during this stage through the use of concrete or real objects as opposed to hypothetical situations or places.

You must constantly keep in mind, however, that telling is not teaching. You should structure the learning setting so that children have experiences at their level with real objects, things, and people. Providing activities at the child's level cannot be overstressed. Teachers often provide activities that are too easy rather than activities that are too difficult; for example, instead of just giving the children a basket of small plastic colored beads to play with, ask them to sort the beads into a red group, a blue group, a yellow group, and a green group.

A characteristic of the concrete operational child is the beginning of the ability to conserve. Unlike the preoperational child, who thinks that because the physical appearance of an object changes it therefore follows that its quality or quantity changes, the concrete operational child begins to develop the ability to understand that change involving physical appearances does not necessarily change quality or quantity (see Figure 4–3).

The child also begins to reverse thought processes, by going back over and "undoing" a mental action she has just accomplished. At the physical level, this relates

FIGURE 4–3   Test of Child's Ability to Conserve.

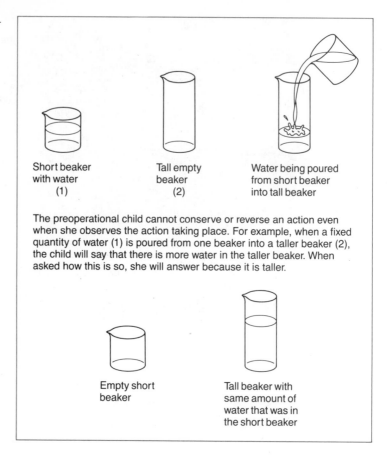

Short beaker
with water
(1)

Tall empty
beaker
(2)

Water being poured
from short beaker
into tall beaker

The preoperational child cannot conserve or reverse an action even
when she observes the action taking place. For example, when a fixed
quantity of water (1) is poured from one beaker into a taller beaker (2),
the child will say that there is more water in the taller beaker. When
asked how this is so, she will answer because it is taller.

Empty short
beaker

Tall beaker with
same amount of
water that was in
the short beaker

to conservation. In the example of two rows of soliders, the child indicated there
were more soldiers in the spread-out row. The child who can reverse an operation
can undo it by mentally returning the soldiers to their original position and is then
able to determine that there are not more soldiers in a longer row. The concrete
operational child begins to manipulate mentally rather than depend only on physical
appearances or concrete objects. Whereas the preoperational child cannot "put back"
the soldiers mentally, the concrete operational child can. Other mental operations
the child is capable of during this stage are

☐ One-to-one correspondence
☐ Classification of objects, events, and time according to certain characteristics
☐ Classification involving multiple properties of objects
☐ Class inclusion operations
☐ Complementary classes

During the concrete operations stage, children are less egocentric. They learn that
other people have thoughts and feelings that can differ from their own. One of the
more meaningful methods of helping a child develop beyond this innate egocentrism

is through interaction with other individuals, especially peers. The teacher's role is not to "teach" children to share or tell them when to apologize from something they've done. It is through involvement with others, interacting and talking about social encounters, that children gradually become less egocentric. This stage does not represent a period into which the child suddenly emerges, after having been a preoperational child. The process of development is not that of Athena stepping from the head of Zeus, but rather a gradual, continual process occurring over a period of time and resulting from maturation and experiences. No simple sets of exercises will cause the child to move up the developmental ladder. Experiences with people and objects result in activities that lead to conceptual understanding.

Formal Operations Stage.   The next stage of development, the second part of operational intelligence, is called *formal operations.* It begins at about eleven years of age and extends to about fifteen years. During this period, the child becomes capable of dealing with increasingly complex verbal and hypothetical problems, and is less dependent upon concrete objects to solve problems. The child becomes free of the world of "things" as far as mental functioning is concerned. Thinking ranges over a wide time span that includes past, present, and future. The child in this stage develops the ability to reason scientifically and logically, and can think with all the processes and power of an adult. How one thinks is thus pretty well established by the age of fifteen, although the child or adolescent does not stop developing new schemes through assimilation and accommodation.

EDUCATIONAL CURRICULA BASED ON PIAGET

The High/Scope Early Elementary Program:
Cognitively Oriented Curriculum

The High/Scope Educational Research Foundation is a nonprofit organization that sponsors and supports the cognitively oriented curriculum. The program is based on Piaget's intellectual development theory and "is an 'open framework' approach that places both the teacher and the child in active, initiating roles. It attempts to blend the virtues of purposeful teaching with open-ended, child-initiated activities."[9]

Since part of the Piagetian theory of intellectual development maintains that children must be actively involved in their own learning through experiences and encounters with people and things, the cognitively oriented curriculum promotes the child's active involvement in his own learning. The program lists these objectives to facilitate the learning process:

☐ An ability to make decisions about what they are going to do and how they are going to do it
☐ An ability to define and solve problems
☐ Self-discipline, ability to identify personal goals, and capacity to pursue and complete self-chosen tasks
☐ An ability to engage with other children and adults in group planning, cooperative effort, and shared leadership

A GLOSSARY OF PIAGETIAN TERMS

Accommodation   Changing one's ideas, or scheme, of reality to fit the new knowledge one is trying to assimilate.

Adaptation   The processes of assimilation and accommodation.

Assimilation   Fitting or adding new knowledge into already existing schemes of reality.

Concrete Operations   The beginning of operational thought. In concrete operations, the child deals with real things. The operations usually associated with concrete operations are classification, seriation, numerations, and correspondences.

Conservation   Piaget uses this term to describe the judgment that the quantity remains the same after a transformation. When the child is capable of reversing thought processes, he is able to conserve.

Constructivism   The process of continually organizing, structuring, and restructuring experiences into existing schemes of thought.

Egocentric   Centering around the child himself. The young child is literally bound by his own thinking. He understands only one point of view, his own. Also, the child can perceive only one aspect of a situation at a time.

Object Permanency   A child constructs the belief that when something (an object, a parent) disappears from his sight, it doesn't cease to exist, that it has permanency. The young child thinks that when he no longer can see an object, it no longer exists. In the sensorimotor stage, the child begins to learn that when his mother leaves the room she still exists and that when his ball rolls out of his sight, it still exists.

Operation   A thought process capable of being reversed and combined with other operations. Operations as conceived by Piaget are also reversible, i.e., $4 - 2 = 2$. The preoperational child is not capable of mentally reversing these operations.

Scheme   A unit of knowledge, an idea. The child begins life with only reflexive motor actions that develop into schemes. All other thoughts and ideas build on these primitive ones.

☐ Expressive abilities—to speak, write, dramatize, and graphically represent their experiences, feelings, and ideas

☐ An ability to comprehend others' self-expression through spoken, written, artistic, and graphic representations

☐ An ability to apply classification, seriation, spatial, temporal, and quantitative-mathematical reasoning in diverse life situations

☐ Skills and abilities in the arts, science, and physical movement as vehicles with which to engage their personal talents and energy

☐ Openness to the points of view, values, and behaviors of others

☐ Spirit of inquiry and a personal sense of goals and values

☐ Long-term interests or avocations which can be cultivated both in and outside of school throughout life.[10]

Achievement of these objectives depends on the child's involvement in the key experiences of action, representation, conceptual relations, and curriculum. *Action* includes planning, working, evaluating, and social interactions. *Representation* includes dramatic activity, drawing and painting, speaking, listening, writing, and reading. *Conceptual relations* consist of classification, seriation, number, space, time, causality, and measurement, which includes length, area, weight, volume, and time. *Curriculum content* consists of language arts, mathematics, art, play and drama, construction, sewing and pattern design, music, movement, media, social studies, and science.

The adult's role in the cognitively oriented curriculum encompasses behaviors in three broad areas. Adults must (1) know where the child is starting from; (2) provide an environment where children can become self-initiating, decision makers and problem solvers; and (3) guide the child. These aspects of the teacher's role are supported by cooperation with adults similarly concerned with children's education.[11] Working in these three areas enables the teacher to come to know each child well. It is important in a cognitively oriented curriculum, as in any other good program, that teachers know at what developmental level each child is functioning. Children benefit most from experiences that match their developmental capacities.

By knowing the developmental stages, teachers can involve the child in appropriate activities. For example, if the child is at the preoperational level, the teacher might use a classification activity involving how objects are similar and different, whereas if the child were at the concrete operational level, a classification activity involving sorting objects into increasingly higher order of classes would be more appropriate. The teacher can thus provide an individualized program for each child. These are ways to identify a child's developmental level:

1. Observe what children are doing, things they make, and pictures they draw
2. Question children about their work, actions, and activities
3. Simulate an activity designed to reveal how the child acts, works, behaves, and interacts

The teacher must also continually encourage and support children's interests and involvement in activities, which occurs within an organized environment and a consistent routine. The teacher must plan what and how children will learn and involve children in planning for their own learning. Teachers plan from key experiences through which children's emerging abilities may be broadened and strengthened. Children generate many of these experiences on their own; others require adult guidance. Many key experiences arise naturally throughout the daily routine. Key experiences are not limited to specific objects or places; they are natural extensions of children's projects and interests. Table 4–2 lists some key experiences that support learning.

A team-teaching concept provides children and adults with greater support, involvement, ideas, attention, help, and expertise. Just as children plan and work in the cognitively oriented classroom, so does the teaching team plan daily for the classroom. The recommended adult-child ratio is one to ten, so a cognitively oriented classroom of thirty children would have three adults—perhaps one teacher, one paid aide, and a volunteer, or one teacher, one assistant teacher, and one aide.

In the cognitively oriented curriculum, the learning process is based on matching children's developing levels of intellectual ability to learning tasks and activities. There is no effort made to push children, speed up the learning process, teach for achievement of a developmental level, or teach facts as a substitute for thinking. The children's emerging abilities are "broadened and strengthened" rather than "taught" in the conventional sense. To match learning tasks with developmental levels, children are involved in activities according to their interests, in a framework based partly on ideas

TABLE 4–2   Key Experiences to Match Developmental Capacities of Children
Between Ages of Four and Six

Active learning

Exploring actively the attributes and functions of materials with all the senses.
Discovering relations through direct experience.
Manipulating, transforming, and combining materials.
Identifying personal interests by choosing materials, activities, and purposes.
Acquiring skills with tools and equipment.
Using small and large muscles.
Taking care of one's needs.
Predicting problems and devising ways of solving them.

Speaking and listening to language

Talking with others about personally meaningful experiences.
Describing relations among objects, people, events, and ideas.
Talking with others about needs, interests, ideas, and feelings.
Having one's own spoken language written down by an adult and read back.
Having fun with language: rhyming, making up stories, listening to poems and stories.
Imitating and describing sounds from the environment.
Listening to others.
Responding to others by asking questions.
Following directions given by others.
Telling stories from pictures and books.
Solving problems or conflicts.

Representing experiences and ideas

Recognizing objects by sound, touch, taste, and smell.
Pantomiming actions.
Relating pictures, photographs, and models to real places and things.
Representing personal experiences through: role play, pretending, and dramatic activities; making models out of clay, blocks, etc.; drawing and painting; graphing, mapping, and using objects to make prints.
Sharing and discussing representations.
Interpreting representations of others.

Writing

Dictating, tracing, copying, or writing stories about personally meaningful experiences.
Expressing ideas and feelings by dictating or writing original stories, poems, songs, riddles.
Including descriptive detail in dictation or writing by describing attributes of objects and relations among objects, people, and events.
Using phonics for spelling words.
Writing simple information such as name, address, etc.

TABLE 4–2 *continued*

Reading

Reading back dictation with an adult.
Matching letters and words that are alike.
Recognizing familiar words such as own name, name of common objects, places, and actions.
Hearing likenesses (rhyming sounds) and differences in words.
Recognizing familiar words such as own name, name of common objects, places, and actions.
Identifying letters in own name and familiar words.
Reading one's own dictated or written story.

Developing logical reasoning

Classification
Investigating and labeling the attributes of things.
Noticing and describing how things are the same and how they are different.
Sorting and matching.
Using and describing something in several different ways.
Describing what characteristics something does not possess or what class it does not belong to.
Holding more than one attribute in mind at a time. (Example: Can you find something that is red and made of wood?)
Sorting objects and then resorting them using different criteria.
Distinguishing between "some" and "all."

Seriation
Comparing objects using a single criterion: Which one is bigger (smaller), heavier (lighter), rougher (smoother), louder (softer), harder (softer), longer (shorter), wider (narrower), sharper, darker, etc.
Comparing and sorting objects into two groups based on a particular criterion (big/little, tall/short, hard/soft, etc.).
Arranging several things in order along some dimension and describing the reactions (the longest one, the shortest one, etc.).
Arranging things into three groups along some dimension and describing the relations (big, bigger, biggest; long, longer, longest; etc.).

Number concepts
Comparing number and amount: more/less, same amount; more/fewer, same number.
Enumerating (counting) objects, as well as counting by rote.
Identifying and writing numerals to twenty.
Representing number information by talking, drawing, or writing numerals.

Understanding time and space

Spatial Relations
Fitting things together and taking them apart.
Rearranging a set of objects or one object in space (folding, twisting, stretching, stacking, tying) and observing the spatial transformations.

TABLE 4-2 *continued*

Observing things and places from different spatial viewpoints.

Experiencing and describing the positions of things in relation to each other (e.g., in the middle, on the side of, on, off, on top of, over, above).

Experiencing and describing relative distances among things and locations (close, near, far, next to, apart, together).

Experiencing and representing one's own body: how it is structured, what various body parts can do.

Learning to locate things in the classroom, school, and neighborhood.

Interpreting representations of spatial relations in drawings and pictures.

Distinguishing and describing shapes.

Identifying parts of objects and identifying an object from one of its parts.

Identifying and representing the order of objects in space.

Developing an awareness of symmetry in one's own representations and representations of others.

Time

Planning and completing what one has planned.

Describing and representing past events.

Anticipating future events verbally and by making appropriate preparations.

Starting and stopping an action on signal.

Noticing, describing, and representing the order of events.

Experiencing and describing different rates of movement.

Using conventional time units when talking about past and future events (morning, yesterday, hour, etc.).

Comparing time periods (short, long; new, old; young, old; a little while, a long time).

Observing that clocks and calendars are used to mark the passage of time.

Observing seasonal changes.

Science

Caring for animals

Planting seeds and caring for growing plants.

Observing, describing, and representing weather changes.

Observing, describing, and representing transformations, i.e., cooking activities (making popcorn, apple sauce, pudding), carving pumpkins, freezing liquids, melting snow, sinking and floating activities.

Exploring the natural environment.

Collecting objects from the natural environment.

Social Studies

Interacting with people of many ages and backgrounds in a variety of situations.

Representing family, school, and community roles and events through socio-dramatic play.

Taking field trips.

Representing field trips by writing experience stories, building models, and drawing pictures.

Utilizing community resources as a basis for classroom activities.

Source: Donna McClelland, consultant, High/Scope Educational Research Foundation.

A key experience for kindergarten children is the chance to care for animals. The children learn to become responsible, which enhances their sense of competence and self-esteem. They also learn nurturance, kindness, and empathy—qualities that are necessary for optimal social functioning.

from open education (see Chapter 2). Open education need not occur in an open space, but can occur in a self-contained classroom. In the open framework, children are involved in decision making, self-direction, and problem solving.

The basic instructional/learning model of the cognitively oriented curriculum is the Plan-Do-Review model. Children plan their activity, work at it, and represent the activity in some way, as they review or recall how they carried out their plan. Table 4–3 shows sample schedules for children in a variety of programs using the cognitively oriented curriculum.

A Cognitively Oriented Curriculum in the Okaloosa County (Florida) Public Schools

The Okaloosa County (Florida) Follow Through Program has adopted the Cognitively Oriented Curriculum described by High Scope Foundation in its K–3 classrooms.[11] This model is one of several used in elementary schools throughout the county. The Okaloosa County program uses the Plan-Do-Review management system model. In addition, many teachers identify and use certain themes as a context or organizing structure for action, representation, conceptual relations, and curriculum content. The themes evolve from the children's interests, social studies, health, and science, and reflect the program's objectives.

Plan.   Children plan for the work they will do; for example, a child may plan to

TABLE 4–3   Sample Schedules of a Cognitively Oriented Curriculum

Preschool Program, Half Day	Day Care Center, Full Day
8:30 Greeting/Circle time	7:30 Free choice/Breakfast
8:45 Planning time	8:00 Outside time
9:00 Work time	8:45 Bathroom
9:45 Clean-up time	9:00 Circle/Planning time
10:00 Recall time	9:15 Work time
10:10 Snack time	10:15 Clean-up time
10:30 Small-group time	10:30 Recall/Snack time
10:50 Circle time	11:00 Small-group time
11:00 Outside time	11:30 Outside/Lunch preparation
	12:00 Lunch
Head Start Program, Half Day	12:30 Circle time
8:30 Greeting/Circle time	1:00 Nap time
8:45 Breakfast, toothbrushing	2:00 Planning time
9:15 Planning time	2:15 Work time
9:30 Work time	3:15 Clean-up time
10:15 Clean-up time	3:30 Recall time
10:30 Recall time	3:45 Outside time
10:45 Snack time	4:30 Departure time
11:00 Small-group time/Circle time	
11:20 Outside time	
11:45 Lunchtime	

Source: Warren Buckleitner, "A Trainer's Perspective: Six Steps to High/Scope Curriculum Implementation." *High/Scope Resource,* Fall, 1989, Vol. 8, No. 3, pp. 4–9. Published by the High/Scope Educational Research Foundation, 600 N. River St., Ypsilanti, MI 48198

plant a cutting she has rooted, her interest aroused by a science unit on plants. Other related activities are available in the science center. During the planning process, children are asked to think about, communicate verbally or in pictures, and/or write about these items:

- ☐ The area where one will implement the plan
- ☐ The kind and amount of materials one will need
- ☐ The sequence one will follow in completing the plan
- ☐ How long it will take to complete the plan and the problems one might encounter

The planning format of the Plan-Do-Review process progresses through several stages as children develop their ability to communicate. The youngest children simply tell the group where they plan to go and what they plan to do. As the children begin to learn letter formation and sounds, they are encouraged to use a combination of invented spelling and drawings to put their plans on paper. They may use words found in the classroom (labels) or look for words in their individual dictionaries. As writing and spelling skills emerge, the children become more independent plan writers.

Do.   Children then carry out the activity in the classroom's learning centers, in this case by planting the cutting, labeling it, and beginning a journal to record the plant's growth. They may also represent their activities or products. In the case of the plant, the child writes and tells about the activity of planting the cutting and beginning the journal. The teacher tries to move the child through a hierarchy of thinking levels during the representation: taking photographs, making tape recordings; building a model with paper, clay, sticks, or spaghetti, and telling about it; drawing a picture, cartoon sequence, puzzle, or painting; writing stories, books, songs, puppet shows, plays, and journals; and making graphs with real objects, pictures, or symbols. Language is incorporated into all these activities; for example, children are asked to label parts and tell about what they are doing (see Figure 4–4).

Review.   Children then participate in an evaluation or review of their activities. In small or large groups, they describe the attributes and details of their products and relate what they have done and how they have done it. The teacher also encourages the child in evaluating the activity, asking whether there were any problems to solve, what steps were followed during work time, and what follow-up, if any, is planned. Children also have many opportunities to ask questions about other children's projects, so that the children as well as the teacher engage other children in the review process.

Room Arrangement

The organization of materials and equipment in the classroom supports the Plan-Do-Review process in that the child knows where to find materials and what materials can be used, which encourages development of self-direction and independence. Small group tables are used for seating, independent work space, center time activities, and teacher-directed instruction. Flexibility and versatility contribute to the learning function. The floor plan in Figure 4–5 shows how room arrangement can support and implement the program's philosophy, goals, and objectives, and how a center

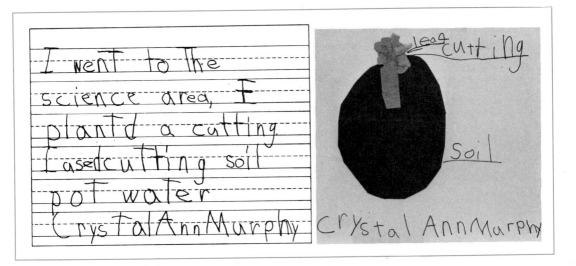

FIGURE 4–4   Representation.

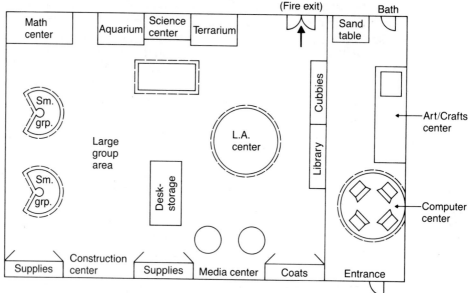

FIGURE 4–5   Floor Plan for High Scope Model.

approach (math, computers, language arts, construction) provides space for large group activities and meetings, small group activities, and individual work. In a classroom where space is a problem, the teacher must work at making one area serve many different purposes. The teacher selects the centers and activities to use in the classroom based on several considerations:

☐ Interests of the children (kindergarten children, for example, are interested in blocks, housekeeping, and art)
☐ Opportunities for facilitating active involvement in seriation, number, time relations, classification, spatial relations, and language development
☐ Opportunities for reinforcing needed skills and concepts and functional use of those skills and concepts

Implementing the Plan-Do-Review model in the classroom depends on:

☐ The teacher's understanding of the cognitively oriented curriculum and the Plan-Do-Review process
☐ The teacher's knowledge and understanding of child development and intellectual development
☐ The teacher's knowledge of subject areas
☐ Materials available
☐ How the teacher views children
☐ The teacher's personal philosophy of education

Small Group Time

The cognitively oriented curriculum in Okaloosa County balances teacher-initiated and student-initiated activities. During Plan-Do-Review, the student-initiated portion

A KINDERGARTEN STUDENT IN THE PLAN-DO-REVIEW PROCESS

This account of a kindergarten child, Carol, in a kindergarten that uses the Plan-Do-Review process, is typical of how a child and teacher interact.[12]

Plan

Carol plans to go to the quiet area to make a train out of unifix cubes (or inch cubes) and count the number of cubes she uses.

Do

Carol makes a train with a long line of cubes. The teacher, Ms. Smith, supports Carol in counting the cubes by removing each cube as Carol counts. The teacher wants to see if Carol can count all the cubes one by one.

Carol successfully counts the 30 cubes in her train. Ms. Smith asks Carol if she knows how to write the number 30. Carol writes 03. Ms. Smith then writes 30 for Carol, and asks Carol to trace the numeral. Then she asks Carol if she can make another train with the same number of cubes. Carol finds more cubes and matches cubes one-to-one until the second train is the same as the first. The teacher asks Carol if her train has an engine. Carol says yes; it has an engine, two boxcars, and a caboose. Ms. Smith asks Carol to show her, using the cubes in the second train, how many cubes are in each car. Carol removes cubes from the train, lines them up in four rows, one below the other, and counts eight for the engine, seven for each of the two boxcars, and eight for the caboose, accounting for all 30 of the cubes.

The teacher writes a label for each car and asks Carol to write after each name the numeral for the number of cubes in each car. Carol is able to do this. The teacher wants to see if Carol understands that the counted number of cubes in the train (30) remains the same when the cubes have been rearranged into train cars. She asks Carol if she thinks there are still the same number of cubes in her train. Carol counts the cubes to check the number (demonstrating that she does not realize that since she has not added or taken away, the number remains the same). The teacher knows Carol does not fully understand this concept and needs more experience counting objects and comparing amounts.

Carol represents her activity by drawing the row of cubes on a large piece of graph paper. Ms. Smith asks Carol to count the number of squares for each car of her train and color each car a different color. Carol does this. To give Carol practice writing numerals, Ms. Smith then asks Carol to write the numbers to 30 above her rows of squares, giving each square a number.

Review

When the children are finished representing, they gather in a circle and share their ideas, products, and what they have done. If Ms. Smith's focus is sequencing, she may ask a child what he did first, second, and third. Emphasis may be on different aspects of an activity according to individual needs, interests, or points inherent in the activity or representation. Children are also encouraged to ask questions and make comments. Following the evaluation, the representation can be displayed or taken home. Carol decides to take hers home. Ms. Smith has a clothesline hung low in the classroom so children can display their work at eye level.

of the day, the teacher and the aide make mental (and sometimes written) notes concerning individual children's skill needs. Observed needs are coupled with more formally diagnosed needs in the basic skills areas and form the basis for planning small group instruction in the communication and mathematics areas.

During small group instruction for language arts and math, children are grouped both heterogeneously and homogeneously. The heterogeneous groups rotate to activity tables and the computer center, where activities have been planned to extend and enrich skills. At the same time, the teacher pulls small homogeneous groups for direct instruction. These instructional periods are called "Math Workshop" and "Language Workshop." The balance of teacher-initiated and student-initiated activities supports and encourages active involvement at an appropriate instructional level. The success of this approach shows up in test scores and in the enthusiasm of both students and teachers.

COMMON THEMES OF PIAGET-BASED CURRICULA

Four recurring themes appear in curricula based on Piaget's ideas. One is that a child's thinking is substantially different from that of the adult, and adults must not try to impose their way of thinking on the child. Adults should provide a setting in which the child can think her own ideas and construct her own model of the world. Appropriate teacher behaviors include tolerance, support, acceptance of wrong answers, and encouragement to make hypotheses. A second recurring theme is that children must be actively involved in learning. A child who is a passive recipient of information does not have the proper opportunity to develop intelligence to its fullest. A third theme is that learning should involve concrete objects and experiences with many children and adults, particularly at the sensorimotor and preoperational stages. Children are too often asked to deal with abstractions such as words and numbers when they have no idea what these symbols represent. The fourth common theme of Piagetian programs pertains to the quality and relatedness of experiences. What a child is like at a particular stage is largely a function of past experiences. Good experiences lead to intellectual development. Our job as teachers and parents is to maximize the quality of experiences. In addition, a child's comprehension of an event depends greatly upon the proximity of the event to the concepts involved. If the child has nothing to associate an experience to, it is meaningless. Assimilation and accommodation cannot function unless experiences closely parallel each other.

Issues

There are a number of issues associated with a comprehensive understanding of Piaget's theory. First, some difficulties associated with Piaget and his theory of intelligence arise from the complexity of his writings, which can be difficult to read and interpret. As a result, it takes a great deal of time, effort, and energy to determine their implications for education. One is never sure of interpreting Piaget correctly, so individuals must be willing to change their interpretations and constantly strive to improve the understanding and conceptualization of his theory.

Second, some people think that Piaget's theory of intellectual development is an educational theory, and some educators confuse Piagetian experiments with a Piagetian curriculum. Well-meaning teachers often believe that by having students replicate Piagetian experiments, they are "teaching Piaget." The experiments do have merit as a diagnostic process for determining how children think; the results, however, should be used to develop meaningful experiences. As Duckworth points out, "Piaget has no answer to the questions of *what* it is children ought to learn. But once, as educators, we have some sense of what we would like children to learn, then I think that Piaget has a great deal to say about *how* we can go about doing that."[13]

A third issue relates to early childhood curricula that call themselves Piaget-based. Educators run the risk of blindly accepting and adopting such programs without thorough knowledge and understanding of Piaget's theory. To accept a curriculum without understanding its inherent concepts can be as ineffectual as applying a curriculum that has no theory as its foundations. The issue here is the same as that regarding Montessori programs; simply naming a program after Piaget does not guarantee it is based on his theory.

Finally, some people would like to teach more at an earlier age, in the hope of "speeding up" development. Piaget called this "the American issue." Piaget's stages are not designed to challenge teachers or students and should not be viewed as something to master as quickly as possible. Programs that seek to implement a Piaget-based curriculum should provide classroom environments rich in materials and opportunities for children to actively participate in learning. Teachers who understand Piaget and who are willing to support and stimulate children in their efforts to construct their own knowledge are essential to any quality early childhood program. Piaget's theory has much to offer parents and teachers who believe that children can and are the major players in the process of cognitive development.

FURTHER READING

To someone without a specialized interest in Piaget, reading his works can be somewhat difficult. Undergraduate students will probably have more success in understanding Piaget if his works are read with the help of one of these books.

Brief, Jean Claude. *Beyond Piaget: A Philosophical Inquiry* (New York: Teachers College Press, 1983)

A significant contribution to Piagetian interpretation, this book summarizes Piaget's work in cognitive and genetic psychology and genetic epistemology. Several chapters are geared to helping early childhood educators deal with Piaget's findings about the child's intellectual growth.

Butterworth, George. *Infancy and Epistemology: An Evaluation of Piaget's Theory* (New York: St. Martin's Press, 1982)

A current trend is to view babies as competent individuals. This work discusses Piaget's theory of intelligence in relation to child development and the psychology of learning.

Hohmann, Mary, Bernard Banet, and David T. Wiekart. *Young Children in Action: A Manual for Preschool Educators* (Ypsilanti, Mich.: The High Scope Press, 1979)

Excellent guide to understanding and implementing the Cognitively Oriented Curriculum.

Kamii, Constance. *Number in Preschool and Kindergarten* (Washington, D.C.: National Association for the Education of Young Children, 1982)

Excellent, easy-to-read discussion of applying Piaget's theory to teaching numbers by one of the leading Piagetian interpreters. Contains many practical ideas and activities for teaching numerical thinking. The appendix on "Autonomy as the Aim of Education: Implications of Piaget's Theory" should be read by every teacher and parent.

Kamii, Constance, and Georgia DeClark. *Young Children Reinvent Arithmetic* (New York: Teachers College Press, 1985)

A must for those who are serious about Piaget's theory and about young children, this book translates Piaget's theory into a program of games and activities.

Weber, Evelyn. *Ideas Influencing Early Childhood Education: A Theoretical Analysis* (New York: Teachers College Press, 1984)

A theoretical analysis of various theorists, philosophers, and psychologists from Plato to Piaget. Outstanding ideas for new trends that influence early childhood education.

FURTHER STUDY

1. How would you respond to someone who said, "Children can't really learn unless the teacher corrects their wrong answers"?

2. Observe three children at the ages of six months, two years, and four years. Note in each child's activities what you consider typical behavior for that age. Can you find examples of behavior that correspond to one of Piaget's stages?

3. Observe a child between birth and eighteen months. Can you cite any concrete evidence, such as specific actions or incidents, to support the view that the child is developing schemes of the world through sensorimotor actions?

4. Interview early childhood teachers to determine their impressions of how effectively Piaget's theory is applied to early childhood settings. Compare their impressions with yours.

5. The High Scope program is very popular in early childhood programs. What accounts for this popularity? Would you implement this curriculum in your program? Why?

6. Suggest practical ways you might include Piaget's theory in your classroom.

7. Compare Piaget's theory of intellectual development to another theory, such as Montessori's. How are they similar and different?

8. Develop a list of learning activities for young children. Label the activities according to whether they would best suit a sensorimotor or preoperational child.

9. Observe a first-grade classroom. Give specific examples to illustrate that the activities did or did not match the children's levels of intellectual development.

10. Examine textbooks and learning materials for young children. Identify those you feel show the influence of Piaget.

11. List five (5) concepts/ideas about Piaget's theory that you consider most significant for how to teach/rear young children.

12. What concepts/ideas of Piaget's theory do you disagree with? Why?

13. Interview a trainer for the High Scope program and identify the key issues in training caregivers in the philosophy and methods of the High Scope curriculum.

14. Why does the application of Piaget's theory to education generate so many different options? Why isn't there *one* application of Piaget's theory?

15. Do you think you would like to teach in the Okaloosa County Public Schools and implement Piaget's theory as they do? Why or why not?

16. List all the ways you consider children's thinking to differ from adult thinking.

17. Visit an early childhood classroom and find examples of egocentrism and conservation. Also, identify any other characteristics of children's thinking as described by Piaget.

18. Why are errors and "wrong" answers important in children's learning?

19. List at least six (6) activities teachers can use to promote children's autonomy.

20. If an early childhood teacher said he didn't think it was important to know about Piaget's theory, how would you respond?

NOTES

1. Mary Ann Spencer Pulaski, *Understanding Piaget* (New York: Harper and Row, 1980), p. 9.

2. P.G. Richmond, *An Introduction to Piaget* (New York: Basic Books, 1970), p. 68.

3. Richmond, *An Introduction to Piaget,* p. 68.

4. Deanna Kuhn, "The Role of Self-Directed Activity in Cognitive Development," in *New Directions in Piagetian Theory and Practice,* ed. Irving E. Sigel et al. (Hillsdale, N.J.: Lawrence Erlbaum, 1981), p. 353.

5. David M. Brodzinsky et al., "New Directions in Piagetian Theory and Research: An Integrative Perspective," in *New Directions in Piagetian Theory and Practice,* ed. Irving E. Sigel et al. (Hillsdale, N.J.: Lawrence Erlbaum, 1981), p. 5.

6. Constance Kamii, "Application of Piaget's Theory to Education: The Preoperational Level" in *New Directions in Piagetian Theory and Practice,* ed. Irving E. Sigel et al. (Hillside, N.J.: Lawrence Erlbaum, 1981), p. 234.

7. Hans G. Furth, *Piaget for Teachers* (Englewood Cliffs, N.J.: Prentice-Hall, 1970), p. 15.

8. Jean Piaget, *Genetic Epistemology,* trans. Eleanor Duckworth (New York: Columbia University Press, 1970), p. 21.

9. *The High Scope Early Elementary Program* (Ypsilanti, Mich.: High Scope Educational Research Foundation, 1973), p. 1.

10. Richard Lalli, *An Introduction to the Cognitively Oriented Curriculum for the Elementary Grades* (Ypsilanti, Mich.: High Scope Educational Research Foundation), pp. 2-3.

11. Ms. Patti Boyles, Follow Through Director, helped to prepare this section on a cognitively oriented curriculum in the Okaloosa County Public Schools.

12. The sections Plan, Do, and Review were contributed by Donna McClelland, senior consultant, High Scope Educational Research Foundation.

13. Eleanor Duckworth, "Learning Symposium: A Commentary," in *New Directions in Piagetian Theory and Practice,* ed. Irving E. Sigel et al. (Hillsdale, N.J.: Lawrence Erlbaum, 1981), p. 363.

CHAPTER 5
Child Care
Taking Care of the Nation's Children

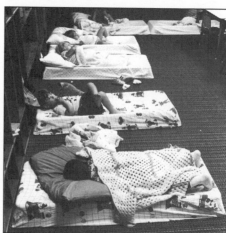

As you read and study:
- ☐ Determine the extent of parents' need for child care services
- ☐ Become conversant with the terminology of and definitions for child care
- ☐ Evaluate and critique the purposes of child care programs
- ☐ Develop an understanding of the meaning of child care and how quality programs operate
- ☐ Determine the nature and types of available child care services and programs
- ☐ Identify criteria associated with quality child care
- ☐ Identify the sources and nature of child care funding
- ☐ Compare and evaluate the effectiveness of child care programs in meeting the needs of children, parents, and families
- ☐ Review proprietary child care and the reasons for its growth
- ☐ Examine and understand the importance of CDA training for early childhood professionals and programs
- ☐ Examine issues associated with the care of the nation's children
- ☐ Consider future trends in child care services and needs
- ☐ Examine the various types of child care settings
- ☐ Become familiar with research studies that examine the effects of child care

POPULARITY OF CHILD CARE

The demand for child care continues to grow. Demand comes primarily from several sources: families in which both parents work, single parents, the mini-baby boom, and changing family patterns. Approximately 57 percent of mothers with preschool-age children are employed or looking for work, and approximately 11.5 million children are in need of care. Divorce also creates a greater demand for child care services.

The high divorce rate and its resulting increase in single-parent families creates additional demand on the need for affordable quality child care, as we discussed in Chapter 1. The need for affordable child care is further influenced by the fact that half the families headed by single mothers aged 25 to 44 are poor. A current trend indicates that people with higher levels of education are having fewer children, while those with less education are having more children. The implication of this trend is that more and more poor children are in school (see Figure 5–1). The responsibility

FIGURE 5–1   Families with Related Children Under 18 that are Below the Poverty Level (Source: Bureau of the Census, "Changes in American Family Life," *Current Population Reports,* Series P–23, No. 163, August, 1989.)

for meeting the needs of such families has spawned legislation, such as the Act for Better Child Care, designed to subsidize the high cost of child care.

Recent years have witnessed an increase in the need for child care for babies. Although 50 percent of mothers with children under one year of age are in the work force, infant care is not readily available; when it is available, it is expensive. By the year 2000, 70 percent of preschoolers' mothers and 80 percent of all women between the ages of 25 and 54 will be working![1]

Although more programs are available for three-, four-, and five-year-olds, many of the programs operate on a part-time basis. Because most parents do not work only part time, the availability of such programs necessitates alternate care arrangements in the course of a day. This situation is inconvenient as well as expensive and disruptive to children's need for continuity in their environment.

There has been an increase in the birthrate among women between the ages of 30 and 34. Many women who postponed childbearing for careers or because of the need to work now want to have children before it is too late. Changing family patterns also create a need for child care (see Chapter 1). Both men and women are deciding to become parents—natural or adoptive—without marrying, and the trend toward single parenthood also generates demand for child care arrangements. The implications of these social conditions are clear: children need care by people other than their parents, frequently in places other than their homes. As more women enter the labor force and as the demand for child care increases, the number of licensed child care programs will continue to increase.

Child care is often a confusing term, sometimes used interchangeably with other terminology such as family day care, baby-sitting, and early childhood education. The concept of child care differs depending on who uses the term and in what context. (The term *child care* is preferable to "day care," because children should be the central focus of any program provided for them.)

One often-used definition for child care is that of the Child Welfare League of America, as a service provided by the community "because of its concern for children who might otherwise lack the care and protection essential for their healthy development."[2] Two key words in this definition are *care* and *protection,* traditionally interpreted to mean providing for children's physical needs and seeing that they do not harm themselves and are not harmed by others—including their parents. The emphasis of this type of service on physical needs sometimes carries a negative connotation. Some regard it as a "holding action," and it is typically referred to as "custodial child care." These programs may offer opportunities for free play, but are not usually structured for educational purposes.

The currently accepted concept of child care holds that it is both supplemental and comprehensive. Care is *supplemental* in that parents delegate responsibility to the caregivers for providing care and appropriate experiences in their absence, and *comprehensive* in that, although it includes custodial care such as supervision, food, shelter, and other physical necessities, it goes beyond these to include activities that encourage and facilitate learning and is responsive to children's health, social, and psychological needs. A comprehensive view of child care considers the child to be a whole person; therefore, the major purpose of child care is to facilitate optimum development. Bettye Caldwell notes that *professional child care* is a *comprehensive* service to children and families that functions as a subsystem of the child rearing system and *supplements* the care children receive from their families.[3] More and more programs use the designation *child development* to convey the comprehensive nature of their services.

TYPES OF CHILD CARE PROGRAMS

Because child care can be provided in many places, by many types of people and agencies, there is a wide variety of care and services. A program may operate twenty-four hours a day, with the center or home open to admit children at any hour. There are also whole-day programs that usually operate on a 6:30 A.M.–6:00 P.M. schedule to accommodate working parents. Half-day programs, such as those operated in many Head Start centers, usually run from 8:30 or 9:00 A.M. to 1:00 or 2:00 P.M. Parents who work usually supplement this kind of service with a private baby-sitter (see Figure 5–2).

Child Care by Family, Relatives, and Friends

Child care arrangements are often made within the nuclear and extended family or with friends. Parents handle these arrangements in various ways. Some mothers and fathers work different shifts, so that one parent cares for the children while the spouse is at work. These families do not need out-of-home care. In some cases, children are cared for by grandparents, aunts, uncles, or other relatives. These arrangements satisfy

FIGURE 5–2   Who's Minding the Children?

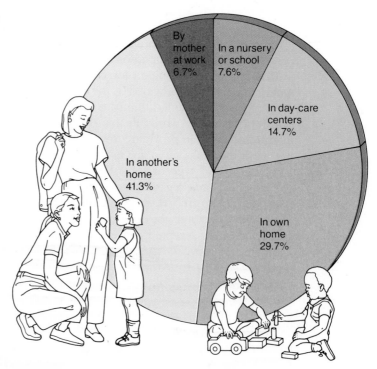

By mother at work 6.7%

In a nursery or school 7.6%

In day-care centers 14.7%

In another's home 41.3%

In own home 29.7%

parents' needs to have their children cared for by people with similar lifestyles and values. The arrangements may be less costly, and compensation may be made in ways other than direct monetary payments; for example, one couple converted part of their house into an efficiency apartment where an elderly aunt lives rent-free in return for caring for the couple's two-year-old child. These types of arrangements allow children to remain in familiar environments with people they know. Child care by family members provides continuity in the young child's life, gives them a sense of safety and security, and is usually more affordable.

The number of children who are cared for through informal arrangements far exceeds the number in centers or family care, primarily because of the lack of available quality child care programs. When people search for child care, they often turn, out of necessity, to people who are available and willing to take care of children—but these two criteria are not the best or only ones people who provide custodial care or baby-sitting services should meet. There is a tremendous difference between placing a child in a high quality, comprehensive program as opposed to placing her with an individual who provides primarily custodial care.

Family child care is the most popular kind, because parents prefer to have their children in a homelike setting. Parents need to have the option of quality family child care available to them.

Family Child Care

By far the most popular type of child care is in a family or familylike setting, known as *family day care* or *family child care*. Fifty percent of the children in child care are in such settings. Family child care involves many kinds of arrangements between parents and care providers, and differs from center care, preschool programs, and care provided to children in their own homes. Generally, family child care consists of three types of settings: homes that are unlicensed and unregulated by a state or local agency; homes that are licensed by regulatory agencies; and homes that are licensed and associated with an administrative agency.[4]

Many parents leave their children at homes that are unregulated and unlicensed, and the kind of care a child receives depends on the skill, background, and training of the person who offers it. Some family care providers are motivated to meet state and/or local standards for child care so they can be licensed. Family child care providers may also be associated with a child care agency. They meet state and agency standards for care and, in return, receive assistance, training, and referrals of parents who need child care. The agency usually subsidizes the cost of the children's care when the parents are eligible for subsidies.

Definitions of Family Child Care.   In Pennsylvania, a family day care home is defined as "any premise other than the child's own home operated for profit or not for profit,

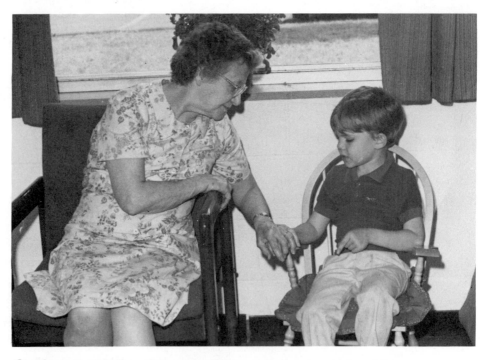

Grandparents and other relatives provide economical and nurturing child care, and many parents feel more comfortable with this type of care.

in which child day care is provided at any one time to four, five, or six children, who are not relatives of the caregiver." In Florida, a family day care home is

> an occupied residence in which day-care is regularly provided for no more than five (5) preschool children and elementary school children from more than one unrelated family including preschool children living in the home and preschool children received for day-care who are related to the resident caregiver. Elementary school siblings of the preschool children received for day-care may also be cared for outside of school hours provided the total number of children including the caregiver's own and those related to her does not exceed ten (10).[5]

Good family child care is much more than baby-sitting. There has been a tendency in the past to equate family care with custodial care, but care providers today are becoming more diligent about interacting with and stimulating the children they care for. The quantity and quality of specific services provided in family homes varies from home to home and from agency to agency, of course, but data compiled through the National Day Care Home Study shows that a substantial amount of caregivers' time (almost 50 percent) is spent in direct interaction with children (see Table 5–1). Undoubtedly, one reason parents prefer family child care is that it offers the opportunity for a family atmosphere, especially for younger children. The states usually define family child care, so you should compare the definitions in this chapter to your state's legal definition.

TABLE 5–1   Distribution of Caregiver Time in Family Day Care Homes

Direct Involvement with Children: Ages One to Five	Percentage of Time	Totals
Teach	13.9	
Play	7.8	
Help	8.9	
Direct	3.7	
Converse	3.3	
Control	3.7	
Interaction with babies less than one year old	3.8	
Interaction with school-age children	1.0	46.1
Indirect involvement with children:		
Direct/Prepare	16.5	16.5
Noninvolvement with children		
Converse with adults	6.3	
Recreation alone	7.8	
Housekeeping	19.4	
Out of range	1.3	34.8
Miscellaneous		2.6

Source: P. Divine-Hawkins, Family Day Care in the United States. Executive Summary (Washington, D.C.: U.S. Department of Health and Human Services, DHHS Publication No. (OHDS) 80-30287, Sept. 1981), p. 27.

FAMILY CHILD CARE PROGRAM

An example of how family child care is sponsored and operated is the program of the Catholic Community Services, Inc. of Dade County Florida (formerly Catholic Service Bureau or Catholic Charities), which provides child care services through center and family programs. Family day care is provided for children ages six weeks to three years old whose parents are working, going to school, or in job training programs. Referrals are also accepted from social service agencies and local court systems, and generally involve cases of child and/or spouse abuse. Referrals also come by word of mouth from friends and relatives.

Parents are served by geographic area, and since Catholic Community Services family child care does not provide transportation, children are placed in family care homes as close to the parents' home as possible.

To be eligible as a family care provider, a person must be over 21, preferably a high school graduate, and have personal characteristics, experience, and skills necessary to work with children, have a first aid certificate and a food handler's permit. A food handler's permit is earned by taking a short course in food preparation and sanitation. To be licensed

as a family child care home, a home must have adequate space for indoor play, an outside fenced play area, a smoke detector, fire extinguisher, telephone, and must be organized and clean. Child care homes must also comply with local zoning ordinances (some municipalities do not permit child care services in certain residential areas) and must meet specific building codes. (Zoning and building ordinances differ from city to city and state to state.) Since individual family child care homes are considered private businesses, a certificate of use and an occupation license may also be required.

Local child care licensing units, such as a state or county health and welfare agency, also have standards that must be met. These standards often include age requirements (over 18); absence of a criminal or child abuse record for all family members; surfaces of the home free of toxic materials such as lead-based paint; outside areas free from hazards and litter; at least one toilet and lavatory; an area for isolating sick children; toys and equipment that are safe and can be safely maintained; and ability to provide nutritious meals.

When family child care providers are associated with an agency such as Catholic

Intergenerational Child Care

Intergenerational programs that integrate children and the elderly into an early-childhood and adult-care facility meet the needs of many. The elderly derive pleasure and feelings of competence from helping to care for and interact with children, and young children receive attention and love from older caregivers. In today's mobile society, families often live long distances from each other, and children may be isolated from the care that grandparents can offer. Intergenerational programs blend the best of both worlds—children and the elderly receive care and attention in a nurturant environment.

Center Child Care

Care of children in center settings, sometimes also called *center child care* or *group child care,* is conducted in specially designed and constructed centers, in churches, YMCAs and YWCAs, and other such settings. In Pennsylvania, center child care is "a facility in which care is provided for seven or more children, at any one time, where

Community Services, they are generally provided with equipment and supplies that will improve the quality of care. This list is representative of equipment and supplies often found in agency-sponsored homes:

Equipment
Portable cribs—children 6 weeks to one year
Cots (folding nursery)
Dressing table
High chairs
Table 54 × 54—plastic laminated top
Stack chairs—10"
Potty chair
Fire extinguishers
Walkers (as needed)
Playpen (as needed)
Infant swing (as needed)
Rocking chair
Infant seats
Slide and climbing toy
Sandbox

Supplies
First-aid box
Crib sheets
Cot sheets
Books
Art supplies

Jumbo pegboard
Play gym
Crib mobiles
Busy Box
Wooden building blocks
Shape sorter
Baby's first blocks
Rock-A-Stack
Turn & Learn Activity Center
Balls/bowl (Johnson & Johnson)
Spin-A-Sound (Johnson & Johnson)
Peek-A-Boo ball (Johnson & Johnson)
Cornpopper, push/pull
Chatter telephone
Poppin Pals
Tupperware animal set
3–4 piece puzzles
Teeter tot (see-saw)
Wheel and riding toys
Balls, tricycles
Safely constructed cars and trucks
Full-length mirrors at child's level
Large Duplo or Lego blocks
Puppets
Playdough
Large beads to string
Plastic containers with lids
Pots and pans

the child care areas are not being used as a family residence. A facility in which care is provided for more than six but less than 12, at any one time, may be licensed/approved as a group day care home if care is provided in a facility where the child care areas are being used as a family residence and the provider meets the requirements of a group day care home."[6] The definition for group or center care in Florida is a little different:

[To] serve groups of six (6) or more children. It utilizes subgroupings on the basis of age and special need but provides opportunity for experience and learning that accompanies a mixing of ages. Group day care centers may enroll children under two years of age *only* if special provisions are made for the needs of the infants to be consistently met by one person, rather than a series of people; and which permits the infant to develop a strong, warm relationship with one mother figure. This relationship should approximate the mothering the infant would receive in a family day care home.[7]

In Texas, on the other hand, "A day care center is a child care facility that provides care less than 24 hours a day for more than 12 children under age 14."[8] Center

Intergenerational child care programs give children an opportunity to interact with senior citizens and benefit both the young and the old.

programs are often comprehensive, but many are baby-sitting programs, and some provide less than good custodial care. Just as the quality of public schools varies among districts, so does the quality of day care services vary among settings. This makes it difficult to arrive at a conclusive definition of child care; variations from state to state make it difficult to do anything but generalize.

FEDERALLY SUPPORTED CHILD CARE

Child care centers often receive federal funds because they serve low-income families who are eligible for cash assistance under Title XX of the Social Security Act. Title XX was passed by Congress in 1974 and is the major source of federal funds to state-operated child care services. How much a state receives is based on its population. A state may be reimbursed for 75 percent of the cost of day care programs that follow Title XX guidelines. Under Title XX, parents are automatically eligible for day care services on the basis of:

Income Maintenance (the parent receives a public assistance check such as Aid to Families with Dependent Children [AFDC])

Supplemental Security Income (SSI) (the parent is receiving a supplement to Social Security income; for example, a widowed parent of young children is eligible for supplementary Social Security income)

Income Eligible (if the family's gross income is below a figure set by the state, the family is eligible for services)

Group Eligibility (members of some groups are automatically eligible, such as children of migrant workers; a child who is under the protective care of the state can also qualify for Title XX child care, without regard to income)

Florida admits children to child care supported by Title XX funds according to these priorities:

1. The child is at risk because of abuse or neglect.
2. The parent is involved in a state or federally supported work incentive program (WIN).
3. The parent is income maintenance and/or the child is group eligible.
4. The parent is income eligible.

A second source of federal support comes through the U.S. Department of Agriculture Child Care Food Program (CCFP). The USDA provides monies and commodities (for example, cheese, dry milk, and butter) to child care centers and homes to support their nutritional programs. In lieu of commodities, programs can choose to receive cash equal to 11¼ cents per child for each lunch or supper served, in addition to the regular reimbursement. Children 12 years of age and younger are eligible for participation. In fiscal 1989, the USDA provided $687,266,850 of support through CCFP. In December 1989 alone, $58,508,750 was spent on CCFP.[9] A third federal source of support is the child care tax credits for individuals and corporations. The federal tax code provides employers with certain "tax breaks" or benefits for providing child care services to their employees.

Since 1975, parents have been able to itemize the cost of child care as a credit against their federal income taxes. Currently, the amount that can be deducted is based on a sliding scale. From $0 to $10,000 of annual adjusted income, 30 percent of the cost of child care can be deducted. As income increases by $2,000, the percentage decreases by one percent until it reaches 20 percent. The maximum amount that a family can credit is $2,400 for one child and $4,800 for 2 children.

Funding

The most common sources for funding and support for child care are

☐ Parents, who pay all or part of the cost
☐ State programs, especially Health and Human Services
☐ Federal agencies—Administration for Children, Youth and Families; Social Security Administration; and Child Care Food Program (USDA)
☐ Private and charitable foundations, such as United Way or the Easter Seal Society
☐ Organizations such as the YMCA, YWCA, YMHA, and religious groups who provide care to members and the public, usually at reduced rates
☐ Employers
☐ Parent cooperatives

EMPLOYER-SPONSORED CHILD CARE PROGRAMS

"America has become a society in which everyone is expected to work—including women with young children. But many of society's institutions were designed during

DAY CARE AT THE HERITAGE MANOR NURSING HOME

Heritage Manor Day Care Facility is located at the Heritage Manor Nursing Home. The day care is fully licensed by the state of Maine and provides services as a benefit to employees and the general public. The educational program is for children ages three months to five years. The staff believes they are responsible for helping each child develop the sense of trust that leads to a healthy self-concept and growing independence. The staff also believes that children learn by using their five senses in active play and through interaction with people as appropriate to their ages and developmental levels.

Exposure of the children to nursing home residents is universal, but interaction is voluntary. Some children choose to mingle only insofar as they walk through the residents' dayrooms on the way to the playground, while others look forward to warm hugs and handshakes and even wheelchair rides. Most children do, however, become accustomed to the patients and come to see them as friends.

Holidays provide an opportunity for young and old to help each other prepare special treats or seasonal dishes such as apple sauce,

cranberry relish, or Christmas cookies, and have parties together, with a patient playing Santa in a wheelchair at Christmas or the friendly treat-distributor on Halloween. Other activities patients and preschoolers share include listening to stories, watching movies, bowling with plastic balls and pins, singing, some creative movement, and special crafts projects. Children also visit from room to room, bringing their warmth and vitality to patients along with special holiday or birthday greetings. The experience of sharing time and space has been beneficial for both the children and the patients, and many "barriers" have been broken.

One day, several four-year-olds asked to go to the recreational area of the nursing home. Allegra found a likely audience to listen to her read from her favorite book. Nikki walked over to a woman in a wheelchair and shyly said "hello." The woman reached out her hands and Nikki gave her a warm embrace. Jamie, who had brought a piece of artwork done at home, showed it to a mentally disabled person who was unable to show any response. Elizabeth and Heather went beyond the recreational area and visited bedridden patients. Later in the

an era of male breadwinners and female homemakers. What is needed is a . . . reform of the institutions and policies that govern the work place, to ensure that women can participate fully in the economy and that men and women have the time and resources to invest in their children."[10]

New trends in child care arise as the number of parents in the work force grows. Corporate- or employer-sponsored child care is one trend that has arisen to meet a need. The trend of women entering the labor force is expected to continue. Projections by the Bureau of Labor Statistics indicate that over 80 percent of women aged 25 to 54 will be in the work force by 2000. More than half of working women are mothers. The most rapidly growing segment of the work force is married women with children under one year of age. To meet the needs of working parents, employers are increasingly called upon to provide affordable, accessible, quality child care. Corporate supported child care is one of the fastest growing employee benefits, as identified by the U.S. Chamber of Commerce.

During the last decade, employer-sponsored child care has become one of the more talked-about and most frequently implemented child care programs. Although not new (the Stride-Rite Corporation started the first on-site corporate child care

morning, the entire group of preschoolers brought a birthday cake to a ninety-year-old woman who could not hold back the tears of joy.

The young children exhibit a great deal of compassion as well as curiosity and interest in the world around them. Even though they may not be able to conceptualize age as a life process, they are beginning to acknowledge the physical characteristics associated with it. They can "feel" that people may not all look and sound the same but that a meaningful relationship is still possible despite physical differences.

When they are first introduced to the residents, the children do not visit for very long, and they are often found to be staring—at a face with unfamiliar wrinkles, or at someone whose walk is very labored. After a few days of encouragement, their involvement with the residents begins to be spontaneous.

The children contribute their vitality to the home and interact in an atmosphere that they might otherwise never know. They do not share adults' aversion to a nursing home. They accept the elderly and infirm; they do not seem to be afraid of people with physical or mental disabilities, who may be unattractive or sometimes offensive. In their innocence, they can overlook the distasteful aspects of sickness and focus on qualities they relate to.

The children and residents have been instrumental in helping each other confront and accept death as a natural part of the life cycle. The children's favorite "grandma" often had fruit or candy for them; when she was close to death, the teachers tried to prepare the children. They commented on and asked the children how Mary seemed to them on their daily visits. Adults and children talked openly with Mary about her feelings whenever she or the children introduced the subject. The children saw Mary, their teachers, and their peers laugh, love, and weep, with the freedom to give expression to their feelings. When Mary died, there was anger and sadness, which later gave way to gladness that "Mary doesn't hurt anymore, and she still loves us." The interaction and bonding of old and young proved mutually beneficial.

program in Boston in 1971), there is a surge in these services. The number of employer-sponsored child care programs has grown from 110 in 1972 to over 3500 in 1989. Part of this growth is attributable to the number of mothers in the work force, but a major reason for the popularity of employer-sponsored child care is the realization that child care is good business. Yet, despite its numerous advantages, child care remains the least frequently offered employee benefit. Only an estimated 3500 of the 44,000 employers with 100 or more workers currently offer any type of child-care support to their employees.

Delivery of specific child care services takes many forms. There are a number of ways employers provide child care services:

□ Use of an information and referral service; counseling for parents on the selection of quality care; and referrals to local child care providers who meet individual family needs. Some corporations provide these services in house, and some contract with separate agencies.

□ Corporations maintain a list of family day care homes and contract with the day care provider for spaces in the home. They may also assist in equipping the providers' homes for child care services.

☐ Corporations provide on-site or near-site child care centers for their employees' children. The corporation provides space, equipment, and child care workers. Some corporations contract with an agency (as described in the account of the Forbes Metropolitan Health Center later in this chapter).

A DAY IN THE LIFE OF AN INFANT AT THE OPEN DOOR INFANT CENTER IN AUSTIN, TEXAS*

Center Schedule for Children and Staff
Center open: 7:30–5:30, Monday–Friday
Teachers and hours:
Shawn: 7:15–1:15
Marie: 7:45–12:45
Rong: 9:00–12:00
Beckie: 11:30–5:30
Teresa: 12:30–6:00
Tanya: 1:00–5:30
Infants and ages:
Cason, 9 mos.
Alex, 8 mos.
Jando, 6 mos.
Colleen, 7 mos.
Piper, 7 mos.
Alyson, 4 mos.
Emily, 3 mos.
Jared, 2 mos. (twin)
Justin, 2 mos. (twin)

The center is dark and quiet when I arrive at 7:15 A.M. I have 15 minutes to prepare the room. I turn on lights, unlock doors, then begin to ready the infant room. We need hot water in the "coffee maker" to heat bottles, wet paper towels for diapering, a trash bag in the can, a blanket on the floor for the babies, and a variety of toys—noisemakers, soft squeeze toys, cause-and-effect boxes, balls, and some paper towel rolls. Toys hang from the bottom of the cribs, because the babies crawl around underneath them; the mirror is at baby height; the swings, high chairs, and rocking chairs are clean and ready to go. The daily record sheet is ready for the parents to begin and the teachers to complete. I put a tape of cheerful morning music on the tape player and the door opens as the first family arrives. It is 7:30 A.M. Cason and

*Contributed by Shawn Michaud, site director, The Open Door Infant Center, Austin, Texas.

his dad come in, with Emily and her mom close behind. Both infants are put on the blanket with toys while the parents put away diapers, bottles, food, and daily supplies. I listen as they tell about the previous night, the sleeping schedule, and morning routine. My coteacher arrives along with three more babies and their parents. Two children have not had their bottles yet, so Marie begins to prepare them. I check diapers, then sit on the floor and visit. Both babies who need bottles are older than six months, so they can sit in infant seats and hold their own bottles. Alex is beginning to make fussy sounds, so I check the chart. He has had no cereal, so I mix it and feed him in the high chair. Colleen arrives and needs a snack. I turn the two babies in high chairs to face each other, with a window at their sides. They babble and watch each other. When I open the window, the breeze blows in, and they smile. Marie has four babies on the floor when our two-month-old twins arrive. We sit them in infant swings so they won't get crawled over while we get all their belongings put away. Alyson and Emily are showing sleepy signs, so I put Emily in her crib and Alyson in the swinging bassinet. I wind the bassinet and pat Emily to sleep. Marie begins cereal for Jando, who has just arrived. Our aide, Rong Fong, arrives, and we are all glad to see her. Piper, the ninth and last infant of the day, arrives as well. It is 9:00 A.M. We prepare the rest of the needed bottles and breakfast. One teacher is at the high chairs, one is on the floor, and one is giving an infant a bottle. At about 10:00 A.M., some babies are ready for a morning nap. We know by individual signals—whining, putting her head on the floor, pulling an ear, rubbing eyes, or crying—all signals we have come to recognize. We put four sleeping babies in their cribs and, one at a time, jiggle or pat them to sleep. One baby is

☐ Through a voucher system, corporations give employees vouchers with which to purchase services at existing child care centers.

☐ Through a vendor system, corporations purchase slots at existing child care centers and make them available to employees either free or at reduced rates.

---

swinging and each of us has one baby now to rock, sing, and tickle. It's a quiet time, 10:30 A.M. As the older babies begin to awaken, around 11:15 to 11:30, the younger infants seem ready to rest. When babies awaken in their cribs, we get them up, kiss, cuddle, and change diapers. I wind up some music toys on the floor. The tired, tiny infants begin to cry, unable to fall asleep. I pull the cribs close and pat one baby while jiggling the other's crib. They drop off in about four minutes. Now comes an active time. One afternoon staff member, Beckie, arrives, and we roll the ball, pull the "see and say" sounds, play patty-cake, and do some infant massage. We prepare lunches for those who will need them soon and change diapers. Alex and Cason get lunch in the high chairs, Colleen and Jando take bottles in the infant seats. I give a bottle to Alyson. The twins and Emily are still asleep. Piper is chewing a teething toy. We anticipate Emily's waking soon and call her mom to plan for her lunchtime breast-feeding. She will come at 12:30 unless we call to say Emily needs her sooner. Warm water will be given if she needs it to help her wait. Teresa, another afternoon staff member, arrives; Rong Fong has left; and Marie is about to leave. We exchange anecdotes and information about the morning. Our times are staggered so the change for the babies can be gradual. The noon hour tends to be somewhat loud with greetings and activity. Jared begins to cry; he is not hungry, sleepy, or wet—from his clenched fists and drawn-up knees, it seems like gas. I pat him and carry him on my shoulder. He does not improve. We call his mom and get permission to give him Mylicon. He burps soon and settles down comfortably. Emily's mom had come in to breast-feed during the busy time; mother and baby spend their time in the rocking chair. Lunches get finished and Alex and Cason go outside with Beckie.

They play in the infant area and swing in the infant swing. Inside, Teresa blows bubbles and holds the stick in front of the fan. The room fills with bubbles, and the babies' eyes follow the bubbles everywhere. Afternoon juice and formula bottles are prepared. Alex and Cason return from outside hot and tired. They both accept juice in cups in the high chairs. Several babies show sleepy signs and go down for afternoon naps. Beckie takes time to do Jando's "exercises" recommended by his therapist. Teresa dances to Chuck Berry with Alyson. One baby claps hands. Emily rolls over for the first time and we all laugh and clap. A prospective family comes to visit. Alex cries and needs to sit on a lap while they are in the room. Cason needs afternoon medicine. He then falls asleep while having his bottle in Tanya's arms. Jared wakes up and lies on the floor over a rolled blanket. He is beginning to hold up his head. Justin lies on his back and watches the musical mobile. Alyson is in the infant seat with the rainbow bars over her. She bats at Mickey Mouse. As parents arrive, they read the babies' charts and pick up bottles while we help get the baby ready. We tell parents of a happy incident during the day and kiss the baby good-bye. Beckie helps the twins' parents carry them to the car with all their belongings. When only two babies remain, Teresa begins to wash the toys with soap and water, then sprays them with a solution of water and bleach. The swings, chairs, and large toys are sprayed and the sink is wiped down. When the last baby has gone, the windows are locked, the blinds pulled down, hot water emptied, diapers restocked, table washed, lights turned out—and the room is dark and quiet once more.

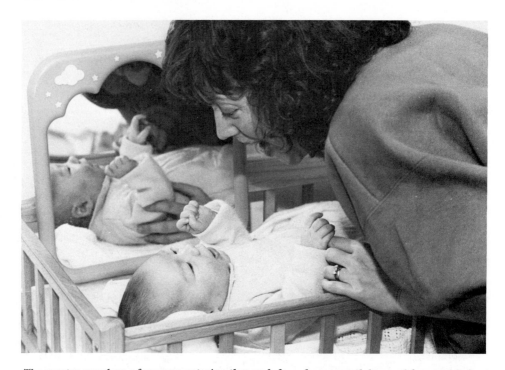

The greater numbers of women entering the work force has created demand for good infant care, which includes nurturing caregivers and an enriched environment.

☐ In a consortium approach, two or more corporations share the cost of an on-site or near-site child care.
☐ A corporation can contribute to a child care center where many of its employees place their children. The subsidy results in reduced rates for employees and/or priority on a center waiting list.
☐ A corporation provides a paid or subsidized leave of absence for the parent in lieu of specific child care services.

In addition, federal tax law allows payroll deductions for child care. The employee reimbursement system works either as a salary reduction plan or as a direct employee benefit. As a benefit, the employee sets aside a certain amount of salary to be paid directly by the employer to the child care provider. More common are employee salary reductions that allow child care payments to be made from pre-tax earnings, often at a considerable discount for most employees. The type of child care the employee can use is not limited. This plan provides a significant benefit to workers in higher tax brackets. Present tax law requires that employees forfeit any of the amount specifically set aside that they do not spend on child care by the end of the calendar year. The current maximum salary reduction allowed for child care is $5000 a year.

If they do not provide direct child care benefits, employers can make child care arrangements easier for their employees in other ways. They can offer a flexible work

Since over 50 percent of women with children under six are in the work force, corporations are finding the need to provide on-site, supported care. One benefit of on-site care is the chance for parents to visit with their children at mealtimes.

schedule, so parents may not need child care, or as much of it. Other possibilities are maternity leave extensions, paternity leaves, and use of sick leave to include absence from work for a sick child. After food, housing, and taxes, child care is the fourth largest budget item for a working family. Many families spend at least 10 percent of their income on child care, and the average single mother may spend up to one-third of her income.

Advantages of Employer-Sponsored Child Care

Many advantages accrue to corporations that sponsor or support child care. The presence of a corporate child care program can be an excellent recruiting device—hospitals, in particular, find child care services an added incentive in recruiting personnel. Other claims for corporate-sponsored child care are that it promotes employee morale and reduces absenteeism. A possible side benefit is that the corporation may be eligible for a variety of tax benefits through business expenses, charitable gifts, and depreciation. Knowing they need not worry about child care may motivate employees to stay with a company; in fact, corporate child care can be viewed as a family support system, which tends to encourage positive feelings toward the company and perhaps offset negative feelings about other factors such as pay and working conditions. Employees may also be more inclined to work different shifts when child care is available.

FORBES METROPOLITAN HEALTH CENTER: EMPLOYER-CONTRACTED CHILD CARE SERVICES*

Employers who provide child care/cognitive program services are not new in the Pittsburgh, Pennsylvania area. The Forbes Metropolitan Health Center, with over 300 employees, has contracted with The Learning Tree Association, a nursery-school development company, for more than ten years. Another Health Center of the Forbes Health System family, located about fifteen miles east of the city, has had a child care center designed and managed by the same development company since 1983. The schools are located on hospital property, and the services to employee/parents are provided in exchange for child care subsidies from the hospital. The Learning Tree schools provide the license, equipment, materials, supplies, faculty, and staff for the care of children ranging in age from six weeks to six years. Since the school is licensed by the Department of Welfare and the Department of Education, the school provides a prekindergarten and a kindergarten, so that children may be involved with the school for as long as six years. Parents pay approximately $75 per week for an infant and $70 for a child over three. The school is open from 6:30 A.M. to 6:00 P.M., five days a week. The school has care for mildly ill children in the planning stages, so that parents will have additional assistance.

The scene hardly ever changes . . . three-year-old Amy stands on tiptoe and pushes the button for herself, with some complaints from her older brother, Eddie. Eddie has been at the school since he was six weeks old, and so has Amy. They are both anxious to see their friends and to share a "show and tell" article, because this is Friday and the day to share special things. Their mother is always patient with them and gently moves them into the elevator that will go up to their floor. The school now occupies an entire floor and has grown from 35 children to 110. The staff remembers how hesitant this mother was six years ago when she first enrolled her as yet unborn child, and how she and the school have developed a firm

*Contributed by Jamie MacIntyre-Southworth, president of The Learning Tree Association, Pittsburgh, Pennsylvania.

partnership, with the father an integral part of the involvement. After her mother has said good-bye—partings are much easier than they were in the beginning—Amy is encouraged to select from several activities available to the early-morning children. These can include having breakfast at school, finishing sleep, or choosing a certain toy or area of play. The children in each Learning Tree School are encouraged to identify with whomever they feel comfortable. All staff, degreed or not, are thought of as "teachers." Amy finds the teacher she wants to be with this particular morning and shares information about a "boo-boo" she acquired overnight. The day moves easily through play, morning meeting, story time, cognitive/idea materials, and hands-on activities that are occasionally thematic. Themes might include social learning and living and other aspects developed through sharing processes.

Lunch is a great social mixer, as well as an opportunity to talk about what we did in the morning. Amy is very verbal and needs help, on occasion, to temper her overt behaviors. This is one day that she will not forget an injustice done to her in the morning and decides to berate another child for the "problem." There is a quiet time of stories and music as the children wind down for the nap period. The teachers make sure everyone goes into the bathroom, washes hands, and then settles down for rest. Kindergarten children may elect to rest, which also includes soft music, or they may select activities in the tutoring room, which is away from the napping area.

The rest of the afternoon consists of snacks (which are nonsugar, nonadditive, and usually fruit or vegetable, along with juice or milk); fun activities that include stories, games or projects, and individual help in cognitive areas. Exploring the neighborhood, visiting the library, and sometimes taking a field trip are all in the schedule for the children at the school. Parents participate in many ways so as to understand the process used in working with their children. This partnership is important to everyone and the commitment is great.

Similarly, there are advantages to employees. Parents can be more relaxed and confident about their children's care. Many parents can visit their children during breaks or even eat lunch with them. Being near their children is particularly advantageous for nursing mothers. Also, if a child becomes ill, the employee is immediately available. Especially when parents have long commuting distances, parents and children get to spend more time together.

Financial factors include the possibility of deducting the cost of child care from an employee's salary, representing a forced means of budgeting; employers can usually provide high quality care at reasonable cost; and when child care is provided as part of an employee's work benefits package, the cost is not taxable.

Proprietary Child Care

Some day care centers are run by corporations, businesses, and individual proprietors for the purpose of making a profit. Some for-profit centers provide custodial services and preschool and elementary programs as well. Many of these programs emphasize their educational component and appeal to middle-class families who are willing to pay for the promised services. About half of all child care centers in the U.S. are operated for profit, and the number is likely to grow. Child care is a big service industry, with more and more entrepreneurs realizing that there is money to be made in caring for the nation's children. Figure 5–3 shows the largest national chains operating child care programs.

Foster Child Care

Almost every state uses foster child care. Children are placed in foster care because their parents can't or won't take care of them, or because they have been abused or abandoned. As many as 250,000 children live in foster care homes or foster group homes. Many children in foster care facilities have physical handicaps or some learning problem that makes them less attractive for adoption. A growing phenomenon in America is the number of *hand-me-down children*; many parents find they cannot afford to raise their children or can no longer discipline them effectively, so they simply turn them over to the juvenile courts, which in turn place them in foster care.

Baby-sitters

Children are their parents' most valuable assets, so parents should not seek the lowest common denominator either in quality or pay when deciding about the kind of person to whom they will entrust their children. These are important qualities for anyone who acts as a baby-sitter:

The necessary age and maturity to provide basic care for children. While no particular chronological age makes a person qualified to give basic care, a certain degree of maturity is necessary.

Education in providing child care. Training might come through a course offered by a school or service organization, or through caring for younger brothers and sisters. In any case, a sitter should know how to diaper, feed, and interact with children.

Basic training in first aid and emergency procedures.

Trustworthiness.

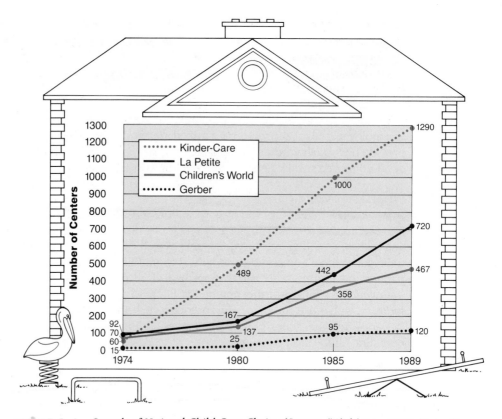

FIGURE 5–3   Growth of National Child Care Chains (Source: "Child Care 1989: Status Report on For-Profit Child Care," *Exchange*, 65, [February, 1989] 20)

Child rearing values that agree with those of the parents. Parents must tell baby-sitters how they want certain situations handled, and how they want their children disciplined.

Personal qualities of neatness, good grooming, and acceptable verbal skills.

Good recommendations and references from others who know and/or have used the sitter.

Drop-in or Casual Child Care

Many parents with part-time jobs or flexible schedules need a place to leave their children. Services that have arisen in response to such needs are in the form of storefront child care centers, child care services in shopping centers, and parents who do occasional baby-sitting in their homes. These services are convenient, but they do have some drawbacks. First, the quality of care may be low simply because the children are transient, and it is difficult to build continuity into a program whose population base is unstable. A second drawback is that sporadic contact with strangers can be stressful to a child.

FAIR PLAY: CHILD CARE FOR SHOPPERS

Parents who shop for groceries at the County Fair Super Market in Carbondale, Illinois, have more than a choice of what kinds of foods they want to buy. The also have a choice of what to do with their young children—take them down the aisle while shopping for the family groceries or leave them at Fair Play, the in-store child care program.

Fair Play is open six days a week (the program is closed on Thursdays) from 9:00 A.M. to 9:00 P.M. for children between the ages of six months to six years. Parents get up to two hours of free child care. Parents who leave their children at Fair Play for longer than two hours—and few seldom do—are charged $5 per hour. Children spend an average of 45 minutes in Fair Play. According to Fair Play coordinator Sandra Overstreet, "The customer-parents are very positive about Fair Play and the services we provide. We have a safe, comfortable center in which each child is treated with love and respect."

At any one time, there are about five children in Fair Play, with about 1,500 "visits" a month. In addition to Sandra, who has a bachelor's degree, the staff includes four part-time child care workers who are students in early childhood education at Southern Illinois University.

These are guidelines that govern Fair Play's operation:

- ☐ The same person who checks the child into Fair Play must check her out.
- ☐ Parents must remain on the premises of County Fair.
- ☐ Parents must supply their own diapers and bottles.
- ☐ Parents are called to pick up children who have trouble adjusting to the facility (this is a rare occurrence).

During a typical day, some of the activities a child can engage in are "cooking" at the play kitchen, drawing a picture to take home (markers, crayons, scissors, and paper are always available for the children), helping grown-ups make play dough, watching the fish in the 55-gallon aquarium (and maybe help feed them, too), having a "bubble storm" (blowing bubbles from the fan), building a castle out of blocks, reading a story from the reading corner, and watching for Mom and Dad from the "Climber."

Today, for example, three-year-old Emma drew several pictures with markers (washable, of course), and then we put them all together into a book for her to take home. She also made breakfast in the housekeeping area. Just before Emma's mother picked her up, we fed the fish together and watched them gobble the food.

Sandra feels that a unique feature of Fair Play is that parents can shop in peace and take their time, knowing that their children are well cared for in a safe place. Also, Sandra points out, "It has given our store a personality that other stores don't have. But best of all, the kids love to come here." Not all parents with eligible children who come to County Fair leave their children at Fair Play. As Sandra points out, "Some parents are here for just a little while. Others want to use shopping as a learning experience, which is great. Also, some days a child may want to shop with his mom or dad and another time he may not."

For their part, the customer/parents like leaving their children at Fair Play. As one parent said, "My kids love it and I feel they are being treated well by Sandra and her helpers." Another parent explains her satisfaction this way; "Every time I bring my son there is something different for him to do—it is a great experience."

Fair Play is exempt from Illinois state licensing requirements because it is located in a shopping center and the parents are on the premises—they are not supposed to leave the store. But as Sandra says, "I work closely with the licensing people and we have a good relationship."

ILL CHILD CARE

One of a working parent's constant dreads is having a child get sick. Balancing the demands of a job and the obligations of parenthood is manageable as long as children are healthy, but when a child is sick, parents must find someone who will take care of the child or stay home. Fortunately, more and more working parents have flexible employee benefits that enable them to stay home with sick children, but many do not. Also, when children are only mildly ill or do not have a contagious illness, parents feel there should be other options to losing a day's work. Child care providers have begun to respond to parent's needs; some centers provide care for sick children as part of their program, and other providers are opening centers exclusively for the care of ill children.

These are some of the ways to manage care of an ill child:

☐ In the home—child care aide goes into homes to care for ill children
☐ Hospital based
☐ Center based (ill child care is part of a center's program of services, usually in a separate room)

A fast-growing and greatly needed area of child care is that of services for mildly ill—and in some cases, chronically ill—children. Many child care programs recognize that when children are sick, parents often face a crisis in their jobs and careers that cannot be casually dismissed by saying that parents should stay home with an ill child.

☐ Separate facility

☐ Family care—ill children are provided for in a family day care home

Staff training for those who provide care for ill children is also a critical concern. Some factors in training include

☐ How to care for ill children according to their different kinds of illnesses

☐ When to exclude the child from ill child care

☐ Curriculum—how to provide learning opportunities for ill children within the limits of their illness

☐ Process

☐ What caregivers and parents can expect in behaviors and symptoms of typical childhood illnesses

☐ How to respond to the needs of ill children

☐ Administering first aid and CPR

RAINBOW RETREAT—"R AND R" FOR ILL CHILDREN

Rainbow Retreat in Newport Beach, California, is one of only a few programs that provide care for mildly ill children. Before using its services, parents preregister their children while they are well. Rainbow Retreat provides care for children between the ages of 2 and 12. After they have registered, parents call the center when they need care for their ill children. Susan Boisvert, director of Rainbow Retreat, or one of her staff members, goes over a checklist to determine whether the child can be admitted directly from the home to the center or if he or she must first see a physician. When parents bring their children in, a staff member does a health assessment regarding the nature of the illness and confirms whether they can attend. Care at Rainbow Retreat costs $5 an hour with a four-hour minimum stay.

Rainbow Retreat will not admit children with measles, mumps, or chicken pox; otherwise, children with almost any other illness are admitted as long as the child's physician feels he can be in the program. Rainbow Retreat will accept children with fevers, ear infections, vomiting, diarrhea, or colds; it will also accept an asthmatic child who has seen a doctor and whose asthma is under control, postsurgical children who have had, for example, an

appendectomy or tonsillectomy, and children in casts who have sprains or fractures.

Although children can stay at Rainbow Retreat for as long as they need ill care, the average stay is two days. Some children stay only one day. Rainbow Retreat can care for 10 children at one time; the daily average is six children. During their stay, children are involved in developmentally appropriate activities that take into consideration their illness and physical condition. At the end of each day, parents receive a report that includes temperature, diet, output, activity participation, and recommendation for future care.

National Pediatric Support Services is the parent organization of Rainbow Retreat as well as a number of regular child care centers. Rainbow Retreat shares a site with each of the child care centers. In addition to Susan, who is a registered nurse, the staff includes a licensed practical nurse and a teaching assistant. The staff takes special precautions to assure that furniture, equipment, and materials are disinfected daily to control infections, yet at the same time allow children freedom to use the center. As a further precaution to limit the spread of germs, no one wears shoes into Rainbow Retreat.

BEFORE- AND AFTER-SCHOOL CARE

In many respects, the public schools are logical places for before- and after-school care. They have the administrative organization, facilities, and staff to provide care. Some have always felt that school buildings should not sit empty in the afternoons, evenings, holidays, and summers, so using the resources already in place for child care seems to make good sense. So in many communities, public schools are helping to alleviate the need for after-school child care.

The Dade County, Florida, public schools provide after-school care for 14,000 students in 162 of the elementary schools. The school district operates 73 after-school centers with its own personnel; 51 are operated by the YMCA, 18 by the YWCA, and 20 by the Family Christian Association of America. The district also operates 74 before-school care sites at 74 centers; 29 are operated by the YMCA, 4 by the YWCA, 40 school based, and one by the Family Christian Association of America. Special needs students are mainstreamed at 76 schools with 760 students in after-school care. Parents pay from $10 to $22 per week depending on the per-child cost at the individual school. Because the programs are school-based and -managed, the costs of services vary depending on the nature and cost of each program. Services begin at day school dismissal and end at 6:00 P.M. The curriculum of the child care programs includes Boy and Girl Scouts, 4-H, fun activities based on skills and concepts measured by the state assessment tests for grades 3 and 5, drama, and ballet.

In other localities, after-school care may be no more than baby-sitting, with large groups of children supervised by a few adults. The cost of after-school care may be more than parents can afford, and when the child care program follows the school calendar, parents are left to find other care when school is not in session.

Latchkey Children

Every day, many children stay home by themselves until it is time to go to school or return from school to empty houses. Children who care for themselves before and/or after school are referred to as *latchkey* or *self-care* children. Some agencies offer support services to latchkey children, such as training them how to answer the phone or deal with strangers at the door. They also work with parents to help them make the home safer and more secure for the children. Parents also form telephone hot lines so children can call someone if they need help, have questions, or just need to talk to someone. Regardless of the support systems, however, latchkey children deal with many uncertainties when they come home by themselves. Many parents find this arrangement quite satisfactory, however, and feel that it promotes independence, autonomy, and responsibility. Some states have laws against leaving children under a certain age (usually twelve) alone without supervision. Many parents may not be aware of these laws, or may feel they really have no choice.

MILITARY CHILD CARE

The Army, Navy, Air Force, Marine Corps, and Coast Guard operate Child Development Programs at 686 locations throughout the world and within the U.S. The armed services are the largest providers of employer child care services. The programs provide care of all kinds—hourly, part-day, full day, before and after school, evening and weekend—to children of military families and other Department of Defense personnel. These programs help family members meet their military responsibilities secure in the knowledge that their children are receiving quality care. Military child care programs are funded through Defense Department appropriations, parent fees, and funds from local programs. Department of Defense funds usually cover the costs of facilities, utilities, supplies, and equipment; parent fees cover the cost of staff salaries.

The armed services have also started a program of family child care services. At Presidio, California, for example, the Army operates 31 family child care homes to service about 112 children of military parents. The Army has determined that family child care is a cost-effective way to provide services to parents. Military personnel are discovering that the availability and quality of child care affects job performance.

During times of high civilian unemployment rates, the number of people in the military services tends to grow, creating a greater demand for child care. Military personnel face problems that many civilians do not, such as frequent relocation, sudden mobilization to active duty, and jobs that require irregular shifts. At the same time, problems of military child care are no different from those of civilian: variation in quality of facilities from base to base; the need for more comprehensive as opposed to custodial care; safe facilities; and training for child care personnel.

THE NANNY MOVEMENT

Nannies are the latest rage in child care. More and more parents, especially the upwardly mobile who can afford a nanny (or *manny,* as males are called) are creating a demand for this type of child care. Although an *au pair,* the traditional mother's helper (often from Europe) has always been part of the child care scene, today's parents want someone more highly skilled. A *nanny,* trained in child development, infant care, nutrition, grooming, manners, and family management, meets this need. The intensive training separates the nanny from baby-sitters and *au pairs.* The American Council of Nanny Schools and other agencies are upgrading nanny curricula. In 1986, there were about 18 nanny schools in operation, and many colleges offer two-year training programs.

Nannies' living arrangements, compensation, and duties vary greatly from family to family. Some live and work in the home twenty-four hours a day, while others work an 8- to 10-hour day and have their own homes. Some nannies have responsibility for child care only; others also assume household responsibilities, including meal preparation; others include teaching their charges as part of their responsibilities. In addition to a salary, some nannies receive paid vacations, medical benefits, and use of a car. Besides providing quality child care, a nanny is a constant presence in a child's life and a trained nanny is a valuable addition to the family and provides more than just child care.

TRAINING AND CERTIFICATION FOR EARLY CHILDHOOD PERSONNEL

A major challenge facing all areas of the early childhood profession is the training and certification of those who care for and teach young children. Training and certification requirements vary from state to state, but more states are tightening standards for child care, preschool, kindergarten, and primary personnel. Many states have mandatory training requirements that an individiual must fulfill before being certified as a child care worker. The curriculum of these training programs frequently specifies mandatory inclusion of topics. For example, in Florida, all child care personnel must complete the Department of Health and Rehabilitative Services' 20-hour child care training course. The course is composed of four modules that include

1. State and local rules and regulations governing child care
2. Health, safety, and nutrition
3. Identifying and reporting child abuse and neglect
4. Child growth and development

In addition, all child care personnel must complete an annual 8-hour inservice training program.

Certificate Programs
Many high schools and vocational education programs conduct training leading to an entry-level certificate. This training certifies people to act as child care aides.

Associate Degree Programs
Many community colleges provide training in early childhood education that qualifies recipients to be child care aides, primary child care providers, and assistant teachers.

Baccalaureate Programs
Four-year colleges provide programs that result in teacher certification. The ages and grades to which the certification applies vary from state to state. Some states have separate certification for prekindergarten programs and nursery schools; in other states, these certifications are "add-ons" to elementary (K–6, 1–6, 1–4) certification.

Master's Degree Programs
Depending on the state, individuals may gain initial early childhood certification at the master's level. Many colleges and universities offer master's level programs for people who want to qualify as program directors or assistant directors or who may want to pursue a career in teaching.

The CDA National Credentialing Program
Fortunately, at the national level, the Child Development Associate (CDA) National Credentialing Program offers early childhood educators the opportunity to develop and demonstrate competencies for meeting the needs of young children. The CDA Program began in 1971 and is a major national effort to evaluate and improve the skills of caregivers in center-based, family day care, and home visitor programs. The CDA National Credentialing Program is operated by the Council for Early Childhood Recognition.

The Council for Early Childhood Recognition has been part of the movement to recognize what quality early childhood education is and what professionals should be. In keeping with this recognition, the Council has introduced a new model as an option for obtaining the CDA credential. This option, known as the CDA Professional Preparation Program, allows the candidate the opportunity to work in a postsecondary institution as part of the credentialing process. A second option is the Direct Assessment method, which has been part of the CDA Credential process since 1971.

Both options have specific eligibility requirements, yet the primary concentration is their definition of a CDA: the Child Development Associate (CDA) is a person who "is able to meet the specific needs of children and who, with parents and other adults, works to nurture children's physical, social, emotional, and intellectual growth in a child development framework."

A candidate for the CDA Credential in any setting must first meet these eligibility requirements:

☐ Be 18 years old or older
☐ Hold a high-school diploma or GED

Following are the requirements for obtaining the CDA National Credential, the Direct Assessment, and the CDA Professional Preparation Program.

The Direct Assessment Method.   To obtain the CDA National Credential, candidates under the direct assessment option must meet these additional eligibility requirements:

☐ 480 hours of experience working with children from ages birth through five years
☐ Complete 120 hours of formal training in early childhood education

The candidate must then feel competent in the six CDA Competency Areas (see Appendix A) by:

Having been formally observed working with children in a child care setting

Distributing and collecting Parent Opinion Questionnaires

Completing work on a Professional Resource File

Being ready to complete the written assessment and interview by a Council Representative

The last two steps of this option include submitting a completed application to the Council for Early Childhood Recognition and completing the oral and written assessments conducted by a council representative. The Council then notifies the candidate of its final decision after reviewing all data collected as evidence.

The CDA Professional Preparation Program.   To obtain credentialing by means of this new option, the candidate must meet the two general eligibility requirements and must also identify an Advisor to work with during the year of study, which is made up of three phases.

The first phase of this model is the Field Work phase. It involves study of the Council Model Curriculum through guided experiences in a child care setting. This curriculum includes six competency goals:

1. To establish and maintain a safe, healthy learning environment.
2. To advance physical and intellectual competence.
3. To support social and emotional development and provide guidance.

4. To establish positive and productive relationships with families.
5. To ensure a well-run, purposeful program responsive to participant needs.
6. To maintain a commitment to professionalism.[11]

These units are completed by the candidate with the guidance of a Field Advisor and are aimed at stimulating the candidate intellectually in the area of early childhood education.

The second phase is the course work, wherein the candidate participates in seminars offered in community colleges and other postsecondary educational institutions. These seminars are designed to supplement the curriculum and are administered by a Seminar Instructor. At the conclusion of this second phase, the Seminar Instructor monitors an Early Childhood Studies Review to test the candidate's knowledge.

The third and last phase is the Final Evaluation, which takes place in the candidate's work setting or field placement. Here a seventh curriculum unit is introduced: "Where You Go From Here: Becoming an Early Childhood Education Professional So You Can Run a Great Program." The candidate works closely with the Field Advisor to determine if there is a full understanding of the scope of responsibilities associated with being a child care professional. The Field Advisor uses a structured observation and interview instrument, with additional input from a Parent Opinion Questionnaire. After careful consideration of these instruments, the Field Advisor determines whether the candidate is ready for verification of performance by the council representative.

The council representative then meets with the candidate to conduct (1) an interview to assess the candidate's knowledge of good early childhood practice; (2) a review of the results of the Parent Opinion Questionnaire and the candidate's Professional Resource File; and (3) a review of additional evidence of the candidate's competence. These results are then sent to the Council Office for review and determination of whether the candidate has successfully completed all aspects of the CDA Professional Preparation Program.

To date, more than 31,600 people have been awarded the CDA Credential. The CDA attests to an individual's competence in the specified areas, and many certified teachers complete the credentialing process to further their skills in working with young children. (Additional information about CDA can be obtained from the Council of Early Childhood Professional Recognition, Suite 500, 1718 Connecticut Ave. N.W., Washington, DC 20009. The toll free number is 1-800-424-4310; the fax number is 202-265-9161).[12]

WHAT CONSTITUTES QUALITY CHILD CARE?

It is easy to say that parents should seek out and insist on quality care, but many parents don't know what to look for, and unfortunately, not all care providers know what constitutes quality care. The following guidelines may give parents and professionals a deeper understanding of the indicators of quality care.

Good child care provides for children's needs and interests at each developmental stage. For example, infants need good physical care as well as continuing love and affection, and sensory stimulation. Toddlers need safe surroundings and opportunities to explore. They need caregivers who support and encourage active involvement.

At all age levels, a safe and pleasant physical setting is important, and should include a safe neighborhood free from traffic and environmental hazards; a fenced play area with well-maintained equipment; child-sized equipment and facilities (toilets, sinks); and areas for displaying the children's work, such as finger painting and clay models. The environment should also be attractive and cheerful. The rooms, home, or center should be clean, well lighted, well ventilated, and bright.

The ratio of adults to children should be sufficient to give children the individual care and attention they need. For infants, the ratio of caregivers should be 1:3; for toddlers, the adult-child ratio should be 1:5, and for preschoolers, 1:8 or 1:9, depending on group size. The program should have a written, developmentally based curriculum for meeting children's needs. The curriculum should specify activities for children of all ages that caregivers can use to stimulate infants, provide for the growing independence of toddlers, and address the prereading and writing skills of four- and five-year-olds. The program should go beyond good physical care to include good social, emotional, and cognitive care. It should include a balance of activities, with time for indoor and outdoor play and for learning skills and concepts. There should be parent involvement to help parents learn about the child care setting and their children's growth and development. Parents need to be encouraged to make the child care services part of their lives, so they are not detached from the center, its staff, or what happens to their children.

Whether in a family or center setting, child care providers should be involved in an ongoing program of training and development. The CDA is a good way for staff members to become competent and maintain the necessary skills. Program administrators should have a background and training in child development and early childhood education. A director of a child care program or agency should have a bachelor's degree in early childhood education, certification, or, at least, special college work in this area. Knowledge of child growth and development is essential for caregivers. Films, books, training in clinical settings, and experiences with children help caregivers know about development. Caregivers need to be developmentally and child-oriented, rather than self- or center-oriented.

Child care providers, especially those of infants, should be sensitive to the adjustments children make when they come into a child care setting. The environment and the people are new to them. A baby who has been the only child at home and cared for only by his mother or father has a lot to adapt to in a center setting, where there are more infants and more caregivers. Many center infant programs make sure that one care provider takes care of the same infants, to give them the security that comes from familiarity. Likewise, new caregivers must also adjust when they come into the home or center, since every child has a unique personality, preferences, and ways of responding to the world.

Quality in Center Programs

The final report of the National Day Care Study, *Children at the Center,* came to these conclusions about quality in child care centers:

> Qualitatively, these findings imply that smaller groups, especially those supervised by lead care givers with preparation relevant to young children, are marked by activity and harmony. Care givers are warm and stimulating. Children are actively engaged in learning and get

along well with others. Presumably as a consequence of this type of day care experience, children also make rapid strides in acquiring the skills and knowledge tapped by standardized tests. Larger groups, especially those supervised by care givers without education or training specifically oriented toward young children, present a contrasting picture. Care givers fall into a passive posture, monitoring activities of many children at once, without active intervention. In such an environment, some children "get lost." Apathy and conflict are somewhat more frequent than in small groups. Gains on standardized tests are less than they might otherwise be in day care settings.[13]

The report also makes some interesting conclusions about class size and the ratio of caregiver to students. Whereas many people have always felt that the smaller the ratio the better, the report concludes that this is not necessarily so, and supports a 1:7 ratio with a group size of 14. This raises some interesting questions about the time-honored 1:5 adult-pupil ratio used in Head Start, but for infants and toddlers, the report supports the 1:5 ratio.

Policy recommendations and the reality of state laws governing child/adult ratios in child care programs are frequently at odds with each other. As Table 5–2 indicates, the ratios vary greatly from state to state and are often higher than child care professionals prefer. The recommendations of NAEYC regarding staff/child ratios are shown in Table 5–3.

Quality and Accreditation

Many professional organizations are involved in determining criteria for quality programs. The Southern Association on Children Under Six issued a position statement listing the fundamental needs that must be met in child care.

☐ The child needs to feel that the situation is a safe and comfortable place for him to be
☐ The child needs to learn to feel good about himself
☐ A child needs to be fully employed in activities that are meaningful to him— that support him in his full-time quest to learn
☐ A child needs to develop ability to live comfortably with other children and adults
☐ A child needs to have his physical development supported and be helped to learn health, nutritional, and safety practices
☐ The child in care needs to feel that there is consistency in his life and a shared concern for him among the important people in his life—his parents and his caregivers[14]

In any discussion of quality, the question invariably arises, "Who determines quality?" Fortunately, the National Association for the Education of Young Children has addressed the issue of a standard in its Center Accreditation Project (CAP). The CAP is a national, voluntary accreditation process for child care centers, preschools, and programs that provide before- and after-school care for school-age children. Accreditation is administered through NAEYC's National Academy of Early Childhood Programs. NAEYC cites these benefits of accreditation:

☐ Accredited programs are recognized as quality programs
☐ Parents will seek out accredited programs
☐ The staff learns through the accrediting process

The criteria addressed in the accreditation project are interactions among staff and children, curriculum, staff and parent interactions, administration, staff qualifications

TABLE 5–2 Child:Staff Ratio Requirements Compared

Source: Gwen Morgan, The National State of Child Care Regulation 1986, Watertown, MA: Work/Family Directions, 1987.

Age of Children in Center Care	CA	KS	MA	NC	OH	TX
			States			
Under 6 weeks	4:1	3:1	3:1	7:1	6:1	5:1
12 months	4:1	5:1	3:1	7:1	6:1	6:1
24 months	4:1	7:1	4:1	12:1	7:1	11:1
36 months	12:1	12:1	10:1	15:1	12:1	15:1
48 months	12:1	12:1	10:1	20:1	14:1	18:1

TABLE 5–3 Staff/Child Ratios and Group Size

Age of Children*	6	8	10	12	14	16	18	20	22	24
					Group Size					
Infants (birth–12 mos.)	1.3	1.4								
Toddlers (12–24 mos.)	1.3	1.4	1.5	1.4						
Two-year-olds (24–36 mos.)		1.4	1.5	1.6**						
Two- and three-year-olds			1.5	1.6	1.7**					
Three-year-olds					1.7	1.8	1.9	1.10**		
Four-year-olds						1.8	1.9	1.10**		
Four- and five-year-olds						1.8	1.9	1.10**		
Five-year-olds						1.8	1.9	1.10		
Six- to eight-year-olds (school age)								1.10	1.11	1.12

*Multi-age grouping is both permissible and desirable. When no infants are included, the staff-child ratio and group size requirements shall be based on the age of the majority of the children in the group. When infants are included, ratios and group size for infants must be maintained.

**Smaller group sizes and lower staff-child ratios are optimal. Larger group sizes and higher staff-child ratios are acceptable only in cases where staff are highly qualified.

Source: *Accreditation Criteria and Procedures of the National Academy of Early Childhood Programs* (Washington, D.C.: National Association for the Education of Young Children, 1984), p. 24.

and development, staffing patterns, physical environment, health and safety, nutrition and food service, and program evaluation.[15]

FINDING CHILD CARE: INFORMATION AND REFERRAL SYSTEMS

A reality that many parents face when they decide they need child care is locating the care they want. There has never been a systematic way to match parents' needs with the care available. Much of child care, especially family care, is hidden from the public. One solution to this mismatch between consumer demand and existing services is a network of child care information and referral systems that is springing up across the country. These systems, usually computer-based and operated by municipal governments, universities, corporations and nonprofit agencies, are designed to help parents gain access to information about competent, convenient, and affordable care. Information supplied to parents includes names, addresses, and phone numbers of providers and basic information about the services, such as hours of operation, ages of children cared for, and activities provided.

ACCREDITING A PROGRAM*

The Decision

The idea of getting our two centers, Open Door Preschools, accredited by NAEYC was exciting for all of us. Accreditation requires higher standards than licensing. The accreditation process would provide a good way to evaluate and improve our centers' programs. We had always felt that we were providing excellent care for our children; accreditation would confirm this belief. This would also be an excellent opportunity for the staff, parents, and teachers to work together toward a major goal. The decision to apply for accreditation was made, and as educational director of Open Door, I would oversee the accreditation process.

Preparation

Following the guidelines that NAEYC set up, we examined and evaluated our programs in various areas, such as goals and philosophy, long-range written curriculum plan, interaction among staff and children, staff-parent communication, policies, staff-training plans, and so on. After a comprehensive evaluation of all these aspects, we identified their strengths

*Contributed by Dr. Nira Changwatchai, site director, The Open Door (South Location), Austin, Texas.

and weaknesses. Also, through weekly staff meetings, we came up with a set of plans to accomplish our goal.

We looked for areas in which to strengthen our programs, including health and safety, environment, and nutrition. We also added several pieces of playground equipment and rearranged the classroom environment. To better prepare our teachers, we invited special speakers to meet with the staff and had our staff attend conferences and workshops. Among the topics were providing appropriate activities for the children, interacting with the children, handling inappropriate behavior, and promoting communication among parents and staff.

Also at this time we had the staff evaluate the program and themselves, and I conducted classroom observations of the teachers, followed by evaluations and discussions of their performance. Parents as well as teachers of both centers answered questionnaires. We had some difficulty getting questionnaires back from parents and realized that we should have communicated better with the parents. We would have received better response if we had gone over items in the questionnaires with the parents and made them aware of the whole process. Also, we should have taken more time at each step in the process to make sure that

CHILD CARE ISSUES

As in any profession, child care is not without controversies and issues. Some issues that confront child care workers and the profession are who child care is for, whether parents should stay home, whether there should be state and/or national licensing standards, who should bear the cost of child care, and whether or not child care is harmful to children.

Who is Child Care For?

One issue concerns whether child care should benefit parents or children. There is a tendency to interpret child care as a service to parents, which critics feel has caused the quality of child care programs to suffer. The needs of children should not be secondary to the needs of parents, and our first concern should be the quality of care children receive. Another aspect of this issue relates to which children should receive services. Ultimately, a system of child care should be available to all parents and their

teachers were prepared for self-evaluation, the staff questionnaires, and classroom observation.

Occasionally during this self-study, the teachers became worried about being observed (after we submitted the materials to NAEYC, validators would come to observe the teachers and centers). After all, what would we do if something went wrong or if somebody were sick? In this case, at the end of the day, validators would talk with the director and staff to clear up these points. I also worried about the paperwork that needed to be compiled and organized. However, we overcame these worries and were ready to move on with all the support from our Board of Directors and parents.

After the improvements were made and the documents prepared, I mailed all the documentation, which included Program Description and Center Profile, summary sheets of classroom observation, staff questionnaires, and parent questionnaires, to NAEYC in March 1986.

Validator Visiting Day

About a month later, the validators arrived. Everyone was excited and nervous at the same time. Even though the validators were very friendly, we each felt as if we were once again student teachers—the difference was that this time we had volunteered to participate. However, things went smoothly. Everyone tried to be calm and act as we normally would. As the days went by, we began to relax. It wasn't as hard as we had anticipated.

Success

After the visits, we had to wait for the results. The validators were here only to confirm our evaluation of our center; the actual decision would be made by a commission. Finally, in June we were informed that both centers, Open Door North and Open Door South, had received accreditation. We were two of the first five centers in Austin to be accredited. It was certainly worthwhile to go through the process, although everyone had to work hard. We were proud to be recognized as having high quality programs by the early childhood profession, and we were proud to provide quality care and education for children. After accreditation, centers must report any changes or improvements to NAEYC annually until it is time to reaccredit again in three years. Having learned a lot our first time around, we had our third center accredited in February 1988, one year after it opened. From now on, accreditation should not be as hard.

children. Until this is possible, we need priorities. Should child care be aimed at low-income parents who need to work or to engage in work-training programs? Or should priority be given to abused and neglected children? Some questions are not easy to answer.

Should Parents Work or Stay Home?

Another issue is the lack of agreement as to the real need for child care. Some feel the availability of child care encourages women to seek employment rather than stay home to care for their children, which, critics contend, leads in turn to a deterioration of family values and the ultimate breakdown of the family. They also argue that readily available child care erodes traditional values of parenthood and family by giving control of the nation's children to state and federal agencies and encouraging parents to relinquish their parental roles.

On the other hand, others consider child care a right, and women agree that child care helps them gain equal access to the workplace. This growing tension between the advocates of working parents and those who feel that a parent's place—usually the mother's— is at home with her children is likely to continue. Pediatrician T. Berry Brazelton, among others, thinks that women can handle two roles at one time and that it is time for our country to recognize this fact as a national trend.[16] Deborah Fallows, on the other hand, believes children are treated with benign neglect in child care programs and children bear the brunt of being left in the care of others.[17] Burton White maintains that full-time care for children under the age of three is not in their best interest.[18]

In reality, the issue is not whether parents should work; rather, it is what kind of care children receive. The issues of employment and parenthood rest on these factors:

☐ The quality of care children receive in their parents' absence. There is bad care, custodial care, and quality care. Parents who work should make every effort to find and use quality care. On the other hand, society has the obligation to up-grade quality.
☐ Parents' attitudes toward work. Some parents want to work more than they want to rear their children. Some parents cannot provide the emotional and social interchanges that form the basis of effective care. These parents are probably happier working and entrusting their children to quality child care.

Evidence does not support the conclusion that working *per se* is bad for children. As Belsky and Steinberg point out:

> With regard to children's intellectual development, the available evidence indicates, in general, that day care has neither beneficial nor deleterious effects. For children growing up in high risk environments, however, experience in center based care does appear to attenuate the declines in IQ frequently observed in youngsters from economically disadvantaged backgrounds. With regard to emotional development, the weight of evidence indicates that day care is not disruptive of the child's emotional bond with his mother, even when day care is initiated in the first year of life. In addition, there is no indication that exposure to day care decreases the child's preference for his mother in comparison with an alternative familiar caregiver. Finally, with respect to social development, the existing data indicate that day-care reared children, when compared with age-mates reared at home, interact more with peers in both positive and negative ways.[19]

Interactions among the Home, the Workplace, and Child Care

Child care professionals are increasingly aware that the family and workplace environments are critical to the final outcome of children's well-being. Accordingly, professionals are seeking ways to help parents in their demanding and stressful roles as modern parents and employees. These interactions take many forms, as we have discussed in this chapter, but the link between the home and the child care program must be strengthened as a means of providing both quality family life situations and quality child care. More and more, child care providers must recognize that child care is a family support system and not a substitute for the home and family. The parenting and developmental information child care programs provide and the skills they help parents develop are as important as the quality of the care they render.

Likewise, what happens in the workplace and the benefits parents have or don't have affects their performance both as employees and as parents. A corporation that has a program of benefits that helps support families—for example, leave for caring for sick children and flexible work schedules—has more productive workers as it simultaneously contributes to an enhanced quality of life for its parent/employees.

The Effects of Child Care on Different Children

Quite often in discussions about and conceptualization of child care, we have a homogenized view of what it is and what it should be—that is, we think there is one universal kind of quality child care that is good for all children. And, in a sense, this is exactly true; the profession can and does maintain, for example, that low caregiver-child ratios and small group size are indicators of quality child care. But is the same kind of child care necessarily good for all children? As we become more knowledgeable about the effects of child care on children in general, we must pay more attention to the effects it has on different children. Caregivers must continue to think about how to tailor different kinds of child care services based on children's individual differences, cultures, and family situations. This is precisely the kind of response professionals are taking with special needs children (Chapter 13), and which will become increasingly necessary for all children in child care. We must become more conscious of and sensitive to the needs of all children, the care they receive, and the effects it has on them and their families.

We must also recognize that to a large extent, how parents view child care is a product of their culture, upbringing, and education. Some parents see child care as a service they should use only for the least amount of time, while other parents may consider child care a major contributor to their children's rearing and are perfectly willing to have their children in a program most of the day.

The "Mommy Track"

As more women enter the work force and become major factors in corporate organizations, there are growing conflicts as to how corporations should respond to the needs of working women. A major source of conflict is working women's responsibilities to children and families. Women more often than not assume primary responsibility for their children's care; for example, when a child is ill, a working mother must find an alternative source of care or must stay home with her ill child. At the same time, many corporate managers maintain that when women put their children and families first, the corporation suffers.

One of the latest suggestions for a corporate response to women in the workplace is Felice Schwartz's proposal of a "Mommy Track."[20] Schwartz suggests that employers divide their women employees into two differentiated career paths based upon whether they are willing to "put their career first" or whether they want to "divide themselves between jobs and family." In essence, the career track is for women who remain childless or who turn over the major responsibility for child rearing to others. They will work late and on weekends and will put the corporation first. The Mommy Track parents, on the other hand, put family first. Those on the career track will receive the promotions and other career benefits, while Mommy Track parents forgo promotions and other benefits in favor of flexible schedules and leaves as necessary to care for their children.

As might be expected, proposing a separate career track for working mothers has created a firestorm of protest from working mothers and women's advocate groups who don't want to see women treated as second-class citizens. The Mommy Track controversy illustrates the conflicts that will continue to occur in corporate life as employers seek to adjust their needs to the needs of working parents. Early childhood educators and other professional groups, however, must not allow women with children to be treated as second-class citizens in corporate America. Rather, what is needed is a national policy of parent and family support to recognize that women need not and should not forgo the opportunities, benefits, and contributions of the workplace or career simply because they have children.

Improving the Quality of Child Care

One obvious way to improve the quality of child care programs and pesonnel is through more stringent facility-licensing requirements and increased training requirements. Parents can and should be educated to the need for quality child care. Parents often help perpetuate poor child care by accepting whatever kind of care they can find. If they are properly educated and involved in programs, they can help make child care better for everyone.

Quality Child Care for All

Although we talk a great deal about quality child care and identify the criteria that constitute quality, the fact remains that quality child care is not widely available to the majority of families and children. One challenge facing early childhood professionals and the nation is how to provide families and children with quality programs that will enhance and promote their optimum development. Not only does the quality of child care differ from program to program, it also differs from one state to another, as we see in the variations in mandated adult/child ratios and the guidelines for training required as a condition for employment.

Furthermore, families and children at risk are generally more likely to receive the poorest quality child care, thus placing the children in double jeopardy. While all children must have quality care, those who are at risk will benefit the most from quality care because quality child care helps moderate the effects of risk factors. A constant challenge to all involved in the education and development of young children must be to upgrade child care programs in every town and city in America.

The comprehensive nature of good child care programs has to be extended. Many still believe that if a program provides germ-free custodial care, it is a good one. Unfortunately, some of these programs are also sterile in the philosophies and activities they provide to parents and children.

Who Should Pay for Child Care?

Who should pay for child care services is a perennial issue. The federal government's support for child care services has been shrinking over the past decade. This means that the three other available sources for child care support—state agencies, private agencies, and consumers—will, of necessity, have to increase their support. The abilities of states to support child care is, however, a function of their wealth and population. In this sense, the more populous and wealthy the state, the more able it is to support child care. Table 5–4 shows the amount of financial support that ten states give to child care.

As fewer and fewer federal dollars become available, more parents will be called upon to help pay the real cost of their children's care. Yet the fact remains that most parents who have to work probably cannot and will not be able to afford the cost of quality child care programs. Efforts to have child care subsidized by employers, foundations, and charitable groups will have to increase.

How Much Should Child Care Cost?

Traditionally, child care has been a low-cost and low-paying operation. Many programs emphasize keeping costs low so that working and low-income parents will not be overburdened, which has resulted in a very low pay scale for child care workers. Thus, the cost of child care is kept low, and the true cost is subsidized by low-paid workers. Yet, if child care costs rise to provide workers with fairer wages, many families who can hardly afford what they now pay would be priced out of the services. Also, as more public schools offer programs for four-year-olds, many child care workers with degrees will be attracted to these programs by the higher salaries. This shift could tend to lower the quality of child care programs and further decrease salaries.

Making Child Care More Humane

Many child care facilities are not good places to leave children; they are sometimes located in dark and dreary basements, and are depressing to both care providers and children. Those who operate child care programs must strive to improve the physical environments of homes and centers. Child care programs can be stifling if children never go anywhere or see anyone besides their caregivers. Good programs take children places and do things with them. They encourage and actively solicit the involvement of grandparents, senior citizens, and other adults so children can be involved with others.

Agreement between Parents and Care Providers

The number of parents who turn over their children to outside child care providers continues to increase each year. Many parents entrust their children to people they

TABLE 5–4 Title XX Child Care Spending in Ten States, 1988

Source: *State Child Care Fact Book— 1988* (Washington, D.C.: Children's Defense Fund, 1988), pp. 86-87.

State	Child Care Expenditures
1. California	$330,000,000
2. New York	$185,000,000
3. Massachusetts	$ 81,218,765
4. Pennsylvania	$ 68,435,000
5. Florida	$ 54,531,877
6. Illinois	$ 50,863,300
7. New Jersey	$ 36,671,050
8. Texas	$ 35,200,000
9. Ohio	$ 30,200,000
10. North Carolina	$ 28,076,857

know very little about. They may be reliable and trustworthy, or they may not. Parents are now better informed as to what constitutes quality child care. Although they are becoming more selective, they still leave their children with people who are relative strangers. It is therefore extremely important for quality child care providers to work closely with parents from the time of their initial contact, usually at registration. Caregivers must demonstrate to parents their competence in areas such as child development, nutrition, and an appropriate curriculum. They must also assure parents that they will maintain daily communication about the child's progress.

Parents and caregivers need to agree on discipline matters, and child care providers and social service agencies need to guide parents as to what constitutes good child rearing and appropriate discipline practices.

FUTURE TRENDS IN CHILD CARE

What does the future hold for child care? These are some trends we can anticipate as we approach the twenty-first century:

☐ The number of women who attach themselves in one way or another to the labor force, in full- or part-time capacities, will increase. The rapidity and ease with which this increase occurs will depend in large measure on what child services are available and how parents adjust their work and lives to the need for child care.
☐ The number of employer-sponsored or assisted child care programs will increase. The growth of these programs will accelerate because of employees' demands for child care and the obvious advantages to employers. The greater the benefits to the employer, the more likely they will increase their involvement in child care.
☐ Public schools will participate in child care, especially after-school care, at a greater rate. They will also be more inclined, and perhaps even forced, to provide preschool programs.
☐ Good child care, especially the kind provided by many corporations, will have an effect on poor child care. Parents will become more aware of what constitutes good child care and demand it of other programs.
☐ The number of information and referral systems will increase because of the gap between the demand for child care and its availability.
☐ For-profit programs will provide child care services for more families. While these services will not be financially available to all families, those who can will pay what is necessary. Fortunately, the quality of for-profit child care is improving.
☐ There will be a proliferation of child care services sponsored by clubs, religious organizations, and neighborhood groups. Many will not necessarily meet licensing standards, but will satisfy parents' needs.
☐ The federal government's role in child care will become less significant, and the influence of individual states will increase. The federal government will not make comprehensive services available to all children because the expense of a national program of child care would necessitate reordering national budget priorities. The trend in federal support to social service programs is to return

monies to the states in the form of block grants, allowing states greater freedom and autonomy in determining how funds are spent. The block grant procedure also reduces direct federal control of state and local programs.

☐ While existing day care services for low-income, disadvantaged families will continue, there will still not be enough services to meet everyone's needs. At the other end of the economic spectrum, services for those who can afford to pay will become more available. Children of the middle class who don't qualify for day care services based on income and whose parents can't afford the fees of profit-making day care programs will remain the forgotten children.

☐ Futuristic thinking about child care must include alternatives to day care, such as adjusted parenting leaves from work and flexible work schedules. It is conceivable, for example, that rather than paying parents to place their children in a child care program, they could be paid to stay at home with them. This strategy could be combined with a program of training parents in child development and child rearing practices.

☐ There is a critical need for appropriate standards and enforcement of child care licensing. Indicators of quality child care are developmentally appropriate expectations, environment, and curriculum; high quality staff-child interactions characterized by clear communication, nurturance, and an understanding of young children; low caregiver-to-child ratios and small group sizes. It is imperative that such factors be included consistently in licensing standards to provide appropriate care for young children.

FURTHER READING

American Academy of Pediatrics. *Tips on Selecting the Right Day Care Facility* (Elk Grove Village, Ill.: American Academy of Pediatrics, 1985)

Pamphlet provides ten guidelines to follow in selecting quality child care. An ideal resource to distribute at parent meetings and seminars. Guidelines include nature of the child care workers, kinds of activities, cleanliness, and health services.

Burud, Sandra L., et al. *Employer-Supported Child Care: Investing in Human Resources* (Dover, Mass: Auburn House, 1984)

Provides all the information employers need to establish child care programs that will benefit themselves and their employees, based on data from more than 400 employer-supported programs. Also includes many useful charts and forms.

Comfort, Randy Lee, and Constance D. Williams. *The Child Care Catalog* (Littleton, Col.: Libraries Unlimited, 1985)

Excellent resource guide that includes extensive bibliographies, descriptions of unique pro-

grams, names and addresses of people and agencies, and many questions to guide the reader's quest for answers about child care. Also a valuable research tool for anyone who wants a quick overview into the field of child care and a top candidate for inclusion in a parent's resource library.

Gorder, Cheryl. *Home Schools: An Alternative* (Columbus, Ohio: Blue Bird Press, 1987)

Gorder wants parents to realize they have choices about where and how their children are educated. Seeks to help parents make choices on the basis of what they believe about their lifestyles, values, and priorities. The author wants parents to be aware of and consider the option of home schooling. Should be read by all preschool and early childhood teachers for its perspective on home schooling and the obstacles parents encounter.

Hollingsworth, Jan. *Unspeakable Acts* (New York: Congdon and Weed, 1988)

Account of the highly publicized child abuse case in Country Walk, Miami, Florida; should be read by all parents and child care workers. Reviewer Glenn Collins said in the *New York Times,* "In its lurid details, its frustrating complexity and in the agony of the children and families who were victimized, this case would seem to be the paradigm of incidents in Minnesota, California, and elsewhere that have surfaced in recent years. A startling difference, though, is the outcome: the molester was convicted and sentenced to life in prison.

Jaisinghani, Vijay T., and Vivian Gunn Morris. *Child Care in a Family Setting: A Comprehensive Guide to Family Day Care* (Pennsylvania: Family Care Associates, 1986)

Outlines most common areas of concern in defining, organizing, and maintaining a quality family day care home. A must for family day care providers as a resource for childproofing your home, keeping accurate records, and the importance of child development.

Marhoefer, Patricia E., and Lisa A. Vadnais. *Caring for the Developing Child* (Albany, N.Y.: Delmar, 1988)

A comprehensive text that answers basic questions in child care. Interesting and appropriate for those beginning a career in child care.

Oryx Press. *Directory of Child Day Care Centers*

Four volumes list services for the Northeast, North Central, Western, and Southern states, giving name of the center, address and telephone number, contact person, capacity, and ages served. This series is valuable for parents who move to a new city and desperately seek child care services.

Rice, Robin D. *The American Nanny* (New York: Harper & Row, 1985).

Comprehensive guide to finding, assessing, living with, and becoming today's highest quality child care provider.

Thomas, Carol H., ed. *Current Issues in Day Care: Readings and Resources* (Phoenix, Ariz.: Oryx Press, 1986)

Collection of nineteen articles addressing important issues and concerns of parents and caregivers; also guides selection and evaluation of child care programs. In addition, there is information relating to employer-sponsored child care, trends, and environmental and health concerns.

FURTHER STUDY

1. Survey parents in your area to determine how many need child care services. Also, determine what services most parents desire from a child care program. Are most of the parents' child care needs being met?
2. Visit child care center programs for infants and toddlers. What makes each program unique? Which program would you feel most comfortable working in? Why?
3. Determine the legal requirements for establishing center and home child care programs in your state, city, or locality. What kind of funding is available? What are the similarities and differences of establishing home and center programs? What is your opinion of the guidelines?
4. Invite people from child care programs, welfare departments, and social service agencies to speak to your class about child care. Find out who may attend child care programs. Also, find out what qualifications and training are necessary to become a child care employee. How do you feel about training welfare mothers as child care employees?
5. After visiting various child care programs, including center and home programs, discuss similarities and differences. Which of the programs provides the best services? What changes or special provisions need to be made to improve the success of these kinds of programs?
6. Gather information on franchised early childhood programs. What are the similarities and differences? In your opinion, what factors are necessary for the success of these kinds of programs?
7. Design a child care program you feel would meet the needs of children and their parents. How is your program similar to or different from those you visited?
8. Identify five of the most important issues associated with child care. Discuss these with parents, child care teachers, professors, and peers. Which issues are most controversial? How do your opinions differ from those of others?

9. Develop a model training program for baby-sitters. What would you include? What competencies would baby-sitters have to demonstrate before they graduate from your program?

10. Develop a manual for baby-sitters that you could use in your baby-sitter training program.

11. Develop a checklist to show parents what to look for in a quality child care program.

12. Some cities operate a hot line for latchkey children to use while they are home alone. List concerns these children might have and how you might alleviate these concerns over a hot line.

13. Interview a group of parents to determine how you could increase their participation in family and child care programs.

14. Visit an employer-sponsored child care program in your area. Describe the program to your classmates, listing pros and cons for parents and employers you found at that particular center.

15. Survey parents to determine the strengths and weaknesses of the child care programs they use.

16. Conduct a survey to determine the cost of child care services in your area. Arrange your data in a table. What conclusions can you draw?

17. Tell why or why not you would leave your six-week-old infant in center child care, and develop a list of pros and cons for such care. Share this information with your classmates.

18. Do you think politicians always consider the social and personal consequences of their regulations, legislations, and administrative directives? Give specific examples.

19. You have been asked by your state senator to review child care regulations in your state. What suggestions would you make? What are the political and social implications of your suggestions?

20. Compare and contrast child care in Israel, Cuba, and other countries. Compare these systems to your ideas of child care. Could we improve the American system using the ideas of other countries? What determines the type of child care a particular country provides?

21. How will employer-sponsored child care meet the future needs of child care in America? What changes do you feel might result in child care as a result of employer involvement?

22. Is the CDA credential recognized in your state? If yes, find out how many centers are participating in the CDA Program.

23. Interview a CDA candidate and gather information about the work one needs to complete for the CDA Credential. How does the candidate feel about the credentialing process? What are his/her goals for completing the CDA program?

24. What are the child care licensing requirements in your state? Do they require training similar to the CDA Program? If yes, how are they alike? How are they different?

25. Write to the Council for Early Childhood Professional Recognition to gather information on the CDA Program. How do you feel about the CDA Program?

NOTES

1. Children's Defense Fund, *Child Care: Key Facts 1989.*

2. *Child Welfare League of America: Standards for Day Care Services* (New York: Child Welfare League of America, 1973), p. 9.

3. Bettye M. Caldwell, "What is Quality Child Care?" *Young Children* 39, 3 (March 1984), p. 4.

4. P. Divine-Hawkins, Family Day Care in the United States: Executive Summary (Washington, D.C.: U.S. Department of Health and Human Services, DHHS Publication No. (OHDS) 80-30287, Sept. 1981), p. 1.

5. Family Day Care Standards (Florida Department of Health and Rehabilitative Services, 1985), p. 1.

6. Commonwealth of Pennsylvania Department of Public Welfare, Bureau of Child Development Programs, *Regulations for Child Care,* April, 1978, p. 8.

7. *Minimum Standards for Child Care Services* (State of Florida, Department of Health and Rehabilitative Services), p. 4.

8. John H. Winters, Human Services Center, *Minimum Standards for Day Care Centers* (Texas Department of Human Services, May, 1985), p. 2.

9. USDA Preliminary Data, Food and Nutrition Service, Key Data, December 1989.

10. *Work Force 2000: Work and Workers for the 21st Century.* A study by the Hudson Institute for the U.S. Dept. of Labor.

11. Carol B. Phillips, "The Child Development Associate Program—Entering a New Era," *Young Children,* 45 (1990), p. 26.

12. CDA Professional Preparation Program, *Essentials for Child Development Associates,* draft copy (Washington D.C.: Council for Early Childhood Professional Recognition, 1989).

13. *Children at the Center:* Final Report of the National Day Care Study, Executive Summary (Cambridge, Mass: Abt Associates, March 1979).

14. The Southern Association on Children Under Six, *Position Statement on Quality Child Care* (pamphlet).

15. National Association for the Education of Young Children, *Accreditation by the National Academy of Early Childhood Programs,* p. 2.

16. T. Berry Brazelton, *Working and Caring* (Reading, Mass.: Addison-Wesley, 1986).

17. Deborah Fallows, *A Mother's Work* (Boston: Houghton Mifflin, 1986).

18. Burton White, *The First Three Years of Life* (Englewood Cliffs, N.J. Prentice-Hall, 1986).

19. Jay Belsky and Laurence D. Steinberg, "The Effects of Day Care," in *In The Beginning: Readings on Infancy,* ed. Jay Belsky (New York: Columbia University Press, 1982), p. 255.

20. Felice Schwartz, "Management Women and the New Facts of Life," *Harvard Business Review,* 67 (1989), pp. 65 76.

CHAPTER 6
Infants and Toddlers
Rediscovering the Early Years

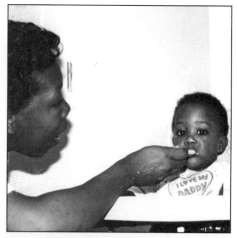

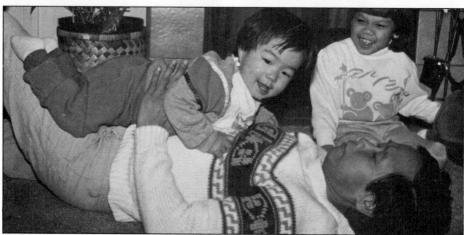

As you read and study:

☐ Identify reasons for increases in the number of programs for infants and toddlers

☐ Understand how infants and toddlers develop in the physical, motor, psychosocial, and language areas

☐ Understand Piaget's cognitive theory as it relates to infants and toddlers

☐ Examine theories about the process of language development and acquisition

☐ Understand Erikson's theory of psychosocial development in the infant and toddler years

☐ Recognize the developmental differences between infants and toddlers and the need to provide developmentally appropriate programs for each

☐ Analyze and understand the features that contribute to quality infant and toddler programs

☐ Identify what constitutes developmentally appropriate curricula for infants and toddlers

☐ Understand issues involved in quality care and education for infants and toddlers

During the last decade of the twentieth century, we will see continuing great interest in and demand for infant and toddler care and education. The growing demand stems primarily from the large numbers of women entering the labor force, the high divorce rate, and the economic need for both parents to work. The demand for early education is also fueled by baby-boom parents who want their children to have an "early start" and get off on the "right foot" so they can have an even better life than their parents. The acceptance of early care and education is also attributable to a changing view of the very young and the discovery that babies are remarkably competent individuals. Parents and early childhood educators are combining forces to give infants and toddlers the quality care and education they need without harmfully and needlessly pushing and hurrying them.

PHYSICAL DEVELOPMENT

The infant and toddler years betweeen birth and age three are full of many important developmental and social events. Infancy, life's first year, includes many firsts—the first breath, the first smile, first thoughts, first words, and first steps. Many significant developmental events also occur during toddlerhood, the period between one and three years. Two events are unassisted walking and rapid language development. Language and mobility are the cornerstones of autonomy that enable toddlers to become independent. These firsts and unique developmental events are significant in children's lives and also in the lives of those who care for and teach them. How adults respond to infants' "firsts" and to toddlers' quest for autonomy helps determine how they grow and develop and master the life events that await them.

To fully understand their roles as educators and nurturers, caregivers need to understand major features of normal growth and development. To begin, we must recognize that infants and toddlers are not the miniature adults many advertisements picture them to be. Children need many years to develop fully and become independent. This period of dependency and caregivers' responses to it are critical for the developing child. Caregivers must constantly keep in mind that "normal" growth and development are based on averages, and the "average" is the middle ground of development. (Table 6–1 gives average heights and weights for infants and toddlers.) To assess children's progress, or lack of it, caregivers must know the milestones of different stages of development. At the same time, to assess what is "normal" for each child, they must consider the whole child. They must look at cultural and family background, including nutritional and health history, to determine what is normal for that child. Caregivers must also keep in mind that when chidlren are provided with good nutrition, health care, and a warm, loving emotional environment, development will tend toward what is "normal" for each of them.

MOTOR DEVELOPMENT

Motor development is an important part of infant and toddler development because it contributes to intellectual and skill development. Human motor development is governed by certain basic principles:

☐ Motor development is sequential. (Table 6–2 lists the sequence of development and major developmental milestones.)

Quality programs provide materials and activities for a wide range of interests and abilities. A good program is not limited to the interests and abilities of the "average" infant or toddler, but addresses each child's individual temperament, likes and dislikes, and style of interaction.

TABLE 6–1   Height and Weight of Infants and Toddlers

Age	Males		Females	
	Height (inches)	Weight (pounds)	Height (inches)	Weight (pounds)
Birth	19.9	7.2	19.6	7.1
3 months	24.1	13.2	23.4	11.9
6 months	26.7	17.3	25.9	15.9
9 months	28.5	20.2	27.7	18.9
1 year	30.0	22.4	29.3	21.0
1½ years	32.4	25.3	31.9	23.9
2 years	34.5	27.8	34.1	26.2
2½ years	36.3	30.1	35.9	28.5
3 years	38.0	32.4	37.6	30.7

Source: P.V.V. Hamill et al., "Physical Growth: National Center for Health Statistics Percentiles," *The American Journal of Clinical Nutrition,* 32 (1979):607-629.

TABLE 6–2   Infant/Toddler
Motor Milestones

Source: William K. Frankenburg, William Sciarillo, and David Burgess, "The Newly Abbreviated and Revised Denver Developmental Screening Test." *The Journal of Pediatrics. 99* (Dec. 1981), pp. 995-999.

Behavior	Age of Accomplishment for 90% of Infants/Toddlers
Chin up momentarily	3 weeks
Arms-legs move equally	7 weeks
Smiles responsively	2 months
Sits with support	4 months
Reaches for objects	5 months
Smiles spontaneously	5 months
Rolls over	5 months
Crawls	7 months
Creeps	10 months
Pulls self to stand	11 months
Walks holding onto furniture	13 months

☐ Maturation of the motor system proceeds from gross (large) behaviors to fine motor. When learning to reach, for example, an infant sweeps toward an object with the whole arm; as a result of development and experiences, gross reaching gives way to specific reaching and grasping.

☐ Motor development is from *cephalo* to *caudal*—from head to foot (tail). This process is known as *cephalocaudal* development. The head is the most developed part of the body at birth; infants hold their heads erect before they sit, and sitting precedes walking.

☐ Motor development proceeds from the *proximal* (midline or central part of the body) to the *distal* (extremities), known as *proximodistal* development. Infants are able to control their arm movements before they can control finger movements.

Toilet Training

Toilet training (or *toilet learning* as it is sometimes called) is a milestone of the toddler period. This process often causes a great deal of anxiety for parents, caregivers, and toddlers. American parents want to accomplish toilet training as quickly and as efficiently as possible, but frustrations arise when they start too early and expect too much of children. Toilet training is largely a matter of physical readiness, and most child rearing experts recommend waiting until children are two years old before beginning. Although some parents claim that their children are trained as early as one year, it is probably the parent rather than the child who is trained.

The principle of toilet training is that parents and caregivers are helping children develop control over an involuntary response. When an infant's bladder and bowel are full, the urethral and sphincter muscles open. The goal of toilet training is to teach the child to control this involuntary reflex and use the toilet when appropriate. Training involves timing, patience, modeling, preparing the environment, establishing a routine, and developing a partnership between the child and parents/caregivers. Another necessary partnership is between parents and child care providers who are

Toilet training is the process of helping children gain control over elimination. It is often not the quick and easy process parents and caregivers would hope for, because so many factors are involved—among them, the child's emotional and physical readiness and the parent's willingness to make it a cooperative experience.

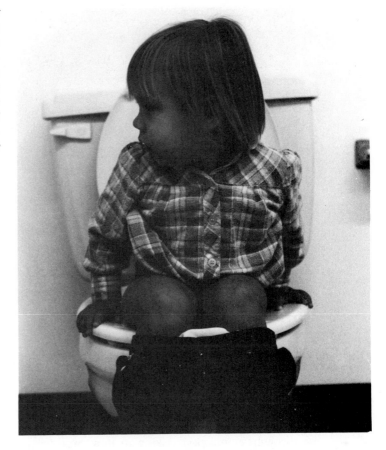

assisting in toilet training, especially when parents don't know what to do or are hesitant about it or want to start too soon.

INTELLECTUAL DEVELOPMENT

As we learned in Chapter 4 in our discussion of Piaget's theory of intellectual development, the first schemes are *sensorimotor*. According to Piaget, infants do not have "thoughts of the mind." Rather, they come to know their world by acting on it through their senses and motor action. According to Piaget, infants *construct* (as opposed to absorbing) schemes using sensorimotor reflexive actions. Sucking, an innate sensorimotor scheme, involves turning the head to the source of nourishment, closing the lips around the nipple, sucking, and swallowing. As a result of experiences and maturation, this basic sensorimotor scheme is adapted or changed to include anticipatory sucking movements and nonnutritive sucking such as sucking a pacifier or blanket.

New schemes are constructed or created through processess of assimilation and accommodation. Piaget believed children are active *constructors* of intelligence

Caregivers in infant and toddler programs plan developmentally appropriate activities for both groups, based on children's interests, that encourage active involvement. Adults guide and encourage children's healthy growth, development, and learning by providing a safe and emotionally supportive environment.

through assimilation (taking in new experiences) and accommodation (changing existing schemes to fit new information), resulting in *equilibrium.* Piaget said children are constantly in quest of a balance between new experiences and old ideas, between what the world is really like and their view of the world. In this sense, humans are programmed to develop their intelligence through active involvement in the environment.

Infants begin life with only reflexive motor actions that are used to satisfy biological needs. By using these reflexive actions on the environment, and in response to the specific environmental conditions, however, the reflexive actions are modified through accommodation and adaptation to the environment. Patterns of adaptive behavior are used to initiate more activity, which leads to more adaptive behavior, which in turn leads to more schemes.

Stages of Cognitive Development

Sensorimotor Intelligence.   Sensorimotor intellectual development consists of six stages, shown in Table 6–3.

Stage I (birth to one month)—During this stage, infants suck and grasp everything. They are literally ruled by reflexive actions and are not in control of their behavior. Reflexive responses to objects are undifferentiated, and infants respond the same way to everything. Sensorimotor schemes help infants learn new ways of interacting with

TABLE 6–3   Stages of Sensorimotor Intellectual Development

Stage	Age	Behavior
Stage I: Reflexive action	Birth to 1 month	1. Reflexive actions of sucking, grasping, crying, rooting, swallowing 2. Through experiences, reflexes become more efficient (e.g., amount of sucking required for nourishment) 3. Little or no tolerance for frustration or delayed gratification
Stage II: Primary circular reactions	1 to 4 months	1. Acquired adaptations form 2. Reflexive actions gradually replaced by voluntary actions 3. Circular reactions result in modification of existing schemes
Stage III: Secondary circular reactions	4 to 8 months	1. Increased responses to people and objects 2. Able to initiate activities 3. Beginning of object permanency
Stage IV: Coordination of secondary schemes	8 to 12 months	1. Increased deliberation and purposefulness in responding to people and objects 2. First clear signs of developing intelligence 3. Continuing development of object permanency 4. Actively searches for hidden objects 5. Comprehends meanings of simple words
Stage V: Experimentation (tertiary circular reactions)	12 to 18 months	1. Active experimentation begins through trial and error 2. Spends much time "experimenting" with objects to see what happens; insatiable curiosity 3. Differentiates self from objects 4. Realization that "out of sight" is not "out of reach" or "out of existence" 5. Beginning of understanding of space, time, and causality
Stage VI: Representational intelligence (intention of means)	18 to 24 months	1. Development of cause-effect relationships 2. Representational intelligence begins; can mentally represent objects 3. Engages in symbolic imitative behavior 4. Beginning of sense of time 5. Egocentric in thought and behavior

the world, and the new ways of interacting promote cognitive development. One infant sensorimotor scheme, for example, is grasping. At birth, the grasping reflex consists of closing the fingers around an object placed in the hand. Through experiences and maturation, this basic reflexive grasping action becomes coordinated with looking, opening the hand, retracting the fingers, and grasping. In this sense, the scheme develops from a pure, reflexive action to an intentional grasping action. As an infant matures, and in response to experiences, the grasping scheme is combined with a delightful activity of grasping and releasing things.

Stage II (one to four months)—The milestone of this stage is the modification of the reflexive actions of Stage I. Sensorimotor behaviors not previously present in the infant begin to appear: habitual thumb sucking (which indicates hand-mouth coordination), tracking moving objects with the eyes, and moving the head toward sounds (which indicates the beginnings of the recognition of causality). Infants begin to direct their own behavior rather than being totally dependent on reflexive actions. The first steps of intellectual development have begun.

Primary circular reactions begin during Stage II. A circular response occurs when an infant's actions cause a reaction in the infant or in another person that prompts the infant to try to repeat the original action. The circular reaction is similar to a stimulus-response, cause-and-effect relationship.

Stage III (four to eight months)—Piaget called this stage that of "making interesting things last." Infants manipulate objects, demonstrating coordination between vision and tactile senses. They also reproduce events with the purpose of sustaining and repeating acts. The intellectual milestone of this stage is the beginning of *object permanence*. When infants in Stages I and II cannot see an object, it does not exist for them—a case of "out of sight, out of mind." During the later part of Stage III, however, there is a growing awareness that when things are out of sight, they do not cease to exist. *Secondary circular reactions* begin during this stage. This process is characterized by infants' repeating an action with the purpose of getting the same response from an object or person; for example, an infant will repeatedly shake a rattle to repeat the sound. Repetitiveness is a characteristic of all circular reactions. "Secondary" means that the reaction is elicited from a source other than the infant. The infant interacts with people and objects to make interesting sights, sounds, and events last. Given an object, the infant will use all available schemes, such as mouthing, hitting, and banging, and if one of these schemes produces an interesting result, the infant continues to use the scheme to elicit the same response. Imitation becomes increasingly intentional as a means of prolonging an interest.

Stage IV (eight to twelve months)—During this stage, the infant uses means to attain ends. Infants move objects out of the way (means) to get another object (end). They begin to search for hidden objects, although not always in the places they were hidden, indicating a growing understanding of object permanence.

Stage V (twelve to eighteen months)—This stage, the climax of the sensorimotor period, marks the beginning of truly intelligent behavior. Stage V is the stage of experimentation. Toddlers experiment with objects to solve problems, and their experimentation is characteristic of intelligence that involves *tertiary circular reactions,* in which they repeat actions and modify behaviors over and over to see what will happen. This repetition helps develop an understanding of cause-and-effect relationships and leads to the discovery of new relationships through exploration and experimentation. Physically, it is also the beginning of the toddler stage, with the commencement of walking. Toddlers' physical mobility, combined with their growing ability and desire to "experiment" with objects, makes for fascinating and often frustrating child rearing. They are avid explorers, determined to touch, taste, and feel all

Through experimentation and interviews, Piaget documented that children construct their own intelligence. It is important for caregivers to provide children with opportunities and materials to actively explore and "experiment," within a safe, supportive environment.

they can. Although the term "terrible two's" was once used to describe this stage, professionals now recognize that there is nothing terrible about toddlers exploring their environment to develop their intelligence. Novelty is interesting for its own sake, and toddlers experiment in many different ways with a given object. They use any available items—a wood hammer, a block, a rhythm band instrument— to pound the pegs in a pound-a-peg toy.

Stage VI (eighteen months to two years)—This is the stage of transition from sensorimotor to symbolic thought. Stage VI is the stage of symbolic representation. Representation occurs when toddlers can visualize events internally and can maintain mental images of objects not present. Representational thought enables toddlers to solve problems in a sensorimotor way through experimentation and trial and error. Representation enables toddlers to more accurately predict cause-and-effect relationships. Toddlers also develop the ability to remember, which enables them to try out actions they see others do. During this stage, toddlers can "think" using mental images and memories, enabling them to engage in pretend activities. Toddlers' representational thought does not necessarily match the real world and its representations, accounting for a toddler's ability to have other objects stand for almost anything: a wooden block is a car; a rag doll is a baby. This type of play is also known as *symbolic play* and becomes more elaborate and complex in the preoperational period.

We need to keep in mind several important concepts of infant and toddler development:

1. The chronological ages associated with Piaget's stages of cognitive development are approximate. Caregivers should not be preoccupied with children's ages, but should focus on cognitive behavior, which gives a clearer understanding of a child's level of development.

2. Infants and toddlers do not "think" as adults do; they come to know their world by acting on it and need many opportunities for active involvement.

3. Infants and toddlers are actively involved in *constructing* their own intelligence. Children's activity with people and objects stimulates them cognitively and leads to the development of mental schemes.

4. Parents and caregivers need to provide environments and opportunities for infants and toddlers to use the basic reflexive actions and their modifications, because environment and opportunity are two important conditions for intellectual development. Reflexive actions form the basis for assimilation and accommodation enabling the development of cognitive structures. Caregivers must ensure that infants and toddlers have experiences that will enable them to do a good job of intellectual construction.

5. At birth, infants do not know that there are objects in the world and, in this sense, have no knowledge of the external world. They do not and cannot differentiate between who they are and the external world. For all practical purposes, the infant is the world. All external objects are acted on through sucking, grasping, and looking. This acting on the world enables infants to construct schemes of the world.

6. The concept of causality, or cause-and-effect, does not exist at birth. Infants' and toddlers' concepts of causality begin to evolve only through acting on the environment.

7. As infants and toddlers move from one stage of intellectual development to another, the previous stage is not replaced by the new; rather, later stages evolve from earlier ones. Schemes developed in Stage I are incorporated into and improved on by the schemes constructed in Stage II, and so forth.

LANGUAGE DEVELOPMENT

S.I. Hayakawa defines language this way:

> Of all forms of symbolism, language is the most highly developed, most subtle, and most complicated. It has been pointed out that human beings, by agreement, can make anything stand for anything. Now, human beings have agreed, in the course of centuries of mutual dependency, to let the various noises that they can produce with their lungs, throats, tongues, teeth, and lips systematically stand for specified happenings in their nervous systems. We call that system of agreements *language*.[1]

This system of agreements has some basic characteristics. First, it is a set of symbols that stand for certain ideas, thoughts, concepts, things, and feelings. The word *chair* is a written and spoken symbol for that object; the word *love* is a symbol for that emotion. Children do not automatically understand this process of assigning symbols to objects. Second, language is arbitrary, since we can make a symbol stand for anything we wish. By convention and custom, we agree upon certain symbols for certain things. Third, language is constantly changing, in both usage and the constant addition of new words to our vocabulary. Fourth, language involving symbols is a human behavior. While baboons have a repertoire of sounds in their communication system, they have never created a new sound. Fifth, because language is a uniquely human phenomenon, it is also an integral part of human society. It becomes a societal instrument for a wide variety of purposes and functions. Language is a social instrument for inducting children into society. Socialization of children would be difficult without language; thus, parents and schools have a responsibility to provide optimum opportunities for language acquisition.

Communication

We find evidence of communication everywhere in nature. Studies of the communication patterns of bees and dolphins make fascinating reading. Your dog wags her tail, and you interpret it as her communicating to you that she is happy. A baby cries,

Quality caregivers recognize that even very young children are capable of engaging in conversation. Attentive adults converse with toddlers and wait for a response, even from children with limited language abilities. The adults label and name objects and feelings and describe events, and expand on children's verbalizations.

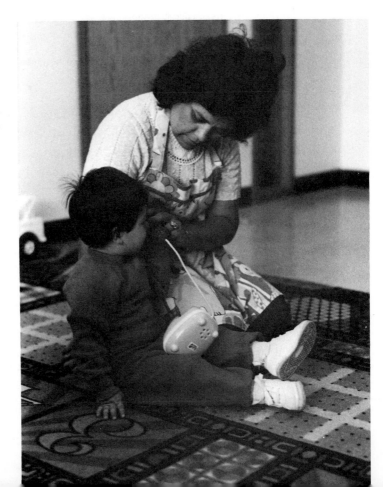

and his mother immediately interprets it as a sign of distress and changes his diaper. A teacher frowns at a child who is talking, and the child ceases, fearing more tangible punishment. These are all examples of communication, but none of them involves what we usually think of as language.

Effects of Language

Language sets parameters for cognitive and social achievement. The language a child learns is generally determined by the society or culture into which she is born and, more specifically, by the home and community. The language style of the child's mother (or primary caregiver) also plays a dominant and important role in the language a child learns and in how she learns to communicate. Factors that influence the mother's language are level of education, language style learned as a child, knowledge of child rearing practices, and time and opportunity to use language with her children.

What and how a child learns affect school achievement and, to a certain extent, self-image. If the child has learned nonstandard English in a nonverbal setting, there will undoubtedly be difficulty with the language of schooling and expectations of the teacher. In the early grades, school achievement is traditionally measured by children's ability to learn to read. Children who do not speak well (generally, standard English is the criterion) often have difficulty learning to write and read, which leads to failure and, in turn, to poor self-image. The roots of school failure and subsequent life failure can often be traced to failure to acquire the vocabulary and language patterns necessary for actively seeking knowledge. Failure to do well in school can often be traced to the language children bring to school.

Language Acquisition

How does language development begin? What forces and processes prompt children to participate in one of the uniquely human endeavors?

Heredity.   Heredity plays a role in language development in a number of ways. First, humans have the respiratory and laryngeal systems that make rapid and efficient vocal communication possible. Second, the human brain makes language possible. The left hemisphere is the center for speech and phonetic analysis and the brain's main language center. But the left hemisphere does not have the exclusive responsibility for the language process. The right hemisphere plays a role in our understanding of speech intonations, enabling us to distinguish between declarative, imperative, and interrogative sentences. Without a brain that enables us to process, language as we know it would be impossible. Third, heredity plays a role in language development in that some theorists believe that humans are innately endowed with the *ability* to produce language.

One proponent of the theory that humans are born with the ability to acquire language is Noam Chomsky. He hypothesizes that all children possess a structure or mechanism called a Language Acquisition Device (LAD) which enables them to acquire language. The young child's LAD uses all the language sounds he hears to process many grammatical sentences, even sentences he has never heard before. The child hears a particular language and processes it to form grammatical rules.

Eric Lenneberg has studied innate language acquisition in considerable detail in many different kinds of children, including the deaf. According to Lenneberg:

> All the evidence suggests that the capacities for speech production and related aspects of language acquisition develop according to built-in biological schedules. They appear when the time is ripe and not until then, when a state of what I have called "resonance" exists. The child somehow becomes "excited," in phase with the environment, so that the sounds he hears and has been hearing all along suddenly acquire a peculiar prominence. The change is like the establishment of new sensitivities. He becomes aware in a new way, selecting certain parts of the total auditory input for attention, ignoring others.[2]

Lenneberg believes that language development runs a definite course on a definite schedule, although he does not entirely dismiss the role of environment. He offers other reasons to support his contention that language is a "biological propensity":

- ☐ Language development begins at about the same time in children's physical development and follows a fixed sequence;
- ☐ Language is learned by all children, even those who have severe handicaps;
- ☐ Nonhuman forms do not have the capacity for language development;
- ☐ All languages are based on the same principles of syntax, semantics and phonology.[3]

The fact that children generate sentences they have never heard before is often cited as proof of innate ability. What would language be if we were only capable of reproducing the sentences and words we heard? The ability of children in all cultures and social settings to acquire language at a relatively immature age tends to support the thesis that language acquisition and use is more than a product of imitation or direct instruction. Indeed, children learn language without formal instruction.

The idea of a sensitive period of language development makes a great deal of sense and had a particular fascination for Montessori, who believed there were two sensitive periods for language development. This first sensitive period begins at birth and lasts until about three years. During this time, children unconsciously absorb language from the environment. The second period begins at three years and lasts until about eight years. During this time, children are active participants in their language development and learn how to use their power of communication. Milestones of language development for infants and toddlers are shown in Table 6–4.

Environmental Factors. Theories about a biological basis of language should not be interpreted to mean that children are born with the particular language they will speak. While the ability to acquire language has a biological basis, the content of the language— vocabulary— is acquired from the environment, which includes other people as models for language. Therefore, development depends on talk between children and adults, and between children and children. Optimal language development ultimately depends on interactions with the best possible language models. The biological process of language acquisition may be the same for all children, but the content of their language will differ according to environmental factors. A child left to his own devices will not learn the language as well as the child reared in a linguistically rich environment. For example, let's take the case of Genie, a modern-day "wild child." During her early days, Genie had minimal human contact, and her

TABLE 6–4   Language Development in Infants and Toddlers

Age	Language
Birth	Crying
1½ months	Social smile
3 months	Cooing
5 months	Ah, goo
5 months	Razzing
6 months	Babbling
8 months	Da-da/Ma-ma (used inappropriately)
10 months	Da-da/Ma-ma (used appropriately)
11 months	One word
12 months	Two words
14 months	Three words
15 months	Four to six words
18 months	One body part name
21 months	Two-word combinations
24 months	Fifty words
24 months	Two-word sentences (Noun/pronoun and verb used inappropriately)
24 months	Pronouns (I, you, me, etc. used inappropriately)

Source: *Clinical Pediatrics*, 17(11), (November 1978).

father and brother barked at her like dogs instead of using human language. She did not have an opportunity to learn language until she was thirteen-and-a-half years old, and even after prolonged treatment and care, Genie remained basically language deficient and conversationally incompetent.[4]

Behaviorism.   One popular view of language development is that language is acquired through associations resulting from stimulus-response learning. Thus, learning theorists see language acquisition as resulting from parents and the environment rewarding children's language efforts. Parents, for example, reward children for their first sounds by talking to them and making sounds in response to the children's sounds. First words are reinforced in the same way with parents (and others) constantly praising and encouraging. Modeling and imitation also play important roles in this view of language acquisition. Children imitate the sounds, words, sentences, and grammar they hear modeled by other children and adults. B.F. Skinner is a leading proponent of the environmental theory of language development. He believes language is mainly a process of reinforcing the child's behavior in certain sounds and sound patterns and not in others. The child's parents reinforce or reward the child when the sounds he makes are a part of the language, and do not reinforce sound patterns not in the language; in this way, the child learns the language of his parents. This helps explain why adults who learn a second language must train their ears to hear new language sounds. They cannot hear many of the sounds in the new language because these sounds were not reinforced in them when they were children.

The question of innate language acquisition versus language acquisition based on environmental factors is similar to the controversy of nature versus nurture in intellectual development. One cannot reject one viewpoint at the expense of the other. We must consider language acquisition as the product of both innate processes and environmental factors.

Caregivers and Language Learning.   People who care for children and who are around them in the early stages of their language learning have a great deal of influence on how and what they learn. Children's language experiences can make the difference in their school success. Many children enter a preschool or child care setting without much experience in talking to and listening to other children or adults in different social settings.

Parents and caregivers should focus on the content of language; learning names for things, learning to speak in full sentences, and how to use and understand language. Many of these language activities relate directly to success in kindergarten and first grade. These guidelines are useful in promoting children's language development:

☐ Treat children as partners in the communication process. Many infant behaviors, such as smiling, cooing, and vocalizing, serve to initiate conversation, and care-givers can be responsive to these through conversation.

☐ Conversations are the building blocks of language development. Attentive and caring adults are infants' and toddlers' best stimulators of cognitive and language development.

☐ Talk to infants in a soothing, pleasant voice, with frequent eye contact, even though they do not "talk" to you. Most mothers and caregivers talk to their young children differently from the way they talk to adults. They adapt their speech so they can communicate in a distinctive way called *motherese*. Mothers' language interactions with their toddlers are much the same as with infants. When conversing with toddlers who are just learning language, it is a good idea to simplify verbalization—not "baby talk," such as "di-di" for diaper or "ba-ba" for bottle— but rather to speak in an easily understandable way, for example, instead of saying, "We are going to take a walk around the block so you must put your coat on," we would instead say, "Let's get coats on."

☐ Use children's names when interacting with them, to personalize the conversa-tion and build self-identity.

☐ Use a variety of means to stimulate and promote language development, includ-ing reading stories, singing songs, listening to records, and giving children many opportunities to interact with other adults and children who have conversations with them.

☐ Encourage children to converse and share information with other children and adults.

☐ Help children learn to converse in different settings. This requires taking chil-dren to different places so they have different places to use their language and different people to use it with. By the same token, going to different places gives children ideas and events for using language.

☐ Have children use language in different ways. Children need to know how to use language to ask questions, explain feelings and emotions, tell what they have done, and to describe things.

☐ Give children experiences in the language of directions and commands. Many children fail in school not because they don't know language, but because they have little or no experience in how language is used for giving and following directions. It is also important for children to understand that language can be used as a means to an end—a way of attaining a desired goal.

☐ Converse with children about what they are doing and how they are doing it. Children learn language through feedback; this includes asking and answering questions and commenting about activities, which shows children that caregivers are paying attention to them and what they are doing.

☐ Talk to children in the full range of adult language, including past and future tenses.

PSYCHOSOCIAL DEVELOPMENT

Erik H. Erikson is noted for his *psychosocial theory* of development. According to Erikson, children's personalities grow and develop in response to social institutions such as families, schools, child care centers, and early childhood programs. Of course, adults are principal components of these environments and therefore play a powerful role in helping or hindering children in their personality development.

Stages of Psychosocial Development

Erikson's theory has eight "stages," which he also classifies as *"ego qualities."* These qualities emerge throughout the human life span; four stages apply to children from birth to age eight and are shown in Table 6–5. Stage I, Basic Trust vs. Mistrust, begins at birth and ends at about 18 months. During this stage, children learn to trust or mistrust their environments and caregivers. Trust develops when children's needs are met consistently, predictably, and lovingly. Stage II, Autonomy vs. Shame and doubt, begins at 18 months and lasts until about 3 years. This is the stage of independence, when children want to do things for themselves. Lack of opportunities to become autonomous and independent and caregiver overprotection result in self-doubt and poor achievement. Stage III, Initiative vs. Guilt, begins at three years and ends at about five years. During this time children need opportunities to respond with initiative to activities and tasks, which give them a sense of purposefulness and accomplishment. Guilt occurs when children are discouraged or prohibited from initiating activities and are overly restricted in attempts to do things on their own. Stage IV, Industry vs. Inferiority, covers the elementary school years. In this period, children display an industrious attitude and want to be productive. They also want recognition for their productivity, and adult response to children's efforts and accomplishments helps develop a positive self-concept. When children are criticized, belittled, or have few opportunities for productivity, the result is a feeling of inferiority.

Characteristics of Caregivers

Regardless of who provides care for infants and toddlers, caregivers should have certain qualities that will enable them to provide for children's *total* needs on all levels—physical, cognitive, language, and social and emotional. These qualities include love of children, caring about children, warmth, kindness, patience, good physical and mental health, compassion, courtesy, dedication, empathy, enthusiasm, hon-

TABLE 6–5   Erikson's Stages of Psychosocial Development in Early Childhood

Stage	Approximate Ages	Characteristics	Role of Early Childhood Educators	Outcome for Child
Basic Trust vs. Mistrust	Birth to 18 months or 2 years	Infants learn either to trust or mistrust that others will care for their basic needs, including nourishment, sucking, warmth, cleanliness, and physical contact.	Meet children's needs with consistency and continuity	Views the world as safe and dependable
Autonomy vs. Shame	18 months to 3 years	Toddlers learn to be self-sufficient or to doubt their abilities in activities such as toileting, feeding, walking, and talking.	Encourage children to do what they are capable of doing; avoid shaming for any behavior	Learns independence and competence
Initiative vs. Guilt	3 to 5 years (to beginning of school)	Children are learning and want to undertake many adultlike activities, sometimes overstepping the limits set by parents and thus feeling guilty.	Encourage children to engage in many activities; provide environment in which children can explore; promote language development	Able to undertake a task, be active and involved
Industry vs. Inferiority	Elementary	Children actively and busily learn to be competent and productive, or feel inferior and unable to do things well.	Help children win recognition by producing things; recognition results from achievement and success	Feelings of self-worth and industry

esty, and intelligence. Parents used to think their children were not capable of learning much in the early years, so it didn't make much difference if those who took care of them did much with them. But we now know that it does matter who takes care of and educates the very young. Alice Honig believes that *nurturing* is a necessary quality for all caregivers: "The high-quality infant caregiver is a special kind of nurturing person, with keen observation skills. Flexible, creative, comforting—she or he has a calm style that radiates secure commitment to an infant's well-being."[5]

Quality caregivers really *know* the children they care for. This knowledge, combined with knowledge of child growth and development, enables them to provide care that is appropriate for *each* child. They also *care* about the children. They accept and respect all children and their cultural and socioeconomic backgrounds. Furthermore, quality caregivers *care about themselves*. This self-caring appears in their commitment to the child care profession and includes learning and developing the skills necessary to be a good care provider. It is further evidenced through good grooming, neatness, and cleanliness.

Programs for Infants and Toddlers

Infants and toddlers are cared for and educated in many kinds of programs and in many different ways. These include child care centers (some of which specialize in the care of infants), family child care homes, baby-sitting cooperatives, mothers' day-out programs, and people who care for children in their own or the child's home. Regardless of the type of program, a good one requires these basic features:

Quality caregivers. It is impossible to have a quality program without a quality staff. Those who are responsible for administering and conducting programs for the very young should make every effort to hire a staff that has the characteristics that contribute to high quality. Patient, warm adults who have an understanding of how infants and toddlers grow and develop are probably the most important factor in a developmentally appropriate child care program.

Acceptable staff/child ratios. Program directors often say they comply with state guidelines for staff/child ratios and are therefore providing a quality program. State regulations for staff-child ratios may, however, be too high to enable caregivers and teachers to do their best. The NAEYC guidelines (presented in Chapter 5) suggest ratios every program should strive to achieve.

Responsive environment. An environment is responsive when it is sensitive to the unique needs of *all* children and is not merely satisfied to meet the needs of the "average" child.

Appropriate curriculum and activities.

The National Association for the Education of Young Children has developed "Guidelines for Developmentally Appropriate Practice" to help staff plan for activities. These are among the suggestions:

☐ A developmentally appropriate curriculum provides for all areas of children's development—physical, emotional, social, and cognitive—through an integrated approach.

Routines such as sleeping, feeding, diapering, washing, and comforting are an important and necessary part of any child care program, and become the context in which a curriculum is developed. Caregivers and parents must keep each other informed about a child's behavior and any deviations in routine.

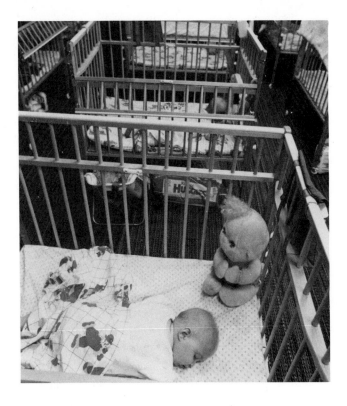

☐ Curriculum planning is based on teachers' observations and recordings of each child's special interests and developmental progress.

☐ Curriculum planning emphasizes an interactive process.

☐ Learning activities and materials should be concrete and real.

☐ Programs should provide for a wider range of developmental interests and abilities than the chronological age range of the group would suggest.

☐ Teachers should offer a variety of activities and materials and increase the difficulty, complexity, and challenge of an activity as children develop understanding and skills.

☐ Adults should provide opportunities for children to choose from among a variety of activities, materials, and equipment and time to explore through active involvement.

☐ The program should offer multicultural and nonsexist experiences, materials, and equipment for children of all ages.

☐ Adults should arrange a balance of rest and active movement for children throughout the program day.

☐ Outdoor experiences should be provided.[6]

As more women enter the work force, more children are placed in child care at earlier ages. While most parents feel they don't have a choice, many privately and publicly wonder, "Is leaving my child at a center all day good for him?" Some early childhood experts expressed their doubts about substitute care for very young children. In *The First Three Years of Life,* Burton White said that "full-time substitute care for babies under three years of age, and especially for those only a few months of age, does not seem to be in the best interest of babies."[7] Generally, however, such cautionary admonitions have been ignored, mainly because of economic and career concerns.

There is now a growing debate about how much child care is good for children and the effects it has on them. The controversy associated with infant care was brought to a boil with the research revelation that "twenty or more hours of such care [non-maternal] per week were associated with significantly increased risk of the development of insecure infant-mother attachment relationships."[8] The fallout over this research was significant and vociferous. The researchers were quick to add that the attributes of the mother, the characteristics of individual children, and the nature of the care arrangements form a "complex ecology" that has to be more fully understood and researched. The nature of children's attachments to their mothers is affected by a number of factors, including (1) the positive relationships children have with their caregivers, and (2) the stability and characteristics of the caregiver.[9]

So, when considering the effects of child care on their young children, it would be wise for parents and others to consider the quality of the program and the quality of the caregivers who will provide primary care to their child.

CURRICULA FOR INFANTS AND TODDLERS

The curriculum for infants and toddlers consists of all the activities and experiences they are involved in while under the direction of caregivers. Consequently, caregivers and teachers plan for *all* activities and involvements: feeding, washing, diapering/toileting, playing, learning and stimulation interactions, outings, involvements with others, and conversations. Caregivers must plan the curriculum so it is developmentally appropriate. In addition to the ideas that caregivers and teachers can extrapolate from the NAEYC guidelines for a developmentally appropriate curriculum, these concepts can also be included: self-help skills, ability to separate from parents, problem solving, autonomy and independence, and assistance in meeting the developmental milestones associated with physical, cognitive, language, personality, and social development. Table 6–6 is a cognitive activity chart that shows how a curriculum for infants and toddlers can be developed for the cognitive domain. In addition, Table 6–7 shows a sample curriculum for eight- to twelve-month-olds and for eighteen- to twenty-four-month-olds.

Childproofing Homes and Centers

Home

☐ Remove throw rugs so toddlers don't trip
☐ Put breakable objects out of toddler's reach
☐ Cover electrical wall outlets with special covers
☐ Remove electrical cords
☐ Install gates in hallways and stairs (make sure gates are federally approved so the toddlers cannot get their heads stuck and strangle)

It is imperative that caregivers and parents provide an environment in which infants and toddlers can grow and explore free from harmful safety hazards.

☐ Take knobs off stoves

☐ Purchase medicines and cleaners that have childproof caps

☐ Store all medicines and cleaning agents out of reach; move all toxic chemicals from low cabinets to high ones (even things like mouthwash should be put in a safe place)

☐ Place safety locks on bathroom doors that can be opened from the outside

☐ Cushion sharp corners of tables and counters with foam rubber and tape or cotton balls

☐ If older children in the home use toys with small parts, beads, etc., have them use these when the toddler is not present or in an area where the toddler can't get them

☐ When cooking, turn all pot handles to the back of the stove

☐ Avoid using cleaning fluids while children are present (because of toxic fumes)

☐ Place guards over hot water faucet in bathrooms so toddlers can't turn them on

TABLE 6–6   Cognitive Activity Chart, Birth to 30 Months

Cognitive Stage	Blocks	Books
Reflexive actions (primary circular reactions) (1–4 months) to suck to get hands to mouth to track and follow movement to provide variety of experiences for modification of reflexive actions	Soft, plastic, bright colors to watch to develop eye muscle to arouse curiosity to motivate movement	Soft, cardboard, bright colors to mouth to grasp with hands to observe contrast in colors and pattern to promote social contact with adult
Secondary circular (4–8 months) to promote eye/hand coordination manipulation to reproduce interesting experiences to initiate activities	Soft, plastic, bright colors to mouth to bang together to coordinate eye and hand movements	Soft cardboard to turn pages to explore with mouth to listen to encourage language
Coordination of secondary schemes (8–12 months) cause/effect object permanence means to ends	Large duplo, square, wooden to stack and knock down to experiment to experience cause and effect	Old magazines, cardboard books to point to label to open and close to take off the shelf to promote language development

	Play		
Music	Mobiles	Sensory Materials	
Caregiver voice, records, radio to listen to range of sounds to locate sounds to be aware of sounds	Homemade or commercial, hands or faces, bright colors to provide visual stimulation to bat at with hands and feet to become aware of self	Lambskin, flannel, silk to provide experiences with different textures to promote reaction to tactile stimulation to soothe emotionally to associate an object with comfort	
	Mirrors	Rattles	Water
Rattles, bells, shaking, clapping to make sounds to cause things to happen to imitate	Floor level, individual to lay in front of to hold look at self look at caregiver to learn about self	Wrist, ankle, commercial to hear a variety of sounds to experience variety of textures to cause things to happen to practice holding to encourage manipulation	Warm and cool to experience water on hands, whole body to use cups for splashing to pour to see what happens if . . .
	Pull Toys	Foods	Peek-A-Boo
Records, instruments to dance to sing to play instruments to bang to shake to encourage simple imitation	With strings to pull and wheels to spin to hear variety of sounds to be able to cause movement	Jello puffed rice yogurt To experience texture and taste	Experience pop 'n pals, to experience surprise jack-in-the-box, to see what happens hiding small toys under a blanket, to learn about the existence of something when not visible

TABLE 6–6 *continued.*

Cognitive Stage	Blocks	Books
Experimentation (12–18 months) to imitate to provide for active experimentation	All kinds to build up to knock down to experience cause and effect to integrate fine motor, cognitive, and emotional development (through practice and mastery)	Nursery rhymes, animals, familiar objects and places to experience the flow and rhythm of language to provide opportunity to imitate sounds to encourage receptive and productive language
Representational intelligence (18–24 months) represent invent	All kinds vertical construction horizontal construction to practice construction of spatial relationships with concrete objects	Nursery rhymes and poems, objects and relationships (in/out/over/under), familiar objects and places to encourage productive language
Preoperational intelligence (24–30 months) to represent the world	Large wooden, Lego; use with props (cars, people, animals) to facilitate imagination and language development	Simple short stories to encourage language production, story telling, and sequencing to encourage the child to relay his or her own story

☐ Keep wastebaskets on tops of desks
☐ Keep doors to washer and dryer closed at all times
☐ Keep all plastic bags, including garbage bags, stored in a safe place
☐ Shorten cords on draperies; if there are loops on cords, cut them
☐ Immediately wipe up any spilled liquid from the floor

Music	Imitation	Manipulatives	Sensory Materials
Singing nursery rhymes to encourage language production to listen to and produce the rhythm and flow of language	Familiar scenarios; play with dolls, stuffed animals, hats, scarves, purses to reenact caregiving routines to encourage imitation of everyday experiences	Object relationships; play with containers, lids, nesting blocks, buckets and tubs to relate parts to each other and the whole to experiment with objects	Object properties to explore and use senses through tubs filled with water, puffed cereal to take in new information through the senses
	Imitation	Manipulatives	Sensory Materials
Simple songs and finger plays to encourage language production to practice production of sounds through repetition of rhythm and rhyme	Familiar scenarios; play with stove, sink, pots, pans, empty food containers to facilitate imaginative play	Object relationships; play with shape sorter, simple puzzles to integrate fine motor and cognitive skills to relate parts to the whole	Object properties; sensory table or tubs with water, rice, sand to discover properties: sink/float; empty/full; hard/soft; dry/wet
	Imitation	Manipulatives	Sensory Materials
Songs, fingerplays to follow directions to understand spatial concepts, prepositions to practice producing words and sounds	Expanding scenarios; play with dolls and dolls' clothes, dress up clothes to experience community roles (fire fighters, doctors, bakers) to expand imitation and imagination through play	Object relationships; play with pegboard (color coding), playdough, with cookie cutter, rolling pins to integrate imagination, fine motor, and language development	Object properties; cooking activities: to discuss and experience smooth, crunchy, wet, sticky, hot to experience sequencing and transformation to integrate cognitive, fine motor, and language opportunities

Source: Developed by Anne DeHaan, St. Joseph Mercy Hospital Learning Center, Pontiac Michigan, and Harriet Jo Midgett, Americare Systems, Inc., Pontiac, Michigan.

☐ Cover toddler area floors with carpeting or mats
☐ Make sure storage shelves are anchored well and won't tip over; store things so children cannot pull heavy objects off shelves onto themselves

TABLE 6–7   Suggestions for Implementing an Infant Curriculum (8–12 months old)

Child Behavior	Materials	Examples of Caregiver Strategies
Hand		
Uses thumb and forefinger	Toys, dolls	Provide objects small enough to pinch and lift.
Uses thumb and two fingers	Toys, dolls	Provide objects small enough to pinch and lift.
Brings both hands to middle of body	Banging objects, pie pans, blocks	Play clapping, banging games with infant; play Pat-a-cake.
Uses finger to poke	Pillow, ball, small box	Provide soft objects to poke into; watch that infant does not poke other children's face, eyes, etc.
Carries objects in hands	Attractive objects small enough to grasp but too big to swallow	Provide objects that can be carried. Play game of moving objects from one place to another nearby place.
Holds and uses pen, crayon	Flat surface, fat felt marker, fat crayon, paper	Provide materials and space. Demonsrate where marks go (on paper, not on floor or table). Remain with infant when child is using marker or crayon. Allow child to make the kind and number of marks he or she wants to. Praise child for interest and effort. Put materials away when child decides he or she is finished.
Reaches, touches, strokes objects	Textured objects	Provide objects of different textures. Infants can stroke, not just grasp and pinch. Demonstrate gentle stroking. Describe the texture, e.g., "the feather is soft." Allow infant to gently stroke many objects.
Uses one hand to hold object, one hand to reach and explore	Objects small enough to grasp	Provide several objects at once that stimulate infant's interest.
Stacks blocks with dominant hand	Blocks, small objects	Allow infant to choose which hand to use in stacking objects
Takes off clothes	Own clothes with big buttonholes, zippers	Infants fingers are beginning to handle buttons, zippers. Allow infant to play with these. Infant does not understand when to undress and when to keep clothes on. Discourage undressing when you want infant to stay dressed.

TABLE 6–7   *continued*

Child Behavior	Materials	Examples of Caregiver Strategies
Muscular Control *Locomotion* Walks forward Walks backward Walks sideways	Floor, ground, clear of toys Area clear of toys	Keep area clear of toys or caution child about obstacles. Play with child: walk sideways, forward, backward.
Runs with stops and starts	Clear area	Provide *flat* running space; on incline, child may run down too fast and fall on face
Jumps with both feet	Low steps, box, block, plastic crate	Keep other children away from jumping spot when one child is jumping to the floor. Sometimes catch child as he or she jumps. Release and steady child so he or she can climb and jump again.
Kicks objects	Large ball: beach ball, Nerf ball, soccer ball, volleyball, rubber ball	Provide space where child can kick ball and it will not go too far, e.g., into a big cardboard box or into a corner.
Walks upstairs and downstairs holding railing	Steps and rail	Provide equipment and time for child to safely walk up and down.
Pushes and pulls objects while walking	Small wagons, strollers, pull toys, push toys that make noise, attract visual attention	Provide clear space for walking where pushed and pulled toys have room to move without bumping and catching on equipment, furniture, rug.
Climbs	Sturdy box, cubes, footstool, low climbing gym	Provide equipment. Remain close by to assist getting down if needed.
Pedals cycle	Low riding cycle; not high tricycle	Provide space for fast and slow riding, for turning curves and in circles. Keep away children on foot.

Source: Reproduced by permission. *Infants and Toddlers Curriculum and Teaching,* 2/E by LaVisa Cam Wilson. Delmar Publishers, Inc., Copyright 1990.

☐ Use only safe equipment and materials, nothing that has sharp edges or is broken
☐ Store all medicines in locked cabinets
☐ Cushion sharp corners with foam rubber and tape
☐ Keep doors closed or install gates
☐ Fence all play areas

Parent-Child Enrichment Programs

Fifteen-month-old Brian Weisbard has already earned two certificates and is working on a third. The certificates, neatly framed and hung in his bedroom, attest to his accomplishments while attending the Family Center at Nova University's Infant Awareness Program in Ft. Lauderdale, Florida. Brian and his mother, Denise, have been attending parent-child awareness programs for eleven months. Brian's certificates were awarded after participating in activities that involve rocking, spinning, rolling, mirror play, and musical games. Although activities for his third certificate are more demanding, Brian is always excited about going to class, and Denise has no doubt that he will be successful. "Brian is a smart child, and these sessions help me discover just how much he is able to do," Denise says. "He needs these sessions to challenge him and unlock his natural abilities. It's also a good way for him to express himself."

Once a week Brian and Denise, a full-time working mother, spend an hour at the local YWCA. Brian plays and learns in a brightly colored room full of balls, hoops, bolsters, fabric tunnels, and other equipment designed to stimulate young children's physical and intellectual growth. Exploratory play is one of Brian's favorite activities. He giggles, laughs, and frequently screams as he climbs stairs,

goes down slides, and jumps in a colorful parachute with twelve other children, all to the strains of "happy music." Brian also likes sensory awareness time, when he gets a chance to help blow soap bubbles. As the bubbles float through the air, he never tires of trying to catch them. Brian hugs and squeezes dolls of different textures. He likes the sticky, slippery feel of cooked spaghetti as he picks up handfuls piled in a big plastic bowl.

Brian's teacher, Marcia Orvieto, provides Denise with parenting information and suggests ways she and Brian can spend "quality time" together. Denise has read and heard a lot about spending time with children. "As a working parent I don't have a lot of time to spend with Brian. I'm determined to make the most of it by doing things together that will help nurture and guide him. Some parents think that just spending time with their children is all that matters. I like to think that if I can spend thirty minutes a day with Brian in activities like reading to him, helping him make a collage of various colors and shapes, and playing games, then we have made good use of our time together."

Denise, vice president of a savings and loan company, wants Brian to socialize with other children and have a chance to learn. This is the major reason she takes him to the parent-child

Developmentally Appropriate Infant and Toddler Programs

Many of the issues we have discussed in earlier chapters, particularly Chapter 5, relate to the area of infant and toddler education. First is the issue of developmental appropriateness. All who provide care for infants and toddlers—indeed, for all children—must understand and recognize this important concept, which provides the solid foundation for any program. The National Association for the Education of Young Children defines "developmentally appropriate" as having two dimensions:

☐ *Age appropriateness.* Human development research indicates that there are universal, predictable sequences of growth and change during the first nine years of life. These predictable changes occur in all domains of development—physical, emotional, social, and cognitive.

☐ *Individual appropriateness.* Each child is unique, with an individual pattern of growth as well as individual personality, learning style, and family background.[10]

awareness program. Denise's friends sometimes laugh when she tells them Brian goes to school, "But, reading begins at birth," she tells them. "And I want to make sure Brian gets the physical and neurological stimulation necessary for learning." Denise does not believe she is "pushing" Brian; she feels she is building the foundation to get him ready for school and a successful life. "With my work schedule, going to the parent-child center gives us a chance to do things together, and I get a lot of useful child development information, too. I think these programs are great!" Denise is not the only parent who is determined to give her child a good start in life. All over America, parents and their young children are enrolling in record numbers in parent-child programs designed to enhance children's natural learning abilities through play. These programs capitalize on what parents and early childhood educators have known for years: a lot of learning in the early years occurs through play.

But there is more to it than play, as Joan Barnes, founder of Gymboree, points out: "Early childhood educators might describe what we do as sensory motor development. We prefer more informal expressions such as movement education play or growth play. Much of early learning is based on physical activity and play

is the child's natural way of being involved in physical activity. Gymboree and other programs provide a place where children can learn by doing." Preschool parent-child enrichment programs are beneficial to parents and children in a number of ways. First, they give parents the opportunity to actively participate in their children's development. Second, many of the programs are planned to combine learning and fun. They integrate ideas from early childhood education, child development, physical education, recreation, physical therapy, and educational psychology into meaningful activities that enhance learning. Third, the programs help parents become better parents. They offer valuable parenting information and insight into child development and behavior. As Linda Rasmussen, senior vice president, Franchise Operations for Gymboree says, "Parents tell us that as a result of Gymboree they have become more tolerant and understanding. If they find their child jumping off a sofa onto the coffee table, they understand the child is not trying to be bad, but filling a basic sensory need. He wants to feel a hard surface and a soft surface, he wants to feel what it's like to move through the air. An understanding parent will figure out a way for the child to fulfill that need without getting hurt."

Based on these dimensions, caregivers must provide different programs of activities for infants and toddlers. To do so, early childhood professionals must get parents and other caregivers to realize that infants, as a group, are different from toddlers and need programs, curricula, and facilities specifically designed for them. Based on this recognition, it is then necessary to design and implement developmentally appropriate curricula. The early childhood profession is leading the way in raising consciousness about the need to match what caregivers do with children to the children's development as individuals. There is a long way to go in this regard, but part of the resolution will come with training caregivers in child development and curriculum planning.

Finally, we will want to match caregivers to children of different ages. Not everyone is emotionally or professionally suited to provide care for infants and toddlers. Both groups need adults who can respond to their particular needs and developmental characteristics. Infants need especially nurturing caregivers; toddlers, on the other hand, need adults who can tolerate and allow for their emerging autonomy and independence.

FURTHER READING

Balter, Lawrence, and Anita Shreve. *Dr. Balter's Child Sense: Understanding and Handling the Common Problems of Infancy and Early Childhood* (New York: Poseidon Press, 1987)

Covering the period from birth to age five, provides many answers for parents and teachers of young children. Includes responses to problems of the young infant up to concerns of the preschool child, such as another baby, a divorce in the family, and other family considerations.

Biber, Barbara. *Early Education and Psychological Development* (New Haven, Conn.: Yale University Press, 1987)

Biber, a leading proponent of the developmental-interaction approach to early childhood education, advocates a "whole child" approach that encourages children to exercise control over their learning with teachers as guides for interactions between students and staff. Valuable insight into the development of the child-centered approach at Bank Street College.

Dittman, Laura L., Ed. *The Infants We Care For* (Washington, D.C.: National Association for the Education of Young Children, 1984)

Members of the NAEYC Commission on the Care and Education of Infants in 1969 identified three goals for care of infants: development of a healthy body, development of an active mind, and development of wholesome feelings. This book raises issues relating to these goals so that caregivers can develop the best possible programs.

Greenman, Jim. *Caring Spaces, Learning Places* (Redmond, Wash.: Exchange Press, 1988)

This book discusses important aspects of indoor and outdoor environments for infants and young children. It covers safety, age appropriateness, aesthetics, planning and design, comfort, different surfaces, remodeling, storage, ideas for setting up a classroom, and the impact of the environment on children and staff.

Harmes, Thelma, and Richard M. Clifford. *Early Childhood Environment Rating Scale* (New York: Teachers College Press, 1980)

Rating scale for use with all types of child care or early childhood settings.

Hass, Carolyn Buhai. *Look at Me: Activities for Babies and Toddlers* (Chicago: Chicago Review Press, 1987)

Easy-to-use activities: Toys to Make, Learning Games, Indoor/Outdoor Fun, Books and Reading, Positive Self-Image, Imaginative Play, Arts and Crafts, Easy and Nutritious Recipes, etc.

Karnes, Merle B. *Small Wonder!* (Circle Pines, Minn.: American Guidance Service, 1981)

Activities emphasizing play and language of infants.

————. *You and Your Small Wonder: Activities for Parents and Toddlers on the Go* (Circle Pines, Minn.: American Guidance Service, 1982)

156 activities to help caregivers of toddlers, covering physical, emotional, intellectual growth, and language development. Information on health and safety and child development. Excellent resource for parents and other caregivers.

Leavitt, Robin Lynn, and Brenda Krause Eheart. *Toddler Day Care; A Guide to Responsive Caregiving* (Lexington, Mass.: Lexington Books, 1985)

Practical information in toddler care by operators of the Developmental Child Care Program at the University of Illinois at Urbana-Champaign. Topics from play to assessment are developmentally based. Focuses exclusively on toddler care and education and easy to read and understand.

Maxim, George. *The Sourcebook: Activities for Infants and Young Children* (Columbus, Ohio: Merrill, 1990)

Activities to encourage infants and young children in physical, emotional, motor, and creative development; guidelines for evaluations.

Morrison, George S. *The Education and Development of Infants, Toddlers, and Preschoolers* (Glenview, Ill.: Scott, Foresman, 1988)

Developmental theory and practical applications caregivers need to provide developmentally appropriate curriculum; includes charts and vignettes. One reviewer said it qualifies as both a textbook and a "good" read for parents.

Wilson, LaVisa Cam. *Infants and Toddlers: Curriculum and Teaching,* Second Edition (Albany, N.Y.: Delmar, 1990)

Comprehensive discussion of infants and toddler caregiving programs. Provides solid, practical advice on how to implement developmentally appropriate curriculum.

White, Burton. *The First Three Years of Life: The Revised Edition* (Englewood Cliffs, N.J.: Prentice-Hall, 1987)

White is convinced that parents and caregivers should focus most of their attention on the first three years of life; takes the reader step-by-step through all stages of development during the first three years.

FURTHER STUDY

1. Visit at least two programs that provide care for infants and toddlers. Observe the curriculum to determine if it is developmentally appropriate. What suggestions would you make for improving the curriculum? Explain what you liked most and least about the program.
2. What five things can caregivers do to promote children's basic trust needs?
3. You have been asked to speak to a group of parents about what they can do to promote their children's language development in the first two years of life. Outline your presentation and list five specific suggestions you will make to the parents.
4. Observe children between the ages of birth and eighteen months. Identify the six stages of sensorimotor intelligence by describing the behaviors you observed in the children. Cite specific examples of secondary and tertiary reactions. For each of the six stages, list two activities that would be cognitively appropriate.
5. What evidence can you provide to support the theory that language is primarily an innate process?
6. In addition to the caregiver qualities cited in this chapter, list and explain five other qualities you think are important for caregivers of infants and toddlers.
7. Why is motor development important in the early years? What are five things early childhood educators can include in their programs to promote motor development?
8. Most of Sylvia's friends and family members criticized her for sending her 3-week-old baby, Katrina, to a child care center. Sylvia honestly weighed the pros and cons of this decision and believes this was the best one for her and her child. List the positive and negative factors involved in putting a 3-week-old infant in a child care center program. Does the law in your state specify how old a child has to be before enrolled in a child care center? If so, what is this age and what other standards must be followed when providing care for infants?
9. Identify infant/toddler programs in your area. Outline their basic services and curricula. What changes would you recommend and why?
10. Dianne is constantly trying to teach her 18-month-old son Brad how to behave in the house. Basically, she wants him to be good and leave things alone. Yet, as soon as she leaves him alone for a minute, he begins to make a mess of the house. How can Dianne keep Brad from making a mess of the house? What would be reasonable expectations for Brad? Is Brad's behavior expected or unexpected for his age-group?
11. Identify customs that are passed down to infants and toddlers as a result of the family's cultural background. How do these customs affect young children's behavior?
12. Visit centers that care for young children of different cultures. List the differences you find. What areas are most similar?
13. Interview parents of young infants from different cultures. What are their five top expectations for their babies? How do expectations differ and how are they alike?
14. Develop a list of recommended items for adults to carry when traveling with young children. How can such a list help parents?

15. Exercising with young babies is a current trend. Express your view on this, and compare your views to those of a mother who attends an infant/exercise program.

16. Interview caregivers who work in family day care homes and others who work in child care centers. How does the care for infants and toddlers differ in the two settings? In which kind of program would you prefer to be a caregiver? Why?

17. Develop a set of activities for mothers and their infants to use at home. Try these activities out with parents and infants, and tell what went well and what you would change.

18. Prepare a panel discussion to present the pros and cons of the trend to teach young babies how to read.

19. Every morning, Maria, the caregiver of an infant group, reads a story to the children. But one day, a new parent went storming to see the program director. The parent claimed that Maria's very heavy Spanish accent would negatively affect his son's language development. Do you think the parent was right or wrong? Why? What would you do if you were the program director?

20. Interview mothers about their concerns in leaving their infants in the care of others. Identify the concerns of fathers in relation to the same situation. Do parents' concerns differ according to the age or sex of their children?

21. Identify at least ten games or activities that are beneficial to the developing infant and the growing toddler. Describe the benefits of each of the games or activities you list.

Notes

1. S.I. Hayakawa, *Language in Thought and Action,* 3rd ed. (New York: Harcourt Brace Jovanovich, 1975, p. 30.

2. Eric H. Lenneberg. "The Biological Foundations of Language," in Mark Lester, *Readings in Applied Transformational Grammar* (New York: Holt, Rinehart and Winston, 1970), p. 8.

3. Eric H. Lenneberg, "A Biological Perspective of Language," in *New Directions in the Study of Language,* ed. Eric H. Lenneberg (Cambridge, Mass.: M.I.T. Press, 1964), pp. 66-68.

4. Susan Curtiss, *Genie: A Psycholinguistic Study of a Modern-Day "Wild Child"* (New York: Academic Press, 1977).

5. Alice S. Honig, "High Quality Infant/Toddler Care," *Young Children,* 4 (November 1985): 40.

6. National Association for the Education of Young Children, "Position Statement on Developmentally Appropriate Practice in Early Childhood Programs Serving Children from Birth Through Age 8," *Young Children* 41:1 (September 1986): pp. 4-29.

7. Burton White. *The First Three Years of Life* (Englewood Cliffs, N.J.: Prentice-Hall, 1987), p. 267.

8. J. Belsky and M.J. Rovine "Non-Maternal Care in the First Year of Life and the Security of Infant-Parent Attachment," *Child Development,* 59 (1988), p. 164.

9. C. Howes "Peer Interaction of Young Children," *Monographs of the Society for Research in Child Development,* 53 (1988), Serial No. 217.

10. Sue Bredekamp, ed., *Developmentally Appropriate Practice in Early Childhood Programs Serving Children from Birth Through Age 8* (Washington, D.C.: NAEYC, 1987), p. 2.

CHAPTER 7
The Preschool Years
Readiness for Learning

As you read and study:
- ☐ Understand preschoolers' basic growth and development
- ☐ Trace the history of preschool and nursery education from the McMillan sisters to the present
- ☐ Discuss various definitions and purposes of play in preschool education
- ☐ Consider how play can be used in program learning
- ☐ Understand reasons for the current interest in preschool programs
- ☐ Examine reasons for developing preschool programs for four-year-olds
- ☐ Examine goals and objectives for preschools
- ☐ Examine and critique preschool curricula and schedules
- ☐ Analyze issues concerning preschool programs
- ☐ Identify trends in preschool education

This chapter is about the preschool years, when children are between the ages of three and five. While the term *preschool years* describes the years before children enter school, this designation is rapidly becoming obsolete. Today, it is common for many children to be in a school of some kind beginning as early as age two and three. And child care beginning at six weeks is becoming *de rigueur* for children of working parents. Additionally, with states such as Texas, Florida, California, New York, and North Carolina developing preschool programs for four-year-olds, the term preschool hardly applies to "threes" and "fours" anymore.

Many parents view this period as the time that children "get ready" to enter kindergarten or first grade, the beginning of what they consider "formal" schooling. Early childhood teachers view the events of the preschool years as the cornerstone of later learning. Some parents, however, still think of this period as a time in which children should be unburdened by learning and allowed to play and enjoy life, perhaps, as some feel, for the last unstructured time. For many, however the preschool years are the beginning of a period of at least fourteen years during which their lives will be dominated and directed by teachers and the process of schooling.

For our purposes, preschools are programs for two- to five-year-old children, before kindergarten. In this chapter we will also discuss what are often called *nursery schools,* programs for three- and four-year-old children.

Early childhood educators generally distinguish between preschool and child care. Applying the term *preschool* to a program usually means it has an educational purpose and a curriculum designed to involve children primarily in learning activities. Parents usually enroll their children in preschools because they believe in early learning and want their children to learn. Child care is primarily intended to provide care for children so parents can work. The purposes of child care and preschool are not mutually exclusive, however, and the better programs of either emphasize both quality care and learning. Some preschools have broadened their programs to include child care components. The preschool program may be conducted in the morning, with a child care program in the afternoon; the preschool may have a before-school and afternoon child care program; or child care and preschool programs may be conducted in the same building but as separate programs.

HISTORY OF PRESCHOOL EDUCATION

The history of preschool education is really the history of nursery education, which cannot be separated from the history of kindergarten education. The origin of nursery schools as it affects the United States was in Great Britain. In 1914, Margaret and Rachel McMillan started an open-air nursery with an emphasis on health care and healthy living. They did not ignore cognitive stimulation, and also began a program of visiting homes to work with mothers. Their work led to the passage, in 1918, of the Fisher Act, which provided national support for nursery education. This led to the establishment of the first public nursery schools in Great Britain.

In 1914, Caroline Pratt opened the Play School (now the City and Country School) in New York City. One of the nation's first truly progressive schools, it was patterned on the philosophy of John Dewey and designed to take advantage of what Miss Pratt called children's "natural and inevitable" desire to learn. The school, currently located at West 13th Street and with an enrollment of 130 students between the ages of two and thirteen, began and continues as an example of a child-centered, learning-by-doing approach to education.

Patty Smith Hill was a champion of the nursery school movement in the U.S. and started a progressive laboratory school at Columbia Teachers College in New York in 1921. Abigail Eliot, another nursery school pioneer, studied in Great Britain for six months with the McMillan sisters, then started the Ruggles Street Nursery School in Boston in 1922. Meanwhile, also in 1922, the Merrill-Palmer Institute Nursery School opened in Detroit, under the direction of Edna White. The Institute and White were responsible for training many nursery school teachers.

A temporary impetus to nursery education occurred in 1933, when the Federal Works Progress Administration provided funds to hire unemployed teachers in nursery school programs. In 1940, the Lanham Act provided money for child care to mothers employed in defense-related industries. This support ended with the war in 1945. From the 1940s to the present, preschools have been mainly private, sponsored by parent cooperatives, churches, and other agencies. Federal involvement in preschool education has been through Head Start and support for child care programs directed at low-income families and children.

THE GROWING POPULARITY OF PRESCHOOLS

We have witnessed an acceleration of a trend that began with the Head Start Program in 1965—children's entrance into preschool programs at earlier ages. This trend continues to grow, with greater numbers of four-year-olds entering preschools, many operated by public schools, as shown in Table 7–1.

Reasons for the rapid increase in and demand for preschool programs for three- and four-year-old children can be understood within the context of societal changes over the last two decades and current societal problems and concerns. You must constantly remember that societal events, issues, and concerns determine the nature and kinds of current educational programs and those we can expect to see in the next decade. Whenever we ask "why" about a particular educational program, we can always find the answer in societal needs, because society traditionally and legitimately looks to the educational establishment to help it address its short- and long-term goals. In fact, it is fair to say that education is one of the principle "handmaidens" of

TABLE 7–1   Preschool Enrollment

	Ages 3–4	Age 5
Total number of children	7,318,000	3,676,000
Number in nursery	2,379,000	242,000
Number in public nursery	780,000	72,000
Number in kindergarten	415,000	2,941,000
Number in public kindergarten	285,000	2,590,000

Source: U.S. Bureau of the Census, *Current Population Reports,* Series P-20, (April 1990). School Enrollment—Social and Economic Characteristics of Students.

society. With these concepts in mind, we can identify the following reasons to explain the modern popularity of preschool programs, particularly public preschool programs for three- and four-year-olds.

1. Changing family patterns, especially regarding single-parent families.
2. Changing economic patterns that have pushed more women into the work force.
3. Changing attitudes toward work and careers. The shift away from a homemaking career to outside employment pressures the early childhood profession to provide more programs and services, among which are programs for threes and fours.
4. The view of public policy planners and researchers that intervention programs (to deal with such problems as substance abuse) work best in the early years. Parents and public policymakers are also influenced by research reports that verify the positive short- and long-term benefits of quality preschool programs to children and society.
5. Growing concern on the part of corporations and businesses as to the quality of the contemporary and future work force.
6. Advocacy for publicly supported and financed preschools as a means of preventing the exclusion of poor children and their families from the early education movement.
7. The increasingly popular notion that three- and four-year-old children are ready, willing, and able to learn.

WHO IS PRESCHOOL FOR?

Whenever we discuss educational programs of any kind, the question sooner or later arises as to who should attend the programs. Preschool programs are no different. At the moment, there is a great deal of discussion about who should attend preschools. A quick and easy answer is that all three- and four-year-old children should attend schools; given unlimited resources, this is the appropriate solution. In fact, the national trend is toward universal public education for three- and four-year-olds; however, we will probably not see this trend become a reality before the first decade of the twenty-first century. So for now, the children who attend public preschools are generally those who are members of a particular risk group—that is, children of low-income parents, children of teenage parents, and special needs children. At the other end of the economic spectrum, parents who *can* afford to send their children to private preschools do so, especially to academically oriented preschools. Such parents will continue to seek out and pay for the best for their children.

Purposes of Preschools

Another facet to the discussion of public preschools always involves that of aims and purposes. It is easy to say that the preschool should stress teaching the basic skills—reading, writing, and arithmetic—however, given the needs of today's at-risk children and the fact that more children are becoming at risk all the time, a purely academic curriculum hardly meets their needs. For the majority of children, an academically oriented program with ample opportunities for social interactions meets their needs and the needs of their parents. A more appropriate response for at-risk children seems to be a program that combines education with a broad range of social services. In fact, a trend in preschool and early childhood programming is to focus on the social services approach as a way to meet all needs of the child and family. Head Start is considered a model for providing comprehensive services (see Chapter 10).

Who Should Provide Preschool Services?

Many agencies provide services for preschool children. These include child care programs, Head Start, cooperative preschools, and others (see Chapter 1). There is a growing consensus, however, that the public schools should provide for three- and four-year-olds. This preference for having the public schools provide services is based on several factors. First, public schools and the infrastructure (teachers, cafeteria workers, custodians, and administration) are already in place; it makes sense, therefore, for them to open their doors, facilities, and services to this younger population. Also, as long as parents pay taxes to support the public schools, they logically and economically conclude that the public schools should provide services for their children rather than their paying other programs to provide services. Second, the public schools are viewed as institutions that can offer all children equal access to educational and other services, and if the public schools enroll three- and four-year-old children, other programs that traditionally offer programs to this age-group will turn their attention to serving the needs of children from birth to age two.

WHO IS THE PRESCHOOLER?

Today's preschooler is not like the four-year-old of previous decades. Many have already attended one, two, or three years of child care or nursery school. Many have traveled widely. Many have experienced the trauma of family divorces, and many have experienced the stress, trauma, and psychological effects of abuse. Both collectively and individually, then, the experiential backgrounds of preschoolers are quite different from those of previous generations. But it is precisely this background of experiences, its impact, and the implications for caregivers that preschool teachers must understand to effectively meet preschoolers' needs.

Physical and Motor Development

A noticeable difference between preschoolers and their infant and toddler counterparts is that preschoolers have lost most of their baby fat and taken on a leaner, lankier look. This "slimming down" and increasing motor coordination enables the preschooler to participate with more confidence in the locomotor activities so vitally necessary during this stage of growth and development. Both girls and boys continue to grow several inches per year throughout the preschool years. At age three, the average boy weighs about 32 pounds and the average girl is about a pound and a half lighter (see Table 7–2).

Preschool children are in an age of rapid motor skill development. They are learning to use and test their bodies. It is a time for learning what they can do and how they can do it as individuals. *Locomotion* plays a large role in motor and skill development and includes activities of moving the body through space—walking, running, hopping,

TABLE 7-2 Height and Weight of Preschoolers

	Males		Females	
Age	Weight (pounds)	Height (inches)	Weight (pounds)	Height (inches)
3 years	32.4	38.0	30.7	37.6
4 years	36.8	40.5	35.2	40.0
5 years	41.2	43.3	38.9	42.7

Source: Adapted from P.V.V. Hamill et al., "Physical Growth: National Center for Health Statistics Percentiles," *The American Journal of Clinical Nutrition,* 32 (1979), pp. 607-629.

jumping, rolling, dancing, climbing, and leaping. Children use these activities to investigate and explore the relationships between themselves, space, and objects in space. Preschoolers demonstrate the principles of cephalocaudal and proximodistal development mentioned in Chapter 6. The cephalocaudal development enables the preschooler to participate in many physical activities; likewise, the concentration of motor development in the small muscles of the arms and hands enables them to participate in fine motor activities such as drawing, coloring, painting, cutting, and pasting. Consequently, preschoolers need programs that provide action, activity, and play, supported by proper nutrition and healthy habits of plentiful rest and good hygiene.

Good educational practices also dictate that a preschool curriculum deemphasize activities that require preschoolers to wait or sit for extended periods of time. Although learning self-control is part of preschoolers' socialization process, developmentally appropriate practices call for activity. It is also important to incorporate health education into programs for four- and five-year-olds. Children should receive information about hygiene and nutrition; because bad habits are almost impossible to break, preschool and elementary curricula should incorporate lifelong goals and objectives for healthy living.

Cognitive Development

Preschoolers are in the preoperational stage of intelligence. As we saw in Chapter 4, these are characteristics of the preoperational stage: (1) children grow in their ability to use symbols, including language; (2) children are not capable of operational thinking (an *operation* is a reversible mental action), which explains why Piaget named this stage preoperational; (3) children center on one thought or idea, often to the exclusion of other thoughts; (4) children are unable to *conserve;* and (5) children are *egocentric.*

Characteristics during the preoperational stage have particular implications for teachers. Because the preschool child is egocentric, he believes everyone sees what he sees and thinks as he thinks. This egocentrism influences how he responds to things and how he interacts with others. Piaget believed the underlying reason for many of the preoperational child's "errors" of reasoning stemmed from his inability to see viewpoints other than his own. This egocentrism is not selfishness, but, rather,

Society and parents often demand quality preschools for four-year-olds because the preschool years are considered a valuable time for learning and getting ready for formal schooling.

a lack of awareness. Early childhood educators recognize that many children are able to engage in cognitive activities earlier than Piaget thought and that many do not demonstrate a characteristic at the age or to the degree Piaget maintained.

Language Development

The preschool years are a period of rapid language growth and development. Vocabulary increases, and as children continue to master syntax and grammar, sentence length increases. The first words infants or toddlers use are *holophrases,* one word that conveys the meaning of a sentence. For example, Amy may say "milk" to express "I'd like some more milk, please."

At one year, the infant knows two or more words; by the age of two, she knows about 275. During the second year of life, the toddler's language proficiency increases to include "telegraphic" speech—combining two- or three-word utterances to act as a sentence. "Amy go," for example, can mean that Amy wants her mother to take her for a walk in the stroller. During the third year of life, children add helping verbs and negatives to their vocabulary, for example, "I don't want milk." Sentences also become longer and more complex. During the fourth and fifth years, children use noun or subject clauses, conjunctions, and prepositions to complete their sentences. During the preschool years, children's language development is diverse, comprehensive, and constitutes a truly impressive range of learning. An even more impressive feature of language acquisition during the preschool years is that children learn intuitively, without a great deal of instruction, the rules of language that apply to words, phrases, and the utterances they use.

PRESCHOOL PLAY

The notion that children can learn through play begins with Froebel, who built his system of schooling on the educative value of play. As discussed in Chapter 2, Froebel believed that natural unfolding (development) occurred through play. Since his time, most early childhood programs have incorporated play into their curricula, or have made play a major part of the day. (Recall also the importance Piaget placed on the contribution of play to intellectual growth.)

Play usually occupies a major part of children's lives. Play activities are essential to the environment in which children learn concepts, develop social and physical skills, master life situations, and practice language processes. Children learn through play. Without the opportunity for play and an environment that supports it, a child's learning is limited. Early childhood programs that provide opportunities for play increase and enhance the limits of children's learning.

Play can be thought of as children's work, and the home and preschool as "work-places" where learning occurs through play. Children engage in play naturally and enjoy it; they do not select play activities because they want to learn. For example, a child does not choose to put blocks in order from small to large because he wants to learn how to seriate, nor does he build an incline because he wants to learn the concept of "down" or the principles of gravity; however, the learning outcomes of his play are obvious. Children's play is full of opportunities for learning, but there is no guarantee that, because children play, they will learn. But providing opportunities for children to choose among well-planned, varied learning activities enhances the probability that children will learn through play.

John Dewey felt that play helps prepare children for adult occupations. This may explain why curriculum developers and teachers base many activities around adult roles; a frequent justification for a dress-up corner is that it helps children try out adult roles.

To expend surplus energy has historically been a popular theory about why children play. This theory resembles the cathartic theory, which holds that children use play as a means of relieving frustrations and emotions. Play is certainly an excellent means of relieving stress, and early childhood educators now recognize that play is one antidote for stressful situations and events.

Piaget believed that play serves an assimilative function; through play, children are able to take in information that assists in the development of schemes. Building on this concept, George Foreman and Fleet Hill believe that play contributes to the constructive process, and coined the term *constructive play* to denote that which "builds on itself to increase the competence of the child."[1] They believe the competence children learn through play makes even more creative acts possible. In other words, competence leads to more and higher levels of competence.

Kinds of Play

Most of a child's play occurs with or in the presence of other children. *Social* play occurs when children play with each other in groups. The most comprehensive

Special projects such as woodworking offer children many opportunities to learn.

description and classification of children's play was applied by Mildred Parten in 1932; her classifications and terminology are still the most common and remain valid today.

☐ Unoccupied play—the child does not play with anything or anyone; he merely stands or sits, without doing anything observable

☐ Solitary play—although involved in play, the child plays alone, seemingly unaware of other children

☐ Onlooker play—the child watches and observes the play of other children; the center of interest is others' play

☐ Parallel play—the child plays by himself, but in ways similar to and with toys or materials similar to those of other children

☐ Associative play—children interact with each other, perhaps by asking questions or sharing materials, but do not play together

☐ Cooperative play—children actively play together, often as a result of organization of the teacher (the least frequently witnessed play in preschools)[2]

Social play allows children to interact with others, enabling them to talk to other children and learn about other points of view. Second, it provides a vehicle for communication. Children have others with whom to practice language and learn from. Third, it helps children learn impulse control; they realize they can't always do whatever they want. And fourth, in giving a child other children with whom to interact, social play negates isolation and helps children learn the interactions so vital to society. In Table 7–3, William Fowler identifies five kinds of play.

Value of Play

Play enhances social interaction and the development of social skills—learning how to share, getting along with others, taking turns, and generally learning how to live in a community. Play promotes physical development and body coordination and

TABLE 7–3   Play in Infancy and Early Childhood

Type of Play	Name of Play	Characteristics of Play	Critical Factors of Play	Examples of Play
Type I	Exploratory-Manipulatory (object and pattern play)	Exploration of single objects; sensorimotor enjoyment, responses to environmental stimulation—forms basis for all play	Variety and complexity of toys; adult attention; relation to peers	Looking, listening, touching, feeling, tasting, smelling, moving
Type II	Instrumental (means-ends)	Plays to purposely accomplish things; how objects can be used as tools; object-object manipulation; employing objects to produce effects	Variety of materials; freedom to try things out; adults who encourage children to develop relationships	Puzzle activities, form boards, using objects as instruments
Type III	Construction-Creative	No single set of combinations or organization. Media-materials determine the organization; no predetermined goals; creation of a new form of structure	General learning experiences (a result of adult guidance and child's own activity); specific experiences in creative and building play	Building with blocks, tinker toys, etc.; painting; constructing; using clay
Type IV	Symbolic and Socio-dramatic	Mental play, use of language to symbolize things; visual imagery, use of words and phrases to carry ideas of things through play	Language development; props for play; opportunity to play	Using a tricycle as a truck; dress-up activities, make-believe roles
Type V	Language	Play with language; trying out language: rules of sound, grammar, and how words represent things	Use of language activities—stories, nursery rhymes, etc., with children; literary and conversational stimulation	Play with grammar forms and with meanings (calling a dog a cat)

Source: William Fowler, *Infant and Child Care: A Guide to Education in Group Settings* (Boston: Allyn and Bacon, 1980), pp. 148-58. Used by permission.

In solitary play, the child focuses on what she is doing. Onlooker play is merely observing the play of others. Children engaged in parallel play are doing what others are doing but are not really playing together; the same is true of associative play, but there is some interaction.

develops and refines small and large motor skills. Play helps children discover their bodies: how they function and how they can be used in learning.

Lifetime attitudes toward play develop in early childhood. Children learn motoric skills they will use as adults and learn that play can be restful, therapeutic, and satisfying. If children are taught that play is something one does only after all one's work is finished, or that it takes away from productive work, or is only for special occasions, children will have a negative attitude toward play, feel guilty about participating in it, and have a hard time integrating it into their adult lives.

Play assists in personality and emotional development, since children can try out different roles, release feelings, express themselves in a nonthreatening atmosphere, and consider the roles of others. Play enhances and promotes development in the cognitive, affective, and psychomotor areas. It helps children learn, acquire information, and construct their own intelligence. Through play, children develop schemes, find out how things work (and what won't work), and lay the foundation for cognitive growth. Because play activities are interesting, play becomes naturally, or intrinsically, rewarding, and children engage in it for its own value. The interest of the child in his play also leads to a continually lengthened attention span.

The Role of the Teacher in Play

Teachers are the key to whether meaningful play, and therefore learning, occurs in the preschool. What teachers do and the attitudes they have toward play determine the quality of the preschool environment and the events that occur there. Teachers have these responsibilities in a quality play curriculum:

Planning to implement the curriculum within a framework of play, integrating specific learning activities with play to achieve specific learning outcomes. Play activities should match children's developmental needs and be free of sex and cultural stereotypes.

Providing time for learning through play—including it in the schedule as a legitimate activity in its own right.

Creating environments and structuring time for learning through play— designing indoor and outdoor learning environments to encourage play and support the role of play in learning.

Providing materials and equipment—materials and equipment should be appropriate to the children's developmental level and should support a nonsexist and multicultural curriculum.

Training assistants and parents in how to promote learning through play.

Supervising play activities—by participating in play, teachers help, show, and model when appropriate, and refrain from interfering when appropriate.

Observing children's play—teachers can learn how children play and the learning outcomes of play to use in planning classroom activities.

Informal or Free Play

Proponents of learning through spontaneous, informal play activities maintain that learning is best when it occurs in an environment that contains materials and people with whom children can interact. Learning materials may be grouped in centers with similar material and equipment—a kitchen center, a dress-up center, a block center, a music and art center, a water or sand area, and a free play center (usually with equipment such as tricycles, wagons, and wooden slides for promoting large muscle development).

The atmosphere of this kind of preschool setting tends to approximate a home setting, where learning is informal, unstructured, and unpressured. Talk and interactions with adults are spontaneous. Play and learning episodes are generally determined by the interest of the child and, to some extent, that of the teacher, based on what she thinks is best for children. The expected learning outcomes are socialization, emotional development, self-control, and tolerance for a school setting.

Three problems can result from a free play format. One is that many teachers interpret it to mean that children are free to do whatever they wish with whatever materials they want to use. Second, aside from seeing that children have materials to play with, teachers don't plan for special play materials, how they will interact with the materials, or what they are to learn while playing. Third, children are sometimes not held accountable for learnings from free play. Some teachers rarely question children about concepts or point out the nature of the learning. Teachers such as these are seldom part of the process. They act as disinterested bystanders, with their primary goal to see that children don't injure themselves while playing. In a good program of free play indoors and outside, teachers are active participants; sometimes they observe, sometimes they play with the children, sometimes they help the children, but they never intrude or impose. Avoiding the possible pitfalls of the "free play" format will enable children to learn many things as they interact with interesting activities, materials, and people in their environment.

Dramatic Play

Dramatic play allows children to participate vicariously in a wide range of activities associated with family living, society, and the culture of which they are a part. Dramatic play centers often include areas such as housekeeping, dress-up, occupations, dolls, school, and other situations that follow the children's interests. A skillful teacher can

An important function of play is to allow children to role-play adult occupations, through which they develop skills and interact with other children.

think of many ways to expand their interest. As this happens, she replaces old centers with new ones; for example, after a visit to the police station, a housekeeping center might be replaced by an occupations center.

In the dramatic play area, children have an opportunity to express themselves, assume different roles, and interact with their peers. Dramatic play centers thus act as a nonsexist and multicultured arena in which all children are equal. Teachers can learn a great deal about children by watching and listening to their dramatic play. For example, one teacher heard a child remark to the doll he was feeding that "you better eat all of this 'cause it's all we got in the house." Further investigation resulted in the teacher's linking up the family with a social service agency that helped them with emergency food and money.

Teachers must assume a proactive role in organizing and changing the dramatic play areas. They must set the stage for dramatic play and participate in play with the children. They must also encourage those who "hang back" and are reluctant to play and involve those who may not be particularly popular with the other children. Surprisingly, because of their background and environment, some children have to be taught how to play. In other words, as in all areas of early childhood education, teachers must deal with children's dramatic play in an individual and holistic way.

Medical Play

Medical play is the symbolic reproduction of medical procedures that will be used with a child. Materials include play medical furniture and supplies as well as real medical equipment and supplies. Medical play is used to reduce anxiety, correct misconceptions, teach about medical problems and provide emotional support. Children use dolls as patients, with real stethoscopes and syringes, and pretend to perform procedures such as listening to the heartbeat and giving injections. This type of play is becoming popular with parents and medical personnel, who see it as an excellent way to meet the special needs that arise from the necessity of medical care.

Outdoor Play

What happens to children outside in a play or recreation area is just as important as what happens inside. However, outdoor play is often considered relatively unimportant, an opportunity for children to let off steam or excess energy. Children do need to relieve stress and tension through play, and outdoor activities provide this opportunity, but we should plan what we allow children to do and the equipment we make available. Outdoor time should not be merely a chance for children to run wild.

Outdoor environments and activities promote large and small muscle development and body coordination as well as language development and social interaction. Teachers should plan for a particular child or group of children to move through progressively more difficult levels of running, climbing, and swinging. The outdoor area is a learning environment, and as such, the playground should be structured and designed according to learning objectives. Many teachers also enjoy bringing the indoor learning environment "outdoors," using easels, play dough, or dramatic play props to further enhance learning opportunities. In addition, taking a group of children outdoors for story or music time, sitting in the shade of a tree, brings a fresh perspective to daily group activities.

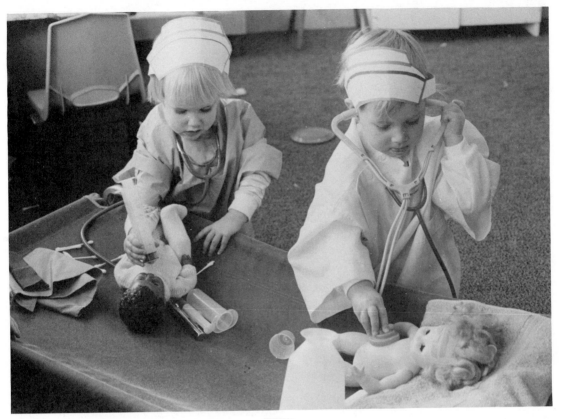

Medical play allows children to symbolically engage in health care procedures and can help alleviate their fears of doctors, nurses, other health practitioners, and medical settings.

THE PRESCHOOL CURRICULUM

How do we determine an appropriate curriculum for three- and four-year-olds? Some say society should decide the curriculum according to what it thinks children should learn and do. For example, Western society values knowing how to read and getting along with others; therefore, activities that help children do these things are included in the curriculum. Others say the public schools should guide the curriculum according to what children will have to learn and do in kindergarten and first grade. That kind of preschool curriculum would therefore include many "readiness" activities. (We will discuss readiness in Chapter 8.) Still others say the individual child should determine the curriculum according to what each knows or doesn't know; therefore, the starting place is the needs and interest of children.

Play as Curriculum

In the continuing debate about what the preschool curriculum should be, many people respond that play is the most appropriate curriculum. However, play is the *process* by which the curriculum is implemented. Although it is true that children learn *through* play, to say play is the curriculum begs the issue of what children are to learn.

Literacy is an important topic throughout education. Giving preschool children opportunities to listen to stories helps to prepare them for later reading and writing.

What good preschool programs do—what any good educational program does— is to take each child at whatever point she is in her development and provide a set of guided experiences that enables her to go as far as possible *without* pushing, hurrying, bullying, belittling, or overstressing. The essence of early education is a set of guided experiences—both cognitive and affective. Unfortunately, some early educators respond to the issues of pushing and hurrying by either doing nothing or by saying that the solution is play. The answer lies between the two.

Early childhood educators should always start with children and base their curriculum on them. What we teach is and should be based on child development, the needs of children, and what they are like as individuals. If this is done, then the curriculum will be child-centered and developmentally appropriate.

PRESCHOOL GOALS

All programs should have goals to guide activities and on which to base teaching methodologies. Without goals, it is easy to end up teaching just about anything without knowing why. Goals of individual preschools vary, but all programs should have certain essential goals. Simply because programs have goals, however, does not necessarily mean their teaching methods support or achieve those goals. This is a weakness of many preschools—there is a difference between what they say they do and what they actually do. Most good preschools, however, set minimum goals in at least a few of these areas: social and interpersonal skills, self-help and intrapersonal skills, building self-image, academics, thinking, learning readiness, language, and nutrition.

Social and Interpersonal Goals

☐ Helping children learn how to get along with other children, with adults, and how to develop good relationships with teachers

☐ Helping children learn to help others and develop caring attitudes

Self-help Skills/Intrapersonal Goals

☐ Modeling for children how to take care of their personal needs such as dressing (tying, buttoning, zipping) and knowing what clothes to wear

☐ Eating skills (using utensils, napkins, and a cup or glass, setting a table)

☐ Health skills (how to wash and bathe, how to brush their teeth)

☐ Grooming skills (combing hair, cleaning nails)

Self-image Goals

☐ Promoting self-help skills to help children develop good self-image and high self-esteem

☐ Helping a child learn about himself, his family, and his culture

☐ Developing a sense of self-worth by providing experiences for success and competence

☐ Teaching about body parts and their function

Academic Goals

☐ Teaching children to learn their names, addresses and phone numbers

☐ Facilitating children's learning of colors, sizes, shapes and positions such as under, over, and around

☐ Facilitating children's learning of numbers and prewriting skills, shape identification, letter recognition, sounds, and rhyming

☐ Providing for small-muscle development

Thinking Goals

☐ Providing an environment and activities that enable children to develop the skills essential to constructing schemes in a Piagetian sense—classification, seriation, numeration, and knowledge of space and time concepts

Learning Readiness Goals

☐ Facilitating readiness skills related to school success, such as following directions, learning to work by oneself, listening to the teacher, developing an attention span, learning to stay with a task until it is completed, staying in one's seat, and controlling impulses

Language Goals

☐ Providing opportunities for interaction with adults and peers as a means of developing oral language skills

☐ Helping children increase their vocabularies

☐ Helping children learn to converse with other children and adults
☐ Building proficiency in language

Nutrition Goals

☐ Providing experiences that enable children to learn the role of good nutritional practices and habits in their overall development
☐ Providing food preparation experiences
☐ Introducing children to new foods, a balanced menu, and essential nutrients

Developing Independence

Above and beyond the goals of promoting the skill areas, but subsumed in them, are two other goals of the preschool experience—to foster independence and a positive attitude toward learning. In many respects, the major goal of all education from preschool to university is to help students become independent. In addition, they should develop an attitude of liking to learn and wanting to come to school. In a sense, the entire school program should help children do things for themselves, to become autonomous. Unfortunately, some preschool programs and teachers foster an atmosphere of dependence, helplessness, and reliance on others by doing things for the children instead of helping children learn to do things for themselves. A good rule of thumb for all preschool educators is to avoid doing anything for a child that he can do or learn to do for himself. We can encourage independence by having children take care of their own environment. Children should be responsible for dusting, cleaning, washing, wiping, polishing, emptying waste baskets, vacuuming, sweeping, and helping to care for classroom pets. Whether programs promote dependence or independence can be ascertained by comparing them to the scale in Table 7–4.

Developing the Whole Child

Preschool educators have always been concerned with the development of the whole child. This concern requires providing activities and experiences that promote growth and development in the physical, emotional, social, and cognitive areas. These areas are not separate and mutually exclusive—they are interrelated, and good programs try to balance activities to address these areas.

THE STATES AND PRESCHOOL

More and more, individual states are assuming responsibility for funding and implementing preschool programs. As this trend continues, the curricula of preschools becomes more oriented toward basic skills. As of 1985, for example, the Texas prekindergarten program includes elements and subelements in five curricular areas: communication development, cognitive development, motor development, fine arts, and social development. These are cognitive elements in the Texas program:

Cognition development, prekindergarten, shall include the following essential elements:

Identifying. The student shall be provided opportunities to:
☐ match objects in a one-to-one correspondence such as a cup to saucer, napkin to plate (mathematics);

TABLE 7—4   Preschool Environment Rating Scale for Independence

Practices that Foster Dependence	Practices that Encourage Independence
1. Teachers put children's wraps on	1. Teachers teach children how to put on their own wraps
2. Adults set table, put out napkins, pour drinks	2. Children set tables, put out napkins, pour own drinks
3. Adults serve children lunch, snack	3. Children serve themselves; preferably eat family style
4. Adults clean up after children	4. Children clean up after themselves
5. Adults feed children	5. Children are taught how to feed themselves
6. Children have to ask adults for materials and equipment	6. Children have reasonably free access to equipment and materials
7. Adults pass out and collect materials	7. Children are responsible for passing out, collecting, and organizing materials

□ orally identify the number of objects in a group (mathematics);
□ recognize the empty set (concept of zero: mathematics);
□ discuss ways people can help each other (social studies);
□ know and practice rules of safety at home and school (social studies, science);
□ learn social skills appropriate to group behavior (social studies);
□ identify basic economic wants of people (food, clothing, shelter: social studies);
□ discuss how and why people celebrate special events, including those that are culturally related (birthdays, holidays: social studies);
□ know and observe rules of the home, classroom, and school (social studies);
□ know terms related to direction and location (up/down, near/far, above/below: social studies);
□ identify individuals who help students learn (family members, teachers: social studies);
□ demonstrate awareness of self in terms of name, age, and gender (social studies);
□ discuss what families do together (play, work: social studies);
□ use the senses to gain information about the environment using taste, smell, touch, sight, and sound (science); and
□ describe phenomena in the environment (science).

Comparing and contrasting. The student shall be provided opportunities to:
□ use vocabulary to designate quantities such as more than, less than, equal to, as many as (mathematics);
□ use vocabulary to designate relationships such as under, over, above, below, in front of, far away from (mathematics);
□ learn the vocabulary to compare sets or groups (same as, different from, alike: mathematics);

Giving children some responsibility for the care and maintenance of the environment is one way to help them develop independence.

- [ ] demonstrate concepts of part and whole with manipulative materials (mathematics);
- [ ] use vocabulary to compare objects (taller/shorter, heavier/lighter: social studies, science, mathematics); and
- [ ] compare similarities and differences among objects using taste, smell, touch, sight, and sound (science).

Classifying. The student shall be provided opportunities to:
- [ ] form groups by sorting and matching objects according to their attributes (mathematics);
- [ ] combine and separate groups of objects to form new groups (mathematics);
- [ ] identify property as "his/hers/mine/ours" (social studies);
- [ ] classify acceptable/unacceptable behavior at home and school (social studies); and
- [ ] sort objects from the environment according to one or more characteristics (use, composition, location: science).

Sequencing and ordering. The student shall be provided opportunities to:
- [ ] repeat a simple pattern using objects (mathematics);
- [ ] order two or three objects by size (length, height: mathematics);
- [ ] count orally (mathematics);
- [ ] describe sequences in basic family and school routines (social studies); and
- [ ] sequence events in order of their occurrence (science).

Predicting cause/effect relationships. The student shall be provided opportunities to know and discuss the consequences of actions in social relationships (sharing, hitting, disturbing others: social studies).[3]

The Daily Schedule

Although there are various ways to implement a preschool's goals, most preschools operate according to a system of "free play"—self-selection of activities and learning centers. A daily schedule in a preschool program might go like this:

Opening activities: As children enter, the teacher greets each individually. Daily personal greetings make the child feel important, build a positive attitude toward school, and provide an opportunity to practice language skills. They also give the teacher a chance to check each child's health and emotional status. Children usually don't arrive all at one time, so the first arrivals need something to do while others are arriving. Free selection of activities or letting children self-select from a limited range of quiet activities, such as puzzles, pegboards, or markers to color with are appropriate. Some teachers further control this procedure by having children use an "Assignment Board" to help them make choices, limit the available choices, and help them practice concepts such as colors, shapes, and recognizing their names. Initially, the teacher can have the board beside her when children come and tell each child what the choices are. She can hand the child's name tag to her and let her put it on the board. Later, children can find their own names and put them up. At the first of the school year, each child's name tag can include his picture (use an instant camera) or a symbol or shape he has selected.

Group meeting/planning: After all the children arrive, children and teacher plan together and talk about the day ahead. This is also the time for announcements, sharing, and group songs.

Learning centers: After the group time, children are free to go to one of various learning centers, organized and designed to teach concepts. Table 7–5 lists types of learning centers and the concepts each is intended to teach.

Bathroom/handwashing: Before any activity in which food is handled, prepared, or eaten, children should wash and dry their hands.

Snacks: After center activities, a snack is usually served. It should be nutritionally sound, and something the children can serve (and sometimes prepare) themselves.

Outdoor activity/play/walk: Ideally, outside play should be a time for learning new concepts and skills, not just a time to run around aimlessly. Children can practice skills of climbing, jumping, swinging, throwing, and body control. Many walking trips and other events can be incorporated into outdoor play.

Bathroom/toileting: Bathroom/toileting time provides a chance to teach health, self-help, and intrapersonal skills. Children should also be allowed to use the bathroom whenever necessary.

Lunch: Lunch should be a relaxing time, and the meal should be served family style, with teachers and children eating together. Children should set their own tables and decorate them with placemats and flowers they can make in the art

TABLE 7–5   Learning Centers

Center	Concepts	Center	Concepts
Housekeeping	Classification Language skills Sociodramatic play Functions Processes	Woodworking (pinewood; cardboard; styrofoam)	Following directions Functions Planning Whole/part
Water/Sand	Texture Volume Quantity Measure	Art	Color Size Shape Texture
Blocks	Size Shape Length Seriation Spatial relations	Science	Design Relationships Identification of odors
Books/Language	Verbalization Listening Directions How to use books Colors, size Shapes Names	Manipulatives	Functions Measure Volume Texture Size Relationships Classification
Puzzles/Perceptual Development	Size Shape Color Whole/part Figure/ground Spatial relations		Spatial relationships Shape Color Size Seriation

center or as a special project. Children should be involved in cleaning up after meals and snacks.

Relaxation: After lunch, children should have a chance to relax, perhaps to the accompaniment of stories, records, and music. This is an ideal time to teach the children breathing exercises and relaxation techniques.

Naptime: Children who want or need to should have a chance to rest or sleep. For those who don't need it or can't sleep on a particular day, quiet activities should be available. Under no circumstances should children be "forced" to sleep or lie on a cot or blanket if they cannot sleep or have outgrown their need for an afternoon nap.

Bathroom/toileting

Snack

Centers or special projects: Following naptime is a good time for center activities or special projects. (Special projects can also be conducted in the morning, and some may be more appropriate then, such as cooking something for snack or lunch.) Special projects might be cooking, holidays, collecting, work projects, art activities and field trips.

Group time: The day can end with a group meeting to review the day's activities. This serves the purpose of developing listening and attention skills, promotes oral communication, stresses that learning is important, and helps children evaluate their performance and behavior.

This preschool schedule is for a whole-day program; there are many other program arrangements. Some preschools operate half-day programs five days a week with only a morning session; others operate both a morning and afternoon session; others operate only two or three days a week. In still other programs, parents can choose how many days they will send their children. Creativity and meeting parent needs seem to be hallmarks of preschool programs.

SELECTING A GOOD EARLY CHILDHOOD PROGRAM

Parents often wonder how to select a good early childhood program. You may want to add to the following guidelines, but these should enable you to help others arrive at an enlightened decision.

☐ What are the physical accommodations? Is the facility pleasant, light, clean, and airy? Is this a physical setting one would want to spend time in? If not, children won't want to, either.

☐ Do the children seem happy and involved or passive? Is television used as a substitute for a good curriculum and good teachers?

☐ What kinds of materials are available for play and learning?

☐ Is there a balance of activity and quiet play, and of individual, small group, and group activities? Child-directed and teacher-directed activities? Indoor and outdoor play?

☐ Is the physical setting safe and healthy?

☐ Does the school have a written philosophy and objectives? Does the program philosophy agree with the parents' personal philosophy of how children should be reared and educated?

☐ Does the staff have written plans? Is there a smooth flow of activities or do children wait for long periods "getting ready" for another activity? Does the curriculum provide for skills in self-help, readiness for learning, and cognitive, language, physical, and social-emotional development? Lack of planning indicates lack of direction. Although a program whose staff doesn't plan is not necessarily poor, planning is one indicator of a good program.

☐ What is the adult-child ratio? How much time do teachers spend with children on a one-to-one or small group basis? Do teachers take time to give children individual attention? Do children have an opportunity to be independent and do things for themselves? Are there opportunities for outdoor activities? Are children treated in a nonsexist manner? Are all children encouraged to participate in all activities?

☐ What kind of education or training does the staff have? The staff should have training in the curriculum and teaching of young children. The director should have at least a bachelor's degree in childhood education.

☐ How is lunchtime handled? Are children allowed to talk while eating? Do staff members eat with the children?

☐ Can the director or a staff member explain the program? Describing a typical day can be helpful.

☐ How does the staff treat adults, including parents?

☐ Is the program affordable? If a program is too expensive for the family budget, parents may be unhappy in the long run; however, parents should inquire about scholarships, reduced fees, fees adjusted to income level, fees paid in monthly installments, and sibling discounts.

☐ Are parents of children enrolled in the program satisfied?

☐ Do the program's hours and services match parents' needs?

☐ How does the staff relate to children? Are the relationships loving and caring?

☐ How do staff members handle typical discipline problems, such as disputes between children? Are positive guidance techniques used? Are indirect guidance techniques used, as through room arrangement, scheduling, and appropriate activity planning? Is there a written discipline philosophy that agrees with the parents' philosophy?

☐ What are the provisions for emergency care and treatment? What other procedures are there for taking care of ill children?

Quality Programs in Public Schools

Among other organizations, the Southern Association on Children Under Six is concerned about the effects of public preschools for four-year-olds and has issued a position statement on quality four-year-old programs in public schools. The statement includes the following quality standards and procedures to avoid:

☐ The administrator or building principal should have a minimum of nine semester hours of early education courses with a focus on developmental characteristics of young children and appropriate programming.

☐ The teacher must hold a valid early childhood certificate; training must have included work with pre-kindergarten children; the training should meet the criteria of the NAEYC guidelines adopted as NCATE Standards for programs in four-year institutions.

☐ The child must be age four by the same date identifying eligibility for entrance in kindergarten.

☐ The adult-child ratio should be 1:7, not to exceed 1:10; enrollment that exceeds ten requires the assignment of an additional responsible adult with training in early childhood education/child development.

☐ The session for the child should not be less than one half-day.

☐ The daily schedule must be flexible, include a balance of free-choice and teacher-initiated large and small group activities, and reflect the developmental needs of the whole child.

☐ The early childhood curriculum must be designed specifically for four-year-olds and must be appropriate for their developmental level and interests.

☐ The learning environment must be arranged in interest centers that provide for individual and group learning experiences.

☐ Materials, equipment, and supplies appropriate for a developmental curriculum must be available in sufficient quantities.

☐ The classroom must be equipped with movable furniture of correct size, have a water supply available and restroom facilities to accommodate four-year-old children.

☐ The outside play area must be accessible for flexible use; be properly equipped for climbing, riding and gross motor activities; and designed for the safety of the child including fencing.

☐ Minimum space requirements should be based on fifty square feet per child inside and one hundred square feet per child outside.

☐ The program must include a parent component: education, classroom visitation, and regular conferences to support the child's educational experience.

☐ A process must be established to provide communication among the early childhood programs in the school: four-year-olds, kindergarten, and primary grades.

☐ Appropriate developmental evaluation and observations must be conducted periodically to provide information for effective planning for meeting the individual needs of children.

Quality programs should avoid:

☐ The reassignment of upper elementary teachers who have no specialized training in early childhood education.

☐ The elimination of play and the opportunity for child-selected activities.

☐ The use of watered-down first grade curriculum that includes formal readiness activities, workbooks, and ditto sheets.

☐ The placement of children in desks or rows of chairs that inhibit an active learning environment.

☐ The accommodation of young children in facilities such as classroom, playground, cafeteria, and bathrooms that are designed for older children.

☐ The use of standardized skill tests rather than observations and informal evaluations to assess the needs of the young child.[4]

EFFECTIVENESS OF PRESCHOOL PROGRAMS

The eternal question about early childhood programs is, "Do they do any good?" During the last several years, a number of longitudinal studies were designed to answer this question. The Perry Preschool Study came to this conclusion:

Results to age 19 indicate lasting beneficial effects of preschool education in improving cognitive performance during early childhood; in improving scholastic placement and achievement during the school years; in decreasing delinquency and crime, the use of welfare assistance, and the incidence of teenage pregnancy; and in increasing high school graduation rates and the frequency of enrollment in post-secondary programs and employment.[5]

From an analysis of seven exemplary preschool programs, Schweinhart and Weikart reached this conclusion:

> The documented effects of early childhood education may be organized according to the major outcomes for participants at each period of their lives. These outcomes and the ages at which they occurred are: improved intellectual performance during early childhood; better scholastic placement and improved scholastic achievement during the elementary school years; and, during adolescence, a lower rate of delinquency and higher rates of both graduation from high school and employment at age 19. The best-documented preschool effect is an immediate improvement in intellectual performance as represented by intelligence test scores.[6]

ISSUES OF PRESCHOOL EDUCATION

A major issue of preschool education is whether programs operated by public schools are appropriate or "good." More and more four-year-olds are enrolled in preschool programs operated by the public schools, and many of the programs are academic in nature; the curriculum consists of many activities, concepts, and skills traditionally associated with kindergarten and first grade. Critics of public school programs for four-year-olds think this kind of program puts pressure on children because they aren't developmentally ready. The issue of "pushing" children is persistent and long-standing in early childhood education, which usually revolves around overemphasis on learning basic skills and other skills associated with school success. The issue is complex; first, we need a precise understanding of what it means to push children. Some children are able to do more than others at earlier ages; some respond better to certain kinds of learning situations than others. Some parents and children are able to be involved in more activities than are others. So, we must always relate the topic of "pushing" to individual children and their family contexts. (Of course, when we feel parents may be pushing their child, we need to counsel and advise them of the potential harm they may be doing.)

Research is emerging about the effects of pushing young children. Researchers at Temple University, for example, found that children of mothers "who pushed them to attain academic success in preschool were less creative, had more anxiety about tests, and, by the end of kindergarten, had failed to maintain their internal academic advantage over their less-pressured peers."[7] Given this kind of data, both parents and early childhood educators must remember to provide opportunities for children to learn and develop at their own rates.

Another issue is whether public schools are the appropriate agencies to provide schooling for four-year-olds. Many feel that public school teachers lack the training to meet the unique needs of this age-group, and that the public schools are motivated by a desire to gain control of this segment of education rather than to serve pre-schoolers' educational needs. The placement of preschools in the public schools and the resulting tension between public school personnel and early childhood educators over what are and are not appropriate educational programs for young children is another critical issue. In response to this issue, many public schools and early childhood educators are calling for a restructuring of preschool early childhood programs that would result in an early childhood unit. (See also Chapter 16.) Such a recommendation comes from "The Report of the NASBE Task Force on Early Childhood Education"; titled *Right from the Start,* the report states

> We recommend that early childhood units be established in elementary schools, to provide a new pedagogy for working with children ages 4-8 and a focal point for enhanced services to preschool children and their parents.[8]

Another issue is the problem of providing quality caregivers and teachers. The growing number of preschools for three- and four-year-olds has created a need for more teachers and caregivers. Unfortunately, programs often hire unqualified personnel. In some cases this brings new revelations of child abuse in centers and programs and makes more apparent our inadequacy in screening people who work with children. In our rush to provide programs, we must not cut corners or compromise standards. Professionals have moral, ethical, and legal obligations to protect children and provide them with teachers of the highest quality. Part of this issue involves teacher certification—people who work with or teach preschoolers should have specific training and/or certification for that age-group. To allow someone with inappropriate certification to teach preschoolers does an injustice to the concept of a developmentally appropriate curriculum. Quality in preschool programs is an issue in another way, focusing on how to provide a balance between the best of those characteristics we define as quality; desirable teacher-child ratios, encouraging independence, and a learning environment that promotes child-centered learning while providing children with the skills necessary for future academic success. There is a tendency on the part of some preschool proponents to focus almost exclusively on the basic skills of reading, writing, and arithmetic, with an accompanying tendency to minimize the importance of nurturing development in children's social and emotional areas. As early childhood educators, we must strive to provide a balance between academics and social development.

Should four-year-olds be in public preschools? This is another issue facing early childhood educators. Despite the trend toward earlier schooling for 3- and 4-year-old children, there is another group that feels school can wait:

> Above all, the preschool years are a time for play. Let your child enjoy them. Parents today are being bombarded with advice and suggestions about ways in which, if they just do the right thing, they can make their children smarter and quicker and altogether more effective than they would have been without these special efforts.
>
> "Maybe I don't spend enough time with him," "Maybe I ought to do more about teaching him to read," "Maybe I'm losing time when I just let him grow up naturally," are doubts that worry many young parents today. Even if you don't read the books that tell you how to increase your child's intelligence or how to raise a brighter child, there is a feeling in the air that parents ought to be doing something special about their children's minds.
>
> We assure you, no matter what you read or what anybody tells you, it is not necessary to push your preschooler.[9]

A final issue is how to conduct a preschool program that is developmentally appropriate. Unfortunately, some preschool curricula are more suited to the kindergartener or first grader. Many programs operate under the false assumption that if it is good for kindergarten or first grade, the watered-down version is suitable for preschool.

Professional and public organizations are calling public attention to the need to match the curriculum and activities of preschool programs to preschoolers' developmental levels, physically, cognitively, socially, and emotionally.

FURTHER READING

Ames, Louis Bates, and Joan Ames Chase. *Don't Push Your Preschooler* (New York: Harper and Row, 1981)

Tells parents about the dangers of pushing their children. Points out that children learn to do a great many things without adult interference. Authors advise parents to relax and enjoy their children in the years before school and offer suggestions for helping children become ready for school and life. Explains the practical application of the maturation approach to development.

Beaty, Janice J. *Skills for Preschool Teachers,* 3rd ed. (Columbus, Ohio: Merrill, 1988)

Excellent guideline for fulfilling CDA requirements. Helpful to anyone involved with early childhood education.

Brown, Janet F., ed. *Curriculum Planning for Young Children* (Washington, D.C.: National Association for the Education of Young Children, 1982)

Collection of articles from *Young Children,* the journal of the National Association for the Education of Young Children. The articles help early childhood educators keep up with research and apply implications of research to everyday practice. Topics included are play, communication, exploring the world, and integrating the arts; final section presents techniques for implementing an effective curriculum.

Burtt, Kent Garland, *Smart Times: A Parent's Guide to Quality Time With Preschoolers* (New York: Harper and Row, 1984)

Helps parents and early childhood educators put "quality" into "quality time." Contains over two hundred activities classified into 23 categories, from "Kitchen Companions" to "Skills for Writer-To-Be."

Furman, Erna, ed. *What Nursery School Teachers Ask Us About: Psychoanalytic Consultations in Preschools* (Madison, Conn.: International Universities Press, 1986)

Deals with questions nursery teachers ask; answers them in straightforward and nonauthoritarian way. The suggestions can be included in daily routines of programs. Chapters are easy to read and free from psychoanalytic jargon. Discussions of "The Roles of Parents and Teachers in the Life of the Young Child," "Separation and Entry to Nursery School," "Stress in the Nursery School," and "Discipline" are particularly interesting and insightful.

Green, Bernard. *Your Child is Bright: Make The Most of It* (New York: St. Martin's Press, 1982)

Program for helping parents help their children achieve their best. Chapters on nutrition, communication, and "mind games." A variation on the traditional theme that parents are their children's best teachers.

Griffin, Elinor Fitch. *Island of Childhood: Education in the Special World of Nursery Schools* (New York: Teachers College Press, 1982)

An alternative to the emphasis of the back-to-basics movement. Author believes achieving relationships and healthy self-concepts are more important than early teaching of reading skills. Presents many ideas popular during the pre-Head Start years, which some feel need to be rediscovered.

Houle, Georgia Bradley. *Learning Centers for Young Children* (West Greenwich, R.I.: Tot-Lot Child Care Products, 1984)

Wide variety of usable, practical learning centers for young children, each teacher-created and tested by the author. All utilize existing classroom materials and props. Each description is accompanied by a drawing of the center and the author's ideas of the educational values of the center and materials.

Mitchell, Anne, Michelle Seligson, and Fern Marx. *Early Childhood Programs and the Public Schools: Between Promise and Practice* (Dover, Mass.: Auburn House, 1989)

A comprehensive look at all aspects of early childhood public school programs: history, results of state and district surveys, administration, financing, regulation, eligibility criteria, coordination of programs, staffing, types of programs, responsiveness to families, and a look toward the future. A good guide for anyone interested in early childhood programs.

Warner, Cynthia. *A Resource Guide to Public School Early Childhood Programs* (Alexandria, Va.: Association for Supervision and Curriculum Development, 1988)

A guide to issues and concerns that surround the decisions administrators and teachers make regarding preschool programs.

FURTHER STUDY

1. Visit preschool programs in your area. Determine their philosophies and find out what goes on in a typical day. Which would you send your children to? Why?
2. Many people, including parents and teachers, think all learning occurs in school or schoollike settings. How do out-of-school and home activities contribute to children's learning?
3. Observe children's play to identify the types of social play listed in the chapter.
4. Piaget believed that children construct schemes through play. Observe children's play, and determine how schemes develop through play.
5. How early do you think children should be enrolled in a preschool program? Interview parents and other educators for their opinions.
6. What do you think should be the basic purposes of a preschool program? Find out what your classmates think. How do your responses differ from theirs?
7. Observe children's play in a preschool program. How would you improve it? What other materials and equipment would you use?
8. There is a trend toward enrolling three-year-olds in public school. What are the reasons for this trend? Do you think the trend will continue? Do you think that even younger children will be enrolled in public schools? Why or why not?
9. Survey preschool parents to learn what they expect from a preschool program. How do parents' expectations compare to the goals of preschool programs you visited?
10. Tell how you would promote learning through a specific preschool activity. For example, what learning outcomes would you have for a sand/water area? What, specifically, would be your role in helping children learn?
11. Develop goals and objectives for a preschool program. Write a daily schedule that would support your goals.
12. Visit a preschool program and request to see their program goals. How do they compare to those listed in this chapter? What would you change, add, or delete?
13. Outline what you would expect to see in a preschool program based on its program goals. Also list at least five things you would like to see in a typical preschool classroom.
14. Review the information you gathered on your visit to a preschool program and assess how this program is preparing children for their school experience.
15. Compare the philosophies of a day care center, a nursery program, and a preschool program. How are they alike? How are they different?
16. Read articles that define today's trend in establishing quality preschool programs. What are the first three issues discussed? Do you agree with these issues? If not, why?
17. Develop an activity file for a preschool program. Is it easier to find materials for some areas than for others? Why?
18. Gather information both for and against early schooling and learning. Which do you now favor? Why?
19. Interview parents of young children to determine what they look for in a good preschool program. How does what parents look for compare to the guidelines in this chapter?
20. How do parents "push" children? How can pushing harm children? Do you think some children need a push? What is the difference between constructive and destructive pushing?

NOTES

1. George Foreman and Fleet Hill, *Constructive Play: Applying Piaget in the Preschool* (Monterey, Calif.: Brooks/Cole, 1980), p. 2.

2. Mildred Parten, "Social Play Among Preschool Children," *Journal of Abnormal and Social Psychology,* 27 (1932), pp. 243-69.

3. Texas Education Agency, *Priority '86: A Guide for Prekindergarten Education* (Austin, Tex.: Texas Education Agency, 1986), pp. 6-7.

4. "Position Statement on Quality Four-Year-Old Programs in Public Schools" (Little Rock, Ark.: The Southern Association on Children Under Six).

5. John R. Berrueta-Clement, et al., *Changed Lives: The Effects of the Perry Preschool Program on Youths Through Age 19* (Ypsilanti, Mich.: The High Scope Press, 1984), p. 1.

6. Lawrence J. Schweinhart and David P. Weikart, "Evidence That Good Early Childhood Programs Work," *Phi Delta Kappan,* 66 (8), p. 547.

7. Chris Raymond, "New Study Reveals Pitfalls in Pushing Children to Succeed Academically in Preschool Years, *The Chronicle of Higher Education* (Nov. 1, 1989), p. A4.

8. National Association of State Boards of Education, *Right from the Start: The Report of the NASBE Task Force on Early Childhood Education* (Alexandria, Va.: National Association of State Boards of Education, 1988), p. vii.

9. Louis Bates Ames and Joan Ames Chase, *Don't Push Your Preschooler* (New York: Harper and Row, 1980), p. 2.

CHAPTER 8
Kindergarten Education
More Than ABC's

As you read and study:

- ☐ Trace the history of kindergarten programs from Froebel to the present
- ☐ Identify and critique goals and objectives for kindergarten programs
- ☐ Understand the concept of and issues surrounding readiness for learning
- ☐ Understand the benefits and disadvantages of different entrance ages for kindergarten
- ☐ Become familiar with issues of full-day and half-day kindergarten programs
- ☐ Examine and critique kindergarten programs and schedules
- ☐ Understand the nature of developmentally appropriate and inappropriate kindergarten curricula
- ☐ Examine and critique kindergarten screening and assessment programs
- ☐ Understand the nature and importance of transitions for kindergarten children
- ☐ Identify and examine issues confronting kindergarten education
- ☐ Conceptualize and articulate a personal philosophy of kindergarten education

Froebel's educational concepts and kindergarten program were imported into the U.S. virtually intact by individuals who believed in his ideas and methods. Froebelian influence remained dominant for almost half a century, until John Dewey and his followers challenged it in the early 1900s. While Froebel's ideas seem perfectly acceptable today, they were not acceptable to those in the mid-eighteenth century who subscribed to the notion of early education. Especially innovative and hard to accept was that learning could be based on play and children's interests—in other words, child-centered. Most European and American schools were subject-oriented and emphasized teaching basic skills. In addition, Froebel was the first to advocate a communal education for young children *outside* the home. Until Froebel, young children were educated in the home, by their mothers. Although Froebel advocated this method too, his ideas for educating children as a group, in a special place outside the home, were revolutionary.

Credit for establishing the first kindergarten in the U.S. is accorded to Margarethe Schurz. After attending lectures on Froebelian principles in Germany, she returned to the U.S. and, in 1856, at Watertown, Wisconsin, opened her kindergarten. Schurz's program was conducted in German, as were many of the new kindergarten programs of the time, since Froebel's ideas of education appealed especially to bilingual parents. Schurz also influenced Elizabeth Peabody, the sister-in-law of Horace Mann, when, at the home of a mutual friend, Mrs. Schurz explained the Froebelian system. Peabody was not only fascinated, but converted.

Elizabeth Peabody opened her kindergarten in Boston in 1860. She and her sister, Mary Mann, also published a book, *Kindergarten Guide*. Peabody almost immediately realized that she lacked grounding in the necessary theory to adequately implement Froebel's ideas. She visited kindergartens in Germany, then returned to the U.S. to popularize Froebel's methods. Elizabeth Peabody is generally credited as the main promoter of the kindergarten in the U.S. An event that also helped advance the kindergarten movement was the appearance of appropriate materials. In 1860, Milton Bradley, the toy manufacturer, attended a lecture by Elizabeth Peabody, became a convert to the concept of kindergarten, and began to manufacture Froebel's gifts and occupations.

The first *public* kindergarten was founded in St. Louis, Missouri, in 1873 by Susan E. Blow, with the cooperation of the St. Louis superintendent of schools, William T. Harris. Elizabeth Peabody had corresponded for several years with Harris, and the combination of her prodding and Susan Blow's enthusiasm and knowledge convinced Harris to open a public kindergarten on an experimental basis. Endorsement of the kindergarten program by a public school system did much to increase its popularity and spread the Froebelian influence within early childhood education. In addition, Harris, who later became the U.S. commissioner of education, encouraged support for Froebel's ideas and methods.

Training for kindergarten teachers has figured prominently in the development of higher education. The Chicago Kindergarten College was founded in 1886 to teach mothers and train kindergarten teachers. In 1930, the Chicago Kindergarten College became the National College of Education. In 1888, in Boston, Massachusetts, Lucy Wheelock opened a kindergarten training program. Known as the Wheelock School, it became Wheelock College in 1949.

The kindergarten movement in the United States was not without growing pains. Over a period of time, the kindergarten program, at first ahead of its time, became rigid, and methods- and teacher-centered rather than child-centered. By the turn of the century, many kindergarten leaders thought kindergarten programs and training should be open to experimentation and innovation, rather than rigidly follow Froebel's ideas. The chief defender of the Froebelian status quo was Susan Blow. In the more moderate camp was Patty Smith Hill, who thought that, while the kindergarten should remain faithful to Froebel's ideas, it should nevertheless be open to innovation. She believed that to survive, the kindergarten movement would have to move into the twentieth century. She was able to convince many of her colleagues and, more than anyone else, is responsible for the survival of the kindergarten as we know it today.

Patty Smith Hill's influence is evident in the format of many present-day preschools and kindergartens. Free, creative play, where children can use materials as they wish, was Hill's idea, and represented a sharp break with Froebelian philosophy. She also introduced large blocks and centers where children could engage in housekeeping, sand and water play, and other activities as they wished, rather than as the teacher dictated.

Many preschool activities have their basis in adult "occupations." Froebel had children engage in building, carpentry, sewing, and sweeping; many Montessori activities (see Chapter 3) were conceived for the same purpose. They chose these activities because many adult activities, such as "building" with blocks and carpentry, appeal to children; educators have also long believed that learning materials and activities could be used to introduce children to the world of work. For example, William Harris was interested in the kindergarten because he thought children could be better prepared for industrial society if they had some understanding of adult occupations.

Were Froebel alive today, he would probably not recognize the program he gave his life to developing. Many kindergarten programs are subject-centered rather than child-centered as Froebel envisioned them. Furthermore, Froebel did not see his program as a "school," but as a place where children could develop through play. Although kindergartens are evolving to meet the needs of society and families, we must not forget the philosophy and ideals on which the first kindergartens were based.

WHO IS KINDERGARTEN FOR?

Froebel's kindergarten was for children three to seven years of age; in the U.S., kindergarten has been considered the year before children enter first grade. Since the age at which children enter first grade varies, however, the ages at which they enter kindergarten also vary. People tend to think that kindergarten is for five-year-old children rather than four-year-olds, and most teachers tend to support an older rather than a younger entrance age because they think "older" children are more "ready" for kindergarten and learn better. Whereas in the past children had to be five years of age prior to December 31st for kindergarten admission, today the trend is toward requiring an older admission age; for example, both Florida and Texas require that children be five years of age by September 1st of the school year for admission to kindergarten.

The entrance age for kindergarten often creates controversy, usually because parents want an earlier entrance age and teachers want a later entrance age. Some states and districts make exceptions to age requirements by testing children for early admittance, which creates further controversy over what test to use and what score to use as a cutoff point. Decisions for early entrance are sometimes based on children's behaviors in a kindergarten setting. Children and their parents may attend a special kindergarten day during the summer or early fall, before the beginning of school, so teachers can judge children's readiness for school and learning. Their judgments determine whether children are admitted to kindergarten early.

There is wide public support for tax-supported public kindergartens *and* for making kindergarten attendance compulsory. A Gallup Poll showed that 80 percent of the respondents favored "making kindergarten available for all those who wish it as part of the public school system"; 71 percent favored compulsory kindergarten attendance; and 70 percent think children should start school at ages four or five (29 percent favored age four and 41 percent favored age five).[1] In keeping with this national sentiment for universal availability of kindergarten, more states are making it a compulsory experience for five-year-olds. As of 1990, 34 states and the Virgin Islands have compulsory attendance laws. The question today is not so much whether a child will attend kindergarten, but when.

Universal Kindergarten

Kindergarten has rapidly become universal for the majority of the nation's five-year-olds. Today, kindergarten is either a whole or half-day program and within the reach of most of the nation's children. As with four-year-olds, the number of five- and six-year-olds projected to attend preschool or kindergarten is dramatic, as we saw in Table 7–2.

SCHOOL READINESS: WHO GETS READY FOR WHOM?

In discussions of preschool and kindergarten programs, no issue generates as much heat as school readiness. Raising entrance ages for admittance to kindergarten and first grade is based on the reasoning that many children are "not ready," and teachers therefore have difficulty teaching them. There is renewed emphasis on what getting children ready for life events and schooling means. The early childhood profession is reexamining "readiness," its many interpretations, and the various ways the concept is applied to educational settings and children.

For most parents and early childhood educators, readiness means the child's ability to participate and succeed in beginning schooling. Readiness includes a child's ability, at a given time, to accomplish activities and engage in processes associated with schooling, whether nursery school, preschool, kindergarten, or first grade. *Readiness* is thus the sum of a child's physical, cognitive, social, and emotional development at a particular time. Readiness does not exist in the abstract—it must relate to something. Increasingly, in today's educational climate, readiness is measured against the process of formal public schooling. By the same token, a child's lack of readiness may be considered a deficit and a detriment, because it indicates a lack of what is needed for success in kindergarten and first grade.

Today's kindergarten is really part of the first year of school, and is no longer considered to be pre-school. What was once taught in first grade is now taught in kindergarten.

The Role of Maturation

Some early childhood educators and many parents believe that time cures all things, including lack of readiness. They believe that as time passes, a child grows and develops physically and cognitively and, as a result, becomes ready to achieve. This belief is manifested in school admissions policies that advocate children's remaining out of school for a year if they demonstrate lack of readiness as measured by a readiness test. Assuming that the passage of time will bring about readiness is similar to the concept of unfolding, popularized by Froebel. Unfolding implies that development is inevitable and certain and that what a child will be, the optimum degree of development, is determined by heredity and a maturational timetable or biological clock. Froebel likened children to plants and parents and teachers to gardeners whose task is to nurture and care for children so they can mature according to their genetic inheritance and maturational timetable. The concept of unfolding continues to be a powerful force in early childhood education, although many challenge it as an inadequate and outmoded concept.

The modern popularizer of the concept of unfolding was Arnold Gesell (1880–1961), whose ideas and work continue at the Gesell Institute of Human Development in New Haven, Connecticut. Gesell made fashionable and acceptable the notion of inherent maturation that is *predictable, patterned*, and *orderly*.[3] He also created a number of tests to measure this development, from which he constructed a series of developmental or behavioral norms that specify in detail children's motor, adaptive, language, and personal-social behavior according to chronological age. Gesell also coined the concept of *developmental age* to distinguish children's developmental growth from chronological age; for example, a child who is five years old may have a developmental age of four because he demonstrates the behavioral characteristics of a four-year-old rather than a five-year-old. Gesell believed that parents make their greatest contribution to readiness by providing a climate in which children can grow without interference to their innate timetable and blueprint for development. The popularity of this *maturationist view* has led to a persistent sentiment that children are being hurried to grow up too soon. More critics of early education say that we should let children be children, and not push them into readiness for learning.

Self-Education Through Play

In addition to time and maturation, self-education through play and appropriate activities also promotes readiness. The self-education viewpoint stresses the roles children play in their own learning. In most discussions of readiness, people talk as though children take no part in it, giving all the credit to maturation and heredity. All great educators, however, have stressed the role children play in their own development. Froebel talked about unfolding, Maria Montessori advocated auto- or self-education, and Piaget stressed the active involvement of the child in the process of cognitive development. The primary pedagogical implication of self-readiness is that children must be involved in developing their own readiness. Time alone is not sufficient to account for or provide children with the skills they need for school success.

For Froebel, play was the energizer, the process that promotes unfolding. Froebel developed his "gifts" and "occupations" to help teachers involve children in play. Montessori believed the prepared environment, with its wealth of sensory materials specifically designed to meet children's interests, is the principle means to help children educate themselves. For Piaget, the physically and mentally active child in an environment that provides for assimilation and accommodation develops the mental schemes necessary for productive learning.

Self-education is child-centered, not subject- or teacher-centered. Children play the star roles in the drama of learning; teachers are the supporting cast. Child-centered readiness programs provide children with enriched environments of material and human resources where they can play and enhance their own development while they construct the cognitive schemes essential for readiness and, ultimately, school success. Concerning self-education, Caroline Pratt said about her famous Play School, "The attempt in the play school has been to place children in an environment through which by experiment with that environment they may become self-educated."[4]

For some children, the home is such an environment; other children lack the enriched environment necessary to fully support their efforts of self-education. Unfortunately, some five-year-olds are denied admission to kindergarten programs because they are not "ready" and spend another year in a sterile home or program environment that has failed to support the growth and development necessary to be ready for the schooling experience.

Quality Programs

Providing young children with *quality* preschool programs is another way to promote and assure their readiness. As more and more kindergarten teachers see that children are not ready for basic skills curricula, agencies such as Head Start, child care centers, and public schools have implemented programs for three- and four-year-olds to provide the activities and experiences necessary for kindergarten success.

What Constitutes Readiness for Learning?

In all the rhetoric associated with readiness, readiness skills and behaviors are frequently overlooked. The areas of readiness skills and behaviors include language, independence, impulse control, interpersonal skills, experiential background, and physical and mental health.

Language.   Language is the most important readiness skill. Children need language skills for success in school and life. Important language skills include receptive language, such as listening to the teacher and following directions; expressive language, demonstrated in the ability to talk fluently and articulately with teacher and peers, the ability to express oneself in the language of the school, and the ability to communicate needs and ideas; and symbolic language, knowing the names of people, places, and things, words for concepts, and adjectives and prepositions.

Independence.   Independence means the ability to work alone on a task; the ability to take care of oneself; and the ability to initiate projects without always being told what to do. Independence also includes mastery of self-help skills, including but not limited to dressing skills, health skills (toileting, handwashing, using a handkerchief, and brushing teeth), and eating skills (using utensils, napkins, serving oneself, and cleaning up).

Impulse Control.   The ability to control impulses includes a cluster of behaviors that make it possible for children to become meaningfully involved in the learning process. Children who are not able to control their impulses are frequently (and erroneously) labeled hyperactive or learning disabled. Controlling impulses includes working cooperatively with others and not hitting others or interfering with their work; developing an attention span that permits involvement in learning activities for a reasonable length of time; and the ability to sit and stay seated for a period of time.

Interpersonal Skills.   Interpersonal skills are those of getting along with and working with others, including peers and adults. Asked why they want their child to attend a preschool program, parents frequently respond, "To learn how to get along with others." Any child care or preschool program is an experience in group living, and children have the opportunity to interact with others so as to become successful in a group setting. Interpersonal skills include cooperating with others; learning and using basic manners; and most important, learning how to learn from others.

Experiences.   Experiential background is important to readiness because experiences are the building blocks of knowledge, the raw materials of cognitive development. They provide the context for mental disequilibrium, which enables children to develop higher levels of thinking. Children must go places—the grocery store, library, zoo—and they must be involved in activities—crafts, building things, painting, coloring, experimenting, and discovering. Children can build only on the background of information they bring to a new experience. If they have had limited experiences, they have little to build on and cannot build well.

Health.   Children must have the physical and mental health necessary to participate in a full day of learning activities. They must have good nutritional and physical habits that will enable them to fully participate in and profit from any program. They must also have positive and nurturing environments and caregivers so as to develop a self-image for achievement.

There are also other concepts to keep in mind about readiness:

Readiness is a never-ending process. It does not exist only in the preschool and kindergarten years, although we often think of it this way. Children are always in need of new knowledge, skills, experiences, and understanding that will help them learn about and participate in the next learning event. We should not think of readiness as something a child does or does not have, but should view it as a continuum throughout life—the next life event is always just ahead.

All children are always ready for some kind of learning. Children always need experiences that will promote learning and get them ready for the next step in the process of schooling. As early childhood educators, we should constantly ask such questions as: "What does the child know? What can I do to help him move to the next level of understanding?"

Schools and teachers should get ready for children, not the other way around. Rather than make children get ready for a predetermined curriculum and notions of what learning is about, early childhood educators should rededicate themselves to the ideal that schools are for children. Public schools that want children to be ready for predetermined and preconceived programs have their priorities reversed. Schools should provide programs based on the needs of children, not on preconceived notions of what children ought to be able to do. Teachers should provide whatever program is necessary for children to learn.

WHAT HAPPENS WHEN WE RETAIN A CHILD?

I'm sure you can remember back to your early elementary school years. More than likely there were children in your classes who were repeating the same grade over again. You probably remember them because they were bigger than you, or they were behavior problems, or they were in the "low" reading group. You took the presence of these children for granted and assumed children who had been retained were a natural part of the typical classroom. You concluded then, as you perhaps do now, that nonpromotion or retention is a good pedagogical device because it exposes children once again to the same material they have previously failed to learn. The fact that you can remember children who were repeating a grade is evidence that retaining children at least once, and perhaps two or three times in a school career, has a long and strong tradition in American public and parochial education. That tradition continues.

Along with the benefits of early education and universal kindergarten come disturbing and potentially disastrous side effects for children. Retained children, instead of participating in kindergarten graduation ceremonies with their classmates, are destined to spend another year in kindergarten. Many of these children are retained or failed because teachers judge them to be immature, or they fail to measure up to the district's or teachers' standards for promotion to first grade. Children are usually retained in the elementary years because of low academic achievement or low IQ. (In comparison, reasons for retention are different at the junior high level, where students are generally retained because of behavioral problems or excessive absences.)

With the pressure on the schools to teach basic skills in the early years comes additional pressure to fail the children who don't master these skills. When well-meaning teachers fail children, they do so in the belief that they are doing them and their families a favor. Teachers believe that children who have an opportunity to spend an extra year in the same grade will do better the second time around. Teachers' hopes, and consequently parents' hopes, are that these failed children will go on to do as well as—many teachers hold out the promise that they will do even better than—their nonretained classmates. But is this true? Do children do better the second time around?

Despite our intuitive feelings that children who are retained will do better, the research evidence is unequivocally to the contrary: children don't do better the second time around. They don't achieve better than their nonretained classmates in spite of having spent a year trying to make up for their failure. In addition, parents report that retained children have a more pessimistic attitude toward school, with a consequently negative impact on their social emotional development.[5]

There are other factors in retention that teachers, parents, and the entire educational community must consider. First, retention in kindergarten and other grades increases the cost of education to the public. In the Dade County Public Schools during the 1987–1988 academic year, 7.7 percent of the 20,554 kindergarten children, or 1583 children, were not promoted to first grade. The average kindergarten class is 25.8 pupils, so this retention rate means that 61 additional teachers must be added to the school district's payroll to teach the retained kindergartners. The average teacher salary in the Dade County Public Schools for 1987–1988 was $29,171; therefore, the cost to the district for retention in the kindergarten was $1,779,431 for one year. A second factor is a link between retention and later school dropout, and third, many of the children who are retained come from low socioeconomic groups.

Despite evidence for its detrimental effects, retention as an antidote to lack of achievement is still a popular solution. In fact, one survey showed that 65 percent of teachers, 74 percent of principals, and 59 percent of parents support retention.[6]

The ultimate issue of retention and promotion is how to prevent failure and promote success. To achieve those goals, educators will have to change their views about what practices are best for children and how to prevent the risk factors that create a climate for unsuccessful school experiences. As alternatives to retaining children in a grade, many school districts are implementing two kinds of programs.

One is the developmental kindergarten, which, in essence, gives children two years to complete one year of kindergarten work. The second is transitional classes between kindergarten and first grade.

DEVELOPMENTAL KINDERGARTENS

The developmental kindergarten is a prekindergarten for developmentally or behaviorally delayed kindergarten children. It is seen as one means of helping the "at-risk" child succeed in school. There is a specific procedure and rationale for placing children in such a program:

- ☐ Test kindergarten-eligible children prior to their entrance to kindergarten to determine which children are "at-risk" (developmentally delayed).
- ☐ Give at-risk children an extra year to develop by placing them into a less cognitively oriented kindergarten classroom where developmental needs can be addressed.
- ☐ Promote them to a regular kindergarten classroom the following year.
- ☐ As a result of having had an extra year to mature in the developmental kindergarten, a reduction in later school failure will be achieved.[7]

TRANSITIONAL CLASSES

A transition class is one that is situated between two classes. The concept and practice of transition classes implies and should involve linear progression. A child is placed in a transition class so that he can continue to progress at his own pace. The curriculum, materials, and teaching practices are appropriate for the child's developmental age or level. Figure 8–1 shows the linear progression intended by transitional programs.

Proponents of transitional programs believe they offer the following advantages:

- ☐ Placement in a transition program promotes success, whereas retention is a regressive practice that promotes failure.
- ☐ The program provides for children's developmental abilities.
- ☐ Children are with other children of the same developmental age.
- ☐ The program provides children with an appropriate learning environment.
- ☐ The program puts children's needs ahead of the need to place a child in a particular grade.
- ☐ The program provides time for children to integrate learning.

WHAT SHOULD KINDERGARTEN BE LIKE?

To decide what the kindergarten should be like, it is instructive to go back to Froebel:

The Kindergarten is an institution which treats the child according to its nature; compares it with a flower in a garden; recognizes its threefold relation to God, man and nature; supplies the means for the development of its faculties, for the training of the senses, and for the strengthening of its physical powers. It is the institution where a child plays with children.[8]

But comparing Froebel's vision of the kindergarten to today's kindergartens, we find them light years apart. Today's kindergarten is centered on basic skills, learning

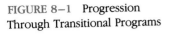

FIGURE 8–1 Progression
Through Transitional Programs

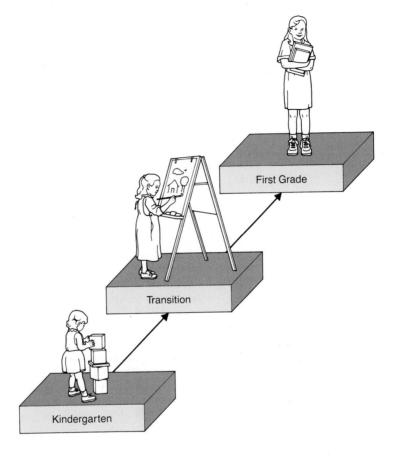

objectives, tests, checklists, and state minimum standards. As the public and professional debate goes on over the appropriate purposes and content of kindergarten
programs, more organizations and agencies issue statements for refocusing attention
on what is best for children. The Nebraska Department of Education offers these
suggestions for a good kindergarten program:

☐ Parents and school personnel work cooperatively to build a partnership between
   home and school that will support the child throughout the school experience...
   ...not a place where the expectations of the parents and the school are in conflict or
   where parents feel isolated from their child's experience.
☐ Children experience a planned, child-centered environment that encourages learning
   through exploration and discovery...not a sit-down-be-quiet classroom dominated by
   desks, paper and workbooks.
☐ Children have access to multilevel experiences and activities of varying degrees of
   complexity. They should be able to use concrete materials which allow for individual
   differences and natural variations in each one's ability to perform...
   ...not a place where all children are expected to perform the same task, reach the
   same level of performance, and accomplish the same objectives.

☐ Children can make choices and decisions within the limits of the materials provided...

...not a largely teacher-directed room where children seldom choose.

☐ Children learn there is often more than one right answer. Divergent thinking is developed and encouraged through use of open-ended materials and many informal conversations among the children and with adults...

...not a place where the day's activities are largely dominated by worksheets and discussions with predetermined answers.

☐ The children's own language, experiences, and stages of development form the basis of reading and writing activities...

...not the almost universal use of commercial, formal pre-reading and early-reading programs.

☐ Children learn to enjoy books and to appreciate literary language through a daily storytime, creative dramatics and repeated opportunities to hear and learn simple rhymes and other poems...not a place where the day is too short for storytime and the opportunity to appreciate literature comes only by way of educational television.

☐ Children participate in daily, planned activities fostering both gross and fine motor development, including such activities as running, jumping, bouncing balls, lacing cards, hammering nails, playing with clay, etc....not a place where children are expected to sit quietly for long periods of time and perform the motor skills beyond the current ability of many of them.

☐ Children develop mathematical understanding through use of familiar materials such as sand, water, unit blocks and counters...not a place where children are asked to mark an X on the right answer in a workbook.

☐ Children's curiosity about natural, familiar elements forms the basis of scientific observations, experimentation and conclusions. Both planned and spontaneous interaction with plants, animals, rocks, soil, water, etc., is considered to be essential...not a place where science is included only when time permits or where the books tell outcomes and the teachers do the experiments.

☐ Experimentation, enjoyment and appreciation of varied forms of music are encouraged on a daily basis...not a place where music is included only when time permits.

☐ Art expression is encouraged through the use of a wide assortment of media integrated within the daily curriculum...not a place where art usually consists of copying a model, coloring a ditto or cutting and pasting a pattern, and/or where art is delegated to the specialist.

☐ All the activities are planned to promote a positive self-image and attitude toward school and peers...not a place where the child's worth is measured only by his/her ability to conform to expectations.

☐ Play is respected for its value as an appropriate learning medium for children of this age...not a place where play is deemphasized because the child "played enough" in preschool and should be ready for "real" learning.[9]

Basic Skills Orientation

There is a great deal of tension between those who advocate a readiness-play orientation to kindergarten and those who advocate a basic skills orientation. For example, Florida, the first state to mandate compulsory kindergarten education for all five-year-olds, has a Primary Education Program that requires the screening of all children within the first six weeks of school for placement into one of three instructional groups: developmental (normal grade level); enrichment (above grade level); and preventative (below grade level). In Dade County, Florida, the nation's fourth

Many kindergartens have a basic-skills orientation; however, such an approach should not dominate a kindergarten classroom, because play and other activities are important at this age.

largest school district, the kindergarten program operates according to a "balanced curriculum," where basic objectives and minimal instructional times are specified for subject matter areas. These are among the objectives for language arts in the specific area of language development:

Listen and respond to simple oral directions.

Repeat short sentences in correct order.

Associate pictures with text read aloud.

Expand speaking vocabulary using new words correctly.

Describe in an oral sentence objects, pictures, or events he/she has experienced.

Demonstrate understanding of positional prepositions, adverbs (i.e., above, below, on, etc.).

Identify differences between questions and statements and respond appropriately.

Read simple words.

Read simple sentences/stories developed in language experience activity.[10]

These are two areas in the Dade County mathematics objectives for kindergarten:

Geometry

Identify figures: circle, square, triangle, rectangle.

Compare size, shape: same, different.

Identify positions: over, under, above, below, between, in the middle of, up, down, bottom, top, on, off, next to, beside, around, in front of, behind, in back of, to the right of, to the left of, inside, outside.

Measurement

Compare length: longer (est), shorter (est), farther (est), near (est).

Compare area: more, less, smaller (est), larger (est).

Compare volume: empty, full, more, less, least, most.

Compare weight: lighter (est), heavier (est).[11]

Rest in the Kindergarten

Some people think kindergarten-age children tire easily and, especially in an all-day kindergarten, need a chance to rest or sleep. Others believe that most kindergarten children have more energy and stamina than we give them credit for. Besides, the kindergarten curriculum is usually so full that there really isn't time for rest.

There are several ways to handle the issue of rest periods. First, parents can be encouraged to have their children get enough rest at home so they can participate in a full day's activities. Through newsletters and personal notes, teachers can tell parents how important it is for their children to get eight or more hours of sleep a night, or however much a child needs so as not to be tired during the day. Second, the teacher can explain the importance of rest to the children. Friendly reminders from teachers about the importance of sleep may have more impact than admonishments from parents. Third, every early childhood program should allow time for relaxation through quiet activities. Young children need time to pause and listen to stories, look at books, converse, and refresh themselves. Teachers should build resting/reflective times into their programs. Listening to the teacher read a story is a pleasant way to rest and unwind.

If kindergarten teachers and administrators believe in a rest time, it should be individualized for each child. A child should not be forced to remain on a cot or mat long after it is apparent that he isn't going to sleep. Also, a sensitive and observant kindergarten teacher knows which children need a nap and which do not. If the policy is not to nap, there may be occasions when a particular child needs to sleep and should be allowed to do so. Likewise, if the policy is to nap or rest, children who don't need to should be given alternative activities.

Teachers also need to keep in mind that what is appropriate at the beginning of the school year may not be appropriate later; children who need a nap at the beginning of the school year may quickly outgrow the need. More importantly, teachers must recognize the necessity of providing children with a curriculum and range of activities that incorporates both active and quiet times. Children should also have opportunities to engage in group and individual activities that accommodate their learning styles and temperaments. Individualizing the curriculum addresses many questions about what is appropriate for children, including the need for rest.

Representative Schedules

Table 8–1 shows a sample schedule of a half-day, socially and cognitively oriented kindergarten program. Figure 8–2 is the schedule one teacher has worked out for her kindergarten.

Also, in a poll of state education directors, 88 percent responded that the kindergarten programs in their state offered a "balanced" curriculum of academics and social goals. California, Minnesota, and Ohio reported an "academics" focus on programs. Although it is certainly true that individual programs in a state differ widely from the official state pronouncement of their purposes, the trend toward basic skills teaching in the kindergarten, while much criticized by traditional kindergarten educators and early childhood educators, will continue. More and more parents and teachers contend that "kindergarten is no longer a year of milk and cookies; it is the first year of the school experience." We can no longer consider kindergarten part of the preschool experience. With compulsory attendance laws and the popularity and universality of kindergarten, it is now an integral and accepted part of the public school experience. In another decade, we will say the same about programs for four-year-olds.

Full- or Half-Day Kindergarten

There are both half-day and full-day kindergarten programs. A school district that operates a half-day program usually offers one session in the morning and one in

TABLE 8–1 Possible Half-Day Kindergarten Schedule

Time	Activity
8:30	Arrival-free time—children select an activity from a group of prearranged activities such as puzzles, games, books, and records which stress cognitive learning.
9:00	Circle time–conversation which emphasizes plans for the day's activities. Can also include discussion of previous day's work.
9:15	Language development program–can be either teacher-designed or a commercial kit, such as Peabody Language Kits, and Alpha-Time.
9:45	Storytime–the children are read stories and discuss them. Children select books from library to take home.
10:15	Activity centers and learning centers–these can deal with any topic, such as science, art, ecology, and writing. All children participate in all the centers, usually on a rotating basis.
10:45	Free choice of games and puzzles selected by teacher for their ability to teach concepts such as size, shape, or number. This period can also be used for outdoor walks in which concepts being developed are extended and reinforced.
11:15	Group discussion–day's activities are reviewed and discussed. The next day's activities are anticipated.
11:45	Dismissal
	Snack, rest, and toilet opportunities may be offered at scheduled times or on an "as needed" basis for each child.

8:00–8:10 — Morning Announcements, Pledge, National Anthem. Take up lunch and snack money.

Schedule

8:10–9:40 — LANGUAGE ARTS

Morning Routine:
Everyone says the following together as I point to pictures or charts on our classroom walls:
- Calendar
- Days of the weeks
- Seasons
- Months of the year
- Colors
- Alphabet Song
- Count by 1's to 100
- Count by 10's to 100
- Count by 5's to 100
- Our Letter People & their Sounds
- Nursery Rhymes
- Shapes

Language Arts Curriculum:
- Alpha Time
- Lippincott Letterbooks
- Getting Ready to Read by Houghton Mifflin
- Developmental Learning Materials (DLM)

Morning Recess 9:40–9:50

9:50–10:50 — MATH

Workbooks: Mathematics Today by H.B.J.

DLM

Thursday: The Children go to the Computer Lab 10:00–10:40

Lunch 10:50–11:30

Storytime 11:30–12:00

P.E. 12:00–12:30

12:30–12:55 — SOCIAL STUDIES & FINE ARTS

Units:
1. All about Me
2. Home & Family
3. Pets
4. School Helpers
5. Community Helpers
6. Fall/Woodland Animals
7. Farm
8. Circus/Fair
9. Columbus Day
10. Halloween
11. Early Times
12. Thanksgiving
13. Christmas
14. Transportation
15. Telephone
16. Ground Hog Day
17. Abe Lincoln
18. Valentine's Day
19. Washington
20. Texas
21. St. Patrick's Day
22. Zoo
23. Spring
24. Easter
25. Plants
26. Insects
27. Birds
28. Sea
29. Review All Units

Snack Recess 12:55–1:15

1:15–1:35 — HEALTH SAFETY SCIENCE

- Monday: Health
- Tuesday: Safety
- Wednesday: Science
- Thursday: Mr. McGruff's Elementary School Puppet Program
- Friday: Films

1:35–2:20 — CENTERS (Monday, Tuesday & Wed.)

Our centers are:
1. Home
2. Sand
3. Number & Game
4. Science & Library
5. Listening
6. Easel
7. Art
8. Flannelboard Bean Bag Toss Puppet
9. Tree House Puzzles
10. Blocks
11. System 80 Language Master Folder Games

Thursday: The children go to the Elem. Library 1:30–2:10
Librarian reads them a story, then they check out a book to take home

FIGURE 8–2 Brenda McDaniel's Kindergarten Schedule at Evadale Elementary School, Evadale, Texas

the afternoon, so that one teacher can teach two classes. Although many kindergartens are half-day programs, there is not general agreement as to whether this system is best. Those who argue for the half-day session say that this is all the schooling the five-year-old child is ready to experience and that it provides an ideal transition to the all-day first grade. Those in favor of full-day sessions generally feel that not only is the child ready for and capable of a program of this length, but that it also allows for a more comprehensive program.

Regardless, the trend is toward full-day kindergarten programs for all five-year-old children. There are, however, essentially two factors that stand in the way of a more rapid transition to full-day programs—tradition and money. Kindergartens are historically and traditionally half-day programs, although there is ample evidence of full-day programs for four- and five-year-old children. Tradition is usually changed by societal needs and passage of time. So as time passes and as the needs of society begin to point to full-day programs to prepare children for living in an increasingly complex world, more kindergarten programs will become full day.

Money is the most important obstacle to the growth of full-day kindergarten programs. Without a doubt, it takes twice as many teachers to operate full-day programs as half-day programs. But as society continues to recognize the benefits of early education and as kindergartens and early childhood programs are seen as one means for solving societal problems, more funding will be forthcoming.

Individualized learning activities focus on specific needs and abilities and allow teachers to continually assess children's achievement. Individualized attention also helps keep children at the center of the teaching/ learning process. Individualization is an important part of a developmentally appropriate curriculum.

A Day in the Kindergarten at Highland Oaks Elementary School

Jennifer Kirk attends kindergarten in the Highland Oaks Elementary School with 911 other children in grades K–6.[12] The 81 kindergarten children are taught by four teachers, parent volunteers, and a varying number of sixth-grade student helpers. A suite (or pod) is shared by three kindergarten classes and three sixth-grade classes. While each class has its own designated area, no walls separate one area from the other. There are portable screens for arranging a self-contained classroom if the teachers so desire.

The curriculum in the four kindergarten classrooms is the same, using cooperative planning and some team teaching. Each teacher is free to teach in her own way and according to her own teaching style. The management system the four teachers use is the same. Children are grouped randomly at the beginning of the year. Each class consists of three groups, designated the circle group (O), the square group (□), and the triangle group (△), which serve as a basis for reading instruction. The morning is devoted almost entirely to the reading process. While one group is taught a reading lesson by the teacher, the second group does seatwork, and the third group, independent activities.

The program described here occurs in April of the school year, and is a much different program from the kind that would be conducted in September. For example, in September, readiness exercises such as sizes, shapes, and colors would be taught. Before the opening of school, the children are given an orange juice party, at which they meet all the teachers and visit the classroom, while the principal gives their parents school information.

When Jennifer arrives at school at 8:10 A.M. (most of the children come by carpool or walk), she puts her lunch box on a shelf and sits in her designated seat. (At the beginning of the year, the children did not have assigned seats, but could sit wherever they wished; getting to know other children was part of the socialization process.) At 8:30 A.M. the whole school (K–6) participates in opening exercises, announced over the intercom system—the Pledge of Allegiance, the national anthem, school announcements, and birthday announcements. Opening exercises last about twenty minutes.

Jennifer's teacher then conducts a calendar activity with the twenty children sitting on the floor in an arc around her. Days of the week and months of the year are reviewed, and the clock (on the calendar) is set for lunch time. They also talk about what yesterday was and what tomorrow will be. A sharing activity is next. Jennifer brought in a puppet and a book to share. Children are encouraged to share important news, such as the birth of a new brother or sister, going on a trip, a parent's achievement, or a new purchase. They are not allowed to bring toys to share. This time is also used to tell the children about the planned activities for the day. There is always a writing activity on the board. Sometimes this lesson, about which the children will "write" and draw a picture, is written by Jennifer's teacher. The story may be from the basal reader or the children dictate a story or sentence to their teacher.

Jennifer then goes to the reading group. She immediately begins to copy the writing already on the board. When the writing is completed, she will put her paper next to her teacher, who will correct it right away so the children can immediately see their mistakes. Jennifer will then take a SWRL booklet and begin to read silently while she waits for the other children to finish their writing. Reading class lasts about thirty minutes. After reading, Jennifer goes to the seatwork station and draws a picture on the back of the writing paper she previously completed. Afterward, she gets a worksheet, prepared by her teacher, and colors the picture and traces over the letters that make the title for the picture. During this time, Jennifer is free to talk quietly with her friends. When she finishes the writing activity, Jennifer shows the paper to her teacher. The teacher checks quickly to see if it has been completed correctly. If so, Jennifer puts her paper in her folder. Each child has his own folder for his work. By this time of the year, the children are working independently and know the routine of the class, so they know to write their name on all papers, how to fold their papers, and to put them in the folders.

At about 10 A.M., Jennifer goes to the independent activities station, where she can choose from many learning activities. Some of these activities are storybooks, writing with paper and pencil, a cut and paste table, a molding clay table, puzzles, a math table with games, books with numbers, sequence cards, sand box, and housekeeping area and the computer. At about 10:30 A.M., a record is played as the children's signal to clean up. When they have put away the things they were working with, the children sit down quietly at their seats. Jennifer and her classmates go to lunch at 10:40 A.M. While walking to the cafeteria, they sing a song, and hop from stepping-stone to stepping-stone as they go.

Jennifer has a half-hour for lunch. She sits where she wants. This again provides an opportunity for socialization. The children are responsible for cleaning up their eating area. This includes wiping the tables off and picking up papers from the floor. When they are finished, the children line up outside the cafeteria where they are met by their teacher, who also had a thirty-minute lunch period. At 11:15 A.M., Jennifer comes back from lunch. She has about fifteen minutes to go the restroom, rest, or get a drink of water.

At 11:30 A.M., Jennifer begins math. Today the children are reviewing number words. Jennifer's teacher writes f-o-u-r on the board and Jennifer writes the numeral 4 beside it. This procedure is followed for all of the number words. When this activity is completed, the children are given a teacher-made worksheet on which to match numerals with number words. Following math, at 12:10 P.M., the teacher reads stories to the children. The children usually bring the books from home or check them out of the school library. The children will make a picture about one of the stories, and will also write words to help illustrate or tell about the

pictures of their stories. When storytime is over at 12:35 P.M., the children go outside. During this time they have the opportunity to participate in an organized activity conducted by the teacher, or an independent activity such as jumping rope, running races, or reading a book. The children are outside for about half an hour. Today Jennifer plays Farmer in the Dell with her teacher and several classmates. At this time the children are also free to get a drink, go to the restroom, and socialize with other children.

At 1 P.M., Jennifer and her classmates come in. They continue their learning of the sign language alphabet and "signing," a special project of the kindergarten class. Learning sign language was begun only after the children had learned the alphabet. This activity began in January with a visit by a staff member of the local association for the deaf, who introduced the children to sign language and signing. This person also acts as a resource person to the class throughout the year. Jennifer's teacher has the group "sign" the writing lesson, and the activity ends by singing and signing the alphabet in sign language.

At about 1:30 P.M., the kindergarten children get ready to go home. There are announcements of interest to the children over the school intercom. Today, the children are reminded about some of the events for the coming week, and are told to have a good weekend. When the announcements are over, the children clean up their classroom. Getting ready to go home includes passing out papers from their folders and putting their chairs on their tables. Jennifer's teacher sings good-bye to each of the children with a hand puppet. All the children are given a hug and kiss by the puppet. Many of the children also reach up to hug and kiss their teacher.

In Jennifer's classroom, mobiles, pictures, and collages are hung on the walls and from the ceiling. The hangings are made by the children, and are changed monthly. This is one of the ways Jennifer's teacher makes the classroom appealing.

continued.

A Day in the Kindergarten at Highland Oaks Elementary School—continued

Sixth-Grade Student Helpers

Today, one of the helpers in Jennifer's kindergarten is Adam, a sixth-grade student. The fifth- and sixth-grade classes are given an opportunity to help with kindergarten activities during their independent work time. Adam comes to Jennifer's class to read stories, put reading materials in order, and help with other activities. Adam says he likes to work with the kindergarten children because they are nice, easy to work with, and have "good personalities." Adam feels that working with the kindergarten children helps him learn how to work with other people and how to assume responsibility. He also feels it gives him an opportunity to learn things that he doesn't know; for example, during the year, he learned sign language along with the kindergarten children.

Homework

Each child gets one homework assignment each week as part of their reading program. They receive another assignment from their teacher that relates to concepts being taught in class. For example, when studying the sense of touch, a paper on which to attach various textures was sent home for each child. After completion, the paper was returned and displayed in the classroom.

Spanish

Jennifer and her class are taught Spanish for 20 minutes a day, usually right after lunch. (Spanish then takes the place of storytime on the schedule.) A native speaker of Spanish uses only Spanish to speak to the children and the children role play, sing songs, and converse with each other and the teacher. Jennifer learns Spanish quickly, since she is at the sensitive stage for language learning. Her tongue is not stiff, like that of an adult who tries to learn a second language. Jennifer and her classmates are also acquiring an awareness for other people, cultures, and languages.

Computers

The computer curriculum allows children to have fun while learning. Initially, the children are introduced to the parts of the computer through group discussions, matching games, paper-and-pencil activities, and specific computer programs such as *Kids on Keys*. Through individualized instruction, each child learns to load the computer by following simple directions. Commercial software enhances academic skills such as letter and number recognition and reading readiness. Specific programs such as *Kindercomp, Monkey Business,* and *Facemaker* reinforce perceptual skills. The emphasis is on important process areas—visual recognition, memory, sequencing, and reasoning ability. The children's familiarity

FIGURE A   Me and My Mommy

with and enjoyment of the computer results in self-motivated and computer-literate enthusiasts.

Outstanding Features of Jennifer's Kindergarten
The emphasis in Jennifer's kindergarten is on learning the basic skills of reading, writing, and arithmetic. Teaching and learning occur in an academic atmosphere full of fun and joy. The teachers plan for and teach their program well, knowing what they want to accomplish and how they want to accomplish it.

One of the outstanding features of Jennifer's kindergarten program is the great amount of affection and caring shown by teachers and staff for the children in the program. Their caring attitude is reflected in the high level of concern for children's achievement and well-

being. Caring shown to the children is in turn reflected in the kindness, courtesy, and affection children show for each other. Such a high-quality, affective climate provides a humane balance to the basic skills orientation of the program.

The classrooms in which teachers and children live and learn are pleasant to be in, because the teachers and children make them so. Walls and bulletin boards are attractively filled with children's work. The teachers encourage high-quality work for the children, and the children are proud to display their achievements. One child's work is shown in Figures A and B.

FIGURE B   My Family

ASSESSMENT IN THE KINDERGARTEN

Because of federal mandates and state laws, school districts usually evaluate children in some way before or at the time of their entrance into school. Also, some type of screening occurs at the time of kindergarten entrance to evaluate learning readiness. Unfortunately, children are often classified on the basis of how well they perform on these screenings, but when testing is appropriate and when the results are used as a basis for teaching children what they need to learn, it is valuable and worthwhile. There are basically seven purposes of readiness tests:

1. To identify what children know
2. To identify special needs
3. To assist in referral decisions
4. To determine appropriate placement
5. To help develop lesson plans and programs
6. To identify behavioral and developmental levels as opposed to chronological level
7. To inform parents about their children's developmental status

Screening Processes

Screening measures give school personnel a broad picture of what children know and are able to do, as well as their physical and emotional status. As gross indicators of children's abilities, screening procedures provide much useful information for decisions about placement for initial instruction, referral to other agencies, and what additional testing may be necessary to pinpoint a learning or health problem. Many school districts conduct a comprehensive screening program in the spring for children who will enter kindergarten in the fall. Screening can involve:

☐ Gathering parent information about health, learning patterns, learning achievements, personal habits, and special problems
☐ Health screening, including a physical examination, health history, and a blood sample for analysis
☐ Vision, hearing, and speech screening
☐ Collecting and analyzing data from former programs and teachers, such as preschools and child care programs
☐ Administering a cognitive and/or behavioral screening instrument

Comprehensive screening programs are conducted in one day or over several days. Data for each child are usually evaluated by a team of professionals who make instructional placement recommendations and, when appropriate, referrals and recommendations for additional testing and to other agencies for assistance.

Screening Instruments

Many screening instruments provide information for grouping and for planning instructional strategies. Most screening instruments can be administered by people who do not have specialized training in test administration. Parent volunteers often help administer screening instruments, many of which can be administered in about thirty minutes.

BRIGANCE® K and 1 Screen.   The BRIGANCE® K and 1 Screen is an evaluation instrument for use in kindergarten and grade 1. The Kindergarten Pupil Data Sheet for the BRIGANCE® K and 1 Screen is shown in Figure 8–3. This sheet shows the skills, behaviors and concepts evaluated in the kindergarten portion of the screening instrument. Samples of test items and directions for administration are shown in Figures 8–4 and 8–5.

DIAL-R.   The DIAL-R (Developmental Indicators for the Assessment of Learning-Revised) is a screening instrument for use with prekindergarten children. It is team-administered and involves individual observation for motor skills, concepts, and language skills. The DIAL-R requires approximately 25–30 minutes to administer. The DIAL-R scoresheet is shown in Figure 8–6. The DIAL-R is designed for screening large numbers of children. The screening team consists of a coordinator, an operator for each of the skills areas screened, and aides or volunteers to register parents and children.

Developmentally Appropriate Assessment

There is a great deal of controversy in the early childhood professions about appropriate and inappropriate uses of assessment. According to the National Association for the Education of Young Children, developmentally appropriate assessment of young children should incorporate the following features:

Decisions that have a major impact on children, such as enrollment, retention, or placement, are not made on the basis of a single developmental assessment or screening device, but must take into account other relevant information, particularly observations by teacher and parents.

Developmental assessment of children's progress and achievements is used to adapt curriculum to match developmental needs, to communicate with the child's family, and to evaluate the program's effectiveness.

Developmental assessments and observations are used to identify children who have special needs and/or who are at risk and to plan appropriate curriculum for them.

Developmental expectations based on standardized measurements and norms should compare any child or group of children only to normative information that is not only age-matched, but also gender-, culture-, and socioeconomically appropriate.

In public schools, there should be a developmentally appropriate placement for every child of legal entry age.[13]

COMPUTERS IN THE KINDERGARTEN

Children often come to kindergarten computer-literate, and many are more knowledgeable than their teachers. There is no longer a question of whether we should provide computer-literacy activities in the kindergarten; it is a question of how much and what kind. While some early childhood educators argue that kindergarten children are not developmentally ready for the skills and processes required for computer

BRIGANCE® Pupil Data Sheet

A. Student's Name: Colin Killoran
Parents/Guardian: Kristin and Edmund Killoran
Address: 310 Locke Street

	Year	Month	Day
Date of Screening	81	6	15
Birthdate	76	5	5
Age	5	5	0

School/Program: Vinal School
Teacher: Leslie Feingold
Assessor: Dennis Dowd

B. BASIC SCREENING ASSESSMENTS

Page	Assessment Number	Skill (Circle the skill for each correct response and make notes as appropriate.)	C. SCORING — Number of Correct Responses	Point Value	Student's Score
2	1	**Personal Data Response:** Verbally gives: ① first name ② full name ③ age 4. address (street or mail) 5. birthdate (month and day)	3 ×	2 points each	6/10
3	2	**Color Recognition:** Identifies and names the colors: ① red ② blue ③ green ④ yellow ⑤ orange 6. purple ⑦ brown ⑧ black ⑨ pink 10. gray	8 ×	1 point each	8/10
5	3	**Picture Vocabulary:** Recognizes and names picture of: ① dog ② cat ③ key ④ girl ⑤ boy ⑥ airplane ⑦ apple 8. leaf ⑨ cup 10. car	8 ×	1 point each	8/10
6	4A	**Visual Discrimination:** Visually discriminates which one of four symbols is different: ① ○ ② □ ③ ○ ④ ○ ⑤ ○ ⑥ O 7. I ⑧ P 9. V 10. X	7 ×	1 point each	7/10
8	5	**Visual-Motor Skills:** Copies: ① ○ ② − ③ + ④ □ 5. △	4 ×	2 pts. ea.	8/10
9	6	**Gross Motor Skills:** ① Hops 2 hops on one foot. ② Hops 2 hops on either foot. ③ Stands on one foot momentarily. 8 Walks backward toe and heel 4 steps. ⑤ Stands on either foot for 5 seconds. ⑥ Stands on either foot for 5 secs. ⑦ Walks forward heel and toe 4 steps. 8 Walks backward toe and heel 4 steps. ⑤ Stands on one foot for 5 seconds. 10 Stands on either foot momentarily with eyes closed. ⑨ Stands on one foot momentarily with eyes closed.	8 ×	1 point each	8/10
12	8	**Rote Counting:** Counts by rote to: (Circle all numerals prior to the first error.) ① ② ③ ④ ⑤ ⑥ 7 8 9 10	6 ×	.5 point each	3/5
13	9	**Identification of Body Parts:** Identifies by pointing or touching: ① chin ② fingernails ③ heel ④ elbow ⑤ ankle ⑥ shoulder ⑦ jaw 8 hips ⑨ wrist 10 waist	8 ×	.5 point each	4/5
15	11	**Follows Verbal Directions:** Listens to, remembers, and follows: ① one verbal direction 2. two verbal directions	1 ×	2.5 points each	2.5/5
17	12	**Numeral Comprehension:** Matches quantity with numerals. ② ① ④ ③ 5	4 ×	2 pts. ea.	8/10
21	15	**Prints Personal Data:** Prints first name Reversals: Yes No ✓	1 ×	5 points	5/5
22	16	**Syntax and Fluency:** ① Speech is understandable. ② Speaks in complete sentences.	2 ×	5 pts. ea.	10/10

Total Score 77.5 /100

D. OBSERVATIONS:

1. Handedness: Right ✓ Left ___ Uncertain ___
2. Pencil grasp: Correct ✓ Incorrect ___
3. Maintained paper in the proper position when writing: Yes ___ No ✓
4. Record other observations below or on the back.

Cooperative had difficulty attending to verbal directions and relied on visual clues

E. SUMMARY: (Compared to other students included in this screening)

1. this student scored: _____ Lower
2. this student's age is: _____ Younger
3. the teacher rates this student: _____ Lower
4. the assessor rates this student: _____ Lower

Average ✓ Higher
Average ✓ Older
Average ___ Higher ✓
Average ✓ Higher

F. RECOMMENDATIONS:

Place in: Preschool ___ Low Kindergarten ___ Average Kindergarten ✓ High Kindergarten ___

Other (Indicate) _____

Refer for: (Indicate if needed.) ask nurse to check hearing

FIGURE 8–3 BRIGANCE® Pupil Data Sheet

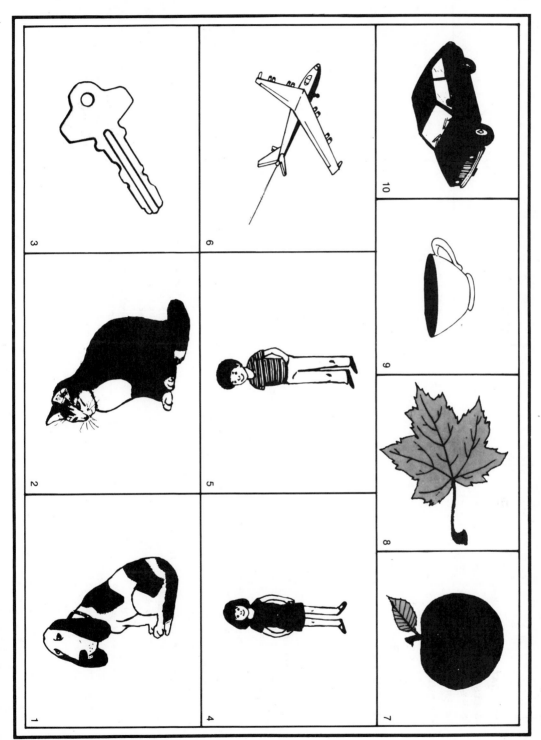

FIGURE 8–4 BRIGANCE® Picture Vocabulary Screening Instrument

Source: © 1987, Curriculum Associates, Inc., reproduced by permission of the publisher.

SKILL: Recognizes and names pictures commonly used in readiness material.

1. dog	2. cat	3. key	4. girl	5. boy
6. airplane	7. apple	8. leaf	9. cup	10. car

PUPIL DATA SHEETS: Kindergarten and First Grade.

ASSESSMENT METHOD: Student performance—individual oral response.

MATERIAL: S-5.

DISCONTINUE: After two consecutive errors.

TIME: Your discretion. Five seconds per picture is recommended.

ACCURACY: Give credit for each correct response.

POINT VALUES: Kindergarten: 1 point each.
First grade: .5 point each.

NOTES:

1. **Possible Observations:** As the student names the pictures, you may wish to observe for the following:

   a. *Articulation Problems:* Are any sounds omitted, substituted, or distorted? See "Articulation of Sounds" on pages S-27 and 27.

   b. *Focusing Difficulties:* Does the student appear to have difficulty focusing on one picture because of being distracted by the other pictures? See **NOTE #5.**

   c. *Interest:* Does the student appear to have an interest in looking at and talking about the pictures? Does the student want to talk about a particular picture?

   d. *Syntax and Fluency:* Is the student's speech understandable and are some of the responses in sentences? See "Syntax and Fluency" on page 22.

2. **Supplemental Assessments:** The pictures may be used to informally assess the student's comprehension and language development. This may be accomplished by asking questions such as the following:

   a. Which two are pets?
   b. Which two are people?
   c. Which two grow on trees?
   d. Which two can we ride in?
   e. Which two have four legs?
   f. Which two can talk?
   g. Why do we have keys? airplanes? cars? cups?
   h. Which ones do you have at home?

DIRECTIONS: This assessment is made by pointing to each picture on S-5 and asking the student to name it.

Point to each picture and

Ask: **What is this?** or **What do you call it?**

Give encouragement if needed.

3. **Assessing the Student with Limited Speech or Who Is Reluctant to Respond Verbally:** If there is difficulty in getting the student to respond verbally, you may wish to ask the student to point to each picture as you name it.

4. **Referencing:** The objects used in this assessment are common to the reading readiness materials of the following publishers:

   Addison-Wesley Reading Program. Reading, Mass.: Addison-Wesley Publishing Company, Inc., 1979.
   HBJ Bookmark Reading. New York: Harcourt Brace Jovanovich, Inc., 1979.
   The Houghton Mifflin Reading Series. Boston: Houghton Mifflin Company, 1979.
   Pathfinder. Boston: Allyn and Bacon, Inc., 1979.
   Reading 720 Rainbow Edition. Lexington, Mass.: Ginn and Company, 1979.
   Scott, Foresman Reading. Glenview, Ill.: Scott, Foresman and Company, 1981.
   Series r. New York: Macmillan Publishing Company, 1980.
   Young American Basic Series. Skokie, Ill.: Rand McNally and Company, 1978.

5. **Screen if Needed:** If it appears that the student is having difficulty focusing on one item at a time because of the visual stimuli of the entire page, you should cover the other items on the page by using blank sheets of paper.

6. **Advanced Skills:** The "Response to Picture" assessment on page 26 in the Advanced Section assesses more advanced skills. You may wish to use it to informally assess the skill level of the more capable student.

FIGURE 8–5   BRIGANCE® Picture Vocabulary Screening Instrument

Source: © 1987, Curriculum Associates, Inc., reproduced by permission of the publisher.

DIAL-R
SCORESHEET

Child's Name _____
LAST   FIRST   NICKNAME

Address _____
NUMBER   STREET   CITY/STATE/ZIP

Phone Number (____) _____
AREA CODE

Parents' Names
MOTHER   FATHER
1 2 3   Language

School _____
Class _____

Today's Date _____
Birth Date _____
C.A. _____

YEAR   MONTH   DAY

Hearing + —
Vision + —

Boy ___ Girl ___

MOTOR (red)

	SCALED SCORE			
	0 under 2 yrs.	1 2-3 yrs.	2 3-4 yrs.	3 4-5 yrs.	4 5-6 yrs.
1. Catching	0	—	1	2	3
2. Jumping, Hopping, and Skipping	0	1-2	3-8	9-12	13-16
jumps: 0 1					
+ hops: (right) 0 1 2 3 4 5 6					
+ hops: (left) 0 1 2 3 4 5 6					
+ skip:					
0-any 1-slide 2-step/hop 3-skip					
3. Building	0	1	2	3	4
4. Touching Fingers	0	1	2	3	4
5. Cutting	0-1	1-7	8-9	10-11	12
6. Matching	0	1-7	8-11	12-18	19-24
I O + □ ◇ E 0 1 2 N 0 1 2 D 0 1 2 S 0 1 2 ≠ 0 1 2 ≠ 0 1 2					
7. Copying	0	—	1	2	
8. Writing Name	0	—	—	1	2

TOTAL (Max.=31)

OBSERVATIONS
1 2 3 4 5 6 7 8

CONCEPTS (green)

	SCALED SCORE				
	0 under 2 yrs.	1 2-3 yrs.	2 3-4 yrs.	3 4-5 yrs.	4 5-6 yrs.
1. Naming Colors	0	1-7	8-15	16-18	
R O W G BL Y B BR P					
2. Identifying Body Parts	0	1-9	10-12	13-15	16-18
nose neck chin ankle hair stomach shoulder hip ear knee chest waist teeth thumb heel tongue elbow wrist					
3. Counting (Meaningful)	0-2	3-4	5-8	9-10	11
4. Counting (Rote)	0	1	3	5-7	9
1 3 5 7 9					
5. Positioning	0	1-2	3	4	5
on under corner between middle					
6. Identifying Concepts	0	1-14	15-20	21-26	27-28
biggest big hot empty night long longest more most fast fastest little littlest cold day short shortest less least slow slowest					
7. Naming Letters	0	—	—	1-10	11-16
O B P E R W Y G					
8. Sorting Chips	0	—	—	1-4	5-8
by color: R B Y by size: big little by shape: ○ □ △					

TOTAL (Max.=31)

OBSERVATIONS
1 2 3 4 5 6 7 8

LANGUAGE (purple)

	SCALED SCORE				
	0 under 2 yrs.	1 2-3 yrs.	2 3-4 yrs.	3 4-5 yrs.	4 5-6 yrs.
1. Articulating	0	1-14	15-26	27-29	
pin truck rabbit dress bed chair cup knife sandwich towel thumb leg mouth/teeth hand fish					
2. Giving Personal Data	0	1-3	4	5	6-7
first name sex phone # last name street age city/state					
3. Remembering	0	1-3	4-5	6-7	8-9
clapping A B C numbers A B C sentences A B C					
4. Naming Nouns	0	1-15	16	17	18
cat phone comb plane TV pencil car clock ambulance					
5. Naming Verbs	0	1-9	10-14	15-16	17-18
sleep call comb fly watch write drive time go to hospital					
6. Classifying Foods	0	1-2	3-4	5-6	7-8
Tally_____					
7. Problem Solving	0	1	2-3	4-5	6-8
hungry 0 1 2 dark room 0 1 2 rain 0 1 2 broken 0 1 2					
8. Sentence Length	0	1-2	3	4	5-8

TOTAL (Max.=31)

OBSERVATIONS
1 2 3 4 5 6 7 8

Motor score _____
Concepts score _____
Language score _____
Total score _____
# of Observations _____

(see page 58 for Cut-off Points by Area Scores)
(see page 15 for Cut-off Points by Total Score)
(see page 50 for Cut-off Points by Observations)

DECISION

CHILDCRAFT
EDUCATION CORP

Copyright © 1983 Carol Mardell-Czudnowski and Dorothea S. Goldenberg. All rights reserved.

FIGURE 8-6 DIAL-R Scoresheet
Source: Carol Mardell-Czudnowski and Dorothea S. Goldenberg, DIAL-R Scoresheet. Edison, N.J.: ChildCraft Corp., 1983. Reproduced by permission.

273

use, others think just the opposite. Three researchers examined how computer use in the home and kindergarten affected children's readiness skills. The kindergartners in the program received one hour a week of instruction in the areas of reading readiness, mathematics, Piagetian cognitive operations, and keyboard skills. The researchers found large gains in reading readiness and keyboard skills, but little gain in math readiness and Piagetian operations. The findings were somewhat affected by the greater availability of software in reading readiness and keyboard skills than in the other two areas. Also, children who had use of computers in their homes and school did better than those who had use of computers only in school. The researchers concluded: "We found no indication that computing experiences interfere with the normal cognitive development of preschoolers."[14]

Two basic goals for computer literacy in the kindergarten should be to have children learn what computers are and to learn to use them. Objectives of a kindergarten computer literacy program should include the following:

☐ Naming the different parts of a computer
☐ Telling what a computer does and what it can be used for
☐ Loading and running a basic software program

Computer literacy and involvement with computers should begin in the preschool and continue in kindergarten. Children can learn many skills and concepts with computers.

☐ Using the computer keyboard to operate a software program
☐ Typing words and a simple story using a word-processor software program

These objectives should be integrated with normal classroom activities. For example, children can listen to stories about computers, take a field trip to a business that uses computers, make a computer model in the art center, cut out letters from magazines and make a computer keyboard, and use a typewriter to write their names.

READING IN THE KINDERGARTEN

Most elementary schools and many kindergartens focus on reading readiness and teaching reading. Students and teachers spend much of their time and energy in this process and related activities. Methods of organizing the classroom, such as grouping and scheduling, are frequently based on reading, and social patterns are often established according to membership in reading groups.

Learning to read in kindergarten and the primary grades is not an unreasonable expectation, and children look forward to it. Parents assume that when their children enter school, they will be taught to read. Learning to read is not only a social dictate, it is an academic necessity; how well a child reads often determines how successful he is in school. But with the greater emphasis on early schooling and basic skills, the teaching of reading is being pushed down to the kindergarten. Many parents and early childhood educators question a number of factors associated with early reading: first, its appropriateness and advisability; second, the teaching methods; and third, the pressure on children and the consequent stress it can cause.

Effective Approaches

As a first step in teaching, teachers should demystify the reading process. Many teachers do a good job of teaching reading through processes and procedures that are easy to understand and implement, and which can lead to a child's almost spontaneous ability to read. Activities that interest children can be a means for teaching them to read. Performances, storytelling, writing, conversations with peers and adults, and field trips provide a natural approach that can be *supplemented* by reading instruction. Reading is, after all, an *extension* of oral language and writing.

We must also stop making nonreaders of children by asking them to perform reading tasks and activities they are not capable of. A child does not suddenly develop a reading problem in kindergarten or first grade; reading problems occur when children come to school and are confronted with tasks for which they are not developmentally ready. The Texas Association for the Education of Young Children has issued descriptions of developmentally *appropriate* and *inappropriate* kindergarten reading programs. These are the recommendations for an appropriate program:

1. Young children learn through experiences that provide for all of the developmental needs—physical, socioemotional, as well as intellectual.
2. Young children learn through self-selected activities while participating in a variety of centers which are interesting and meaningful to them. (Learning Centers include: socio-dramatic, block, science, math, manipulatives, listening, reading, writing, art, music, and construction.)

Turtle in the Kindergarten*

Five-year-old Jane has just finished an activity-time lesson during which she has drawn a picture of something she likes to climb—she has made a picture of the climbing bar. Then she goes to a corner of the room called "The Turtle's Corner" where there are three computers and a large chart displaying the commands for operating the computer program. She is going to draw her picture on the computer.

Since the beginning of the school year, Jane has been using an Apple II-E computer and a series of commands to make a small white triangle, called a turtle, move forward and right on the computer screen. She has been using a Logo program called Instant to draw squares, half-circles, and rectangles. Her teacher has programmed the system so Jane and her classmates can make the turtle execute one of these commands simply by pressing one key. Today she is ready to start to draw on the computer screen a picture about something she likes to do at school.

Jane has in front of her the Instant chart that gives all the commands for the computer program. If Jane makes a mistake as she draws her picture, she presses the "U" key, a command that erases the entire picture and redraws it except for the mistaken last step. Jane finishes in ten or fifteen minutes. Her teacher saves the picture on a disk and will print it for Jane to use as an illustration in a book she is writing about what she does in the classroom.

Other days, Jane makes designs or patterns. Earlier in the year, when the class was studying farms, she made a picture of a lamb. Her friend, Rob, made a horse, and Claire drew a barn. All the classmates' pictures were put into a farm book, and each child received a copy of the book.

When Jane is not using the Instant program on the computer, she and Claire choose to move the "floor turtle," or robot, around the floor, using commands similar to those she used to move the screen turtle. They instruct the robot to visit some pictures that they and their classmates have painted, or direct it through a tunnel and make its eyes blink on the way. Or, Jane and Claire use its touch sensors to let it work its way through a maze that Pat and Rob built.

Some days Jane uses the Puppet Theatre program that the class is piloting for some researchers at MIT. Here she and Rob choose the puppets' clothes and the background

3. Young children are encouraged to talk about their experiences with other children and adults in the classroom.
4. Young children are involved in a variety of psychomotor experiences, including music, rhythms, movement, large and small motor manipulatives and outdoor activity.
5. Young children are provided with many opportunities to interact in meaningful print contexts: listening to stories, participating in shared book experiences, making language experience stories and books, developing key word vocabularies, reading classroom labels, and using print in the various learning centers.

And this is the description of an inappropriate program:

1. Formal kindergarten reading programs usually focus upon whole group instruction in visual-motor and phonics lessons with commercially prepared workbooks and ditto sheets.
2. Formal kindergarten reading programs usually include reading instruction in a basal reading series. This process frequently involves the learning of *rules* with emphasis upon the *form* rather than the *meaning* of written language.

scene. Next, they write a dialogue for the puppets on the screen. She and Rob have fun experimenting with sounds and their own invented spelling to write the words. The computer says the words as they sound phonetically, and Jane laughs when a word sounds different from what she expected. She may try other invented spelling for the misspelled word or she simply continues with the dialogue. When the dialogue is finished, Jane and Rob print it out and enjoy reading it to each other and their classmates. Jane's teacher prefers Puppet Theatre to other early writing and talking programs because, rather than using a controlled vocabulary, Jane is able to write and hear any combination of letters she chooses. The immediate feedback lets Jane know just what the letter combinations sound like and allows her to learn by experimenting and discovery. The program offers Jane a great deal of flexibility, and at the same time, gives her control over her own learning.

On other days, Jane uses pieces of commercial software the teacher has chosen for the class, after carefully reviewing many software programs.

For their reading readiness work, Jane and her classmates are often given an opportunity to write a story on the computer using the word-processing capability of Logowriter. At first Jane's stories were very short — only one line, in fact—but now she often writes six or eight lines, using invented spelling with ease. She especially enjoys illustrating her stories, reading them to her classmates, and then taking them home to read to her family.

Each of the twenty-three children in the kindergarten gets a turn to use the computer before anyone can have a second turn. In this way, everyone has equal access to this powerful teaching and learning tool.

Jane's teacher has chosen Logo for the computer program because it allows the children to be in control. They draw the pictures and graphics they want to draw. Logo is an excellent way to teach computer skills. Jane's teacher also feels she can learn a lot about the children's learning styles and how they solve problems by how they approach drawing their pictures.

*Contributed by Louisa Birch, a kindergarten teacher at Meadowbrook School, Weston, Massachusetts.

3. A formal kindergarten reading program often requires children to sit for inappropriately long blocks of time in teacher-directed activities with overemphasis upon table work and fine motor skills.
4. A formal kindergarten reading program focuses upon isolated skill-oriented experiences which include repetition and memorization.[15]

LITERACY AND THE NATION'S CHILDREN

Literacy is an "in" word; we hear it in virtually all educational circles, and almost every early childhood educator is talking about how to promote it. It has replaced reading readiness as the primary objective of many kindergarten and primary programs. *Literacy* means the ability to read, write, speak, and listen, with emphasis on reading and writing well. To be literate also means reading, writing, speaking, and listening within the context of one's cultural and social setting.

Literacy is a hot topic in educational circles for a number of reasons. First, it is estimated that over 50 million Americans are functionally illiterate—at or below a fifth-grade reading level. Furthermore, when we compare the U.S. literacy rate to that of other countries, we don't fare too well—many industrialized countries have higher literacy rates than the U.S. Consequently, educators and social policy planners are always concerned about the inability of the schools to teach all children to read at more than a functional level.

Second, as we discussed in Chapter 1, businesses and industry are concerned about how unprepared the nation's work force is to meet the demands of the workplace. Critics of the educational establishment maintain that many high school graduates don't have the basic literacy skills required for many of today's high-tech jobs. Therefore, schools, especially at the early grades, are feeling the pressure to adopt measures that will give future citizens the skills they will need for productive work and meaningful living.

A third reason for the interest in children's literacy relates to a theme that recurs often in this book—the pendulum of change. Every fifteen or twenty years or so, a wave of reform sweeps the public schools. Usually reform movements contain elements of previous movements, as is the case with literacy. Many of the practices advocated in the name of making the nation literate are those used in and advocated by the open education movement of several decades ago.

Cultural and Social Processes

Literacy is also viewed as a process that involves *both* cognitive and social activities. Presently, many reading and writing practices focus primarily on the cognitive—they are designed to give children mental skills such as word recognition or sound/word relationships. Teachers teach children to read using methods such as whole-word and phonetic analysis; these methods constitute the major portion of the reading program. Reading and writing are frequently taught as isolated, separate subjects and skills. Furthermore, reading and writing are often taught in ways that give them little meaning to children. Treating reading and writing as processes and skills that are separate from children's daily and immediate lives can lead to failure and retention.

Emergent literacy themes, however, emphasize using the environment and social contexts to support and extend children's reading and writing. Children want to make sense of what they read and write. The meaningful part of reading and writing occurs when children talk to each other, write letters to grandparents and others, and read good literature or have it read to them. All of this occurs within a print-rich environment; one in which the child sees others read, make lists, and use language and the written word to achieve goals. Proponents of whole language maintain that this environment is highly preferable to dry drills or stereotypical sentences in a basic reading book, such as "Look, Amy, look."

Emergent Literacy

Today, early childhood educators use the term *emergent literacy* when talking about reading, writing, speaking, and listening. They use this term because it is now fashionable for educators to view literacy as a process that begins at birth, and perhaps before, especially when you consider the effects of parents' literacy status on their children's literacy. Thus, with the first cry, children are considered to be beginning the process of language development. This viewpoint takes literacy as a never ending process, a continuum across the school years and into adulthood. The process of becoming literate is also viewed as a *natural* process; reading and writing are processes that children participate in naturally, long before they come to school. No doubt you have participated with or know of toddlers and preschoolers who are literate in many ways. They "read" all kinds of signs (McDonalds) and labels (Campbell's Soup) and scribble with and on anything and everything.

The concept of emergent literacy, then, is based on the following beliefs about literacy and about how children learn:

☐ Reading and writing involve cognitive and social abilities that children employ in the processes of becoming literate and gaining meaning from reading, writing, speaking, and listening.

☐ Most children begin processes involved in reading and writing long before they come to school; they do not wait until someone teaches them. They should not have to wait to be taught. (Remember what Montessori said about early literacy.)

☐ Literacy is a social process that develops within a context where children have the opportunity to interact with and respond to printed language and to other children and adults who are using printed language. In this context, children bring meaning to and derive meaning from reading and writing. Teachers and classrooms should encourage discussing and sharing knowledge and ideas through reading and writing.

☐ The cultural group in which children develop literacy influences how literacy develops and the form it takes. Children should also have opportunities to read the literature of many cultural groups in addition to their own.

Whole Language

Literacy is certainly a worthy national and educational goal. But how do educators go about accomplishing this agenda? The practice of choice in many school districts is the use of "whole language" approaches to reading, writing, and speaking. *Whole language* is the use of all aspects of language—reading, writing, listening, and speaking—in the process of becoming literate. Children learn about reading and writing by speaking and listening; they learn to read by writing; and they learn to write by reading. These are common practices in implementing the whole language approach.

The use of *assisted reading,* in which the teacher first reads a story to the children, then on the second and following readings, pauses to allow the children to predict words and phrases. This process is repeated until children are reading the story themselves.

Making literacy *child-centered,* whereby reading and writing are purposeful and meaningful to the children.

Accepting children's errors as indicators of their developing literacy rather than of their failure to read and write. As they write, for example, teachers encourage children to spell words as they think they should be spelled. "Invented spelling" is part of the language learning process, based on the theory that it is acceptable for a child to orally misread a word as long as comprehension and meaning is maintained.

The use of *"quality" literature* that is interesting and exciting as both a motivation for reading and as a model for children's own writing.

WRITING TO READ*

Writing to Read is a multidimensional computer-based reading and writing program for kindergarten and first grade students. It combines advanced technology with educational techniques based on extensive research to provide an active and motivating learning system. Developed by Dr. John Henry Martin, an educator who has worked in the area of children's learning for more than thirty-five years, Writing to Read is based on the premise that children best learn to read by being taught how to write. With this program, young children learn to write what they can say and read what they have written. The program builds on a child's natural language growth, which typically includes a 2000- to 4000-word vocabulary when entering kindergarten. In many traditional programs, the kindergartner is expected to learn to read only six to eight words, but in Writing to Read, the child is able to write any word in his vocabulary in a "risk-free" environment.

This instructional method builds writing and reading skills before a youngster has mastered all the intricacies of spelling. A phonemic spelling system is used in which the sounds of spoken English are represented by a selected set of forty-two phonemes. To learn these phonemes, five learning stations are provided that address visual, auditory, and tactile modalities. Once a child has learned these phonemes, he can write anything he can say. Children can write and read motivating words such as *tyrannosaurus rex, boa constrictor,* or *skateboarding*. A distinction is made between

*Contributed by Kathie W. Dobberteen, kindergarten teacher, South Bay Union School District, Imperial Beach, CA.

invented spelling and standard spelling, but while in the Writing to Read Center, children spell words the way they sound without worrying about correct spelling. Children make a natural transition to conventional spelling as they read standard spelling in textbooks and literature.

There are a number of expected outcomes for children involved in this program. First, children become fluent and productive writers. Students are expected to write words, sentences, or stories every day while in the Center. By the end of first grade, a number of children are writing multichapter books in several writing styles. They are able to communicate in ways that were not possible before Writing to Read. Children become confident about their writing ability, and writing becomes a part of their basic repertoire of skills at a very young age. With this advanced competence, children are able to write across the curriculum, which enhances learning throughout the school day. They develop a greater curiosity about language because they can use any of the words they have heard spoken and are not restricted to the small vocabulary in the basal text.

Five learning stations work together to provide an active and motivating learning environment. The stations include Computer, Work Journal, Writing/Typing, Listening Library, and Make Words.

We'll follow a typical kindergarten child during her daily hour in the Writing to Read Center. Cecilia began the program in December after a two-week orientation. She is in a class of 33 kindergarten children in South Bay Union School District, located in California on the

The use of *predictable reading material;* for example, in the book *Goodnight Moon,* the phrase "goodnight moon" appears repeatedly throughout the text, so that when teachers and parents read this book to children, they can pause to let the children finish the pattern: "goodnight chair, . . . " after which the child should—and usually does—respond "goodnight moon."

The *integration of language with all subject areas,* so that children read and write across the curriculum—in science, social studies, math, and other areas—not just during reading class.

Amanda Torres and her teacher, Kathie Dobberteen, at the Writing to Read Center. Today's teachers emphasize writing as a means of promoting reading and overall literacy development.

Mexican border in the most southwesterly corner of the U.S. The district has a substantial percentage of low-income, single-parent families, as well as a high level of limited English-speaking students. (Students who are being taught in Spanish participate in the Spanish version of Writing to Read called Voy a Leer Escribiendo, or VALE.) Despite these circumstances, South Bay has high expectations for all students, and six of its 12

schools are represented as State of California Distinguished Schools.

The Writing to Read Center is located in a separate room not far from the kindergarten. Mrs. Dobberteen, Cecilia's teacher, had already passed out the small consumable books called Work Journals to all the children in the classroom before they entered the Center. The children have been assigned their first station while in the classroom, so they walk into Writing

Writing is used as a way to help children communicate, with emphasis on helping children make sense of what they write rather than on the mechanics of writing.

The use of a *thematic approach,* such as "Who Am I," to provide a context for language learning and a means of integrating all the content areas. (In this particular theme, use science to explain their circulatory systems and math to determine their average heart rates.)

WRITING TO READ—continued

to Read and proceed directly to that station to begin work. Cecilia and her partner John have been assigned first to the Computer Station. Ms. Allas, the lab assistant, has already loaded the correct disk into the computer. At this station, Cecilia will interact with her partner while responding to instruction given by the computer "voice." The computer will instruct the partners to say and type the sounds of one of the 30 words included in the ten instructional cycles. Cecilia will work at this station for approximately 15 minutes, which provides enough repetition to learn the sounds in a Cycle Word such as "cat." Sometimes at this station, the partners work on several other pieces of software included in the program. These include "Silly Sentences," in which children practice correct spelling and sentence structure by typing amusing sentences such as, "Did you ever see a pig in a bed?" and two motivating games.

After Cecilia and John have completed their Cycle Words at the Computer Station, they proceed to the Work Journal Station. Here they listen to a taped lesson that reinforces the sounds they have just learned in the software program. They write sounds and words in their Work Journal. After the partners have completed the Computer and Work Journal Stations, they are free to choose their next station. An important goal of the Writing to Read program is to help children become responsible for their own learning. Independent movement from station to station is one of the ten Vital Practices that make up a model Writing to Read Center.

Cecilia decides she would like to write something on the computer today, so she goes to the typing section of the Writing/Typing Station, which contains eight word-processing computers. She finds her own story disk and loads it into the computer. She just recently had a birthday and wants to write about the ring she received as a gift. Cecilia is a very independent kindergartner and writes her story without assistance. When she has finished, she prints her story on the printer, removes her disk, and puts it away. The next stop is the Writing Table, where Cecilia proudly reads her story to Mrs. Dobberteen. Cecilia receives a lot of specific praise for her creation, but no red pencil marks, because this is a risk-free environment where children do assisted self-editing. (See Figure A.)

Mrs. Dobberteen asks Cecilia if she can post her wonderful story on the board. Today, permission is granted, although most of the time a second story has to be printed for posting because boys and girls want to take their stories home to read to their parents.

Cecilia has just enough time to go the the Make Words Station where she can choose manipulatives to form words. Today she chooses letter stamps and a stamp pad to write her mom a note. She stamps "I love you, Mom" and draws lots of hearts around the edge of the paper.

There are usually groans when Mrs. Dobberteen signals that it is time to clean up the Center to go back to the classroom. Children, while actively learning, are having a great deal of fun because in this system, they become producers rather than consumers. Dr. Grignon, the superintendent of South Bay, says

To support whole language learning, classroom procedures include these:

☐ Providing quality literature: books, poems, and other types of language arts activities

☐ Pointing out uses of print materials, such as lists, books, greeting cards, magazines, menus, and phone books

☐ Journal writing

☐ Labeling classroom objects

☐ Having children dictate stories that are written down and reread to them

FIGURE A   Cecilia's Story

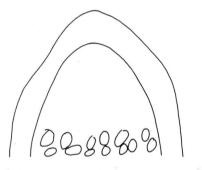

cecilia June 9 a roobe is red and a
dimin is cler sum peple find dimins
in cavs and in tunls and mostle
dimins go with enetes I hav regs with
dimins and i dont wair them becus
thair icspensiv and tha fol vair ese
the end

☐ Encouraging children to write, draw, and label their work
☐ Establishing an environment that encourages talking, listening, and interpretation of written and oral language

Implications of Whole Language

Whole language has a number of implications for children and early childhood teachers. First, whole language represents a move away from subject-centered basic skills approaches to reading, writing, and learning. This leads to a second implication—

WRITING TO READ—continued

Writing to Read is one of his favorite places to visit because children are usually so involved they don't pay attention when visitors enter the Center—except to ask them to listen to their stories.

Tomorrow, when the class comes to Writing to Read, Cecilia will probably be assigned to the Listening Library Station first because she did not have time to go to that station today. At this station, she will listen to high-quality children's literature while tracking the story in the book. This process helps to reinforce the sound-symbol relationship in context and in learning standard spelling because children see correct spelling in the books. Cecilia will also have a chance to go to the Writing Table, which is part of the Writing/Typing Station. Here, she will work with pencil and paper while Mrs. Dobberteen encourages her writing. She can also illustrate her writing or work on different sections of her Work Journal. In addition to these two stations, she will probably return to the Computer and Work Journal with her partner.

Mrs. Dobberteen sees many strengths in the Writing to Read program. First, it provides for all the readiness levels of the students in her kindergarten class by encouraging developmentally appropriate activities that can be adjusted to meet students' needs. Self-esteem is enhanced because children are not categorized into high, middle, and low groups, and because students develop a "can do" attitude. Youngsters can progress and review at their own rate because the computer allows for individualized learning. In an area of high transience such as South Bay, it allows a child to come into the program and be placed immediately at an appropriate level of instruction. Mrs. Dobberteen says it is wonderful to watch children become so enthusiastic about breaking the alphabetic code while they are writing and reading about things that are important to them. Many smiles and hugs are given in this exciting environment.

Mrs. Dobberteen also points out that several challenges have arisen in implementing the Writing to Read Program in South Bay. The first is that, as exciting and motivating as they are, computers will not teach writing and reading on their own. They work in tandem with a well-trained and committed teacher who understands the philosophy of the program and follows the model of the system. It allows children to soar into the stratosphere in terms of reading and writing, but takes a lot of down-to-earth work to make it happen.

The second challenge is a result of the effectiveness of the program. South Bay has found that the philosophy- and language-rich environment must be continued throughout the grades; this cannot be a program just for kindergarten and first grade. In South Bay Union School District, this problem has been solved by installing a distributed network that provides three computers in every second through sixth grade classroom. The computers are linked to a central file server in the Writing to Read Center. Every student spends 20 minutes per day on the computer using a variety of software.

that whole language is child-centered, not subject-centered. Third, "good" literature is used to help children learn to read and write. Fourth is a deemphasis on phonics instruction as a primary focus of reading and a shift to using phonics as it evolves naturally, when necessary for sense. A fifth factor is the use of integrated/thematic approaches to provide a context and vehicle for promoting, nourishing, and developing children's literacy.

BILINGUAL EDUCATION

For most people, *bilingual education* means that children (or adults, or both) will be taught a second language. Some people interpret this to mean that the child's

Children in Kathie Dobberteen's class using the Writing to Read Center. Dobberteen believes children need involvement in literacy activities that will provide success and a basis for learning to read and write well.

Children are encouraged to do much fluent word-processing at the computer on a daily basis.

Writing to Read has made a significant impact on this district not only at the kindergarten and first grade levels, but throughout all the elementary grades. Children are truly being prepared to take an important role in our highly technological society.

native language, whether English, Spanish, Urdu, or any of the other 125 languages in which bilingual programs are conducted, will tend to be suppressed. For other people, bilingual means the child will become proficient in a second language. Title 11 of Public Law 98-511, the Bilingual Education Act, sets forth the federal government's policy of bilingual education:

> The Congress declares it to be the policy of the United States, in order to establish equal educational opportunity for all children and to promote educational excellence (A) to encourage the establishment and operation, where appropriate, of educational programs using bilingual educational practices, techniques, and methods, (B) to encourage the establishment of special alternative instructional programs for students of limited English

proficiency in school districts where the establishment of bilingual education programs is not practicable or for other appropriate reasons, and (C) for those purposes, to provide financial assistance to local educational agencies.[16]

Diversity is a positive aspect of American society. Ethnic pride and identity have caused renewed interest in languages and a more conscious effort to preserve children's native languages. Sixty years ago, foreign-born Americans and their children wanted to camouflage their ethnicity and unlearn their language because it seemed unpatriotic or un-American; today, however, we hold the opposite viewpoint.

Another reason for interest in bilingual education is the emphasis on civil rights. Indeed, much of the concept of providing children with an opportunity to know, value, and use their heritage and language stems from people's recognition that they have a right to them.

Types of Programs

Schools have several potential responses to a child's linguistic deficiency. They can hope the child will learn English merely by exposure to it in the classroom. Second, they can provide a program of *Teaching English to Speakers of Other Languages* (TESOL), which emphasizes teaching the child English as quickly as possible so as to conduct the program of schooling in English. A third response is to provide a *tran-*

Bilingual education is an important part of many early childhood programs, given the upsurge in immigration and the number of families for whom English is not their native language.

sitional program, in which the child studies in the native language until he becomes proficient in the second language. The goal in this type of program is to help the child acquire concepts and skills through his native language while he is becoming proficient in English. English is still the dominant language of the U.S., although some cities that have a large number of speakers of other languages are officially bilingual.

P.L. 98-511 defines a program of *transitional bilingual education*—most of the bilingual programs are transitional—this way:

> The term "program of transitional bilingual education" means a program of instruction, designed for children of limited English proficiency in elementary or secondary schools, which provides, with respect to the years of study to which such program is applicable, structured English language instruction, and, to the extent necessary to allow a child to achieve competence in the English language, instruction in the child's native language. Such instruction shall incorporate the cultural heritage of such children and of other children in American society. Such instruction shall, to the extent necessary, be in all courses or subjects of study which will allow a child to meet grade-promotion and graduation standards.[17]

Bilingual-Multicultural Preschool Curriculum Models. In 1975, the Administration for Children, Youth and Families authorized development and implementation of bilingual and multicultural programs at the preschool level. The goal of these programs is to develop bilingual/multicultural early childhood curriculum approaches that provide instruction in two languages, foster children's cognitive and social growth through multicultural references, and to provide for individualization of instruction based upon children's linguistic needs.

KINDERGARTEN CHILDREN AND TRANSITIONS

Young children face many transitions in their lives. They are left with baby-sitters, enter child care programs, preschools, and kindergarten and first grade. Depending on how adults help children make these transitions, they can be unsettling and traumatic or happy and rewarding experiences. The transition from home to preschool to kindergarten influences positively or negatively children's attitudes toward school. A transition is a passage from one learning setting, grade, program or experience to another. Under no circumstances should the transition from preschool to kindergarten or from kindergarten to first grade be viewed as the beginning of "real learning." Leaving kindergarten to enter first grade is a major transition. The transition may not be too difficult for children whose kindergarten classroom is housed in the same building as the primary grades. For others whose kindergarten is separate from the primary program or for children who have not attended kindergarten, the experience can be unsettling, traumatic, or rewarding. Children with special needs who are making a transition from a special program to a mainstreamed classroom need extra attention and support, as we will discuss in Chapter 11. There are ways parents and kindergarten teachers can help children make transitions easily and confidently:

> Educate and prepare children ahead of time for any new situation. For example, children and teachers can visit the kindergarten or first grade program the children will attend. Also, toward the end of the preschool or kindergarten year, or as time to enter the kindergarten or first grade approaches, children can

practice certain routines as they will do them when they enter their new school or grade.

Alert parents to new and different standards, dress, behavior, and parent/teacher interactions. Preschool teachers, in cooperation with kindergarten teachers, should share curriculum materials with parents so they can be familiar with what their children will learn. Kindergarten teachers can do the same with first grade teachers.

Provide parents of special needs children and bilingual parents with additional help and support during the transition process.

Visit programs children will attend to better understand the physical, curricular, and affective climates of the new programs. Teachers can then incorporate methods into their own program that will help children adjust to new settings.

Cooperate with the staff of any program the children will attend, to work out a "transitional plan." Continuity between programs is important for social, emotional, and educational reasons. Children should see their new setting as an exciting place where they will be happy and successful.

The nature, extent, creativity, and effectiveness of transitional experiences for children, parents and staff will be limited only by the commitment of all involved. If we are interested in providing good preschools, kindergartens, and primary schools, then we will include transitional experiences in the curricula of all the programs.

WHAT LIES AHEAD?

The trend in kindergarten education is toward full-day, cognitive-based programs. Kindergartens give public schools an opportunity to provide children with the help they need for later success in school and life. Children come to kindergarten programs knowing more than their counterparts of twenty years ago. Children with different abilities and a society with different needs require that kindergarten programs change accordingly.

FURTHER READING

Balaban, Nancy. *Starting School* (New York: Teachers College Press, 1985)

Sensitive and practical suggestions to help teachers and caregivers ease the separation process for young children starting their early childhood program experiences.

Frombarg, Doris P. *The Full-Day Kindergarten* (New York: Teachers College Press, 1987)

Views young children as active, responsible, inquiring learners whose flexible thinking processes and social-emotional life must be encouraged and enhanced. Guidelines for creating unique kindergarten experiences combining academic instruction with nurturance to promote all areas of development.

Hakuta, Kenji. *Mirror of Language: The Debate on Bilingualism* (New York: Basic Books, 1987)

Controversies in bilingualism, second-language literacy, and the teaching of second languages.

Spodek, Bernard, ed. *Today's Kindergarten: Exploring the Knowledge Base, Expanding the Curriculum* (New York: Teachers College Press, 1986)

Collection of topics from bilingual education to socialization; focuses on concepts, ideas, and issues relating to young children.

FURTHER STUDY

1. Interview parents to determine what they think children should learn in kindergarten. How do their ideas compare to the ideas in this chapter?
2. Critique the kindergarten skills objectives of the Dade County Public Schools. What would you add or delete? Why?
3. Do you think you are a cognitive-skills-oriented teacher or a social-emotional-play-oriented teacher? Explain your reasons, and compare your response to those of your classmates.
4. List what you think should be the goals of a kindergarten program. Explain your reasons.
5. Draw a floor plan for a kindergarten program and develop a daily schedule to support your teaching goals.
6. As a teacher, would you support an earlier or later entrance age to kindergarten? If your local legislator wanted specific reasons, what would you tell him or her? Ask other teachers, and compare their viewpoints.
7. How might culture, socioeconomic background, and home life affect what should be taught to children in kindergarten?
8. Give examples from your observations of kindergarten programs to support one of these opinions: Society is pushing kindergarten children, or many kindergartens are not teaching children enough.
9. List special services school districts should provide to kindergarten children.
10. Compare the curriculum of a for-profit kindergarten, a parochial school kindergarten, and a public school kindergarten. What are the similarities and/or differences? Which would you send your child to? Why?
11. Do you think kindergarten should be mandatory for all 5-year-old children? At what age should it be mandatory?
12. Should the results of a readiness test be the final word on whether a child is admitted to kindergarten? Explain your answer.
13. Critique the State of Nebraska statements as to what constitutes a good kindergarten. What would you add or change? Why?
14. What are reasons for the current interest in helping children make transitions from one setting or agency to another? What are other transitions that early childhood educators should help children make, besides those mentioned in this chapter?
15. Visit a kindergarten that uses one of the practices mentioned in this chapter. Determine what the teachers think are the strengths and weaknesses of the program. How do the children like the program? Would you use the program? Why or why not?
16. Do you think the schools should teach programs of bilingual education? Why?
17. You have been asked to speak to a parent's group about the pros and cons of teaching reading in kindergarten. What major topics would you include?
18. How would you advise parents to promote literacy in the home?
19. List five reasons children should be computer-literate.
20. What are the issues facing kindergarten education in your hometown school district?

NOTES

1. Alec M. Gallup, "The 18th Annual Gallup Poll of the Public's Attitudes Toward the Public Schools," *Phi Delta Kappan,* 68, 1, pp. 55–56.
2. Sandra L. Robinson, "The State of Kindergarten Offerings in the United States," *Childhood Education,* 64 (1987), pp. 23–28.
3. Arnold Gesell and Catherine Amatruda, *Developmental Diagnosis: Normal and Abnormal Child Development* (New York: Harper and Row, 1941).
4. Caroline Pratt and Lucile C. Deming, "The Play School," in *Experimental Schools Revisited,* ed. Charlotte Winsor (New York: Agathon Press, 1973), p. 23.
5. Lorrie A. Shepard and Mary Lee Smith, "Effects of Kindergarten Retention at the End of First Grade," *Psychology in the Schools,* 24 (1987), pp. 346–357.
6. Deborah Byrnes and Kaoru Yamamoto, "Views on Grade Repetition," *Journal of Research and Development in Education,* 20 (1986), pp. 14–20.

7. Jeffrey Burkart, "Developmental Kindergarten—In the Child's Best Interest? *National Association of Early Childhood Teacher Educators,* 10 (1989), pp. 9–10.

8. Friedrich Froebel, *Mother's Songs, Games and Stories* (New York: Arno Press, 1976), p. 136.

9. Reprinted by permission of the Nebraska Department of Education, Division of School Assistance and Support.

10. School Board of Dade County, Florida.

11. School Board of Dade County, Florida.

12. Highland Oaks Elementary School is in Dade County, Florida, the fourth largest school district in the United States.

13. Sue Bredekamp, Ed., *Developmentally Appropriate Practice in Early Childhood Programs Serving Child from Birth through Age 8,* Expanded Edition (Washington, D.C.: National Association for the Education of Young Children, 1987), p. 13.

14. Linda Garvey, Yukari Okamoto, and Teresa McDivitt, Stanford University.

15. Texas Association for the Education of Young Children, *Developmentally Appropriate Kindergarten Reading Programs: A Position Statement,* p. 1.

16. Statute 2372, Section 703.

17. Statute 2372, Section 4A.

CHAPTER 9
The Primary Years
The Process of Schooling

As you read and study:
- [ ] Compare and contrast the differences between preschool and kindergarten children and children in the primary grades
- [ ] Explain the physical, cognitive, language, psychosocial, and moral characteristics of primary children
- [ ] Understand cooperative learning, including its benefits, disadvantages, and the implications for schooling
- [ ] Be knowledgeable about curricular areas emphasized in the primary grades
- [ ] Identify and discuss basic skills and basic skills tests
- [ ] Cite ways the basic skills curricula influence primary children and their teaching and learning
- [ ] Understand how to teach children to "think" and the implications of critical thinking
- [ ] Analyze computer curricula for the primary grades and understand their essential features
- [ ] Identify issues relating to primary education
- [ ] Think about the future of primary education

In contrast to the renewed interest in infants, one might almost say that the years from six to eight are the forgotten years of early childhood, and primary children are frequently overlooked in terms of early childhood education. Although the profession defines early childhood education as from birth to age eight, children from birth through kindergarten receive most of the attention; primary grade children are more often thought of as belonging to the elementary years. Indeed, the years from six to twelve are often referred to as the *middle years* or *middle childhood,* the years between early childhood and adolescence.

WHAT ARE PRIMARY CHILDREN LIKE?

Physical Development

Two words describe the physical growth of the primary age child—*slow* and *steady.* Children at this age do not make the rapid and obvious height and weight gains of the infant, toddler, and preschooler. This is instead a time of continual growth during which children develop increasing control over their bodies and explore the things they are able to do. Boys continue to be taller and heavier than girls during this period; average height and weight gains are two-and-a-half inches and five pounds per year. Wide variations appear not only in individual rates of growth and development, however, but also among the sizes of children in each classroom. The wide differences in physical appearances result from genetic and cultural factors, nutritional intake and habits, health care, and experiential background.

Someone who has not been around primary children for many years might notice of a first grade class "how much bigger the children are today!" The perception that children today are larger than children of 50 years ago is accurate; children today *are* bigger than they were in the past. This comparison is a *secular trend* that occurs in industrialized, developed countries with high standards of health care and nutrition. This secular trend does not continue indefinitely, because there are genetic determinants beyond which humans as a species cannot develop. In fact, the secular trend in the U.S. has diminished, but is just beginning in some developing countries. Figure 9–1 shows that five-year-old boys and girls in the U.S. in 1965 were about two inches taller than five-year-olds in 1905, and nine-year-olds in 1965 were three inches taller than children in 1905.

Motor Development

The primary child is adept at many motor skills. The six-year-old is in the *initiative* stage of psychosocial development; seven- and eight-year-old children are in the *industry* stage. Not only are children intuitively driven to initiate activities, they are also learning to be competent and productive individuals. The primary years are thus a time to use and test developing motor skills. Children at this age should be actively involved in projects and creative activities that enable them to use their bodies to learn and to develop feelings of purpose and competence. Their growing competence and confidence in their physical skills is reflected in games of running, chasing, and kicking. A nearly universal characteristic of children in this period is their almost constant physical involvement.

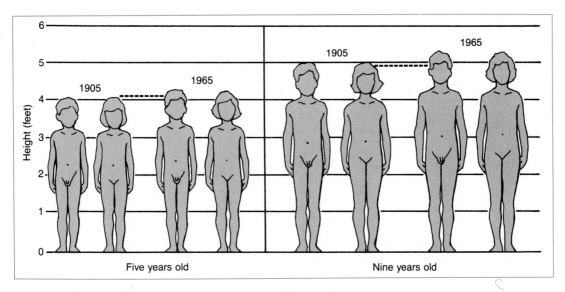

FIGURE 9–1   Early Maturation (From "Earlier Maturation in Man," by J. M. Tanner. Copyright © 1968 by SCIENTIFIC AMERICAN, Inc.

Differences between boys' and girls' motor skills during the primary years are minimal; their abilities are about equal. One implication for teachers is that they should not try to limit either boys' or girls' involvement in activities based on gender. Also, children should not be organized into leagues and activities that require physical and motor skills beyond their abilities or that are too competitive. We see evidence of the continuing refinement of fine motor skills in the primary years in children's abilities to do many of the tasks they were previously unable to do or could do only with difficulty. They are now able to dress themselves relatively easily and attend to most of their personal needs, such as using utensils, combing their hair, and brushing their teeth. They are also more proficient at school tasks that require fine motor skills, such as writing, artwork, and use of computers.

Cognitive Development

Children's cognitive development during the elementary school years enables them to do things as fifth and sixth graders that they could not do as first and second graders. A major difference between these two age-groups is that the older child's thinking has become less egocentric and more logical. The cognitive milestone that enables children between seven and eleven to think and act as they do is *concrete operational thought;* their reasoning, however, is still tied to the concrete. Logical operations are possible with concrete objects and referents in the here and now. Abstract reasoning comes later, in the *formal operation stage* during adolescence.

Moral Development

The leading proponents of a developmental concept of children's moral growth are Jean Piaget and Lawrence Kohlberg. Piaget identified the two stages of moral thinking typical of children in the elementary grades as the stage of *heteronomy*—being governed by others regarding right and wrong—and the stage of *autonomy*—being governed by oneself regarding right and wrong. As Piaget points out:

> Society is the sum of social relations, and among these relations we can distinguish two extreme types: relations of constraint, whose characteristic is to impose upon the individual from outside a system of rules with obligatory content, and relations of cooperation whose characteristic is to create within people's minds the consciousness of ideal norms at the back of all rules. Arising from the ties of authority and unilateral respect, the relations of constraint therefore characterize most of the features of society as it exists, and in particular the relations of the child to its adult surrounding. Defined by equality and mutual respect, the relations of cooperation, on the contrary, constitute an equiliberal limit rather than a static system.[1]

The stage of heteronomy is characterized by "relations of constraint." In this stage, the child's concept of good and bad and right and wrong is determined by the judgments pronounced by adults. An act is "wrong" because one's parents or teacher say it is wrong. The child's understanding of morality is based upon the authority of adults and those values which "constrain" her.

Gradually, as the child matures and has opportunities for experiences with peers and adults, moral thinking may change to "relations of cooperation." This stage of personal morality is characterized by exchange of viewpoints between children and between children and adults as to what is right, wrong, good, or bad. This level of moral development is not achieved by authority, but rather by social experiences within which one has opportunities to try out different ideas and discuss moral situations. Autonomous behavior does not mean that children agree with other children or adults, but that autonomous people exchange opinions and try to negotiate solutions.

The stage of relations of constraint is characteristic of children up through first and second grades, while the stage of relations of cooperation is characteristic for children in the middle and upper elementary grades. The real criterion for determining which developmental stage a child is operating in, however, is how she is thinking, not how old she is.

Lawrence Kohlberg, a follower of Piaget, also believes children's moral thinking occurs in developmental levels. The levels and substages of moral growth as conceptualized by Kohlberg are preconventional, conventional, and postconventional.[2]

Level I, Preconventional Level (Ages 4-10).   Morality is basically a matter of good or bad, based on a system of punishments and rewards as administered by adults in authority positions. In Stage 1, the punishment-and-obedience orientation, the child operates within and responds to physical consequences of behavior. Good and bad are based upon the rewards they bring, and the child bases judgments on whether an action will bring pleasure. In Stage 2, the instrumental-relativist orientation, the child's actions are motivated by satisfaction of needs. Consequently, interpersonal relations have their basis in arrangements of mutual convenience based on need satisfaction. ("You scratch my back; I'll scratch yours.")

Level II, Conventional Level (Ages 10-13).   Morality is doing what is socially accepted, desired, and approved. The child conforms to, supports, and justifies the order of society. Stage 3 is the interpersonal concordance or "good boy—nice girl" orientation. Emphasis is on what a "good boy" or "nice girl" would do. The child conforms to images of what good behavior is. In Stage 4, the "law-and-order" orientation, emphasis is on respect for authority and doing one's duty under the law.

Level III, Postconventional Level (Age 13 and Beyond).   Morality consists of principles beyond a particular group or authority structure. The individual develops a moral system that reflects universal considerations and rights.

Stage 5 is the social-contract legalistic orientation. Right action consists of the individual rights agreed upon by all society. In addition to democratic and constitutional considerations, what is right is relative to personal values. At Stage 6, the universal-ethical-principle orientation, what is right is determined by universal principles of justice, reciprocity, and equality. The actions of the individual are based on a combination of conscience and these ethical principles.

Just as Piaget's cognitive stages are fixed and invariant for all children, so too are Kohlberg's moral levels. All individuals move through the process of moral development beginning at Level I and progress through each level. No level can be skipped, nor does an individual necessarily achieve every level. Just as intellectual development may become "fixed" at a particular level of development, so may an individual become fixed at any one of the moral levels.

Implications for Classrooms

The theories of Piaget, Kohlberg, and programs for promoting affective education have these implications for classroom practice:

☐ The teacher must like and respect children.
☐ The classroom climate must be accepting of individual values. Respect for children means respect for and acceptance of the value system the child brings to school. It is easy to accept an individual with a value system similar to one's own; it takes more self-discipline and maturity to accept an individual with a different value system.
☐ Teachers and schools must be willing to deal with issues, morals, and value systems other than those they promote for convenience, such as obedience and docility.
☐ Kohlberg maintains that a sense of justice must prevail in the schools, instead of the injustice that arises from imposing arbitrary institutional values.
☐ Children must have opportunities to interact with peers, children of different age-groups, and adults to enable them to move to the higher levels of moral functioning.
☐ Students must have opportunities to make decisions and discuss the results of decision making. One does not develop a value system through being told what to do or through a solitary opportunity at decision making.

SIGNIFICANCE OF THE PRIMARY YEARS

The primary years of early childhood education are significant because children are inducted into the process of formal schooling. The preschool experience is often viewed as preparation for school; with first grade, the process of schooling begins. How this induction goes will, to a large extent, determine whether children like or dislike the process of schooling. Children's attitudes toward themselves and their lives are determined at this time. The degree of success now will set limits on life-long success as well as school success. Preparation for dealing with, engaging in, and successfully completing school tasks begins long before the primary grades, but it is during the primary grades that children encounter failure, grade retention, and negative attitudes. Negative experiences during this period have a profound effect on their efforts to develop positive self-image. Primary children are in Erikson's *industry vs. inferiority* stage. They want and need to be competent; faced with school failure, they can develop feelings of inferiority and a feeling that they will never be able to do anything well.

In the primary years, children encounter the academic-oriented, basic-skills-based, achievement-test-centered, accountability-conscious, pressure-filled process that characterizes modern schooling. Many states prescribe minimum basic skill for grades one, two, and three, with achievement measured by state examinations. In Florida, a student can be retained twice in the primary grades for failure to achieve; results of a third grade achievement examination given at the *beginning* of the school year are used to make decisions regarding promotion to the fourth grade.

REASONS FOR THE BACK-TO-BASICS MOVEMENT

Schooling in the elementary years has become a serious enterprise for which it is possible to identify political, social, and economic reasons. First, educators, parents and politicians are realizing that solutions to illiteracy, a poorly prepared work force, and many social problems begin in the first years of school, not after the problems have gone beyond correction. A second reason is that the public will not tolerate further decline in educational standards. The public wants the schools to do a better job teaching the basic skills because of declining SAT scores, the need for remedial reading courses for college freshmen, the high rate of adult illiteracy, and the inability of many high school graduates to fill out a job application. Third, parents and the general public believe a return to "old fashioned" schooling that emphasizes basic skills and discipline will alleviate and perhaps cure the apparent decline of traditional American values.

Basic Skills and Teaching Methodology

The back-to-basics movement is more than a return to the "three Rs." It affects the methodology of teaching and the classroom environment. We see its effects several ways:

1. Emphasis on drill, memorization, and a teacher-directed and -controlled learning environment
2. More homework as an aid to learning. We now take it for granted that children will have homework in the primary grades; some school districts prescribe a certain amount of homework for each subject and grade level. Parents support the emphasis on homework because they see it as a way to keep children involved in the learning process.

3. Renewal of the teacher's role as disciplinarian. Teachers are rediscovering their role in managing and guiding behavior (see Chapter 12), and parents and the public expect teachers to maintain an atmosphere of no-nonsense learning.
4. Higher standards for grade promotion. Promotion is often tied to or based on results of achievement test scores, and promotion standards based on age and level of socialization are coming under tighter public scrutiny.
5. Redefining the curriculum of the primary grades by state legislatures, which specify minimum basic skills for each grade level.
6. Use of tests to measure student achievement, determine promotions, judge teacher performance, and measure the quality of schools.

CURRICULUM FOR THE PRIMARY GRADES

Whether or not we approve of the basic skills emphasis in the primary grades, the fact remains that the present curriculum centers around reading, writing, and arithmetic. The curricular emphasis in the primary grades *is* the basic skills. Other content areas—science, social studies, art/music, health and physical education—are often included only when and if there is time, which means that in actual practice, they may not be taught at all.

The emphasis on testing and assessment has influenced how and what teachers teach in grades 1-3. Efforts are under way to reduce the emphasis on tests and testing; nonetheless, the primary grades will continue to have basic skills teaching as one of their essential missions.

With the emphasis on basic skills and teaching/learning accountability, many states specify minimum basic skills that form the basis for the primary curriculum. Many of these states also produce assessment instruments to test student achievement of these skills. Figure 9–2 shows a sample assessment item for mathematics at the beginning of grade three. These are sample assessment items for reading for grade three:

DIRECTIONS: Read the story and choose the sentence that best tells the <u>main idea</u>, or what the story is about.

> The baby has a basket of toys. He has a toy duck. He has a doll. He has a train and a truck. He likes his duck.

1. Which sentence best tells the <u>main idea</u>?
   - A. ☐   He likes his duck.
   - B. ☐   He has a doll.
   - C. ☐   He has a train and a truck.
   - D. ☐   The baby has a basket of toys.

> The children at school had a picnic. They played games. They ran in the grass. They went up a hill. They had good things to eat.

2. Which sentence best tells the <u>main idea</u>?
   - A. ☐   The children at school had a picnic.
   - B. ☐   They ran in the grass.
   - C. ☐   They went up a hill.
   - D. ☐   They had good things to eat.[3]

Figure 9–3 is an example of the Dade County writing assessment.

Special Primary Curricula

Despite the preoccupation with basic skills, from time to time other curricula receive attention for possible inclusion in the primary grades. There is, for example, a growing feeling among early childhood educators that solutions to many societal problems, including war and conflict, should begin in the primary and preschool years. Consequently, there is emphasis on *prosocial behaviors*—teaching children the fundamentals of peaceful living, kindness, helpfulness, and cooperation. Teachers can do several things to foster development of prosocial skills in the classroom.

- ☐ Be a good role model for children. Teachers must demonstrate in their lives and relationships with children and other adults the behaviors of cooperation and kindness that they want to encourage in children.
- ☐ Provide positive feedback and reinforcement when children perform prosocial behaviors. When children are rewarded for appropriate behavior, they tend to repeat that behavior. For example, you might say, "I like how you helped Tim get up when you accidentally ran into him. I bet that made him feel better."

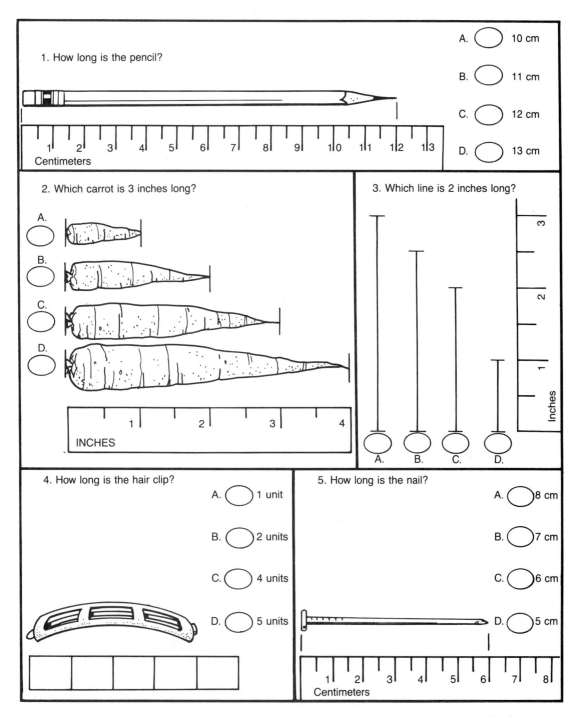

1. How long is the pencil?

A. ◯ 10 cm
B. ◯ 11 cm
C. ◯ 12 cm
D. ◯ 13 cm

Centimeters

2. Which carrot is 3 inches long?

A. ◯
B. ◯
C. ◯
D. ◯

INCHES

3. Which line is 2 inches long?

A. ◯ B. ◯ C. ◯ D. ◯

Inches

4. How long is the hair clip?

A. ◯ 1 unit
B. ◯ 2 units
C. ◯ 4 units
D. ◯ 5 units

5. How long is the nail?

A. ◯ 8 cm
B. ◯ 7 cm
C. ◯ 6 cm
D. ◯ 5 cm

Centimeters

FIGURE 9–2 Sample Assessment Items: Mathematics, Grade 3 (From the School Board of Dade County, Florida)

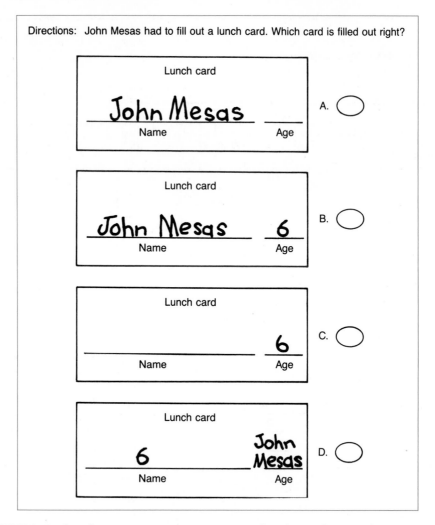

Directions: John Mesas had to fill out a lunch card. Which card is filled out right?

FIGURE 9–3   Sample Assessment Items: Writing, Grade 3 (From the School Board of Dade County, Florida)

☐ Provide opportunities for children to help and show kindness to others. Cooperative programs between primary children and nursing and retirement homes are excellent opportunities to practice helping and kind behaviors.

☐ Conduct classroom routines and activities so they are as free as possible of conflict. At the same time, teachers can provide many opportunities for children to work together and practice skills for cooperative living. Learning centers and activities can be designed for children to share and work cooperatively.

☐ When real conflicts occur, provide practice in conflict resolution skills. These skills include taking turns, talking through problems, compromising, and apologizing. A word of caution regarding apologies: too often, an apology is a per-functory response on the part of teachers and children. Rather than just saying the often empty words "I'm sorry," it is far more meaningful to help the child understand how the other child is feeling. Encouraging empathic behavior in children is a key to the development of prosocial behavior.

☐ Conduct classroom activities based on multicultural principles (see Chapter 11) and free from stereotyping and sexist behaviors (see Chapter 14).

☐ Read stories to children and provide literature for them to read that exemplify prosocial behaviors.

☐ Counsel and work with parents to encourage them to limit their children's television viewing, especially of programs that are violent.

☐ Help children feel good about themselves, build strong self-images, and be competent individuals. Children who are happy, confident, and competent feel good about themselves and behave positively toward others.

Teaching Thinking

The back-to-basics movement has been a dominant theme in American education for the past 20 years and is likely to continue as a curriculum force. When we think of the basic skills, we generally think of reading, writing, and arithmetic, and many elementary schools allot these subjects the lion's share of time and teacher emphasis. Yet some critics of education and advocates of basic education do not consider the 3 Rs the ultimate "basic" of sound education. Rather, the real basic of education is *thinking*. The rationale is that if students can think, they can meaningfully engage in subject-matter curriculum and the rigors and demands of the workplace and life. As a result, teachers are including the teaching of thinking in their daily lesson plans.

In classrooms that emphasize thinking, students are encouraged to use their "power of analysis," and teachers ask higher-level questions. Teachers are being encouraged to challenge their children to think about classroom information and learning material, rather than merely memorize acceptable responses. So, instead of asking children to recall information, teachers are asking them to think critically about information, solve problems, and reflect.

Cooperative Learning

You can probably remember how, when you were in third or fourth grade—or any other grade, for that matter—you competed with the other kids. You probably tried to see if you could be the first to raise your hand. You leaned out over the front of your seat, frantically waving for your teacher's attention. In many of today's primary classrooms, however, the emphasis is on cooperation, not competition. Cooperative learning is seen as a way to boost student achievement and enhance self-esteem.

Cooperative learning is an instructional and learning strategy that focuses on instructional methods in which students are encouraged or required to work together on academic tasks. Students work in small, mixed-ability learning groups of usually four students who are themselves responsible for learning and for helping their group members learn. In one form of cooperative learning, called "Student Teams—Achievement Division," four students—usually one high achiever, two average students, and one low achiever—participate in a regular cycle of activities.

TEACHING THINKING WITH TEAM*

TEAM (Teaching Enrichment Activities to Minority Students) is a program designed to teach thinking skills, vocabulary development, and various enrichment activities in all subject areas to high-achieving minority students. Students are selected for the program according to teacher recommendation; test scores have nothing to do with the selection process. The purpose of the TEAM program is to compensate for environmental factors that might have hindered the child's ability and performance. The program is also designed to improve these students' thinking skills to enhance their prospects for access to academic excellence and/or gifted programs. The success rate of TEAM students entering a gifted program is 40 to 70 percent. The TEAM program is being implemented, for the first time, at Charles R. Hadley Elementary in Miami, Florida, with a group of 24 second grade students.

In a TEAM classroom, students' skills are improved by using a structured cognitive stimulation program, with highly sequential activities designed to stimulate thinking at the analytical level. Students also develop verbal reasoning skills, ability to make judgments, and strategies for questioning.

There is never a right or wrong answer in the TEAM classroom. If the student can justify an answer and sufficiently back it up, it is considered correct. Students are, however, consistently challenged to go beyond simple "yes" and "no" answers.

A primary vehicle for TEAM program implementation in our classroom is provision of a comfortable environment. We have pillows where the children can go to read while lying down. We let them know they can accomplish whatever they put their minds to. We let the children know they will not be ridiculed, no matter what answer they give. They know that every question and answer is valued. We always emphasize the positive in our classroom. We feel that reinforcing the negative makes a child feel bad about herself, and without positive self-regard, she is less likely to try to succeed. Most of our children come from an environment filled with negative feelings. Instead of adding to the negative feelings the child already has, we try to change those feelings into positive ones.

We set high standards and expectations for our students—it seems that minimal expectations have been the norm in many of these children's previous classroom experiences. We couldn't help but wonder why. We have found that by raising our expectations for our students, we see a high level of accomplishment. It is our belief that teachers have the power to control student achievement by setting high expectations. If we want the best from our students, we should expect nothing but the best.

Our students are consistently involved in situations that require creative and imaginative responses. For Columbus Day, for example, we did a writing activity in which the students had to imagine that they were on one of the three ships. We first gave them facts about the voyage and the discovery, then they had to picture themselves as part of the crew. What

☐ The teacher presents the lesson to the group.
☐ Students work to master the material using worksheets or other learning materials. Students are encouraged not only to complete their work, but to explain their work and ideas to group members.
☐ Students take brief quizzes.[4]

Children in a cooperative learning group are assigned certain responsibilities; for example, there is a group *leader,* who announces the problems or task; a *praiser,*

were the weather conditions? How did they eat? What kind of foods did they have? Was it a hard or easy voyage? Why? These types of activities get the children thinking, creating, and imagining. In this way, social studies and language arts are also incorporated into the curriculum. Subject areas in primary curricula tend to be isolated, so we strive to integrate all areas whenever possible.

We also incorporate the use of journals. Every morning, the children complete a journal entry using five or more sentences; for example, "My family is. . . ." The children express whatever feelings they wish. At the end of the week, we collect the journals, read them, and write back to the children. The children look forward to reading what we have written.

Another technique we use is brainstorming. This is an excellent way for students to share answers and express themselves. Students who have difficulty reading and writing can express themselves in this way—orally. Brainstorming is used in every subject. The students know their contribution will always be valued. Through this collaboration of thoughts and ideas, students are motivated for the lesson.

Cooperative learning is another facet of the TEAM program. Students are asked to work in pairs and groups to come up with solutions to problems. Structure in classrooms has generally been strict with regard to discipline and isolates children so that they work individually. Is this the way our society works? In our opinion, it is not. On the contrary, a well-functioning society is composed of members who share and work together toward a common goal. What better

place to begin to learn the concept of cooperation than in the classroom? This is why we feel cooperative learning is crucial to a child's success in the outside world. Our students work in groups, share their ideas and thoughts, and evaluate each other. In our classroom, which is composed of a writing center, pillows, a computer, a listening station, magazines, books, newspapers, math kits, and SRA kits, you see children circulating freely from center to center. Of course, there is an overall structure to classroom organization and scheduling, but the children are free to go to the center of their choice.

Any teacher, in any classroom, can teach children to think. As teachers, we need to be flexible and change with the times. Teachers cannot expect to do the same thing year after year, with different students who have different needs. A good teacher who sets high standards can accomplish anything. Motivation is the key to all learning. If the teacher motivates the students, and the students are truly excited about learning, the process can begin. A teacher needs to build self-confidence and self-esteem in students. Teachers need to challenge students, let them take risks, provide for a comfortable environment, and expect the best from them. After all, the teacher is the *key* to any program, whether it succeeds or fails.

*Contributed by Sara P. Grillo, student teacher, and Maria de la Torre, Supervising teacher, Charles R. Hadley Elementary School, Miami, Florida.

who praises group members for their answers and work; and a *checker*. Responsibilities rotate as the group engages in different tasks. Children are also encouraged to develop and use interpersonal skills, such as addressing classmates by their first names, saying "Thank you," and explaining to their groupmates why they are proposing an answer. On the classroom level, five basic elements must be incorporated into the instructional process for cooperative learning to be successful.

☐ Positive independence—The students have to believe they are in the learning process together and that they care about one another's learning.

A major trend in the primary curriculum is to provide time, opportunities, and activities for children to learn how to think—the most basic of the "basics."

☐ Verbal, face-to-face interaction—Students have to explain, argue, elaborate, and tie what they are learning now to what they have previously learned.
☐ Individual accountability—Every member of the group has to realize that it is his or her own responsibility to learn.
☐ Social—Students must learn appropriate leadership, communication, trust-building, and conflict-resolution skills.
☐ Group processing—The group has to assess how well its members are working together and how they can do better.[5]

These are benefits of cooperative learning:

☐ It motivates students to do their best.
☐ It motivates students to help one another.
☐ It significantly increases student achievement.[6]

Supporters of cooperative learning maintain that it enables children to learn how to cooperate, and that children learn from each other. And because schools are usually such competitive places, it gives the children an opportunity to learn cooperative skills they will need later in life. Not all teachers agree that cooperative learning is a good idea, however. They maintain that it is too time-consuming, because a group may take longer than an individual to solve a problem. Other critics charge that time spent on cooperative learning takes away time from learning the basic skills of reading, writing, and arithmetic.

Given the pressure on the public schools for accountability, it makes sense that teachers would want to use a humanistic approach that increases student achievement. Furthermore, school critics say that classrooms are frequently too competitive and that students who are neither competitive nor high achievers are left behind. Cooperative learning would seem to be one of the better ways to reduce classroom competitiveness and foster "helping" attitudes.

Implications for Teachers and Parents

Teachers and parents who want to promote creative thinking in children need to be aware of several things. First, children need the freedom *and* security to be creative thinkers. Many teachers and school programs focus on helping children learn the *right* answers to problems, so children soon learn from the process of schooling that there is only one right answer. Children may be so "right-answer"-oriented that they are uncomfortable with searching for other answers or consider it a waste of time.

Second, the environment must support children's creative efforts. Teachers must create classroom settings in which children have the time, opportunity, and materials with which to be creative. Letting children think creatively only when all their subjects are completed, or scheduling creative thinking for certain times, does not properly encourage it.

Third, creative *and* critical thinking must be *integrated* into the total curriculum, so that children learn to think critically and creatively across the curriculum, the school day, and throughout their lives.

COMPUTERS IN THE PRIMARY GRADES

Computers are an integral part of society, and they are here to stay. Three problems confront early childhood teachers in their search to implement an effective program of computer instruction: their personal acceptance of computers; decisions about how to use computers in the classroom; and assuring themselves that computers do not have a negative influence on children. Teachers cannot afford to decide *not* to use computers; in fact, they must promote access to computers and come up with creative ways to involve students.

Children and their teachers need to be computer literate, and this goal should direct the computer program of the primary grades. You can develop an effective program of computer literacy with the following guidelines:

1. Computer literacy must be defined comprehensively, including two general areas: learning *with* computers and learning *about* computers.

Teaching children to use computers deserves more emphasis in grades 1–3. Computers help children extend and enrich skills and learn new ones. The teacher, of course, should be computer literate.

2. However, decisions concerning what children learn about computers should be made not by asking "What can we teach kids about computers?" but by asking "What understandings about computers, their impact on our world, and their uses are *developmentally appropriate* for, and *educationally relevant* to, young children." This implies that lectures on the history of computers or rote memorization of computer components terminology should not be included in the curriculum. Only when meaningful concepts can be actively learned should they be considered for inclusion.

3. For both general areas, educators should (a) decide first how and when to use computers to accomplish the goals of early education, and (b) integrate these uses into the curriculum, while (c) remaining consistent with the beliefs, principles, and practices of the program. These guidelines have several important ramifications. For example, they imply that (a) the development of the "whole child" will be given first and primary consideration; (b) there will not be a "computers" unit that is separate from work in social studies, science, language arts, and so on; and (c) *individual children will have different needs, interests, and abilities and, therefore, will learn different things about computers and will use them in different ways.* This should be welcomed as well as accepted; no effort should be made to force all children to "master" all aspects of computer literacy. Instead of one definition on computer literacy for all, teachers should determine what computers can do to help a particular child reach a particular goal.[7]

A suggested scope and sequence of topics and skills for preschool, kindergarten, and the primary grades is outlined in Table 9–1.

TABLE 9–1   Teaching Young Children *About* Computers: A Suggested Outline

	Preschool	Kindergarten	Grades 1	2	3
I. Hardware, Software, Outerwear, and Underwear: What Should Young Children Understand?					
A. What is a computer? How does a computer work?					
1. Models for understanding hardware and software	I	I	I	D	D
2. Computers need instructions	I	I	D	D	D
3. Computers can do many jobs	I	D	D	D	D
4. Computers work with letters, words, numbers, sound and pictures	I	D	D	D	D
B. What are the parts of a computer? What do they do?					
1. Computer systems and components (parts)		I	D	D	D
2. Models for understanding parts of a computer and what they do		I	D	D	D
C. What different kinds of computers are there?					
1. History					I
2. Types of computers		I	I	D	D
D. Capabilities and limitations					
1. What computers can and cannot do	I	I	D	D	D
2. Artificial intelligence			I	I	D
II. How Are Computers Used in the Neighborhood?					
A. Local applications of computers		I	D	D	D
B. Impact of computers		I	D	D	D
III. How Can *We* Use Computers?					
A. Getting started: using computers, typing, and problem solving	I	I	D	D	D
B. Computer programming: now we teach the computer	I	D	D	D	D
C. Using computers as tools: learning what is in the curriculum with computers	I	D	D	D	D

I = Incidental, Informal, Introduction

D = Directed activities, Discussions

Source: Douglas H. Clements, *Computers in Early and Primary Education* (Englewood Cliffs, N.J.: Prentice-Hall, 1985) p. 54.

CHARACTERISTICS OF A GOOD PRIMARY TEACHER

When all is said and done, it is the teacher who sets the tone and direction for classroom instruction and learning. Without a quality teacher, there will not be a quality program. A quality primary teacher must possess all the personal qualities of a humane, loving, caring person. In addition, the teacher must be capable of dealing with young children who are full of energy. Unlike upper elementary children, who are more goal- and self-directed, primary children need help in developing the skills and personal habits that will enable them to be self-directed and independent learners. To help them develop these skills and habits should be the primary teacher's foremost goal. These guidelines will help implement that goal:

1. Plan for instruction. Planning is the basis for the vision of what a teacher wants for herself and for the children. Teachers who try to operate without a plan are

No matter what the content, the key to successful teaching and learning is a well-prepared, child-oriented teacher.

like builders without a blueprint. Although planning takes time, it saves time in the long run, and it provides direction for instruction.

2. Be the classroom leader. A quality teacher *leads* the classroom. Some teachers forget this, and although children at all ages are capable of performing leadership responsibilities, it is the teacher who sets the tone, direction, and guidelines within which effective instruction occurs. Without strong leadership—not overbearing or dictatorial leadership—classrooms don't operate well. Planning for instruction helps a teacher lead.

3. Involve children in meaningful learning tasks. To learn, children need to be *involved.* To learn to read they must read; to learn to write, they must write. Although these guidelines may seem self-evident, they aren't always implemented. To learn, children need to spend time on learning tasks.

4. Provide individualized instruction. In a classroom of 25 to 30 or more children, there is a wide range of differences. The teacher must provide for these ranges in abilities and interests if children are going to learn to their fullest. There is a difference between *individual* and *individualized* instruction; it is impossible to provide individual attention to all children all the time, but providing for children at their individual levels is possible and necessary. Educators are often accused of teaching to the average, boring the more able, and leaving the less able behind. This criticism can be addressed with individualized instruction.

ISSUES IN PRIMARY EDUCATION

Testing

Much of the primary school child's life is influenced by testing. What children study, how they study it, and the length of time they study it are all determined by testing. Decisions about promotion are also made from test results. With so much emphasis on tests, it is understandable that the issue raises many concerns. Critics maintain that the testing movement reduces teaching and learning to the lowest common denominator—teaching children what they need to know to get the right answers.

Promotion

It should not be surprising that a central issue of the back-to-basics movement is whether a child should be promoted if he doesn't demonstrate competence in the skills specified for his grade. Retention as a cure for poor or nonachievement is popular, especially with the public pressure for tougher standards and greater accountability. Despite the use of retention as a panacea for poor achievement, "the evidence to date suggests that achievement-based promotion does not deal effectively with the problem of low achievement."[8] Better and more helpful approaches to student achievement include strategies such as these:

☐ Promotion combined with remedial instruction
☐ Promotion to a transition class in which students receive help to master the skills they don't know

☐ Use of after-school and summer programs to help students master skills

☐ Providing children specific and individualized help in mastery of skills

☐ Working with parents to teach them how to help their children work on mastery skills

☐ Identifying children who may need help before they enter first grade so that remedial services can be provided early

Any effort to improve student achievement must emphasize helping children rather than practices that threaten to detract from their self-image and which make them solely responsible for their failure.

Homework

Many parents and teachers consider homework essential to the back-to-basics movement and the redefinition of primary education. Unfortunately, however, homework is often assigned on the assumption that it will help children, and the more homework, the better. When assigning homework, teachers should keep in mind the purpose of the homework, the child's ability to do the assigned work, and the relation of the homework to curriculum goals. These additional guidelines will also prove helpful:

1. What happens in the classroom is the real ballgame. That is where achievement test scores are going to go up or down. Homework can enhance the game, but doesn't really change it.
2. More isn't better. Increasing the quantity of homework without addressing curriculum issues will produce minimal results. The homework curriculum must be carefully planned so that it is integral to the classroom learning.
3. Good teaching. Reinforcement is an essential element in motivating and instructing students. A teacher who gives homework should also give reinforcement. Feedback must be a part of the homework scheme.
4. School isn't everything. Both the quantity and timing of homework must be considered in light of the student's total life.[9]

Child-Centered Teaching and Learning

There has always been a tension between subject-centered teaching and child-centered teaching. Whenever subject matter becomes the center of focus in an educational system, as is presently the case, there is a danger that children's needs and developmental characteristics will be moved to the background. Educators must constantly remind themselves and the public that schools are for children, and their best interests must have priority. It makes little sense for a school to raise the average of its achievement tests scores at the cost of lowering children's self-esteem and intrinsic self-worth.

HOME SCHOOLING

One hundred fifty years ago, home schooling was rather widespread. With the advent of compulsory public schooling in 1836, home schooling went into decline. During the last decade, however, there has been a remarkable increase in the number of parents who are taking their children out of school to teach them at home. It is difficult to determine exactly how many parents are using home schooling, but Susannah Sheffer of Holt Associates, a support agency to the home schooling movement in Boston, Massachusetts, estimates that 20,000 families are educating 50,000 children at home.

John Holt (1923–1985) was a leading proponent of home schooling and an early popularizer and supporter of the open education movement. In his books *How Children Learn* and *How Children Fail,* he stressed the need for children to learn in

Thea and Nathan Wheeling: Learning at Home

Thea Wheeling of Franklin, Pennsylvania, has home-schooled her seven-year-old son, Nathan, for the past three years. Thea is not happy about the age at which children go off to school for formal learning. As she explains, "All the reading I was doing indicated that children are not ready for formal learning until between the ages of eight to ten. I wanted to delay Nathan's formal learning until that time. I didn't want him to enter a public school setting where he would be forced to learn. In a public school there is too much competition and aggression. These are the kinds of things that affect a child's self-esteem. My husband, Greg, and I wanted the best for Nathan and we believe I am providing the best for him at home."

Although some people perceive of home schooling as children's sitting all day at the kitchen or dining room table, this is certainly not true for Thea and Nathan. "We don't have typical days," says Thea. "We usually begin by doing math—Nathan's favorite—and writing and language activities for about half an hour or so. We also read a lot. I read to Nathan and he reads to me. He also really enjoys reading to his baby sister Leslie, who is two years old." Nathan says the best part of his home school days are the times he and his mother read to each other.

Thea believes that good learning and teaching are integrated with real-life activities. Nathan, who is quite advanced in math, helps Thea pay her monthly bills, helps balance the checkbook, and addresses and mails family correspondence. Many of Nathan's learning experiences occur outside the home in the community. "We do a lot of things with nature, so we are always going on walks and field trips. Nathan is a member of the Junior Naturalist Club, and he learns a lot by participating in it."

Once a week, Nathan visits and stays overnight with his great-grandmother, who is 82. He helps her with household chores and yard work. According to Thea, "This is the kind of activity Nathan wouldn't be able to do if he were in school. I believe he has learned many prosocial skills by being involved with a wide range of other adults. As a result, he has learned a lot about helping others, sharing, and human interactions."

Thea believes that home schooling gives Nathan opportunities to learn in natural, un-hurried ways, free from pressure to learn and achieve. "We can wait for certain kinds of learning to occur. When he made his P backward, I didn't worry about it. He didn't have to do it like everyone else in the class. We went on and read stories and wrote poetry. He soon learned how to make a P the right way, and I didn't have to scold or nag him to do it."

Thea and Greg plan to enter Nathan in public school beginning with third grade. "He has a good foundation," says Thea. "Scholastically, he is ahead of where he should be for his grade level. He also knows how to learn on his own. His vision and hearing have had more time to develop and he has reached the age of cause-and-effect reasoning. Now he is ready for formal learning. I don't think he will have any problems adjusting to public schooling."

environments that were free from undue pressure and where they could control their own learning. As Holt became increasingly disenchanted with the public schools as places that are conducive to children's best interests, he championed home schooling as an option for parents who wanted to provide an optimal education for their children. These are some of the motivations for parents' educating their children at home:

Some parents like being home with their children and believe it is best if one parent stays home. In most cases, this parent is the mother. They also believe that having children living and learning in the home enhances family cohesiveness and unity. Proponents of strengthening the family unit see home schooling as a contributor to family stability.

Some parents don't want to give up the educating of their children to other people or agencies. As one parent expresses it, "Why should I let someone else have all the fun and joy of teaching my children?"

Some parents believe children learn best when they decide themselves what they will learn, and when and how they will learn it. With evidence of the "hurried child" and the current push in preschool and primary grades for basic education, some parents think home schooling is a natural alternative to the pressures of public schooling.

Some parents prefer home schooling as an appropriate way to inculcate religious values of their choice, since the public schools, of course, must steer away from religion.

Some parents believe that before the age of eight or ten, children are not physically or cognitively ready for the pressures and demands of formal, public schooling.

Issues of Home Schooling

Socialization.   Almost without exception, the first issue raised in regard to children schooled at home is whether they are being properly socialized. Most people believe one of the primary functions of preschools, public schools, and play groups is to socialize young children; consequently, they think that if children don't go to school, they will miss opportunities for socialization. Thea Wheeling, however, believes that young children's socialization occurs best in the family setting. "We can provide for Nathan's socialization better than the public schools. In the public schools, there are 20 to 30 children all the same age with only one adult, the teacher. This is not a real situation nor a natural way to socialize. Opportunities for socialization are limited in a public school classroom. In the real world, children interact with adults of all ages who live by different rules and have different relationships. The best socialization occurs in a family setting. As a family, we interact with other families, the church, community agencies, other adults, the elderly, and with children of all ages. Nathan has more opportunities for real socialization than children who stay in a classroom all day with one adult. We don't prevent him from socializing with other children and adults; on the other hand, in a school setting children are frequently prevented from interacting with others."

Lack of Learning.   The public—especially the segment that believes true learning occurs only in a school setting—wonders if children really learn anything at home. The Wheelings submit a learning/teaching plan to the school district each year. The plan includes specific learning goals and objectives for all the curriculum areas Nathan's peers will cover.

Many home schoolers use prepackaged curricula available from commercial publishers. Others use a combination of commercial materials and materials loaned by the public schools. Many public school principals and teachers are supportive of home schoolers' efforts and provide material and advice and encourage children and their families to participate in special activities and events. Thea, on the other hand, prefers to base Nathan's learning activities on the events and activities of daily living, although she is careful to ensure that Nathan learns the information and skills he needs for the end-of-year achievement tests he takes each year at the school. "So far he has done very well," says Thea. "He scores at or above his age level in many areas." She also has frequent conferences with the public school teachers to be sure she is providing Nathan with equivalent instruction in her home schooling program.

Teacher Certification.   Critics of the home schooling movement question whether people who are not certified teachers can do a good job of teaching their children at home. Some think home schooling should be taught by a certified teacher. Thea responds to such criticism by saying, "I am a literate person. I read a lot in books and professional journals, seek advice from others, attend meetings with other home school parents and follow the curriculum of the public school. I agree with those who say that a parent is the child's first and best teacher."

Parent Rights.   There is a tension between parents who believe they have the right to provide an alternative but equivalent education for their children and those who believe strongly in compulsory public school attendance. Critics think the home school movement undermines the traditional role of the public schools. It is unlikely that the issues of home schooling will ever be resolved to everyone's satisfaction; at the same time, home schooling is a reality for a growing number of children whose parents believe they have the right and ability to teach their children at home and that learning occurs best at home.

THE FUTURE OF PRIMARY EDUCATION

The educational system is slow to meet the demands and dictates of society, so it is unlikely that there will be dramatic changes in the next decade. The direction will be determined by continual reassessment of the purpose of education and attempts to match the needs of society to the goals of the schools. Drug use, child abuse, the breakup of the family, and illiteracy are some of the societal problems the schools are being asked to address in significant ways. At the same time, national leaders are articulating their visions for America's elementary schools, and they provide useful information about what the future may hold. One notable example is reported by William Bennett, former secretary of education. In this first study of the nation's elementary schools in three decades, Bennett said the schools were doing a good job, but could do a better job by implementing some of these suggestions:

☐ There should be greater parent involvement, with parents taking a central role in educating their children

☐ All adults must accept responsibility for educating children

☐ Teachers should be more involved in curriculum decisions

☐ The elementary curriculum should be "unified" or integrated so that one subject area reinforces another

☐ Elementary schools need more time to devote to learning, perhaps with a 12-month school year

☐ Corporations should provide money to elementary schools to help them achieve their goals

☐ All elementary schools should have a disciplinary code

☐ Elementary schools must help save children from drugs

☐ Elementary children should be promoted on the basis of mastery of skills rather than according to a "chronological lockstep"

☐ Curricular reforms should include the "sublime and most solemn responsibility" of all elementary schools—to teach children to read; emphasis on writing; hands-on experiences in science; emphasis on problem solving in math; social studies that encompasses geography, history, and civics as well as the habits of life in a democratic society; arts programs; computer literacy; and every school should have a library, and every child should have a library card.[10]

These suggestions are worthy of consideration, although they raise questions about implementation, costs, and their influence on children and the educational process. Above all, however, all schools must help children and youth develop the skills necessary for life success. After all, even with the trend toward having children spend more time in school, we know that learning doesn't end with school and that children don't learn all they will need to know in an academic setting. It makes sense, therefore, to empower students with skills they can use throughout life in all kinds of interpersonal and organizational settings. These skills include:

☐ The ability to communicate with others, orally and in writing.

☐ The ability to work well with people of all races, cultures, and personalities.

☐ The ability to be responsible for directing one's behavior.

☐ The desire and ability for success in life—not as measured by how much money one will earn, but as a productive member of society.

☐ The desire and ability to continue learning throughout life.

FURTHER READING

Black, Howard, and Sandra Black. *Building Thinking Skills—Book 1* (Pacific Grove, Calif.: Midwest Publications, 1984)

First in a series of books to help teachers and others teach children thinking skills, with inexpensive and effective ways to do so.

Clements, Douglas H. *Computers in Early and Primary Education* (Englewood Cliffs, N.J.: Prentice-Hall, 1985)

Practical guide to computers and their use; shows how to integrate computers into the various curriculum areas.

Crompton, Rob. *Computers and the Primary Curriculum 3–13* (London: Falmer Press, 1989)

Comprehensive, up-to-date, and practical guide to the use of computers across a wide age range. Extensive use of color and samples of children's work to demonstrate the versatility of computers in schools.

Hoot, James L., and Steven B. Silvern, Eds. *Writing with Computers in the Early Grades* (New York: Teachers College Press, 1988)

Computers are rapidly changing educational life. Leaders in the field of computer application in early childhood examine issues inherent in word-processing programs designed for children. Up-to-date information for teachers about software materials for helping children to become better writers. Includes availability of programs, problems, and practical ideas for classroom use.

Kamii, Constance. *Young Children Continue to Reinvent Arithmetic, 2nd Grade. Implications of Piaget's Theory* (New York: Teachers College Press, 1989)

Based on Piaget's theory and four years of research in public school. Traditional arithmetic teaching has been based on the assumption that arithmetic consists of rules that children must internalize. Kamii extends the theory from her earlier volume and provides new activities for second grade.

Paul, Richard, A.J.A. Brinker, and Marla Charbonneau. *Critical Thinking Handbook: K–3.* (Rohnert Park, Calif.: Center for Critical Thinking and Moral Critique, 1987)

Designed to help teachers understand the process of critical thinking and how it can be taught. Provides general strategies for teaching thinking and shows how to adapt existing lesson plans to incorporate critical thinking activities.

FURTHER STUDY

1. Interview parents and teachers to determine their views pro and con of nonpromotion in the primary grades. Summarize your findings. What are your opinions on retention?
2. Visit elementary schools to determine their computer literacy curricula. Do you think the schools are doing as much as they can to promote computer literacy in the primary grades?
3. Are you computer literate? Could you implement a program of computer literacy in a first grade? Why or why not?
4. Survey children in a first, second, and third grade to determine how many have computers in the home. Find out what software is most popular, whether the children like working on computers, and what suggestions they would make for using computers in the school. List five implications of your findings for you as an early childhood teacher.
5. List at least six reasons that early childhood teachers should know about child growth and development.
6. Critique Bennett's recommendations for the public schools. Which recommendations do you agree and disagree with?
7. Do you think the public and the public schools are too caught up in the back-to-basics movement? Why or why not?
8. List five things primary teachers can do to minimize the negative effects of the testing movement on young children.
9. In addition to the characteristics of primary teachers listed in this chapter, what others do you think are desirable? Recall your own primary teachers. What characteristics did they have that had the greatest influence on you?
10. You have been asked to submit ten recommendations for changing and improving primary education in the U.S. Offer a rationale for each of your recommendations.
11. What other issues of primary education would you add to those mentioned in this chapter? How would you suggest dealing with them?
12. Do you think the primary grades are the neglected years of early childhood education? Why or why not?
13. Identify five contemporary issues or concerns facing society, and tell how teachers and primary schools could address each of them.
14. Why do many educators and parents think assigning homework is one way to improve the

process of education and children's achievement? Do you agree?

15. Survey the homework practices and policies of school districts and teachers in your area. What conclusions can you draw? What recommendations would you make?

16. Explain how first grade children's cognitive and physical differences would make a difference in how they were taught. Give specific examples.

17. Of the three primary grades, decide which you would most like to teach, and explain your reasons.

18. What do you think are the most important subjects of the primary grades? Why? What would

you say to a parent who thought any subjects besides reading, writing, and arithmetic were a waste of time?

19. Give your views pro and con for "social" promotion. What would you say to a state legislator who said that all children should be failed until they learned what they were supposed to in each grade?

20. Write about primary education in the year 2010. Tell what schools will be like, what children will learn, and how teaching will occur. Explain how you will prepare yourself for this future.

NOTES

1. Jean Piaget, *The Moral Judgment of the Child,* trans. Marjorie Gabin (New York: The Free Press, 1965), p. 395.

2. Lawrence Kohlberg, "The Claim to Moral Adequacy of a Highest Stage of Moral Judgment," *The Journal of Philosophy,* vol. 70, no. 18 (October 25, 1973): 630–646.

3. The School Board of Dade County, Florida, *Sample Assessment Items: Reading, Grade 3* (1983), p. 9.

4. R.E. Slavin, "Cooperative Learning and the Cooperative School," *Educational Leadership,* 45 (1987): 7–13.

5. R. Brandt, "On Cooperation in Schools: A Conversation with David and Roger Johnson," *Educational Leadership,* 45 (1987): 14–19.

6. R.E. Slavin, pp. 8–9.

7. Douglas H. Clements, *Computers in Early and Primary Education* (Englewood Cliffs, N.J.: Prentice-Hall, 1985), pp. 52–53.

8. Monica Overman, "Practical Applications of Research: Student Promotion and Retention," *Phi Delta Kappan* 67 (April 1986): 612.

9. R.A. Pendergrass, "Homework: Is It Really A Basic?" *The Clearing House* 58 (March 1985): 314.

10. William J. Bennett, *First Lessons: A Report on Elementary Education in America* (Washington, D.C.: Department of Education, 1986).

CHAPTER 10
The Federal Government and Early Childhood Education
Helping Children Win

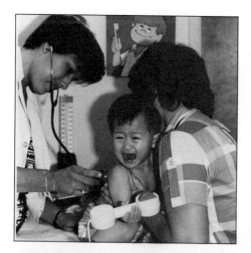

As you read and study:

☐ Examine the objectives of Head Start and other federal programs

☐ Describe and understand the full range of services that Head Start provides to children and their families

☐ Describe the nature and purposes of the home-based program option

☐ Discuss the purposes and function of the Head Start Measures Project

☐ Analyze and understand the Head Start Migrant program

☐ Clarify your personal values regarding involvement of the federal government in educational programs

☐ Analyze the impact of Head Start on children and families

☐ Examine the results of federally supported programs for children and their families

☐ Examine current attitudes toward federal support for early childhood programs

Evidence from many sources indicates that when parents' incomes are inadequate to meet social and educational needs, children are impaired in their ability to become contributing members of society. One of the most damaging consequences of poverty, however, is the effect of that lack of opportunity on self-image.

It is estimated that upwards of fifty million children live in poverty, meaning that their families' incomes are below the poverty guidelines set by the U.S. government. The effects of poverty are debilitating for both children and families. Being poor means more than being eligible for a free school lunch. It means these children as a group are less healthy, live in inadequate housing, and do not have the opportunities for activities and experiences their wealthier counterparts have. Divorce brings economic consequences as well as social ones. A child in a household headed by a single female has a greater chance of being poor; the majority of low-income families are headed by females. Poverty, in a sense, has become feminized.

By federal definition, being poor means that you and your family do not have an income that allows you to purchase adequate health care, housing, food, clothing, and educational services. As of 1990, the federal government used the income levels in Table 10–1 (adjusted to family size and farm or nonfarm residence) to define the poverty level. (These figures change annually because of changing rates of inflation and the cost of living.)

Many children are at risk for developmental delays and educational failure. A poor environment is a major contributor to risk factors for both rural and urban children. Head Start helps reduce the effects of such risks.

HEAD START: HISTORY AND OPERATING PRINCIPLES

To help overcome the negative effects of poverty on the lives of adults and children, the federal government, in 1964, passed the Economic Opportunity Act. One of the main purposes of this act was to break intergenerational cycles of poverty by providing educational and social opportunities for children from low-income families. The Economic Opportunity Act created the Office of Economic Opportunity, and from this office Project Head Start was developed and administered. Head Start was implemented during the summer of 1965, and approximately 550,000 children in 2,500 child-development centers were enrolled in the program.

Today, the National Head Start program has a budget of $1,386,315,000 and serves 488,470 children, or about 20 percent of those eligible. There are 1,283 Head Start programs, including 106 Indian and 24 Migrant programs, for a total of 24,026 classrooms at an average cost per child of $2,767 annually. A total of 11,394,800 children have been served by Head Start since it began.[1] Table 10–2 shows the racial and ethnic composition of Head Start programs.

Table 10–3 shows the ages of children served. Head Start was established and operates according to the following premises:

1. Children who come from low-income families often have not received the cognitive, social, and physical experiences normally associated with success in first grade.
2. Many problems created by poverty can be alleviated or compensated for if children receive these experiences before they start school.
3. Intergenerational poverty cycles can be broken by providing educational and social opportunities for children early in their lives.

TABLE 10–1 1990 Family Income Guidelines for All States Except Alaska and Hawaii

*For family units with more than 8 members, add $2,340 for each additional member.

Source: Code of Federal Regulations 1305.2(b)6.

Size of Family Unit*	Income
1	$ 5,980
2	$ 8,020
3	$10,060
4	$12,100
5	$14,140
6	$16,180
7	$18,220
8	$20,560

TABLE 10–2 Racial and Ethnic Composition of Head Start

Source: Administration for Children, Youth and Families, "Project Head Start Statistical Fact Sheet" (Washington, D.C.: Jan. 1990), p. 1.

Racial/Ethnic Group	Percentage of Enrollment
American Indian	4%
Hispanic	22%
Black	38%
White	33%
Asian	3%

TABLE 10–3 Ages of Children Served by Head Start

Source: Administration for Children, Youth and Families, "Project Head Start Statistical Fact Sheet" (Washington, D.C.: Jan. 1990), p. 2.

Age	Percentage of Enrollment
5 years old and older	8%
4 years old	64%
3 years old	25%
Under 3 years of age	3%

In our discussion of Head Start children, we often lose sight of the families from which they come. These are typical characteristics of Head Start families:

☐ 51% are headed by a single parent
☐ 52% have one or two children
☐ 51% have an annual income below $6000
☐ 62% have a primary caretaker between the ages of 20 and 29
☐ 55% have a primary caretaker with a GED or less education
☐ 67% belong to a minority group
☐ 74% are receiving some type of welfare
☐ 47% have heads of households who are unemployed[2]

The Economic Opportunity Act required communities to create community action agencies to coordinate programs and money for Project Head Start. The act further specified that any nonprofit organization could apply for operational money, develop a program, and operate a Head Start center; thus, organizations such as churches, parent groups, and public schools could design a Head Start program and apply to the community action agency for funds. Later it was also possible for an agency to apply directly to the federal offices of Project Head Start for financing rather than to the community action agency. Many organizations currently receive their money this way and are therefore known as single-purpose agencies. While many Head Start programs were initially established by public school systems, most operated for only six to eight weeks during the summer. Presently, at the federal level, funding for Head Start comes through the Administration for Children, Youth and Families (ACYF). Figure 10–1 shows the organizational structure that governs the operation of Head Start programs.

Head Start is intended to provide a comprehensive developmental program for preschool children from low-income families. The project is also committed to helping children achieve a positive outlook on life through success in school and daily life activities. The overall general goal is to promote social competence by providing children with opportunities to achieve their potential in cognitive, language, socio-emotional, and physical development.

Agencies are permitted and encouraged to consider several program models and select the option best suited to the needs of the children and the capabilities and resources of the program staff. Available program options are the center-based program option, the home-based program option, or approved locally designed variations.

The overall goal of Head Start is to bring about a greater degree of social competence in disadvantaged children. By social competence is meant the child's everyday effectiveness in dealing with his environment and later responsibilities in school and life. Social competence

Head Start is devoted to helping children and their families break intergenerational cycles of risk, poverty, and hopelessness. The nation must resolve to provide all eligible children with a Head Start experience.

FIGURE 10–1   Organizational Structure of Head Start

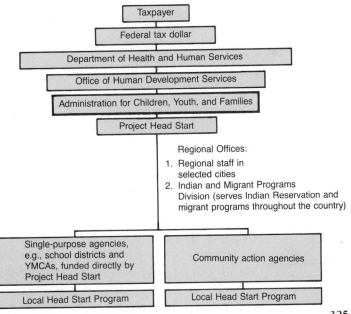

Taxpayer

Federal tax dollar

Department of Health and Human Services

Office of Human Development Services

Administration for Children, Youth, and Families

Project Head Start

Regional Offices:
1. Regional staff in selected cities
2. Indian and Migrant Programs Division (serves Indian Reservation and migrant programs throughout the country)

Single-purpose agencies, e.g., school districts and YMCAs, funded directly by Project Head Start

Community action agencies

Local Head Start Program

Local Head Start Program

takes into account the interrelatedness of cognitive and intellectual development, physical and mental health, nutritional needs, and other factors that enable a child to function optimally. Head Start is a comprehensive developmental approach to helping achieve social competence. To this end, Head Start goals provide for:

A. The improvement of the child's health and physical abilities.
B. The encouragement of self-confidence, spontaneity, curiosity, and self-discipline which will assist in the development of the child's social and emotional health.
C. The enhancement of the child's mental processes and skills with particular attention to conceptual and verbal skills.
D. The establishment of patterns and expectations of success for the child, which will create a climate of confidence for his present and future learning efforts and overall development.
E. An increase in the ability of the child and his family to relate to each other and to others in a loving and supporting manner.
F. The enhancement of the sense of dignity and self-worth within the child and his family.

Head Start's approach is based on the philosophy that: (1) a child can benefit most from a comprehensive, interdisciplinary program to foster his development and remedy his problems, and (2) the child's entire family, as well as the community, must be involved.[3]

Implementation of these objectives occurs through Head Start child development centers, which provide a wide range of social, economic, educative, and physical services for children and their families.

HEAD START COMPONENTS

Head Start has the following program components: education, parent involvement, health service (including psychological services, nutrition, and mental health), social service, and career development for staff, parents, and administration.

Education

Objectives.   The educational program of Head Start is guided by the following objectives:

1. Provide children with a learning environment and the varied experiences which will help them develop socially, intellectually, physically, and emotionally in a manner appropriate to their age and state of development toward the overall goal of social competence.
2. Integrate the educational aspects of the various Head Start components in the daily program of activities.
3. Involve parents in educational activities of the program to enhance their role as the principal influence on the child's education and development.
4. Assist parents to increase their knowledge, understanding, skills and experience in child growth and development.
5. Identify and reinforce experiences which occur in the home that parents can utilize as educational activities for their children.[4]

These educational objectives guide local programs in developing their own programs that are unique and responsive to the children, families, and communities they serve. Thus, there is really no national Head Start curriculum, although some people mistakenly believe there is. Many Head Start centers stress activities generally typical of nursery school/kindergarten programs and include activities associated with success in school, such as taking and following directions, listening, and becoming accustomed to the routines and materials of learning, such as books.

Programmatic Direction. One problem many Head Start centers have with the educational component of their programs is translating the national goals into meaningful local goals. This in turn results in uncertainty about the kind of program the center will conduct, making it difficult for teachers to select appropriate activities. Head Start's educational objectives are sufficiently comprehensive to permit a grantee to conduct just about any kind of educational program it considers appropriate; however, herein lies the problem. If a Head Start Program director has adequate preparation and is able to conceptualize what a good program should include, then working within the guidelines of the Head Start educational objectives can be a strength. If directors do not have adequate preparation, the program may be full of directionless activities.

The Administration for Children, Youth and Families defines a part-day Head Start Program as one in which children attend less than six hours a day; full-day programs are those in which children attend six or more hours a day. Keep in mind that local grantees are free to develop their own programs within Head Start guidelines. This is a schedule for a relatively unstructured, full-day program (activities in parentheses should be scheduled according to the children's needs):

Teachers and assistant teachers arrive
  (plan for day)
  (set up room for day)
Children arrive, greeted individually, health inspection
Early morning activities
Breakfast
Brush teeth
(Group time)
Free choice of activities in learning areas (1 hour)
  art, building, dramatic, reading, manipulative
(Group time)
(Snack)
Outdoor activities (1 hour)
  organized games and exercises
(Group time)
Lunch
Brush teeth
Nap time (30 minutes—1 hour)
(Snack)
(Outdoor activities)
Children leave

(Teachers and assistant teachers evaluate and plan)
  Assistant teachers leave
  Teacher leaves
  Home visits[5]
This schedule is typical of a more structured program:
  7:30 Arrival, individual activities
  8:00 Breakfast, toothbrushing, toileting
  8:45 Planning time (individually as children complete health needs)
  9:00 Work time
  9:40 Clean-up, toileting
  10:00 Recall time and snack (children assist with snack)
  10:25 Small group time
  10:40 Circle time (health activities, songs and games—planned experiences in
        either health, safety, or nutrition *must* be provided on a weekly basis, as a
        part of the daily routine activities, i.e., small group time, circle time)
  11:00 Outside activity time
  11:30 Preparation for lunch (handwashing, table setting)
  12:00 Lunchtime
  12:30 Circle time (stories, finger plays, nursery rhymes—opportunities must be
        provided for children to engage in a fifteen-minute activity prior to napping)
  12:45 Rest time, teacher breaks (removal of children's shoes is required at rest
        time)
  1:45 Snack
  2:00 Dismissal, individual activities
  2:30 Team planning[6]

Performance Standards.   Since 1973, Head Start programs have had performance standards or requirements that must be met to continue receiving federal funds. For example, according to the standards, educational objectives must be written to incorporate activities and services for meeting the needs of all children in the Head Start Program. Each objective in all the component areas has a corresponding performance standard. Linking objectives to minimum standards of performance represents an admirable attempt by Head Start to strengthen its program of services.

Coordination with Public Schools.   The attitude among some Head Start personnel has been that whatever the public schools included in their programs, Head Start would not. Unfortunately, the crucial issues of personalizing instruction and doing what is best for children may have been overlooked. Head Start is now beginning to adopt the position that it will provide what the child needs and rely on the public school to extend and go beyond this. Obviously, this philosophy calls for more coordination and liaison between Head Start and the public schools.

Educational Skills Project.   To strengthen its educational component, the Administration for Children, Youth and Families in 1978 launched its Basic Educational Skills Program to place greater emphasis on teaching basic skills. As a pilot project, the program looked for effective ways to teach Head Start children communication and problem-solving skills and to help them acquire positive attitudes toward learning. It sought to link basic skills instruction in Head Start and elementary programs, through collaborative efforts with public schools, to ensure the outcomes would be beneficial to Head Start children in the center programs and in the elementary schools they later attended. The Basic Educational Skills Program concluded in 1982.

Parent Involvement

From the outset, Head Start has been committed to the philosophy that if children's lives are to improve, corresponding changes must be made in their parents' lives. One cannot hope to change children's lives without involving parents, so part of the Head Start thrust is directed toward that end. Objectives for this program are to:

1. Provide a planned program of experiences and activities which support and enhance the parental role as the principal influence in their child's education and development.
2. Provide a program that recognizes the parents as:
   A. Responsible guardians of their children's well-being.
   B. Prime educators of their children.
   C. Contributors to the Head Start Program and to their communities.

Head Start helps parents learn child rearing and caregiving skills.

3. Provide the following kinds of opportunities for parent participation:
    A. Direct involvement in decision making in program planning and operations.
    B. Participation in classroom and other program activities as paid employees, volunteers or observers.
    C. Activities for parents which they have helped to develop.
    D. Working with their own children in cooperation with Head Start staff.[7]

Employment.   It is required that parents and community members be given first chance at all entry-level positions. Therefore, it is not uncommon to find parents employed as aides and teachers in Head Start. The belief is that by helping parents learn, you also help their children learn. For example, parents who learn in the Head Start center that mealtime is a time for conversation are more likely to model this behavior by talking to their children at home. In this respect, there is a great deal of emphasis on the Head Start teacher's modeling appropriate behavior for parents so that parents will tend to model for their children.

Increasing Parent Income, Responsibility, and Pride.   Employing parents in Head Start centers is also a way to increase family incomes. Many parent volunteers have later been hired as bus drivers, cooks, and aides. As a result of seminars and training programs, some parents have gained the skills necessary to assume positions of increased responsibility, such as assistant teacher, teacher, and program director. To make this process a reality, each Head Start center must create and implement a career development ladder, whereby employees and volunteers, through training and involvement, can move from one position to another with increased responsibility and pay. Jobs in Head Start are not viewed as dead-end positions. Of course, pay and responsibility are not the only benefits; self-image, an important factor in personal life, is also enhanced.

Policy Council.   Every Head Start program operates under policies established by a council that includes parents. If an agency receives money to operate three Head Start centers, each local center has a *parent committee,* and representatives from the parent committees serve on the Policy Council for the three programs. Half the Policy Council members are selected from among parents with children in the program, and half from interested community agencies (day care, family services) and parents who have previously had children in Head Start. Policies established by the Council include determining the attendance area for the center, determining the basis on which children should be recruited, helping develop and oversee the program budget, and acting as a personnel and grievance committee.

The philosophy inherent in involving parents in a Policy Council is twofold. First, in many instances the people for whom programs are developed are the last to be consulted about them. The Policy Council system ensures that parents will have a voice in decisions. The second rationale for the Policy Council is to give parents an opportunity to develop skills for operating programs and meetings. A basic concept of Head Start is to place people who lack certain skills in positions where they can develop these skills, which they can transfer to other settings and from which they gain self-confidence. Those who question the disadvantaged parent's ability to make Head Start decisions must remember that lack of formal education does not mean one cannot make good decisions, and also that the Policy Council does not operate in a vacuum—it has the advice and guidance of the center director as well as educational consultants and the center teachers. Fifty-one percent of the Policy Council is made up of parents, and the other 49 percent of members represent agencies in the larger community.

Often, Head Start staff attend policy advisory committee meetings and offer comments, recommendations, and opinions, but do not vote. Not all Head Start policy comes directly from the Policy Council. The Administration for Children, Youth and Families requires grantees to observe its performance standards and guidelines. In this sense, the Policy Council works within a framework designed by child development and human service experts. While staff make certain recommendations to the council about policy and procedures, the ultimate decisions as to how the program will operate, within the framework of the performance standards, is the responsibility of the Policy Council. Consequently, the council does not necessarily do anything it wishes; rather, a group of people learn responsible action through making decisions about things that affect them.

Positive View of Education.   Through involvement, parents who have previously had a poor concept of education come to appreciate the power and value of education in their lives and their children's. This changed attitude toward education is reflected in parental attitudes and interaction with children, and research shows that the attitude of the child's parents toward education plays a major role in determining the child's attitude.

Health Services
Head Start's health services component delivers a comprehensive developmental program of medical, dental, mental health, and nutrition services to the child. Objectives for the medical and dental components are to:

1. Provide a comprehensive developmental health services program which includes a broad range of medical, dental, mental health, and nutrition services to preschool children, including handicapped children, to assist the child in his physical, emotional, cognitive, and social development toward the overall goal of social competence.
2. Promote preventive health services and early intervention.
3. Provide the child's family with the necessary skills and insight and otherwise attempt to link the family to an ongoing health care system to ensure that the child continues to receive comprehensive developmental health care even after he leaves the Head Start program.[8]

Direct Service.   Child health services in public school settings usually consist of examinations and reports to the parent; corrective and remedial care are often left to the discretion of the parent. Head Start, however, assumes a much more active role. The child's current health status is monitored and reported to the parent and, in cooperation with the parent, corrective and preventive procedures are undertaken. For example, if the child needs glasses, corrective orthopedic surgery, or dental care, services may be provided through the Head Start budget, although the program usually works with social service agencies to provide services or money for health needs.

Regardless of the procedure, the parents' role in providing health care for the child is never bypassed. Although Head Start employees may take the child to the doctor or dentist, every effort is made to see that the parent receives support and assistance for securing appropriate services. For example, the community worker for the Head Start program might provide transportation for the parent, or if the parent has difficulty arranging an appointment with a specialist, the community worker might make arrangements. The philosophy inherent in this process supports the right of the parent as the primary caregiver; an associated rationale is that through involvement in providing health services, parents learn how to provide for future needs.

Daily Health Education.   In addition to arranging medical examinations and care, each Head Start program also teaches children how to care for their health, including the importance of eating proper foods and care of their teeth.

Mental Health Objectives.   The mental health portion of the Head Start health services component has these objectives:

1. Assist all children participating in the program in emotional, cognitive and social development toward the overall goal of social competence in coordination with the education program and other related component activities.
2. Provide handicapped children and children with special needs with the necessary mental health services which will ensure that the child and his family achieve the full benefits of participation in the program.
3. Provide staff and parents with an understanding of child growth and development, and appreciation of individual differences, and the need for a supportive environment.
4. Provide for prevention, early identification and early intervention in problems that interfere with a child's development.
5. Develop a positive attitude toward mental health services and a recognition of the contribution of psychology, medicine, social services, education and others to the mental health program.
6. Mobilize community resources to serve children with problems that prevent them from coping with their environment.[9]

Reading the objectives, we see that the Head Start concept of mental health focuses on early detection and prevention. Since detecting problems depends upon the abilities of Head Start staff members, training programs are initiated for that purpose. A Head Start program might hire a psychologist to help design and implement a diagnostic program through observation. The staff and parents would be trained to detect children's problems, and the psychologist would help the staff develop a set of prescriptions for dealing with particular behaviors. Thus, for example, a program to modify the behavior of an overly aggressive child would be developed and implemented under expert guidance. In addition, follow-up activities for use with the child in the center and home would also be developed.

Head Start programs also seek to direct children and parents to existing mental health delivery systems such as community health centers. It is not the intent of Head Start programs to duplicate existing services, but to help its clientele become aware of and utilize available services.

Social Services

The social services worker (or family services coordinator) also works with families to analyze and find solutions to problems. The purpose of the social services component is to help families find the services that will enable them to lead full and meaningful lives. Solutions generally come through liaison with existing agencies, such as welfare departments, health agencies, and school systems. For example, if a family is not receiving its full welfare benefits, or if it could benefit from family counseling, the social services worker would handle these problems through linkage with an appropriate public agency. Objectives for the social services component are to:

1. Establish and maintain an outreach and recruitment process which systematically insures enrollment of eligible children.
2. Provide enrollment of eligible children regardless of race, sex, creed, color, national origin, or handicapping condition.
3. Achieve parent participation in the center and home program and related activities.
4. Assist the family in its own efforts to improve the condition and quality of family life.
5. Make parents aware of community services and resources and facilitate their use.[10]

Eligibility.   It is also the function of the social services component to enroll those who are eligible for Head Start. After eligibility has been determined, the children must be enrolled. The basic criterion for admission to Head Start is family income level. Ninety percent of the children enrolled in a Head Start program must come from families that meet poverty guidelines; 10 percent may come from families above poverty levels.

Nutrition
Head Start provides nutritious meals as well as nutrition education for children and their families. Objectives for the nutrition component are to:

1. Help provide food which will help meet the child's daily nutritional needs in the child's home or in another clean and pleasant environment recognizing individual differences and cultural patterns and thereby promote sound physical, social, and emotional growth and development.
2. Provide an environment for nutritional services which will support and promote the use of the feeding situation as an opportunity for learning.
3. Help staff, child and family to understand the relationship of nutrition to health, factors which influence food practices, variety of ways to provide for nutritional needs and to apply this knowledge in the development of sound food habits even after leaving the Head Start program.
4. Demonstrate the interrelationships of nutrition to other activities of the Head Start program and its contribution to the overall child development goals.
5. Involve all staff, parents and other community agencies as appropriate in meeting the child's nutritional needs so that nutritional care provided by Head Start complements and supplements that of the home and community.[11]

A basic premise of Head Start is that children must be properly fed to have the strength and energy to learn. This philosophy also calls for teaching children good nutrition habits that will carry over for the rest of their lives and be passed on to their children. In addition, mothers are given basic nutritional education so they, in turn, can continue the nutritional program of the Head Start center. Nutrition education for parents includes seminars on buying food and reading and comparing grocery advertisements.

One Head Start program in consumer education for parents and staff emphasized can sizes, number of servings per can, comparison of prices, nutritional value, and specific foods that can maximize dollar value.

Nutrition programs consist of a breakfast, snack, and lunch at the center. The menus are not traditional school cafeteria fare, but include food children like as well as foods indigenous to their ethnic background. Table 10–4 illustrates a typical weekly Head Start menu. Generally, Head Start centers serve food family style—the food is served in bowls and children help themselves whenever possible. Of course, there are variations from center to center, but whatever the style, a meal is a vehicle for teaching skills and knowledge.

Staff Development

Staff development is one of the major program goals of Head Start, and remains a part of the project that involves parents. Many teachers and aides in Head Start centers have no previous college training, and many are parents. Much of the parent training in child development and educational practices occurs through staff development programs. Generally, before Head Start employees begin teaching, they receive intensive training with on-the-job experiences as a volunteer, aide, bus driver, or cook. They have contact with children, know about the program and are familiar with its goals and objectives, and have an experience base for training. Inservice training is usually conducted by professionals hired at the local level or by representatives of the Head Start regional offices whose duties include assistance in designing training

TABLE 10–4   A Typical Weekly Menu for a Head Start Program (breakfast, lunch, and snack)

Monday	Tuesday	Wednesday	Thursday	Friday
cinnamon toast fruit milk	hot biscuits with butter scrambled eggs juice milk	french toast applesauce milk	cheese omelette toast with butter juice milk	farina with raisins milk
hot dog baked beans coleslaw muffin with butter pears milk	fried chicken yams broccoli cranberry sauce milk brown/serve rolls butter	spaghetti with meatballs celery & carrot stick french bread with butter milk apple	tuna/noodle casserole peas & carrots raisin cup milk bread & butter	roast beef mashed potatoes lima beans choc. sundae milk hot biscuits
melba toast boiled egg juice	dried cereal milk	pineapple chunks milk pretzels	mini-cheesecake milk	variety snack corn-rice-wheat chex party snack milk

Source: Tri-County Head Start, Hughesville, Maryland. Used with permission.

programs. Head Start programs also provide CDA training for their staffs (see Chapter 5).

Administration

The Head Start administration component is designed to help local programs strengthen their administrative and management capabilities to bring about effective delivery of services. This component covers five major areas: program planning and management; personnel management; financial management; procurement and property management; and eligibility and enrollment.

HEAD START IMPROVEMENTS AND INNOVATIONS

Traditionally, Head Start services have been delivered in five half- or whole-day programs, but there is a trend toward local options in service delivery. Under this approach, local Head Start programs are encouraged to plan, develop, and implement alternative ways to deliver services to children and parents. Grantees can, for example, have children attend centers on an "as needed" basis, instead of five days a week; a child might attend only one or two days a week depending upon his needs, capacities, and abilities.

All Head Start programs are encouraged to explore ways to deliver services directly to the child in the home. This approach is based on the premise that the parent is the most important person in the child's life and the home the optimum place for growth and development. In brief, the local option encourages Head Start staff to plan programs that fit their needs and the needs of children and parents, while also taking into consideration the characteristics of the community they serve.

Home-Based Option

Home-based programs are a Head Start option that local agencies may choose as a means of delivering Head Start services. Home-based programs began in 1972 with the three-year Home Start Demonstration project. Skilled home visitors assist parents in providing support services and developmental activities that children would normally receive in a center-based program. Presently, 3000 home visitors provide services to over 35,000 children and their families by working through 500 Head Start programs. The primary difference between a center-based option and a home-based option is that the home-based option focuses on the parent in the home setting and is designed to help the parent participate in activities with the child. The home-based option is augmented by group socialization activities conducted at the center, in one of the family's homes, or somewhere else, such as a community center. The home-based option has these strengths:

1. Parent involvement is the very keystone of the program.
2. Geographically isolated families have an invaluable opportunity to be part of a comprehensive child and family program.
3. The individualized family plan is based on both a child and family assessment.
4. The family plan is facilitated by a home visitor who is an adult educator with knowledge and training related to all Head Start components.
5. The program includes the entire family.[12]

Nutritious meals and snacks and nutritional information are important components of all Head Start programs.

The Bear River Head Start program in Logan, Utah, has developed a training manual to help home visitors work with parents. This is an excerpt for the fourth week of the program:

> Small muscle development means the use of hands and fingers. It is important to eye-hand coordination. A child must first see a target then be able to hit it. An example of this would be pouring milk into a glass. When your child enters school, he needs small muscle skills.
>
> 1. Encourage your child to dress himself and fasten his clothes.
> 2. Let your child spread his bread or pour milk from a small pitcher or bottle.
> 3. Make your own puzzles. Use magazine pictures and cardboard. Be careful not to make them too hard. Beginning puzzles may only have three or four pieces.
> 4. Let your child practice lacing shoes.
> 5. Play a game of dropping clothes pins into a jar or can.
> 6. *Above all, have patience.* Learning these skills takes time.[13]

According to Glenna Markey of the Bear River Head Start, there are several keys to making a home-based option work:

☐ The home visitor must work with the parent, *not* the child. When *parents* work with their children, we achieve the intended results of the home-based option.

☐ The home visitor must help the parent become a "child development specialist," ultimately benefiting the parents' children and grandchildren.

☐ The home visitor must try to do such a good job that the parent can do without her. In this sense, the home visitors put themselves out of a job!

The Head Start Measures Project

The Head Start Measures Project is a federally funded program to help local Head Start programs assess and match curricular activities, instruction, and services to children's individual needs. The project was developed and is conducted by the College of Education at the University of Arizona. Since the project began in the 1984–85 program year, it has served well over 100,000 children.

A central feature of the Measures Project is the *Head Start Measures Battery* (HSMB), designed for assessment and planning with Head Start preschool children in the areas of language, math, nature and science, perception, reading, and social development. The areas of prereading and fine and gross motor skills are presently under development. Children are assessed at the beginning and end of the program year. The assessment results provide teachers with information about each child's fall and spring developmental levels, developmental growth throughout the year, what skills they learned, and the extent to which educational goals were met.

The measures approach views each child as progressing along an individual *developmental path* and focuses on what children are able to do as opposed to what they cannot do. Using the results of the Measures Battery, teachers match learning and teaching episodes to children's skills and developmental levels. Assessment and activity planning are linked through the use of *path referencing*. Information is provided for each child's developmental path in each of the six areas. The teacher knows what skills the child has mastered and can plan activities he is ready to learn on his path of develpment. The HSMB provides a developmental level score for each child, the child's performance or mastery level on each skill, and a teaching level score, indicating the level of skills taught to the child. Results of the HSMB are provided to individual programs in three ways: developmental profiles for the class and for each child, developmental profiles in conjunction with a planning guide to assist in developing plans for learning activities, and skill level progress reports showing the child's improvement in each skill area.

Using the HSMB assessment and planning system, teachers are able to *assess* children's developmental levels; *screen* children to locate those who need special attention; *plan,* using the HSMB planning guide, to identify what skills children are ready to learn; *update* plans as children learn; *communicate* to parents what their children can do and what they are ready to learn; and *document* each child's progress. Research findings for the first year of implementation for the Measures Project (1984–85) indicate that "Children show improvement in Developmental Level (DL) over what would be expected from maturation alone; that children who participated in the planning portion of the system showed more improvement than those who did not; that children improved more if teachers had more accurate knowledge of the children's Developmental Levels; and that an analysis of the overall results of the HSMB assessment in the Head Start Program shows evidence that teachers are individualizing activities for their children."[14]

A test item from the Head Start Measures Battery is shown in Figure 10–2. The HSMB Classroom Activity Guide was developed for Head Start by Child Inc. with the cooperation of the University of Arizona.

Services to Handicapped Children

Since at least 10 percent of Head Start enrollment consists of handicapped children, there may be some handicapped children in each classroom. Head Start defines handicapped children as "mentally retarded, hard of hearing, deaf, speech impaired, visually handicapped, seriously emotionally disturbed, crippled, or other health-impaired children, who by reason thereof require special education and related services."[15] To provide adequately for these children, staff and parents receive training in methods and procedures related to the particular disabilities. Head Start also provides staff training in identification, treatment, and prevention of child abuse and neglect. (See Chapter 11 for more information on educating the handicapped.)

Public School Involvement

Should the public schools become involved in Head Start and day care? Not everyone agrees that they should; however, there appears to be a large-scale effort on the part of the public schools and national teacher's organizations to gain control of existing social service agencies, day care, and Head Start programs. There is growing recognition that the number of families who need Head Start programs is much greater than the number of families served. The ability of social service organizations to meet the needs of families is limited, and the demand for services greater than currently available resources. Therefore, many professionals and legislators feel that, since public schools already exist in every community, it makes sense to give them the responsibility for delivering services to preschool children and their families.

There are many strong arguments against public school involvement in social services. One is that public schools are not doing a good job in their traditional role

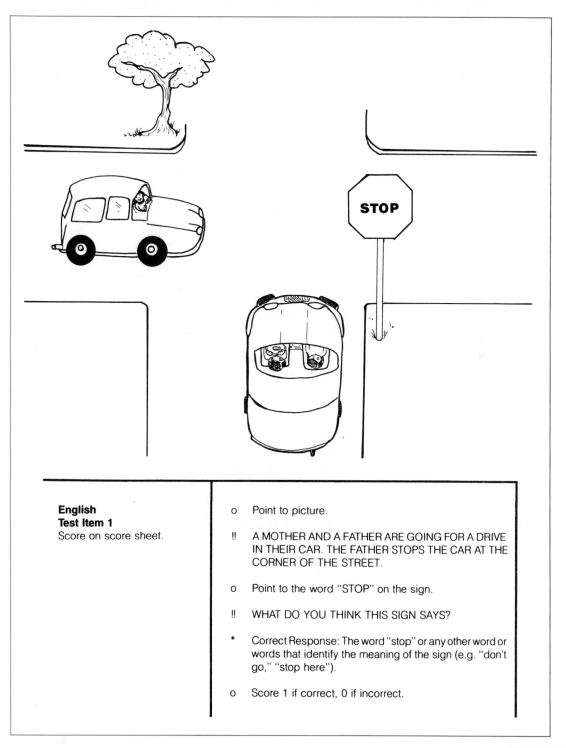

English **Test Item 1** Score on score sheet.	o Point to picture. ‼ A MOTHER AND A FATHER ARE GOING FOR A DRIVE IN THEIR CAR. THE FATHER STOPS THE CAR AT THE CORNER OF THE STREET. o Point to the word "STOP" on the sign. ‼ WHAT DO YOU THINK THIS SIGN SAYS? * Correct Response: The word "stop" or any other word or words that identify the meaning of the sign (e.g. "don't go," "stop here"). o Score 1 if correct, 0 if incorrect.

FIGURE 10–2 An Item from the Head Start Measures Battery (Source: *Head Start Measures Battery,* University of Arizona.)

Ten percent of Head Start enrollment must include children with special needs, and Head Start is a leader in providing services for these children. Even greater effort will be directed toward meeting their needs as identification of and concern for special needs children grows.

of teaching the basic skills of reading, writing, and arithmetic. Critics cite the dropout rate, illiteracy figures, and declining achievement test scores as evidence that the schools have failed. Therefore, the argument continues, if the schools are already failing, how can we expect them to succeed at another job? Second, critics of public school involvement in preschool and family affairs point to the historic reluctance of the schools to take responsibility for this area of education. Many teachers, administrators, and taxpayers feel that preschool and family education does not represent the legitimate function of the public schools. This argument will probably be the most persuasive in determining whether public schools will become more involved than they already are. The third argument against public school involvement is that teachers and administrators are not trained to assume responsibilities for working with pre-school children and their families because colleges of education have not trained teachers for this role. On the other hand, the colleges respond that they could initiate retraining programs for teachers and design new training programs. Fourth, if a greater number of certified teachers were employed in early childhood programs, there would be fewer positions for people without college degrees. This would have a negative effect on people already employed in these programs, some of whom are parents. One of the reasons many child care agencies and Head Start centers are in operation is to provide low-income parents with an opportunity to earn money. Many of the employment opportunities available in early childhood programs that do not require certification should be filled by individuals without the four-year degree.

Does Head Start Make a Difference?

No question in early childhood education has been debated, discussed, considered, and examined more than whether Head Start makes a difference in the lives of children. The most conclusive evidence that serves to answer this question comes from well-designed and well-conducted research projects—for example, the Perry Preschool Project, an experiment designed to reveal the effects of early educational intervention on disadvantaged youth. Describing the causes and effects of this project, the authors found that early education programs significantly reduced the number of children assigned to special education; significantly reduced the number of children retained in grade; and significantly increased children's scores on fourth grade math-ematics achievement tests with a suggestive trend toward increased scores on fourth grade reading tests. In addition, low-income children who attended preschools sur-passed their controls on the Stanford-Binet I.Q. test for up to three years after the program ended. Also, children who attended preschool were more likely than control children to give reasons of achievement for being proud of themselves.

To the question, "What do we know so far about Head Start?" Schweinhart and Weikart respond:

1. Short-, mid-, and long-term positive effects are available.
2. Adequately funded Head Start programs run by well-trained, competent staff can achieve the level of quality operation that will lead to positive effects.
3. Equal educational opportunity for all people is a fundamental goal of the great Ameri-can experiment and good Head Start programs can make a sound contribution to the achievement of the goal.[16]

Additionally, in a study of children attending Head Start with other children, the researchers concluded:

As a result of these analyses, we may conclude that participation in Head Start appeared to provide significant 1-year gains on some measures of ability for low-income children. These gains, which could reasonably be attributed to children's participation in the Head Start program, were considerably more likely to accrue to Black children than to White children. Moreover, among Black children cognitive gains attributable to Head Start participation were more likely to occur in children with lower initial cognitive ability. It is important that the significant "Head Start advantage" was found in analytical designs that either controlled for

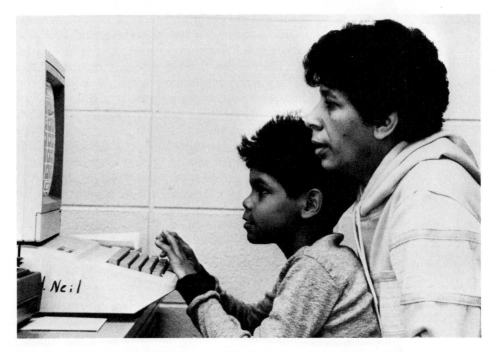

Head Start promotes family literacy, and local programs are using computers toward this end.

test-specific ability or for general ability assessed at program entry, contrasting Head Start children with children of statistically comparable backgrounds who either had no preschool experience or who attended a non-Head Start preschool. Although the advantage of Head Start participation was clearer compared with no preschool experience, we conclude that there is evidence to support the superiority of Head Start over other preschool experience as well.[17]

HEAD START: NEW INITIATIVES, FUTURE DIRECTIONS

Head Start always has been and remains in the vanguard of agencies involved in new and innovative programs. The following represent some of Head Start's current bold new ventures.

Comprehensive Child Development Program (CCDP)

The CCDP program is Head Start's latest involvement in infant-toddler programming. The purpose of this effort is to encourage intensive and comprehensive services to enhance the physical, social, emotional, and intellectual development of low-income children from birth to compulsory school age, including the provision of necessary support to their parents and other family members. Services to infants and young children under this program include

☐ Health services (including screening and referral)
☐ Child care that meets state licensing requirements

☐ Early intervention services
☐ Nutritional services

Services for parents and other family members are intended to contribute to their children's healthy development and include

☐ Prenatal care
☐ Education in infant and child development
☐ Health, nutrition, and parenting services
☐ Assistance in securing adequate income support, health care, nutrition assistance and housing

Family Literacy

Head Start has historically been involved in and concerned about issues of family literacy. Today many Head Start programs are promoting family literacy through a number of unique programs; for example, Head Start and IBM have joined forces in a program to promote intergenerational literacy. The objectives of the Head Start/ IBM Partnership Project include

☐ Identifying quality software for programs for young children
☐ Developing curriculum integration strategies to enhance the appropriate use of technology within the preschool classroom
☐ Determining an optimal hardware configuration for young children
☐ Evaluating the response of Head Start children, staff, and parents to the use of technology
☐ Determining training and support requirements
☐ Using community volunteers to support access and integration of technology in Head Start programs

At the St. Bernardine Head Start in Baltimore, a Computers in the Classroom project is offering literacy training to Head Start parents as part of an ongoing initiative to involve parents in adult education. The parents in the program have developed an Afro-Centric Holistic Intergenerational Model, as shown in Figure 10–3.

MIGRANT EDUCATION

In 1965, Congress authorized Title I of the Elementary and Secondary Education Act (ESEA) to provide public school programs for disadvantaged children. These funds, however, did not provide adequate services for the children of migrant workers; consequently, in 1966, ESEA Title I was amended by P.L. 89–750 to provide money specifically for education of migrant children.

> Currently "migratory child" means a child (a) whose parent or guardian is a migratory agricultural worker or migratory fisherman; and (b) who has within the past twelve months moved from one school district into another (or, in a state comprising a single school district has moved from one school administrative area into another) in order to enable the child, the child's guardian, or a member of the child's immediate family to obtain temporary or seasonal employment in an agricultural or fishing activity.[18]

Historically, the migrant child has suffered educationally because his family seldom lives in one place for any length of time; public schools have not always been willing

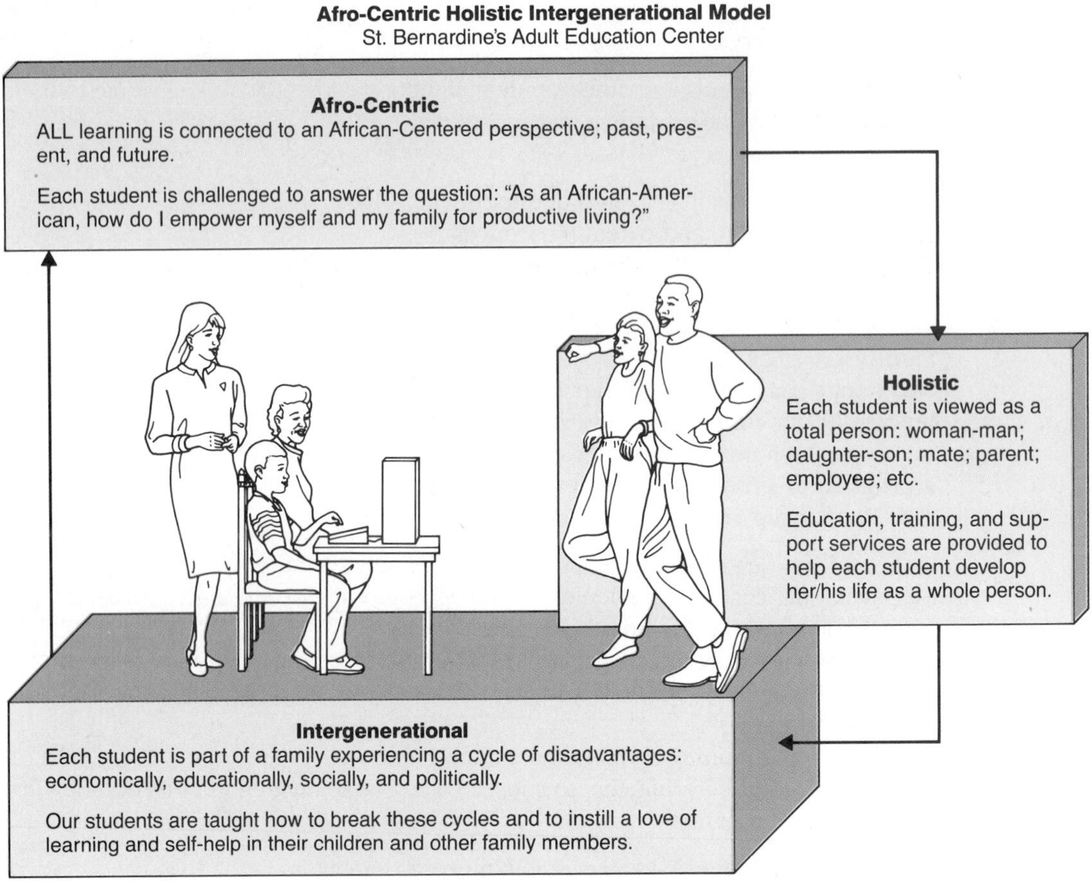

Afro-Centric Holistic Intergenerational Model
St. Bernardine's Adult Education Center

Afro-Centric
ALL learning is connected to an African-Centered perspective; past, present, and future.

Each student is challenged to answer the question: "As an African-American, how do I empower myself and my family for productive living?"

Holistic
Each student is viewed as a total person: woman-man; daughter-son; mate; parent; employee; etc.

Education, training, and support services are provided to help each student develop her/his life as a whole person.

Intergenerational
Each student is part of a family experiencing a cycle of disadvantages: economically, educationally, socially, and politically.

Our students are taught how to break these cycles and to instill a love of learning and self-help in their children and other family members.

FIGURE 10–3   An Afro-Centric Holistic Intergenerational Model, St. Bernardine's Adult Education Center. (Source: *Head Start/IBM Partnership: A Project in Intergenerational Literacy* by Linda Tsantis, 1989, U.S. Administration for Children, Youth, and Families.)

to give migrant children the special attention they need; and migrant children have had to work to supplement their families' incomes. Without an education, migrant children are caught in the trap of illiteracy and inadequate job skills that prevents their escaping the cycle of poverty.

CHAPTER 1

Chapter 1 of the Hawkins-Stafford Elementary and Secondary Improvement Act of 1988 serves about five million children in about 30 percent of the nation's public schools; for fiscal year 1987–1988, it had a budget of 3.5 billion dollars. Two-thirds of the participating children are in grades K–6. The purpose of this program is to improve the educational opportunities of educationally deprived children by helping

DAISY GIRL SCOUTS: A HEAD START ON LITERACY

Daisy Girl Scouts—A Head Start on Literacy: Playing in the World of Words is a demonstration project designed for girls to become Daisy Girl Scouts after their Head Start experience and thus continue to enhance the development of their potential and social competence. Like all other girls in the scouting program, Head Start graduates will be encouraged to continue in Girl Scouting throughout their school years and to enjoy the life-long benefits from participation in a supportive environment like Head Start.

By initiating this coordinated effort with Head Start, Girl Scouts are acting on a national commitment to increase pluralism, reaching out with opportunities to girls from underserved, low-income populations. In this project, Head Start girl graduates will begin exploring the overall Girl Scout program. With an additional emphasis on getting "a head start on literacy," age-appropriate activities will encourage preliteracy skill development. Through the fun of "playing in the world of words"—active listening, storytelling, singing, dramatic play, dancing, drawing, and making things like their own Daisy Girl Scout scrapbooks—girls will be learning to express themselves and to understand others. Activities like these will help them look forward to learning to read and succeed in school and to enjoy interacting with their ever-widening world.

Head Start and Girl Scouts of America have joined forces to further the program goals of both agencies. Their cooperation is an excellent example of interagency involvement to benefit low-income children and their families.

them succeed in the regular program of the local educational agency, attain grade-level proficiency, and improve achievement in basic and more advanced skills. These purposes are accomplished through such means as supplemental education programs, schoolwide programs and the increased involvement of parents in their children's education.

FEDERAL SUPPORT FOR EARLY CHILDHOOD PROGRAMS

In addition to Head Start, Migrant Education, and Chapter 1, the federal government plays a major role in funding other programs that involve and affect young children and their families.

A DAY IN THE LIFE OF A CHILD IN THE MIGRANT PRESCHOOL EDUCATION PROGRAM IN MABTON, WASHINGTON

Carlos Trevino, age four, migrates with his parents, five brothers, and a younger sister from Texas to Washington in April. His family comes to the Yakima Valley to cut asparagus. The labor camp where he lives is provided by the asparagus growers.

Carlos's family gets up at 3 A.M. and gets Carlos and his younger sister ready for their day at the Mabton Child Development Center. The bus arrives for Carlos at 3:30, and he is transported to the Mabton Child Development Center, supported with funds from Chapter 1, Migrant, Washington State Title XX Day Care, and the United States Department of Agriculture (for meals and snacks). Carlos lives six miles from the center and arrives at 4:15 A.M. Upon his arrival he is immediately put to bed by a Title XX worker. Carlos goes right to sleep and wakes at 7 A.M., when all the children are awakened. Carlos washes his face and hands, combs his hair, and gets ready for breakfast. Today, his breakfast consists of migas (corn tortilla with egg), milk, and a quarter of an orange.

The menu for breakfast and other meals is approved by the U.S. Department of Agriculture and is culturally related to the Mexican-American children in the Mabton program. After eating breakfast, Carlos helps clean up the table. Today it is his job to wipe the table. He then brushes his teeth.

There are twenty children in Carlos's class, taught by one teacher and two assistants.

Today, Carlos begins his day with a free choice of activities. He can select from one of the following learning areas: kitchen area, block area, art, or manipulative area.

Carlos chooses the manipulative area, where there are materials and games that will help him learn to tie his shoes. Other materials such as puzzles will help with visual memory, pegboards will help him learn colors, and other materials are designed to promote readiness for learning to read and write. During his free choice time, one of the teachers will help Carlos to make sure he is learning the manual dexterity he will need to learn to tie his shoes, hold a pencil, and perform other tasks requiring manual dexterity and fine motor control.

At 9 A.M., Carlos goes outside, where he can swing, slide, play in the sand, and use a tricycle. His teacher encourages him to play in the sand. She believes the sandbox toys will help him with his manual dexterity. At 9:30, Carlos has a snack of milk and banana. This snack is served by the children themselves. They prepare the tables, pour their own milk, peel their own bananas, and clean up. At 9:45 A.M., Carlos goes into his classroom, where he receives instruction in the individualized bilingual education curriculum. During this lesson, the room is arranged so there are three tables with six to seven children at each table. Each teacher teaches a group lesson lasting from ten to fifteen minutes. Each group rotates from one table to another, so they receive a

Child Care

The federal government is one of the largest supporters of child care. The government supports child care in five ways. One way is through state agencies. Title XX of the Social Security Act provides monies to states in the form of "block grants." These monies are used to provide certain groups and classes of parents and children with child care. Some eligibility criteria under Title XX are that the parent receives Aid to Families with Dependent Children (AFDC); the parent receives a social security payment supplement; the gross income of the parent is below an eligibility level established by the state; or, the parent belongs to a particular group (such as migrant farm

total of thirty or forty-five minutes of language instruction. At 10:30 A.M., Carlos again has a free choice activity, and chooses to go to the block area. At 11 A.M., he goes outside and plays on the swings. At 11:15, Carlos goes inside and washes his hands and face and combs his hair before lunch. (The staff taught him to do these acts of personal hygiene for himself.) Then he helps set the table.

After the tables are set, the children seat themselves, and the food is placed on the table in bowls for the children to pass and serve themselves. Mealtimes help the children learn manners, the use of eating utensils, and decision making. The teachers eat with the children.

After lunch, Carlos has a play period outside before his nap at 12:45 P.M. While the children are sleeping, the teachers plan the next day's activities.

Carlos wakes from his nap at 3 P.M. and has a snack of guacamole con tortilla (avocado with tortilla) and milk. Carlos helps clean up from the snack time, then chooses to take part in a planned art activity, making a collage. Each child's collage is hung on the bulletin board. At 3:45, the bus arrives and Carlos goes home.

Carlos's older brother Roberto, who is in the third grade, also gets up at 3 A.M., but he prepares for the daily cutting of asparagus rather than school. Asparagus harvesting begins about April 1 and ends about June 25

every year. At 4 A.M., after a breakfast of eggs, chorizo (ground beef and sausage), tortillas, and milk, Roberto goes with his father to the asparagus fields. He cuts about eighty pounds of asparagus from 4:15 until 10:00 A.M. Roberto's family is paid seven cents a pound for the asparagus. What Roberto earns will be paid to his father. By state law, Roberto is allowed to miss one hour of school per day, with his parent's permission, to cut asparagus. Since the family needs the money Roberto is able to earn, they readily give their permission. Someone from Roberto's family takes him from the fields to the labor camp where one of the other migrant workers takes him and other children to school. This way, only one worker has to lose time in the fields.

Roberto arrives at school at about 10:30 A.M. Classes have already begun, and he continues with the regular curriculum and schedule until after lunch. During the afternoon, Roberto spends up to two hours in a migrant resource room. Here his teacher has developed an individual skills program based on information she received from the Migrant Student Record Transfer System and the schools' own testing program. Roberto receives a complete program in mathematics, reading, and oral language. Skills learned in this program should bring him up to grade level with other students in the school.

workers) that is automatically eligible for child care services. Monies for child care under Title XX programs amount to over 700 million dollars.

A second source of federal support for child care is the U.S. Department of Agriculture Child Care Food Program. The USDA provides monies and commodities to child care centers and homes to support their nutrition programs. Children twelve years old and younger are eligible. The USDA provided nearly $700 million for the food program in fiscal 1989.

A third source of federal support for child care is child care tax credits. Since 1975, parents have been able to itemize the cost of child care as a deduction against their federal income taxes. Currently, the amount that can be deducted is based on a sliding scale. Beginning at $10,000 of annual income, 30 percent of the cost of child care can be deducted. As income increases, the percentage decreases until it reaches 20 percent. The maximum amount a family can deduct is $2400 for one child and $4800 for two children.

A fourth source of federal support to child care is employer support or employer sponsorship. The federal tax code allows employers certain tax breaks or benefits for providing child care for employees.

Last, a source of federal support comes through the government's role as an employer. Many federal agencies, including the CIA and the Internal Revenue Service, provide child care services for employees. Remember the federal government's role in supporting military child care (see Chapter 5).

The federal government will continue to play an influential role in all of education, ranging from services to pregnant women to higher education. While some are critical of the federal presence, which they see as federal control, others believe that without even greater federal support, issues of equality and quality cannot be adequately addressed. Regardless, the federal government's presence in the education fabric of American life and its early childhood programs is well established. The federal government will continue to play a dominant role in deciding who gets what kind of services. The challenge for early childhood educators is to serve as advocates on behalf of children and their families and to influence federal policy so that programs, services, and monies are put to their best use.

FURTHER READING

Beaty, Janice J. *Skills for Preschool Teachers,* 3rd ed. (Columbus, Ohio: Merrill, 1988)

Designed specifically for the Head Start, day care, and kindergarten worker, content parallels the Child Development Associate Competencies; helpful for anyone contemplating this training program.

Living and Teaching Nutrition (College Park, Md.: Head Start Resource and Training Center, University of Maryland, 1983)

Inservice training guide featuring nine workshops; chapters include: What's New in Nutri-tion? How's Your Diet? Economical Nutrition; Fresh Fruits and Vegetables; Dental Health and Sugar; Planning Menus and Planning Snacks; Family-Style Eating; Cooking Experiences for Young Children; Nutrition Activities for Young Children.

Morrison, George S. *Parent Involvement in the Home, School and Community* (Columbus, Ohio: Merrill, 1978)

Practical approach to involving parents; reality-based and full of useful information.

FURTHER STUDY

1. Accompany a Head Start worker when she visits homes. How do you think qualities of the homes you visited affect the children's learning ability?
2. Discuss the range of cultural differences in your community. Give an example of a classroom problem that may result from cultural variations.
3. Interview parents of Head Start children to find out what they feel has been the impact of Head Start on their family.
4. Visit a local school district and gather information about its federally supported programs. What kind of federal education programs does the district have? How is the money spent? Do you approve or disapprove of what you saw?
5. Visit several Head Start programs and compare

and contrast what you see. How are they similar and different? How do you account for this?

6. After reviewing current literature and interviewing children, parents, and Head Start personnel, briefly state your opinion concerning the success or failure of the present Head Start program. Give reasons for your comments and discuss with your peers.

7. Interview Head Start workers to determine their opinions about the future of the program. What changes do they suggest?

8. Examine the latest poverty income guidelines published by the federal government. Do you feel these incomes are sufficient for rearing a family? Why or why not? What solutions would you propose to the problem of substandard incomes for a large number of American families?

9. Compare the schedule of a Head Start center in this chapter with a Head Start center in your community. Also compare the Head Start schedules to those of preschools. What would you change? Be specific, and include your reasons.

10. Develop a list of pros and cons for involving parents in early childhood programs. What implications does this list have for teachers of young children? For Head Start programs? How do you feel about parent involvement in early childhood programs?

11. Develop a questionnaire you could give to parents to find out their needs and ideas about home-based and center-based early childhood programs. Which do they prefer?

12. Collect magazine articles about working with parents. Save only those that give specific ideas and tips. What is their major emphasis? Could parents use them?

13. Develop a set of criteria for deciding which families would be eligible for a home-based education program.

14. Conduct a poll of parents to find out how they think early childhood programs and schools can help them in educating their children; how they think they can be involved in early childhood programs; what specific help they feel they need in child rearing and educating; and what activities they would like in a home visitation program.

15. Survey parents to determine their views and beliefs about federal cutbacks to social programs and early childhood programs. Analyze their opinions as they correlate to income level, cultural background, and educational level.

16. What effects have federal cuts in social services had on particular families and children in your area? Give specific examples.

17. Contact the migrant education office in your area. What are the occupations of migrant parents? What are the major problems faced by the children and families? What services are being provided for them? Do you think the services to migrants are as effective and comprehensive as they should be?

18. Write a position paper supporting or rejecting federal support to early childhood programs.

19. Interview the director of the Follow Through program in your school district. After this interview, visit a Follow Through classroom. Do you support the purposes of Follow Through? Why? What three things impressed you most and least about the program?

20. Would you want to teach in a Head Start/Follow Through program? Why or why not?

NOTES

1. Administration for Children, Youth and Families, "Project Head Start Statistical Fact Sheet" (Washington, D.C.: January 1990), pp. 2–3.

2. Esther Kresh, *National Head Start Bulletin,* 28 (May, 1989), p. 9.

3. U.S. Department of Health and Human Services, *Head Start Program Performance Standards* (45-CFR 1304) (Washington, D.C.: U.S. Government Printing Office, November, 1984).

4. *Head Start Program Performance Standards,* pp. 8–9.

5. Schedule from Franklin-Vance Warren Opportunity, Inc., Head Start Program, Henderson, North Carolina.

6. Sample daily schedule of the Metropolitan Dade County, Florida, Head Start.

7. *Head Start Program Performance Standards,* p. 58.

8. *Head Start Program Performance Standards,* p. 16.

9. *Head Start Program Performance Standards,* pp. 30–31.

10. *Head Start Program Performance Standards,* p. 53.

11. *Head Start Program Performance Standards,* p. 38.

12. E. Dollie Wolverton, "The Home-Based Option: Reinforcing Parents," *Head Start Bulletin* 12 (October/November, 1986), p. 1.

13. From *Home Start Curriculum Guide,* Bear River Head Start Program, Logan, Utah.

14. John R. Bergan et al., *The Head Start Measures Project: A Summary Report on Full-Year Implementation, 1984–1985* (Tucson, Ariz.: The Center for Educational Evaluation, The University of Arizona), p. 15

15. *Head Start Newsletter,* 7, no. 2, DHEW Publication no. OHD 74-1068 (November-December 1973).

16. Lawrence J. Schweinhart and David P. Weikart, "What Do We Know So Far?: A Review of the Head Start Synthesis Project." *Young Children,* 41, no. 2 (January 1986), p. 50.

17. Valerie E. Lee, J. Brooks-Gunn, and Elizabeth Schnur, "Does Head Start Work? A 1-year Follow-Up Comparison of Disadvantaged Children Attending Head Start, No Preschool, and Other Preschool Programs," *Developmental Psychology,* 24 (2), pp. 210–222. © 1988 American Psychological Corporation.

18. *Federal Register,* July 13, 1977, p. 36080.

CHAPTER 11
Teaching Children with Special Needs
Developing Awareness

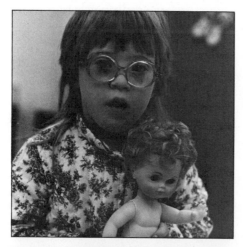

As you read and study:
- [ ] Identify and learn the terminology and legal definitions of children with special needs
- [ ] Assess the legal, political, moral and social bases for mainstreaming children in early childhood programs
- [ ] Develop and evaluate a personal philosophy about teaching in the mainstream
- [ ] Identify reasons for current interest in special needs children
- [ ] Understand the major provisions of P.L. 94–142 and P.L. 99–457
- [ ] Determine the implications of P.L. 94–142 and P.L. 99–457 for children, families, and teachers
- [ ] Identify and evaluate issues relating to mainstreaming and teaching handicapped children
- [ ] Examine and review what is involved in an Individual Education Program
- [ ] Understand the reasons for and basic components of an Individual Family Service Plan
- [ ] Examine and understand the basis of programs for the gifted
- [ ] Develop methods for involving parents of special needs children in educational programs
- [ ] Develop an understanding of multicultural education
- [ ] Develop a philosophy of teaching for multicultural awareness and understanding

Educators and the public are very much involved in providing all children with an education appropriate to their physical, mental, social, and emotional abilities. In particular, there is a great deal of emphasis on educating children who have needs that other children do not. There are special needs children in every classroom of every school. These children are handicapped, gifted, and children with multicultural heritages. They require teaching strategies and approaches designed to meet their individual special needs.

Handicapped Children

To understand programs for the handicapped, it is important to know the federal government's definition of handicapped children:

> The term "handicapped children" means those children evaluated . . . as being mentally retarded, hard of hearing, deaf, speech impaired, visually handicapped, seriously emotionally disturbed, orthopedically impaired, other health impaired, deaf-blind, multi-handicapped, or as having specific learning disabilities, who because of those impairments need special education and related services.[1]

Several facets of the government's definition differ from the public's general conception of the handicapped. First, the federal definition is more comprehensive. Second, the public generally thinks of the handicaps as mainly physical disabilities and not so much in terms of the emotionally or orthopedically impaired. Table 11–1 shows the number of handicapped children in the various categories; about 10 to 12 percent of the nation's children are handicapped.

Gifted and Talented Children

The Jacob K. Javits Gifted and Talented Students Education Act of 1988 defines gifted and talented children as those who "give evidence of high performance capability in areas such as intellectual, creative, artistic, or leadership capacity, or in specific academic fields, and who require services or activities not ordinarily provided by the

TABLE 11–1 Handicapped Children and Youth Served Under P.L. 94-142 and P.L. 89-313, 1985–1986

Source: Office of Special Education and Rehabilitative Services, U.S. Dept. of Education, National Summary of Handicapped Children Receiving Education and Related Services under P.L. 94-142 and P.L. 89-313, 1985-1986.

Type of Handicap	Total Served, Ages 0–21, U.S. and Insular Areas
Mentally Retarded	686,007
Hard of Hearing and Deaf	68,413
Speech Impaired	1,128,471
Visually Handicapped	29,026
Emotionally Disturbed	376,943
Orthopedically Impaired	59,000
Deaf-Blind	2,133
Multi-handicapped	89,701
Learning Disabled	1,872,339
Other Health Impaired	58,141
Total for year	4,370,244

school in order to fully develop such capabilities." The definition distinguishes between *giftedness,* characterized by above-average intellectual ability, and *talented,* referring to individuals who excel in such areas as drama, art, music, athletics, and leadership. Students can have these abilities separately or in combination. A talented five-year-old may be learning disabled, and an orthopedically handicapped student may be gifted.

Multicultural Children

Multicultural students are those whose home culture differs from that of the general population and/or school. These children are members of minority cultures such as Asian American, Native American, African American, or Hispanic. Multicultural children may or may not have special learning needs; quite often, however, they have special language needs. Other children may need help because of differences in behavior based on cultural customs and values. All children in every classroom, regardless of their cultural background, need teachers who are multiculturally aware and who promote multicultural understanding.

TEACHING IN THE MAINSTREAM

Many children are taught in the mainstream when they enter the public schools. *Mainstreaming* is the social and educational integration of special needs children into the general instructional process, usually the regular classroom. This practice implies that such children will be identified and that the services of special educators and other professionals as well as regular teachers will be utilized. Mainstreaming means the special needs child will be educated in the regular school classroom for part or all of the school day. Removal from the regular classroom should occur only if the regular classroom cannot offer appropriate instruction; then instruction is usually provided by a special educator such as a resource teacher.

Mainstreaming can be interpreted to mean that children with special needs will be a part of the system of education that has traditionally meant "normal" children and regular classrooms. In another sense, mainstreaming means the schools are returning special needs children to the system from which they have been excluded for over three-quarters of a century. Until recently, it was acceptable, and thought to be educationally sound, legal, and humane, to provide separate (but not always equal) education for special needs children outside the regular classroom. It is no longer justifiable to do so if the child can benefit from an educational program in the regular classroom. In mainstreaming, emphasis is on the concept of *normalcy.* This means that children will be treated normally and educated as normally as possible. These are guidelines for preparing to teach in a mainstreamed classroom:

☐ Have a well thought-out philosophy of education. This is important no matter what kind of children you teach; however, it is absolutely necessary to think through your attitudes toward the handicapped.
☐ Know the nature of the handicapped children you will be teaching. Just as it is important to know normal childhood growth and development, it is essential for you to know about the different handicaps and how to account for them in the teaching-learning process.

355

Mainstreaming integrates the handicapped child into the least restrictive environment, often the regular classroom. Special needs children also include those of different cultures, and multicultural activities should be part of every early childhood classroom.

Because P.L. 94–142 requires individualized education for the handicapped child and P.L. 99–457 requires an Individualized Family Service Plan, it is important to know what these consist of and the procedures for completing them. Although developing a program for the individual child and/or family is not the same as individualized instruction, it is important to know the differences between the two and how to conduct both processes.

☐ Methods and techniques of diagnostic and prescriptive teaching are essential as a basis for writing and implementing the Individualized Educational Program and the Individualized Family Service Plan.

☐ Working with parents is an absolute must for every classroom teacher. You should learn all you can about parent conferences and communication, parent

involvement, and parents as volunteers and aides. In a sense, P.L. 94–142 and
P.L. 99–457 mainstream parents as well as children.

☐ Working with paraprofessionals offers a unique opportunity for the classroom
teacher to individualize instruction. Since it is obvious that the regular classroom teacher needs help in individualizing instruction, it makes sense to use
paraprofessionals in this process. You should become knowledgeable about and
adept in working with paraprofessionals.

☐ As more individual education becomes a reality, teachers will need skills in assessing student behavior. Therefore, training in tests and measurements and observational skills are a necessity.

☐ Teachers must know how to identify sources of, and how to order and use, a
broad range of instructional materials, including media. One cannot hope to individualize without a full range of materials and media. The learning modalities
teachers must regularly be concerned with are visual, auditory, and tactile/kin-
esthetic. Some children in a classroom may learn best through one mode; other
children may learn best through another. The classroom teacher can utilize media, in particular, to help make teaching styles congruent with children's learning modalities.

☐ Every teacher in a mainstreamed classroom (and even those who are not)
should be familiar with P.L. 94–142 and P.L. 99–457 and their implications.

INTEREST IN SPECIAL NEEDS CHILDREN

There are several reasons for the present interest in education of special needs
children. First, court cases and legal decisions have extended to special needs children
the rights and privileges enjoyed by everyone. To ensure that these rights and privileges are accorded to their children, parent involvement is a necessity. In some
instances, court decisions have encouraged or ordered this involvement. In the absence of the special needs child's ability to be his own advocate, the courts, agencies,
and parents assume that function.

Legislation enacted at the state and federal levels has specified that handicapped
children must receive a free and appropriate education. In essence, this legislation
promotes and encourages development of programs for education of the handicapped.
This legislation also provides for parent involvement. Thus, educators are involving
parents of handicapped children because they must.

Second, there is federal money available to create programs for special needs
children, and greater social consciousness toward children with special needs. People
recognize that the handicapped have often been treated as second-class citizens and
have been victims of oppression and degradation, so there is an effort to make
reparations for past behavior and attitudes.

Third, many young people see teaching special needs children as a rewarding
profession, with unlimited opportunities to contribute. These young people feel they
can best serve society, children, and themselves by teaching, and many preservice
professionals feel that most children will learn on their own, but the special needs
child needs help and training. Consequently, many bright, young educators are de-
voting their lives to helping these children.

Fourth, American education emphasizes meeting the needs of individual children, and special needs children require special attention and accommodation.

Public Law 94–142

The landmark legislation providing for the needs of the handicapped is P.L. 94–142. Section 3 of this law states:

> It is the purpose of this Act to assure that all handicapped children have available to them, within the time periods specified in section 612(2)(B), a free appropriate public education which emphasizes special education and related services designed to meet their unique needs, to assure that the rights of handicapped children and their parents or guardians are protected, to assist States and localities to provide for the education of all handicapped children, and to assess and assure the effectiveness of efforts to educate handicapped children.[2]

P.L. 94–142 provides for a free and appropriate education (FAPE) for all persons between the ages of three and twenty-one. The operative word is *appropriate;* the child must receive an education suited to his age, maturity, handicapping condition, past achievements, and parental expectations. The common practice was to diagnose children as handicapped and then put them in an existing program, whether or not that program was specifically appropriate; now, the educational program has to be appropriate to the child, which means that a plan must be developed for each child.

The child's education must occur within the least restrictive educational environment. *Least restrictive* means that environment in which the child will be able to receive a program that meets his specific needs—the regular classroom, if that is the environment in which the child can learn best. The least restrictive educational environment is not always the regular classroom; however, this law provides more opportunity to be with regular children (see Figure 11–1).

The law requires *individualization of instruction* and *diagnosis.* Not only must the child's education be appropriate, it must also be individualized, taking into consideration his specific needs, handicapping conditions, and preferences, as well as those of his parents. The key to the individualization process is another feature of the law that requires development of an individual educational plan (IEP) for each child. This plan must specify what will be done for the child, and how and when it will be done. The plan must be in writing. In developing this educational plan, a person trained in diagnosing handicapping conditions, such as a school psychologist, must be involved, as well as a classroom teacher, the parent, and, where appropriate, the child himself.

There are several implications associated with this educational plan. One is that for the first time, on a formal basis, parents and children are involved in the educational determination of what will happen to the child. Second, the child must have a plan tailor-made or individualized for him. This individualization assures accurate diagnosis and realistic goal setting, as well as responsible implementation of the program. This brings an element of personalization to the process, and increases the possibility that the teaching-learning process will be more humane.

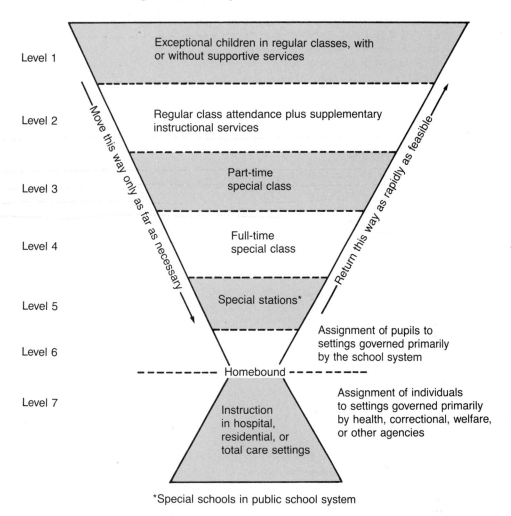

Level 1 — Exceptional children in regular classes, with or without supportive services

Level 2 — Regular class attendance plus supplementary instructional services

Level 3 — Part-time special class

Level 4 — Full-time special class

Level 5 — Special stations*

Level 6 — Homebound

Level 7 — Instruction in hospital, residential, or total care settings

Move this way only as far as necessary

Return this way as rapidly as feasible

Assignment of pupils to settings governed primarily by the school system

Assignment of individuals to settings governed primarily by health, correctional, welfare, or other agencies

*Special schools in public school system

FIGURE 11–1 The Cascade System of Educational Placement (Source: "Proposed CEC Policy Statement on the Organization and Administration of Special Education," *Exceptional Children,* 1973, 39, 495. Copyright by the Council for Exceptional Children. Reprinted with permission.)

The legislation specifies that parents and child will have a role in diagnosis, placement, and development of the individualized educational plan. Parents can state their desires for the child, and information parents have about the child's learning style, interests, and abilities can be considered in developing the educational plan. This process was not always possible or even considered necessary before passage of P.L. 94–142.

The law also provides for parents to initiate a hearing if they do not agree with the diagnosis, placement, or educational plan. This provision gives the parents "clout" in encouraging public school personnel to provide a free and appropriate education for the child.

Implications for Parents.   While the implications of P.L. 94–142 are far-reaching for children and adults with handicaps, its implications for involving parents in the educational process are especially important. To receive money under the provisions of the law or to continue receiving federal money for other programs, school districts must involve parents in the development of the educational program of their handicapped child. Involvement becomes the right of every parent of a handicapped child. The second implication of this act is that parents' knowledge of the child must be included in the development of the educational plan. Third, parents are assured of continued involvement in their child's education because the plan has to be reviewed and revised at least annually, and because of the law's due process features, which stipulate that if the parents are not satisfied with the child's placement or with the educational plan, they have the right to appeal to higher authorities in the schools and, ultimately, to the courts. Child advocate organizations, organizations for handicapped citizens, and civil rights groups advise parents of their rights and responsibilities under the provisions of this act.

Parents' Rights.   Under the provision of P.L. 94–142, parents have these rights regarding their child's education:

1. The parent must give consent for evaluation of the child.
2. The parent has the right to "examine all relevant records with respect to the identification, evaluation, and educational placement of the child."
3. The parent must be given written prior notice whenever a change in "the identification, evaluation or educational placement of the child" occurs.
4. This written notice must be in the parent's native tongue.
5. The parent has an "opportunity to present complaints with respect to any matter relating to the identification, evaluation, or educational placement of the child."
6. The parent has the right to a due process hearing in relation to any complaint.
7. The parent has the right to participate in development of the individual educational program for the child.
8. Meetings to develop the IEP must be conducted in the parent's native tongue.
9. Meetings to develop the IEP must be held at a time and place agreeable to the parent.

    P.L. 94–142's most obvious benefit is to give the handicapped child access to the regular classroom. As mainstreaming continues, there will be more peer interaction among the handicapped and nonhandicapped. The concept of *least restrictive environment* offers a great deal of opportunity for handicapped children, assuring that the child will be educated and cared for in the environment that best meets his needs. Figure 11–1 illustrates the process of establishing a least restrictive environment.

Child Find

Public Law 94–142 provides for Child Find agencies to facilitate identification of handicapped children. Child Find programs are operated by state and local agencies, including school districts. The major purposes of Child Find are to:

☐ Locate and identify handicapped children and youth
☐ Conduct screening and assessment tests
☐ Recommend educational and therapeutic services
☐ Refer parents to appropriate social service agencies

Public Law 99–457

Congress in 1986 passed P.L. 99–457, the Education of the Handicapped Act Amendments—landmark legislation relating to handicapped infants, toddlers, and preschoolers. P.L. 99–457 amends P.L. 91–230, the Education of the Handicapped Act (EHA), which was passed in 1970. P.L. 99–457 authorizes two new programs: Title I, Program for Infants and Toddlers with Handicaps (birth through age two years) and Title II, Preschool Grants Program (ages three through five years). The Preschool Grants Program extends to handicapped children between the ages of three and five the rights extended to the handicapped under P.L. 94–142. By the 1990–91 school year, states applying for P.L. 94–142 funds will have to assure that they are providing a free and appropriate public education to all handicapped children ages three to five. This age-group was included in P.L. 94–142, but often did not receive public school services because states had discretion as to whether to provide services to this age-group. Beginning with the 1990-91 school year the states can no longer choose not to provide services if they want to continue to receive funding under P.L. 94–142.

The legislation recognizes that families play a large role in delivery of services to preschool handicapped children; consequently, P.L. 99–457 provides that, whenever appropriate and to the extent desired by parents, the preschooler's individualized IEP will include instruction for parents. The legislation also recognizes the desirability of variations in program options to provide services to handicapped preschoolers. Variations may be part-day, home-based, and part- or full-day center-based.

The Program for Infants and Toddlers authorized by P.L. 99–457 establishes a state grant program for handicapped infants and toddlers from birth to two years who: (1) are experiencing developmental delays in one or more of the following areas: cognitive, physical, language and speech, psychosocial, or self-help skills; or (2) have a physical or mental condition that has a high probability of resulting in delay (e.g., Down syndrome, cerebral palsy), and (3) are at risk medically or environmentally for substantial developmental delays if early intervention is not provided. This program provides for early intervention for all eligible children. Early intervention services provided under 99–457 include:

☐ A multidisciplinary assessment and a written individualized Family Service Plan (IFSP) (see Appendix C) developed by a multidisciplinary team and the parents. Services must meet developmental needs and can include special education, speech and language pathology and audiology, occupational therapy, physical therapy, psychological services, parent and family training and counseling services, transition services, medical diagnostic services, and health services.
☐ An Individualized Family Service Plan, which must contain a statement of the child's present levels of development; a statement of the family's strengths and needs in regard to enhancing the child's development; a statement of major ex-

P. L. 94–142 and P. L. 99–457 give more young children and their families access to services they need. The emphasis in early childhood programs is to mainstream children into a least restrictive environment.

pected outcomes for the child and family; the criteria, procedures, and timeliness for determining progress; the specific early intervention services necessary to meet the unique needs of the child and family; the projected dates for initiation of services; the name of the case manager; and transition procedures from the early intervention program into a preschool program.

FUNCTION OF THE IEP

The use of an individualized educational program with all children, not just the handicapped, is gaining acceptance with teachers. Individualizing objectives, methodology, and teaching can ensure that the teaching process will become more accurate and accountable. Figure 11–2 shows an IEP form developed by Dade County, Florida. The format of the IEP may be different in each state, but all plans must include annual goals and instructional objectives.

The IEP has several purposes. First, it protects the child and parent by assuring that planning will occur. Second, the IEP assures that the child will have a plan tailored to his individual strengths, weaknesses, and learning styles. Third, the IEP helps teachers and other instructional and administrative personnel focus their teaching

DADE COUNTY PUBLIC SCHOOLS   EXCEPTIONAL STUDENT EDUCATION
INDIVIDUALIZED EDUCATION PLAN (IEP) AND AUTHORIZATION FOR PLACEMENT

NAME _____ BIRTHDATE _____ SCHOOL _____ CONFERENCE DATE _____

ADDRESS _____

Present Levels of Educational Performance

Special Education Placement
and Related Services; Persons Responsible

Annual Goals	Instructional Objectives/Evaluation Criteria	+ or −	Date

Projected: Date of Initiation _____ Anticipated Duration _____

Extent of participation in regular program: _____ MIS-12075 (05-78)

TEAM CHAIRPERSON: _____ LEA REPRESENTATIVE: _____

Ethnic Origin—*Circle One*

1. White
2. Black
3. Hispanic
4. Asian
5. Indian, American

Committee Members   Title

1. _____
2. _____
3. _____
4. _____
5. _____
6. _____

Language Proficiency—*Circle One*

A. Monolingual - No English
B. Intermediate - Some English
C. Bilingual - Both English & another
          language equally well
D. Independent - Mostly English
E. Monolingual - English exclusively

Parent Involvement: YES ☐   NO ☐
Notification Dates: _____ _____ _____
Notification Method: _____ _____ _____
Date of Annual Review: _____

Recommendation for Placement for _____ *(Year)*

☐ Terminate Special Class Placement (refer to Placement Committee)
    Comment: _____

Additional Information/Comments:

☐ Continue Special Class Placement
    Parent signed <u>New</u> IEP: YES ☐   NO ☐

DADE COUNTY PUBLIC SCHOOLS
EXCEPTIONAL STUDENT EDUCATION

STUDENT'S WEEKLY CALENDAR

	Monday	Tuesday	Wednesday	Thursday	Friday
7:30					
8:00					
8:30					
9:00					
9:30					
10:00					
10:30					
11:00					
11:30					
12:00					
12:30					
1:00					
1:30					
2:00					
2:30					
3:00					
3:30					
4:00					
4:30					

Student Name _____

I.D.# _____

R = Regular Education
E = Exceptional Education

ADDITIONAL NOTES:

____ % Exceptional Education Time plus
____ % Regular Education Time =
100% Program Time

A current calendar must be maintained to account for all program aspects (100% total) of the child's school time, including regular education.

Signature _____
Exceptional Education Classroom Teacher

Program   Date of this Calendar
LEA Representative _____
Position _____

FIGURE 11–2   Individualized Educational Plan or IEP (Source: Dade County, Florida, Public Schools.)

and resources on the child's specific needs, and promotes the best use of everyone's time, efforts, and talents.

Fourth, teachers can be more confident in their teaching because they have planned what and how they will teach. Parents can be confident that the instructional processes for their child have been planned in advance and that individual differences and needs have been considered. Fifth, the IEP assures that the handicapped child will receive a broad range of services from other agencies. The plan must not only include an educational component, but must also specify how the child's total needs will be met. If the child can benefit from physical therapy, for example, it must be written into the IEP. This provision is beneficial not only for the child, but for the classroom teacher as well, because it broadens her perspective of the educational function. Sixth, the IEP helps to clarify and refine decisions as to what is best for the child—where he should be placed, how he should be taught and helped. It also assures that the child will not be categorized or labeled without discussion of his unique needs. Seventh, review of the IEP at least annually forces educators to consider how and what the child has learned, whether what was prescribed is effective, and to prescribe new or modified learning strategies.

TEACHING THE HANDICAPPED

As an early childhood educator, you will have children with special needs in your classroom. Learning disabled students constitute the majority of handicapped children. These are some of the general types of handicaps you will encounter in your classroom:

- ☐ Visual impairment—loss of visual functions sufficient to restrict the learning process
- ☐ Hearing impairment—slightly to severely defective hearing
- ☐ Physical handicap—a condition that impedes normal development of gross or fine motor abilities
- ☐ Speech impairment or communication disorder—disorders of expressive or receptive language; stuttering, chronic voice disorders, or serious articulation problems affecting social, emotional, and educational achievement
- ☐ Health impairment—illnesses of a chronic and prolonged nature such as epilepsy, hemophilia, asthma, cardiac conditions, severe allergies, blood disorders, diabetes, and neurological disorders
- ☐ Serious emotional disturbances—dangerous aggressiveness, self-destructiveness, severe withdrawal and uncommunicative, hyperactive to the extent that it affects adaptive behavior, severely anxious, depressed, psychotic, or autistic
- ☐ Specific learning disabilities—disorder in one or more of the basic psychological processes involved in understanding or using language, spoken or written, that may manifest itself in imperfect ability to listen, think, speak, read, write, spell, or perform mathematical calculations

Resource Room

One method of providing for the handicapped child in a mainstreamed setting is the *resource room*. As the name implies, this classroom is an instructional setting that

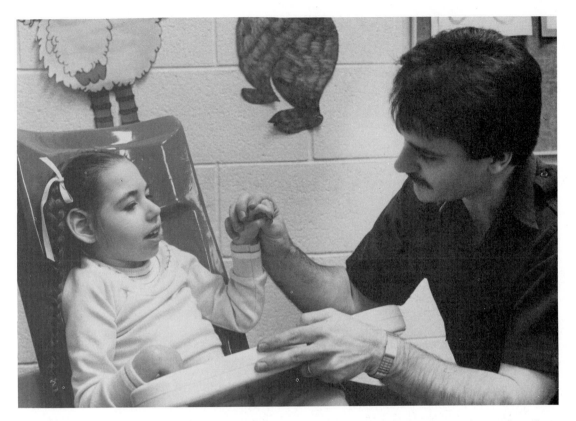

To integrate special needs children into a regular classroom, schools must make adjustments in human and educational resources, and the Match-Up Matrix can help teachers and caregivers make adjustments.

provides resources for handicapped students and their teachers. A student who participates in the resource program is enrolled in the regular educational program and goes to the resource room on a regular basis for special support, usually of an academic nature. The regular classroom teachers of the exceptional student receive support from materials and ideas shared by the resource teacher. In this way, teachers discover different approaches or alternative methods for dealing with the student's problem. The *resource teacher* has training in special education and experience in teaching handicapped students. The resource teacher shares ideas with the other faculty members to promote positive attitudes toward exceptional learners.

The Transdisciplinary Team

The *transdisciplinary team approach* to special needs children consists of *interdisciplinary* involvement across and among various health and social services disciplines. Members of the team can include any of these professionals: early childhood educator, physical therapist, occupational therapist, speech therapist, psychologist, social worker, and pediatrician. The rationale for the transdisciplinary approach is that a unified and

THE OPEN DOOR PRESCHOOL, AUSTIN, TEXAS*

The Open Door Preschool is a child care center that has successfully offered mainstreamed care since 1975. Addressing the problems created by the educational segregation of the disabled preschooler was the school's founding principle. The opportunity to play and learn with nondisabled children helps prepare the disabled child for life in the mainstream of society. A mainstreamed preschool experience provides the opportunity to develop social skills as well as a strong self-concept; both of these help the disabled child participate successfully with her nondisabled peers.

Twenty-five to 30 percent of the enrollment of the Open Door are disabled or children in need of special care. A broad definition for "special needs" results in a great variety of skill levels. Children's skill level as well as their chronological age are considered when creating the composition of each class. Further, the nature of each special need is considered so that each class is manageable in terms of supervision and routine care. These considerations result in classes that are defined more by developmental level than by age.

Jeffrey first came to the Open Door when he was 23 months old. His parents described him as a normal, active toddler, but they did report some problems at his previous preschool. Jeffrey's teacher, however, immediately saw reason for concern about Jeffrey's abilities. When the family finally agreed to obtain some evaluations, Jeffrey was determined to be functioning at a 15- to 18-month-old level. A year later, Jeffrey is still in the Bluebird room, our youngest classroom. He is receiving speech and occupational therapy twice each week. Jeffrey's vocabulary has increased to over 20 words; he participates in many group activities; he loves music—the louder the better; and he enjoys drawing, painting, and water play. Jeffrey is well liked and accepted by his classmates, all of whom are a year younger than he is. He is very at home with his two-year-old classmates, and he seems to function close to their level.

Emma came to the Open Door when she was 4½. Her early childhood teachers and therapists placed her on an 18-month-old level. Because of her size, Emma was placed in our Sunshine room, which is primarily three-year-olds. Emma spent a year and a half in the Sunshine room. When she arrived each afternoon, she played quietly with toys. As the other children awoke from their naps, she greeted them with exuberant hugs and a twinkly-eyed smile. By the time Emma graduated to the Rainbow room with her classmates, she was 1½ years older than the others in the class. Despite her vocabulary of only four words, Emma's size required that she be with the oldest children in our school. The other children in the class knew Emma very well. She had been with most of them for at least a year. Her difficulties with speech, fine motor tasks, and coordination did not prevent Emma from being included in many classroom activities. She enjoys being with her classmates. She scribbles as they draw, she struggles up the climber as they race up and down it, and she is right in the middle of any water play. Emma's loving hugs to all visitors are the finest greetings we can possibly give. Emma has helped many of the others at the Open Door learn to see how much everyone has to offer regardless of seemingly insurmountable hurdles.

Success stories at the Open Door are many. In our 15 years of operation, we have turned away only one child, whose violent outbursts were uncontrollable. That was an incredibly painful experience for the staff. It is not only possible to mainstream children on the preschool level, but it is also beneficial to all involved. The disabled children learn to interact with other children with whatever abilities they have; the nondisabled children learn to see the abilities people have rather than to focus on the abilities that are lacking or are lagging behind. All in all, everyone benefits from this exposure to a variety of skill levels.

*Contributed by Elizabeth Sears, executive director, The Open Door, Austin, Texas.

holistic approach is the most effective way to provide resources and deliver services to children and their families. Members of the transdisciplinary team diagnose, prescribe, share information, and work cooperatively to meet children's needs. One of the members, usually the early childhood educator, heads the team, and other members act as consultants. The team leader carries out the instructions of the other team members. A variation of this model is to have members of the team, such as the physical therapist, work directly with the child at specified times (for example, twice a week) and provide activities and suggestions for the early childhood educator to implement at other times.

Handicapped Children in Head Start Programs
Head Start services to handicapped children consist of the following:

1. *Outreach and recruitment.* This effort is directed toward locating, identifying and recruiting handicapped children into Head Start. The most common sources for outreach are parents, public health departments, school systems, and newspaper articles.
2. *Diagnosis and assessment of handicapped children.* Head Start staff members work with private diagnostic consultants to achieve this service.
3. *Mainstreaming and special services.* Special services include individualized instruction, parent counseling, and psychological and physical therapy.
4. *Teaching and technical assistance.* This includes working with staff and parents to provide training for working with handicapped children.
5. *Coordination with other agencies.* Head Start staff work closely with other agencies to identify, recruit, and provide services to handicapped children and their families.
6. *Summer Head Start.* Many Head Start children who would otherwise probably not receive services before entering public school are served in summer programs.

Guidelines for Teaching the Handicapped
Teachers of the handicapped can improve their teaching by emphasizing children's abilities rather than focusing on their handicapping conditions. Handicapped children have many talents and abilities and are capable of a wide range of achievements, and teachers can help them fulfull their potentials as they would any other child. Teaching methods that are effective with the nonhandicapped may be equally effective with the handicapped. Conversely, many instructional activities that special educators use with the handicapped work just as well with the nonhandicapped. Teachers first need to diagnose what children are able to do. Diagnosis can occur informally, through observation, examination of work samples, teacher-made tests, discussions with parents, examination of cumulative records, and discussions with other teachers.

Use of concrete examples and materials and multisensory approaches to learning are also important in teaching the handicapped. And, as with the nonhandicapped, it is important to involve children in learning activities. The teacher must also model what children are to do, rather than just tell them what to do. A good procedure is to tell children what they are to do; model a behavior or have a child who has already

COLLABORATIVE INTERVENTION: A MOBILE TEAM APPROACH TO THERAPY NEEDS OF INFANTS AND CHILDREN IN COMMUNITY-BASED PROGRAMS

In 1974 Alberta Children's Hospital in Calgary, Alberta, Canada, initiated a unique outreach program to provide therapeutic intervention by mobile therapy teams for children with special needs in mainstreamed community settings.

Four mobile teams, each staffed by a speech/language pathologist, a physiotherapist, and an occupational therapist, travel daily throughout the city from their hospital base. Although some direct treatment is provided, the main focus is toward a collaborative approach wherein goal setting and program implementation is a joint venture involving primary caregivers—parents, teachers, and aides. The teams receive support from a psychologist who consults with the therapists and the nonspecialized community day care centers.

The program caseload consists of 150 infants and children having a broad range of disabilities and functioning levels. Intervention takes place in homes, family day homes, child day care centers, nursery schools, and in preschool and school programs.

A significant feature of the program is the collaborative network established with 25 high-quality community-based day care centers. A solid four-way partnership exists between the hospital teams, the families, the day care centers, and the government funding agencies involved with special services for handicapped children.

Philosophy
Central to the program philosophy is the belief that minimal separation from family and community life affords the best opportunity for children with disabilities to reach their maximum potential. The merging of knowledge and skills offered by therapists and primary caregivers facilitates the transfer of responsibility to family and community for the integration of therapy techniques into the child's daily activities.

Objectives
Objectives of the outreach program are to
☐ Provide therapeutic intervention by direct treatment, demonstration teaching, and consultation
☐ Share knowledge and skills with primary caregivers and facilitate transfer of responsibility for therapy carry-over to family and community
☐ Help primary caregivers integrate treatment into daily routines
☐ Provide inservices, one-to-one consultation, and dialogue leading to increased knowledge and skills for parents, educators, and related community staff
☐ Support, educate, and encourage parents to become informed advocates for their children
☐ Provide educational presentations directed at increasing public awareness, knowledge, and involvement.

Community Education
Educational presentations are targeted in two directions: one is inservice sessions for regular day care workers to increase specific skill levels; the other is community presentations to increase public awareness and knowledge of children's disabilities leading to the development of community understanding and advocacy for the life-long integration process.

Program Model
The purpose, the quantity, and the type of assessment and intervention vary according to the needs of each child. It is essential, therefore, that the program and model of service delivery remain flexible. The broad range of intervention, however, including therapy, education, family support, community support, and case management is timely and coordinated.

A collaborative model is consistently followed and everyone involved with the child is an integral member of the team. The team approach varies between interdisciplinary and transdisciplinary, according to the circumstances of each child, family, and community placement. To achieve maximum integration of the child's program into daily routine, the Mobile

Outreach programs such as the Alberta Children's Hospital Mobile Team take services to special needs children in centers and homes, rather than wait for children and families to come to them.

Team emphasizes teaching the necessary skills to parents and community caregivers. Over the past 15 years, the Program has assisted in the development of a strong cadre of community day care and preschool program staff whose enthusiasm and dedication to excellence is outstandinig.

The mutual teaching/learning component of the model encompasses an exchange of skills and information within the team disciplines and between the teams and primary caregivers, as well as with the staff of community agencies and recreational programs. Sharing knowledge takes the form of demonstration teaching, writing skill-specific programs, and providing disability-specific materials. At times, the use of videos encourages mutual evaluation of skill acquisition. Sharing practical alternatives and creative responses to programming problems are the essence of frequent, short, and specific teaching sessions.

The Mobile Team Program pioneered the concept of integration of children with special needs into regular nonspecialized community settings. Although the model was initially developed for an urban setting, it has been adapted to the needs of several smaller regional cities and rural areas.

Overall, the program has broadened horizons, challenged traditions, and provided incentives to enhance the futures of children with special needs by reaching out and sharing the expertise of a long-established tertiary care institution.

*Contributed by Ruth Cripps, director, Community Outreach Services, Alberta Children's Hospital, and Shirley Crozier, coordinator, Mobile Team Program, Alberta Children's Hospital.

MATCHING CHILDREN'S CHARACTERISTICS TO SETTING RESOURCES

Mary Wilson has developed a Match-Up Matrix to help educators make decisions about necessary human and materials resources, facilities, and special arrangements for integrating the handicapped into regular classroom settings.

Adam

Two-and-a-half-year-old Adam has diplegia (involvement of the lower extremities) and a seizure disorder resulting from a head injury he received in a car accident at 18 months of age. Shortly after the accident, Adam received physical therapy through the hospital's out-patient services. On the recommendation of his therapist, Adam's parents are seeking to enroll him in a preschool.

Adam uses a walker to maneuver in his environment. Though he is able to do many things with minimal effort, he often asks for help. His language and cognitive skills have been assessed at or above age level; however, self-help skills have been affected by his gross motor delays. Though seizures occurred frequently after the accident, with daily medication there has been no recurrence except with a high fever. Adam relates well to adults, though he sometimes appears unnecessarily dependent upon them. Adam has limited opportunities to interact with children his own age. He has a teenage brother, both parents work, and a housekeeper/baby-sitter sees to his needs. Both parents are concerned about Adam's care and want him "to be happy."

In the Match-Up Matrix of Adam's needs and the preschool's resources, we see a match in nearly every area; nevertheless, a few adjustments are necessary (Table A). The greatest concern involves motor and, secondarily, self-help skills. The walker in a busy classroom requires attention to traffic patterns, seating and mobility into and out of areas, especially the small bathroom. The hospital's physical therapist has offered to visit the school and share suggestions for Adam's independence. As with many young children who have not attended school, Adam will need help to learn independent play skills and interactive social skills. A final concern is Adam's seizure disorder. Though the staff members have been assured that they are unlikely to observe a seizure at school, the team feels it is important to know what to expect and what to do.

His parents decide to enroll Adam in the Sunshine Preschool. When they visit the program after the first two months, they are amazed by how much Adam can do for himself. As a result, they are beginning to demand more independence in daily routines at home. His therapist reports an increase in his progress and, particularly, in his motivation since he started school.

Sally

Sally is a 3-year-old girl with cerebral palsy described as "spastic quadriparesis," which indicates involvement in all extremities. She is learning to use an adapted wheelchair with help. She reaches for objects, but is often inaccurate. She controls her head and trunk, but requires support for sitting. Sally seems to understand all that is said to her; however, her motor impairment affects the intelligibility of her speech and her ability to demonstrate what she knows. Though she can make her immediate needs known through simple words and gestures, the use of a picture board helps her to express concepts. Sally smiles, laughs, and approaches adults and children, but her participation is limited. She needs help to dress, undress, and feed herself. Sally may throw

mastered a skill model it for others; have children perform the skill or task under supervision and give them corrective feedback; let children practice or perform the behavior; and involve the children in evaluating their performance. Make learning interesting. Dolls, for example, can help teach concepts of body parts and hygiene. Make the learning environment a pleasant and rewarding place to be. A dependable

TABLE A   Match-Up Matrix for Adam at Sunshine Preschool

Setting	Training	Specialists	Equipment and Materials	Appropriate Peers	Aide/ Helper	Action
Motor	− Traffic Seating Mobility	+ Therapist from hospital	+	− Not independent	N.A.	*1
Language	+	N.A.	N.A.	+	N.A.	
Cognitive	+	N.A.	N.A.	+	N.A.	
Social	− Sharing Independent play	N.A.	N.A.	+	N.A.	*3
Self-help	− Independent dressing, toileting	N.A.	− Traffic	+	N.A.	*2
Behavior	+	N.A.	N.A.	+	N.A.	
Medical	− Information on seizures	+ Family doctor/ neurologist	N.A.	N.A.	N.A.	*4
Home	+ Teenage brother	N.A.	N.A.	N.A.	N.A.	

Note: A + indicates a child's needs can be met with current setting resources; a − indicates a setting resource need followed by action/resource need. The numbers in the action column indicate priority; #1 is what staff will do first.

tantrums to control certain situations, particularly at home. Sally's parents are eager to get services for their daughter. She has not been in school before, though her mother now feels she is "ready." Her parents believe Sally's strengths are in social and cognitive skills and feel that

classroom schedule is easier for handicapped children because it gives them a sense of security and consistency.

Parent involvement is one of the most effective ways to increase student achievement. Parents can help with the instructional process both at home and in school. The teacher also needs to make a special effort to involve all children in all classroom

TABLE B   Match-Up Matrix for Sally at Rainbow Preschool

Setting	Training	Specialists	Equipment and Materials	Appropriate Peers	Aide/ Helper	Action
Motor	− Handling Positioning	− Hospital therapist? Doctor refers?	− Wheelchair Toys Utensils	− Independent mobility	− Mother volunteers peers? para?	*1
Language	− Poor speech Use of picture board	+ School consultant/ parents	− Pictures of school activity/ needs	− Need training	− Needs help with board	*2
Cognitive	+	N.A.	− Adaptive toys, tools	+	N.A.	*4
Social	+	N.A.	N.A.	− Help peers understand	− Help child participate, interact	*5

any classroom could easily handle their daughter's needs. Nevertheless, Sally's mother has offered to volunteer several days per week at lunch to help her daughter at that time.

Sally's matrix presents a complex situation. Motor is the area of most concern, but the extent of the handicap affects several areas. The team has also identified language as an area lacking a match. Though Sally has strengths in cognitive and social areas, equipment or an adult presence would be required to facilitate Sally's participation. Sally's behavior and the lack of experience in school settings suggest the need for consistent, individualized programming.

Through the Match-Up Matrix, the parents and school agreed that the Sunshine Preschool was not the appropriate program to serve Sally's needs at that time (Table B). However, the matrix allowed the team to identify what services were required and made an informed referral. The team was also able to identify what

activities. With a few modifications, most activities conducted in early childhood programs can be made appropriate for the handicapped. In addition, a goal of every early childhood program should be to have children become independent of others, especially teachers and parents. Table 11–2 offers specific procedures for adapting teaching methods to handicapped children's special needs.

TABLE B   *continued*

Setting	Training	Specialists	Equipment and Materials	Appropriate Peers	Aide/ Helper	Action
Self-help	– Dressing Toileting Feeding	– Hospital therapist? Doctor refers?	– Clothing Potty chair Utensils	– Have peers help	+ Mother volunteers	*3
Behavior	+	N.A.	– Progam for tantrum at home and school	+	+ Trained parapro-fessionals	*6
Medical	+	N.A.	N.A.	N.A.	N.A.	
Home	– Under-stands child needs	– Social worker? Parent support group	– Information on cerebral palsy	N.A.	+ Mother volunteers	*7

Note: *indicates order of priorities.

resources or skills would enable successful enrollment at Sunshine Preschool in the future.

Sally's parents decided to enroll her at Rainbow Preschool, an interdisciplinary program for eight multihandicapped youngsters of all cognitive levels. Located in an elementary school, the preschool and the kindergarten classes have frequent contact. Sally's parents participate in the parent group which provides information, training, and support to its mem-bers. Sally's parents have indicated interest in reapplying to Sunshine next year. The team looks foward to that application, confident that Sally will have made progress and may indeed be "ready" for their school, and the school for her.

*Contributed by Mary Wilson, Director of the Early Childhood Program at Sullivan County (New York) Community College.

INTEGRATION OF NONHANDICAPPED WITH HANDICAPPED CHILDREN IN EARLY CHILDHOOD PROGRAMS

Integration of handicapped and nonhandicapped children is becoming more popular as a way of providing better education and support services. Special education programs use two kinds of integration. The first is a type of *reverse mainstreaming,* in

TABLE 11–2 Adapting to the Child with Special Needs

Impairment	Characteristics	Specific Teaching Approaches
Any disability		Accept the child
		Create real experiences to develop the sense of touch, taste, hearing, sight, or smell
		Adapt environment to accommodate needs
		Model appropriate behavior and language
		Encourage independence
		Allow ample time to complete tasks
		Facilitate participation in all class activities
		Remove hazards
		Apply same standards of behavior for all children, when possible
		Capitalize on children's talents, skills, interests
		Practice emergency procedures
		Confer frequently with child's therapist/ physician/parents
		Maintain accurate records of progress or observed changes
		Respond appropriately to other children's fears or questions about the disability
Language/ speech	Use of single words and/or gestures	Describe ongoing activities
	Severe articulation problems, making it difficult to understand the child	Use phrases and short sentences
		Restate rather than correct
	Difficulty following directions	Provide abundant opportunities to talk
		Listen and respond to content of language
		Show interest; maintain eye contact
		Use speech rather than gestures
		Provide daily oral experience in singing and regular language activities
Mental	Few communication skills	Provide consistent, brief directions
	Poor motor skills	Plan for much repetition
	Lack of self-help skills	Reinforce successful efforts

TABLE 11–2 *continued*

Impairment	Characteristics	Specific Teaching Approaches
	Learning at slower rate Short attention span	Praise appropriate social behavior and participation Use multisensory experiences Break tasks into small components if necessary
Hearing	Limited communication skills (usually) Inability to understand others' speech and language May be learning hand signs in addition to speech reading and use of residual hearing	Learn child's hearing capacity Use child's name when directing speech to her/him Articulate clearly with moderate speed; avoid exaggeration, loud voice, or mumbling Seat child for good visibility of activity, teacher, or other children Learn to change hearing aid battery and/or cord (See language/speech section for additional suggestions)
Visual	Some children may see shadow forms, colors, or even large pictures Peripheral vision may be best (turned-away face does not indicate inattentiveness)	Orient child to classroom layout and materials locations Give directions related to child's body and orientation Describe objects and activities completely Give notice of change in activities Encourage other children to identify themselves and describe what is happening Acknowledge child when she/he enters room Provide activities to develop motor skills, listening skills, moving about, and use of senses
Physical	May use crutches or wheelchair Poor fine and/or large motor control and coordination May have speech delay Tenseness or stress may increase spasticity	Change child's position frequently (20–30 min.) Allow space for movement Keep change of clothing available Determine child's most comfortable floor sitting position

Source: Dorothy Morgan and May Elizabeth York, "Ideas for Mainstreaming Young Children," *Young Children,* 36, no. 2 (January, 1981), pp. 22–23.

which nonhandicapped children are placed in programs for the handicapped. In this model, the handicapped are the majority of children in the program. Usually, a group of two-thirds handicapped children and one-third nonhandicapped works as well, but the optimum ratio for any program varies. The other type of integration occurs when the handicapped are *mainstreamed,* or placed in a program for nonhandicapped children, so that the nonhandicapped constitute the majority of the class.

Reverse mainstreaming is receiving a lot of attention in early childhood education today, and a number of assumptions are implicit in any model of reverse mainstreaming: (1) the instructional program and activities will be appropriate for both handicapped and nonhandicapped; (2) integration will have a positive rather than negative effect on both groups; (3) the program is pedagogically and administratively manageable. These are issues to consider in a program of reverse mainstreaming:

☐ Recruitment, identification, and selection of children to participate in the program
☐ Working with all parents, especially parents of the nonhandicapped, to assure them that their children are receiving a good—even an above-average—educational experience
☐ Identification of services, equipment, materials, and necessary special training

The principal advantages of integrating a classroom that was previously for only the handicapped are that the nonhandicapped provide role models for behavior and skill development and the teacher is able to maintain perspective on normal growth and development.

MAKING TRANSITIONS

Transitional experiences from one setting to another are a must for the special needs child, especially for children who have attended preschool in a special setting or in a separate public school facility from the elementary school. To help the special needs child make a transition from one setting to another, the staffs of the sending agency and the receiving agency must cooperate in arrangements, activities, and plans; for example:

☐ Try to approximate certain features of the receiving environment. If the new classroom has a larger ratio of children to adults, gradually get the child used to working and functioning in larger groups.
☐ Help the child become accustomed to social skills appropriate to the new environment. If the child has been using a restroom inside the classroom but will have to go outside the classroom in the new school, help her practice this new routine.
☐ Use materials and activities as the child will encounter them in the new setting. Get a set of textbooks the child will use and familiarize her with the format and activities.
☐ Approximate the kind and length of instructional activities the child will be expected to participate in and complete.
☐ Visit the new school with the child and her parents.
☐ Communicate with the receiving teacher to share information about the child.

☐ Structure a social setting in the receiving classroom. Arrange a "buddy system" with a child in the new classroom.

☐ After the child has made the transition, visit the classroom to demonstrate a supportive, caring attitude to the receiving teacher, parents, and child.

☐ The receiving teacher has reciprocal responsibilities to make the transition as stress-free and rewarding as possible. Successful transitions involve all concerned: parents, children, teachers, administrators, and support personnel. (Other suggestions for transitional experiences are described in Chapter 8.)

GIFTED CHILDREN

Practitioners Ann and Elizabeth Lupkowski believe young gifted children may display the following behaviors:

☐ **Long attention span.** The attention span of gifted children is often longer than that of their peers . . . . Some young gifted children are able to work on projects for blocks of time as long as 45 minutes to 2½ hours.

☐ **Creativity and imagination.** Gifted children may have unique and innovative ideas for the use of common materials or unique names for possessions . . . . These children may also design unusual dramatic play situations, such as astronauts landing on the moon, and they often have imaginary friends or companions.

☐ **Social relationships.** All children have varied social skills, and gifted children are no exception. They may be leaders of other children, with advanced social skills for their age, or they may prefer to be alone to work on their own interests . . . . Some gifted children may find innovative ways to settle disputes. Also, young gifted children may prefer to interact with older children and adults rather than with their same-age peers.

☐ **Number concepts.** Some gifted children seem to be fascinated with numbers before they begin formal schooling.

☐ **Verbal skills.** Gifted preschoolers may recognize letters early and show an early interest in printed matter. They may be interested in foreign languages and also exhibit correct pronunciation and sentence structure in their native language. Young gifted children may show an advanced vocabulary and may begin reading before they start school, although the significance of early reading as an indicator of giftedness has not been established.

☐ **Memory.** Gifted children may show exceptional memories.

☐ **Specific interests.** The young gifted child may show an in-depth interest in one or more areas and spend a great deal of time developing a collection of a class of objects, such as rocks or plastic animals.

☐ **Attention to detail.** Gifted children often notice "insignificant" details in pictures and situations. They also enjoy making things more complex—elaborating on rules for games, for example.

☐ **High energy level.** Some gifted children have been called hyperactive because of the high level of energy they show. These children also seem to need little sleep.

☐ **Reasoning ability.** The ability to form analogies at a young age and to justify those responses may be another indicator of giftedness . . . . Perhaps the ability to successfully complete and justify this type of task is an indicator of advanced cognitive development.

☐ **Insight ability.** Exceptional insight ability has been postulated as another characteristic of the intellectually gifted. They may be superior in insight ability because of the ability to sift out relevant information, blend those pieces of information, and add new information to appropriate information acquired in the past. These children have the ability to find solutions to complex problems.[3]

Pediatrician Michael Lewis has found four signs that most—but not all—gifted young children display during the first year of life:

1. **Sleep Problems.** These children either don't go to sleep easily, they wake up early, or they don't sleep long amounts of time. Any or all of these patterns may be present. While these kids give the impression that they are having some problems with sleeping, we don't think this is actually the case. Evidently, these children are exhibiting individual differences in sleep patterns: the only *problem* is that the parents don't get enough sleep.

2. **Alertness and Attentiveness.** One of the outstanding signs that parents report is that these children always look interested in what is going on around them. They are usually alert—their eyes are open, scanning the field, and they listen attentively. Indeed, they give you the feeling there is an inquisitive mind at work, even though it is the mind of a five-week-old.

3. **Early Stranger Fear or Recognition.** Normally, by eight months of age, children are smart enough to remember who they know and who they don't know. When they see a stranger they can compare the image of that person against the images of people they know. When it doesn't match anyone familiar, they become inhibited. Some of these children (about 70 percent) go on to become frightened and upset, a reaction we call stranger anxiety. This pattern normally shows itself in babies at about eight or nine months. In a large proportion of gifted children, we are seeing stranger anxiety showing itself in the third to fourth month of life.
Not all gifted children we have seen show fearfulness; some just show interest. But, one way or another, all show early *recognition* that they see a stranger.

4. **Early Language Usage.** Many children speak what seem to be intelligent sounds—"mama," "dada" and other words such as these—somewhere in the last quarter of the first year. However, we don't really consider them true words or true noun usage. It is the most complicated words, such as "boat" or "tree" or "dog" that we consider true noun usage. We have noticed that many gifted children start to produce these terms in the last quarter of the first year, when most children are still saying "mama," "dada," "cup," or other simple words.[4]

Gifted children may not display all these signs, but the presence of several of them can alert parents and early childhood teachers to make appropriate instructional, environmental, and social adjustments.

Mainstreaming the Gifted

There is a tendency among professional educators to provide special classes and programs and sometimes schools for the gifted and talented, which would seem to be a move away from providing for these children in regular classrooms. Regular classroom teachers can provide for the gifted in their classrooms through enrichment and acceleration. Enrichment provides an opportunity for children to pursue topics in greater depth and in different ways than they normally might. Acceleration permits children to progress academically at their own pace. In the regular classroom, a teacher can encourage children to pursue special interests, as a means of extending and enriching classroom learning. She can use parents and resource people to tutor and

Gifted children need differentiated programs and activities, and teachers must extend and enrich learning activities.

work in special ways with the gifted and talented children, and provide opportunities for the children to assume leadership responsibilities. They may be interested in tutoring other students who need extra practice or help. Tutoring can cut across grade and age levels. Students can also help explain directions and procedures to the class. The teacher can encourage them to use their talents and abilities outside the classroom by becoming involved with other people and agencies, and encourage creativity through classroom activities that require divergent thinking (for example, "Let's think of all the different uses for a paper clip"). The teacher must challenge children to think through the use of higher-order questions that encourage them to explain, apply, analyze, rearrange, and judge.

Many schools have resource rooms for the gifted and talented, where children can spend a half-day or more every week working with a teacher who is interested and trained in working with the gifted. There are seven ways to provide for the needs of gifted and talented children; of the seven, the *resource room-pullout* is the most popular and common method.

☐ *Enrichment classroom.* The classroom teacher conducts a differentiated program of study without the help of outside personnel.

☐ *Consultant teacher.* A program of differentiated instruction is conducted in the regular classroom with the assistance of a specially trained consultant.

☐ *Resource room-pullout.* Gifted students leave the classroom for a short period of time to receive instruction from a specially trained teacher.

☐ *Community mentor.* Gifted students interact with an adult from the community who has special knowledge in the area of interest.

☐ *Independent study.* Students select projects and work on them under the supervision of a qualified teacher.

☐ *Special class.* Gifted students are grouped together during most of the class time and are instructed by a specially trained teacher.

☐ *Special schools.* Gifted students receive differentiated instruction at a special school with a specially trained staff.[5]

CHILDREN WITH MULTICULTURAL HERITAGES

Backgrounds and languages reflect society's cultural pluralism. Children are influenced in many ways by the cultures in which they are reared. They learn distinctive ways of communicating, both verbal and nonverbal; develop a preference for certain foods; dress in certain kinds of clothing; develop ways of interacting with others, and subscribe to a particular value system. Children need to learn about each other's cultural differences.

As an early childhood educator you will want to promote multicultural awareness in your classroom. In its simplest form, *multicultural awareness* is the appreciation and understanding of other people and their cultures, as well as one's own culture. The terms and concepts for describing multicultural awareness are not as important as the methods, procedures, and activities for developing a meaningful program. Educators and the public often assume they are promoting multicultural awareness when they are actually presenting only a fragment of the concept. Multicultural awareness in the classroom is not the presentation of other cultures to the exclusion of the cultures represented by children in the class. Rather, a multicultural awareness program should focus on other cultures while at the same time making children aware of the content, nature, and richness of their own. Learning about other cultures concurrently with their own enables children to integrate commonalities and appreciate differences without inferring inferiority or superiority of one or the other.

Ideas and Activities for Multicultural Awareness in Early Childhood Programs

☐ One's own culture—children study their own cultural background, and are able to understand others' cultures as they come to know more about their own.

☐ People puzzles—paste pictures of children and adults of different cultures from magazines and old books on cardboard and cut them up to make puzzles

☐ Puppets—have students make puppets in ethnic dress and put on class plays

☐ Stamp and postcard collections—have students compile stamps and postcards of different nations and display them in the classroom after discussions

☐ Family trees—begin with students' own family trees; also, make a "family tree" of the class members

☐ Artifact collection—have students collect items of interest that depict different cultures, including the American; discuss the items and analyze and compare to each other

☐ Easy food recipes—supervise the students in making foods from different cultures

☐ Arts and crafts—make jewelry, mosaics, or headdresses of other lands

☐ Songs and dances—have students learn easy songs and dances of other cultures

☐ Clothing—collect old pieces of fabric that students can make into ethnic clothing; they can paint, color, or embroider old sheets

☐ Maps—make a large, simplified world map and pin students' names to show where they or their families originated; colored strings from the various places may all lead to your city

☐ Class mural—toward the end of the year, have all students contribute their drawings and interpretations of the cultures they study throughout the year; display the mural in the classroom or hallway

☐ Special events—celebrate a special holiday or event as it is done in a particular culture; a UNICEF calendar is a good source of ideas

☐ Human resources—invite a member of the community to present and discuss a particular aspect of his or her native culture

Teachers use many different kinds of activities to help gifted and talented children go beyond what they would normally experience.

- [ ] Games—have students learn games children play in another part of the world
- [ ] Parents—parents can come to the school or center to share customs, crafts, and foods
- [ ] Field trips—children can visit other schools or centers and take field trips to ethnic neighborhoods or stores
- [ ] Multicultural learning center—a learning center can be devoted to books, magazines, media, and cultural objects
- [ ] Role playing—role playing can help students get a feel for another culture
- [ ] National, state, and local resources—many agencies offer materials and assistance in multicultural instruction; an excellent source is the U.S. Committee for UNICEF, United Nations Children's Fund, 331 East 38th Street, New York, NY 10016

The Role of the Teacher in Multicultural Education

The teacher is the key to a multicultural classroom. These guidelines can help teachers become more effective in teaching multiculturalism:

- [ ] Treat the children in your class as unique individuals, each with something special to contribute
- [ ] Promote uniqueness as a positive attribute; use the word "unique" often
- [ ] Become familiar with the cultural backgrounds of the children you teach; ask their parents about special family customs and holidays, and if possible, visit their neighborhoods
- [ ] Use the above information in your lesson planning; through the language arts, music, art, and classroom cooking, you can include a number of different cultural customs in your curriculum, calling special attention to the class members who celebrate these events in their homes
- [ ] Share your own heritage with your class; tell them old family stories, and show them old photographs
- [ ] Be aware of what you say and what you do regarding other cultures and cultural groups
- [ ] Exhibit accepting and respectful behavior toward visitors and volunteers in your classroom
- [ ] Familiarize yourself with the ethnic resources in your center/school and community; another teacher may have a child whose parent would be willing to share his cultural heritage with your class as well
- [ ] Attend multicultural events in your community—international festivals, ethnic fairs, or holiday parties related to one cultural group, such as Oktoberfest[6]

Anti-Bias Curriculum

The goal of an *anti-bias* curriculum is to help children learn to be accepting of others regardless of gender, race, ethnicity, or disability. Children participating in an anti-bias curriculum are comfortable with diversity and learn to stand up for themselves and others in the face of injustice. Additionally, in this supportive, open-minded environment, a child learns to construct a knowledgeable, confident self-identity.

Young children are learning to be aware of differences and need a sensitive teacher to help them form positive, unbiased perceptions about variations among people. As children color pictures of themselves, for example, you may hear a comment such as "Your skin is white and my skin is brown." Many teachers are tempted, in the name of equality, to respond, "It doesn't matter what color we are, we are all people." While this comment does not sound harmful, it fails to help the child develop positive feelings about *herself*. A more appropriate response might be "Tabitha, your skin is a beautiful brown, which is just right for you; Christina, your skin is a beautiful white, which is just right for you." A comment such as this positively acknowledges each child's different skin color, which is an important step for developing a positive concept of self.

Through the sensitive guidance of caring teachers, children learn to speak up for themselves and others. By living and learning in an accepting environment, children find that they have the ability to change intolerable situations and can have a positive impact on the future. It is important that the anti-bias curriculum start in early childhood and continue throughout the school years.

INVOLVING SPECIAL NEEDS FAMILIES

Many of the procedures for involving parents can also be used with parents of children with special needs; however, teachers must consider the entire context of family life. The family's total needs must be met, and educational, social, and medical problems addressed. It is important to work cooperatively with community agencies that can assist in delivery of these services. Parents of children with special needs frequently lack the support systems necessary for dealing with their and their children's needs. It is up to educators to be supportive, to help create support systems, and provide linkage to support systems.

Parents Need Help

Parents of special needs children need help, not sympathy, and help is often best when it is *self-help*. One barrier to self-help is the feeling of the handicapped child's parent toward his child, himself, and society. Hopelessness and helplessness may prevail. Parents may feel guilty, fearing they did something to cause the handicap. They need support to escape from and deal realistically with their feelings of guilt. Sometimes parents feel ashamed of their child and themselves and react to this feeling by withdrawing from society, consciously or unconsciously attempting to protect themselves and the child from attention. Parents need help to see that there is nothing "wrong" with their children and that they are unique and interesting.

Mainstreaming has helped not only handicapped children and their parents, but all parents and all children. By extending certain basic rights and processes to the handicapped, all special needs children will be assured of these rights. It will not be long before every child will have an IEP written for him.

FURTHER READING

Banks, James A., and Cherry A. McGee Banks, Eds. *Multicultural Education: Issues and Perspectives* (Needham Heights, Mass.: Allyn and Bacon, 1989)

Provides teachers and caregivers with knowledge, insight, and understanding for working effectively with students from both gender groups, with exceptional students, and with students from various social-class, religious, ethnic, and cultural groups. This book is based on the assumption that schools need reform to effectively provide for diverse groups.

Bricker, Diane D. *Early Education of At-Risk and Handicapped Infants, Toddlers, and Preschool Children* (Glenview, Ill.: Scott, Foresman, 1986)

A comprehensive and readable text providing a contemporary view of the field. Offers concrete intervention strategies.

Cook, Ruth E., Annette Tessier, and Virginia B. Armbruster. *Adapting Early Childhood Curricula for Children With Special Needs, Second Edition* (Columbus, Ohio: Merrill, 1987)

Useful and helpful insights into early childhood curriculum and special needs children. Early childhood educators can benefit greatly by learning how to adapt curriculum to the special needs of all children.

Davis, Gary A, and Silvia B. Rimm. *Education of the Gifted and Talented, Second Edition* (Englewood Cliffs, N.J.: Prentice-Hall, 1989)

Designed to help all who work with the gifted to meet their special needs and problems. Helps the reader understand the great national resource that exists in the gifted and talented.

Essa, Eva. *A Practical Guide to Solving Preschool Behavior Problems* (Albany, N.Y.: Delmar, 1990)

Combines many approaches and theories of child management, and deals with many specific behavior problems.

Gallagher, James J., Pascal Trohanis, and Richard M. Clifford, Eds. *Policy Implementation and PL 99-457: Planning for Young Children with Special Needs* (Baltimore, Md.: Paul H. Brookes, 1989)

Offers state-of-the-art guidelines and action plans for helping all who work with young children to move toward full compliance with the law. An excellent resource guide.

Gaylord-Ross, Robert, Ed. *Integration Strategies for Students with Handicaps.* (Baltimore, Md.: Paul H. Brookes, 1989)

Explains current practices of integration in special education. Describes pupils, settings, materials, procedures, evaluation, design, and practical techniques for successfully integrating individuals with handicaps into school, work, and community settings.

Gollnick, Donna M., and Philip C. Chinn. *Multicultural Education in a Pluralistic Society, Third Edition* (Columbus, Ohio: Merrill, 1990)

Provides an overview of the microcultures to which children belong and gives specific ideas for how educators can use pluralism to implement multicultural education.

Haring, Norris G., and Linda McCormick, Eds. *Exceptional Children and Youth, Fifth Edition* (Columbus, Ohio: Merrill, 1990)

Focuses on the diversity of topics and issues facing teachers and all who work with exceptional children. Explores such areas as full integration of the handicapped, prevention through early intervention, peer tutoring and social interaction, self-monitoring, and academic learning time.

Kendall, Frances E. *Diversity in the Classroom* (New York: Teachers College Press, 1983)

Outlines resources and multicultural approaches to teaching and learning; also gives ideas for setting up a multicultural classroom environment.

Lerner, Janet, Carol Mardel-Czudnowski, and Dorothea Goldenberg. *Special Education for the Early Childhood Years* (Englewood-Cliffs, N.J.: Prentice-Hall, 1987)

Provides current information about young handicapped and at-risk children. Emphasis on teaching skills is particularly useful for both pre- and inservice teachers.

Lewis, Rena B., and Donald H. Doorlag, *Teaching Special Students in the Mainstream* (Columbus, Ohio: Merrill, 1983)

Clear and informative account of providing for children with special needs; tips and practical advice.

Marozas, Donald S., and Deborah C. May. *Issues and Practices in Special Education* (White Plains, N.Y.: Longman, 1988)

Designed to heighten awareness of the problems, issues, and practices affecting special populations and special educators. It will also stimulate critical thinking and discussion through its use of current literature, classic articles, and case histories.

McGuinness, Diane, *When Children Don't Learn: Understanding the Biology and Psychology of Learning Disabilities* (New York: Basic Books, 1985)

Challenges educators to examine how individual children learn and to develop programs, not labels, to help them reach their potential; also prompts reexamination of traditional assumptions about sex differences in learning and their implications for classroom learning.

Mercer, Cecil D., and Ann R. Mercer. *Teaching Students with Learning Problems* (Columbus, Ohio: Merrill, 1989)

Prepares regular classroom teachers, resource room teachers, remedial education teachers, and other professionals for the challenges of individualized programming for students with behavior problems. Contains an in-depth discussion of peer tutoring, motivational techniques, teacher coaching, and computer-assisted instruction.

National Center for Clinical Infant Programs. *Equals in This Partnership: Parents of Disabled and At-Risk Infants and Toddlers Speak to Professionals* (Washington, D.C.: National Center for Clinical Infant Programs, 1984)

In 1984, a conference on "Comprehensive Approaches to Disabled and At-Risk Infants and Toddlers" was held in Washington, D.C. This booklet contains proceedings of that conference. Premise is that parents and families, not professionals and consultants, have to be in charge of education and care of their handicapped children.

Pelton, Leroy, H., Ed. *The Social Context of Child Abuse and Neglect* (New York: Human Sciences Press, 1985)

Pelton believes child abuse has been overly "psychologized," meaning that in their orientation to abuse, too many professionals adopt the medical model of "disease, treatment, and cure." Instead, Pelton says caregivers must examine social and economic reasons for abuse and the need for social services to address the situational context of abuse. Focuses on the role of poverty in abuse.

Peterson, Nancy L. *Early Intervention for Handicapped and At-Risk Children: An Introduction to Early Childhood-Special Education* (Denver, Col.: Love, 1987)

Comprehensive and readable introduction to the field; good descriptions of children with special needs and programs for providing services.

Pueschel, S.M., J.C. Bernier, and L.E. Weidenman. *The Special Child: A Source Book for Parents of Children with Developmental Disabilities* (Baltimore, Md.: Paul H. Brookes, 1988)

People who work with young children but have not been trained specifically in special education will find this book an excellent tool for understanding the needs of children and families with whom they work.

Ramsey, Patricia G. *Children's Understanding of Diversity: Multicultural Perspectives in Early Childhood Education* (New York: Teachers College Press, 1986)

How early childhood education can help minimize prejudice; provides actual classroom practice experiences.

Reynolds, Maynard C., and Jack W. Birch. *Adaptive Mainstreaming: A Primer for Teachers and Principals, Third Edition* (White Plains, N.Y.: Longman, 1988)

A practical introduction to the education of handicapped and gifted students. Presents research and philosophical rationales for teaching exceptional students in a least-restrictive environment.

Ross, Robert T., et al. *Lives of the Mentally Retarded: A Forty-Year Follow-up Study* (Stanford, Calif.: Stanford University Press, 1985)

Reports findings of a study to determine status of San Francisco school children forty years after they were identified as "educable mentally retarded." One surprising conclusion of the study was that: "Most of the subjects are little different from persons of 'normal' intelligence who share their social class status. Their work histories were acceptable, marital relationships fairly stable, child rearing practices appropriate . . . . They appeared to be productive, law-abiding citizens of the community." Authors conclude that "except in their school years and except for their place in the school system, they had no identity as retarded persons."

Safford, Philip L. *Integrated Teaching in Early Childhood: Starting in the Mainstream* (White Plains, N.Y.: Longman, 1989)

Demonstrates a teaching philosophy that enables all teachers in public schools and preschools to respond effectively and creatively to the special needs of all children. The practices advocated are all developmentally appropriate and designed to meet individual needs.

Sparks, Louise Derman, and the ABC Task Force. *Anti-bias Curriculum: Tools for Empowering Young*

Children (Washington, D.C.: National Association for the Education of Young Children, 1989)

> Helps early childhood teachers help children learn to think critically, to solve problems, and to discuss difficult issues of justice so as to develop healthy self-images. Also helps teachers examine their own biases.

Townley, Roderick. *Safe and Sound: A Parents Guide to Child Protection* (New York: Simon and Schuster, 1985)

> For parents with children of all ages; useful information on physical abuse, choosing a day care center, and what to do if your child disappears; also a section on topics such as punishment versus rehabilitation for offenders.

FURTHER STUDY

1. Visit parents of a handicapped child. What problems do the parents have to deal with? Are they dealing with them adequately? What suggestions would you make for helping these parents with their problems?
2. Visit several public schools to see how they are providing individualized and appropriate programs for handicapped children. What efforts are being made to involve parents?
3. Review the IFSP in Appendix C. What factors make it unique? Which provisions would be most difficult to implement? Why?
4. Interview parents of handicapped children. What do they feel are parents' greatest problems? What do they consider the greatest needs for their children? List specific ways they have been involved in educational agencies. How have educational agencies avoided or resisted providing for their or their children's needs?
5. What are some assets that many handicapped children possess?
6. Visit and spend some time in a mainstreamed classroom. What specific skills would you need to become a good teacher in such a setting?
7. Visit a resource room. How is this setting different from a regular classroom? Would you want to teach in a resource room? Why or why not?
8. What architectural and structural accommodations are being made in public buildings and schools to provide for people with special needs?
9. Would you want to be a teacher of handicapped children in a setting other than a regular classroom? Why or why not?
10. Visit agencies and programs that provide services for the handicapped. Before you visit, list specific features, services, and facilities you will look for.
11. Visit a multicultural program. Compare and contrast this to other special programs. What changes would you make, if any? Why or why not?
12. Compare and contrast a gifted program to a regular classroom setting.
13. What programs does the federal government support for children with special needs in your area? Give specific information.
14. Identify the special needs of children in a mainstreamed classroom. What would you do to improve the program?
15. Visit with handicapped adults. From their school experiences, what do they suggest for improving classrooms, teaching, and attitudes toward the handicapped?
16. Discuss with people of another culture their culture's attitudes toward the handicapped. How are they similar or different from your attitudes?
17. John was convinced his 2-year-old son was gifted. His wife, Yvonne, disagreed; she said their son was not independent enough. John insisted that the boy's advanced language development was the mark of a bright child. What suggestions would you make to help these parents settle their disagreement about their son's giftedness? Why might some parents think their children are gifted while other parents might not?
18. Use Mary Wilson's match-up matrix with a handicapped child and the primary classroom he or she will attend. Report your findings to your classmates.
19. List the pros and cons of the transdisciplinary approach to meeting the needs of handicapped children.
20. Volunteer to teach a gifted child for six weeks. What special experiences did you provide? What did you learn? Would you want to teach the gifted? Why or why not?

NOTES

1. *Federal Register,* Tuesday, August 23, 1977, p. 42478.

2. U.S., *Statutes at Large,* vol. 89.

3. Ann E. Lupkowski, and Elizabeth A. Lupkowski, "Meeting the Needs of Gifted Preschoolers, *Children Today* (March/April 1985), pp. 10-14.

4. Michael Lewis with Leslie Kane, "Early Signals of Gifted," *Mothers Today* (January/February 1985), p. 14.

5. J. Gallagher, P. Weiss, K. Oglesby, and T. Thomas, *The status of gifted/talented education: United States survey needs, practices, and policies.* Los Angeles: National/State Leadership Training Institute on the Gifted and Talented, 1983.

6. Carol Johnson Parker, "Multicultural Awareness Activities," *Dimensions,* 10, no. 4 (July, 1982), p. 112.

CHAPTER 12
Guiding Behavior
Helping Children Become Responsible

As you read and study:

☐ Distinguish among guidance, discipline, and punishment
☐ Understand the basis for children's behavior and why they behave as they do
☐ Understand the importance of helping children develop an internal locus of control
☐ Understand the importance of guiding children's behavior and helping them become responsible
☐ Identify acceptable and inappropriate classroom and home behaviors
☐ Determine the effectiveness of positive reinforcement in developing appropriate behaviors in children
☐ Consider different reinforcement systems for managing behavior
☐ Analyze contingency management systems in parent-child and teacher-child relationships
☐ Develop a philosophy of guiding children's behavior
☐ Compare and contrast different theories of guiding children's behavior
☐ Identify the essential characteristics of effective behavior guidance
☐ Become conversant about issues related to behavioral guidance of young children
☐ Identify appropriate child guidance principles

Guiding children's behavior at home and in the early childhood classroom is a concern of educators and parents. Many parents tend to interpret children's misbehavior as a sign that educators have gone "soft" on discipline and are demanding that schools and teachers return to a more fundamental system where control and authority prevail. Modern society is in a great deal of turmoil. There is national concern about the breakup of the American family, widespread substance use, rampant crime, and general disrespect for authority. These are seen as evidence of parental and societal erosion of authority and discipline beginning in the earliest years. In fact, many believe that current social ills are caused by parents' failure to discipline their children. These people believe a primary way to instill renewed respect for traditional values is to return to strict discipline, including physical punishment.

BEHAVIOR: WHAT IS IT?

Behavior is the sum total of a child's actions. When we talk about behavior management and guidance, we are generally referring to behavior we can observe. We are concerned with what we see a child doing—not completing work, walking aimlessly around the room, or going for a drink of water—as opposed to what the child is thinking. The same is true for behavior at home. Parents should focus on the behaviors they can see, not what they think is going on in their children's minds. Focusing on overt behavior does not mean teachers and parents should ignore children's hopes, dreams, fears, and worries. They need to attend to emotions, too, because observable behaviors are often the outward manifestation of inner thoughts and turmoil. But it is the external behaviors to which teachers and parents usually respond. External behaviors are the focus of discussion in this chapter.

DISCIPLINE DEFINED

Discipline generally refers to correcting and directing children toward acceptable behavior. Other concepts of discipline have to do with getting children to obey, do what they are told to do, and "listen" to whomever is giving instructions. Results from a Gallup Poll indicate that when the public uses the word *discipline,* it means: "obeying rules/regulations, authority/control by teachers and respect for teacher."[1] This is a somewhat negative view of discipline that focuses on *control* rather than on helping children build positive behaviors. In this chapter, our emphasis is not on learning how to discipline children; rather, it is on developing insights and skills to help children develop appropriate behaviors.

From this perspective, then, *behavior guidance* is a process of *regulating,* so that children can control their own behavior and become independent. In this view, behavior guidance is a process of helping children develop skills. Teachers' and parents' roles are to guide children toward developing self-control, encouraging them to be independent, meeting their intellectual and emotional needs, establishing expectations for them, organizing appropriate behaviors, arranging environments so self-discipline can occur, and, when necessary, changing their own behavior. Thus, effective guidance of children's behavior at home and school consists of these essential elements:

1. Helping children build new behaviors and skills of independence and responsibility
2. Meeting children's needs
3. Establishing appropriate expectations
4. Arranging and modifying the environment so that appropriate, expected behavior and self-control is possible
5. Modifying our own behavior and expectations where and when appropriate
6. Avoiding creating or encouraging behavior problems

The goal of most parents and teachers is to have children behave in socially acceptable and appropriate ways. Since this goal is never really fully achieved, we should view guidance as a process of learning by doing. A child cannot learn to discipline himself by being told to sit still and behave. Just as no one learns to ride a bicycle by reading a book on the subject, children do not learn to discipline themselves by being told what to do all the time. Maria Montessori often remarked that "Discipline is not telling." Children must be shown and taught through precept and example. Children need encouragement and opportunities to practice self-discipline. They must be given opportunities to develop, practice, and perfect their abilities to control and guide their own behavior.

Locus of Control

We have been talking about what is generally referred to as *locus of control*—the source or place of control. The preferred and recommended locus of control for young and old alike is internal. We want children to control their own behavior. If the locus of control is external, the child is controlled by others; she is always told what to do and how to behave. We try to avoid developing an external locus of control in children.

It would be naive, however, to think that a child is born with this desired inner-directed locus of control. Instead, the process of helping children develop an internal locus of control begins at birth and continues through the early childhood years. In fact, developing an inner locus of control is a never-ending process that goes on throughout our lives.

Helping Children Build New Behaviors

Helping children build new behaviors creates a sense of responsibility and self-confidence. As children are given responsibility, they develop greater self-discipline, so that teachers and parents have to provide less guidance and children are less of a "discipline problem." Ironically, many teachers and parents hesitate to let children assume responsibilities, and without responsibilities, children are bored, frustrated, and become discipline problems—the very opposite of what is intended. Guidance is not a matter of getting children to please the teacher by remarks such as "Show me how perfect you can be," "Don't embarrass me by your behavior in front of other teachers," "I want to see nice groups," or "I'm waiting for quiet." Rather, it is important to instill in children a sense of independence and responsibility for their own behavior. For example, you might say, "You have really worked a long time cutting out the flower you drew. I like how you kept working on it until you were finished. Would you like some tape to hang it up with?"

Meeting Children's Needs

Abraham Maslow (1890–1970) felt that human growth and development was oriented toward *self-actualization,* the striving to realize one's potential. He felt that humans are internally motivated by five basic needs that constitute a hierarchy of motivating behaviors progressing from physical needs to self-fulfillment. Maslow's hierarchy moves through physical needs, safety and security needs, belonging and affection needs, and self-esteem needs culminating in self-actualization. Let's look at an example of each of these stages and behaviors.

1. *Physical needs*—children's ability to guide their behavior depends in part on how well their physical needs are met. Children do their best in school, for example, when they are well nourished. Thus parents should provide for their children's nutritional needs by giving them breakfast. Teachers should also stress the nutritional and health benefits of eating breakfast. The quality of the

Children have a basic need for love and affection, and are more capable of responsible behavior when this need is met.

environment is also important. If classrooms are dark, smell of stale air, and are noisy, children cannot be expected to "behave." Children also need adequate rest to do their best and be their best. The amount of rest is an individual matter, but many young children need eight to ten hours of sleep. A tired child cannot meet many of the expectations of schooling.

2. *Safety and security*—children should not have to fear their teacher or principal and should feel comfortable and secure at home. Asking or forcing children to do school tasks for which they don't have the skills makes them feel insecure, and when children are afraid and insecure, they are under a great deal of tension. Consider also the dangers many urban children face, such as crime, drugs, and homelessness, or the insecurity of children who live in an atmosphere of domestic violence.

3. *Belonging and affection*—children need love and affection and the sense of belonging that comes from being given jobs to do, from being given responsibilities, and from helping to make classroom and home decisions. Love and affection needs are also satisfied when parents hold, hug, and kiss their children and tell them "I love you."

4. *Self-esteem*—when a child views himself as worthy, responsible, and competent, he will act that way. Children's views of themselves come primarily from parents and teachers. Experiencing success gives them feelings of high self-esteem, and it is up to parents and teachers to give all children opportunities for success.

5. *Self-actualization*—children want to use their talents and abilities to do things for themselves and to be independent. Teachers and parents can help children become independent by helping them learn to dress themselves, go to the restroom by themselves, and take care of their environments. They can also help children set achievement and behavior goals ("tell me what you are going to build with your blocks") and encourage them to evaluate their behavior ("let's talk about how you cleaned up your room"). So it is important for teachers and parents to consider the children's basic needs in the process of helping them guide and develop responsibility for their behavior.

Establishing Appropriate Expectations

Teachers and parents need to know what their expectations are for children. When children know what parent and teachers expect, they can better achieve those expectations. Up to a point, the more we expect of children, the more and better they achieve. Generally, teachers and parents expect too little of most children.

Arranging the Environment

Environment plays a key role in children's ability to guide their behavior. For example, if parents want a child to be responsible for taking care of his room, they should arrange the environment so he can do so, by providing shelves, hangers, and drawers at child height. Similarly, a teacher should arrange the classroom so children can get and return their own papers and materials, use learning centers, and have time to work on individual projects.

Modifying Adult Behavior and Expectations

Changing adult behavior is often one of the easiest ways to change children's behaviors. When the level of expectations is beyond children's abilities to achieve, we see a greater probability of misbehavior. When teachers show children how to do a task and then have them practice the skill under supervision, there is a greater possibility that they will learn the skill. A teacher, therefore, may have to change her behavior from telling to showing and demonstrating.

Avoiding Problems

Parents and teachers actually encourage a great deal of children's misbehavior. Teachers see too much and ignore too little. Parents expect perfection and adult behavior. If parents and teachers focus on building responsible behavior, there will be less need to solve behavior problems.

PRINCIPLES OF BEHAVIOR MODIFICATION

A popular approach to guidance based on behavior rather than on feelings is *behavior modification*. An important concept of behavior modification is that all behavior is caused. Everyone acts the way they do for reasons, although the reasons may not always be apparent; in fact, a child does not always know why he behaves a certain way. How often have you heard the expressions, "He didn't know what he was doing," "I don't know why he acts like he does," "I can't understand why I did that," and "I didn't know what I was doing"?

A second basic concept is that behavior results from reinforcement received from the environment. American psychologist Edward L. Thorndike (1874–1949) observed that the consequences of one's behavior influence future behavior. The stimulus-response associations depend on response outcomes. He formalized this observation in his learning principle, the *law of effect*. If a satisfying condition follows a behavior, the individual tends to repeat that behavior, and the strength of the stimulus-response connection increases. If an unsatisfying condition follows a behavior, the individual tends not to repeat that behavior, and the stimulus-response connection weakens or disappears. The law of effect points out how important the quality of feedback is for behavior. This law has gradually come to be known as the Imperial Law of Effect, which says that the consequences of particular responses determine whether the response will be continued and therefore learned. In other words, what happens to an individual after he acts in a particular way determines whether he continues to act that way. If a child cries and is immediately given a cookie, he will probably learn to cry to receive cookies. Receiving cookies reinforces crying behavior. We should understand that this behavior is not always planned; a child does not necessarily say to himself, "I'm going to cry because I know my mother will give me a cookie." The child may have cried, and his mother, to stop the crying, gave the child a cookie. The child then came to associate the two events.

Figure 12–1 shows how a young child might be conditioned to have a fear of dogs (or anything else, for that matter). The child and mother are walking through the park. The mother, who has a fear of large dogs, screams when she sees a large dog. The scream frightens the child. Although the child may or may not have seen the dog

FIGURE 12–1   Fear Conditioning

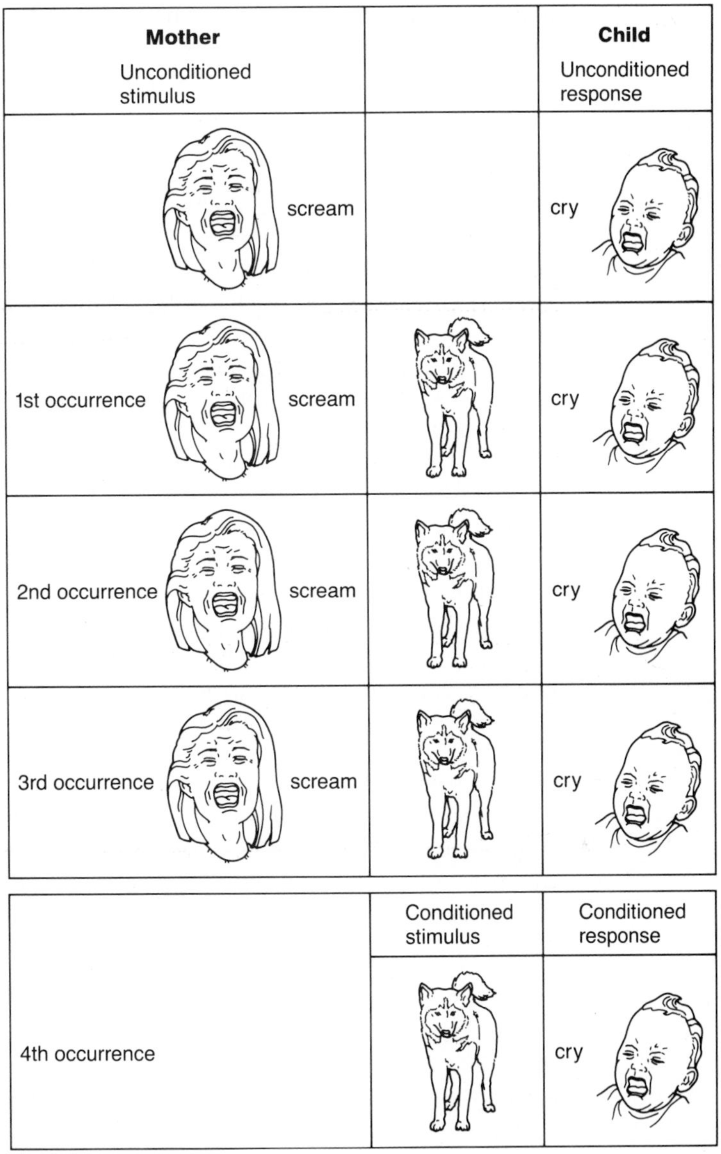

Mother Unconditioned stimulus		Child Unconditioned response
scream		cry
1st occurrence scream		cry
2nd occurrence scream		cry
3rd occurrence scream		cry

	Conditioned stimulus	Conditioned response
4th occurrence		cry

the first time, on subsequent walks through the park, he associates his mother's screams with the dog, until after a number of occurrences, he, too, is afraid of dogs.

B. F. Skinner (1904–) is given credit for many of the technological and pedagogical applications of behavior modification, including programmed instruction. Skinner also emphasizes the role of the environment in providing people with clues that reinforce their behavior.

In behavior management, we are concerned with behavior modification, or changing behavior. As used in this chapter, behavior modification means the *conscious* application of the methods of behavioral science, with the intent of altering child behavior. Teachers and parents have always been concerned with changing children's behavior, but it is implicit in the term *behavior modification* that we mean the conscious use of techniques to change behavior. Behaviorists maintain that all behavior is learned and, in this sense, that all behavior is caused by reinforcers from which individuals gain pleasure of some kind. The problem, however, is that teachers and parents have usually changed children's behavior without realizing it. Teachers and parents should be more aware of the effect they have on children's behavior. To use power ignorantly and unconsciously to achieve ends that are basically dehumanizing to children is not good teaching practice. For example, when a child first comes to school, he may not understand that sitting quietly is a desirable behavior that many schools and teachers have established as a goal. The teacher may scold the child until he not only sits quietly, but sits quietly and bites his nails. The teacher did not intentionally set out to reinforce nail biting, but this is the child's terminal behavior, and the teacher is unaware of how it happened.

Reinforced Misbehavior

We must recognize that teacher and parent behavior, attitude, predisposition, and inclination can cause a great deal of child misbehavior. Many children misbehave because their misbehavior is reinforced. For example, children enjoy receiving attention; therefore, when a child receives any kind of attention, it reinforces the behavior the child exhibited to get that attention. A child who is noisy receives teacher attention by being scolded. The chances of his exhibiting the same behavior (talking to the child beside him) to elicit attention from the teacher is greatly increased because he was reinforced.

We sometimes encourage children to do sloppy work or hurry through an activity when we emphasize finishing it. We may give the child a worksheet with six squares to color and cut out, and say, "After you color all the squares, I will give you a pair of scissors so you can cut the squares out." The child may hurry through the coloring to get to the cutting. We would do better to concentrate on coloring first, then cutting.

Positive Reinforcement

When we talk about positive reinforcement, we are talking about providing *rewards* or *reinforcers* that promote behaviors teachers and parents decide are desirable. *Positive reinforcement* is maintaining or increasing the frequency of a behavior following a particular stimulus. What the child receives, whether candy, money, or a hug, is the *reinforcer,* the *reinforcement,* or the *reward*. Generally, a positive reinforcer is any stimulus that maintains or increases a particular behavior. These are verbal reinforcers: "Good," "Right," "Correct," "Wonderful," "Very good," "I like that," "Good boy/girl," "Hey! That's great!" and "I knew you could do it." Teachers can also use nonverbal behavior to reinforce children's behavior and learning; for example, a nod, smile, hug, pat on the head or shoulder, standing close to someone, eye contact, paying attention, or even a wink show a child that you approve of his behavior or are proud of what he is doing. The classroom can be set up to provide a positively reinforcing environment. If it is organized to help make desired behaviors possible, provides opportunities for novelty, gives children opportunities for control over their environment, and reflects children's desires, interests, and ideas, they will tend to try to live up to the expectations the setting suggests.

Understanding Behavior

Another extremely important concept of behavior modification focuses on external behavior rather than on the causes of behavior; that is, teachers and parents should generally not be concerned with *why* a child acts as he does. This idea usually takes some getting used to, because it is almost the opposite of what we have been taught. Teachers particularly feel it is beneficial to know why a child acts the way she does, and spend a great deal of time and effort trying to determine motivations. If Gloria is fidgety and inclined to daydream, the teacher may spend six weeks investigating the causes. He learns that Gloria's mother has been divorced three times and ignores her at home. On the basis of this information, he concludes that Gloria needs help, but is no closer to solving her problem than he was six weeks previously. A teacher's time and energy should be spent developing strategies to help children with their

Very young children can begin to learn responsibility by picking up and putting away their toys, but parents and caregivers must arrange the environment to promote that kind of responsibility. Although this child may be putting his toys in the basket as a kind of game, caregivers and parents can reinforce this type of behavior through positive responses.

behavior. Sometimes underlying causes help us deal with the behavior we wish to modify, but we need to recognize that the behavior a child exhibits is the problem, and it is behavior that we need to attend to.

Punishment

Is it possible to guide behavior without punishment? Most parents and teachers have punished children at one time or another; sometimes it seems necessary for the children's safety. In general, however, punishment does not guide children toward building new behavior. If punishment is necessary, make sure you explain why, and offer guidance for good behavior. Punishment also tends to build negative feelings in both individuals. If one must punish, the incident should be immediately put behind one—forgive and forget.

Teachers and parents sometimes seem to think a child behaves a certain way because he is innately bad. They also sometimes feel children do the things they do to disturb adults. Both attitudes show a lack of understanding of child development. Children are not born with a tendency to do bad things, nor do they spend their time plotting against teachers and parents. The responsibility for changing and directing behavior rests with adults.

Ignoring Behavior

Ignoring inappropriate behavior is probably one of the most overlooked strategies for managing an effective learning setting. Ironically, many teachers feel guilty when they use this strategy. They believe that ignoring undesirable behaviors is not good teaching. Although ignoring off-task behavior may be an effective strategy, ignoring behavior must be combined with positive reinforcement of desirable behavior. Thus, one ignores inappropriate behavior and at the same time reinforces appropriate behavior. A combination of positive reinforcement and ignoring can lead to *extinction* of the undesired behavior.

Providing Guidance

A child is generally not capable of acting or thinking his way out of undesirable behavior. Parents and teachers may say, "You know how to act," when indeed the child does not know. Teachers also often say, "He could do better if he wanted to." The problem, however, is that the child may not know what he wants to do, or may not know what's appropriate. In other words, he needs an organized procedure for how to act. Thinking does not build new behavior; acting does. Building new behavior, then, is a process of getting children to act in new ways.

A common approach to behavior control is "talking to" and reasoning. As children often do not understand abstract reasoning, it doesn't generally have the desired effect. The child is likely to behave the same way, or worse. This often leads to a punishment trap, in which the teacher or parent resorts to yelling, screaming, or paddling, to get the desired results. The behavior we want children to demonstrate must be within their ability. A child cannot pay attention to and be interested in a story that is based on concepts that are too advanced for his comprehension or is read in a monotonic, unenthusiastic voice. Although *Tom Sawyer* is a children's classic,

Helping children and warmly supporting their efforts is the most effective and humane kind of guidance.

we cannot expect a group of three-year-olds to sit still and listen attentively as it is read aloud.

REINFORCING BEHAVIOR

Appropriate Reinforcers

A reinforcer is only as effective as the child's desire for it. In other words, if the reinforcer has the power to reinforce the behavior that precedes it, then it will work. A method used to determine the nature of a reinforcer is the *Premack Principle*. David Premack determined that behaviors with a high probability of occurrence can be used to reinforce behaviors with a low probability of occurrence. For example, activities children participate in when they have free time are often what they like to do best. Teachers can use these activities to reinforce desired behaviors.

Using the chalkboard or easels is a highly desirable activity in many early childhood classrooms. Therefore, teachers can provide time to use the chalkboard or the art easels to reinforce desired behavior. Rewards that children help select are most likely to have a desired effect on behavior. Privileges children often choose are getting the teacher's mail, watering the plants, feeding classroom pets, washing chalkboards, running errands, going outside, bringing books from home to read, playing games with friends, leading games, extra recess, passing out papers and supplies, using audiovisual equipment, watching TV, doing flash cards, and cutting and pasting. Table 12–1 shows typical reinforcers in an early childhood setting.

Praise as a Reinforcer

Praise is probably the most frequent method of rewarding or reinforcing children's behavior. Praise is either general or specific. Specific praise is more effective because it describes the behavior we want to build. The child has no doubt that he is being praised and what he is being praised for. For example, if a child picks up her blocks and you say "good, Laura," she may or may not know what you are referring to, but

TABLE 12–1   Reinforcers Used in Early Childhood Settings

Primary Reinforcers		Conditioned Reinforcers	
Reinforce behavior without the respondent's having much previous experience with the item		Reinforce as a result of experiences the respondent has had with the reinforcer	
Food		**Verbal—praise**	
Juice	Raisins	I like the way you ...	
Peanuts	Cheese	Great — Fine	A-Okay — Tremendous
Celery	Fruit	Right on — Wow	Excellent
Carrots		Beautiful — Way to go	Fantastic
		Terrific — Super	Fine job
		Nonverbal	
		Facial — *Gestures*	*Proximity*
		Smile — Clapping of hands	Standing near someone
		Wink — Wave	Shaking hands
		Raised eyebrow — Forming an A-Okay sign (thumb + index finger)	Getting down on a child's level
		Eye contact — Victory sign	Hug, touching
		Nod head	Holding child's arm up
		Shrug shoulders	
		Social (occur in or as a result of social consequences)	
		Parties	
		Group approval	
		Class privileges	

if you say "Laura, you did a nice job of putting your blocks away," Laura knows exactly what you are talking about.

Parents and teachers should approach children positively. A positive approach builds self-esteem. We help build positive self-images and expectations for good behavior by complimenting children and praising them for the things they do well. Every child has praiseworthy qualities.

Contingency Management

Teachers frequently find it helpful to engage in *contingency contracting* or *contingency management* to reinforce behavior. With this strategy, the child might be told, "If you put the materials away when you're done with them, you can use the chalkboard for five minutes." Sometimes contingency management is accompanied by a written contract between teacher and student, depending, of course, on the child's age and maturity.

When parents or teachers manage a contingency, they must be sure they have thought through its consequences. For example, if a parent says, "If you don't clean up your room, you have to stay there until you do," the child may choose not to clean up his room but to stay there and play with his toys. In this case, he doesn't have to do as he was told and is rewarded for not doing it.

Token System

Reinforcement works best when it occurs at the time of the behavior we want to reinforce. Also, the sooner reinforcement follows the desired behavior, the better it works. Particularly when building new skills or shaping new behaviors, it is important to reinforce the child immediately. To provide immediate reinforcement, some teachers use tokens, such as plastic discs, buttons, trading stamps, or beans, which the child later trades for an activity. If the children like to use the art easel, the teacher might allow a child to exchange ten tokens for time at the easel. When a child performs appropriate tasks and exhibits teacher-specified behavior, he receives a token.

Time Out

Another practice teachers in early childhood classrooms often use is *time out*. A teacher should use time out only when it is appropriate to children's developmental levels. Time out is the removal of a child from an activity because he has done something wrong. Presumably, the time out gives him an opportunity to think about his misbehavior. After a set amount of time or when the child says he can behave (which, of course, *all* children say), he is allowed to return to the activity. This strategy is inappropriate for infants' and toddlers' developmental levels, but infrequent use is sometimes effective with preschoolers. "Time out" is generally not effective as a guidance technique, because it is debatable whether a young child will "think" about what he did wrong. Additionally, time out is usually irrelevant to the inappropriate behavior, so the child doesn't make a connection between what he did "wrong" and the punishment.

Children are energetic and impulsive, so it is effective to use *preventive guidance* techniques that catch problems before they happen—or "prevent" them. Examples

THE WAUKEGAN EFFECTIVE SCHOOLS APPROACH FOLLOW-THROUGH MODEL PROGRAM, WAUKEGAN, ILLINOIS*

The Waukegan Demonstration Center is a nationally validated Follow-Through Program in the Effective Schools Approach. The Waukegan Follow-Through Program has four basic goals:

1. Increased academic achievement and improvement in school and home environments for many children
2. Advances in development of comprehensive instructional approaches
3. Creation of alternatives for training and support of school faculty and staffs
4. Progress in involving parents in the educational and political process of schooling

These four goals are implemented through these major components:

☐ *Motivation*—The Effective Schools Approach is designed to motivate students to learn through two systems, a token exchange system in grades K–1 and a contracting system in grades 2–3.
☐ *Curriculum*—Emphasis is on teaching the basic skills of reading, math, spelling, and handwriting.

☐ *Team teaching*—All behavior classrooms are staffed by a lead teacher and a paraprofessional.
☐ *Continuous program measures*—Every month, students' progress is analyzed and progress prescriptions are written.

This analysis is conducted in cooperation with the University of Kansas. Standardized tests are also used to assess student achievement.

The Waukegan program not only demonstrates the Effective Schools Approach model, but also provides technical assistance to school districts and programs that want to implement the model. So far, program adaptations have been introduced in St. Francis, Wisconsin; Midland, Texas; Milwaukee, Wisconsin; Sanford, Maine; Berwyn, Illinois; Marlin, Texas; Calumet Park, Illinois; Dallas, Texas (Wilmer-Hutchins I.S.D.); Zion, Illinois

*Contributed by Isabelle L. Buckner, principal, Carmen Elementary School

of preventive guidance are room arrangement, scheduling, minimizing waiting time, and an interesting, active curriculum. These approaches are far more effective than using "band-aid" approaches to guidance such as "time out."

Beginning when the child is about three years old, caregivers should explain to the child why he has been removed and what would be an acceptable way to act. Not getting to play in the block center because he knocked over someone's building may be just what a child needs to learn how to regulate his behavior.

The Classroom as a Reinforcer of Behavior

As mentioned earlier, behavior modification strategies can also be applied to the physical setting of the classroom. The classroom should be arranged so that it is conducive to the behaviors the teacher wants to reinforce. If a teacher wants to encourage independent work, there must be places and time for children to work alone. Disruptive behavior is often encouraged by classroom arrangements that force children to walk over other children to get to equipment and materials. A teacher may find that the classroom actually contributes to off-task behaviors. The atmosphere

(Y.W.C.A. Key Kids); Cassopolis, Michigan; and Waukegan, Illinois (Lake County Head Start).

An Effective Schools Approach classroom has elements of a number of educational strategies, including team teaching, individualized teaching, and a reinforcement system utilizing a token system or contracting. Instructional objectives are written for all children based on what they know and what they should learn.

The Effective Schools Approach model rests on the assumption that many children are not naturally motivated to learn, but need to be taught. There are many things in a classroom and school day that children find rewarding, but these activities, such as recess, are not always immediately available to them. A reward is much more reinforcing when it immediately follows the desired or target behavior.

The Effective Schools Approach classroom uses a token exchange system to create and maintain a high level of motivation. Tokens are given immediately to every child for good behavior. The teacher and staff determine what they are going to reward the children for,

and rewarded behaviors change constantly, depending on the child and the objectives of the learning program. For example, a child may be rewarded for making straight lines on his writing paper. After he has learned to do this consistently, however, his learning objectives (target behavior) will change. In the same way, the things for which children exchange tokens change according to preferences and instructional needs.

Children who are engaged in on-task behavior are not interrupted, and continue to work until their tokens can be exchanged for enjoyable activities (called *backups*) of their choice. A token system motivates children, keeps them interested in their work, and teaches independence, because each child is free to earn the opportunity to engage in backup activities. A token can be any object, but it is best if it is something children can hold and put in their pockets. In the Effective Schools Approach program, children wear aprons similar to a carpenter's apron with several large pockets in which they can put their tokens quickly and easily. The aprons have the

of the classroom or the learning environment must be such that new behaviors are possible.

Although teachers want to encourage independence, they often make the children ask for materials, which the teacher must then locate. This practice discourages independence. To promote independence, materials should be readily available. The same situation applies in the home. If a parent wants a child to keep his room neat and clean, it must be possible for the child to do so. The child should also be shown how to take care of his room. The parent may have to lower shelves or install clothes hooks. When the physical arrangement is to the child's size, the child can be taught how to use a clothes hanger and where to hang certain clothes. A child's room should have a place for everything; these places should be accessible and easy to use.

TEACHING BY PRECEPT AND EXAMPLE

We have all heard the maxim that "telling is not teaching." Nevertheless, we tend to teach by instructions and directions. The teacher of young children soon realizes,

THE WAUKEGAN EFFECTIVE SCHOOLS APPROACH FOLLOW-THROUGH MODEL PROGRAM, WAUKEGAN, ILLINOIS —Continued

children's names on them, so whoever is instructing them can always use first names when reinforcing.

Children are given or earn tokens only during an "earn" period. The behavior for which children receive tokens depends on the individual child and what each is being taught. Since children are working at many different levels, they are rewarded for many different behaviors. The procedure and rationale is the same for all, however—every child is reinforced, that is, given tokens. A token system won't work unless children have tokens to spend! All children should also have similar amounts of tokens to exchange. The implications for teachers are to have children involved in tasks they can accomplish and to work individually with them so they can succeed. The period when children can earn tokens (the "earn period") generally occurs when they are engaged in academic work; they are thus motivated to stay on task and work diligently to earn tokens.

Merely earning tokens does no good unless children have opportunities to exchange their

tokens for items or activities that are attractive to them. How many tokens an activity is worth depends upon its value to children. If children prefer to have a story read to them rather than go out for recess, then the story time activity would cost more tokens. Children must exchange their tokens during each "spend" period; they cannot carry over tokens from one day to the next, otherwise they could conceivably spend a day doing nothing but spend tokens on pleasurable activities.

Motivation is also kept high by varying the activities for which tokens can be exchanged, the length of the earn period, and the time when exchanges occur. In this way, children won't tire of the activities and won't be tempted to earn a certain number of tokens and then stop working.

The purpose of a token system is to give children positive reinforcement for good behavior. Children enjoy the Effective Schools Approach classroom because they can earn the opportunity to do things they find pleasurable. Also, since the emphasis is on achievement and positive reinforcement, the classroom is free

however, that actions speak louder than words. We encourage children to be discourteous by being discourteous to them. When we want them to move, we say, "Move!" instead of "Would you please move?" How will students learn what it means to be courteous if they are not shown courtesy?

The leading proponent of the modeling approach to learning is Albert Bandura, who believes that most behavior people exhibit is learned from the behavior of a model or models. A model may be someone whom we respect or find interesting and whom we believe is being rewarded for the behavior he exhibits. Bandura sees behavior modeling as similar to Skinner's concept of reinforcement. For example, children tend to model behavior that brings rewards from parent and teacher, and affection is a powerful reward.

Children see and remember how other people act. The child then tries the act, and if this new action brings a reward of some kind, the child repeats it. Groups as well as individuals serve as models. For example, it is common to hear a teacher in an early childhood classroom comment "I like how Cristina and Carlos are sitting quietly and listening to the story." Immediately following such a remark, you can see the group of children settle down to listen quietly to the story. Models children emulate don't necessarily have to be from real life; they can come from television

from punishment, negative attitudes, and threats.

The second and third grade contract classrooms use a procedure called *contingency contracting*. Children select an activity they would like to participate in contingent on completing a certain amount of work. The amount of work a child contracts for and the length of time for completing it depends on the individual. Contracting provides incentives by giving children the opportunity to engage in pleasurable activities in exchange for a certain amount of work. It also involves children in planning and goal setting and helps them become more responsible for their work and behavior.

The Language of an Effective Schools Approach Classroom

☐ *Earn*—period of time children are working with academic materials (instruction in books)

☐ *Spend*—time to use tokens to buy games and activities in the classroom

☐ *Token*—a chip the teacher gives the child for good work or good behavior

☐ *Exchange*—period when activities are announced, child counts tokens, and chooses an activity

☐ *Backup*—activity or game offered during a spend time and at the end of a contracting period

☐ *Contract*—a written agreement between teacher and student for pages to be done (used in second and third grades)

☐ *Red line*—a mark to show completion of an assignment; time when teacher questions the child as to what he/she has done

☐ *Time out*—three to five minutes when, because of poor behavior, a child cannot earn or spend tokens (kindergarten and first grade), or participate in contracting or backups (second and third grades)

and reading. In addition, the modeled behavior does not have to be socially acceptable to be reinforcing. The teacher should use the following techniques to help children learn through modeling:

☐ *Showing*. The teacher shows children where the block corner is and how and where the blocks are stored.

☐ *Demonstration*. The teacher performs a task while students watch. For example, the teacher demonstrates the proper way to put the blocks away and how to store them. Extensions of the demonstration method are to have the children practice the demonstration while the teacher supervises and to have a child demonstrate to other children.

☐ *Modeling*. Modeling occurs when the teacher practices the behavior she expects of the children. Also, the teacher can call children's attention to the desired behavior when another child models it.

☐ *Supervision*. Supervision is a process of reviewing, insisting, maintaining standards, and following up. If children are not performing the desired behavior, it will be necessary for you to *review* the behavior. You must be consistent in your expectations of desired behavior. Children will soon learn they don't have to

A CULTURAL BASIS FOR CLASSROOM MANAGEMENT

It is easy for teachers to believe that behavior and discipline are separate aspects of classroom management. This feeling goes along with the notion that children are children and through their energetic, active involvement in their environment and their lack of experience and maturity, misbehavior inevitably occurs. We must recognize, however, that it is almost impossible to separate the child and how he behaves from the cultural environment in which he is reared. Environment determines to a great extent the kind of behavior management the child expects and will respond to. Unless the teacher or caregiver is aware of these cultural conditions, she may not discipline the child appropriately, and the child will respond negatively to the discipline.

Some examples will help us understand this cultural reality. In a third grade classroom, a teacher asks Jorgé to sit in his seat and finish a writing project he began earlier in the day. His friend Roberto sneers at him and whispers, "Don't let the teacher walk on you." For fear of appearing subservient to the female teacher, Jorgé refuses to write, and taps his pencil on the desk as a further sign of his determination not to do what the teacher wants. Rather than force Jorgé to do his work, the teacher could assure him that he is not being "walked on"; discuss with the whole class the necessity for doing classwork and following directions; invite Jorgé's parents to talk with him and her about the situation; and manage her own behavior so that she is more sensitive to her students' culturally determined attitudes. It is always advisable for teachers to become aware of the cultural backgrounds of the children they are teaching. While it is true that awareness will come through teaching, some can also come through training programs conducted by colleges, universities, and other agencies.

In a second grade classroom, Ms. Gonzalez, a new teacher, has difficulty controlling the class. The class as a whole does not listen to her, although she uses many of the techniques taught in her college classes. She believes her colleagues are firmer with their students than she feels she should be. Finally, in frustration, she asks the teacher in the next classroom, "What am I going to do?" Her friend tells her that one reason for her difficulty is that the children come from families in which a "heavy hand" is the natural way of punishment, and the children are accustomed to feeling that an adult is not serious unless some form of physical punishment accompanies a command. The friend goes on to explain to Ms. Gonzalez that, while it is not necessary for her to punish the children, it will be necessary, at least in the beginning, for her to be firmer in following up her directions. She cannot ask that something be done and expect it to be done until she is able to build a basis for this kind of behavior.

In a child care classroom, Ms. Chan is concerned about the three-year-old children's lack of independence. Many are still on bottles and cannot dress themselves, and some cannot use eating utensils. During a conference with the director, Ms. Chan learns that it is customary in the culture of the children's homes for parents to overprotect and extend the period of dependency. A mother is viewed as a good parent when she does many of the things for her child that other cultures expect the child to do for himself after he reaches three or four years of age. These parents value extended dependency.

In conferences with parents and staff, Ms. Chan will have to decide which areas are most important for the children's successful functioning in the center and will have to teach those skills and behaviors. Although it is important that she understand the parents' attitudes, she must explain the necessity of certain independent behaviors in the center. She should also solicit the parents' help. She will concentrate her efforts in the beginning on helping the children dress themselves and learn how to feed themselves.

put away their blocks if you allow them not to do it even once. Remember, you are responsible for setting up the environment to enable the child's learning to take place.

Guidance Tips for the Early Childhood Educator

Many of these ideas for guiding behavior apply to the home as well as the classroom, so parents should also find them helpful. The first rule in guiding children's behavior is to *know yourself.* Unless you know your attitudes toward discipline and behavior, it will be hard to practice a rational and consistent program of management and discipline. So, develop a philosophy of discipline. What do you believe about child rearing, discipline, and punishment?

Another important rule is to *know your children.* A good way to learn about the children you teach is through home visits. If you do not have an opportunity to visit the home, a parent conference is also valuable. Either way, some of the information you should gather is a health history; interests of the child; the parents' educational expectations for the child; what school support is available in the home (for example, books and places to study); parents' attitudes toward education, schooling, and discipline; parents' support of the child (for example, encouragement to do well); parents' interests and abilities; home conditions that would support or hinder school achievement (such as where the child sleeps); parents' desire to become involved in the school; and the child's attitude toward schooling.

The visit or conference offers an opportunity for the teacher to share some of her ideas and philosophy with the parent. You should, for example, express your desire for the child to do well in school; encourage the parents to take part in school and classroom programs; suggest (if asked) ways to help the child learn; describe some of the school programs; give information about school events, projects, and meetings; and explain your beliefs about discipline.

Plan classroom guidelines from the first day of class. As the year goes on, you can involve children in establishing classroom rules, but in the beginning, children want and need to know what they can and cannot do. Rules might relate to changing groups and bathroom routines. Whatever rules you establish, they should be fair, reasonable, and appropriate to the children's age and maturity. Keep rules to a minimum; the fewer the better. For example, in Cindy Rominger's classroom of four-year-olds at the Texas Women's University Nursery School, the rules are simple, few, and consistently enforced.

1. Be gentle with your friends.
2. Use an inside voice.
3. Keep your feet on the floor.
4. Use your words when you have a problem.

The children are reminded of these rules and helped to conform with them. Four-year-old children can realistically be expected to follow these guidelines, so there is less chance for misbehavior. A child is able to become responsible for her own behavior in a positive, accepting atmosphere within which she knows what the expectations are for her. Review the rules, and have children evaluate their behavior against the rules. You can have expectations without having rules. If you have activities ready for children when they enter the classroom, you establish the expectation that upon entering the classroom, they should be busy.

Establish a classroom routine. Children need the confidence and security of a routine that will help them do their best. A routine also helps prevent discipline problems, because children know what to do and can learn to do it without a lot of disturbance. Parents need to establish routines in the home; if the child knows the family always eats at 5:30 P.M., he can be expected to be there. A teacher must also be consistent. Consistency plays an important role in managing behavior in both the home and classroom. If children know what to expect in terms of routine and behavior, they will behave better.

When possible, ignore off-task behavior. By ignoring off-task behavior, you are not reinforcing or rewarding it. Some authorities feel that by ignoring off-task behavior, teachers run the risk of also ignoring good behavior; however, a behaviorally aware teacher or parent *knows* what behavior to ignore and plans for the behavior he will reinforce. Make the classroom reinforcing. The classroom should be a place where children can do their best work and be on their best behavior. Components of an environmentally rewarding classroom are:

☐ Opportunities for children to display their work
☐ Opportunities for freedom of movement (within guidelines)
☐ Opportunities for independent work
☐ A variety of work stations and materials based on children's interests

Use positive reinforcement. When a child does something good, when he is on-task, reward him. Use verbal and nonverbal reinforcement and privileges to help assure that the appropriate behavior will continue. "Catch children being good"— look for good behavior. This helps improve not only individual behavior but group behavior as well. It can also be helpful to write contracts for certain work experiences. Contracting is a great way to involve the child in planning his own work and behavior. Rules to follow in contracting are to keep contracts short and uncomplicated; make an offer the child can't refuse; make sure the child is able to do what you contract for; and pay off when the contract is completed.

Be a good role model. Don't ask children to behave in a way you don't want to or are not willing to behave. Treat the children the way you want them to behave. But don't be afraid to be firm; in some instances, being firm may require physically punishing a child, and if you judge this to be necessary, do it.

Use many techniques for positive guidance of children's behavior. Some of these include keeping children busy and involved in a variety of interesting activities; developing and maintaining a good relationship with children; talking over classroom problems with the children; talking with the child who has a problem; and making and managing contingencies.

Seek help. Ask other teachers, parents, administrators, and experts in child behavior for advice. You will be surprised how much good help is available when you ask. Learning, teaching, and discipline go hand-in-hand. A teacher's success depends upon her attitude toward and methods of guidance and discipline. Teachers who master skills of effective discipline and promote opportunities for children to acquire self-discipline will be able to engage in individualized instruction and creativity.

Development of Autonomous Behavior

Implicit in guiding children's behavior is the assumption that they can be, should be, and will be responsible for their own behavior. The ultimate goal of all education, according to Constance Kamii, is to develop *autonomy* in children, which means "being governed by oneself."

Early childhood educators need to conduct programs that promote development of autonomy. One aspect of facilitating autonomy is exchanging points of view with children.

> When a child tells a lie, for example, the adult can deprive him of dessert or make him write 50 times "I will not lie." The adult can also refrain from punishing the child and, instead, look him straight in the eye with great skepticism and affection and say, "I really can't believe what you are saying because . . . ." This is an example of an exchange of points of view that contributes to the development of autonomy in children. The child who can see that the adult cannot believe him can be motivated to think about what he must do to be believed. The child who is raised with many similar opportunities can, over time, construct for himself the conviction that it is best eventually for people to deal honestly with each other.[2]

The ultimate goal of developing autonomy in children is to have them regulate their own behavior and have them make decisions about good and bad, right and wrong (when they are mature enough to understand these concepts), and how they will behave in relation to themselves and others. Autonomous behavior can be achieved only when a child considers other people's points of view, which can occur only if they are presented with viewpoints that differ from their own and are encouraged to consider them in deciding how they will behave. The ability to take another person's point of view is largely developmental. It is not until around age eight, when the child becomes less egocentric, that she is able to decenter and see things from other people's points of view. Autonomy is reinforced when teachers and parents allow sufficient time and opportunities for children to practice and perform tasks for themselves. Independence is also nurtured when children are allowed to use problem-solving techniques and permitted to learn from their mistakes.

Rewards and punishment tend to encourage children to obey others without helping them understand how their behavior was appropriate or inappropriate. Even more importantly, they have not had an opportunity to develop rules of conduct to govern their behavior. Children can be encouraged to regulate and be responsible for their own behavior through what Piaget referred to as "sanctions by reciprocity." These sanctions "are directly related to the act we want to sanction and to the adult's point of view, and have the effect of motivating the child to construct rules of conduct for himself, through the coordination of viewpoints."[3] Examples of sanctions by reciprocity include exclusion from the group, whereby the child has a choice of staying and behaving or leaving; taking away from children the materials or privileges they have abused, such as not allowing them to use certain materials while leaving open the opportunity to use them again if they express a desire to use them appropriately; and helping children fix things they have broken and clean up after themselves. A fine line separates sanctions by reciprocity and punishment. The critical ingredient that balances the scales on the side of reciprocity is teachers' respect for children and their desire to help them develop autonomy rather than blind obedience.

To become self-directive and autonomous, children should be encouraged to do things for themselves from an early age. This includes allowing them to practice and develop self-help skills such as drinking from a cup.

Self-Regulation

Self-regulation is the ability to comply with a request, to initiate and cease activities according to situational demands, to modulate the intensity, frequency, and duration of verbal and motor acts in social and educational settings, to postpone acting upon a desired object or goal, and to generate socially approved behavior in the absence of external monitors.

Self-regulation is a life-long goal, not necessarily something that children achieve in the early years in the twinkling of an eye. We are always in the process of refining our ability to self-regulate our behavior.

The stages of development of self-regulation in the early years are outlined in Table 12–2. The table also illustrates the behavioral features of each stage as well as parent and teacher behaviors that promote self-regulation.

Giving Children Choices

Life is full of choices. You make choices every day—some require thought and decisions, others don't. But every time you make a decision, you are being responsible and exercising your right to decide. Children like to have choices, and choices help

TABLE 12—2   The Development of Self-Regulation

Phases in the Development of Self-Regulation	Age	Features	Caregiver Roles
Neurophysiological modulation	Birth to 2 or 3 months	Development of clearly defined periods of wakefulness; development of schemes to self-soothe, e.g., nonnutritive sucking.	Provide interactions and opportunities for stimulation; provide routines of eating and sleeping.
Sensorimotor modulation	3 months to 1 year	Ability to engage in sensorimotor acts and change an act in response to events. Modulations help infants become aware of their *own* actions in holding, reaching, and playing. When infants differentiate their own actions from those of others, the potential for self-regulation emerges.	Provide caregiver–infant interactions; provide activities for the infant.
Control	1 year to 18 months	Shows awareness of social and task demands defined by caregiver. Can initiate, maintain, modulate, or cease physical acts, communication, and emotional signals.	Provide patterns of communication and interaction. Provide opportunities for toddlers to notice the effects of their actions. Call attention to expectations. Channel the toddler into desired activities.
Self-control	2 years or older	Compliance and emergent abilities to delay an act or request and to behave according to caregiver and social expectations in the absence of external monitors.	Continue to provide and call attention to expectations. Avoid "controlling" toddlers' behaviors. Avoid being critical of behaviors.
Self-regulation	3 years or older	Growing ability to adapt and regulate behavior to set behavioral demands.	Continue to provide and call attention to expectations. Encourage independence, provide verbal interaction, and give reasons for behavior.

Source: Adapted from Claire B. Kopp, "Antecedents of Self-Regulation: A Developmental Perspective," *Developmental Psychology,* 18 (March 1982): 200. Copyright 1982 by the American Psychological Association. Adapted by permission.

them become independent. Making choices develops confidence and self-discipline. Learning to make choices early in life lays the foundation for decision making later. These are some guidelines for giving children choices:

☐ Give children choices when there are valid choices to make. When it comes time to clean up the classroom, don't let children choose whether they want to participate, but let them choose between collecting the scissors or the crayons.
☐ Help children make choices. Rather than say "What would you like to do today?" say "Sarah, you have a choice between working in the woodworking center or the computer center. Which would you like to do?"
☐ When caregivers don't want children to make a decision, they should not offer them a choice.

Physical Punishment

Whether parents and teachers should spank or paddle as a means of guiding behavior is an age-old controversy. Many parents spank their children, following a "No!" with a slap on the hand or a spank on the bottom. This form of punishment can be an effective means of controlling a child's behavior when used in moderation immediately following the misbehavior. Some parents advocate physical punishment based on religious beliefs. Yet what parents do with their child in the home is not acceptable for others outside the home, where spanking is considered an inappropriate form of guidance. In fact, in some places, such as Florida, physical punishment in child-care programs is legislatively prohibited.

There are a number of problems with spanking and other forms of physical punishment. First, physical punishment is generally ineffective in building behavior in children. Physical punishment does not show children what to do or provide them with alternative ways of behaving. Second, adults who use physical punishment are modeling physical aggression. They are, in effect, saying that it is permissible to use aggression in interpersonal relationships. Children who are spanked are more likely to use aggression with their peers. Third, spanking and physical punishment increase the risk of physical injury to the child. Spanking can be an emotionally charged situation, and the spanker can become too aggressive, overdo the punishment, and hit the child in vulnerable places. The best advice regarding physical punishment is to avoid it; use nonviolent means for guiding children's behavior. In the long run, parents and early childhood professionals determine children's behavior. In guiding the behavior of children entrusted to their care, teachers and others must select procedures that are appropriate to their own philosophies and children's particular needs. Guiding children to help them develop their own internal system of behavior control benefits them more than a system that relies on external control and authoritarianism. Developing self-discipline in children should be a primary goal of all teachers.

FURTHER READING

Bluestein, Jane, and Lynn Collins. *Parents in a Pressure Cooker: A Guide to Responsible and Loving Parent/Child Relationships* (Albuquerque, N.M.: I.S.S. Publications, 1983)

Helps caregivers rear responsible children who are self-regulated rather than dependent on others for external control. One premise is that to rear responsible children, one has to begin with responsible adults, so there is a chapter devoted to modeling; another useful chapter deals with expectations.

Canter, Lee, and Marlene Canter. *Assertive Discipline: A Take-Charge Approach for Today's Educator* (Santa Monica, Calif.: Canter and Associates, 1986)

Lee Canter is the leading proponent of "assertive discipline"; based on principles of assertiveness training, this approach encourages teachers and parents to take charge of the discipline process; derives its popularity from the self-help movement of the '70s and '80s.

Charles, C.M. *Building Classroom Discipline* (New York: Longman, 1985)

Seven models of classroom discipline. Helps the reader develop a personal system of discipline.

Essa, Eva. *A Practical Guide to Solving Preschool Behavior Problems, 2nd Edition.* (Albany, N.Y.: Delmar, 1990)

Based on the behaviorist approach to guiding behavior, provides practical ideas for caregivers, addresses specific behavior problems such as hitting, biting, tantrums, and whining. One section is devoted to social behaviors such as nonparticipation in play and group activities.

Fontenelle, Don. H. *Understanding and Managing Overactive Children* (Englewood Cliffs, N.J.: Prentice-Hall, 1983)

Caregivers always have questions about how to guide the behavior of children they assess as overactive. Often, children are incorrectly labeled overactive; the first two chapters provide insight into the nature and causes of overactivity. Good section on general management techniques.

Kostelnik, Marjorie J., Laura C. Stein, Alice Phipps Whiren, and Anne K. Soderman. *Guiding Children's Social Development* (Cincinnati, Ohio: South-Western, 1988)

Helps relate to children in ways that will help them maximize their potential. Describes generic principles and skills adaptable to any early childhood setting.

Marion, Marian. *Guidance of Young Children, 2nd Ed.* (Columbus, Ohio: Merrill, 1987)

A practical guide for helping early childhood educators and others guide young children. Examines the three critical factors in guidance: the child, adults who work with children, and the environment.

Miller, Darla Ferris. *Positive Child Guidance* (Albany, N.Y.: Delmar, 1990)

Emphasizes the role of positive child guidance in preparing young children to become competent, confident, and cooperative citizens. Presents developmentally appropriate methods for guiding children, along with effective strategies and suggestions for preventing and handling misbehaviors.

Schaefer, C.E., and H.L. Millman, *How to Help Children with Common Problems* (New York: Van Nostrand Reinhold, 1981)

Information and strategies for helping parents deal with children's everyday problems. Addresses lying, stealing, shyness, overactivity, bedwetting.

FURTHER STUDY

1. What are the advantages and disadvantages of using rewards to stimulate and reinforce desired behaviors?
2. Some critics argue that teachers need to devote so much time to managing student behavior because pupils are forced to engage in contrived learning. Discuss this claim.
3. What is the difference between normal behavior and acceptable behavior? Give an example of a case where normal behavior may not be acceptable and another where acceptable behavior may not be normal.
4. Visit a classroom that uses behavior modification. Interview parents, teachers, and students to find out how they feel about the program.
5. Observe an early childhood classroom. What reinforcement system (implicit or explicit) does the teacher use to operate the classroom? Do you think the teacher is aware of the systems of reinforcement in use?
6. Interview children to determine what they find reinforcing. How do their selections compare to the reinforcers mentioned in this chapter?
7. Behavior modification is practiced by parents and teachers without their being aware of what

they are doing or the processes they are using. Observe a mother-child relationship for examples of parental behavioral management. What rewards does she offer? What was the child's resultant behavior? After further observation, answer these questions for the teacher-child relationship. In both situations, what are some ethical implications of the adult's actions?

8. Observe an early childhood classroom to see which behaviors earn the teacher's attention. Does the teacher pay more attention to positive or negative behavior? Why do you think the teacher acts the way he does?

9. A mother says her four-year-old daughter will not keep her room neat; it is always a mess, and she can't get the child to put anything away. Develop specific strategies you could give a parent to use in helping her keep the child's room in order. Design a floor plan and show furnishings that would help a child keep her room neat.

10. While observing in a primary classroom, identify and examine aspects of the physical setting and atmosphere that could influence classroom behavior. Can you suggest improvements?

11. List ten behaviors you think are desirable in kindergarten children. For each behavior, give two examples of how you would encourage and promote development of that behavior.

12. Interview five parents of young children to de-termine what they mean when they use the word *discipline*. What implications might these definitions have for you if you were their children's teacher?

13. How does a parent's behavior influence and affect a child's behavior? Give specific examples.

14. List five methods for guiding children's behavior. Tell why you think each is effective, and give examples.

15. Does a child's age make any difference in the method of discipline used and the kind and nature of guidance techniques? Give specific examples pro and con.

16. Do you believe in the adage, "spare the rod and spoil the child"? Where does this saying come from? What does it mean? Do you think the implications of this saying are appropriate for today's children?

17. Why is it important for caregivers and parents to agree on a philosophy of behavioral guidance?

18. Why is some children's behavior easier to guide than other children's?

19. Write a children's Bill of Rights relating to their care, guidance, and discipline in a child care center.

20. Interview parents who believe in physical punishment. Why do they believe what they do? Do you think they are justified in their beliefs? Why?

NOTES

1. George H. Gallup, "The 14th Annual Gallup Poll of the Public's Attitudes Toward the Public Schools," *Phi Delta Kappan,* 64 (September 1983).

2. Constance Kamii, *Number in Preschool and Kin-dergarten* (Washington, D.C.: National Association for the Education of Young Children, 1982), p. 23.

3. Kamii, *Number in Preschool and Kindergarten,* p. 77.

CHAPTER 13
Parent Involvement
Key to Successful Programs

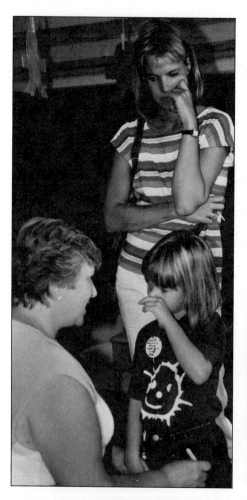

As you read and study:
☐ Identify current changes in contemporary families and the influences of these changes on children, parents, and early childhood education
☐ Examine the implications changing family and parenting patterns have for early childhood educators
☐ Examine reasons for the importance of parent involvement programs
☐ Define parent involvement
☐ Develop a personal philosophy of parent involvement
☐ Identify why early childhood professionals and others encourage and support programs for involving parents
☐ Understand the importance of involving all the different kinds of parents, such as teenage parents, who are represented in early childhood programs

PARENT INVOLVEMENT—A PROCESS WHOSE TIME HAS COME

As recently as a decade or so ago, there was much talk about parent involvement, but not much of it was going on. But times have changed, and now early childhood educators not only talk about the importance and benefits of parent involvement, they also seek and implement significant ways to involve parents. Parent involvement has come into its own in early childhood education.

WHO IS A PARENT?

A parent is anyone who provides children with basic care, direction, support, protection, and guidance. Accordingly, a parent can be single, married, heterosexual, homosexual, a cousin, aunt, uncle, grandparent, a court-appointed guardian, a brother, a sister, an institution employee, a surrogate, a foster parent, or a group such as a commune. These changing patterns of who parents are have important implications for early childhood teachers, because these are individuals whom they seek to involve.

WHAT IS A FAMILY?

Just as we have changed our thinking about parents, so too must we change our thinking about families. Families have undergone radical changes since the '70s. Children are born into many different kinds of families, and parents create for children a wide variety of living arrangements. These family structures affect, in obvious and subtle ways, children's development and how early educators relate to them.

For statistical and reporting purposes, the U.S. Census Bureau classifies family households into three types: married couple families, families with male householders (no wife present), and families with female householders (no husband present). A *household* is defined as the person or persons who comprise a family unit. A *family* is defined as two or more persons living together who are related by birth, marriage, or adoption. The term *householder* has replaced "head of family." Table 13–1 illustrates how families have changed over the years.

TABLE 13–1   Eight Ways Families Have Changed

	1981	1984	1988	Percent of Change, 1981–1988
1. Married couples	49,294,000	50,090,000	51,809,000	+1.6%
2. Married couples with children	24,927,000	24,339,000	24,600,000	−1.3%
3. Male householder (no spouse) with children	666,000	799,000	1,047,000	+57.0%
4. Female householder (no spouse) with children	5,634,000	5,907,000	6,273,000	+11.3%
5. Marriages	2,438,000	2,487,000	111,456	− 95%
6. Divorces	1,219,000	1,155,000	13,968	− 99%
7. Average size per household	2.73	2.71	2.64	−3.3%
8. Average size per family	3.27	3.24	3.17	−3.1%

Source: Bureau of the Census

Types of Families

Nuclear Family. Our concept of the family is undergoing radical redefinition. The *nuclear family,* consisting of two parents and one child or more, is no longer the unit in which many children live. We must recognize that as society changes, so do families.

Extended Families. An extended family consists of parents, grandparents, aunts, uncles, brothers, sisters, and sometimes cousins, living together as a unit or sharing feelings of kinship through close geographical proximity and shared concern and responsibility for family matters. In an extended family, children may be reared by any other family members, particularly grandparents. In an extended family situation, it is not uncommon for a grandparent to respond to a note from a teacher for a conference about a child's school progress. Sometimes an unperceptive teacher interprets this as a sign that parents don't care, when it is actually a normal state of affairs in a family where everyone is willing to be responsible for children's growth and development. The extended family may well be the type to which more and more divorced spouses will turn as a means of support and assistance in child rearing.

Single-parent Families. With the increase in the divorce rate and new attitudes toward child rearing, single parent families are increasing, and single fathers rearing dependent children are no longer rare. Also, some people choose to be single parents through adoption, artificial insemination or one of the other procedures that are possible through the latest reproductive technology.

Stepfamilies and Blended Families. A stepfamily is one parent with children of his or her own and a spouse. When two people, each with children of their own, marry, they form *blended, merged,* or *reconstructed* families. These families have "his" children and "her" children; if they have children together, a third level of sibling relationships is added with "their" children.

Foster Parent Families. Foster parents are those who care for, in a family setting, children who are not their own. Foster parents are usually screened by the agencies that place children with them, and sometimes the children are relatives. Foster parents occasionally adopt the children they care for, but even if not, the children sometimes remain in the foster home for extended periods. A major crisis facing many social service agencies today is a lack of qualified foster care families. Many agencies are vigorously attempting to recruit, identify, and train parent families, especially from minority groups.

IMPLICATIONS OF FAMILY PATTERNS FOR EARLY CHILDHOOD EDUCATORS

Support Services

There are many ways for teachers to help children and parents in these days of changing family patterns. They may, for example, help develop support services for families and parents. Support can extend from being a "listening ear" to organizing support groups and seminars on single parenting. Teachers can help parents link up

The number of single-parent families continues to grow. Early childhood educators must take into account the concerns of these families and work with them to meet their particular needs.

with other agencies and groups, such as Big Brothers and Big Sisters and Parents Without Partners. Through newsletters and fliers, teachers can provide parents with specific advice on how to help children become independent and how to help them meet the demands of single parenting, stepfamilies, and other family configurations.

Child Care

Another way teachers can help is to make arrangements for child care services. More families need child care, and early childhood personnel are logical advocates for establishing child care where none exists, extending existing services, and helping to arrange cooperative babysitting services.

Avoiding Criticism

Teachers should be careful not to criticize parents or place extra demands on them. They may not have extra time to spend with their children, or know how to discipline them. Regardless of their circumstances, parents need help, not criticism. Similarly, teachers should not be judgmental; they should examine and clarify their attitudes and values toward family patterns and remember that there is no "right" family pattern from which all children should come. Teachers also need to address the issue of changing family patterns in the educational experiences they arrange. They need to offer experiences children might not otherwise have because of their family organization. For example, outdoor activities such as fishing trips and sports events can be interesting and enriching learning experiences for all children who don't have such opportunities.

Classroom Adjustments

Teachers need to adjust classroom or center activities and plans to account for how particular children cope with their home situations. Children's needs for different kinds of activities depend on their experiences at home. There are many opportunities for role-playing situations, and such activities help bring into the open situations that children need to talk about. Use classroom opportunities to discuss family patterns, parents, and the roles parents play. Make it a point in the classroom to model, encourage, and teach effective interpersonal skills.

Sensitivity

There are also specific ways to approach today's changing family patterns. For example, avoid making presents for both parents and awarding prizes for bringing both parents to meetings. Avoid father-son and mother-daughter affairs. Replace terms like "broken home" with "single-parent family." Be sensitive to the demands of school in relation to children's home lives. For example, when a teacher sent a field trip permission form home with the children and told them to have their mothers or fathers sign it, one child said "I don't have a father. If my mother can't sign it, can the man who sleeps with her sign it?" Seek help, guidance, and clarification from parents about how they would like specific situations handled; for example, ask whether they want you to send notices of school events to both parents.

Seeking Training

Request inservice training to help you work with parents. Inservice programs can provide information about referral agencies; guidance techniques; how to help parents deal with their problems; and child abuse identification and prevention. Teachers need to be alert to the signs of all kinds of child abuse, including sexual.

Increasing Parent Contacts

Finally, teachers should encourage greater and different kinds of parent involvement through home visits, talking to parents about children's needs, providing information and opportunities to parents, grandparents, and other family members, gathering information from parents (such as interest inventories), and keeping in touch with parents. Make parent contacts positive, not negative.

Why is Parent Involvement Important?

By now you have probably asked yourself, "Why should I be bothered with parent involvement?" The most compelling reason for involving parents is the effect it has on improving children's achievement: "According to recent studies, parent involvement in almost any form improves student achievement."[1] When children have a quality school program and supportive and involved parents, they do better on academic and social skills.[2] Children see parent involvement as a sign that their parents value education. When their parents are involved in their program, they recognize that their parents are not just "leaving them off" and forgetting them.

Many teachers realize that they more effectively achieve their teaching and classroom goals when they encourage parent assistance and involvement. In turn, parents are more inclined to join the effort to improve the teaching-learning process. Every parent has a duty to be involved in some way in his or her children's educational program or in any program that provides a major service to them and their children. In fact, specific legislation, especially as it relates to programs that receive federal and state funds, mandates parent involvement, particularly for parents with special needs children (see Chapter 11) and for programs such as Head Start.

Evidence shows that parents are more supportive of programs with which they have direct and meaningful involvement. If early childhood educators want support for quality programs, parent involvement is a certain way to achieve it. The rediscovery of the relationship between parents and schools is partly the result of political and societal forces. The consumer movement of the last several decades convinced parents that they should no longer be kept out of their children's schools. Parents believe that if they have a right to demand greater accountability from industries and government agencies, they can also demand effective instruction and care from schools and child care centers. Parents have become more militant in their demand for quality education, and schools and other agencies have responded by seeking ways to involve parents in the quest for quality. Teachers and parents realize that mutual cooperation is in everyone's best interest.

WHAT IS PARENT INVOLVEMENT?

Parent involvement is a threefold process; it is "a partnership between parents and teachers and their helpers in the community, . . . a developmental process that is built over a period of time through intentional planning and effort of every team member, and a process by which parents and teachers work, learn and participate in decision making experiences in a shared manner"—a developmental process based on partnership and shared decision making.[3]

Based on this developmental approach, then, parent involvement is: *a process of helping parents use their abilities to benefit themselves, their children, and the early childhood program.* Parents, children, and the program are all part of the process; consequently, all three parties should benefit from a well-planned program of parent involvement. Nonetheless, the focus in parent/child/family interactions is the parent, and early childhood educators must work with and through parents if they want to be successful.

Three Approaches to Parent Involvement

Task Approach.   The most common and traditional way to approach parent involvement is through a task orientation, aimed at completing specific tasks to support the school or classroom program. In this orientation, faculty, staff, and administration work to involve parents as tutors, aides, attendance monitors, fund raisers, field trip monitors, and clerical helpers. This is the type of parent involvement most teachers are comfortable with, and the type that usually comes to mind when planning for parent involvement. It can also include getting parents to help with areas the school traditionally has trouble with, such as asking parents to monitor homework assignments and for assistance with inappropriate school behavior.

Process Approach.   In a process orientation, parents are encouraged to participate in certain activities that are important to the educational process, such as curriculum planning, textbook review and selection, membership on task forces and committees, teacher review and selection, and helping to set behavior standards. This orientation is only now becoming popular, because professional educators have traditionally been reluctant to share these responsibilities with parents. Also, parents need preparation and support for this kind of involvement. Teachers often think parents lack the necessary skills to help in certain areas, but with some preparation, assistance, and opportunity to participate, many parents are extremely effective.

Developmental Approach.   A developmental orientation helps parents develop skills that will benefit themselves, children, schools, teachers, families and, at the same time, enhance the process of parent involvement. This humanistic orientation is exemplified in cooperative preschools, community schools, and Head Start programs. Ideally, an effective and comprehensive program of parent involvement includes all three orientations. Diagrammatically, it would look like Figure 13–1.

Methods for Involving Parents
The first and primary prerequisite for effective parent involvement is the right attitude. Teachers have to *want* parent involvement in early childhood and school programs; otherwise, parent involvement won't be as effective as it could be. A teacher must not feel threatened by parents, and must sincerely believe that parent involvement will increase opportunities for all.

FIGURE 13–1   Parent/Citizen Involvement

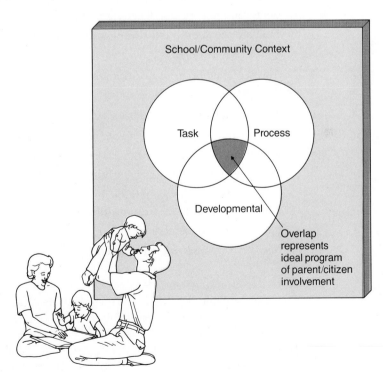

Also, the school and center administration must be ready for parents. When a program of parent involvement receives continuous support and recognition, it tends to be successful; without support, success is limited. Success also depends on how well teachers involve parents. Parents must have meaningful involvement, not the kind they feel is wasting their time and talents.

Planning is a critical factor for a successful program of parent involvement. Determine what parents will do before they become involved, but be willing to change plans after determining parent strengths, weaknesses, and needs. Seek creative ways to involve *all* parents. Some parents, regardless of their level of education, are threatened by school and schoollike settings. Help them overcome these fears. It may be unrealistic to expect all parents to participate, but it is not unrealistic to give all parents a chance. Be willing to go to the parents through home visitations; don't always make them come to you.

Provide for all levels of abilities, desires, and needs. Don't expect the same participation from every parent, nor all parents to want to do the same thing. Regardless of how much or little a parent can or wants to be involved, give them the opportunity to participate.

Let parents help organize and operate the program of parent involvement. In such an approach, the teacher's functions will be to

Develop a program rationale and structure, including philosophy and goals

Train parents for effective involvement

Supervise the program, including planning with the parent helpers and demonstrating specific teaching methods and tasks

Evaluate the overall effectiveness of the program, including each parent's performance

A well-planned parent involvement orientation session should include discussion of these topics:

The philosophy of the school

The teacher's philosophy of teaching/learning

Goals and objectives for the classroom and the children

Rules and regulations of the school and classroom

Specific tasks of the volunteers, how to perform them, and any necessary special preparations, limits of responsibilities, and duties

Classroom management techniques

A survey of parent interests and abilities

Activities for Involving Parents

There are unlimited possibilities for parent involvement, but a coordinated effort is required to build an effective and meaningful program that can bring about a change in education and benefit all concerned: parents, children, teachers, and community. Parents can make a significant difference in their children's education, and with the teacher's assistance, they will be able to join teachers and schools in a productive partnership. The following are examples of activities that allow for significant parent involvement.

Schoolwide activities

1. Workshops—to introduce parents to the school's policies, procedures, and programs. Most parents want to know what is going on in the school, and would do a better job of parenting and educating if they knew how.
2. Family nights, cultural dinners, carnivals, and potluck dinners—to bring parents and the community to the school in nonthreatening, social ways.
3. Adult education classes—to provide the community with opportunities to learn about a wide range of subjects.
4. Training programs—to give parents skills as classroom aides and as club and activity sponsors.
5. Support services such as car pools and baby-sitting—to make attendance and involvement possible.
6. Fairs and bazaars—to involve parents in fund raising.
7. Performances and plays—programs in which children have a part tend to bring parents to school; however, the purpose of children's performances should not be to get parents involved.

Communication activities

1. Telephone "hot lines"—hot lines staffed by parents can help allay fears and provide information relating to child abuse, communicable diseases, and special events.
2. Newsletters—newsletters planned with parents' help are an excellent way to keep parents informed about program events. Newsletters can also include curriculum information and activities. Newsletters in parents' native languages also help keep minority-language parents informed.
3. Home learning materials and activities—a monthly calendar of activities is one good way to keep parents involved in their children's learning.

Educational activities

1. Participation in classroom and center activities—while not all parents can be directly involved in classroom activities, those who can should be encouraged. Parents must have guidance, direction, and training for these involvements. Involving parents as paid aides is an excellent way to also provide employment and training. Many programs, such as Head Start, actively support such a policy.
2. Involvement of parents in writing individual educational programs (IEPS)—for special needs children. Involvement in writing an individualized education plan is not only a legal requirement, but also an excellent learning experience (see Chapter 11).

Service activities

1. Resource libraries and materials centers—parents benefit from books and other materials relating to parenting. Some programs furnish resource areas with comfortable chairs to encourage parents to use them.

2. Child care—parents may not be able to attend programs and become involved if they do not have child care for their children. Child care makes their participation possible and more enjoyable.
3. Respite care—some early childhood programs provide respite care for parents, enabling them to have periodic relief from the responsibilities of parenting a handicapped or chronically ill child.
4. Service exchanges—service exchanges operated by child care programs and schools help parents in their needs for services. For example, one parent provided child care in her home in exchange for having her washing machine repaired. The possibilities in such exchanges are endless.
5. Parent support groups—parents need support in their roles as parents. Support groups can provide parenting information, community agency information, and speakers.
6. Welcoming committee—a good way to involve parents in any program is to have other parents contact them when their children first join a program.

Decision activities

1. Hiring and policy making—parents should serve on committees that set policy and hire staff.
2. Curriculum development and review—Parent involvement in curriculum planning helps them learn about and understand what constitutes a quality program and what is involved in a developmentally appropriate curriculum. When parents know about the curriculum, they are more supportive of it.

Parent-Teacher Conferences

Significant parent involvement occurs through parent-teacher conferences, which are often the first contact many parents have with school. Conferences are critical from a public relations point of view and as a vehicle for helping parents and teachers accomplish their goals. These guidelines will help teachers prepare for and conduct successful conferences.

☐ Plan ahead. Be sure of the reason for the conference. What are your objectives? What do you want to accomplish? List the points you want to cover and think about what you are going to say.
☐ When you meet the parent, spend some time getting to know him. This is not wasted time; the more effectively you establish rapport with the parent, the more you will accomplish in the long run.
☐ Avoid an authoritative atmosphere. Don't sit behind your desk while the parent sits in a child's chair. Treat parents like the adults they are.
☐ Communicate at the parent's level. Do not condescend or patronize. Instead, use words, phrases, and explanations the parent understands and is familiar with. Do not use jargon or complicated explanations, and speak in your natural style.
☐ Accentuate the positive. Make every effort to show and tell the parent what the child is doing well. When you deal with problems, put them in the proper perspective: what the child is able to do, what the goals and purposes of the learn-

ing program are, what specific skill or concept you are trying to get the child to learn, and what problems the child is having in achieving. Most important, explain what you plan to do to help the child achieve and what specific role the parent can have in meeting the achievement goals.

☐ Give parents a chance to talk. You won't learn much about them if you do all the talking, nor are you likely to achieve your goals. Teachers are often accustomed to dominating a conversation, and many parents will not be as verbal as you, so you will have to encourage parents to talk.

☐ Learn to listen. An active listener holds eye contact, uses body language such as head nodding and hand gestures, doesn't interrupt, avoids arguing, paraphrases as a way of clarifying ideas, and keeps the conversation on track.

☐ A conference must be followed up. It is a good idea to ask the parent for a definite time for the next conference as you are concluding the current one. Another conference is the best method of solidifying gains and extending support, but other acceptable means of follow-up are telephone calls, written reports, notes sent with children, or brief visits to the home. While these types of contacts may appear casual, they should be planned for and conducted as seriously as any regular parent-teacher conference.

☐ Develop an action plan. Never leave the parent with a sense of frustration, not knowing what you are doing or what they are to do. Every communication with parents should end on a positive note, so that everyone knows what can be done and how to do it.

These are advantages of parent-teacher conference follow-up:

Parents see that you genuinely care about their children

Everyone can clarify problems, issues, advice, and directions

It encourages parents and children to continue to do their best

It offers further opportunities to extend classroom learnings to the home

You can extend programs initiated for helping parents and child and formulate new plans.

Telephone Contacts. When it is impossible to arrange a face-to-face conference as a follow-up, a telephone call is an efficient way to contact parents. (Some families, however, do not have a telephone.) The same guidelines apply as to face-to-face conferences; in addition, remember these points:

☐ Since you can't see someone on a telephone, it takes a little longer to build rapport and trust. The time you spend overcoming parents' initial fears and apprehensions will pay dividends later.

☐ Constantly clarify what you are talking about and what you and the parents have agreed to do, using such phrases as: "What I heard you say then . . ." or "So far, we have agreed that . . . ."

☐ Don't act hurried. There is a limit to the amount of time you can spend on the phone, but you may be one of the few people who cares about the parent and the child, and your telephone contact may be the major part of the parents' support system.

INVOLVING SINGLE PARENTS

Sometimes, parent involvement activities are conducted without much regard for single parents. Teachers sometimes think of single parents as problems to deal with rather than people to work with. One-parent families need not be a problem in involvement if teachers remember some simple points.

First, most adults in one-parent families are employed during school hours, and may not be available for conferences or other activities during that time. Teachers must be willing to accommodate parents' schedules by arranging conferences at other times, perhaps early morning (breakfast), midmorning, noon (lunch), early afternoon, late afternoon, or early evening. Some employers, sensitive to parents' needs, give released time to participate in school functions, but others do not. Teachers and principals need to think seriously about going to parents, rather than having parents always come to them. Some schools have set up parent conferences to accommodate parents' work schedules, some teachers find that home visitations work best.

Second, teachers need to remember that working parents have a limited amount of time to spend on involvement with their children's school and with their children at home. When teachers confer with single parents, they should make sure (1) the meeting starts on time, (2) they have a list of items (skills, behaviors, achievements) to discuss, (3) they have sample materials available to illustrate all points, (4) they make specific suggestions relative to one-parent environments, and (5) the meeting ends on time. One-parent families are more likely to need child care assistance to attend meetings, so child care should be planned for every parent meeting or activity.

Parents can be involved and informed through telephone conferences. For many of today's busy working parents, the telephone is an ideal means of communication between home and school.

Third, illustrate for single parents how they can make their time with their children more meaningful. If a child has trouble following directions, show parents how to use home situations to help in this area—children can learn to follow directions while helping parents run errands, get a meal, do the wash, or help with housework.

Fourth, get to know parents' life styles and living conditions. It is easy for a teacher to say that every child should have a quiet place to study, but this may be an impossible demand on some households. Teachers need to visit some of the homes in their community before they set meeting times or decide what parent involvement activities to implement, or what they will ask of parents during the year. All educators, particularly teachers, need to keep in mind the condition of the home environment when they request that children bring certain items to school or carry out certain tasks at home. When asking for a parent's help, the teacher needs to be sensitive to the parent's talents and time constraints.

Fifth, help develop support groups for one-parent families within the school, such as discussion groups and classes on parenting for singles. Teachers must include the needs and abilities of one-parent families in their parent involvement activities and programs. After all, single parents may be the majority of parents represented in the program.

LANGUAGE MINORITY PARENTS

The developmental concept of parent involvement is particularly important when working with language minority parents. Programs for promoting parental involvement must consider this group. Language minority parents are individuals whose English language proficiency is minimal, and who lack a comprehensive knowledge of the norms and social system, including basic school philosophy, practice and structure. Language minority parents often face language and cultural barriers that greatly hamper their ability to become actively involved, although many have a great desire and willingness to participate in their children's education.

Because the culture of language minority parents often differs from the majority in a community, those who seek a truly collaborative community, home, and school involvement must take into account the cultural features that can inhibit collaboration. Traditional styles of child rearing, family organization, attitudes toward schooling, organizations around which families center their lives, life goals and values, political influences, and methods of communication within the cultural group all have implications for parent participation.

Language minority parents often lack information about the American educational system, resulting in misconceptions, fear, and a general reluctance to respond to invitations for involvement. Furthermore, the American educational system may be quite different from what language minority parents are used to in a former school system. Language minority parents may have been taught to avoid active involvement in the educational process, with the result that they prefer to leave all decisions concerning their children's education to teachers and administrators.

The American ideal of a community-controlled and -supported educational system must be explained to parents from cultures where this concept is not as highly valued. Traditional roles of children, teachers, and administrators also have to be explained.

Many parents, and especially language minority parents, are quite willing to relinquish to teachers any rights and responsibilities they have for their children's education, and need to be educated to assume their roles and obligations toward schooling.

TEENAGE PARENTS

At one time, most teenage parents were married, but today the majority of teenage parents are not. Also, most teenage parents elect to keep their children rather than put them up for adoption and are rearing them as single parents. Teenage parents frequently live in extended families, and the child's grandmother often serves as the primary caregiver. Regardless of their living arrangements, teenage parents have the following needs:

Support in their role as parents. Support can include information about child rearing practices and child development. Regardless of the nature and quality of the information given to teenage parents, they frequently need help in implementing the information in their interactions with their children.

Support in their continuing development as adolescents and young adults. Remember that younger teenage parents are really children themselves. They need assistance in meeting their own developmental needs as well as those of their children.

Help with completing their own education. Some early childhood programs provide parenting courses as well as classes designed to help teenage parent drop-outs complete requirements for a high school diploma. Remember that a critical influence on children's development is the mother's education level.

As early childhood programs enroll more children of teenage parents, they must be attentive to creatively and sensitively involving these parents as a means of supporting the development of parents and children.

INVOLVING FATHERS

More caregivers recognize that fathering and mothering are complementary processes. Definitions of nurturing are changing to include the legitimate and positive involvement of fathers in children's lives. Many fathers are competent caregivers. More fathers, as they discover or rediscover their roles in parenting, turn to caregivers for support and advice. Fathers' roles are extremely important in parenting. Fathers provide direct supervision to children, help set the tone for family life, provide stability to a relationship, support the mother in her parenting role and career goals, and provide a masculine role model for the children.

There are many styles of fathering; some fathers are at home while their wives work; some have custody of the children; some are single; some dominate home life and control everything; some are passive and exert little influence in the home; some are frequently absent because their work requires travel; some take little interest in their homes and families; some are surrogates. Regardless of the roles fathers play in their children's lives, early childhood educators must make special efforts to involve them.

INVOLVING OTHER CAREGIVERS

Often children of two-career families and single parents are cared for by nannies, au pairs, baby-sitters, and housekeepers. Whatever their titles, these adults usually play significant roles in children's lives. Many early childhood programs and schools are reaching out to involve them in activities such as teacher conferences, help with field trips, and supervision of homework. The involvement should occur with parents' blessing and approval for a cooperative working relationship.

FAMILY SUPPORT PROGRAMS

There is a movement in early childhood education to develop family support programs that look at the total family and design programs to help all members. These programs are not necessarily new; Head Start, through many of its programs, considers the family the focus of its services. Now, more early childhood programs recognize that working only with children leaves the family—a critical factor in the child's development—out of the process.

COMMUNITY INVOLVEMENT

A comprehensive program of parent involvement has, in addition to parents, teachers, and schools, a fourth important component: the community. More childhood educators realize that neither they alone nor the limited resources of their programs are sufficient to meet the needs of many children, parents, and families. Consequently, early education professionals are seeking ways to link parents to community services and resources. For example, if a child is in need of clothing, a teacher who is aware of community resources might contact the local Salvation Army for assistance.

These are some things teachers and caregivers can do to increase their effectiveness in parent-community involvement:

☐ Become familiar with the community and community agencies by walking around the neighborhood to locate resource agencies and meet the people who staff them and by using the telephone book to contact community agencies.
☐ Compile a list of community agencies and contact persons for immediate referral and use.

Only by helping parents meet their needs and those of their families and children will there be opportunities for the nation's children to reach their full potential. For this reason alone, regardless of all the other benefits, parent involvement programs and activities must be an essential part of every early childhood program. Parents should expect nothing less from the profession, and we, in turn, must do our very best for them.

National Organizations

National programs dedicated to parent involvement can be a good resource for information and support. Two of these are:

☐ Parents United for Better Schools, The Maple Square Mall, Philadelphia, PA 19144. (215-829-0442). This is an organization of parents working to help other parents work for better schools.

☐ National Committee for Citizens in Education, 410 Wilde Village Green, Columbia, MD 21944 (800-638-9675). This organization seeks to inform parents of their rights and to get them involved in the public schools.

FURTHER READING

Berman, Claire. *Making It As a Stepparent: New Roles/New Rules* (New York: Harper and Row, 1984)

A guide for those considering the many challenges of creating a stepfamily; includes resources and many practical ideas for every family member.

Brown, S., and P. Kornhouser, *Working Parents: How To Be Happy With Your Children* (Atlanta, Ga.: Humanics, 1982)

Manual for working parents gives effective techniques for enhancing the time they spend with their children.

Brutt, Kent Garland. *Smart Times* (New York: Harper and Row, 1983)

Over 200 appropriate activities for at-home fun and learning; defines "quality time" for today's active parents.

Bundy, Darcie. *The Affordable Baby* (New York: Harper and Row, 1984)

Complete financial examination of having a baby, including charts and tables to demonstrate cost comparisons.

Coletta, Anthony J. *Working Together: A Guide to Parent Involvement* (Atlanta, Ga.: Humanics Limited, 1982)

Based on the premise that parent/teacher partnerships should evince clear communication and reciprocity to help children meet their needs for survival, growth, and happiness; includes plans for parent participation in the classroom.

Ehly, Stewart W., et al. *Working with Parents of Exceptional Children* (St. Louis: Times Mirror/Mosby, 1985)

Helps caregivers know more about what to do and how to do it when working with parents of special needs children. Although main focus is parents of exceptional children, concepts and processes apply to all parents. The last chapter on the gifted is particularly useful.

Harris, Rosa Alexander. *How to Select, Train, and Use Volunteers in the Schools* (Lanham, Md.: University Press of America, 1985)

Concise blueprint for recruiting, selecting, training, and evaluating a school volunteer program.

Kane, Patricia. *Food Makes the Difference: A Parent's Guide to Raising a Healthy Child* (New York: Simon and Schuster, 1985)

Advocates a "nutritional/ecological regime," the process of finding the causes of disturbances in the body and finding answers to these biochemical puzzles; provides useful recipes and diets for parents to help their children overcome illness and behavioral problems.

Metzger, Peg, et al. *Parents Make the Difference* (West Falls, N.Y.: Just Sew Education Publications, 1984)

Stresses parents' role in determining the direction of their children's growth and development. Chapters deal with how parents set the stage for learning and communicating with children.

Miller, Shelby H. *Children as Parents: Final Report on a Study of Childbearing and Child Rearing Among 12- to 15-Year Olds* (New York: Child Welfare League of America, 1983)

Deals with the need for caregivers to know more about the problems of teenage parents (children as mothers) and how to work with them; final chapter suggests how to help teenagers be good parents.

Moyer, Joan, ed. *Selecting Educational Equipment and Materials for Home and School* (Wheaton, Md: Association for Childhood Education International, 1986)

Part I is devoted to "Criteria for Selection of Materials" and provides philosophy and rationale to guide decision making. Part II lists materials needed in infant groups, nursery school groups, kindergartens, and primary and intermediate grades.

Prueit, Kyle D. *The Nurturing Father: Journey Toward the Complete Man* (New York: Warner Books, 1987)

> Relates the experiences of 17 families in which the father stayed home while the mother went to work. How did the kids turn out? Very well. It is worth the time to find out why.

Rodgers, Joann Ellison, and Michael F. Cataldo. *Raising Sons: Practical Strategies for Single Mothers* (New York: New American Library, 1984)

> Looks at new roles of single parents, especially single mothers. Authors believe there are new "contracts" between men and women, and the same follows with mothers and sons. Helps others identify new rules and better meet the needs of their growing sons.

Schaefer, Charles E. *How to Talk to Children About Really Important Things* (New York: Harper and Row, 1984)

> Offers communication skills for parents of children between the ages of 5 to 10; also recommended for parents of preschoolers so they can plan ahead.

Swick, Kevin. *Inviting Parents Into the Young Child's World* (Champaign, Ill.: Stipes, 1984)

> Practical guidelines for facilitating parent involvement.

Tuchscherer, Pamela. *Creative Parent Communication* (Bend, Ore.: Pinnaroo Publishing, 1986)

> Designed to help teachers create effective, attractively written communications for parents. Contains letter shells for common situations, such as invitations to the classroom, rainy-day procedures, and schedule changes.

Yablonsky, Lewis. *Fathers and Sons* (New York: Simon and Schuster, 1982)

> Examination of the roles fathers play and how fathers can develop significant relationships with their sons and families.

FURTHER STUDY

1. Arrange with a local school district to be present during a parent-teacher conference. Discuss with the teacher, prior to the visit, her objectives and procedures. After the conference, assess its success with the teacher.
2. Simulate a parent-teacher conference with your classmates. Establish objectives and procedures for the visit. Analyze this conference. (A good way to analyze the simulation is to videotape it.)
3. Recall from your school experiences instances of parent-teacher conferences or other involvement. What particular incidents have had a positive or negative effect on you?
4. List the various ways teachers communicate pupils' progress to parents. What do you think are the most and least effective ways? What specific methods do you plan to use?
5. You are responsible for publicizing a parent meeting about how the school plans to involve parents. Describe methods and techniques you would use to publicize the meeting.
6. List six reasons that early childhood teachers might resist involving parents.
7. You have just been appointed the program director for a parent involvement program in grade one. Write objectives for the program. Develop specific activities for involving parents in the classroom. How would you train parents? What classroom activities would you have parents become involved with?
8. Visit social services agencies in your area. Describe how they can help meet the needs of parents and families.
9. Invite directors of social services to meet with your class to discuss how they and early childhood educators can work cooperatively to help parents, families, and children.
10. What are your opinions and feelings about parent involvement in early childhood programs? Discuss them with your classmates.
11. Conduct a poll of parents to find out how they think early childhood programs and schools can help them in educating their children; how they think they can be involved in early childhood programs; what specific help they feel they need in child rearing/educating; and what activities they would like in a home visitation program.

12. What functions do you feel the family should exercise but does not? What family functions could be better accomplished by other agencies? Do you think education about sex role and function is better accomplished in the home or by an external educational agency? What functions do you feel the family you came from should have performed but did not? What functions did they perform that you do not agree with?

13. As families change, so, too, do the services they need. Interview parents in as many settings as possible (e.g., urban, suburban, rural), from as many socioeconomic backgrounds as possible, and from as many kinds of families as possible. Determine what services they believe can help them most, then tell how you as a teacher could help provide those services.

14. How will the role of children in the family change? What new roles may be assigned to children?

15. Do you think it is necessary to rear children in a nuclear family? Why or why not?

16. Interview parents with children in child care, preschool, and the primary grades. Ask them what types of parent involvement have been most effective for them.

17. Develop a set of guidelines that a child care center could use to facilitate the involvement of fathers; language-minority parents; and parents with handicapped children.

18. Based on discussion with early childhood educators and your observations of programs, what do you think are the most effective means of parent involvement?

19. What are today's most serious parenting problems? How can early childhood educators help parents with these problems?

NOTES

1. Ann Henderson, ed., *Parent Participation—Student Achievement: The Evidence Grows* (Columbia, Md.: National Committee for Citizens in Education, 1981), p. 1.

2. Irving Lazar, et al., *The Persistence of Preschool Effects: A Summary Report* (Washington, D.C.: U.S. Government Printing Office, 1976).

3. Kevin J. Swick, *Inviting Parents into the Young Child's World* (Champaign, Ill.: Stipes Publishing Co., 1984), p. 115.

CHAPTER 14
Contemporary Concerns
Educating Children in a Changing Society

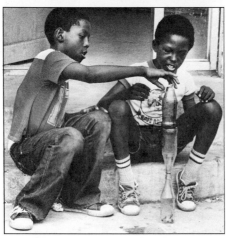

As you read and study:
- [ ] Assess the effects of poverty on children and the implications of these effects for caregivers
- [ ] Discuss what society can do to better meet the total needs of poor children and their families
- [ ] Examine definitions of child abuse and neglect
- [ ] Know and understand the role of the early childhood educator in identifying and reporting child abuse
- [ ] Examine reasons that parents and caregivers abuse children
- [ ] Identify and understand the uses of an abuse prevention curriculum
- [ ] Identify behaviors and attitudes that tend to promote sexual stereotyping
- [ ] Examine humanistic education in the preschool curriculum
- [ ] Identify conditions that promote a humanistic early childhood program
- [ ] Realize the tragic effect of the AIDS epidemic on children
- [ ] Learn how caregivers and teachers can provide for children with AIDS
- [ ] Understand the effects of crack and cocaine on infants
- [ ] Identify the salient features of drug prevention programs for young children
- [ ] Understand the causes of stress in children's lives and what caregivers can do to help children and themselves cope with stress

CHILDREN OF POVERTY

Although everyone imagines America as a land of opportunity, a large number of the nation's children may not realize the dream of becoming all that one can be. More and more children are subject to the disadvantages and long-term destructive consequences poverty engenders. To be poor means that one gets a poor start in life. Thirteen million children in the U.S. live below the poverty level. Nine million children have no access to basic health care; eighteen million have never been to a dentist; and two million children under the age of 15 are not enrolled in school. Over 40 percent of New York City's young children live below the poverty line and the number is growing. New York City alone has 16,000 to 25,000 homeless children, known as *boarder babies,* living in municipal shelters. Table 14–1 gives us an idea of a child's chances of growing up in poverty.

Early childhood educators are seeking ways to provide educational and preventive social services to poor children and their families to enable them to develop their potential so as to lead healthy and successful lives. Certainly, agencies such as Head Start have done many good things for the poor and disadvantaged, but it is not enough. Only about 20 percent of the children who need Head Start services receive them, and Head Start services do not start soon enough. Many children actually need a head start on Head Start.

Although programs such as Project Beethoven offer some children hope and opportunities, what about the rest—the majority? A former U.S. commissioner of education says:

> The overwhelming fact that must be faced regarding children in the U.S. today is that they are losing ground. Efforts to provide children with healthy and rewarding lives are declining even as the needs for such efforts are growing. The self-interest of adults is taking center stage, and the interests of children are being shoved into the wings.[1]

What, then, are the prospects? Will we keep any of our promises to our children? What can we do? Here is one suggestion:

> The problems of income, education, employment, and family functioning cannot be adequately handled piecemeal and through crisis intervention; many believe that there must be a national mandate, a service agenda to enlist the aid of both the public and the private sectors. According to this view, before government and the nonprofit sector can develop

TABLE 14–1 An American Child's Chances of Being Poor

Source: Children's Defense Fund, *A Vision For America's Future.* (Washington D.C.: Children's Defense Fund, 1989.) p. xivi.

If white	1 in 6
If black	4 in 9
If Hispanic	2 in 5
If younger than 3	1 in 4
If 3 to 5	2 in 9
If 6 to 17	1 in 5
If family head is younger than 25	1 in 2
If family head is younger than 30	1 in 3

such complementary service priorities, there must be much greater awareness on the part of not only policy makers but also the general public of the needs of America's children and of the current constraints to fulfilling those needs.[2]

CHILD ABUSE AND NEGLECT

Many of our views of childhood are highly romanticized. We tend to believe that parents always love their children and enjoy caring for them. We also tend to believe that family settings are full of joy, happiness, and parent-child harmony. Unfortunately for children, their parents, and for society, these assumptions are not always true.

Child abuse is not new, although it receives greater attention and publicity than previously. Abuse, in the form of abandonment, infanticide, and neglect, has been documented throughout history. The attitude that children are property is part of the reason for the history of abuse. Parents believed, and some still do, that they own their children and can do with them as they please. The extent to which children are abused is difficult to ascertain, but is probably much greater than most people realize.

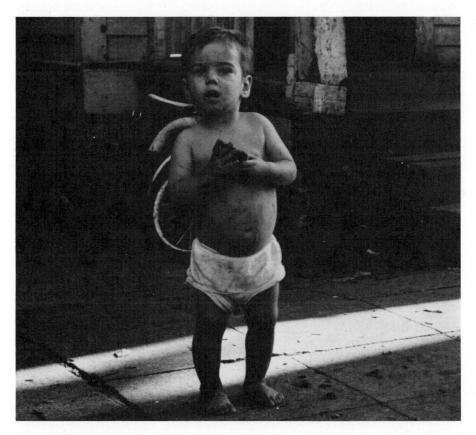

More and more of the nation's children are living in poverty. Poverty has many short-term and long-term consequences for children. Society needs to make many efforts to help children enjoy a reasonable standard of living.

439

THE BEETHOVEN PROJECT

The Center for Successful Child Development (CSCD) in Chicago is a family-oriented early childhood intervention program. CSCD is undertaking an innovative program to provide intensive and comprehensive support services to all children born after January 1, 1987, in the Beethoven Elementary School attendance area. The CSCD, on Chicago's South Side, serves the Robert Taylor Homes—the largest public housing complex in the U.S., with 20,000 residents. The Beethoven Project concentrates on six of the complex's high-rise apartment buildings. Forty-eight percent of the residents of the six buildings are under age 14, and 68 percent are under age 25. Seventy-five percent of the households are headed by women; all residents are black; and at least 90 percent of the program participants are receiving some type of public assistance. Besides poverty, residents face problems of a high crime rate, high unemployment, high drop-out rates from school, health and nutrition problems, drug problems of epidemic proportions, and the highest neonatal mortality rate in Chicago.

The Beethoven Project, according to its director, Gina Barclay-McLaughlin, has two major goals:

1. To promote the healthy growth and development of children from conception through age five in all domains of development (social, emotional, physical, and cognitive), so that they are prepared to achieve when they begin formal schooling. The CSCD staff believes that the most successful and enduring positive child outcomes are gained by recognizing each child's individual strengths, capabilities, and needs, and through the provision of services that are individually tailored to the child.

2. To help parents build on their strengths as individuals and as parents of the child. The CSCD staff believes that optimal child outcomes can only be realized through provision of support to the entire family; children cannot be viewed in isolation from their parents. If adults feel competent and effective as individuals and as parents, they will be better able to foster their children's development.

In support of these major goals, CSCD is committed to a philosophy of service provision based on the following assumptions:

Valid statistics are difficult to come by because the interest in reporting child abuse is relatively new and because the definitions of child abuse and neglect differ from state to state and reports are categorized differently. It is estimated that there are probably as many as one million incidents of abuse a year, but that only one in four cases is reported.

Because of the increasing concern over child abuse, social agencies, hospitals, child care centers, and schools are becoming more involved in identification, treatment, and prevention of this national social problem. To do something about child abuse, those who are involved with children and parents have to know what abuse is. Public Law 93-247, the Child Abuse Prevention and Treatment Act, defines child abuse and neglect:

> The physical or mental injury, sexual abuse, negligent treatment or maltreatment of a child under the age of eighteen by a person who is responsible for the child's welfare under circumstances which indicate that the child's health or welfare is harmed or threatened thereby as determined in accordance with regulations prescribed by the Secretary.[3]

□ Services provided as *early* in life as possible (even before birth) will ultimately be the most effective

□ Services in multiproblem communities need to be *comprehensive*

□ Services need to be *appropriate and relevant* to the specific needs of a community and to the cultural heritage of the families

□ Services need to be *individualized* to meet the unique needs of families even when they are from the same demographic population

As a comprehensive program, CSCD draws on a number of intervention approaches and academic disciplines, including sociology, anthropology, psychology, public health, infant mental health, community development, adult education, early childhood education, and social work. This multiplicity of perspectives and emphases is reflected in CSCD's principal program components.

1. Home-Based Services: recruitment, assessment, social services and child-rearing guidance provided by community family advo-

cates, home visitors, a social worker, and child development specialists.

2. Center-Based Services:
□ Family Drop-In Center—developmental activities for children; recreational and personal development activities for adults

□ Guided Peer Support Groups—Meld's Young Mother (MYM) groups for adolescents and support groups for older mothers

□ Primary Care Health Center—a prevention-oriented maternal and child health care center

□ Infant/Toddler Center—developmental day care for young children

□ Head Start—developmental preschool program

Staff anticipate that through this comprehensive package of medical, social, and child development services, CSCD will make a significant positive impact on children's health and development, on mothers' personal development and parental role functioning, and on the development of strong caregiver-child relationships.

In addition, all states have some kind of legal or statutory definition for child abuse and treatment and many states are defining penalties for child abuse.

Just as debilitating as physical abuse and neglect is *emotional abuse.* Emotional abuse occurs when parents, teachers, and caregivers strip children of their self-esteem and self-image. Adults take away children's self-esteem through continual criticism, belittling, screaming and nagging, creating fear, and intentionally and severely limiting opportunities. Emotional abuse is difficult to define legally and, most certainly, difficult to document. The unfortunate consequence for emotionally abused children is that they are often left in a debilitating environment. Both abuse and neglect adversely affect children's growth and development.

The guidelines in Table 14–2 may help you identify abuse and neglect; however, one characteristic doesn't necessarily indicate abuse. You should observe the child's behavior and appearance over a period of time. Teachers should also be willing to give parents the benefit of the doubt about a child's condition. These are other ways to deal with suspected abuse:

TABLE 14–2   Guidelines for Detecting Abuse and Neglect

Kind of Abuse	Child's Appearance	Child's Behavior	Parent or Caretaker's Behavior
Physical	Unusual bruises, welts, burns, or fractures Bite marks Frequent injuries, explained as "accidental"	Reports injury by parents Unpleasant, hard to get along with, demanding, often disobeys, frequently causes trouble or interferes with others; breaks or damages things; or shy, avoids others, too anxious to please, too ready to let other people say and do things to him/her without protest Frequently late or absent, or comes to school too early or hangs around after school Avoids physical contact with adults Wears long sleeves or other concealing clothing Version of how a physical injury occurred is not believable (doesn't fit type or seriousness of the injury) Seems frightened of parents Shows little or no distress at separation from parents May seek affection from any adult	History of abuse as a child Uses unnecessarily harsh discipline Offers explanation of child's injury that doesn't make sense, doesn't fit injury, or offers no explanation Seems unconcerned about child Sees child as bad, evil, a monster, etc. Misuses alcohol or other drugs Attempts to conceal child's injury or protect identity of responsible party
Emotional	Less obvious signs than other types of mistreatment; behavior is best indication	Unpleasant, hard to get along with, demanding; frequently causes trouble, won't leave others alone Unusually shy, avoids others, too anxious to please, too submissive,	Blames or belittles child Cold and rejecting Withholds love Treats children unequally Seems not to care about child's problems

TABLE 14–2 *continued*

Kind of Abuse	Child's Appearance	Child's Behavior	Parent or Caretaker's Behavior
Emotional—cont'd		puts up with unpleasantness from others without protest Either unusually adult or overly young for age (e.g., sucks thumb, rocks constantly) Behind for age physically, emotionally, or intellectually	
Neglect	Often dirty, tired, no energy Comes to school without breakfast, often does not have lunch or lunch money Clothes dirty or inappropriate for weather Alone often, for long periods Needs glasses, dental care, or other medical attention	Frequently absent Begs or steals food Causes trouble in school Often hasn't done homework Uses alcohol or drugs Engages in vandalism, sexual misconduct	Misuses alcohol or other drugs Disorganized, upset home life Seems not to care what happens Isolated from friends, relatives, neighbors Doesn't know how to get along with others Long-term chronic illnesses History of neglect as a child
Sexual	Torn, stained, or bloody underclothing Pain or itching in genital area Has venereal disease	Withdrawn or engages in fantasy or babyish behavior Poor relationships with other children Unwilling to participate in physical activities Engages in delinquent acts or runs away Says has been sexually assaulted by parent/caretaker	Protective or jealous of child Encourages child to engage in prostitution or sexual acts in presence of caretaker Misuses alcohol or other drugs Frequently absent from home

Source: United States Department of Health, Education and Welfare, Office of Human Development Services, Administration for Children, Youth and Families, Head Start Bureau, Indian and Migrant Programs Div., *New Light on an Old Problem,* DHEW Publication No. (OHDS) 78-31108 (Washington, D.C., 1978), pp. 8-11.

You should be aware of the official policy and specific reporting procedures of your school system, and should know your legal obligations and the protections from civil and criminal liability specified in your state's reporting law. (All states provide immunity for mandated, good-faith reports.)

Although you should be familiar with your state's legal definition of abuse and neglect, you are not required to make legal distinctions in order to report. Definitions should serve as guides. If you suspect that a child is abused or neglected, you should report. The teacher's value lies in noticing conditions that indicate that a child's welfare may be in jeopardy.

Be concerned about the rights of the child— the rights to life, food, shelter, clothing, and security. But also be aware of the parents' rights—particularly their rights to be treated with respect and to be given needed help and support.

Bear in mind that reporting does not stigmatize a parent as "evil." The report is the start of a rehabilitative process that seeks to protect the child and help the family as a whole.

A report signifies only the *suspicion* of abuse or neglect. Teacher's reports are seldom unfounded. At the very least, they tend to indicate a need for help and support to the family.

If you report a borderline case in good faith, do not feel guilty or upset if it is dismissed as unfounded upon investigation. Some marginal cases are found to be valid.

Don't put off making a report until the end of the school year. Teachers sometimes live with their suspicions until they suddenly fear for the child's safety during the summer months. A delayed report may mean a delay in needed help for the child and the family. Moreover, by reporting late in the school year, you remove yourself as a continued support to both the child protective agency and the reported family.

If you remove yourself from a case of suspected abuse or neglect by passing it on to superiors, you deprive child protective services of one of their most competent sources of information. For example, a teacher who tells a [children's protective services] worker that the child is especially upset on Mondays directs the worker to investigate conditions in the home on weekends. Few persons other than teachers are able to provide this kind of information. Your guideline should be to resolve any question in favor of the child. When in doubt, report. Even if you, as a teacher, have no immunity from liability and prosecution under state law, the fact that your report is made in good faith will free you from liability and prosecution.

In the absence of guidance from the protective agency, the teacher can rely on several general rules for dealing with the abused or neglected child:

Try to give the child additional attention whenever possible.

Create a more individualized program for the child. Lower your academic expectations and make fewer demands on the child's performance—he or she probably has enough pressures and crises to deal with presently at home.

Be warm and loving. If possible, let the child perceive you as a special friend to whom he or she can talk. By abusing or neglecting the child, someone has said in a physical way, "I don't love you." You can reassure the child that someone cares.

Most important, remember that in identifying and reporting child maltreatment, you are not putting yourself in the position of autocrat over a family. The one purpose of your actions is to get help for a troubled child and family; the one goal is to reverse a situation that jeopardizes a child's healthy growth and development.[4]

Causes of Abuse

Why do parents and guardians abuse children? Those who have been responsible for a group of young children will better understand the reasons for child abuse than those who do not know young children. Child rearing is hard work; it requires patience, self-control, understanding, and restraint. It is entirely likely that most parents, at one time or another, have come close to behavior that could be judged abusive.

Stress is one of the most frequent causes of child abuse. Stressful situations arise from employment, divorce or separation, income, quality of family life, moving, death of a family member, violations of law, sickness or injury, and other sources. We are learning more about stress and its effect on health and the general quality of life. Training is offered for dealing with and managing stress. Parenting and teaching are stressful occupations, and parents and teachers often need support from professionals to deal with the stress of their roles.

Lack of parenting information is another reason parents abuse or neglect their children. Some parents don't know what to do or how to do it; these cases more frequently result in acts of omission or neglect than in physical violence. Frequently, the child does not receive proper emotional care and support because the parent is ignorant of this need. Lack of parenting information is attributable to several factors. First, in this mobile population, young parents often live apart from their own parents, and there is little opportunity for grandparents to share child rearing information. Second, the greater number of teenage parents means that many parents are neither emotionally or cognitively ready to have children; they are really children themselves. We need a national effort to put parenting information into the curricula of every elementary and high school program. Fortunately, a trend is beginning in this area.

A third reason for child abuse is the parent's cognitive and emotional state. How people are reared and parenting attitudes that are modeled for them have a tremendous influence on how they will rear their children. Methods of child rearing are handed down from generation to generation, and people who were abused as children are often abusive parents.

A fourth cause of abuse relates to unwanted and unloved children. We like to assume that every child is wanted and loved, but this is not the case. Some parents take out their frustration on their children, whom they view as barriers to their dreams and self-fulfillment. Or, a parent may dislike a child because the child is a constant reminder of an absent spouse.

Some people believe a fifth reason for child abuse is the amount of violence in our society. Opponents of violence on television cite it as an example of people's callousness toward each other and poor role modeling for children.

A sixth cause of abuse can be attributed to parental substance abuse. First and foremost, substance abuse creates a chaotic environment in which children cannot tell what to expect from their parents. Second, children of alcohol- or drug-using parents are often neglected because the parent is emotionally absent when drunk or high, or physically absent. Substance-abusing parents are the kind of parents who forget to go to the store to buy food for a week. Because children of drug-using parents may not be physically abused, the signs of abuse may be subtle. A teacher might pick up clues that something is wrong at home if the child isn't bringing lunch, is wearing the same clothes over and over again, or wearing clothes that don't fit, or wearing worn-out shoes because mom and dad haven't noticed that new ones are needed. In general, drug use renders parents dysfunctional and unable to adequately care for their children.

To fully understand the causes and symptoms of abuse of children, we must consider the entire context of the family setting. Most abused children live in families that are *dysfunctional.* Dysfunctional families are characterized by parental mental instability, confused roles (a parent may function in the role of a child, thus necessitating that the child function at an adult level), and a chaotic, unpredictable family structure and environment. The families are not functioning at a healthy level and are generally unable to adequately care for and nurture a child's growth and development.

What can be done about child abuse? There must be a conscious effort to educate, treat, and help abusers or potential abusers. The school is a good place to begin. There are also organizations such as Parents Anonymous, a national, self-help organization that offers nurturing and therapeutic service to prevent child abuse. Parents Anonymous has chapters in every state. A toll-free number (800-421-0353) is maintained for all who want and need help. Another source of help is the federal government's National Center on Child Abuse and Neglect, which helps coordinate and develop programs and policies concerning child abuse and neglect. For information, write to: National Center on Child Abuse and Neglect, Children's Bureau, Office of Child Development, Office of Human Development, Department of Health and Human Services, P.O. Box 1182, Washington, D.C. 20012.

The National Child Abuse Hotline (800-422-4453) handles crisis calls and provides information and referrals to every county in the United States. The National Committee for Prevention of Child Abuse (NCPCA) is a volunteer organization of concerned citizens that works with community, state, and national groups to expand and disseminate knowledge about child abuse prevention. NCPCA has chapters in almost all states; its address is: National Committee for Prevention of Child Abuse, 332 South Michigan Avenue, Suite 950, Chicago, Ill. 60604 (312-663-3520).

Therapeutic Nurseries

How can one help abusing parents and abused children? One long-standing method is to remove the children from the home and place him in foster care; however, this method may not give the child the help he needs to learn new ways of behaving and of relating to others. An approach that is gaining popularity is the *therapeutic nursery,* of which a major goal is to help children learn ways to express themselves without resorting to anger and violence. These nurseries give children guidance needed to learn new methods of responding other than through the anger and violence they have learned from their parents.

Parents receive training in parenting skills, learning how to interact with, discipline, and guide their children without violence. Parents frequently spend time in the nursery observing and interacting with their children under the direction of counselors and teachers, who help parents break old habits of responding and develop new skills of interaction.

Child Abuse Prevention Curricula

Many curricula have been developed to help teachers, caregivers, and parents work with children to prevent abuse. The primary purposes of these programs are to educate children about abuse and to teach them strategies to avoid abuse. Before using an abuse prevention curriculum with children, staff and parents should help select the curriculum and learn how to use it. Parent involvement is essential. As with anything early childhood educators undertake, parents' understanding, approval, and support of a program make its goals easier to achieve. Parents and caregivers should not assume, however, that merely teaching children with an abuse prevention curriculum ends their responsibilities. A parent's responsibility for a child's care and protection never ends. Likewise, teachers and caregivers have the same responsibility for the children entrusted to them.

MISSING CHILDREN

Their faces smile at us from grocery bags, milk cartons, billboards, and utility bills—representatives of the country's lost, missing, strayed, and stolen children. No one really knows how many there are. Many disappear from home; some are stolen by one parent or the other in custody disputes. Some run away from home because of what they feel are intolerable conditions. Others are abducted, abused, and murdered. The tragic death of Adam Walsh in 1981 heightened public awareness of the plight of missing children and precipitated passage of child protection laws, including the Missing Children's Assistance Act of 1984. As a result of this act, the National Center for Missing and Exploited Children was established. The Center, created through a cooperative arrangement with the U.S. Department of Justice, Office of Juvenile Justice and Delinquency Prevention, serves as a clearinghouse for information on missing and exploited children; provides training assistance to law enforcement and child protection agencies; assists individuals, agencies, and state and local governments in locating missing children; and administers a national toll-free hot line (800-843-5678) to report information regarding missing children. The address is: National Center for Missing and Exploited Children, 1835 K Street, N.W., Suite 700, Washington, D.C. 20006.

The Center offers these suggestions to parents to help prevent child abduction and exploitation:

- ☐ Know where your children are at all times. Be familiar with their friends and daily activities.
- ☐ Be sensitive to changes in your children's behavior; they are a signal that you should sit down and talk to your children about what caused the changes.
- ☐ Be alert to a teenager or adult who is paying an unusual amount of attention to your children or giving them inappropriate or expensive gifts.
- ☐ Teach your children to trust their own feelings, and assure them that they have the right to say NO to what they sense is wrong.
- ☐ Listen carefully to your children's fears, and be supportive in all your discussions with them.
- ☐ Teach your children that no one should approach them or touch them in a way that makes them feel uncomfortable. If someone does, they should tell the parents immediately.
- ☐ Be careful about babysitters and any other individuals who have custody of your children.[5]

The Center also offers advice to parents to help them be prepared if their child is missing:

1. **Keep a complete description of the child.** This description must include color of hair, color of eyes, height, weight, and date of birth. In addition, the description should contain their identifiers—eyeglasses or contact lenses, braces on teeth, pierced ears, and other unique physical attributes. The complete description must be written down.

2. **Take color photographs of your child every six months.** Photographs should be of high quality and in sharp focus so that the child is easily recognizable. Head and shoulder portraits from different angles, such as those taken by school photographers, are preferable.

3. **Have your dentist prepare dental charts for your child, and be sure that they are updated each time an examination or dental work is performed.** Make sure that your dentist maintains accurate, up-to-date dental charts and x-rays on your child as a routine part of his or her normal office procedure. If you move, you should get a copy from your former dentist to keep yourself until a new dentist is found.

4. **Know where your child's medical records are located.** Medical records, particularly x-rays, can be invaluable in helping to identify a recovered child. It is important to have all permanent scars, birthmarks, blemishes, and broken bones recorded. You should find out from your child's doctor where such records are located and how you can obtain them if the need arises.

5. **Arrange with your local police department to have your child fingerprinted.** In order for fingerprints to be useful in identifying a person, they must be properly taken. Your police department has trained personnel to be sure that they are useful. The police department will give you the fingerprint card and will *not* keep a record of the child's prints.[6]

SEXISM AND SEX ROLE STEREOTYPING

The reasons for the concern about sex role stereotyping and sexism are essentially the same as those that have promoted our interest in early childhood education. The civil rights movement and its emphasis on equality provided an impetus for seeking more equal treatment for women as well as minority groups. Encouraged by the Civil Rights Act of 1964, which prohibits discrimination on the basis of race or national origin, civil rights and women's groups successfully sought legislation to prohibit discrimination on the basis of sex. Title IX of the Education Amendments Acts of 1972, as amended by Public Law 93-568, prohibits such discrimination in the schools:

> No person in the United States shall on the basis of sex, be excluded from participation in, be denied the benefits of, or be subjected to discrimination under any education program or activity receiving Federal financial assistance.[7]

Since Title IX prohibits sex discrimination in any educational program that receives federal money, early childhood programs as well as elementary schools, high schools, and universities cannot discriminate against males or females in enrollment policies, curriculum offerings, or activities.

The women's movement has encouraged the nation, educational institutions, and families to examine how they educate, treat, and rear children in relationship to sex roles and sex role stereotyping. There have been attempts to examine educational practices and materials for the purpose of eliminating sex-stereotyping content. At

Good early childhood settings are nonsexist and avoid sex stereotyping practices. These programs also help children develop and demonstrate the best qualities and behaviors characteristic of each sex.

the same time, more and more teachers and agencies are developing curricula and activities that will promote a nonsexist environment.

This is how the Federal Register defines *sexism:*

> The collection of attitudes, beliefs, and behaviors which result from the assumption that one sex is superior. *In the context of schools,* the term refers to the collection of structures, policies, practices and activities that overtly or covertly prescribe the development of girls and boys and prepare them for traditional sex roles.[8]

On the basis of sex, parents and society begin at a child's birth to teach a particular sex role. Probably no other factor plays such a determining role in life as does identification with a sex role. It was once thought that certain characteristics of maleness or femaleness were innate; but it is now generally recognized that sex role is a product of socialization, role modeling, and conscious and unconscious behavior modification. Culturally, certain role models are considered appropriate for males and certain roles for females. Traditional male roles center around masculinity; traditional female roles around femininity.

Society imposes and enforces certain sex roles. Schools, as agents of socialization, encourage certain behaviors for boys and different ones for girls. Parents, by the way they dress their children, the toys they give them, and by what they let them do, encourage certain sex role behaviors. Parents also model behaviors for their children and tell them to act "like your mother" or act "like your father." Parents and teachers also modify, shape, and reinforce sex role behavior. "Don't act like a girl," or "Play with this, this is for boys," or "Don't play with that, only girls do that," "Boys don't cry," are a few of the ways they modify behavior toward one sex role or the other.

Educators disagree as to whether children can or should be reared in an unstereotyped environment. Some say children have a right to determine their own sex roles, and should therefore be reared in an environment that does not impose arbitrary sex roles. Rather, the environment should be free from sex-role stereotyping to encourage the child to develop his or her own sex role. Other educators say it is impossible not to assign sex roles. In addition, they argue that development of a sex role is a difficult task of childhood and children need help in this process.

It is too simplistic to say one will not assign or teach a particular sex role. As society is now constituted, differentiated sex roles are still very much in evidence and likely to remain so. Parents and teachers should provide children with less restrictive options and promote a more open framework in which sex roles can develop. These are some ways to provide a less sex-stereotyped environment.

☐ *Provide opportunities for all children to experience the activities, materials, toys and emotions traditionally associated with both sexes.* Give boys as well as girls opportunities to experience tenderness, affection, and the warmth of close parent/child, teacher/pupil relationships. Conversely, girls as well as boys should be able to behave aggressively, get dirty, and participate in what are typically considered male activities, such as woodworking and block-building.

☐ *Examine the classroom materials you are using and plan to use to determine whether they contain obvious instances of sex stereotyping.* When you find examples, modify the materials or don't use them. Let the publishers know your feelings and tell other faculty members about them.

☐ *Examine your behavior to see whether you are encouraging sex stereotypes.* Do you tell girls they can't empty wastebaskets, but they can water the plants? Do you tell girls they can't lift certain things in the classroom because they are too heavy for them? Do you give the female students most of your attention? Do you reward only females who are always passive, well-behaved, and well-mannered?

☐ *Have a colleague or parent observe you in your classroom to determine what sex role behaviors you are encouraging.* We are often unaware of our behaviors, and self-correction begins only after the behaviors are pointed out to us. Obviously, unless you begin with yourself, eliminating sex role stereotyping practices will be next to impossible.

☐ *Determine what physical arrangements in the classroom promote or encourage sex role stereotyping.* Are boys encouraged to use the block area more than girls? Are girls encouraged to use the quiet areas more than boys? Do children hang their wraps separately, a place for the boys and a place for the girls? All children should have equal access to all learning areas of the classroom; no area should be reserved exclusively for one sex.

☐ *Counsel with parents to show them ways to promote nonsexist child rearing.* If society is to achieve a truly nonsexist environment, parents will be the key factor, for it is in the home that many sex stereotyping behaviors are initiated and practiced.

☐ *Become conscious of words that promote sexism.* For example, in a topic on community helpers, taught in most preschool and kindergarten programs at one time or another, many words carry a sexist connotation. *Fireman, policeman,* and *mailman* are all masculine terms; nonsexist terms would be *firefighter, police officer,* and *mail carrier.* You should examine all your curricular materials and teaching practices to determine how you can make them free from sexism.

☐ *Examine your teaching and behavior to be sure you are not limiting certain roles to either sex.* Females should not be encouraged to pursue only roles that are subservient, submissive, lacking in intellectual demands, or low paying.

☐ *Do not encourage children to dress in ways that lead to sex stereotyping.* Females should not be encouraged to wear frilly dresses, then forbidden to participate in an activity because they might get dirty or spoil their clothes. Children should be encouraged to dress so they will be able to participate in a wide range of activities both indoors and outdoors. This is an area in which you may be able to help parents if they seek your advice. Or, you may want to discuss how dressing their child differently can contribute to more effective participation.

MAKING EARLY CHILDHOOD PROGRAMS HUMANE

Some classrooms seem to destroy children's personal dignity. In a dehumanized classroom, a child thinks less of herself than she ought to because of the conditions and atmosphere of the setting. On the other hand, a humane setting encourages children's full development and treats them as good and worthy human beings. A continual challenge to early childhood educators is how to make centers, homes, classrooms, and buildings in which they teach humane settings.

Interrelationship of Intelligence, Emotions, and Behavior

We tend to talk of the cognitive (intellectual), affective (feeling, emotional), and psychomotor (behavioral) domains as though they were separate and distinct. Table 14–3 shows the relationship among the three domains; all three areas must be accounted for in the instructional process and cannot be easily compartmentalized. Neither is it possible to assign topics or activities to one area with absolute assurance that they belong only to that area. Failure to integrate the three domains encourages fragmentation of teaching and usually emphasizes the cognitive domain to the exclusion of the other two, particularly the affective. There has also been a tendency to think education cannot have both achievement and humanistic goals. Now more educators are realizing that we need not choose between teaching the basics (achieve-

TABLE 14–3   Interrelationship of the Cognitive, Affective, and Psychomotor Domains in a Humanized Early Childhood Setting

Domain	Intrapersonal	Interpersonal
Cognitive	Learning about body parts and how the body functions	Identifying likenesses and differences among people
	Learning right from left	
	Identifying the letters of one's name	
	Identifying colors of foods	
Affective	Identifying what foods one likes	Deciding what they want for snack time
	Deciding what one wants for a snack	Group discussions about favorite foods
Behavioral (Psychomotor)	Being able to walk well	Planning a grocery trip
	Playing games requiring knowledge of right and left	Shopping for food
	Writing one's name	Making cookies with everyone helping
	Eating favorite foods	
	Cutting carrots for snack	

ment) or having a humanistic setting (values); it is possible and desirable to have both.

Requirements of Humane Settings

A humanized classroom is not so much a place as a condition or atmosphere in which a series of forces interact to enable meaningful learning and living. Specific items vary according to the social setting, different groups of children, and teacher attitude. We can, however, generalize about humanistic schools, learning settings, teachers, and curriculum. The school is open to the community; encourages community involvement; promotes student freedom; and encourages student growth toward independence. The learning setting is individualized and self-paced; is flexible in time (no rigid time schedule) and space (learning can occur anywhere); and provides an emotionally secure atmosphere. The teacher respects and trusts children; is honest and accepting; believes in, promotes, and provides for individual differences; promotes a feeling of human warmth; and encourages children to express their own ideas. The curriculum is based on children's interests; learning is considered a lifelong process; integrates subject matter with children's interests; is based on the whole student (not just as he exists in school); utilizes real-life problems in place of hypothetical ones; integrates the cognitive, affective and psychomotor; is based on planning by both teachers and children; and provides for development of the affective domain. At the heart of how to make early childhood settings more humane is the issue of child-centered education. When anything gets in the way of children's best

Teachers are the key to making early childhood programs humane, and a sense of humanity should underlie all of our programs for and interactions with young children.

interests, then children are pushed from the center and replaced by whatever is given priority, whether subject matter, testing, accountability, or something else. One of our roles as educators and caregivers is to continue our efforts to promote child-centered learning through humane environments, practices, and interpersonal relationships.

HOMELESS CHILDREN

Walking down a city street, you may have had to walk around homeless men and women occupying heat grates and doorways. You have seen them on television—tattered and toothless men sleeping on park benches, covered with newspapers and cardboard, or bedraggled bag ladies whose shopping bags contain all their worldly possessions. Have you seen a homeless child? Homeless children are the neglected, forgotten, often abandoned segment of the growing homeless population in the U.S. The National Coalition for the Homeless estimates there are between 500,000 and 750,000 homeless youth, most of whom are living in homeless families or on their own.

Homelessness has significant mental, physical, and educational consequences for children. Homelessness results in developmental delays and can produce high levels of distress. Homeless children observed in day care centers exhibited such problem behaviors as short attention spans, weak impulse control, withdrawal, aggression, speech delays, and regressive behaviors. Homeless children are at greater risk for health problems. It is estimated that 40 percent of homeless children do not attend school, and, if and when they do enter school, they face many problems relating to their previous school problems (grade failure) and problems associated with school

EUGENE P. TONE SCHOOL PROJECT, TACOMA, WASHINGTON*

History

The original concept of providing educational services to Tacoma's homeless children began in the early 1980s. School personnel discovered that children who were living with their families in emergency shelters were generally not attending school. Especially affected were those children who, along with their mothers, had fled abusive home situations. Mothers who had experienced domestic violence were less likely to send their children to public schools because they feared the abusive parent might attempt to take their children without their consent.

The discovery that children were not receiving educational services led to the creation of a committee to research the problem and develop possible solutions. The committee, consisting of both Tacoma School District personnel and Tacoma/Pierce County YWCA representatives, determined that a new school program should be established to meet the educational needs of homeless children.

The YWCA was selected as the site for the school for two reasons. First, because the YWCA is the location of the Women's Support Shelter (shelter for victims of domestic violence), committee members felt an on-site school would be more secure for the shelter's children. Second, the YWCA pool and gym provide an ideal setting for the school's physical education component.

Target Population

Homelessness has reached crisis proportions. Estimates place the current homeless population in the U.S. at between 2 and 3 million persons. Further estimates claim that almost 50 percent of the homeless population consists of intact families. The National Academy of Sciences has stated that children are among the fastest-growing homeless group. Of the 500,000 to 750,000 school-age homeless children nationwide, only 43 percent attend school on a regular basis.

Causes of homelessness vary: lack of affordable housing, unemployment, and underemployment are just a few of the reasons people become homeless. Certainly, there is no single cause nor is there a typical story of homelessness. To be homeless means one thing: to lack a regular or adequate place to live.

Program Staff

The purpose of the Tone School Project is to provide a full educational school program for homeless children. The Tone School attempts to have a positive impact on these children who are at great risk of dropping out or falling behind. Students in the Tone School are challenged and stimulated educationally within a safe, supportive, and nurturing atmosphere.

A major function of the school is to assist students in their eventual transition to a mainstream public school program. School support staff work closely with the student's family and new teachers and administrators to facilitate a helpful and healthy transition. In addition, homeless children who are in need of special education services have access to a school psychologist and a communication disorder specialist.

attendance (long trips to attend school).[9] Fortunately, more agencies are responding to the unique needs of homeless children and their families.

CHILDREN WITH AIDS

AIDS, or Acquired Immune Deficiency Syndrome, is a relatively new disease first described in 1981 and named in 1982. AIDS is caused by the Human Immunodeficiency Virus (HIV), which weakens or destroys the immune system, allowing diseases and

Tone School Goals

☐ To provide a safe, supportive educational environment for school-age children who, along with their families, lack a regular or adequate place to live. (They live in emergency shelters, are living out-of-doors, or in cars, or abandoned buildings, etc.)
☐ To provide students with individual assessment and to utilize prescriptive teaching methods.
☐ To provide a full complement of support services to help students and their families cope with the social and emotional impact of their homeless situation. Support services include social work, counseling, and nursing.
☐ To assist with the eventual placement and follow-up of students transferring to a permanent school setting.

Program Staff

Tone School staff functions as a multidisciplinary team. This team consists of two certified teachers, a teacher's assistant, a school social worker, a school counselor, a school nurse, a resource/volunteer coordinator, the YWCA executive director, and the Tacoma School District program administrator.

Staff have been selected according to their degree of experience educating or working with "at-risk" children. To provide services to children who are assessed as requiring special education, one of the school's teachers must be certified in Special Education.

Transportation and Enrollment

The Tacoma School District provides school bus transportation to and from the school. When a family arrives at a Tacoma family shelter, children may attend the Tone School immediately. School enrollment forms are kept at all family shelters to facilitate the enrollment process. Staff will then assist the family in obtaining school records, immunization records, birth certificates, and other documentation required for placing their children in a mainstream school setting.

Nutrition

The Tacoma School District provides breakfast and lunches for the children of the Tone School. In addition, supplemental food is provided for the school by businesses and volunteer donations.

Volunteers

A Citizen Support Committee was formed in October of 1988. Although the Tone School Project is a partnership between the Tacoma School District and the Tacoma/Pierce County YWCA, our program would not be as successful without the support of the community. Individuals, groups, and businesses have done much for this program. Volunteers have helped with the acquisition of donations and resources and have provided valuable individualized instructional assistance. Volunteers have also helped to coordinate special events, provided grant-writing assistance, and worked to raise funds for the school. The Tone School Project will have received approximately 2500 hours of volunteer time and energy during this school year.

*Connie Iverson, Teacher at Eugene P. Tone School Project, Tacoma, Washington

infections to develop. Children and adults with HIV may develop AIDS, or they may develop symptoms not normally associated with AIDS that are referred to as AIDS Related Complex (ARC).

The manifestation of AIDS in children is different from adults; for example, Kaposi's Sarcoma, a form of cancer, is found in about 25 percent of adult AIDS cases, but seldom in children. More commonly, children with AIDS develop infections such as pneumonia and central nervous system disorders. Some children with the AIDS virus are born with facial and cranial abnormalities. As of November 1989, the Centers for Disease Control estimated that 1,908 children below age thirteen have developed AIDS. At least 71 percent of these cases have been transmitted from an infected mother to her fetus or infant during the perinatal period.

A pregnant woman infected with AIDS always passes the AIDS antibodies to the fetus; however, the actual virus is passed only about 40 percent of the time through mixing of blood at birth or through the presence of the AIDS virus on the cervix. It is not until children are about fifteen months old that they start making their own antibodies if they have the virus, because children's immune systems do not fully function until that time and therefore they cannot produce AIDS antibodies. This explains why the HIV virus cannot be determined in babies under fifteen months.

Children at Risk for AIDS

A question that everyone asks about AIDS is, "How do you get it?" These are the ways children are at risk for or can acquire AIDS:

Born to an infected mother

Victim of sexual abuse

Receiving a tainted blood transfusion

Engaging in homosexual practices

Engaging in IV drug use

Being breast-fed by an HIV-infected person

Engaging in heterosexual practices with an HIV-infected person.

Guidelines for Parents and Caregivers

All staff members in early childhood education programs need to be aware of the facts and issues surrounding AIDS and its transmission. Most importantly, they should be aware of the following guidelines on AIDS infection, recommended by the National Association for the Education of Young Children.

HIV-infected children should be admitted to group programs if their health, neurological development, behavior, and immune status are appropriate. Decisions on admittance should be made individually by qualified persons who have expertise regarding HIV infection and AIDS, including the child's physician. This decision should take into account both the efficacy of program participation for the infected child and whether the child poses a potential health threat to others.

More young children face the risks and life-threatening dangers of the AIDS epidemic, and programs must plan to meet their needs sensitively and humanely.

Parents of children attending group programs do not have the "right" to know the HIV status of other children in the program. Caregivers and teachers need to know when a child has immunodeficiency, regardless of cause, so that precautions can be taken to protect the child from other infections. This does not, however, require knowledge of HIV status.

Because it is not always known when children are infected with HIV or other infectious agents, precautions should be taken to reduce the risk of infection. Recommended practices include: promptly cleaning soiled surfaces with disinfectant (1 tablespoon of bleach added to 1 quart water, prepared daily; for blood spills, a dilution of 1 part bleach to 10 parts water is needed), using paper towels and tissues with proper disposal, and avoiding exposure of mucous membranes or any open skin lesion to blood or blood-contaminated body fluid by using disposable gloves, for example.[10]

AIDS Education

Although the majority of early childhood educators recognize the value of educating children about AIDS and its transmission, controversies over how much information and at what age to teach children about AIDS are far from settled. Whatever is done,

one thing is certain. The information should be accurate and developmentally appropriate. The following suggestions by Skeen and Hodson meet these two criteria:

> Many of the younger-than-8-year-olds *we* care for will not ask, "What is AIDS?" and will not say, "I'm afraid I'll get it." But some will. Children who ask need a little information and a lot of reassurance. Tell the child that AIDS is a serious disease. Although some people have died from AIDS, it is still a very rare disease. Tell the child not to worry because the child's chances of getting AIDS are very, very small.[11]

Skeen and Hodson offer common sense advice that makes good sense as well:

> ...*if* a child does ask how a person gets AIDS, it is probable that saying, "It's caused by a virus, a tiny germ," is the best answer. Issues of sexual transmission, the spread of the disease through the sharing of contaminated needles during drug use, and the transmission of AIDS through infected blood mother-to-fetus, are issues that can be discussed when the child is older.[12]

"Double C" Babies

When Lashonda came early into the world, she was jittery, cried most of the time, was tactilely defensive (didn't like to be touched), and was not easily comforted. The behavioral characteristics that describe Lashonda appear increasingly in infants who are born drug-dependent. These children are the unfortunate victims of mothers who use crack and cocaine throughout their pregnancy and even as a means of speeding the birth of the child. Lashonda's plight raises a host of legal, developmental, and educational issues. Juvenile courts are being asked to decide whether parents such as Lashonda's are capable of caring for their children. Crack-using parents are being accused of prenatal child abuse. Children's advocates question whether crack-using parents have the ability to provide the necessary love, care, and protection for normal growth and development. Fetal exposure to crack and cocaine can result in retarded growth, premature birth, smaller head circumference and brain size, and impairments to the nervous system. All these effects can have long-lasting negative influences on developmental outcomes as well as educational performance.

These consequences of the effects of crack and cocaine on infants are only half the story of how substance abuse affects children in the early years. In many urban neighborhoods, it is not uncommon to see seven-, eight-, and nine-year-olds acting as lookouts, drug runners, and intermediaries in drug deals. Many children live in families that put them at risk for later substance abuse. Social environment and parents' child-rearing practices can develop in children risk factors that make them vulnerable to later drug use. In a study of the personality and environmental precursors to later drug use, researchers identified parenting styles and personality correlates that place children at risk.

Parenting Styles.   While parenting styles play an important role in children's attitudes and developmental outcomes, they are particularly powerful for girls as related to later drug use. As for the influence of fathers on their daughter's later drug use, correlates such as the following are significant:

> ... a deemphasis on the daughter's competitiveness, little fostering of the daughter's achievement, a preference that the daughter achieve early autonomy, a relative absence of strict

rules for the daughter, opposition to traditional sex-typing and strict division of the sexes, and permissiveness with respect to the expressiveness of the daughter via crying, negative remarks, or becoming dirty while playing.[13]

In addition, family environmental variables play a significant role in determining whether or not girls will turn to drugs:

Later drug use among girls was correlated with characterizations of the home as: messy, crowded, and unkempt; carelessly maintained; busy and noisy; disorderly; interpersonally informal, and even child-oriented; and with little emphasis on propriety, conventions, and religion. Further correlates included: indulgence of the daughter, direct and open communication, and less pressure on these girls to achieve.[14]

Personality Correlates of Later Drug Use

For both sexes, the constellation of personality characteristics encompassed by the concept of ego undercontrol (inability to delay gratification, rapid tempo, emotional expressiveness, mood lability [instability], overreactivity, etc.) correlationally foretold later drug use: for girls, but not for boys, an absence of ego-resiliency (i.e., adaptational insufficiencies leading to a personal vulnerability) also presaged drug usage in adolescence.[15]

These are family characteristics that can affect children's use of drugs:

Family members feel lonely, isolated, frustrated.

Parents and children communicate poorly, particularly fathers and sons.

Parents demonstrate little sense of ethics.

Parents and children lack self-esteem.

Parents drink heavily.

Children feel rejected.

Parents have low expectations for children.

Family follows rigid, stereotyped sex roles.

Family management is inadequate.

Parents excessively dominate and control their children.

Parents use negative discipline measures (either extremely strict or too permissive).

Adults fight about discipline and other issues.[16]

Conversely, in a different kind of family atmosphere, children are less likely to turn to drugs. These are characteristics of families in which drug abuse is less likely:

Family members have warm, positive relationships.

Parents are committed to education.

Parents believe in society's general values.

Family attends religious services.

Household tasks are distributed among all family members.

Families have high aspirations for children's success.

Strong kinship networks exist in the family.

The family is proud of children's accomplishments.

Affectionate, supportive parent-child relationships meet the children's emotional needs.

Children derive a great deal of satisfaction from their families.

Parents use a reasoned, democratic discipline.[17]

PREVENTION

It is imperative that society seek to win the war on drugs and to reduce or eliminate not only the use but also the subsequent harmful effects of drugs. Society increasingly looks to the public schools to assist with prevention and eradication efforts. And since the roots of later drug use are evident in family environments, parenting styles, and early childhood behaviors, it is logical that early childhood programs are in the forefront of substance abuse prevention programs. These efforts generally take two directions. One is to provide young parents and parents-to-be with the courses, resources, and support services necessary for them to exhibit the parenting styles and create the family environments that will enable children to resist temptations to use addictive substances. The second focus is to provide early childhood educators and caregivers with the knowledge and resources to conduct programs that will help them instill in children the characteristics known to help them avoid later substance abuse. These programs generally include helping children develop the following skills.

☐ *Positive self-concept.* This is probably the most important aspect of all in preventing substance abuse. Self-concept, or self-esteem, is the underlying feeling a person has concerning her worth. When positive, the person feels lovable, worthwhile, confident. When low, or negative, the person may feel incompetent, unworthy, valueless, afraid. The child with a strong, positive self-image is able to take the risks inherent in decision-making, problem-solving, and taking responsibility. She can be assertive, and continues to develop self-control in all the other skills because of her level of self-confidence.

☐ *Self-control.* It is often felt that the person who abuses drugs simply needs to exert self-control. In reality, the person is physically and/or psychologically addicted and it is too late. The time to exert self-control is in the beginning of use, or to prevent use.

☐ *Taking responsibility.* Children must learn that behavior has consequences, and that we are responsible for our own behavior. This is difficult and must be learned bit by bit, over time. Giving children too much responsibility too soon is as counter-productive as not giving enough.

☐ *Decision-making.* Responsibility is a factor in decision-making. Whom will my behavior affect and how? What are my choices? How do I decide?

☐ *Problem-solving.* There are both academic and social problems which must be solved. Cognitive skills are necessary for problem-solving, as are perseverance, divergent thinking, and self-confidence.

☐ *Expressiveness.* Children who can express their feelings articulately, appropriately, and assertively have a much better chance of resisting peer pressure when making decisions.[18]

CHILDHOOD STRESS

The scene of children being left at a child care center or preschool for the first time is familiar to anyone who has worked with young children. Some children quickly become happily involved with new friends in a new setting; some are tense. They cling fearfully to their parents, and cries of despair pierce the air. For many children, separation from the ones they are attached to is a stressful experience that causes them and others a great deal of trauma. Crying, fear, and tension are the *stress responses,* the symptoms or outward manifestations of children's stress.

Young children are subjected to an increasing number of situations and events that cause them fear and stress (see Table 14–4). Some of the *stressors* include their parents' divorce, being left at home alone before and after school, parents who constantly argue, the death of a parent or friend, being hospitalized, living in a dangerous neighborhood, fears of nuclear war, poverty, riots, and child abuse. Children are also subjected to stress by parents who hurry them to grow up, to act like adults, to get into school, and to succeed. Other causes of stress are the rush to early schooling, the emphasis on competency testing, and basic skills learning.

Parents and early childhood professionals are becoming aware of the effects stress can have on children. These can include sickness, withdrawal, shyness, loss of appetite, poor sleep patterns, urinary and bowel disorders, and general behavioral and discipline problems. Many early childhood educators believe that one way to alleviate stress is through play. They feel children should be encouraged to play as a therapeutic antidote to the effects of stress. A second way to relieve stress in children is to stop hurrying and pressuring them. Many think children should be free from parental and societal demands so they can enjoy their childhood. Unfortunately, society is as it is; we cannot and should not want to return to the "old days." The tempo of twentieth-century America is hectic, and demands for individual achievement are increasing. Despite our wishes, the pace of life is not going to slow down. As a result, the emphasis must be on helping children reduce stress and teaching them how to reduce stress in their lives.

From preschool on, children should be taught stress reduction techniques, including relaxation and breathing exercises, yoga, physical exercises, meditation, and regular physical activity. Since we cannot slow the pace of society, we need to teach children coping skills. The amount and kinds of stress on children and its effect are causing more early childhood educators and caregivers to become involved in programs and agencies that work for solutions to societal issues and forces that cause children stress. Reducing stress is one of the premier issues in early childhood education. Events and actions that cause stress in children, and educators' searches for ways to reduce or eliminate stress, help keep young children and early childhood education in the forefront of the educational scene.

TABLE 14–4   Common Fears and When to Expect Them

Source: Mark Rubinstein, M.D., "What Children Fear the Most," *Child,* 4 (July/ Aug. 1989), p. 42.

Infants	Toddlers	Preschool	School-Age
Strangers	Separation	Monsters	School
Separation	Toilets	Animals	Injury
Noises	Noises	Bedtime	Bullies
Falling	Bedtime	Daycare	Teachers
	Daycare	Death	Tests
			Getting Lost

HEALTH ISSUES

The spread of diseases in early childhood programs is a serious concern to all who care for young children (see Figure 14–1). Part of the responsibility of all caregivers is to provide *healthy* care for all children. One of the most effective ways to control the spread of disease in early childhood programs and to promote the healthy care of young children is by washing hands.

These are generally accepted procedures for handwashing:

1. Turn on faucet. In some programs, faucets have control levers that can be turned on and shut off with the elbows. This is the preferable method since it eliminates the spread of germs and fecal matter by the hands.
2. Wet hands, wrists, and forearms.
3. Apply liquid soap. Liquid soap is preferred because cake soap can transmit germs and fecal matter.

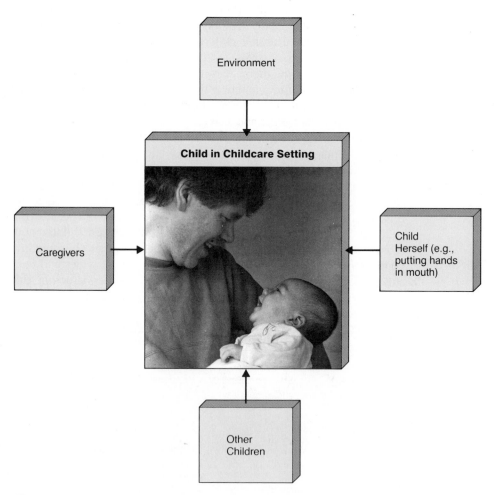

FIGURE 14–1   Spread of Contamination in Child Care Centers

4. Scrub hands, wrists, and forearms, making sure that enough pressure is applied to produce friction.
5. Rinse hands, wrists, and forearms.
6. Dry hands, wrists, and forearms completely with a disposable paper towel.
7. Use a disposable paper towel to turn off the faucet.[19]

The spread of germs can also be greatly reduced through the use of sanitary diapering techniques. Diapering is another prime vehicle for germ transmission. It is imperative that sanitary procedures be followed while diapering children. The National Association for the Education of Young Children's guidelines for sanitary diaper changing are as follows.

☐ **Place** paper or other disposable cover on diapering surface.
☐ **Pick up** the child. If the diaper is soiled, hold the child away from you.
☐ **Lay** the child on the diapering surface. **Never leave the child unattended.**
☐ If you use them, **put** on disposable gloves now.
☐ **Remove** soiled diaper and clothes. Fold disposable diapers inward and reseal with their tapes.

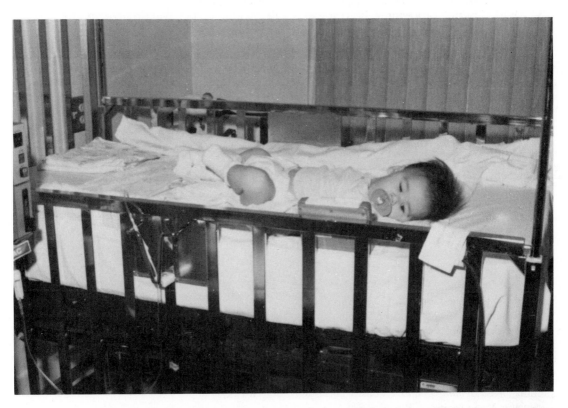

Young children experience greater stress than ever before. Some of this stress results from the benefits of new advances in health care; other stress results from the pressures of living in a fast-paced society.

☐ **Put** disposable diapers in a lined, covered step can. Put cloth diapers in a plastic bag securely tied, then put into a larger, labeled, plastic bag to go home. Do not put diapers in toilet. Bulky stool may be emptied into toilet.

☐ **Put** soiled clothes in double, labeled, plastic bags to be taken home.

☐ **Clean** the child's bottom with a moist disposable wipe. Wipe front to back using towelette only once. Repeat with fresh wipes if necessary. Pay particular attention to skin folds. Pat dry with paper towel. Do not use any kind of powder, as inhaling it can be dangerous. Use a skin care product only on parent request.

☐ **Dispose** of the towelette or paper towel in a lined, covered step can.

☐ **If you used disposable gloves, discard** them now.

☐ **Wipe** your hands with a disposable wipe. **Dispose** of it in the lined, covered step can.

☐ **Diaper** or dress the child. Now you can hold her or him close to you.

☐ **Wash** the child's hands. Assist the child back to the group.

☐ **Remove** disposable covering from the diapering surface.

☐ **Wash** and rinse the area with water (use soap if necessary) and sanitize it with bleach solution made fresh daily.

☐ **Wash** your own hands thoroughly.[20]

It sounds trite, but it is true that health in child care and preschool programs begins with the people who conduct the programs. Hand-washing policies and diapering procedures, however well stated and intended, will do little good if they are not followed. It is important, therefore, for caregivers and teachers to do all that they can to protect and promote the health of children and to follow all procedures and guidelines that will achieve these two goals.

FURTHER READING

Arnet, Ruth P. *Stress and Your Child: A Parent's Guide to Symptoms, Strategies, and Benefits* (Englewood Cliffs, NJ.: Prentice-Hall, 1984)

Comprehensive review and discussion of major factors causing stress in young children; also provides practical and useful suggestions for understanding stress and how caregivers can help alleviate situations that cause stress.

Blom, Gaston E., et al. *Stress in Childhood: An Intervention Model for Teachers and Other Professionals* (New York: Teachers College Press, 1986)

A stress-intervention model for teachers and other caregivers to apply without becoming therapists, also suggests time-efficient interventions adaptable to a teacher's role. Describes children experiencing stress and their behavioral responses to it.

Brenner, Avis. *Helping Children Cope With Stress* (Lexington, Mass.: Lexington Books, 1984)

Describes the many kinds of stress operating on and affecting children and ways that care-

givers and parents can help children cope with stress.

Edwards, Carolyn Pope. *Promoting Social and Moral Development in Young Children: Creative Approaches for the Classroom* (New York: Teachers College Press, 1986)

Describes a creative approach to social-cognitive development of children aged two to six based on Piagetian theory; seven areas of social and moral development.

Fernandez, John P. *Child Care and Corporate Productivity: Resolving Family/Work Conflicts* (Lexington, Mass.: D.C. Heath, 1986)

Summarizes results of a survey of 5000 employees at five corporations regarding views and perceptions of child care; useful data to support decisions about meeting employee needs for child care.

Marotz, Lynn, Jeanettia Rush, and Marie Cross. *Health, Safety, and Nutrition for the Young Child.* (Albany, N.Y.: Delmar, 1985)

Interrelates the areas of health, safety, and nutrition; focuses on prevention.

Miller, M.S. *Childstress: Understanding and Answering Stress Signals of Infants, Children, and Teenagers* (New York: Doubleday, 1982)

Defines child's internal and external resources to cope with stress; lists signals to help adults identify stress in children.

Sarafino, Edward P. *The Fears of Childhood* (New York: Human Sciences Press, 1985)

Describes what children fear, why fears develop, and how parents and caregivers can help children overcome anxieties; presents specific ways to prevent fears from developing and straightforward advice on helping children when fears do arise.

FURTHER STUDY

1. Examine children's readers and supplemental materials to determine instances of sexism. What recommendations would you make to change such practices?
2. Visit child care programs and observe the caregiver's hand-washing and diapering procedures. How closely do they approximate the guidelines listed in this chapter? What suggestions would you make for improvement?
3. Observe children in both school and nonschool settings for examples of how dress reflects sex stereotyping, and how parents' behaviors promote sex stereotyping.
4. Why is the nation so concerned about crack/cocaine babies? What can early childhood educators do to help crack babies and their mothers?
5. Interview child care directors in your vicinity to see if they have policies regarding AIDS children. If some have no policies, why not? How would you improve existing policies?
6. We tend to ignore the role of the environment and materials in promoting sexism, but they do play a powerful role. Examine the environment of classrooms and homes to determine the extent of sexist practices. Make recommendations based on your findings.
7. Become familiar with the child abuse laws in your state. What are the responsibilities of teachers and other school personnel?
8. Interview social workers and other public service personnel who work with abused children and their families. Determine the problems, issues, and frustrations in working with these groups.
9. Interview people in your community to determine typical attitudes toward and means of punishment of children in different cultures. Be specific, so you can be aware of similarities and differences. What implications do these have for the teacher's role in reporting child abuse?
10. Visit child care centers, preschools, and primary grade classrooms. What features in the environments would you consider inhumane? Humane? Explain your opinions. What caregiver/teacher behaviors did you observe that contributed positively and negatively to a humane atmosphere? Provide specific examples.
11. What *effects* of stress have you noticed in children? Give specific examples.
12. Do you agree or disagree that today's children are being "hurried"? What can teachers and caregivers do to relieve or reduce stress in children?
13. What are five reasons for the increase in reported child abuse? Do you think the public's heightened awareness of child abuse will help reduce the causes of abuse?
14. As the director of a child care center, what would you do when hiring staff to assure that a person did not have a history of child abuse? How could you and your staff help parents protect their children from abuse?
15. Review a curriculum for young children designed to protect them from child abuse. Do you think the curriculum content is appropriate for the ages for which it is intended? Would you want the program used with your child? Why or why not?
16. What are six issues and concerns for children, parents, and the early childhood profession that emerge from the national attention to child abuse?
17. Why are substance abuse programs being targeted to ever-younger children? Visit local child care programs, community agencies, and schools to find out what drug prevention programs they use. What are the essential features of these programs?

18. Why does it sometimes seem that this country does not treat children as its greatest asset?

19. List five of the most serious problems young children face today. Identify the causes of and reasons for each problem, and propose realistic solutions for each.

20. Each year injuries kill 8000 and permanently dis-able 50,000 children. Childhood injury is the nation's newest childhood epidemic. This epidemic includes injuries related to bicycling, scalding, burns, choking, poisoning, drownings, and falls. What specific things can parents, care-givers, and early childhood teachers do to help prevent injuries in young children?

Notes

1. Harold Howe II, "The Prospect for Children in the United States," *Phi Delta Kappan, 68* (November 1986), p. 191.

2. Madeleine H. Kimmich, *America's Children: Who Cares?* (Washington, D.C.: The Urban Institute Press, 1985), p. 109.

3. United States Statutes at Large, vol. P. 88 part 1 (Washington, D.C.: United States Government Printing Office, 1976), p. 5.

4. United States Department of Health, Education and Welfare, Office of Human Development, Office of Child Development, Children's Bureau National Center on Child Abuse and Neglect, Child Abuse and Neglect, *The Problem and Its Management,* Vol. 2, *The Roles and Responsibilities of Professionals.* DHEW Publication No. (OHD) 75-30074, pp. 70–72.

5. National Center for Missing and Exploited Children, *Child Protection* (Washington, D.C.), pamphlet.

6. National Center for Missing and Exploited Children, *Just in Case: Parental Guidelines in Case Your Child Might Someday be Missing* (Washington, D.C.), pamphlet.

7. *Federal Register,* Wednesday, June 4, 1975, p. 24128.

8. *Federal Register,* August 11, 1975, p. 33803.

9. Andrea L. Solarz, "Homelessness: Implications for Children and Youth," *Social Policy Report* (Washington, D.C.: Society for Research in Child Development, 1988).

10. "New Guidelines on HIV Infection (AIDS) Announced for Group Programs," *Young Children, 44* (Jan. 1989), p. 51.

11. Patsy Skeen and Diane Hodson, "AIDS: What Adults Should Know About AIDS (and Shouldn't Discuss with Very Young Children," *Young Children 42* (May 1987), pp. 65–71.

12. Skeen and Hodson, pp. 65–71.

13. Jack Block, Jeanne H. Block, and Susan Keyes. "Longitudinally Foretelling Drug Usage in Adolescence: Early Childhood Personality and Environmental Precursors," *Child Development, 59* (1988), p. 346. © The Society for Research in Child Development, Inc.

14. Block, Block, and Keyes, p. 346.

15. Block, Block, and Keyes, p. 349.

16. Ura Jean Oyemade and Valora Washington, "Drug Abuse Prevention Begins in Early Childhood (And is Much More Than a Matter of Instructing Young Children About Drugs!)," *Young Children,* 44 (1989), p. 11.

17. Oyemade and Washington, p. 11.

18. Susan K. Bumgarner, "A Preschool Approach: Substance Abuse Prevention," *Dimensions, 15* (1987), p. 15.

19. "How Seriously Do You Take the Soaps?" *Young Children,* 42 (1987), p. 69.

20. Abby Shapiro Kendrick, Roxane Kaufmann, and Katherine P. Messenger, *Healthy Young Children: A Manual for Programs.* (Washington, D.C.: NAEYC, 1988), p. 44.

CHAPTER 15
Responsible Caregiving and Teaching
Becoming a Professional

As you read and study:

☐ Examine the relationship between an early childhood teacher's attitude and character and the healthy growth of children
☐ Analyze qualities of early childhood teachers that are worthy of emulation
☐ Become aware of and sensitive to the philosophies of early childhood professionals and teachers of the year
☐ Identify important things you can begin to do that can result in a happy and productive career
☐ Identify important themes and concepts that contribute to becoming a good caregiver and teacher
☐ Analyze and understand the roles of early childhood educators
☐ Develop a philosophy of early childhood education
☐ Identify qualities that help someone become a good teacher
☐ Begin to develop a personal plan for becoming a professional

In preparing to undertake the challenges of the next century, many people try to forecast what life will be like. The consensus of the forecasters is that learning will be considered a lifelong process and that more money will be spent on education. As an early childhood educator, you should be prepared to take your place in a world where learning is valued and respected. You should also be prepared to devote your career to continually learning new skills and gaining new knowledge.

Currently, there is a great deal of discussion about quality in early childhood programs. The quality of programs is directly related to the quality of the professionals in these programs. And as you will discover throughout this chapter, merely discussing quality is not sufficient—teachers and caregivers must involve themselves in activities that will promote quality in their lives and the lives of the children they teach and care for.

QUALITIES OF THE EARLY CHILDHOOD EDUCATOR

Anyone who has contemplated teaching has probably asked, "Am I the kind of person who is suited for teaching?" This is a difficult question to answer honestly. These are qualities early childhood teachers need: love and respect for children, caring, compassion, courtesy, dedication, empathy, enthusiasm, friendliness, helpfulness, honesty, intelligence, kindness, motivation, patience, sensitivity, trust, understanding, and warmth. Home and early school experiences are critical for developing these qualities. So if we want these qualities in our future teachers, we need to promote them *now*, in our teaching of young children. Toward that end, teachers might well concentrate on nurturing in themselves what is probably the most important of these characteristics: caring.

As a teacher, you will live and work in a classroom where things don't always go well; where children don't always learn ably and well; where children are not always clean and free from illness and hunger; where children's and parents' backgrounds and ways of life are different from yours. If you truly care, teaching is not easy. Caring means you will lose sleep trying to find a way to help a child learn to read, that you will spend your own money to buy materials, that you will spend long hours planning and gathering materials. Caring also means you will not leave your intelligence, enthusiasm, or talents outside the classroom, but will bring them into the classroom, principal's office, and school board meeting.

PREPARING FOR A CAREER IN EARLY CHILDHOOD EDUCATION

Teaching can be a greatly rewarding career for those who want it to be so. There are some things you can do to make your career happy and productive for both you and the children you will teach.

Go where the jobs are. Sometimes, a person locks herself into a particular geographic area or teaching field. Some areas may have an oversupply of teachers, while other areas, especially urban, have a chronic shortage of teachers and caregivers. These urban areas usually offer challenging and rewarding opportunities. There will always be a job for one who is willing to go where the jobs are.

Seek every opportunity for experiences with all kinds of children in all kinds of settings. Individuals often limit themselves to experiences in public school settings, but there are also opportunities through church schools, child care, baby-sitting, and children's clothing stores to broaden and expand your knowledge of children. These experiences can often be work-related and can be doubly rewarding. Sometimes these positions pay little or nothing, but be willing to volunteer your services, because volunteer positions have a way of leading to paid positions. Many career possibilities and opportunities can become available through the volunteer route. Before committing yourself to training for one teaching specialty, volunteer in at least three different areas of education to find out exactly what age and field of education you are most interested in. Do other volunteer work with children in activities such as recreation, social events, or scouting.

Honestly analyze your attitudes and feelings toward children. Do you really want to teach, or would you be happier in another field? During your experiences with children, you should constantly test your attitude toward teaching. If you decide that teaching isn't for you because of how you feel about children, then by all means don't teach.

Explore the possibilities for educational service in areas and fields other than the public school. Don't limit your career choices and alternatives because of your limited conception of the teacher's role. Students often think teacher education prepares an individual only to teach. Other opportunities for service include religious organiza-

Teaching can be a joyful experience for those who dedicate themselves to it. The profession demands, and young children deserve, the best of teachers and caregivers.

Volunteer activities give one a chance to expand one's vision of working with young children and to learn new skills. You should not hesitate to seek out appropriate volunteer activities as a way to enhance your personal and professional growth.

tions, federal, state, and local agencies, private educational enterprises, hospitals, libraries, and social work. Don't feel pressured to choose a major during your first year or two in college. Take a variety of electives that will help you in career choices, and talk to vocational counselors. Don't make up your mind too quickly about teaching a certain grade level or age range. Many teachers find out, much to their surprise, that the grade level they *thought* was best for them was not. You should remain flexible about a grade or subject level.

Employ every educational opportunity to enhance your training program and career. Through wise course selection, weaknesses can be strengthened and new alternatives explored. For example, if your program of studies requires a certain

Becoming a good teacher requires a lot of hard work and dedication. All who call themselves "teacher" must accept the challenges and responsibilities that are part of the title.

number of social science credits, use them to explore areas such as sociology and anthropology, which have fascinating relationships to education. Electives practicing teachers sometimes wish they had taken in college are typing, first aid, audiovisual aids and media, behavior modification/management, special education, creative writing, and arts and crafts. Of course, a teacher can never have too strong a background in child development.

Start now to develop a philosophy of education and teaching. Your philosophy should be based upon what you believe about children and the learning process, how you think children should be taught, and your present values. A philosophy of teaching serves as a guide for classroom practice. Many teachers fill the school day and children's lives with unrelated activities, without considering whether they match their objectives. So much of teaching is based on no philosophy at all. In fact, your philosophy may be the only guide to help you teach, for as surprising as it may seem, many schools operate without a written philosophy. Basing your teaching on a philosophy will make the difference between filling children's school days with unrelated activities or with activities directed toward helping them learn and develop to their fullest potential. As you develop your philosophy during preservice training, discuss it with friends, professors, and inservice teachers, and be willing to revise your philosophy as you gain new knowledge and insights. Developing a philosophy will not automatically make you a good teacher, but it will provide a foundation on which to build a good teaching career. (An added benefit of developing a philosophy is that it will help you respond well during a job interview.)

Examine your willingness to dedicate yourself to teaching. Acquaint yourself thoroughly with what teaching involves. Visit many different kinds of schools. Is the school atmosphere one in which you want to spend the rest of your life? Talk with many teachers to learn what is involved in teaching. Ask yourself, "Am I willing to work hard? Am I willing to give more time to teaching than a teaching contract may specify? Are teachers the kind of people with whom I want to work? Do I have the physical energy for teaching? Do I have the enthusiasm necessary for good teaching?"

As you enter the teaching profession, several other suggestions will help you find your career more productive and rewarding.

Adjust to the ever-emerging new careers of teaching and society. All careers are molded by the needs of society and the resources available. Many teachers and schools waste potential and miss opportunities because of their unwillingness to adjust to changing circumstances and conditions.

Be willing to improve your skills and increase your knowledge. Many teachers choose to do this by returning to school, which is usually encouraged by state cer-

AS I SEE IT*

I became a child-caregiver after working at Catholic Charities Day Care Center in Washington, D.C., as a summer youth employee in 1974. I enjoyed the job then and I still enjoy it now. What I like about my job is being able to watch children grow mentally, verbally, and physically and knowing that I have some part in their growth.

I think a good teacher is one who is willing to do anything to enhance learning. She should be creative, alert, and able to make learning fun and exciting. She should be able to give hugs and kisses as well as define limits. She should also have a good sense of humor. In day care the caregiver must be able to make a child feel comfortable enough to allow his mother to leave him. Once the child begins to trust you, he will also be willing to learn.

The most important thing about my job is keeping the children safe. There will always be little accidents in day care, like bumps on heads, bruised knees, and cut fingers. The staff must be alert enough to prevent any serious accidents.

A few things make me really mad about the policy makers for child care services. They look at caregivers as people whose role does not matter. There is so much disregard for how caregivers feel. Policy makers do very little to make one feel good about one's job. The pay is so low that many good caregivers must leave day care to survive and take care of their families. Sometimes I think all their talk about children being our greatest asset and making child care workers' pay more decent is so they can be comfortable with doing nothing.

My advice to others wanting to be caregivers is that when you work with young children, you must remember that children are people too, and you are their role model. Therefore, try not to do anything you are ashamed of in the presence of children, and always be conscious of your actions.

*Contributed by Linda Anthony, Toddler I teacher

tification requirements for permanent or continuing certification. Many teachers fulfill the requirements through a master's degree. A trend in teacher certification is to allow accumulation of a specified number of "points," gained through college credits, inservice programs, attendance at professional meetings and conferences, and other professional involvements.

Reading is one method of self-improvement; a less obvious method is to force change by periodically teaching at different grade levels. By changing grade levels, teachers gain new insights into and perspectives on children and teaching. Whatever method you choose for self-improvement, you should recognize the need for constant retraining. While some school districts do provide opportunities for retraining, most of the responsibility will be yours.

Be willing to try new things. Some new teachers get in a rut immediately upon entering the profession. They feel their college education has provided them with the one right way to teach children. This attitude results in a preconceived, fixed notion of what teaching is. These teachers become so preoccupied with fulfilling this image of good teaching that they seldom relax enough to try new ideas. Despite the number of new ideas and methods available, it is surprising how few the average

Becoming a good teacher begins with the initial commitment to the profession and continues throughout life. A good teacher constantly seeks to improve his or her skills.

GROWING FROM A STUDENT TO A PROFESSIONAL*

My first encounter with professionalism occurred as an undergraduate student at Stephen F. Austin State University in Nacogdoches, Texas. I majored in Child Development and Family Living because I enjoyed working with young children and wanted to understand their growth and development. A professor recommended that it was a good professional move to join the National Association for the Education of Young Children. She added that a resumé indicating professional involvement is often useful in interviewing. I joined, but never attended any meetings or functions.

After graduation, I moved to Denton, Texas, to attend graduate school at Texas Woman's University, again majoring in Child Development. While attending graduate school, I taught three- and four-year-old children at the Texas Woman's University Nursery School. The director of the nursery school, Mrs. Barbara Jackson—my supervisor, mentor, and friend—encouraged me to rejoin NAEYC. I joined, but again did not attend any functions the first year. The local affiliate, Denton AEYC, asked Mrs. Jackson to present her wonderful "Science for Preschool Children" session at the Spring Workshop. Mrs. Jackson asked me if I would help her. This was the beginning of my professional involvement! Little did I know what a beginning it was.

Aside from serving as support at the workshop (Mrs. Jackson really *did* everything), I also made the signs to label our activities. For the next workshop, Dr. Velma Schmidt and Dr.

Arminta Jacobson asked me to make signs because they liked the ones I had previously made. Who would have thought signmaking would be my ticket to professionalism? After becoming involved at this minimal level, I was asked to serve as a member of the "Workshop Planning" committee. I played a low-key role, primarily following the lead of others. The next year I was asked to serve as chairperson of the "Week of the Young Child" (WOYC) committee. The Week of the Young Child is designed to bring attention to the needs of young children.

Immediately after receiving my doctoral degree in Child Development, I moved to Austin, Texas, while my husband attended law school. In Austin, I taught at The Open Door, a mainstreaming preschool near the University of Texas. Almost immediately after I began teaching in the four-year-old class, the director, Jill Gronquist, encouraged me to join the Austin Association for the Education of Young Children (AAEYC) as cochair of the "Public Education and Speakers Bureau" committee. The next year, Jill resigned her office as vice president for community relations and asked that I fill her position. Intimidated by the responsibility, I nonetheless attended a summer board meeting. The board was a delightful group of preschool and child care professionals, and I slowly began to feel comfortable in the position. As fate would have it, a primary responsibility of the community relations vice presidency is to plan and implement the Week of the Young Child. Fortunately, Bibi Somyak, who teaches four-

teacher tries—although sometimes, trying something new may arouse opposition from your colleagues.

Be enthusiastic for teaching and in your teaching. Time and again the one attribute that seems to separate the good teacher from the mediocre is enthusiasm. Even if you weren't born with enthusiasm, *trying* to be enthusiastic will help a great deal.

Maintain an open-door policy in teaching. Welcome into your classroom parents, colleagues, college students, and all who want to know what schools and centers are doing. Teaching can be a lonely profession, but it need not be.

year-olds at First English Lutheran Child Development Center, beautifully orchestrated the first WOYC of my term. Writing WOYC information for inclusion in the AAEYC newsletter was essentially the extent of my involvement.

As the second Week of the Young Child during my vice presidency rolled around, the responsibility was mine. I was busy in a new position with the Internal Revenue Service. The IRS Austin Service Center and Compliance Center had been designated by the federal government to implement a model on-site child care center for the employees of the IRS, Department of Veteran Affairs, and the Department of the Treasury. With the assistance of many qualified professionals, I planned and implemented a program to serve 100 children between the ages of six weeks and six years. With the help of my friend Joanne Polasek, we planned and held a successful mall fair during the WOYC for Austin children and their families. We also held our annual "Parade to the Capitol," where youngsters and their parents and teachers march to the capitol and are entertained by children's musicians. At the capitol, a proclamation is read declaring the day as Texas Children's Day during the Week of the Young Child. The events are intended to emphasize to the community the needs of young children and receive local media coverage.

At the IRS, while simultaneously teaching child development at Austin Community College, I feel I accomplished significant professional growth. Through association with professionals such as Elizabeth Sears, director of The Open Door; Sandra Hamilton, department chairperson of child development at Austin Community College, and Gale Spear, a Bank Street College of Education graduate who is director of the Austin Community College Child Care Center as well as a college instructor at ACC, I learned about child advocacy and the importance of vocalizing concerns about quality child care. Through these associations, I have grown in my commitment to young children and to my profession. Such issues now influence my life greatly—whom I vote for, what type of program with which I am willing to be associated, keeping up with legislation that affects children and their families, and keeping up-to-date in our field's professional literature.

The road was long as I evolved into a committed professional but, to me personally, I feel it was worth the wait. Of course, all previous developments in my career affect my present functioning. I've learned a lot as I become increasingly involved in my field and look forward to learning and growing more, in the years to come.

*Contributed by Cindy Haralson, child development specialist, Dade County Public Schools

DEVELOPING A PHILOSOPHY OF EDUCATION

A philosophy of education is a set of beliefs about how children develop and learn and what and how they should be taught. Your philosophy of education will be quite personal. There may be similarities between your philosophy and that of another teacher, but what you believe is unique with you. You should not try to mold your philosophy to match another's; your philosophy should reflect your beliefs.

As we discussed earlier, your philosophy will guide and direct your daily teaching. Your beliefs about how children learn best will determine whether you individualize

TEACHERS OF THE YEAR

Linda S. Lentin, First Grade Teacher, Florida Teacher of the Year, 1989

I believe it is my duty and responsibility to convince my students that they are winners. I accomplish this by offering them a wide range of activities and experiences that are designed to make them more self-confident, more independent, and more responsible. This is not an easy task—it takes dedication, commitment, and elbow grease. But the rewards are so wonderful and special that all the hours spent in planning, conferring, creating, assessing, and reassessing are worthwhile!

I believe that play is a young child's work, and through the use of active hands-on activities, children can learn basic skills, physical and social sciences, art, music, and social skills. My classroom provides experiences in which each and every child achieves a degree of success. Organization is necessary to ensure a good match between the learner and the materials, and to provide an atmosphere in which child-initiated choices of activities will be effective for the learner. My classroom is a busy and businesslike place. My young learners are happily engrossed in their learning centers and groups. They are aware of the growth and learning that happens all around them, helping, supporting, and applauding each other. They truly care about one another! What better reward could any teacher have?

I believe excellent teachers view themselves as true professionals who must continuously update their skills. I have recently received a master's degree in Early Childhood Education, have become certified in Gifted Education, and I have taken several computer courses. I participate in our School-Based Management/Shared Decision-Making Program and serve on its Documentation Committee. It is truly exciting to be on the cutting edge of educational reform and to feel that teachers' ideas have a real impact on what happens throughout their schools.

I believe that a dedicated teacher involves parents and encourages and motivates them to play an active role in the education of their children. I am in close contact with parents and send home notes, reward certificates, and progress reports weekly. Working parents are grateful to have my home phone number and many important decisions are reached during a phone conference. Having been a working parent myself has made me more sensitive to the concerns and needs of working parents. Several parents volunteer in my classroom as "Math Moms" or "Reading Partners." These volunteers become staunch supporters of our school, its goals and programs. A videotape the children and I made of a school day is borrowed by families in the class and shows the importance and value of parental involvement.

It is my belief that a great teacher is flexible and open to new strategies and technology. I have embraced computers as a real asset to learning and have found them to be effective in teaching higher-level thinking skills. As part of my goal to make children independent and self-initiating, I have a child-operated "Tell a Story Place" where children use a tape recorder and dictate a story that is later written and displayed for the child to see and "read." Children and machines work together to enhance learning in activity centers throughout our classroom.

One thing that I believe with all my heart has not changed: a wonderful teacher is nurturing and loving. The most important component in any successful classroom is an attitude of caring and acceptance. I motivate—and, yes, even prod—my young students to strive for excellence, but I also create a climate in which it is all right to make mistakes. How else can they become self-reliant? Sincere praise is the keystone of my philosophy—it turns a small, dependent five-year-old child into a strong, secure, confident, curious "self-starter." This metamorphosis is the greatest reward of all!

Cathy Gust, Kindergarten Teacher, Pennsylvania Teacher of the Year, 1989

As a philosopher once said, "to teach is to touch a life forever." We teachers have an enormous responsibility to the next generation. It is our job to provide our most valuable resource with the best education possible. When I was a child, teachers gave me a sense of security, a desire to learn, and a feeling of self-worth. It is this memory that has helped define my philosophy of education as well as my desire to make learning as positive and as meaningful as possible for all children.

I certainly believe that for true learning to take place, children need to feel good about themselves. It is my responsibility to ensure that children meet success and feel special in the classroom every minute of the day. When children begin to believe in themselves and accept that we all make mistakes, they have unlimited potential. I think the most powerful words a young child can say is "I can do it!"

The learning environment needs to be driven by children not by curriculum. Early childhood educators need to evaluate what they know about children and their natural development and then plan curriculum that takes all of this into account. I think children at a young age need a language-rich environment filled with an integrated approach to reading, writing, math, and all other curricular areas. Children learn best by play, so this must be an integral part of every day. I see myself as a facilitator of an environment that is filled with age-appropriate activities in which children can interact, think, experience, and grow at a pace that is congruent with their own rate of development.

Teachers need to take pride in their role and never lose sight of why they teach. In education, there are no exact formulas to ensure student success, but it is within our power to reach out and truly make a difference in the lives of those we touch every day. It is critical to get to know the total child and to make a commitment to each and every child you have the opportunity to work with. Seeing children enjoy learning and feeling good about themselves is the most significant reward a teacher can receive. Children are our future and our hope for all our dreams of tomorrow.

Harriet Paul Jonquiere, Second Grade Teacher, New York Teacher of the Year, 1989

My personal beliefs about teaching and learning have evolved slowly over the years. They come from many sources. Each book I read, each class I attend, each new person I meet changes my thoughts a little. I am sure that, like most teachers, I will still be extending my thoughts about teaching and learning for many years to come.

I believe there is a developmental pattern to the acquisition of knowledge. It is the teacher's job to understand that pattern and how it affects the way each student learns. I recognize a hierarchy of thinking skills. The teacher should be aware of this hierarchy and constantly seek to bring each student's thinking to a higher level. I believe that language and thought are closely related. The teacher has an obligation to help all students use language well so they will be able to clearly express their thoughts and to acquire precise knowledge of the world.

It is the task of the teacher to stand between the known and the unknown. The teacher must see where the students are and lay the stepping stones to new knowledge surely and safely so

Continued.

TEACHERS OF THE YEAR—continued

that students come to trust themselves, their teachers, and the educational process.

I believe that when a student is having a problem, it is incumbent upon the teacher to question herself, her methods, and her organization, as well as the behavior of the student. It is the teacher's job to make students aware of the goals of each lesson and the steps they will take to accomplish those goals. In this way students gradually learn how to go about the process of acquiring new knowledge for themselves. I believe that students, parents, teachers and administrators working together can solve any educational problem. School staff should lead the way in establishing cordial, mutually supportive relations between the school and the home.

I believe there is a difference between right and wrong and that right consists of sharing, supporting, helping, building, and respecting. It is easy to list these, but it is hard, even for adults, to translate these fine generalities into action. By both word and example teachers should help students learn how to be kind and helpful to others and how to show respect for themselves, each other, and the adults who care for them.

I believe that all students are entitled to have teachers who care about them and who believe they can learn. All students have a right to have their race, religion, and ethnic background not only respected but honored. A healthy American classroom is one in which we glory in our diversity.

Andrea Rochelle Willis, Third Grade Teacher, Michigan Teacher of the Year, 1989

Twenty-four years ago, waiting for my first class of students to arrive, I asked myself two questions: Why was I there, and what did I expect to happen? The four-inch high letters, THINK, individually cut from neon-colored poster board, dominated the space above the front blackboard. Even then, to engage children

in the thinking process was one of my major goals. It never occurred to me to ask myself how I was going to accomplish this task. I just believed with all my heart that if I did a good job of teaching, "thinking" would take place.

I believe teaching is an ongoing learning experience. This ongoing process has given me the opportunity to grow as a person and as a teacher. Every setback, every disappointment, as well as each success has provided me with valuable insights and direction as I have pursued my career in education.

In planning for each year, I have never lost sight of the fact that the world is constantly changing. As educators we must prepare our students to accept these changes; we must give them the skills to face the challenges of tomorrow's world. For this reason we must be actively involved in the learning experience ourselves.

It is my desire to teach every child. Each child comes into the learning situation with a unique set of values, abilities, learning styles, and expectations. I recognize these differences and try to provide instruction by creating a nonthreatening environment that allows students the freedom to explore their own creative resources.

I place a great deal of emphasis on self-growth through self-awareness activities to thus build self-esteem. Through group interaction and hands-on activities, I try to provide students with new opportunities and experiences whenever possible. Through creative problem-solving activities, we learn to appreciate that there are many "right" answers to any given problem.

I am constantly changing, questioning, and searching for answers. I want my students to develop a love of learning and the ability to question. I want them to be able to evaluate their own growth in terms of their feelings and emotions. By guiding them in group involvement situations, I hope to teach them peaceful and humane ways of dealing with conflict, ways and ideas they can carry with them throughout their lifetimes.

I believe in failure as a positive force. We learn from our mistakes. Failure is a negative only if you allow it to stop you from growing. If we reassess each failure and deal with it in terms of learning, we can often turn situations around and come out winners in the end. This is a skill I hope to pass on to my students. It is not enough today to merely teach facts; children need to know how to survive in all situations.

I worry about peer pressure and substance abuse. I think we have to equip our students with the ability to think and make decisions. If we value individuality, perhaps our students will not be afraid to say "no," or to be different and follow their own convictions rather than go along with the crowd.

I set high standards and goals for myself and my students. In doing so I hope to enable each student to reach his or her highest potential. I don't pretend to know all the answers, and I'm still asking myself the same questions I did as a first-year teacher. I do know that I believe in education as the most positive force in our society today.

I take pride in being able to say that I seldom do the same thing twice in the classroom. That is not to say that I haven't taught the same concepts over again or repeated favorite activities. It just seems that each time I do something, it becomes a new and different experience. I enjoy that variety and freshness—it keeps me on my toes and keeps the "spark" in the classroom.

Through the years, in addition to enrichment activities, I've developed several programs that I feel are unique to my classroom. I follow the basic curriculum adopted by the district and supplement it often with activities that give youngsters new opportunities. Sometimes these activities may lead youngsters into discovering hidden personal talents.

I try to instill a sense of independent thinking in each child I come in contact with. I know that you cannot separate parts of a child into neat little compartments of academic, social, physical, and emotional growth. You must deal with the whole child. I consider myself a holistic teacher who puts as much value and emphasis on the affective domain as on the cognitive domain. I have never been afraid to march to a different drummer, and I don't want my students to be afraid to be individuals, either. One of the greatest things I can teach children is to think for themselves and to have confidence in their own abilities. I was shown how to live this way, and I think I have an obligation to give others the same chance.

Gail C. Hartman, Third Grade Teacher, New Mexico Teacher of the Year, 1989

I cannot recall a time when I did not want to be a teacher. My mother was a creative elementary school teacher who used motivational techniques to encourage her three daughters to learn. She was extraordinarily good at encouraging us to be imaginative in amusing ourselves and solving problems. From her I learned the teacher's indispensable skills of improvising teaching aids, decorations, and equipment from the materials at hand. My father was a civil engineer who loved learning and had a natural gift for teaching. My parents developed in us a sense that learning was not only useful, but one of life's great pleasures.

As a church school teacher during high school and as a summer recreation director at a local playground, I came to know that I belonged in the classroom. In college, my part-time job as a library aide in the elementary training school on the campus put me in regular contact with children, and I have found working with children a gratifying career ever since.

Most of my teaching experience has been in kindergarten, though over the last twenty-five
Continued.

TEACHERS OF THE YEAR—continued

years I have taught kindergarten through third grades. I feel that my greatest accomplishment has probably been to make the introduction to education for at least 500 five-year-olds an exciting, creative, positive experience. I believe that attitude toward learning is the most significant factor in determining success or failure in education. Consequently, I work hard at providing a stimulating, nonthreatening environment where children can develop a positive attitude toward themselves as lifelong learners.

If "variety is the spice of life," then my teaching career has been well seasoned. I have taught in classroom situations and as a tutor working one-on-one with children with learning disabilities. I have taught in localities as far apart as New York, Louisiana, and New Mexico. My teaching positions have been in rural communities where children traveled forty miles from isolated ranches to get to school; to multicultural, bilingual neighborhoods in metropolitan areas; in areas of affluence and of poverty; in private and public schools. I have taught in schools equipped with the latest in computer technology and in a classroom crudely converted from an athletic locker room, where equipment and materials were literally nonexistent.

Each position challenged me to adapt methods and materials to the needs of the children in my care. The philosophy I developed as a result of these varied experiences can be stated simply: to accept children exactly the way they come to me, and to move them along in their total development at a pace that is challenging and exciting but not stressful. I hope to develop in children a thirst for learning—not just learning to read, but reading to learn. I hope to give them the will and the skills to be all they can be, to help them find their special talents, and then to challenge them to have the courage to develop those talents.

The rewards I receive from teaching are many: the mental stimulation of working in a profession that grows and changes daily, the relationships that are established with co-workers and parents, the lifelong friendships with students, the affection I receive from children, and the freedom I have to be creative and innovative. But none of these compares to the reward one receives from watching children grow, not only in knowledge and the ability to think and make critical decisions, but also in confidence and self-esteem as they realize they are special in this world—and knowing I had a part in developing that growth.

Edna Loveday, Kindergarten Teacher, Tennessee Teacher of the Year, 1989
Through the years of firsthand experiences at home and at school, my philosophy of education has become my purpose for being. My personal family experiences have been an education in themselves. My husband and I are fortunate to have adopted four children—two adopted as infants and two as older children. Comparing the advantages of the two children who were adopted very young and received good early training against the disadvantages of the two who missed an early sound foundation, I can say I know the real importance of providing a solid education early in life. I have truly seen firsthand the problems that result from poor early childhood experiences and have learned that once a personality is set, it is hard to recapture what has been missed. Those first years set the pattern and foundation that will follow the child throughout the growing years.

My philosophy of education is grounded in my belief that the early years in a child's life are the most important. I believe it is my respon-sibility as a teacher to nurture the child, encourage and promote a good self-concept, and expose him or her to a love of learning that will last a lifetime.

My profession, teaching, is an exciting adventure! This adventure is a never-ending process. I am committed to teaching because I believe there is a desire to grow and a desire to learn in every young child. There is nothing more exciting than to watch the sparkle in the eyes of a young child as new discoveries are made. Teachers hold the future in their hands. One cannot be a teacher and not feel total commitment when faced with such a challenge as this.

The challenge is to help each young child become the very best he or she is capable of becoming. Each child is an individual—an individual who is important, unique, and of great value. Each child has unique needs and abilities. Each child has the right to be addressed as an individual to the extent possible within the limits of the classroom setting. It is my responsibility to see that these needs are met by creating stimulating learning environments that encourage and motivate the child to reach his or her highest potential. This can happen only through a commitment to good planning and preparation for the individual needs of all children—children with normal abilities, special abilities, and disabilities.

To live up to such a commitment means a continual reevaluation of myself and my growth as well as that of my children. I must constantly remind myself of children's individuality. I must not let myself be caught in daily patterns, expecting individuals to behave like robots. I must stop periodically, not only to observe and evaluate the children, but to assess myself as well.

I believe that early childhood is the most important period of a child's intellectual development. I am challenged to make this time of their lives successful and to provide early educational experiences that are exciting, stimulating, and rewarding. During this time, it is vital for the child to build a positive self-concept and to develop a positive attitude toward learning. The child must also learn to face disappointments, overcome them, and use them as positive growth experiences. Education *must*

reach the total child with that "extra something" that makes learning a stimulating challenge, a wanted compulsion, and a joy. To achieve this goal, learning must involve the total child. Education must promote social, emotional, and intellectual growth.

Nothing has given me more strength and determination to succeed in teaching than my fellow teachers. There is nothing like the tremendous collegial support system among faculty members that can inspire you during difficult times and give you instant encouragement to start again. What better lessons can be learned than those taught from the expertise of one teacher and shared with another? This sharing of gifts and exchange of ideas among teachers only contributes to the educational growth of the student.

We, as teachers, plant small seeds of hope in each student. These seeds enable students to achieve life's full potential as individuals develop, mature, and blossom into full growth, serving the community as well as the world. Only then is our effort successful. But to achieve this success, we must expect it.

We ask ourselves why things happen as they do in our lives. I firmly believe my philosophy of education is built on the why of my life. All families have special joys and heartaches, and our family's life experiences have been no exception. Because our two younger children received such poor educational foundations during their early childhood, I am constantly reminded of how important this time in life is to each of my five-year-old students. Each day I feel a tremendous responsibility to use every available opportunity, event, or advantage to give each one a good beginning in education. All children must develop a good self-concept, a positive attitude toward school, and a lifelong love of learning that will continue to influence their lives as they grow into responsible, happy children and adults.

instruction or try to teach the same thing to everyone in the same way. Your philosophy will determine whether you help children do things for themselves or whether you do things for them. These are some ways to go about developing your philosophy:

☐ Read widely in textbooks, journals, and other professional literature to get ideas and points of view. A word of caution: when people refer to philosophies of education, they often think only of the historical influences; this is only part of the information available for writing a philosophy. Make sure you explore contemporary ideas as well, for these will also have a strong influence on you as a teacher and caregiver.

☐ If you have not written your philosophy, these headings will help you get started:

I believe the purposes of education are . . .

I believe that children learn best when they are taught under certain conditions and in certain ways. Some of these are . . .

The curriculum of any classroom should include certain "basics" that contribute to children's social, emotional, intellectual, and physical development. These basics are . . .

Children learn best in an environment that promotes learning. Some of the features of a good learning environment are . . .

All children have certain needs that must be met if they are to grow and learn at their best. Some of these basic needs are . . . . I would meet these needs these ways . . .

A teacher should have certain qualities and behave in certain ways. Qualities I think important for teaching are . . .

☐ Have other people read your philosophy. This helps you clarify your ideas and redefine your thoughts, because your philosophy should be understandable to others. (They don't necessarily have to agree with you.)

☐ Talk with successful teachers and other educators. (The accounts that follow are evidence that a philosophy can help one become an above-average teacher.) Talking with others exposes you to others' points of view and stimulates thinking.

☐ Evaluate your philosophy against this checklist:

Does it accurately relate my beliefs about teaching? Have I been honest with myself?

Is it understandable to me and others?

Does it provide practical guidance for teaching?

Are my ideas consistent with each other?

Does what I believe make good sense?

Have I been comprehensive and stated my beliefs about:

How children learn

What children should be taught

How children should be taught

The conditions under which children learn best

The qualities of a good teacher

BECOMING A PROFESSIONAL

Becoming a professional means you will participate in training and education beyond the minimum needed for your present position. You will also want to consider your career objectives and the qualifications you might need for positions of increasing responsibility. The National Academy of Early Childhood Programs specifies staff qualifications and training appropriate for positions in early childhood programs that you should review to determine how they apply to your career and life goals (Table 15–1).

A Good Teacher: A Lesson from History

It is worthwhile looking at the history of early childhood education for ideas about good teachers; in fact, we need look no further than Froebel, father of the kindergarten:

> I understand it thus. She [the mother] says, "I bring my child—take care of it, as *I* would do"; or "Do with my child what is right to do"; or "Do it better than I am able to do it." A silent agreement is made between the parents and you, the teacher; the child is passed from hand to hand, from heart to heart. What else *can* you do but be a mother to the little one, for the hour, morning or day when you have the sacred charge of a young soul? In hope and trust the child is brought to you, and you have to show yourself worthy of the confidence which is placed in your skill, your experience and your knowledge.[1].

TABLE 15–1   Staff Qualifications and Development

Title	Level of Professional Responsibility	Training Requirements
Early childhood teacher assistant	Preprofessionals who implement program activities under direct supervision of professional staff	High school graduate or equivalent, participation in professional development programs
Early childhood associate teacher	Professionals who independently implement program activities and may be responsible for care and education of a group of children	CDA credential or associate degree in Early Childhood Education/Child Development
Early childhood teacher	Professionals who are responsible for care and education of a group of children	Baccalaureate degree in Early Childhood Education/Child Development
Early childhood specialist	Professionals who supervise and train staff, design curriculum, and/or administer programs	Baccalaureate degree in Early Childhood Education/Child Development; at least three years of full-time teaching experience with young children and/or graduate degree in ECE/CD

Source: From *Accreditation Criteria and Procedures* of the National Academy of Early Childhood Programs, Washington, D.C. (1984), pp. 18–20.

A Good Teacher from the Parents' Viewpoint

In our discussion of becoming a good teacher, we could consider what the public thinks teachers should be. These are reasonable expectations:

1. Parents should expect teachers to teach their children.
2. Parents want well-planned lessons and a well-organized curriculum.
3. Parents want evidence of learning.
4. Parents want children to have an interesting school day.
5. Parents want teachers to be well-educated, literate, and well-spoken.
6. Parents want teachers who care about kids.
7. Parents want teachers to be adults of civility, maturity, and character.
8. Parents think powerful teachers' unions should use some of their muscle to weed out incompetents.[2]

A professional person is an ethical one, and fortunately, we have a set of ethical standards to guide our thinking and behavior. Developed by Evangeline Ward, these standards are both a guide and a challenge.

A Good Teacher from the Profession's Perspective

As an early childhood educator you will want to be a good teacher as judged by the profession. The National Association for the Education of Young Children has developed both a statement of commitment and a Code of Ethical Conduct (Appendix D). This is the Statement of Commitment:

As an individual who works with young children, I commit myself to furthering the values of early childhood education as they are reflected in the NAEYC Code of Ethical Conduct. To the best of my ability I will:

☐ Ensure that programs for young children are based on current knowledge of child development and early childhood education.
☐ Respect and support families in their task of nurturing children.
☐ Respect colleagues in early childhood education and support them in maintaining the NAEYC Code of Ethical Conduct.
☐ Serve as an advocate for children, their families and their teachers in community and society.
☐ Maintain high standards of professional conduct.
☐ Recognize how personal values, opinions, and biases can affect professional judgment.
☐ Be open to new ideas and be willing to learn from the suggestions of others.
☐ Continue to learn, grow, and contribute as a professional.
☐ Honor the ideals and principles of the NAEYC Code of Ethical Conduct.[3]

Preamble

As an educator of young children in their years of greatest vulnerability, I, to the best of intent and ability, shall devote myself to the following commitments and act to support them.

For the child

I shall accord the respect due each child as a human being from birth on.

I shall recognize the unique potentials to be fulfilled within each child.

I shall provide access to differing opinions and views inherent in every person, subject, or thing encountered as the child grows.

I shall recognize the child's right to ask questions about the unknowns that exist in the present so the answers (which may be within the child's capacity to discover) may be forthcoming eventually.

I shall protect and extend the child's physical well-being, emotional stability, mental capacities, and social acceptability.

For the parents and family members

I shall accord each child's parents and family members respect for the responsibilities they carry.

By no deliberate action on my part will the child be held accountable for the incidental meeting of his or her parents and the attendant lodging of the child's destiny with relatives and siblings.

Recognizing the continuing nature of familial strength as support for the growing child, I shall maintain objectivity with regard to what I perceive as family weaknesses.

Maintaining family value systems and pride in cultural-ethnic choices or variations will supersede any attempts I might inadvertently or otherwise make to impose my values.

Because advocacy on behalf of children always requires that someone cares about or is strongly motivated by a sense of fairness and intervenes on behalf of children in relation to those services and institutions that impinge on their lives, I shall support family strength.

For myself and the early childhood profession

Admitting my biases is the first evidence of my willingness to become a conscious professional.

Knowing my capacity to continue to learn throughout life, I shall vigorously pursue knowledge about contemporary developments in early education by informal and formal means.

My role with young children demands an awareness of new knowledge that emerges from varied disciplines and the responsibility to use such knowledge.

Recognizing the limitation I bring to knowing intimately the ethical-cultural value systems of the multicultural American way of life, I shall actively seek the understanding and acceptance of the chosen ways of others to assist them educationally in meeting each child's needs for his or her unknown future impact on society.

Working with other adults and parents to maximize my strengths and theirs, both personally and professionally, I shall provide a model to demonstrate to young children how adults can create an improved way of living and learning through planned cooperation.

The encouragement of language development with young children will never exceed the boundaries of propriety or violate the confidence and trust of a child or that child's family.

I shall share my professional skills, information, and talents to enhance early education for young children wherever they are.

I shall cooperate with other persons and organizations to promote programs for children and families that improve their opportunities to utilize and enhance their uniqueness and strength.

I shall ensure that individually different styles of learning are meshed compatibly with individually different styles of teaching to help all people grow and learn well—this applies to adults learning to be teachers as well as to children.[4]

FUTURE OF TEACHING

What does the future hold for early childhood teachers? As early childhood education changes, the changes will affect teachers as well as children.

Professionalization of Teaching

We will see a stronger movement toward professionalizing teaching. Professionalization of teaching is part of the national effort to improve education. The public recognizes, albeit belatedly, that real and lasting changes in education will occur when teachers are trained as professionals and treated as professionals. The emphasis on professionalism will require teachers to assume more responsibility for their own behavior and their professional development.

Intensifying Teacher Training.   We will see an intensification of teacher training as professionalism demands higher levels of competence. A bachelor's degree may become a five-year program. Early childhood teachers and child care workers will probably have to take additional training through the CDA, inservice training, or college-related courses. Early childhood educators will be challenged and often required to demonstrate professionalism through courses, workshops, and certificate programs.

Minimum Standards for Teaching.   There is a trend toward requiring teacher college graduates to pass minimum basic skills tests before they receive a teaching certificate. Testing for teacher certification is a direct result of the accountability movement, the back-to-basics movement, and the reaction against grade inflation and "soft" or "easy" education courses. Some state tests include items for assessing basic teaching and literacy skills. Critics of education contend that it only makes sense to require teachers to demonstrate that they know the skills we expect them to teach young children.

Closely associated with the testing movement in teacher education is the fifth-year training concept. Teacher training programs find it difficult to provide all the experiences a teacher needs in a four-year program; consequently, five- and six-year training programs are being developed. The fifth year may take place at the college or university, or in a school district as a probationary period. In some programs, the fifth year may result in a master's degree, so people who choose teaching as a career can expect to spend more time learning how to become a good teacher.

Current Changes in Teacher Education

The Demise of Education as a Major.   There is growing pressure from state departments of education, professional groups, and public policymakers to require education colleges to eliminate or greatly reduce the number of education courses at the undergraduate level. In fact, legislation in Texas limits to 15 the number of credit hours an education major can take at the undergraduate level. These kinds of regulations and restrictions are usually made by people who see little value in education courses; they assume that if you know your content area, you can teach it. How much calculus a first grade teacher needs to know is not usually addressed. Nonetheless, efforts to limit education courses will likely continue.

Changing Clientele.   Early childhood programs will begin to serve different types of children in different ways. For example, as a result of P.L. 94-142 and P.L. 99-457, there are more young handicapped children, birth to age five, in programs designed to meet their and their families' needs. This means new programs will be developed and teachers will be trained or retrained to provide appropriate services.

Likewise, the gifted child will receive more attention, which also means retraining teachers and developing new programs. In addition, as we have seen, the extension of preschool programs downward to include younger children will continue. In fact, ten years from now, there will be many new careers in education that will involve working with children and families.

Expanded Teacher Role. A higher degree of professionalism will bring greater responsibility and decision making. The role of the teacher will continue to be conceptualized. Teachers will be trained to work with parents, design curriculum materials, plan programs for paraprofessionals, and work cooperatively with community agencies. Many schools currently operate a system of differentiated staffing and employ teachers and aides with differing role functions, levels of responsibility, training, and salary. Also, as the currently popular school-based management movement grows, more teachers will be involved in decisions about how schools operate and how and what children will learn.

Differentiated staffing will be accompanied by differentiated teaching. There will be closer attention to different learning styles. Greater attention to learning styles will also involve greater use of concrete learning materials, self-selected activities, and use of students as tutors.

Teaching and Community Agencies

Teaching is an integral part of the broader range of human services and helping professions. The sharp lines that have traditionally separated social work, the health professions, and education are gradually blurring; however, members of all three professions are often reluctant to admit that the other professionals can provide meaningful services that complement their own. There is also a trend toward resolving social problems through interdisciplinary programs, to which each profession contributes its particular expertise.

FURTHER READING

Adler, Mortimer J. *The Paideia Proposal: An Educational Manifesto* (New York: Macmillan, 1982)

A call to improve public and basic education; advocates the same course of study and quality education for everyone. (*Paideia* comes from the Greek, meaning "upbringing children.")

Jorde, Paula. *Avoiding Burnout: Strategies for Managing Time, Space and People in Early Childhood Education* (Washington, D.C.: Acropolis Books, 1982)

For early childhood educators who want to manage their total lives.

Kelly, James L., and Mary Jean Kelly, eds. *The Successful Elementary Teacher* (Lanham, Md.: University Press of America, 1985)

For and about beginning teachers, these essays include intellectual development, motivation, humanizing the classroom, mainstreaming, multicultural education, classroom management, characteristics of good teachers, and classroom environment.

Kidder, Tracy. *Among Schoolchildren* (Boston: Houghton-Mifflin, 1989)

This best-selling and highly acclaimed book traces a year in the life of Chris Zajac, an elementary teacher in Holyoke, Mass. The reader shares Ms. Zajac's successes and failures as she teaches her ethnically mixed fifth grade class consisting of many recent Puerto Rican immigrants.

Kohl, Herbert. *Growing Minds: On Becoming a Teacher* (New York: Harper and Row, 1984)

Practical, professional guide for growing into the profession of teaching; thesis is that, regardless of individual's motivations for entering the profession, one still has to learn how to become a good teacher. Author believes competence is acquired through careful and steady effort, self-growth, and experience.

Macrorie, Ken. *Twenty Teachers* (New York: Oxford University Press, 1984)

Told by the teachers themselves, accounts of philosophies of teaching, how they teach, why and how their students do good work.

Williamson, Bonnie. *A First Year Teacher's Guidebook for Success* (Sacramento, Calif.: Dynamic Teaching, 1988)

A useful reference book for beginning and experienced teachers. A good way to help a new teacher get started and for other teachers to get and stay organized.

FURTHER STUDY

1. How important are the classroom teacher's character and attitude to children's healthy growth during their primary years? Explain.
2. Recall the primary teachers who taught you. List which characteristics you would imitate and which you would try to avoid as a teacher.
3. Some educators believe teachers are born, not made. Interview public school teachers and college professors to determine their opinions about this belief.
4. To teach young children, do you think teachers must be trained specifically in early childhood education?
5. For what specific roles do you think early childhood teachers should be educated?
6. Reflecting on your years in the primary grades, what experiences do you consider most meaningful? Why? Would these experiences be valid learning experiences for children today?
7. As a class, brainstorm and compile a list of competencies for early childhood teachers that are (1) generic, that is, applicable to all teaching; and (2) specific for early childhood education. Have professors of education and inservice teachers respond to your list.
8. Talk with other professionals about careers that relate to children and parents. How did they come to their jobs? Is there evidence that they planned for these careers? Do you think you would enjoy an alternative career in education? Why or why not?
9. List advantages and disadvantages of being an early childhood teacher. How will you overcome the disadvantages and capitalize on the advantages?
10. Share your philosophy of education with your classmates. Have them critique it for comprehensiveness, clarity, and meaning.
11. With your classmates, practice interviewing for a job. Develop a list of questions a job interviewer might ask. A good way to gather questions is to interview principals and find out what they ask. You might also want to practice your simulated interview with closed-circuit television so you can evaluate your performance.
12. Videotape yourself teaching a small group of children. You can take this videotape to job interviews as evidence of your teaching abilities.
13. List the reasons you have decided to go into teaching. Share and compare the list with your classmates. What conclusions can you draw from the lists?
14. After reading the accounts of Teachers of the Year, what impressed you most about their accounts? What outstanding qualities do these teachers demonstrate? Why were they able to become Teachers of the Year?
15. List four reasons you decided to become a teacher/caregiver, and rank them in order of importance.
16. List five ways early childhood professionals encourage others to become teachers and caregivers.
17. How can professionals ensure that those who are not committed and dedicated do not enter the profession?
18. List ten characteristics and qualities of an early childhood professional.
19. How can early childhood teachers help "professionalize" the field?
20. How must the training of teachers and caregivers change to meet the changing needs of children, families, and society?

NOTES

1. Friedrich Froebel, *Mother's Songs, Games, and Stories* (New York: Arno Press, 1976), pp. xxxiii.

2. Francis Roberts, "The Ideal Teacher," *Parents* (December 1984), pp. 42-44. Copyright © 1985 Gruner & Jahr USA Publishing. Reprinted from *Parents* Magazine by permission.

3. Stephanie Feeney and Kenneth Kipnis, "A New Code of Ethics for Early Childhood Educators!" *Young Children*, 45 (1989), p. 29.

4. Reprinted by permission from E. Ward, "A Code of Ethics: The Hallmark of a Profession," in L.G. Katz and E.H. Ward, *Ethical Behavior in Early Childhood Education*, pp.20-21. Copyright © 1978, National Association for the Education of Young Children, 1834 Connecticut Ave. N.W., Washington, D.C., 20009.

CHAPTER 16
Future Trends in Early Childhood Education
Where Do We Go From Here?

As you read and study:
- ☐ Define *trend* and explain why trends occur.
- ☐ Explain why it is important for early childhood professionals to know about trends.
- ☐ Identify trends in early childhood education.
- ☐ Identify the sources of and reasons for trends in early childhood education.
- ☐ Tell what significance trends have for learning, teaching, and caregiving in the early years.
- ☐ Predict possible future trends in early childhood education.

Humans have never been content with the present; they have always wanted to know what is going to happen in the future—whether that future is a few hours, a few days, or a few years away. Those who claim to be able to tell the future are given special recognition by peers and press. Modern society abounds with those whose job or pastime it is to predict future events. From weather forecasters to stock market forecasters, from palm readers to horoscope hot lines, from groundhogs on February 2nd to media personalities, everyone wants insight into what the future holds.

Early childhood educators are no different. They too are interested in and concerned about *trends*, current tendencies that influence the direction of future policy and practice. Some trends are more important than others and will significantly influence how things are done in the future. Others are fashionable for a time—a year or two or less—and are soon forgotten in the public's attention to other trends. We can identify trends by reading national newspapers, popular magazines, and professional journals. Clues to the trends in the field of early childhood are all around us. They are apparent in public policy, legislation, and the public interest. Indeed, a long-established trend, which is so ingrained in the public perception that it can hardly be called a trend anymore, is society's fascination for and interest in the field of early childhood education.

You should not be surprised that trends are rather easily discernible in the popular media, for trends are a reflection of the interests, problems, concerns, and issues of society. It should not come as a surprise, either, for example, that as society becomes more concerned about and involved in the "war on drugs," the public schools and early childhood programs would be asked to assist through activities, curricula, and education. Likewise, as more women enter the workplace, it is only natural that issues relating to the care of infants and toddlers should demand our attention.

WHY ARE TRENDS IMPORTANT?

Although we may at first think that knowing about the future is of little importance, future trends involve a great deal of serious business. There are a number of reasons for early childhood educators to know about future trends in the field.

First, as we have seen, trends are "signs of the times," and as such, they highlight the conditions and concerns of society and what society desires for parents, families, and children, Trends thus point the way for future practice. Second, since trends guide future actions, they enable us as early childhood educators to be involved in shaping and defining the programs and policies that will help address the problems, issues, and concerns of society. We are thus able to be major participants in shaping the future. We literally become part of the solution. Third, as we participate in the resolution of society's concerns, we are also able to participate in shaping the profession's response to these issues. We become involved in the education and socialization of the nation's children in such a way that they will be able to live more productive and meaningful lives.

THE NATURE OF TRENDS

A particular trend may not be—and probably is not—separate and distinct from other trends. From one social issue or concern, many trends emerge and parallel each

Early childhood educators must keep up with the trends in their profession and fill the needs of children who will live the longest part of their lives in the 21st century. Old ways were—generally—good for old times, but we need new ways for new times.

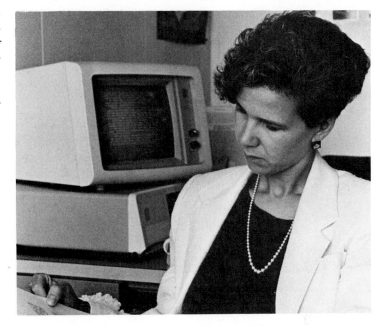

other. For example, changes in the modern American family spawned many trends, such as the need for the infant child care, which in turn helped set in motion our current interest in and fascination for infants, infant development, and infant care. Women's rights and abortion issues have been a major cause for interest in prenatal development and legal issues relating to abortion and fetal rights.

Some trends may seem to contradict each other. For instance, it is likely that as business and industry continue to bemoan the lack of basic skills by high school graduates, pressure will continue on all levels of education from preschool to high school for more emphasis on teaching basic skills. At the same time, early childhood educators will increase their efforts to implement developmentally appropriate curricula that run counter to many of the practices supported by basic-skills advocates.

CURRENT TRENDS AND THEIR SIGNIFICANCE

The following are trends that have important implications for early childhood educators as well as for young children, parents, and families.

Trends Relating to the Care and Education of Children

Trend: Corporate Involvement in Early Childhood Programs. Boardroom directors across the country are interested in babies and all children from the early years through high school. This interest is primarily economic and is based on the philosophy of the Investments in the Future outlined in Chapter 1. Corporations are concerned about the quality of their future work forces. Corporate America is shaken by the bleak prospects of a shrinking pool of skilled workers. As a result, businesses are starting now to invest in their own futures by investing in the futures of the nation's

495

children. Entry-level job skills in business and industry are becoming more sophisticated, and many high school drop-outs are finding themselves left in the dust by their more skilled peers who graduate from high school and technical school. A stark reality of the '90s is that the number of unskilled jobs at which a high school drop-out can be successful is decreasing all the time. Figure 16–1 shows the amount of education that children of today will need to hold the jobs of tomorrow.

New Jersey has a coalition of business groups called "Invest in Children," designed to improve the health and education of the state's youth. The state and businesses have also joined forces to free mothers from welfare. Known as *Reach*—Realizing Economic Achievement—the program provides help for all welfare recipients without children under the age of two in getting a job or enrolling in school or job training programs. South Carolina recently passed a bill called "Target 2000: School Reform for the Next Decade." The bill was passed with the cooperation and support of the state's businesses. The legislation went a step further, however, by mandating the involvement of business in education through the Business Education Partnership, which also includes civic, legislative, and education leaders. In Connecticut, the state and Connecticut Mutual Life Insurance Company joined forces in a "Drugs Don't Work" program to emphasize drug prevention in the public schools. Many programs

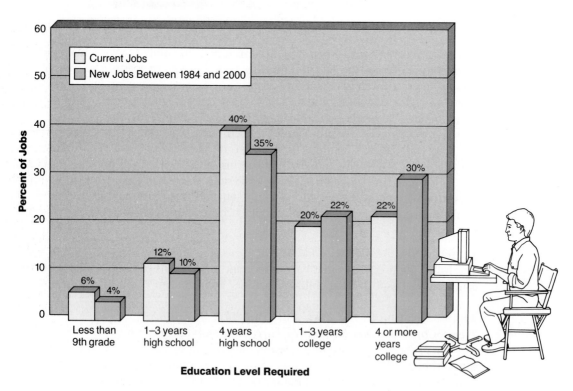

FIGURE 16–1   Amount of Education Children of Today Will Need to Hold Tomorrow's Jobs (Source: Adapted from Hudson Institute, Inc., *Workforce 2000: Work and Workers for the 21st Century,* 1987.)
Note: Totals exceed 100% due to rounding.

similar to these can be found in most states and are becoming commonplace rather than a curiosity.

You may wonder what job training for welfare mothers and drug prevention programs have to do with early childhood education. The answer is straightforward: many problems of early adolescence, such as drug use and delinquency, have roots in the early years. With foresight, businesses are joining with legislators and educators to combat those obstacles that keep America's youth from developing or learning the skills they need to be gainfully employed.

Trend: Federal Involvement in Funding Child Care Programs and in Setting Standards for Child Care.   Federal involvement in child care initiatives is apparent in a number of ways. First is federal legislation, such as the Act for Better Child Care (ABC), P.L. 99-457, relating to special needs children, and others mentioned in previous chapters. Federal involvement will continue to grow, especially as it relates to providing affordable and accessible child care for children. Funding for these initiatives will more than likely be conducted by allocating federal money to the 50 states.

Trends Relating to Professionals and the Profession

Trend: The Legitimizing and Justification of the Developmentally Appropriate Curriculum.   Although the terms *developmentally appropriate* and *developmentally appropriate curriculum* have appeared in the literature for some time, it was not until about 1985 that early childhood educators began to use them as a focus for discussions about what constitutes the best for young children. There were and still are a number of problems regarding the use of developmentally appropriate practices.

As businesses become more involved in early childhood programs, educators must be prepared to provide specific ideas and sound rationales to justify their support.

ABIG LEARNING CENTER—A SATELLITE OF THE DADE COUNTY PUBLIC SCHOOLS

The 73 students in grades K–2 at ABIG Learning Center may not know they are making history, but they are helping write it. They are participating in some of the most interesting and significant events in the current restructuring of American public schools. They are the first students to attend the first satellite learning center in the U.S. operated by a public school system at a worksite for children of employees. ABIG Learning Center in Dade County, Florida, opened on August 28, 1987—the leader in a current wave of innovative programs and monetary support of the public schools by corporate America. ABIG Learning Center is located on the grounds of the 1300-employee international headquarters of American Bankers Insurance Group. A school at a worksite. What a revolutionary idea! As you would expect, a lot of shared responsibility is necessary to make such a unique project work. Both parties are responsible for contributing certain things. American Bankers provides:

☐ A learning facility on corporate property that meets all state and local building and health codes (the 6000-square-foot facility has three classrooms, resource center, conference room, offices, clinic, and an open assembly area; the center cost $375,000 to construct)
☐ Maintenance of the learning center (estimated at $60,000 a year)
☐ All custodial services
☐ All utilities
☐ Building security (there is an alarm system and monitoring by remote television)
☐ Transportation of the children (parents bring their children to the learning center on the way to work and pick them up after work; the worksite is about a quarter of a mile from the learning center)

The Dade County School System provides:

☐ Three teachers for the three classes—kindergarten, a K-1 combination, and a 1-2 combination
☐ Staff, including teachers' aides and cafeteria workers (breakfast and lunch are brought from a nearby elementary school)
☐ Support services and personnel, including a speech clinician, a special education teacher, a teacher for hearing impaired, and specialists in Spanish, physical education, art, and music
☐ Library and media supplies and services
☐ Classroom furniture and learning materials
☐ Classroom supplies and other materials and equipment normally found in the district's elementary schools (a copier, computers [11], and a television set in each room)

This joint venture offers numerous advantages to all parties involved. For American Bankers, these are some of the advantages:

☐ Providing a major fringe benefit to their parent-employees
☐ A means for attracting and recruiting employees
☐ A means of encouraging employee-parent retention
☐ Reduction of employee absenteeism and tardiness
☐ Enhanced morale of employee-parents

First, the general public and many early childhood educators don't know what "developmentally appropriate" means. To many, the term is nothing more than a catchphrase without meaning. Consequently, it is terminology that is used much, but practiced little. Second, early childhood educators have been slow to educate the public to the meaning of the term. Furthermore, some professionals have been impatient with those who don't understand the meaning of the concept. Third, early childhood educators have been slow to implement the concepts inherent in *developmentally appropriate* into a *developmentally appropriate curriculum*. They have

☐ Opportunity to participate in school and community education

☐ Opportunity to directly and positively influence and enhance the skills of the future work force

The advantages to the Dade County Public Schools for participating in ventures such as the satellite learning center are numerous and significant:

☐ An opportunity to participate in and promote school/business partnerships

☐ Direct reduction of capital cost outlay for a new school facility

☐ Relief from overcrowding in the schools (approximately 60,000 *new* students enter the Dade County Public Schools each year)

☐ Assistance in meeting the district's integration goals, since the population of the learning center reflects the integration of the worksite

☐ Community goodwill

☐ Significant parent involvement

☐ Positive local, state, national, and international publicity

Parents also benefit in many ways:

☐ The convenience of being able to bring their children to school at their worksite (in essence, parents have no school transportation problems)

☐ The "comfort" and "peace of mind" that comes from having their children close to their worksite

☐ Freedom from baby-sitting, before and after school child care, and latchkey worries (the learning center is open from 7:00 A.M. to 8:15 P.M.)

☐ Additional time to spend with their children on the way to and from work

☐ The convenience and satisfaction of greater and more accessible parent involvement (there is daily parent-teacher contact; in addition, parents with flexible schedules help chaperon field trips, and some parents use their lunchtime to come to the center)

The children also benefit in many ways:

☐ A small, intimate learning center

☐ An extended family environment and attitude (many of the children have been together since they entered the corporate child care center at six weeks of age, and there is a pronounced neighborhood atmosphere at the learning center)

☐ Increased time spent with their parents

Center director Roberta Keiser is enthusiastic about what she and her staff are accomplishing. As she says, "We are addressing the contemporary needs of parents and children, especially the single parent. Society is changing, so why shouldn't the schools keep up with the needs of society?" This blending of work, education, and family is certainly a wave of the future, and other corporations and school districts throughout the country are climbing on the bandwagon of cooperative working relationships through innovative programs.

paid lip service to the concept but have not implemented it in practice. Now, however, early childhood educators are spending more time and energy explaining to the general public and their colleagues what it means in practical terms and to develop and implement practices that are developmentally and individually appropriate for young children.

Trend: A Return to the Child-Centered Curriculum. The attempts by professional organizations and early childhood educators to explain and implement developmen-

EMPLOYMENT HAS ITS BENEFITS

At the American Express operations center in Plantation, Florida, employment has its benefits. These include:

- ☐ Up to 12 weeks of unpaid leave for a new mother or to care for a family member
- ☐ A child-care referral center, including information on at least three day care centers at a requested price range
- ☐ Reduced cost for nursery care at Pembroke Pines Hospital when a sick child can't attend the regular day care center
- ☐ Prenatal programs on nutrition and exercise
- ☐ Discount programs with certain child care providers

- ☐ A cooperative program with the Broward, Florida, YMCA for group rates at summer camps; children are picked up at the work-site and returned at the end of the day
- ☐ A Back-to-School Program with local school merchants who provide special shopping times exclusively for American Express employees at a 10 percent discount
- ☐ A "Mommy-Daddy and Me" program, an on-site program conducted cooperatively with Broward County Community College
- ☐ An around-the-clock operation, American Express has 17 work schedules, thus allowing employees to adjust their work schedules to fit family needs

tally appropriate curricula and programs will also hasten and promote a return to child-centered programs and practices. While there will continue to be an emphasis on basic skills, the basic-skills orientation will be more mindful of the whole child. This trend is mildly evident in the efforts of some parents and professionals to delay some children's entrance into kindergarten because of lack of readiness. The trend is also evident in the growth of prekindergartens and pre-first-grade programs.

Trend: A Better, More Integrated Definition and Reconceptualization of What Constitutes Early Childhood and Early Childhood Education. Just as early childhood educators increase their efforts to explain the developmentally appropriate curriculum, so will they also increase efforts to define through practice the meaning of *early childhood education.* One current meaning is an integration of the *care* and *education* of young children. Increasingly, child care programs are becoming educational programs as well—and this is as it should be. Rather than distinguishing between the two, it will be assumed that when children are receiving care, they will be educated as well.

Trend: Involvement of Early Childhood Educators with Community Agencies. Early childhood professionals will of necessity become more involved with community and other agencies that can assist them in providing a broad range of services to all children and their families. Teachers and caregivers will have to develop skills at working and cooperating with community agency personnel, learn what agencies are available in their community and what services they provide, and how to link parents and children to these services. Clearly, early childhood educators and others cannot do it all, nor do they have the skills, knowledge, and resources to deal with the full range of problems confronting many contemporary children and families.

The trends toward child-centered and developmentally appropriate curricula call for educators to conduct programs that make these concepts realities.

Trend: Allocation of Additional Time to the Teaching/Learning Process. American educators have always been infatuated with the prospect of solving educational problems through the use of time. For many, time cures all things—including poor achievement and the ability to read and write well. In their search for solutions, educators are quick to see additional time spent in school—longer school days and more time devoted to individual subjects—as quick, easy, and long-term solutions to educational problems.

Extending the "more time" principle to educational issues, educational planners and policymakers are suggesting that schools undertake programs such as year-round school (the 180-day school year is now almost a thing of the past), Saturday schools, longer school days (often designed to accommodate parents' work schedules), and summer schools. These are already realities in many school districts, and many features will become standard in the majority of the nation's school systems in the future. Let us look at one of the options more closely.

Trends Relating to Parents, Families, and the Community

Trend: Community and Parent Involvement in the Public Schools and Early Childhood Programs. Each of Chicago's 600 schools will have an elected council of ten people—six parents, two community residents with no children in the school, and two teachers. The council will be headed by a parent. In a sense, Chicago is turning over the running of its schools to parents!

SATURDAY SCHOOL

Saturday school. Are you kidding? What child would shun Saturday morning cartoons for reading, writing, and arithmetic? As a matter of fact, quite a few! For some children, Saturday school is a routine part of their schedule. Consider the inner-city children at Charles R. Drew Elementary School in Liberty City, Florida. About 400 children attend class from 9:15 A.M. to 11:45 A.M. The curriculum provides a variety of enrichment activities. In a relaxed classroom atmosphere, students practice skills learned throughout the week. Teachers have freedom to develop and refine their teaching styles while trying out new materials and methods.

According to principal Fred Morley, "The students from our school who attend Saturday school do much better on achievement tests than those children of a similar mental ability who choose to stay home and watch cartoons."

Although the idea of children attending Saturday school may sound incredible and futuristic, it is not. It is a part of the trend toward providing more opportunities and time for teachers and children to spend in the learning environment.

Trends Relating to the Prenatal Period and Infancy

Trend: Increasing Interest in the Prenatal Period.   More procedures will be developed to help and protect the developing fetus in the psychosocial, legal, and medical areas. These are some of the areas that are becoming the focus of public attention:

Prenatal diagnosis. Ultrasound, amniocentesis, and other forms of prenatal diagnosis are now almost routine parts of efforts to assess prenatal development. The numbers and kinds of procedures for diagnosing prenatal development will continue to increase.

Prenatal surgery. A frequent outcome of prenatal diagnosis is intervention of some kind. Prenatal surgery is now a reality, and the use of such procedures to correct prenatal problems will become routine.

Legal rights of the fetus. Fetal advocates and legal agencies are testing the current boundaries of the rights of a fetus especially as related to parents' rights.

Environmental factors, particularly maternal nutrition and drug use that adversely affect fetal development.

How to benefit and/or change the course of fetal psychological development. More professionals are convinced that working and counseling with parents before and during pregnancy enhance infants' opportunities for development.

Trend: Greater Emphasis on Learning and Development in Infancy.   Infant stimulation programs will continue to be popular. Early childhood educators will also broaden their examination and discussion of what programs and practices are and are not good for infants in the context of the developmentally appropriate curriculum.

Trend: More Interest in and Programs for Intervention Services at Earlier Ages.   Early childhood educators have always been aware that intervention in the early years can help children and their families overcome problems associated with

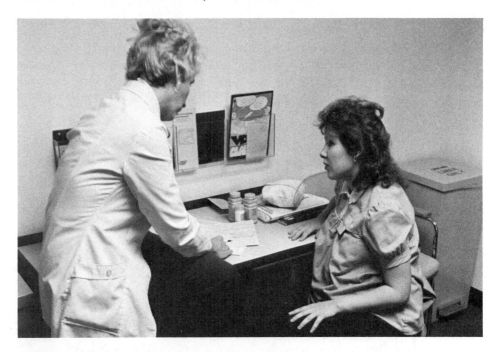

The field of early childhood education is expanding to include the prenatal period.

environmental constraints and deprivations. This was one of the reasons for initiating Head Start. Now, early childhood professionals place more emphasis on identifying the early causes of later developmental and behavioral problems and are seeking ways to intervene to create the family, parenting, and other conditions that prevent, insofar as possible, the conditions that lead to later deficits. One example is the field of infant psychiatry, a purpose of which is to provide for intervention services.

> In a psychiatric assessment of infants, clinicians aim to obtain a data base that allows them to come to a diagnostic understanding of both infants and the people who care for them. The information clinicians obtain should also allow them to say something about the likely future course of any condition at hand and help them in planning appropriate and specific interventions.[1]

Furthermore, researchers are now able to identify many of the early root causes of later delinquent behavior and drug use. For example, in a longitudinal study of the personality and psychosocial correlates of drug use, one group of researchers conclude that:

> Among girls and boys, personality characteristics are identifiable at an early age (3–4 years) that persist over time and are conducive to later involvement with drugs. No important differences were observed, at these earlier ages, between the path to later marijuana use and the path to later hard drug use. For both sexes, the constellation of personality characteristics encompassed by the concept of ego undercontrol (inability to delay gratification, rapid tempo, emotional expressiveness, mood lability, overactivity, etc.) correlationally foretold later drug use.[2]

The researchers go on to recommend that:

> . . . current, social policies seeking to prevent drug use must be broadened. Without discounting current emphasis on the importance of "saying no" to drug-encouraging peers, it may also be worthwhile to support intervention efforts that seek to change early behaviors likely to place the child/adolescent at risk for drug use. Having established a connection between early personality characteristics and later substance use, we can now attempt to undo that condition.[3]

If the early years are critical to later life and learning and if early behavior and personality characteristics are precursors to undesirable and antisocial behavior, then it makes sense to provide intervention programs that will address the root causes responsible for influencing young children's behaviors. Intervention strategies, in order to be effective, must target at least four areas.

1. *Teacher training.* Early childhood educators and caregivers must be trained to identify early behaviors that can lead to later problems. Furthermore, and perhaps more importantly, all who work with young children must sincerely want to help children in whom they identify undesirable attributes and behavior.

Because the roots of later behavior can often be detected in early childhood, teachers and caregivers must learn to identify these causes and design programs and curricula that will avert the behaviors or lessen their impact.

Seeing problems and doing nothing about them is an injustice to children, their parents and families, and society. Teachers can be guilty of malpractice too.

2. *Curriculum development.* Identifying problems in young children is not enough—early childhood educators and caregivers must intervene in some ways. But simply intervening is not sufficient; intervention must occur in the right ways. For intervention to be effective, teachers need a curriculum and support services from school personnel and community agencies. One challenge of the present and future is for early childhood professionals to develop the curricula necessary to help children in all areas, not just in those of basic skills.

3. *Parent training, education, and involvement.* Many of the environmental and social conditions that lay the foundation for later life problems result from parenting patterns and family interactions. Parents need knowledge and skills that will enable them to help their children grow and develop appropriately. As outlined in Chapter 13, working with parents is a necessary role for all who work with children and families.

Trend: Public School Programs as Providers of Services to Three- and Four-Year-Old Children

The role of the public schools as providers of services to four-year-old children will increase. Involvement will include providing for all at-risk children and those not at risk as well. In fact, the public schools will begin to include three-year-old children in their services. Into the next century, public schools will make more initiatives to provide programs for all children, beginning at birth.

Expansion of before- and after-school care programs. This public school trend is already apparent and will be fueled by the constant increase of single parents and women in the work force.

More Head Start programs operated by the public schools. This trend will be especially pronounced as the push continues to identify and provide services for disadvantaged young.

More programs for teenage parents and their children. Efforts will continue to provide more programs for student/parents so they can finish their high school educations.

More services for three-year-old children and their parents. A logical outgrowth of providing services to four-year-old children is to begin to provide them also to three-year-olds.

Trend: Shifting Resources from the Elderly to the Young.
Over the past decade there has been tension between advocates for the elderly and advocates of the young and disadvantaged arising from allocation of resources. In fact, the elderly as a group have been criticized for taking away from children resources such as money and services. No one doubts the legitimate needs of both groups. The American population is growing older, and many elderly lack the resources to obtain adequate health care. Some have to literally declare bankruptcy to become eligible for federal aid. Yet older Americans are viewed through another prism, that of the social critics who see this relatively wealthy group selfishly taking for themselves and ignoring needy children.

Such critics portray a country of haves—wealthy older adults—and have-nots—the poor children of America. Child advocates are quick to point out that one in five children lives in poverty and it is time that children receive their fair share of the country's benefits. More and more members of Congress and others who influence spending and legislation are listening. How well they listen and the impact this listening will have on future programs for children remains to be seen.

Trend: The Increasing Minorities—America's Future Population.   America has always been a country of minorities. What is happening, however, is that two minority groups, blacks and Hispanics, are rapidly becoming the majority. By the year 2030, the proportion of all children who are minority (projected from 1985 data) will increase from 28 percent to 41 percent![4] Some urban areas already have "majority" minority populations. For example, in the school district of Dade County, Florida, 56 percent of students are Hispanic, 32 percent black, and 22 percent white. As we look into the window of the twenty-first century, we see a completely changed picture of what many feel America is today.

In this picture we see three minority groups growing in numbers—the elderly, blacks, and Hispanics, in that order. How we prepare to meet the needs of these groups is very much a part of the anticipating and the excitement with which we prepare for the next century. Early childhood educators will continue to play a leading role in shaping the future. To do so effectively and to confront the shape of things to come, one imperative will be for all early childhood professionals to determine the multiculturally appropriateness of the developmentally appropriate curriculum.

As the public and its leaders become more aware of the impact of the early years on later development, and as parents continue to press for additional benefits, we will eventually see a national policy of family support.

One positive indicator of meeting the needs of the growing minority populations is that we are beginning to see more intergenerational child care programs. A large segment of the staff in these programs is made up of older citizens (usually over age 55), and there is greater emphasis on the needs of the community at large.

Still, we have a long way to go in meeting the needs of blacks and Hispanics. Many feel that the federal government must play a larger role in continued funding of programs (see Chapter 1). Others feel these concerns need to be met by the individual states.

By analyzing the data in Figures 16–2 and 16–3, we can certainly recognize the continued growth in the number of minority children and project the impact it will have on the young work force of the future.

Trend: The Development of a National Family Policy.   This nation does not have a coordinated or comprehensive policy of family support. But this omission is slowly

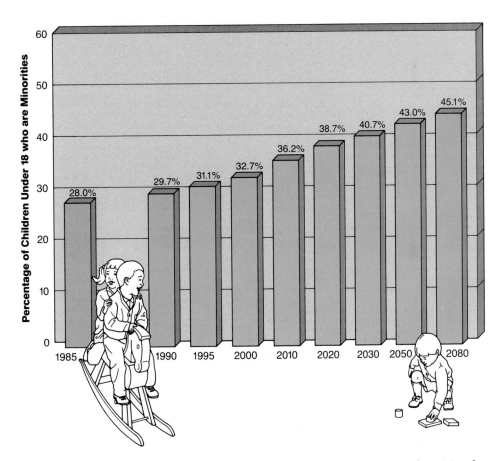

FIGURE 16–2   Minority Children in the U.S. (Source: Children's Defense Fund, *A Vision for America's Future: An Agenda for the 1990s* [Washington, D.C.: 1989], p. 116.)

LONGFELLOW ELEMENTARY SCHOOL FOR THE VISUAL AND PERFORMING ARTS—KANSAS CITY, MISSOURI

An excellent example of restructuring at work in the early childhood arena is Longfellow Elementary School in Kansas City, Missouri, a magnet school for the visual and performing arts. Yvonne Hatfield's 22 kindergartners engage in an all-day program of basic skill instruction and drama, dance, music, and movement. Visual arts include such things as painting, sketching, modeling with clay, photography, and creative writing and the performing arts include music, theater, and dance.

Drama plays a significant role in the curriculum and life of the kindergarten classroom. As Yvonne explains, "Drama and the other performing arts give children exposure to and experience with topics and people they would not otherwise have. Drama is in many ways a mirror of real life events. I use drama to help children learn many important skills, concepts, and values. Drama is also a natural way of helping children learn through their bodies."

Yvonne gives these examples of drama activities in her kindergarten. "One of my groups reads in their basal reader a story of the rabbit and the hare. After the reading, the children acted out the story, and we emphasized expression and how the human voice—their voices—sounds in certain situations. Also, during Black History Month in February, the children did a "Readers Theatre" of the Rosa Parks Story. One group read the story and another group acted out the events. The children had a lot of fun getting ready. They made bus-stop signs, designed and made costumes of out clothing from the Salvation Army, and made a bus out of cardboard boxes with chairs for seats. I revised an existing script for the children and worked with the parents of the children who had reading parts. It was a great learning activity!"

Yvonne teaches readiness skills, reading (many of the children are reading at a first grade level or above by the end of the school year), math, social studies, science, writing, and creative movement—all integrated with drama. Support teachers provide instruction in art, music, physical education, computers, and Suzuki violin.

"I integrate academics into everything I do," explains Yvonne. "The visual and performing arts give children experiences to build their

changing; it may well be that within the next decade a national policy will be in place, either in whole or in part. What would such a family policy include? The keystone will undoubtedly be a comprehensive program of federally supported affordable and quality child care. Other components could include the following:

Provisions for maternity leave following the birth of infants or the adoption of children as well as paternity leave.

Support for two-career and single-parent families. Such support could be in the form of child care referral services, parenting programs to assist in positive parenting and help with parenting problems; counseling services aimed at the resolution of family and marital problems; and support during relocation.

Flexible benefits that would enable the family to select from a range of benefit options (such as child care, family counseling, and medical benefits).

Flexible employee work schedules that enable parents to adjust their work schedules to child care and family needs.

academics on! The arts also give children a chance to appreciate their self-worth at many levels and in different ways. Take, for example, a child like Alex, who struggles in reading. He really excels in dance. The experiences of being good in this area are a great benefit to him."

A number of important activities support the curriculum and make the kindergarten program unique.

Artist-in-Residence Program

The school district has an artist-in-residence program through which artists come into the school and classrooms to perform and teach. For example, a local, well-known puppeteer gave a performance, then taught the children about puppets. He worked with the children in making puppets and helped them give a performance with their puppets. In this way, a specific art activity is integrated into the curriculum and daily classroom activities.

Field Trips

The kindergarten children go three times a month to various performing arts functions.

These include trips to the ballet, symphony orchestra, plays, and other performances throughout the Kansas City area. Following the field trips, children's experiences are integrated into the curriculum. For example, after a trip to the zoo, some children may create an art product and others may choose to write about the experience.

Community support for the Longfellow Magnet School is strong. According to Dee Davis, coordinator, early childhood, for the Kansas City Public Schools, "Families are enthusiastic about schools of choice for their children. They want and like to make choices on behalf of their children. Parents feel children do better in school when they study what interests them most."

The curriculum of the kindergarten program, with its focus on song and dance, is in many ways reminiscent of that supported by Froebel and other great educators. It is also significant that a school named for one of America's most celebrated poets—Henry Wadsworth Longfellow—should be involved in promoting learning through the arts.

Trend: Restructuring the Public Schools. Across America, state and local school districts are restructuring their schools. *Restructuring*, or making over and redesigning how schools operate, is popular for a number of reasons. First is the universal and persistent public dissatisfaction with the schools' poor performance in properly preparing their graduates. Second, society continually looks to the public schools for help in addressing and solving societal problems. The public is tired of the continuing failure of old solutions. Society wants new solutions to what are perceived as threats to civilization—problems of drug abuse and crime. Educational planners and public school personnel recognize that radical and innovative solutions are the order of the day.

Third, restructuring is also seen as a way of integrating the schools. *Magnet* schools, designed to attract students of all races and cultures from all over a district or attendance area, are but one example of using schools and their curricula to desegregate.

Restructuring is apparent in many of the new schools and programs that are a part of the ever-changing educational landscape. Early childhood programs are in the forefront of many of these restructuring innovations.

FIGURE 16–3   Young Minorities in the Work Force (Source: Children's Defense Fund, *A Vision for America's Future: An Agenda for the 1990s* [Washington, D.C.: 1989], p. 117.)

WHERE DO WE GO FROM HERE?

Changes in the public's attitude and changes and development in public policy are usually not radical or sudden. Changes in the nature, context, and intent of early childhood programs do not occur within the blink of an eye. What policies and programs exist today are the result of all our past years of efforts to improve the quality of early childhood programs for young children and their parents. Likewise, what early childhood programs will be like in the future and the nature of public policy toward young children and families will be the culminating effect of policies, programs, and attitudes that are in effect now.

FURTHER READING

Children's Defense Fund. *A Vision for America's Future. An Agenda for the 1990s: A Children's Defense Budget* (Washington, D.C.: Children's Defense Fund, 1989)

Provides startling and significant statistics regarding the state of America's children. Most important, it outlines not only the condition of American children, but also what early childhood educators—and all of society—can do to improve the lives and futures of the nation's children. Must reading for all early childhood professionals.

Olmstead, Patricia P., and David P. Weikart. *How Nations Serve Young Children: Profiles of Child Care and Education in 14 Countries* (Ypsilanti, Mich.: High/Scope Press, 1989)

Fourteen profiles written by researchers in developed and developing countries that give fascinating accounts of historical traditions, national attitudes, and political and economic realities influencing each country's policies toward care and education for young children.

Tobin, Joseph J., and David Y.H. Wu. *Preschool in Three Cultures* (New Haven, Conn.: Yale University Press, 1989)

A study of preschools in three cultures—Japanese, Chinese, and American. Many early childhood educators may find that what they thought were universal practices are not so universal after all.

FURTHER STUDY

1. Interview early childhood professionals in your area to determine what they see as trends in child care, child development, parent involvement, parenting, and preschool programs.
2. Critique the trends in this chapter. What trends do you believe will be integrated and accepted parts of the early childhood field? Identify trends in your area that were not discussed.
3. Find evidence in your community of how corporations and businesses are becoming involved in early childhood and other educational programs. Would you consider this involvement significant?
4. Sometimes you hear the term "maternity backlash" to describe the friction between employed women and their employers over benefits relating to children and families. Interview working mothers to determine what benefits they have and what benefits they feel they should have.
5. Prepare a short presentation for your classmates or a parent group in which you explain, with examples, the concept and implementation of the developmentally appropriate curriculum in an infant child care center.
6. Explain the concept of "child-centered" as you would to a parent.
7. Compile a directory of community agencies in your area that you believe teachers could use to help children and parents. Include the services the agencies provide and how they would meet specific needs.
8. Visit a program that provides services to pregnant teenagers or to teenage mothers and their children. What is the nature of the services, and how are they helping the people for whom they are intended?
9. Read a national newspaper such as *The New York Times* for two weeks and determine: (a) Is there evidence to support trends reported in this chapter? (b) Are any new trends evident? (c) Among children, parents, families, and the elderly, which group receives the most attention?
10. Do you think it is reasonable for the public to expect early childhood professionals to help solve and prevent societal problems? Why or why not?
11. Visit early childhood, preschool, and elementary school programs and identify curricula specifically designed to prevent present or future behavioral problems. How effective do the programs appear to be?
12. Why is there more interest in the prenatal period? Do you think it is appropriate and justifiable for the prenatal period to be included in the field of early childhood education? Why?
13. Visit public preschool programs in your area. What is the focus of their curricula? Why are the public schools becoming more involved in preschool programs? Do you approve of such programs? Why or why not? Do you think that public schools will become involved in programs for infants and toddlers?
14. Find examples from newspapers, journals, and television for a shift in resources from the elderly to the young. Do you agree with this shift? Will the shift be a lasting one? Are there enough resources for both the young and the elderly?

NOTES

1. Klaus Minde and Regina Minde, *Infant Psychiatry: An Introductory Textbook* (Beverly Hills, Calif.: Sage Publications, 1986), p. 53.

2. Jack Block, Jeanne H. Block, and Susan Keyes, "Longitudinally Foretelling Drug Usage in Adolescence: Early Childhood Personality and Environmental Precursors," *Child Development*, 59 (1988), p. 350. © The Society for Research in Child Development

3. Block, Block, and Keyes, p. 353. © The Society for Research in Child Development

4. Children's Defense Fund, *A Vision of America's Future* (Washington, D.C.: CDF, 1989), p. 116.

APPENDIX A
CDA Competency Goals and Functional Areas*

COMPETENCY GOALS	FUNCTIONAL AREAS
I. To establish and maintain a safe, healthy learning environment	1. Safe: Candidate provides a safe environment to prevent and reduce injuries.
	2. Healthy: Candidate promotes good health and nutrition and provides an environment that contributes to the prevention of illness.
	3. Learning Environment: Candidate uses space, relationships, materials, and routines as resources for constructing an interesting, secure, and enjoyable environment that encourages play, exploration and learning.
II. To advance physical and intellectual competence	4. Physical: Candidate provides a variety of equipment, activities, and opportunities to promote the physical development of children.
	5. Cognitive: Candidate provides activities and opportunities that encourage curiosity, exploration, and problem solving appropriate to the developmental levels and learning styles of children.
	6. Communication: Candidate actively communicates with children and provides opportunities for support for children to acquire, and use, verbal and nonverbal means of communicating thoughts and feelings.

*Source: From *CDA Professional Preparation Program: Essentials for Child Development Associates,* copyright 1989, The Council for Early Childhood Professional Recognition.

COMPETENCY GOALS	FUNCTIONAL AREAS
	7. Creative: Candidate provides opportunities that stimulate children to play with sound, rhythm, language, materials, space, and ideas in individual ways and to express their creative abilities.
III. To support social and emotional development and provide positive guidance	8. Self: Candidate provides physical and emotional development and emotional security for each child and helps each child to know, accept, and take pride in himself or herself and to develop a sense of independence.
	9. Social: Candidate helps each child feel accepted in the group, helps children learn to communicate and get along with others, and encourages feelings of empathy and mutual respect among children and adults.
	10. Guidance: Candidate provides a supportive environment in which children can begin to learn and practice appropriate and acceptable behaviors as individuals and as a group.
IV. To establish positive and productive relationships with families	11. Families: Candidate maintains an open, friendly, and cooperative relationship with each child's family, encourages their involvement in the program, and supports the child's relationship with his or her family.
V. To ensure a well-run, purposeful program responsive to participant needs	12. Program Management: Candidate is a manager who uses all available resources to ensure an effective operation. The Candidate is a competent organizer, planner, record keeper, communicator, and a cooperative co-worker.
VI. To maintain a commitment to professionalism	13. Professionalism: Candidate makes decisions based on knowledge of early childhood theories and practices, promotes quality in child care services, and takes advantage of opportunities to improve competence, both for personal and professional growth and for the benefit of children and families.

APPENDIX B
The Key Experiences
Sensorimotor, Preschool, and Kindergarten*

Piaget's sensorimotor period generally refers to the first 18-24 months of life.

Active Learning

☐ Exploring actively and with all senses
☐ Discovering relationships among self and objects through direct experience (by doing)
☐ Using the large muscles: crawling, walking, climbing
☐ Imitating the actions of others
☐ Using the small muscles: grabbing, pointing, feeding self

Language

☐ Listening to sounds, voices, and words
☐ Imitating sounds, voices, and words
☐ Recognizing sounds, voices, and words
☐ Identifying what is happening
☐ Identifying pictures, photographs, and models

Representation

☐ Learning about object permanence (An object continues to exist if it is partially visible or completely hidden.)
☐ Learning about object constancy (Certain aspects of objects do not change even though the objects seem different under different circumstances, e.g., when their position in space is changed or when they are perceived through senses other than sight.)
☐ Imitating the actions of others
☐ Exploring art materials (e.g., scribbling, using blobs of paint, attempting to make a circle)
☐ Using one object to stand for another
☐ Building models (e.g., making a simple tower with one or two blocks)

Classification

☐ Investigating the attributes of objects
☐ Noticing how things are the same, or different

*The Key Experiences © are copyrighted by the High/Scope Educational Research Foundation.

□ Noticing the color, sizes, and shapes of things

□ Noticing how things go together (e.g., ball goes with toys; cow goes with animals)

Seriation

□ Beginning to compare sizes: big/little; qualities heavy/light; quantities: more/less

□ Enumerating (counting) objects, as well as counting by rote

Temporal Relations

□ Developing awareness of beginnings and endings of time intervals: start/stop; morning/night

□ Developing awareness of the ordering of events: first, last, next

□ Developing awareness that within time periods there are different lengths of time: long time/short time

Spatial Relations

□ Body awareness/body concepts; parts of the body and what they can do; feelings

□ Learning to locate objects within environment

□ Position of self and object: on/off; in/out

□ Direction of self and objects: up/down; forward/backward

□ Distance between self and objects: near/far

□ Observing objects and people from different perspectives

PRESCHOOL KEY EXPERIENCES

From the assumption that active learning is at the heart of the developmental process, and with the description from Piaget's theory of the most important cognitive characteristics of "preoperational" children, we have derived approximately fifty "key experiences" to serve as guideposts for planning and evaluating developmentally valid programs for young children.

Key Experiences in Active Learning

□ Exploring actively with all the senses

□ Discovering relationships through direct experience

□ Manipulating, transforming, and combining materials

□ Choosing materials, activities, and purposes

□ Acquiring skills with tools and equipment

□ Using the large muscles

□ Taking care of one's own needs

Key Experiences in Using Language

□ Talking with others about personally meaningful experiences

□ Describing objects, events, and relationships

□ Expressing feelings in words

□ Having one's own spoken language written down by an adult and read back

□ Having fun with language: rhyming, making up stories, listening to poems and stories

Key Experiences in Representing Experiences and Ideas

□ Recognizing objects by sound, touch, taste, and smell

□ Imitating actions

□ Relating pictures, photographs, and models to real places and things

□ Role playing, pretending

□ Making models out of clay, blocks, etc.

□ Drawing and painting

Key Experiences in Developing Logical Reasoning

Classification

□ Investigating and labeling the attributes of things

□ Noticing and describing how things are the same and how they are different

□ Sorting and matching

☐ Using and describing something in several different ways

☐ Describing what characteristics something does not possess or what class it does not belong to

☐ Holding more than one attribute in mind at a time. (Example: Can you find something that is red and made of wood?)

☐ Distinguishing between "some" and "all"

Seriation

☐ Comparing: Which one is bigger (smaller), heavier (lighter), rougher (smoother), louder (softer), harder (softer), longer (shorter), taller (shorter), wider (narrower), sharper, darker, etc.

☐ Arranging several things in order along some dimension and describing the relationships (the longest one, the shortest one, etc.)

Number Concepts

☐ Comparing number and amount: more/ less, same amount; more/fewer, same number

☐ Comparing the number of items in two sets by matching them up in one-to-one correspondence. (Example: are there as many crackers as there are children?)

☐ Enumerating (counting) objects, as well as counting by rote

Key Experiences in Understanding Time and Space

Spatial Relationships

☐ Fitting things together and taking them apart

☐ Rearranging a set of objects or one object in space (folding, twisting, stretching, stacking, tying) and observing the spatial transformations

☐ Observing things and places from different spatial viewpoints

☐ Experiencing and describing the positions of things in relation to each other (e.g., in the middle, on the side of, on, off, on top of, over, above)

☐ Experiencing and describing the direction of movement of things and people (to, from, into, out of, toward, away from)

☐ Experiencing and describing relative distances among things and locations (close, near, far, next to, apart, together)

☐ Experiencing and representing one's own body: how it is structured, what various body parts can do

☐ Learning to locate things in the classroom, school, and neighborhood

☐ Interpreting representations of spatial relations in drawings and pictures

☐ Distinguishing and describing shapes

Time

Planning and completing what one has planned

☐ Describing and representing past events

☐ Anticipating future events verbally and by making appropriate preparations

☐ Starting and stopping an action on signal

☐ Noticing, describing, and representing the order of events

☐ Experiencing and describing different rates of movement

☐ Using conventional time units when talking about past and future events (morning, yesterday, hour, etc.)

☐ Comparing time periods (short, long; new, old; young, old; a little while, a long time)

☐ Observing that clocks and calendars are used to mark the passage of time

☐ Observing seasonal changes

KINDERGARTEN KEY EXPERIENCES

From the assumption that active learning is at the heart of the developmental process and with the description from Piaget's theory of the most important cognitive characteristic of "preoperational" children, we have developed some "key experiences" to serve as guideposts for planning and evaluating developmentally valid classroom activities for young children. They are concepts and experiences to develop logical thinking and reasoning abilities as well as academic skills.

The following key experiences have been found to support learning and development in the Cognitively Oriented Curriculum (and are designed to match the developmental capacities of children between the ages of four and six). There are general types of activities and processes which broaden and strengthen children's emerging abilities.

Active Learning

- ☐ Exploring actively the attributes and functions of materials with all the senses.
- ☐ Discovering relations through direct experience.
- ☐ Manipulating, transforming, and combining materials.
- ☐ Identifying personal interests by choosing materials, activities, and purposes.
- ☐ Acquiring skills with tools and equipment.
- ☐ Using small and large muscles.
- ☐ Taking care of one's own needs.
- ☐ Predicting problems and devising ways of solving them.

Speaking and Listening to Language

- ☐ Talking with others about personally meaningful experiences.
- ☐ Describing relations among objects, people, events, and ideas.
- ☐ Talking with others about needs, interests, ideas, and feelings.
- ☐ Having one's own spoken language written down by an adult and read back.
- ☐ Having fun with language; rhyming, making up stories, listening to poems and stories.
- ☐ Imitating and describing sounds from the environment.
- ☐ Listening to others.
- ☐ Responding to others by asking questions.
- ☐ Following directions given by others.
- ☐ Telling stories from pictures and books.
- ☐ Solving problems or conflicts.

Representing Experiences and Ideas

- ☐ Recognizing objects by sound, touch, taste, and smell.
- ☐ Pantomiming actions.
- ☐ Relating pictures, photographs, and models to real places and things.
- ☐ Representing personal experiences through: role play, pretending, and dramatic activities; making models out of clay, blocks, etc.; drawing and painting; graphing, mapping, and using objects to make prints.
- ☐ Sharing and discussing representations.
- ☐ Intepreting representation of others.

Understanding Time and Space
Spatial Relations

- ☐ Fitting things together and taking them apart.
- ☐ Rearranging a set of objects or one object in space (folding, twisting, stretching, stacking, typing) and observing the spatial transformations.
- ☐ Observing things and places from different spatial viewpoints. Experiencing and describing the positions of things in relation to each other (e.g., in the middle, on the side of, on, off, on top of, over, above).
- ☐ Experiencing and describing the direction of movement of things and people (to, from, into, out of, toward, away from).
- ☐ Experiencing and describing relative distances among things and locations (close, near, far, next to, apart, together).
- ☐ Experiencing and representing one's own body: how it is structured, what various body parts can do.
- ☐ Learning to locate things in the classroom, school, and neighborhood.
- ☐ Interpreting representations of spatial relations in drawings and pictures.
- ☐ Distinguishing and describing shapes.

☐ Identifying parts of objects and identifying an object from one of its parts.

☐ Identifying and representing the order of objects in space.

☐ Developing an awareness of symmetry in one's own representations and representations of others.

Time

☐ Planning and completing what one has planned.

☐ Describing and representing past events.

☐ Anticipating future events verbally and by making appropriate preparations.

☐ Starting and stopping an action on signal.

☐ Noticing, describing, and representing the order of events.

☐ Experiencing and describing different rates of movement.

☐ Using conventional time units when talking about past and future events (morning, yesterday, hour, etc.)

☐ Comparing time periods (short, long; new, old; young, old; a little while, a long time).

☐ Observing that clocks and calendars are used to mark the passage of time.

☐ Observing seasonal changes.

Science

☐ Caring for animals.

☐ Planting seeds and caring for growing plants.

☐ Observing, describing, and representing weather changes.

☐ Observing, describing, and representing transformations, i.e., cooking activities (making popcorn, apple sauce, pudding), carving pumpkins, freezing liquids, melting snow, sinking and floating activities.

☐ Exploring the natural environment.

☐ Collecting objects from the natural environment.

Social Studies

☐ Interacting with people of many ages and backgrounds in a variety of situations.

☐ Representing family, school, and community roles and events through socio-dramatic play.

☐ Taking field trips.

☐ Representing field trips by writing experience stories, building models, and drawing pictures.

☐ Utilizing community resources as a basis for classroom activities.

Writing

☐ Dictating, tracing, copying or writing stories about personally meaningful experiences.

☐ Expressing ideas and feelings by dictating or writing original stories, poems, songs and riddles.

☐ Including descriptive detail in dictation or writing by describing attributes of objects and relations among objects, people, and events.

☐ Using phonics for spelling words.

☐ Writing simple information such as name, address, etc.

Reading

☐ Reading back dictation with an adult.

☐ Matching letters and words that are alike.

☐ Recognizing familiar words such as own name, name of common objects, places and actions.

☐ Hearing likenesses (rhyming sounds) and differences in words.

☐ Identifying letters in own name and familiar words.

☐ Reading one's own dictated or written story.

☐ Making up words of like sounds including nonsense syllables and words.

Developing Logical Reasoning

Classification

☐ Investigating and labeling the attributes of things.

☐ Noticing and describing how things are the same and how they are different. Sorting and matching.

☐ Using and describing something in several different ways.

☐ Describing what characteristics something does *not* possess or what class it does not belong to.

☐ Holding more than one attribute in mind at a time. (Example: Can you find something that is red and made of wood?)

☐ Sorting objects and then resorting them using different criteria.

☐ Distinguishing between "some" and "all."

Seriation

☐ Comparing objects using a single criterion: Which one is bigger (smaller), heavier (lighter), rougher (smoother), louder (softer), harder (softer), longer (shorter), wider (narrower), sharper, darker, etc.

☐ Comparing and sorting objects into two groups based on a particular criterion (big/little, tall/short, hard/soft, etc.).

☐ Arranging several things in order along some dimension and describing the relations (the longest one, the shortest one, etc.)

☐ Arranging things into three groups along some dimension and describing the relations (big, bigger, biggest; long, longer, longest; etc.).

Number Concepts

☐ Comparing number and amount; more/less, same amount; more/fewer, same number.

☐ Enumerating (counting) objects, as well as counting by rote.

☐ Identifying and writing numerals to twenty.

☐ Representing number information by talking, drawings, or writing numerals.

APPENDIX C
Sample Individualized Family Service Plan*
The Crowder Family

The IFSP for the Crowder family was developed by Geneva Woodruff and Chris Hanson at Project WIN in Brighton, Massachusetts, with assistance from Ibby Jeppson of ACCH and Patti Place of NASDSE. The format for this IFSP was developed by Roxane Kaufmann of NEC*TAS and Mary McGonigel and Josie Thomas of ACCH to provide a simple format that includes all the Public Law 99-457 requirements, yet is still "family friendly." This IFSP would have been handwritten to emphasize the informality and flexibility that should characterize IFSPs, but it was necessary to type it for reproduction clarity.

A family with a child who is HIV positive was included in this document to illustrate that some children and families will require services that go beyond those traditionally associated with early intervention and to highlight the collaboration and coordination among agencies that is critical if Public Law 99-457 is to fulfill its promise to these children and families. The transagency model developed at Project WIN is an approach that has proven effective in meeting the multiple needs of families whose children are HIV positive in a way that is respectful of family values and that builds on the strengths and resources already present in families.

*Source: Reprinted with permission of ACCH and NEC*TAS from *Guidelines and Recommended Practices for the Individualized Family Service Plan,* Beverly H. Johnson, Mary J. McGonigel and Roxane K. Kaufman, eds.

Individualized Family Service Plan (IFSP)

Child's Name: Mary Crowder

Birthdate: 10/10/86   **Age:** 23 months

Developmental Levels:

15-18	months	**Fine Motor**	12-15	months	**Gross Motor**
15-18	months	**Cognitive**	18-21	months	**Language**
12-15	months	**Self-Help**	18-21	months	**Social/Emotional**

Child Strengths and Needs:

Mary's developmental strengths are in her ability to communicate and interact with her mother, aunt, and brother and sister. Despite her many health problems, Mary's temperament is sunny, and her disposition makes it easy for her to get the adults around her involved with her.

Mary's physical health varies considerably as a result of her ARC, and this affects her motor development, which is very uneven. Mary has persistent diarrhea and recurring ear infections. Mary is a fussy eater and sometimes throws food she doesn't like or want. She doesn't have many opportunities to play with or be around other young children, which would allow her to make the most of her good language and social skills.

Child's Name: ___Mary Crowder___

Family Strengths and Needs:

Theresa is deeply committed to keeping her family together and to caring for Mary at home as long as she can. Theresa's periods of being sick with ARC make it hard for her, at times, to manage the demands of taking care of Mary. She has a lot of help from Yvonne and Julie, both of whom are great sources of support and can be relied on to help out whenever they are needed. Yvonne goes grocery shopping for the family, helps Julie with her school work, takes Mary and Theresa to medical appointments, and has made a home for Roger with her family. Because Theresa relies so heavily on Yvonne and because Yvonne disapproves of Theresa's drug use so strongly, Theresa wants to enter a treatment program again.

Julie is devoted to her little sister and helps out with her every chance she gets. Julie says she wants to be a very important part of Mary's IFSP team. Theresa praises Julie for her help, but she is also concerned about putting too many burdens on her. Theresa is also worried about the effect her and Mary's illness has on Julie, but Theresa says she has a hard time bringing that up with Julie.

Right now, mealtimes are not good times at the Crowders'. Theresa is often too tired to cook dinner and then coax Mary to eat, but she worries about Mary not getting enough to eat and wants to see her grow stronger. Julie manages dinner whenever Theresa is too tired, but she isn't sure what she can make for dinner that Mary would like and want to eat. Theresa also wants some time alone during the day to rest when she isn't feeling strong, and she hopes Mary will have a chance to be around other young children. Theresa needs a stroller in order for her to be able to take Mary out of the house.

Outcomes:

1. Theresa wants to control her drug addiction in order to maintain her good relationship with her sister.

2. Theresa wants Mary to be in day care, so that Theresa has some time to rest during the day and so that Mary can have a chance to play with children her own age.

3. Theresa and Julie want some help at mealtimes in order for Mary to learn how to eat more foods, be less fussy, and grow stronger.

4. Mary will have physical therapy in order to increase her body strength and mobility and make it possible for Theresa and Julie to take care of her at home.

5. Theresa wants Julie to have someone outside the family to talk to in order for Julie to get the information and support that she needs.

Child's Name: ___Mary Crowder___

Outcome: # 1

Theresa wants to control her drug addiction in order to maintain her good relationship with her sister.

Strategies/Activities:

1.   Theresa, Lizzie (the WIN service coordinator), and Lucy (Theresa's hospital social worker) will discuss Theresa's options for a drug treatment program.

2.   Theresa will choose the option she prefers and will call to refer herself within a week of the discussion.

3.   If there is a waiting list, Lucy will arrange for Theresa to have priority admission status because of her illness.

4.   Theresa will complete the intake process for the treatment option she chooses and will go to treatment sessions as scheduled. Lizzie or Lucy will go with Theresa to her appointments whenever she asks.

5.   Lucy, Lizzie, and Yvonne will help and support Theresa, encouraging her efforts. Theresa will tell Lizzie and Lucy when she feels like using drugs, and they will tell Theresa whenever they think she is using drugs.

Criteria/Timelines:

Theresa will determine if she is making progress overcoming her drug addiction. She suggested that she review her progress with Lizzie every month.

Child's Name: ___Mary Crowder___

Outcome: # 2

Theresa wants Mary to be in day care so that Theresa has some time to rest during the day and so that Mary can have a chance to play with children her own age.

Strategies/Activities:

1. Lizzie and Julie will investigate day care centers within walking distance of the Crowder's house and will talk over the options with Theresa within the next two weeks.

2. Theresa will make a choice from the options, after talking it over with Julie to see what program Julie thinks is best.

3. If the publicly funded day care centers are not available or if they are not appropriate for Mary, Lucy will arrange for Theresa to get financial assistance from the Department of Social Services or for the hospital pediatric AIDS support program to pay the fees.

4. Lizzie and Theresa will enroll Mary together, as soon as possible.

5. Yvonne will try to get a friend to loan Theresa a stroller. If this doesn't work out in the next week, Lucy will ask Social Services to buy a stroller so that Mary can go to day care.

6. Theresa will take Mary every morning to the center when she is well enough to take her. Julie will pick Mary up in the afternoons.

7. Lizzie will arrange right away for a home health aide or visiting nurse to help out with Mary during the day when Mary is ill at home and Theresa is not well enough to manage alone.

8. When Theresa and Mary are both well, Theresa will take Mary in her stroller to the park once a week.

Criteria/Timelines:

The timelines are as listed above in the activities. Theresa will decide if she is satisfied with the way things are going and if her need has been met as specified in the outcome.

Child's Name: ___Mary Crowder___

Outcome: # 3

Theresa and Julie want some help with mealtimes in order for Mary to learn how to eat more foods, be less fussy, and grow stronger.

Strategies/Activities:

1. Lizzie will arrange for a home nutritionist or visiting nurse to come to the Crowder's home five evenings a week, beginning in two weeks.

2. The home visitor will help Theresa and Julie make a list of several finger foods that are good for Mary and that she likes and is able to eat.

3. The home visitor will show Julie how to make several easy-to-prepare dishes that Mary likes and is able to eat.

4. Anna Martinez, the WIN occupational therapist, and Lizzie will do a feeding evaluation of Mary next week, before the home visitor comes. They will do an assessment to determine if Mary has any special feeding problems and will develop a plan with Theresa for remediation, which will become a part of this IFSP, if necessary. The evaluation will be done at home at a regular mealtime.

5. Yvonne will continue to do the grocery shopping for the Crowders, now using a list that Julie has made for her.

Criteria/Timelines:

The timelines are as listed above in the activities. Theresa will decide if she is satisfied with the way things are going and if her need has been met as specified in the outcome.

Child's Name: ___Mary Crowder___

Outcome: # 4

Mary will have physical therapy in order to help prevent loss of her previously attained motor skills and to try to build her body strength and mobility to make it possible for Theresa and Julie to care for Mary at home.

Strategies/Activities:

1.   Virginia Taylor, the hospital physical therapist, will visit Theresa and Mary at home once a week, starting next week, to monitor Mary's motor development for signs of loss of previously attained skills.

2.   Virginia will work with Mary on her balance. She will show Julie and Theresa how to play with Mary in ways that help Mary practice her balance.

3.   When Julie plays with Mary, she will play in the ways that Virginia is teaching her.

4.   Lizzie will come to one of Virginia's sessions every month, starting next month, to learn how Mary is doing and to be able to help Julie and Theresa play with Mary in ways that help Mary maintain her skills or grow stronger.

Criteria/Timelines:

Mary's therapy will begin next week. Virginia will use clinical observation to judge Mary's progress or Mary's maintenance of previously attained motor skills, and will do a formal evaluation of Mary jointly with Lizzie every three months to monitor Mary's motor development.

Child's Name: _____Mary Crowder_____

Outcome: # 5

Theresa wants Julie to have someone outside the family to talk to in order for Julie to get the information and support that she needs.

Strategies/Activities:

1.   Julie will visit Lucy at her office once every two weeks, starting next week, so that they can talk about whatever is on Julie's mind.

2.   In two weeks, Theresa, Lucy, and Julie will visit the support group for brothers and sisters at the hospital. If Julie likes the group, she will start attending the monthly support group sessions, and she will participate in the other group activities.

3.   Theresa will let Lucy know if she has similar concerns about Roger.

Criteria/Timelines:

Theresa and Julie will decide if they are satisfied with the way things are going and if the need has been met.

Child's Name: ___Mary Crowder___

Notes on the IFSP Process:

Lucy Crawford, Theresa's hospital social worker, referred Theresa and Mary to Project WIN. The WIN assessment staff planned a transdisciplinary arena assessment with Theresa, Yvonne, and Julia. Lucy became part of the team for the assessment.

Following the assessment, Theresa decided to enroll in Project WIN with Mary. Lucy is part of Theresa's IFSP team, along with the occupational and physical therapists from the project. Yvonne and Julie are on the team, and Lizzie O'Shea will work with Theresa as her service coordinator.

Because Theresa and Mary have ARC, they may need the services of many agencies other than the hospital and Project WIN. New members will be added to this transagency IFSP team by Theresa, or with Theresa's consent, as the need arises.

Theresa was very clear about the kinds of support she needed and plans to tell Lizzie any time she needs or wants a change in the IFSP for Mary, Julie, Roger, or herself. Because Yvonne may need to take over for Theresa at any time should she become too ill to care for her family, Theresa has asked that Yvonne be a full member of the team and have access to all the records relating to Mary and the Crowders' IFSP.

Back Cover Sheet — IFSP

Project WIN
77B Warren Street
Brighton, MA 02135
(617) 783-7300

Child's Name: Mary Crowder   **Birthdate:** 10/10/86

Address: 1715 NE Adams Street, #527

Boston, MA   **Phone:**   462-4347

Service Coordinator (Case Manager): Lizzie O'Shea, R.N.

IFSP Team Members and Signatures:

Theresa Crowder, mother	*Theresa Crowder*
Yvonne Baker, aunt	*Yvonne Baker*
Lucy Crawford, M.S.W.	*Lucy Crawford, M.S.W.*
Virginia Taylor, L.P.T.	*Virginia Taylor LPT*
Anna Martinez, O.T.R.	*Anna Martinez OTR*
Lizzie O'Shea	*Lizzie O'Shea RN*

Frequency, Intensity, and Duration of Services:

Services will begin immediately and continue until the September after Mary's third birthday when she is eligible for public school preschool. Frequency and intensity will vary; see individual outcomes.

IFSP Review Dates: 12/15/88   6/15/89

3/15/89   9/15/89

Transition Plan:_____X_____ **Not Applicable**   _____ **Yes, (see outcomes)**

Parent Signature(s):

This plan represents our wishes. I (we) understand and agree with it, and I (we) authorize Project KAI to carry out this plan with me (us).

Theresa Crowder   *Sept. 15, 1988*
Parent(s)   **Date**

APPENDIX D
The National Association for the Education of Young Children
Code of Ethical Conduct*

PREAMBLE

NAEYC recognizes that many daily decisions required of those who work with young children are of a moral and ethical nature. The NAEYC Code of Ethical Conduct offers guidelines for responsible behavior and sets forth a common basis for resolving the principal ethical dilemmas encountered in early childhood education. The primary focus is on daily practice with children and their families in programs for children from birth to 8 years of age: preschools, child care centers, family day care homes, kindergartens, and primary classrooms. Many of the provisions also apply to specialists who do not work directly with children, including program administrators, parent educators, college professors, and child care licensing specialists.

Standards of ethical behavior in early childhood education are based on commitment to core values that are deeply rooted in the history of our field. We have committed ourselves to:

□ Appreciating childhood as a unique and valuable stage of the human life cycle

□ Basing our work with children on knowledge of child development

□ Appreciating and supporting the close ties between the child and family

□ Recognizing that children are best understood in the context of family, culture, and society

□ Respecting the dignity, worth, and uniqueness of each individual (child, family member, and colleague)

□ Helping children and adults achieve their full potential in the context of relationships that are based on trust, respect, and positive regard

The Code sets forth a conception of our professional responsibilities in four sections, each addressing an arena of professional relationships: 1) children, 2) families, 3) colleagues,

*This Code of Ethical Conduct and Statement of Commitment was prepared under the auspices of the Ethics Commission of the National Association for the Education of Young Children. The Commission members were Stephanie Feeney (Chairperson), Bettye Caldwell, Sally Cartwright, Carrie Cheek, Josué Cruz, Jr., Anne G. Dorsey, Dorothy M. Hill, Lilian G. Katz, Pamm Mattick, Shirley A. Norris, and Sue Spayth Riley.

531

and 4) community and society. Each section includes an introduction to the primary responsibilities of the early childhood practitioner in that arena, a set of ideals pointing in the direction of exemplary professional practice, and a set of principles defining practices that are required, prohibited, and permitted.

The ideals reflect the aspirations of practitioners. The principles are intended to guide conduct and assist practitioners in resolving ethical dilemmas encountered in the field. There is not necessarily a corresponding principle for each ideal. Both ideals and principles are intended to direct practitioners to those questions which, when responsibly answered, will provide the basis for conscientious decision making. While the Code provides specific direction for addressing some ethical dilemmas, many others will require the practitioner to combine the guidance of the Code with sound professional judgment.

The ideals and principles in this Code present a shared conception of professional responsibility that affirms our commitment to the core values of our field. The Code publicly acknowledges the responsibilities that we in the field have assumed and in so doing supports ethical behavior in our work. Practitioners who face ethical dilemmas are urged to seek guidance in the applicable parts of this Code and in the spirit that informs the whole.

SECTION I: ETHICAL RESPONSIBILITIES TO CHILDREN

Childhood is a unique and valuable stage in the life cycle. Our paramount responsibility is to provide safe, healthy, nurturing, and responsive settings for children. We are committed to supporting children's development by cherishing individual differences, by helping them learn to live and work cooperatively, and by promoting their self-esteem.

Ideals:

I-1.1—To be familiar with the knowledge base of early childhood education and to keep cur-

rent through continuing education and in-service training.

I-1.2—To base program practices upon current knowledge in the field of child development and related disciplines and upon particular knowledge of each child.

I-1.3—To recognize and respect the uniqueness and the potential of each child.

I-1.4—To appreciate the special vulnerability of children.

I-1.5—To create and maintain safe and healthy settings that foster children's social, emotional, intellectual, and physical development and that respect their dignity and their contributions.

I-1.6—To support the right of children with special needs to participate, consistent with their ability, in regular childhood programs.

Principles:

P-1.1—Above all, we shall not harm children. We shall not participate in practices that are disrespectful, degrading, dangerous, exploitative, intimidating, psychologically damaging, or physically harmful to children. ***This principle has precedence over all others in this Code.***

P-1.2—We shall not participate in practices that discriminate against children by denying benefits, giving special advantages, or excluding them from programs or activities on the basis of their race, religion, sex, national origin, or the status, behavior, or beliefs of their parents. (This principle does not apply to programs that have a lawful mandate to provide services to a particular population of children.)

P-1.3—We shall involve all of those with relevant knowledge (including staff and parents) in decisions concerning a child.

P-1.4—When, after appropriate efforts have been made with a child and the family, the child still does not appear to be benefitting from a program, we shall communicate our concern to the family in a positive way and offer them assistance in finding a more suitable setting.

P-1.5—We shall be familiar with the symptoms of child abuse and neglect and know community procedures for addressing them.

P-1.6—When we have evidence of child abuse or neglect, we shall report the evidence to the appropriate community agency and follow up to ensure that appropriate action has been taken. When possible, parents will be informed that the referral has been made.

P-1.7—When another person tells us of their suspicion that a child is being abused or neglected but we lack evidence, we shall assist that person in taking appropriate action to protect the child.

P-1.8—When a child protective agency fails to provide adequate protection for abused or neglected children, we acknowledge a collective ethical responsibility to work toward improvement of these services.

SECTION II: ETHICAL RESPONSIBILITIES TO FAMILIES

Families are of primary importance in children's development. (The term *family* may include others, besides parents, who are responsibly involved with the child.) Because the family and the early childhood educators have a common interest in the child's welfare, we acknowledge a primary responsibility to bring about collaboration between the home and school in ways that enhance the child's development.

Ideals:

I-2.1—To develop relationships of mutual trust with the families we serve.

I-2.2—To acknowledge and build upon strengths and competencies as we support families in their task of nurturing children.

I-2.3—To respect the dignity of each family and its culture, customs, and beliefs.

I-2.4—To respect families' childrearing values and their right to make decisions for their children.

I-2.5—To interpret each child's progress to parents within the framework of a developmental perspective and to help families understand and appreciate the value of developmentally appropriate early childhood programs.

I-2.6—To help family members improve their understanding of their children and to enhance their skills as parents.

I-2.7—To participate in building support networks for families by providing them with opportunities to interact with program staff and families.

Principles:

P-2.1—We shall not deny family members access to their child's classroom or program setting.

P-2.2—We shall inform families of program philosophy, policies, and personnel qualifications, and explain why we teach as we do.

P-2.3—We shall inform families of and, when appropriate, involve them in policy decisions.

P-2.4—We shall inform families of and, when appropriate, involve them in significant decisions affecting their child.

P-2.5—We shall inform the family of accidents involving their child, of risks such as exposures to contagious disease that may result in infection, and of events that might result in psychological damage.

P-2.6—We shall not permit or participate in research that could in any way hinder the education or development of the children in our programs. Families shall be fully informed of any proposed research projects involving their children and shall have the opportunity to give or withhold consent.

P-2.7—We shall not engage in or support exploitation of families. We shall not use our relationship with a family for private advantage or personal gain, or enter into relationships with family members that might impair our effectiveness in working with children.

P-2.8—We shall develop written policies for the protection of confidentiality and the disclosure of children's records. The policy documents shall be made available to all program personnel and families. Disclosure of children's records beyond family members, program personnel, and consultants having an obligation of confidentiality shall require familial consent (except in cases of abuse or neglect).

P-2.9—We shall maintain confidentiality and shall respect the family's right to privacy, refraining from disclosure of confidential information and intrusion into family life. However, when we are concerned about a child's welfare, it is permissible to reveal confidential information to agencies and individuals who may be able to act in the child's interest.

P-2.10—In cases where family members are in conflict we shall work openly, sharing our observations of the child, to help all parties involved make informed decisions. We shall refrain from becoming an advocate for one party.

P-2.11—We shall be familiar with and appropriately use community resources and professional services that support families. After a referral has been made, we shall follow up to ensure that services have been adequately provided.

SECTION III: ETHICAL RESPONSIBILITIES TO COLLEAGUES

In a caring, cooperative work place human dignity is respected, professional satisfaction is promoted, and positive relationships are modeled. Our primary responsibility in this arena is to establish and maintain settings and relationships that support productive work and meet professional needs.

A—Responsibilities to Co-workers
Ideals:

I-3A.1—To establish and maintain relationships of trust and cooperation with co-workers.

I-3A.2—To share resources and information with co-workers.

I-3A.3—To support co-workers in meeting their professional needs and in their professional development.

I-3A.4—To accord co-workers due recognition of professional achievement.

Principles:

P-3A.1—When we have concern about the professional behavior of a co-worker, we shall

first let that person know of our concern and attempt to resolve the matter collegially.

P-3A.2—We shall exercise care in expressing views regarding the personal attributes or professional conduct of co-workers. Statements should be based on firsthand knowledge and relevant to the interests of children and programs.

B—Responsibilities to Employers
Ideals:

I-3B.1—To assist the program in providing the highest quality of service.

I-3B.2—To maintain loyalty to the program and uphold its reputation.

Principles:

P-3B.1—When we do not agree with program policies, we shall first attempt to effect change through constructive action within the organization.

P-3B.2—We shall speak or act on behalf of an organization only when authorized. We shall take care to note when we are speaking for the organization and when we are expressing a personal judgment.

C—Responsibilities to Employees
Ideals:

I-3C.1—To promote policies and working conditions that foster competence, well-being, and self-esteem in staff members.

I-3C.2—To create a climate of trust and candor that will enable staff to speak and act in the best interests of children, families, and the field of early childhood education.

I-3C.3—To strive to secure an adequate livelihood for those who work with or on behalf of young children.

Principles:

P-3C.1—In decisions concerning children and programs, we shall appropriately utilize the training, experience, and expertise of staff members.

P-3C.2—We shall provide staff members with working conditions that permit them to carry out their responsibilities, timely and nonthreatening evaluation procedures, written grievance procedures, constructive feedback, and opportunities for continuing professional development and advancement.

P-3C.3—We shall develop and maintain comprehensive written personnel policies that define program standards and, when applicable, that specify the extent to which employees are accountable for their conduct outside the work place. These policies shall be given to new staff members and shall be available for review by all staff members.

P-3C.4—Employees who do not meet program standards shall be informed of areas of concern and, when possible, assisted in improving their performance.

P-3C.5—Employees who are dismissed shall be informed of the reasons for the termination. When a dismissal is for cause, justification must be based on evidence of inadequate or inappropriate behavior that is accurately documented, current, and available for the employee to review.

P-3C.6—In making evaluations and recommendations, judgments shall be based on fact and relevant to the interests of children and programs.

P-3C.7—Hiring and promotion shall be based solely on a person's record of accomplishment and ability to carry out the responsibilities of the position.

P-3C.8—In hiring, promotion, and provision of training, we shall not participate in any form of discrimination based on race, religion, sex, national origin, handicap, age, or sexual preference. We shall be familiar with laws and regulations that pertain to employment discrimination.

SECTION IV: ETHICAL RESPONSIBILITIES TO COMMUNITY AND SOCIETY

Early childhood programs operate with a context of an immediate community made up of families and other institutions concerned with children's welfare. Our responsibilities to the community are to provide programs that meet its needs and to cooperate with agencies and professions that share responsibility for children. Because the larger society has a measure of responsibility for the welfare and protection of children, and because of our specialized expertise in child development, we acknowledge an obligation to serve as a voice for children everywhere.

Ideals:

I-4.1—To provide the community with high-quality, culturally sensitive programs and services.

I-4.2—To promote cooperation among agencies and professions concerned with the welfare of young children, their families, and their teachers.

I-4.3—To work, through education, research, and advocacy, toward an environmentally safe world in which all children are adequately fed, sheltered, and nurtured.

I-4.4—To work, through education, research, and advocacy, toward a society in which all young children have access to quality programs.

I-4.5—To promote knowledge and understanding of young children and their needs. To work toward greater social acknowledgment of children's rights and greater social acceptance of responsibility for their well-being.

I-4.6—To support policies and laws that promote the well-being of children and families. To oppose those that impair their well-being. To cooperate with other individuals and groups in these efforts.

I-4.7—To further the professional development of the field of early childhood education and to strengthen its commitment to realizing its core values as reflected in this Code.

Principles:

P-4.1—We shall communicate openly and truthfully about the nature and extent of services that we provide.

P-4.2—We shall not accept or continue to work in positions for which we are personally unsuited or professionally unqualified. We shall not offer services that we do not have the competence, qualifications, or resources to provide.

P-4.3—We shall be objective and accurate in reporting the knowledge upon which we base our program practices.

P-4.4—We shall cooperate with other professionals who work with children and their families.

P-4.5—We shall not hire or recommend for employment any person who is unsuited for a position with respect to competence, qualifications, or character.

P-4.6—We shall report the unethical or incompetent behavior of a colleague to a supervisor when informal resolution is not effective.

P-4.7—We shall be familiar with laws and regulations that serve to protect the children in our programs.

P-4.8—We shall not participate in practices which are in violation of laws and regulations that protect the children in our programs.

P-4.9—When we have evidence that an early childhood program is violating laws or regulations protecting children, we shall report it to persons responsible for the program. If compliance is not accomplished within a reasonable time, we will report the violation to appropriate authorities who can be expected to remedy the situation.

P-4.10—When we have evidence that an agency or a professional charged with providing services to children, families, or teachers is failing to meet its obligations, we acknowledge a collective ethical responsibility to report the problem to appropriate authorities or to the public.

P-4.11—When a program violates or requires its employees to violate this Code, it is permissible, after fair assessment of the evidence, to disclose the identity of that program.

APPENDIX E
Journals and Associations Concerning Early Childhood Education

Action for Children's Television
20 University Road
Cambridge, Massachusetts 02138

Administration for Children, Youth and Families
Office of Human Development Services
Department of Health and Human Services
200 Independence Avenue, S.W.
Washington, D.C. 20201

American Academy of Pediatrics
141 N.W. Point Road
Box 927
Elk Grove Village, Illinois 60009

American Alliance for Health, Physical Education, Recreation, and Dance
1900 Association Drive
Reston, Virginia 22091

American Association of Elementary, Kinder-Nursery Educators
1201 16th Street, N.W.
Washington, D.C. 20036

American Association for Gifted Children
200 Madison Avenue
New York, New York 10016

American Baby, Inc.
575 Lexington Avenue
New York, New York 10022

American Child Care Services
532 Settlers Landing Road
P.O. Box 548
Hampton, Virginia 23669

American Home Economics Association
2010 Massachusetts Avenue, N.W.
Washington, D.C. 20036

American Montessori Society
(AMS)
150 Fifth Avenue, Suite 203
New York, New York 10011

Association for Childhood Education International
11141 Georgia Avenue
Suite 200
Wheaton, Maryland 20902

Association for Children with Learning Disabilities
4156 Library Road
Pittsburgh, Pennsylvania 15234

Beechnut Infant Hotline
1-800-523-6633
P.O. Box 127
Fort Washington, Pennsylvania 19103

Big Brothers/Big Sisters of America
230 N. 13th Street
Philadelphia, Pennsylvania 19103

Bureau of Education for the Handicapped (Office of Special Education Programs)
U.S. Office of Education
Room 3086, Switzer Building
330 C Street, S.W.
Washington, D.C. 20202

Child Care Center
22 2nd Street
Fifth floor
San Francisco, California 94105

Child Care Employee News
6536 Telegraph Avenue, Suite A201
Oakland, California 94609-1114

Child Care Information Exchange
P.O. Box 2890
Redmond, Washington 98073-2890

Child Care Quarterly
Human Sciences Publishers
72 Fifth Avenue
New York, New York 10011

Child Development
University of Chicago Press
Journals Division
5720 S. Woodlawn Avenue
Chicago, Illinois 60637

Child Development Associate Credentialing Commission
1718 Connecticut Avenue, N.W.
Washington, D.C. 20009

Child Welfare League of America, Inc.
440 First Street, N.W.
Suite 210
Washington, D.C. 20001

Childhood Education
Association for Childhood Education International
11141 Georgia Avenue, Ste. 200
Wheaton, Maryland 20902

Children Today
Children's Bureau, Administration for Children, Youth, and Families
Office of Human Development Services
U.S. Department of Health and Human Services

P.O. Box 1182
Washington, D.C. 20013

Children's Defense Fund
122 C Street, N.W.
Suite 400
Washington, D.C. 20005

Children's Foundation
815 15th Street, N.W.
Suite 928
Washington, D.C. 20005

Children's Rights Group
693 Mission Street
San Francisco, California 94051

Council for Exceptional Children
1920 Association Drive
Reston, Virginia 22091

Day Care and Early Education
Human Sciences Press
233 Spring Street
New York, New York 10013

Day Care U.S.A. Newsletter
United Communications Group
4550 Montgomery Ave., Ste. 700N
Bethesda, Maryland 20814

Developmental Psychology
American Psychological Association
1200 17th Street, N.W.
Washington, D.C. 20036

Exceptional Children
Council for Exceptional Children
1920 Association Drive
Reston, Virginia 22091

Family Service of America
11700 West Lake Park Drive
Milwaukee, Wisconsin 53224

Foster Grandparents Program
ACTION
806 Connecticut Avenue, N.W.
Room M-1006
Washington, D.C. 20525

Foundation for Child Development
345 East 46th Street
New York, New York 10017

Growing Child
Dunn and Hargitt, Inc.
22 North Second Street
P.O. Box 620
Lafayette, Indiana 47902

Harris Foundation
2 North LaSalle Street
Suite 605
Chicago, Illinois 60603

Head Start Bureau
Department of Health and Human Services
300 C Street, S.W.
Washington, D.C. 20201

High/Scope Educational Research Foundation
600 North River Street
Ypsilanti, Michigan 48197

Instructor
Harcourt Brace Jovanovich, Inc.
7500 Old Oak Blvd.
Cleveland, Ohio 44130

International Concerns Committee for Children
911 Cypress Drive
Boulder, Colorado 80303

Journal of Family Issues
National Council on Family Relations
Sage Publications, Inc.
2111 W. Hillcrest Drive
Newbury Park, California 91320

Journal of Learning Disabilities
5341 Industrial Oaks Blvd.
Austin, Texas 78735

Learning
Springhouse Corporation
1111 Bethlehem Pike
Springhouse, Pennsylvania 19477

Legal Services for Children
1254 Market Street
Third Floor
San Francisco, California 94102

National Association of Homes for Children
1701 K Street, N.W.
Suite 200
Washington, D.C. 20006

National Association for Retarded Citizens (NARC)
P.O. Box 6109
Arlington, Texas 76005

National Black Child Development Institute
1463 Rhode Island Avenue, N.W.
Washington, D.C. 20005

National Committee for Adoption
1930 17th Street N.W.
Washington, D.C. 20009

National Committee for Prevention of Child Abuse
332 South Michigan Avenue
Suite 950
Chicago, Illinois 60604

National Easter Seal Society
70 E. Lake Street
Chicago, Illinois 60601

Office of Early Childhood Development (OECD)
Office of Education
U.S. Department of Education
1200 19th Street, N.W.
Washington, D.C. 20506

Parents
Gruner + Jahr U.S.A. Publishing
685 Third Avenue
New York, New York 10017

Parents Anonymous
6733 S. Sepulveda
Suite 200
Los Angeles, California 90045

Play Schools Association
19 W. 44th Street
Suite 615
New York, New York 10036

Rosenberg Foundation
210 Post Street
Room 911
San Francisco, California 94108

Southern Association on Children Under Six
P.O. Box 5403
Brady Station
Little Rock, Arkansas 72215

Teaching Pre K–8
Early Years, Inc.
325 Post Road West
Box 3330
Westport, Connecticut 06880

Today's Education (Journal of NEA)
National Education Association
1201 16th Street, N.W.
Washington, D.C. 20036

Totline
Warren Publishing House, Inc.
Box 2255
Everett, Washington 98203

USA Toy Library Association
2719 Broadway Avenue
Evanston, Illinois 60201

Young Children (Journal of NAEYC)
National Association for the Education of Young
  Children
1834 Connecticut Avenue, N.W.
Washington, D.C. 20009

Zero to Three
Bulletin for the National Center for Clinical In-
  fant Programs
733 15th Street, N.W.
Suite 912
Washington, D.C. 20005

INDEX

A Day in a Children's House, 98–101
ABIG Learning Center, 498, 499
Absorbent mind, 83, 84
Abuse. *See* Child abuse
Academic materials, 88, 94, 95, 96
Accommodation, 111, 112, 122
Accreditation, 168, 169
Act for Better Child Care, 139
Action, 122
Active learning, 515
Adaptation, 110, 111, 113, 122
Aid to Families with Dependent
    Children (AFDC), 146
AIDS
  children at risk, 456
  children with, 455, 456
  education, 456, 457
  guidelines for treating, 456, 457
Alberta Children's Hospital, 368,
    369
American Association of Elementary,
    Kindergarten, and Nursery
    School Educators, 74
American Council of Parent
    Cooperatives, 76
American Express, 500
American Montessori Society, 104
American Sunday School Union, 74
*An Essay Concerning Human
    Understanding,* 47
Anti-bias curriculum, 382, 383
As I See It, 474
Assessment. *See* Testing
Assimilation, 111, 112, 122
Association Montessori Internationale,
    104
Auto-education, 86, 87
Autonomy, 296, 409

Baby, 13
Baby-sitters, 155, 156

Babysitting cooperatives, 9
Back to basics, 71, 72, 298, 299,
    303
Balanced curriculum, 259
Bandura, Albert, 404
Basic concepts of good teaching, 63,
    474
Basic education movement, 34, 35
Basic needs, 392, 393
Basic skills, 258, 259, 260
Bear River Head Start, 337
Beethoven Project, 440, 441
Behavior
  building new, 391, 392
  defined, 390
  ignoring, 398
  understanding, 397, 398
Behavior guidance, 390
Behaviorism, 194, 195
Behavior management
  arranging environment, 393
  and autonomy, 409
  avoiding problems, 394
  and behavior modification, 391,
    394–98
  contingency management, 401
  cultural basis, 406
  discipline, 390, 391
  environment, 393
  expectations, 393
  guidance, 398
  misbehavior, 394, 396
  modeling, 404, 405
  praise, 400, 401
  principles, 394–98
  punishment, 398, 412
  reinforcement, 396, 397, 399, 400,
    402, 403
  reinforcers, 396, 400
  self-regulation, 410, 411
  tips, 407, 408

Behavior management (*continued*)
  token system, 401
Behavior modification, 391, 394–98
Bell, T. H., 23
Bilingual education, 284, 285, 286, 287
Bilingual Education Act, 285
Blank tablets. *See* Views of children
Block grants, 4, 346
Bloom, B. S., 66, 68
Blow, Susan, 74, 248, 249
Boarder babies, 438
Book for Mothers, 51
BRIGANCE ®, 269, 270, 271, 272
British Primary School, 71
Brofenbrenner, Urie, 13
Bureau of Education for the handi-
    capped, 76

Caregiver, 14
Casa dei Bambini. *See* Children's House
Cascade System of Educational Place-
    ment, 359
Catholic Community Services, 144, 145
Cephalocaudal development, 220
Chapter 1, 344, 345
Chicago Kindergarten College, 144, 145
Child, 13
Child abuse
  causes, 444, 445, 446
  definition, 439, 440
  emotional, 441, 442, 443
  identifying, 441, 442, 443, 444
  neglect, 443
  physical, 442
  prevention, 446, 447
  sexual, 443
  therapeutic nursery, 446
Child Abuse Prevention and Treatment
    Act. *See* P.L. 93-247
Child and Family Resource Program,
    11

Child care
  accreditation, 168, 169
  after-school, 10, 160
  baby-sitters, 155, 156
  center, 144, 145, 146
  church-sponsored, 8
  comprehensive, 139
  definition, 8, 9
  drop-off, 10, 156
  effects of, 171
  employer, 9, 147–55
  examples, 148, 149, 150, 151, 154,
    157, 159, 168, 169
  family day care, 8, 11, 140, 141, 142,
    143, 144, 145
  federally supported, 146, 147
  foster, 155
  health issues, 462, 463, 464
  high school, 10
  ill, 158, 159
  information and referral, 167, 168
  intergenerational, 144
  issues, 168–74, 420
  latchkey, 160
  military, 160, 161
  mommy track, 171, 172
  nanny, 161
  popularity, 138, 139
  proprietary, 155
  quality, 164, 165, 166, 167, 172
  supplemental, 139
  Title XX, 146, 147, 346, 347
  training, 161, 162, 163, 164
  trends, 174, 175
  types, 140
Child Care Food Program (CCFP), 147
Child-centered curriculum, 61, 499, 500
Child development, 140
Child Development Associate (CDA),
    14, 162, 163, 513, 514
Child Education Foundation, 75
Child Find, 360, 361
Childhood, disappearance of, 17, 18
Childhood Education, 75
Childhood stress, 460, 461
Childproofing, 200, 201
Children
  educational practices, 63
  observation, 15, 16
  rights of, 23–26
  views of, 18
Children's House, 59, 74
Child welfare, 139
Child Welfare League of America,
    139

Classical conditioning, 394
Classification, 120, 515, 516
Classrooms, humane, 173, 452, 453
Clinical method, 64
Cocaine babies, 5, 458
Cognitive development, 110, 202–5
Cognitive oriented curriculum, 124,
    125, 126
Collaborative intervention, 368, 369
Comenius, John Amos, 44–46, 53, 74
Common Sense Book of Baby and
    Child Care, 75
Communication 191, 192. See also
    Language development
Community mentor, 380
Competent child. See Views of
    children
Computers
  in kindergarten, 269, 274, 275
  objectives, 269
  in primary grades, 307, 308, 309,
    310
Conceptual relations, 122
Concrete operations, 118, 119, 120,
    121, 122, 295
Conditioned response, 394
Conservation, 122, 220
Constructivism, 113, 122, 185, 186
Consultant teacher, 379
Contingency management, 401
Conventional level, 296
Cooperative learning, 303, 304, 305,
    306, 307
Corporations and early childhood
    education, 4, 5
Curriculum content, 122

Daisy Girl Scouts: A head start on
    literacy, 345
Day care. See Child care
Day Care and Child Development
    Council of America, 76
Department of Children, Youth, and
    Families, 11
Developmental age, 252
Developmental approach, 423
Developmental path, 337
Dewey, John, 35, 60, 61, 62, 63, 70, 73,
    74, 216, 222
DIAL-R, 269, 273
Disappearance of Childhood, 18
Discipline, 390, 391
"Double C" (cocaine and crack)
    babies, 458, 459
Drug prevention, 460

Early childhood
  associate teacher, 485
  associations, 537–40
  definition, 6
  ecology, 12
  journals, 537–40
  popularity of, 2
  program, 9
  specialist, 485
  teacher, 14, 485
  teacher assistant, 485
  terminology, 6
Early childhood education
  basic concepts to good teaching,
    63
  contemporary influences, 26–35
  definition, 6, 500
  preparing for a career in, 470, 471,
    472, 473, 474, 475, 476
Early childhood educators, 470, 500
Early childhood programs, 9
  corporate involvement, 495, 496,
    497
  federal involvement, 497
  making humane, 451, 452
  state involvement, 4
Early childhood settings, definition, 6
Economic Opportunity Act (EOA), 69,
    76, 323, 324
Educational level required for
    tomorrow's jobs, 496
Education Consolidation and
    Improvement Act, 76
Education for All Handicapped
    Children Act. See P.L. 94-142
Education of the Handicapped Act
    Amendments. See P.L. 99-457
Egocentrism, 117, 122, 220
Elementary and Secondary Education
    Act, 76, 343
Eliot, Abigail, 75, 217
Elkind, David, 20
Emergent literacy, 278
Emile, 48, 49, 50, 74
Employer child care, 9
Entrance age, 249, 250
Environment
  effects of, 47
  relation to language development,
    193, 194
Environmentalism, 47, 51
Equilibrium, 111, 112, 186
Erikson, Erik, 75, 196, 197, 298
Ethical conduct, 486, 487

Eugene P. Tone School Project, 454, 455

Fair Play child care, 157
Families
  below poverty level, 138
  blended, 419
  changes in, 418
  divorce, 138
  extended, 419
  foster, 419
  implications for teaching, 419, 420, 421, 422
  nuclear, 419
  single-parent, 419, 428, 429
  step, 419
  support for, 431
  types of, 419
Family day care, 8
Farson, Richard, 24
Fathers, 31, 32
Federal government, 34
First grade
  pre-first, 10
  interim, 10
  junior, 6, 10
First Three Years of Life, 200
Fisher Act, 216
Flesch, Rudolf, 65, 75
Follow Through, 8, 11, 23, 127, 402, 403, 404, 405
Forbes Metropolitan Health Center, 154
Foreman, George, 222
Formal operations, 121, 295
Foster care, 419
Freud, Sigmund, 74
Froebel, Friedrich Wilhelm, 42, 53–58, 59, 70, 74, 222, 248, 249, 251

Gallaudet, Thomas, 74
"Garden of Children", 54
Gesell, Arnold, 75, 251, 252
Gifted children
  definition, 354, 355
  identification, 377, 378
  mainstreaming, 378, 379
  resource room-pullout, 379, 380
Giftedness, 355
Gifts and occupations, 55, 56, 57, 58
Great Didactic, 44, 74
Group child care. See Child care, center
Growing from a student to a professional, 476, 477

Growing plants. See Views of children
Gust, Cathy, 479

Handicapped. See also Mainstreaming
  definition, 354, 355
  integration, 373
  in Head Start, 338, 367
  least restrictive environment, 358
  numbers, 355
  resource room, 364, 365
  resources, 370, 371, 372, 373
  teaching, 364, 365, 367, 370, 371, 372
  transdisciplinary, 365, 366
  transitions, 376, 377
Handicapped Children's Early Education Program, 76
Harris, William T., 250, 251
Hartman, Gail C., 481, 482
Hawkins-Stafford Elementary & Secondary Improvement Amendments of 1988, 344
Hayakawa, S. I., 190
Head Start, 2, 8, 11, 23, 36, 37, 70, 76, 217, 219, 438
  Act of 1981. See P.L. 97-35
  administration, 335
  budget, 323
  definition, 8
  education, 326, 327, 328, 329
  Educational Skills Project, 328, 329
  federal support, 345, 346, 347, 348
  future, 342
  goals, 324, 326
  handicapped children, 338, 367
  health services, 331, 332
  history, 323
  home-based, 335, 336
  innovations, 335
  issues, 341, 342
  Measures Project, 337, 338, 339
  migrant, 343, 344
  nutrition, 333, 334
  organization, 325
  parent involvement, 329
  performance standards, 328
  public school involvement, 328, 338, 339
  racial and ethnic composition, 323
  social services, 332, 333
  staff development, 334
Head Start Measures Battery (HSMB), 337, 338, 339
Health and Human Services, 11

Health and Social Services, 11
Health issues, 462, 463, 464
Heritage Manor Nursing Home, 148, 149
Heteronomy, 296
Highland Oaks Elementary School, 264–67
High Scope Early Elementary Program, 121, 122, 123
Hill, Fleet, 222
Hill, Patty Smith, 75, 217, 249
Holophrases, 221
Home base, 8, 11, 335
Homeless children, 453, 454
Home schooling, 312, 313, 314, 315
Home Start, 8, 11, 76
Home visitor, 14
Honig, Alice, 19
How Gertrude Teaches Children, 51, 74
Hunt, J. McV., 66, 68

Imperial Law of Effect, 394
Income guidelines, 323
Independence, 233, 235
Indpendent study, 380
Individual Educational Plan, 358, 362, 363, 364
Individualized Family Service Plan, 356, 521–30
Industry stage of intellectual development, 294
Industry vs. inferiority stage, 298
Infant, 13
  cognitive development, 186–90
  curricula, 200, 201
  intellectual development, 185, 186
  language development, 190, 191–196
  learning and development, 502
  motor development, 182, 184
  motor milestones, 184
  physical development, 182, 183
  programs, 198, 199, 200, 208, 209
  psychosocial development, 196, 197, 198
  toilet training, 184
Infant Stimulation Programs, 10
Infants and toddlers, 182–210
Initiative stage, 294
Intelligence, 110
Intelligence and Experience, 66
Interdisciplinary, 365
International Kindergarten Union, 74

Intervention services, 502, 503, 504, 505

Jencks, Christopher, 68
Johnson, Harriet, 75
Jonquiere, Harriet Paul, 479, 480
Junior first grade, 6
Junior kindergarten, 9, 10

Kaiser Child Care Centers, 75
Kamii, Constance, 409
Kerckhoff, Richard, 26
Key experiences,
    cognitive oriented, 124, 125, 126
    kindergarten, 517, 518, 519, 520
    preschool, 516, 517
    sensorimotor, 515, 516
Kindergarten
    assessment, 268, 269
    bilingual 284, 285, 286, 287
    computers, 269, 274, 275
    curriculum, 256, 257, 258, 259, 260
    definition, 6
    developmental, 9, 256
    enrollment, 249, 250
    full-day, 261, 263
    half-day, 261, 263
    history, 248, 249
    junior, 9
    key experiences, 517, 518, 519, 520
    literacy, 277, 278, 279
    prekindergarten, 6
    quality programs, 253
    readiness, 250–54
    reading, 275, 276, 277
    rest, 260
    retention, 254, 255
    schedules, 261–63
    senior, 9
    testing, 268, 269
    transitional, 6, 9, 256, 287, 288
    universal, 250
    vignettes, 264–67, 276–77, 280–85
Kindergarten Guide, 248
Kohlberg, Lawrence, 295, 296, 297

Laboratory School, 8, 11
Laissez-faire, 49
Language, 515
Language Acquisition Device (LAD), 192
Language development
    acquisition, 192

Language development (continued)
    behaviorism, 194
    communication, 191, 192
    effects, 192
    environmental factors, 193
    goals, 231, 232
    heredity, 192, 193
    learning, 195, 196
    listening, 124
    speaking, 124
Lanham Act, 75, 217
Latchkey children, 160
Law of Effect, 394
Learning at home, 313
Least restrictive environment, 358
Lekotek, 10
Lennenberg, Eric, 193
Lentin, Linda S., 478
Leonard and Gertrude, 50
Letter to the Mayors and Alderman of All the Cities of Germany in Behalf of Christian Schools, 44, 74
Literacy, 42, 277, 278, 279
Littwin, Susan, 20
Locke, John, 21, 47, 48
Locomotion, 219
Locus of Control, 391
Logical reasoning, 125, 519, 520
Longfellow Elementary School for the Visual and Performing Arts, 508, 509
Loveday, Edna, 482, 483
Luther, Martin, 42–44, 74

Mabton, Washington, Migrant Preschool Education Program, 346, 347
McGuffey, William, 74
McLin, Eva, 75
McMillan, Margaret and Rachel, 75, 216
Magnet school, 11
Mainstreaming
    definition, 355
    least restrictive environment, 358
    normalcy, 355
    reverse, 373
    teaching in, 355, 356, 357
Managing behavior. See Behavior management
Mann, Horace, 74, 248
Maslow, Abraham, 392, 393
Match-up matrix, 371, 372, 373

Matching children's characteristics to setting resources, 370, 371, 372, 373
Maturation, 113, 251
Maturationist view, 252
Merrill-Palmer Institute, 75, 217
Migrancy
    education, 343, 344, 345, 346
    programs, 345, 346, 347, 348
Migrant Preschool Education Program in Mabton, Washington, 346, 347
Miniature adults. See Views of children
Minorities, 506, 507, 510
Missing children, 447, 448
Montessori, Maria, 42, 46, 53, 59, 60, 70, 73, 74
Montessori Kindergarten Program: Natchez-Adams School, 102
Montessori program
    characteristics, 96, 97
    criticism, 97, 102, 103
    definition, 11
    examples, 98–102
    features, 96
    materials, 89–95
    method in practice, 87, 88–95, 96
    principles, 82–87
    selecting, 104
    self-education, 252
    teacher's role, 87
Moral autonomy, 409
Mother's Songs, Games, and Stories, 57
Multicultural children, 355, 380, 381, 382
My Pedagogical Creed, 61

Nanny movement, 161
Naptime, 260
National Academy of Early Childhood Programs, 485
National Association for the Education of Young Children (NAEYC), 6, 76, 486, 487, 531–536
National Association of Nursery Education, 75
National Commission to Prevent Infant Mortality, 76
National Committee on Nursery Schools, 75
National Family Policy, 506, 507
National Defense Education Act, 76

National Organization for Women
    (NOW), 26
Naturalism, 48
Neill, A. S., 49, 75
Neonate, 13
Nongraded, 7
*Normal Child and Primary
    Education, The,* 75
Normalcy in education, 355
Nursery school, 6, 9. *See also*
    Preschool
Nutrition, 232

Object permanency, 122, 188
Observation of children
    advantages, 15
    definition, 15
    steps in, 15, 16
Occupations, 55, 56, 57, 58
Okaloosa County (Florida) Cognitively
    Oriented Curriculum, 127, 128,
    129
Open Door Infant Center, 150, 151
Open Door Preschool, 366
Open education, 11, 70
Operational thinking, 220
Orbis Pictus, 44, 46
Origins of Intelligence in Children, 75
Owen, Robert, 51, 52, 53, 74

P.L. 89-750, 343
P.L. 93-247, 440, 441
P.L. 93-568, 448
P.L. 94-142, 66, 76, 356, 357, 358, 359,
    360, 361
P.L. 97-35, 76
P.L. 98-511, 285, 287
P.L. 99-457, 66, 76, 356, 357, 361, 497
P.L. 100-297, 344
Packard, Vance, 18
Parents
    choices relating to schooling, 5
    and early childhood, 3, 14
    educational practices, 63
    single, 28, 29, 31
    styles, 458, 459
    teenage, 32–34
    working, 27
Parent-Child Enrichment Programs,
    208, 209
Parent Cooperative Preschool, 7
Parent Cooperative Preschools,
    International, 76
Parent involvement
    activities, 424, 425, 426

Parent involvement (*continued*)
    approaches, 422, 423
    bilingual parents, 424
    caregivers, 431
    community, 431
    conferences, 426, 427
    definition, 422
    developmental orientation, 423
    in early childhood programs, 501
    fathers, 430
    handicapped children, 360
    importance, 421, 422
    language minority, 429, 430
    methods, 423, 424
    objectives, 329, 330
    process orientation, 423
    single parent, 428, 429
    special needs parents, 383
    teenage, 430
    training, 505
Path referencing, 337
Pavlov, Ivan P., 394
Peabody, Elizabeth, 74, 248
Perry Preschool Study, The, 240
Pestalozzi, John Heinrick, 42, 49, 50,
    51, 53, 70, 74
Philosophy of education, 477
Piaget, Jean
    accommodation, 111, 112, 122
    adaptation, 110, 111, 113, 122
    assimilation, 111, 112, 122
    concrete operations, 118, 119, 120,
        121, 122
    conservation, 122
    constructivism, 113, 122
    curriculum, 121–32
    educational practices, 63
    egocentrism, 117, 122
    equilibrium, 111, 112
    formal operations, 121
    history, 46, 53, 70
    influence, 53, 70, 73, 75
    intelligence, 110
    issues, 132, 133
    maturation, 113
    moral education, 295
    object permanency, 122
    play, 222
    preoperational stage, 115, 117, 220
    scheme, 112, 113, 122
    sensorimotor stage, 112, 115
    social transmission, 114
Plan-Do-Review, 127, 128–31
Play
    associative, 223

Play (*continued*)
    cooperative, 223
    constructive, 222, 224
    as curriculum, 229
    dramatic, 227, 228
    exploratory, 224
    free, 226, 227, 234, 249
    informal, 226, 227
    instrumental, 224
    kinds, 222, 223, 224
    language, 224
    medical, 228
    onlooker, 223
    outdoor, 228
    parallel, 223
    self-education, 252
    social, 222, 223
    sociodramatic, 224
    solitary, 223
    symbolic, 224
    teacher's role, 226
    unoccupied, 223
    value, 224, 225
Positive reinforcement, 396, 397
Postconventional level, 297
Postman, Neil, 18
Poverty, 138, 438, 439
Practical life, 87, 88, 89
Praise, 400, 401
Pratt, Caroline, 217
Preconventional level, 296
Pre-First Grade, 6
Prekindergarten, 6, 9
Premack, David, 399
Premack Principle, 399
Prenatal period, 502
Preoperational stage, 115, 117, 220
Prepared environment, 85, 86
Prepimary, 6, 9
Preschool, 9
    church related/sponsored, 8
    curriculum, 229, 230
    definition, 6, 216
    effectiveness, 240
    enrollment, 217
    goals, 230, 231, 232
    history, 216, 217
    issues, 240, 241, 242
    key experiences, 516, 517
    parent cooperative, 7, 9
    play, 222–28, 229
    popularity, 217, 218
    purposes, 218, 219
    providers, 219
    qualities, 239, 240

Preschool (*continued*)
  schedules, 234–37
  selecting, 237, 238
  state involvement, 232, 233
Preschooler, 13
  cognitive development, 220, 221
  language development, 221, 222
  motor development, 219, 220
  physical development, 219, 220
Prevention, 460
Preventive guidance, 401
Primary children
  cognitive development, 295
  moral development, 295, 296, 297
  motor development, 294, 295
  physical development, 294
Primary circular reactions, 187, 188, 202
Primary education
  computers, 307, 308, 309
  curriculum, 299
  future, 315, 316
  home schooling, 312, 313, 314, 315
  issues, 311, 312
  significance, 297
  teacher, 310, 311
Primary reinforcer, 394, 395
Primary school, 6, 9
  British, 11
Primary teacher, 310, 311
Private school, 6, 11
Process approach, 423
Professional Code of Ethics, 486, 487
Progressive education, 61, 62
Progressivism, 61
Promotion, 311, 312
Prosocial behaviors, 300
Protestant Reformation, 42
Proximodistal development, 220
Psychosocial development, 196–200, 294
Public policy, 16, 17
Public schools
  corporate involvement, 4, 5
  and early education, 35–37
  restructuring, 509
Punishment, 398

Raikes, Robert, 74
Rainbow Retreat, 159
Ratios, teacher/child, 166, 167
Readiness, 250, 252
  experiences, 253, 254
  health, 254
  impulse control, 253

Readiness (*continued*)
  independence, 253
  interpersonal skills, 253
  language, 253
  learning, 231
Reading approaches, 275, 276, 277
Reinforcement. *See* Behavior management
Representation, 122
Research and Policy Committee for Economic Development, 23
Resource room, 364, 365
Resource room-pullout, 379, 380
Respect, 82, 83
Retention, 254, 255, 256
Reverse mainstreaming, 373, 376
Reversibility, 119
Right from the Start, 241
Room arrangement, 129, 130
Rousseau, Jean Jaques, 42, 48, 49, 53, 74
Ruggles Street Nursery School, 217

Saturday School, 502
Scheme, 112, 113, 122
Schurz, Margarethe, 74, 248
Screening, 268
Secondary circular reactions, 188, 202
Seguin, Edouard, 74
Self-actualization, 392, 393
Self-education. *See* Auto-education
Self-esteem, 393
Self-help, 383
Self-regulation, 410, 411
Sensitive periods, 84, 85
Sensorimotor stage, 112, 115, 185–90, 411, 515, 516
Sensory materials, 87, 91, 92, 93, 94
Sensory training. *See* Montessori
Seriation, 125, 516, 520
Sex roles, 448, 449, 450, 451
Sexism, 448, 449
Single parents. *See* Parents
Skinner, B. F., 194, 394, 395
Social interest, 61
Social Security Income (SSI), 146
Social Security Title XX Day Care. *See* Title XX
Social transmission, 114
Some Thoughts Concerning Education, 47
Southern Association of Children Under Six (SACUS), 239
Spatial relations, 125, 126, 516

Special class, 380
Special needs. *See also* Handicapped; Gifted children; Mainstreaming; Mulicultural children
  adapting to, 374, 375
  interest in, 357–62
  involving families, 383
Special school, 380
Split class, 10
Spock, Dr. Benjamin, 75
Sputnik, 66, 75
Staff-child ratios, 166, 167
Standards for teaching, 488
Stress, 460, 461
Summerhill, 49, 75
Support services, 419
Symbolic play, 190

Tabula Rasa, 21, 47
Task approach, 422
Taste songs, 57, 58
Taylor, Katherine Whiteside, 76
Teacher
  education, 488, 489
  educational practices, 63
  of the year, 478–83
  parent perception of, 486
  qualifications, 485
  qualities, 470
  role, 71, 87
  training, 488, 504
Teaching
  and community agencies, 489
  future of, 487
  intensifying training, 488
  professionalization, 488
Teaching/Learning process, 501
Teaching Enrichment Activities to Minority Students (TEAM), 304, 305
Telegraphic speech, 221
Tertiary circular reactions, 188
Testing, 311
Therapeutic nursery, 446
Thorndike, Edward L., 394
Three Essays of the Theory of Sexuality, 74
Time out, 401, 402
Title I, 343
Title XX, 146, 147, 346, 347
Toddler, 13
  cognitive development, 186–90
  curricula, 200, 201
  intellectual development, 185, 186
  language development, 190, 191–96

Toddler (*continued*)
  motor development, 182, 184
  motor milestone, 184
  physical development, 182, 183
  programs, 198, 199, 200, 208, 209
  psychosocial development, 196,
    197, 198
  toilet training, 184
Token system, 401
Toy library, 8, 10, 75
Transdisciplinary team, 365, 366
Transitional bilingual education, 286,
  287
Transitional classes, 10
Transitional experiences, 376, 377
Transitional kindergarten, 6, 9, 256,
  287, 288
Trends
  child-centered curriculum, 499, 500
  community and parent involvement,
    501
  corporate involvement, 495, 496,
    497
  definition of, 494
  developmentally appropriate
    curriculum, 497, 498, 499
  early childhood education, 500
  early childhood educators and
    community agencies, 500
  federal involvement, 496

Trends (*continued*)
  future of, 510
  importance of, 494
  intervention services, 502, 503, 504,
    505
  learning and development in
    infancy, 502
  minorities, increase of, 506, 507
  minorities, in the work force, 510
  national family policy, 507, 508
  nature of, 494, 495
  prenatal period, 502
  public school programs for three-
    and four-year-olds, 505
  public school, restructuring, 509
  shifting resources from elderly to
    the young, 505, 506
  significance, 495, 496–509
  teaching/learning process, 501

UN Declaration of the rights of the
  child, 24
Unconditioned response, 394
Unconditioned stimulus, 394
Universal education, 42
Unfolding, 49, 222, 251
  children as growing plants, 21, 22,
    256
Utopians, 51

Vernacular, 43
Views of children, 18–23
  blank tablets, 21, 47
  competent child, 20, 35
  garden of children, 54
  growing plants, 21, 22
  miniature adults, 19

Ward, Evangeline, 486
Waukegan Effective Schools Approach
  Follow Through, 402, 403, 404,
  405
White House Conference on
  Families, 76
Whole child, 35, 233, 234
Whole language, 279, 280, 281, 282,
  283, 284
White, Edna Noble, 75
Why Johnny Can't Read, 65, 75
Willis, Andrea Rochelle, 480, 481
Women's movement, 26, 27
Work Projects Administration
  (WPA), 75
Working parents, 27

Young Children, 75
Youth, 76

THE AUTHOR

 George S. Morrison, Ed.D., is professor of early childhood and urban education at Florida International University, where he teaches courses in early childhood education, curriculum development, and urban education. Professor Morrison's accomplishments include a Distinguished Academic Service Award from the Pennsylvania Department of Education and an Outstanding Alumni Award from the University of Pittsburgh School of Education. Dr. Morrison is also the author of several other books on early childhood education and child development. His professional affiliations include the National Association for the Education of Young Children, the Southern Association on Children Under Six, the Society for Research in Child Development, the American Psychological Society, the World Organization for Early Childhood Education, and the Association for Supervision and Curriculum Development.